D0982611

MURRAY'S HANDBOOK
FOR
TRAVELLERS IN SWITZERLAND
1838

THE VICTORIAN LIBRARY

MURRAY'S HANDBOOK
FOR
TRAVELLERS IN SWITZERLAND
1838

WITH AN INTRODUCTION BY

JACK SIMMONS

NEW YORK: HUMANITIES PRESS

LEICESTER UNIVERSITY PRESS

1970

First published in 1838
Victorian Library edition published in 1970 by
Leicester University Press

Distributed in North America by
Humanities Press Inc., New York

Introduction copyright © Leicester University Press 1970

Printed in Great Britain by
Unwin Brothers Limited, The Gresham Press
Old Woking, Surrey, England

Introduction set in Monotype Modern Extended 7

SBN 391 00111 6

THE VICTORIAN LIBRARY

There is a growing demand for the classics of Victorian literature in many fields, in history, in literature, in sociology and economics, in the natural sciences. Hitherto this demand has been met, in the main, from the second-hand market. But the prices of second-hand books are rising sharply, and the supply of them is very uncertain. It is the object of this series, THE VICTORIAN LIBRARY, to make some of these classics available again, at a reasonable cost. Since most of the volumes in it are reprinted photographically from the first edition, or another chosen because it has some special value, an accurate text is ensured. Each work carries a substantial introduction, written specially for this series by a well-known authority on the author or his subject, and a bibliographical note on the text.

The volumes necessarily vary in size. In planning the newly-set pages the designer, Arthur Lockwood, has maintained a consistent style for the principal features. The uniform design of binding and jackets provides for ready recognition of the various books in the series when shelved under different subject classifications.

Recommendation of titles for THE VICTORIAN LIBRARY and of scholars to contribute the introductions is made by a joint committee of the Board of the University Press and the Victorian Studies Centre of the University of Leicester.

EDITOR'S NOTE

The first edition of the *Handbook* is reproduced here complete, except for the omission of the panorama of the Bernese Alps, facing page 1, and of the map at the end of the book: both of them rather poor pieces, which give very little help to the reader today.

I am deeply grateful to Mr John Murray for allowing me to make use of the manuscript of part of the text that is in his possession (including the letter reproduced on page ⟨24⟩) and for supplying me, from the records of his firm, with many of the particulars included in the bibliographical note on page ⟨31⟩.

2 January 1970   J.S.

INTRODUCTION

I

Murray's *Handbook for Travellers in Switzerland*, which is reprinted here in its original form, has several claims on our attention: as one of the earliest major modern guidebooks; as a source of information, not readily to be found elsewhere in English; as a document in the history of taste; and as one of the first volumes in a long and remarkable series.

The guidebook, as we know it, is a product of Romanticism. It made its appearance in Britain in the second half of the eighteenth century, with such works as West's *Guide to the Lakes* (1778) and the early guides to watering-places like Bath, Tunbridge Wells, and Scarborough. Before that century was out the first guidebooks to large English provincial towns had begun to appear, for Newcastle, Bristol, Liverpool, and Leicester. The new interest in the past, so powerfully fostered by Byron and Scott, stimulated the demand for them. Parts of *Childe Harold* and *Don Juan* might indeed be thought themselves to be inspired guidebooks; the notes that Scott appended to his poems and to the Waverley Novels often provide a detailed topographical commentary on the scenes and episodes fictionally treated there. At the same time Wordsworth was moved to write what it might almost be permissible to call an anti-guidebook. His *Guide to the Lakes*, first published in an obscure form in 1810, is a noble effort by one of the supreme Romantics to describe the country he knew and loved, in an almost wholly unromantic way, by a rigorous analysis of the elements of the landscape as he saw them. The cult of the picturesque had encouraged the emergence of the guidebook in the first place; Wordsworth ruthlessly questioned every "picturesque" assumption, to produce a description of the Lakes that is as consistently rational as an account of aesthetic matters can be.

By this time another sort of guidebook was beginning to be demanded in England. The twenty years' war with France had virtually closed the Continent to English travellers. A number made their way across the Channel during the short-lived Peace of Amiens in 1802—and some of them were caught in France when war was suddenly resumed next year. Directly the conflict was ended in 1814–15, the travellers flooded out: pre-eminently to Paris and to the battlefield of Waterloo, where the fate of Europe was at length decided. There was one outstanding reason for going to Paris: it contained at that moment a collection of masterpieces of painting and sculpture, loot assembled with relentless rapacity by the French in their years of triumph. They were on show there for only a very short time, before the Bourbon government hastened to put itself right with the opinion of the civilized world by restoring some at least of these priceless treasures to their former owners.

Nevertheless Paris had, then as now, an attraction for foreign visitors quite independent of any such temporary exhibition; the legitimate possessions of the Louvre would draw any lover of art from the end of the world. Now that peace was restored—in an Englishman's eyes, with a reasonable hope of lasting—it became possible to think of foreign travel as regular and easy. In the past it had been practicable for only two classes of people: the rich and noble, who moved majestically on their way, at great expense; and people of modest means, who might have to be prepared to undertake much of their journey on foot. Now a third group appeared, a genuine middle class. They could benefit by the immeasurably improved roads of north-western Europe, for which they owed thanks primarily to the French, and by the multiplication and improvement of light vehicles for travelling on them, as well as of public services by *diligence* and coach.

Inside Great Britain such travellers had long been provided with useful roadbooks, giving practical information about the route, the tolls to be paid, and the accommodation offered by the inns on the way. Similar roadbooks had been produced in Continental countries—the best, as might be expected, in

France; but none of them really met the demands of these middle-class travellers, who were now coming to use the Continental roads in ever-increasing numbers. Some attempts were made to meet this need, especially by Mrs Mariana Starke in her *Travels on the Continent: Written for the Use and Particular Information of Travellers*, which was published by John Murray in 1820 and ran through eight editions down to 1833. But this work, like its fellows, was cumbrous and diffuse. What was wanted was a book of a new kind: filled with practical information, like the roadbooks, but supplying also an account of the country, its people, antiquities, and landscape, on a scale large enough to satisfy the curiosity of a well-educated man.

II

Among the ordinary English travellers of the middle class who set out in these years to explore the Continent was John Murray III—so one must name him, in the unique publishing dynasty already established, as it still is today, at No. 50, Albemarle Street, in London. Murray was just twenty-one, fresh from his education at Charterhouse and Edinburgh, when he first set foot on the Continent at Rotterdam in 1829, adequately supplied by his father with the money he needed for his travels, on the understanding that he mastered the German language. He was immediately struck by the difficulty of getting the kind of information he wanted, as an intelligent visitor, concerning the history, economy, and society of the countries he was visiting; and he soon began to assemble notes of his observations, for his own practical use and perhaps for the benefit of others too. "I travelled thus", he says, "note-book in hand, and whether in the street, the *Eilwagen*, or the picture gallery, I noted down every fact as it occurred."[1] On his return home he worked over these notes, arranged his material in Routes, compiled general accounts of the history, architecture, and geology of the countries concerned, and then showed the whole to his father. The elder Murray—one of the

1 *Murray's Magazine*, vi (1889), 624. This article, by John Murray III himself, gives the fullest account of the origin of the *Handbooks*.

leading European publishers of his time, the friend of Scott and Byron—thought well of his son's effort and suggested a title for it: a *Handbook*. This was the first time that the word had been used in English.[1]

Here was no more than the beginning, however, of the first *Handbook*. The younger Murray himself made several more journeys in aid of it, and he lent proof-sheets of his drafts to friends to use and test out on journeys of their own. Not until 1836 was the book published, as *A Handbook for Travellers on the Continent*, comprising Holland, Belgium, the Rhine, and North Germany. Next year a second volume appeared, devoted to Southern Germany, Austria, Hungary, and the Danube out to the Black Sea.

These first two volumes were written wholly by John Murray III himself—though, like all writers of guidebooks, he was indebted to earlier books and personal informants and, like the honest man he was, he said so. Long before this first large task was completed, he had made up his mind that he would like to add further volumes, covering other countries, to the first two. He already regarded a *Switzerland* as a complement to them;[2] but he was also travelling and assembling material for *Handbooks* to France, to Scandinavia and Russia, and—the biggest task of all—to Italy. It must have been evident from an early stage that he could not possibly prepare the whole series himself. He was not, after all, a professional writer, but a publisher. Though John Murray II was still the

1 The orthography of the word was never consistently maintained, even by Murray himself. It appears as "Hand Book" on the title-page of the first of the series, in 1836, and as "Handbook" on that of the second in 1837. The first edition of the *Switzerland* (1838) has "Hand-book"; the second, of 1842, has "Hand Book". The form "Handbook" has been used consistently here throughout. The word may well have been coined from the German *Handbuch*, which dates back at least to the sixteenth century.

John Murray II, moreover, devised the red cloth cover that quickly became standard for the whole series. But his son did not at first take to the idea of a uniform colour. He pressed for making the cover of the *Southern Germany* green; and though that plea did not succeed, his father consented to allow the first edition of the *Switzerland* to be bound in blue. But the uniform red prevailed thereafter. (John Murray IV, *John Murray III*, 1919, 63–4, 67.)

2 In the preface to the *Handbook for Travellers on the Continent* (1836) he writes (p. iv) that if the work proves successful it will be followed by a *Handbook for Southern Germany*: "The *Handbook for Switzerland* will form a third volume—the materials for which are already collected, while the second volume is even now in the press."

very active head of the firm, he was already nearing sixty when the first of the *Handbooks* was published in 1836, and in the normal course his son would soon have to succeed him. (In fact the old man died not long afterwards, in 1843.) If the young John Murray was to realize the great prospect opened up by the success of the first volumes and the planning of the series that was to follow them, he must clearly seek help. That might take one of three forms. He could employ assistants to provide him with notes and drafts, which he could then work up into the finished text; he could commission another writer to make himself wholly responsible for a *Handbook*; or he could divide the work with a collaborator.

He rejected the first solution, and quite rightly: for in the kind of book he was set on producing, there was no substitute for the personal visit, the personal recommendation—or discommendation—of inns and public services. Directly the books began to emerge as a series, they carried with them certain certificates: one, which soon appeared explicitly in every volume, to the effect that the text contained no advertising matter, in favour of individual inns or other interests;[1] the other declaring that they were based on a personal inspection of the country they described, and that when the information included in them had been secured at second hand, this would be specifically stated.

Murray was evidently reluctant, at first, to adopt the second solution to his problem. The danger in it was that a book might result, by a competent authority, quite different from the others in the series. He already wanted them all to employ certain standard practices, and to confine each *Handbook* within reasonable limits of length. If he gave an able author his head, it might be difficult for him to enforce these controls—as, indeed, he found only too plainly when he did adopt this plan with Richard Ford in the famous *Handbook for Travellers in Spain*. That was a masterpiece of a very rare kind—a guidebook that can still be read with absorption as a work of literature today, when it is a century and a quarter old; but its preparation nearly drove Murray distraught, so

---

1 This first appeared in 1842 (in the *North Italy* and the second edition of the *Switzerland*). It reached a standard form, repeated in the *Handbooks* over many years, in the *France* of 1843.

little idea had his author of the economic realities, or even the common sense, of producing a book like this.

For the *Switzerland* he had already adopted the third plan: of dividing the work between himself and a collaborator whom he knew and could rely on. A number of books had recently been published in England that were concerned with the exploration of the Alps: notably those of C. J. Latrobe and William Brockedon. Murray was himself no mountaineer, and apt to be a trifle impatient with those who had taken up that pastime. As he tartly puts it in his introduction here (p. xxvii): "The passion for climbing mountains, so ardent in a young traveller, soon cools; and they who have surmounted the Righi, the Faulhorn, and the Dôle may fairly consider any further ascents a waste of time and labour." Why not divide the book, then, so as to leave the Alps in the hands of one of those who had more sympathy for the subject than he had? Latrobe was abroad in these years, in America, the West Indies, and Australia. Murray's choice fell on Brockedon, to whom he pays anonymous tribute in his preface. Brockedon was a man very unlike himself, and the conjunction of the two authors produced a piquant diversity of approach that is one of the charms of the book in the original form it wears here.

Brockedon differed from Murray in two important respects. He was twenty years older, a man of the previous generation; and though he had once been in business, as a watchmaker in his native town of Totnes, he was not in any sense a business man, but an artist. He made some reputation for himself as a painter, primarily of historical subjects in the fashion of the day, but also of portraits. In 1824 he paid a visit to the Alps, to investigate the route adopted by Hannibal in crossing them. At once he was captivated by the spectacle they presented, and in this and four subsequent journeys undertaken in 1825–9 he crossed the mountain chain fifty-eight times, passing in and out of Italy by more than forty different routes. The result was the publication of his *Illustrations of the Passes of the Alps*, issued in twelve parts in 1827–9, followed by his *Journals of Excursions in the Alps* in 1833.[1]

These books established him as one of the leading inter-

---

1 For Brockedon see the *Dictionary of National Biography* and the *Transactions of the Devonshire Association*, ix (1877), 243–9.

preters of Alpine scenery to the Englishmen of his time. Much of what he had discussed in them he now distilled for the second part of the *Handbook*. Since his contribution was anonymous, he was able without awkwardness to incorporate in it half-a-dozen substantial passages from his earlier books. Though he necessarily includes a good deal of historical information, and is not blind to the economic and social state of the country he is describing—see, for instance, his account of the industries of Annecy (pp. 309–10) or the salt-works of Moutiers (pp. 315–16)—his chief concern is with the visual, one may fairly say with the picturesque. He can still use, quite naturally, the language of the eighteenth century. The object of the excursion from Chamonix to the Jardin is, he tells us, "to enter more into the heart of Mont Blanc, to penetrate into its profound valleys, and witness scenes of wilder horrors and more savage solitude" (p. 294). Again, on the descent from the Col de Viso: "At length, however, all these sublime horrors are passed, and vegetation is soon after reached, in a beautiful little plain covered with the richest herbage" (p. 345).

Nor is this attitude an inappropriate one, since the country Brockedon was concerned with was widely different from that which had been described by Murray in the first part of the *Handbook*. It was very much larger in area, stretching from Geneva to the Mediterranean, from Grenoble to Lake Maggiore—for the book comprehended, in addition to Switzerland, the whole of Savoy and Piedmont; but most of this huge tract was sparsely peopled, or barren mountain. It contained only two towns of any size, Chambéry (with a population of 10,000) and Annecy (6,000)—except Nice (20,000), already established as the largest resort on the Riviera, but clearly marginal to the territory Brockedon was chiefly concerned with.[1] Brockedon's main duty to his reader was to describe the physical features of the country; Murray had to deal in much larger measure with the human geography and the interesting peculiarities of Swiss society.

It is here, perhaps, that Murray startles us most. He has something sharp to say about the villainies of waiters and

[1] Routes 136 and 137 were removed from the *Handbook for Switzerland* in the third edition of 1846 and thereafter, being transferred to the *Handbook for North Italy*, first published in 1842.

couriers (pp. xiv, xx); but he pays resounding tribute to the merits of Swiss guides, and he defends the innkeepers against the common charge of extortion (pp. xvii, xxi). Up to p. xxx his account of the country—still, after all, very little known to Englishmen, and some parts of it exceedingly remote from all foreigners—is a favourable one. Then he comes to *"the moral condition of the Swiss"*, and he suddenly plunges into a fierce indictment of their venal character, their penchant for begging, the deplorable influence of the Roman Catholic church, the rigid petty tyranny exerted by close oligarchic governments in many of the cantons. Some of this may be set down to insular, and especially Protestant, prejudice, and to misunderstanding of a society vastly different from Murray's own. Gradually, in subsequent editions of the book, the sharpness of these comments was reduced, until in the nineteenth and last edition of 1904 the verdict has, on balance, quite changed (p. lxxxv):

On the subject of the *moral condition of the Swiss*, and of their character as a nation, there is much variety of opinion. The Swiss with whom the ordinary traveller comes into contact, especially the German portion of them, are often either polyglot waiters, grasping landlords, or slow-witted and churlish peasants. This disposes the superficial traveller to dislike and to take very little interest in the people amongst whom he is travelling; he has also perhaps heard something of their time-serving, their love of money, and their readiness to fight for any paymaster in former times, while he knows little of the most interesting portions of Swiss history, and is absolutely ignorant of the nature of the Swiss constitution. But a deeper acquaintance with the Swiss, treated as men and citizens and not as mere servants of the passing traveller, will lead to a better appreciation of their sterling qualities, even beneath a rough exterior, as in the case of the peasants. Looked at as a nation, the Swiss are deserving of our study and admiration, as the heirs of a freedom which has, like our own, been handed down from father to son through many centuries.

Murray described Switzerland at an interesting juncture in its history. He was writing in the uneasy interlude that followed the furious upheavals unleashed by the French Revolution. The country had been neutralized, by agreement between the great powers, in 1815; but its internal political structure was still disturbed, until the making of the settlement of 1848, which established the constitution of the state we know today, fully federal, balanced internally between competing racial, linguistic, and religious groups. Again and again, in his introduction and in the course of the text, he has occasion to remind us of the bitter feuds that had divided Swiss neighbours from one another in the past. Those feuds were by no means dead—witness the nasty fight at Liestal in 1833 (pp. 8–9). The cantons were still, collectively, little more than a loose alliance of very small organisms, each deeply distrustful of one or more of its neighbours. Their relationship was symbolized in their determination to retain separate currencies, which demand four pages of explanation from Murray to the bewildered traveller (pp. viii–xii).

In reading the *Handbook* it is important to bear in mind the state of Switzerland at the particular time when Murray was writing. Profound changes had been set going by the revolution that had begun there in 1798. They were still working themselves out in the 1830s, to an end that could hardly be foreseen.

The description that Murray gives of the country is somewhat uneven. Consider, for example, what he has to tell us about the Swiss towns. He begins his book with a description of Basle that might be taken as a model of its kind. As a brief introduction it is almost as good for the traveller of the 1970s as it was for his predecessor in the 1830s. He is rather less good on Berne—though it must be remembered that what he chiefly saw was the old town, from the church of the Holy Ghost along the tongue of land washed by the Aare to the Nydegg bridge. Beautiful as that was, and happily still is, it was not yet girdled by the whole series of terraces and the majestic high bridges that give it so singular a distinction today. For the small towns he seems to have scarcely any feeling whatever. One could hardly expect him to appreciate Solothurn—which a modern visitor may well think one of the most ravishing small towns in northern Europe—for its quality derives largely from the fusion of Gothic and Baroque, and like nearly all Englishmen of his time Murray regarded the Baroque with contempt and dislike. But he has nothing interesting to say of the highly picturesque fortified hill-top towns. He recommends the traveller to avoid Romont altogether, on account of the badness of the road through it; he omits all reference to Rue; he has only tepid commendation for Aarburg. When he comes to Morat, he rightly gives space to the critically important battle fought there in 1476. But he dismisses the place itself—perhaps the most complete example of a walled town in Switzerland—in this single sentence (p. 117): "Its narrow and somewhat dismal streets are overlooked by an old castle; and it is still partly surrounded by feudal fortifications—the same which, for ten days, withstood the artillery of Charles the Bold." This sentence, as we shall see, gave some offence in Morat itself.

III

During the century and a half since Murray wrote, Switzerland has changed very greatly. In his general account of the country, seven lines suffice for what he has to tell us of its industry. The reference is appreciative, in the midst of long passages that are unfavourable to the Swiss character, but it is brief and generalized. Nor has he anything extensive to say of the industrial and commercial growth of individual towns, except when he writes of the watches of La Chaux de Fonds (p. 125) and Geneva (p. 136) and of the salt-mines of Bex (p. 151). This is not because he is uninterested in such matters, or thinks his readers will not wish to hear about them. His *Handbook for France*, which was already in preparation when this book was written and was published only five years afterwards, is interesting for just these things—the account he gives of the coal-working and textile manufactures of the north-east of the country, for example. The reason why he does not describe them in Switzerland is that there they were relatively unimportant. Muslins and cottons, watches and clocks, are briefly referred to from time to time, and that is all. Today, anyone who set out to write a book like Murray's (but who, alas, would ever do so now?) would feel obliged to describe the country's remarkable industrial growth. Winterthur was for Murray (p. 27) "an industrious manufacturing town", concerned with textiles. What would he have thought of it now, of Sulzer and the Swiss Locomotive Company—or of Oerlikon at Zürich or Brown Boveri at Baden? In his time this development was only just beginning. In ours Switzerland has become one of the most important industrial and financial centres of Western Europe, and she has done so largely by concentrating on those things that she is unquestionably able to make well, like chemicals and electrical goods, watches and foodstuffs and textiles.

Switzerland's most famous industry today, however, remains tourism, as it has been for almost the whole of the last hundred years. Here things have not gone quite as Murray might have expected. For him, in the 1830s, Swiss tourism had two components. Historically, the more important and interesting was that which was centred on the watering-places: the restoration of invalids to health by means of the mineral springs in which Switzerland abounds. The newer industry of providing for those who came, in rude health, merely as visitors, in order to sample its natural beauties, is also dealt with in the *Handbook*, and especially in Part II; but this second element, important though it was, takes a lower place in the book as a whole than the first.

What are we to say on this matter now? The watering-places are still there, and many of them remain in business—more than twenty are still officially classified as mineral spas. But none of them could begin to compare in popularity today with Lucerne or Interlaken or Lugano. In England most of the older watering-places have either almost gone out of business as such—like Woodhall and Droitwich—or turned over to another livelihood: to popular tourism, like Scarborough and Margate and Torquay, or to the accommodation of commuters and conferences, like Harrogate. For Murray "the most frequented watering-place in Switzerland" is Schintznach Bad, between Aarau and Zürich. "In May and June", he tells us (p. 17), "300 people often dine here in the splendid saloon." Go there today, and what do you find? A watering-place still, and a delightful one. From the most frequented spa in Switzerland, however, it has become one of the least frequented in Europe. It lies on the main railway line from Zürich to Berne; but only the slowest trains stop there. Arrive by car, and you will find it stands in a cul-de-sac.

Even the huge green torrent of the Aare runs at a distance
from it now; modern waterworks have left it on a stagnant arm
of the river, a large pond. An express train roars by, an air-
liner overhead, bound for Zürich. The motor-cars that arrive
there are almost all Swiss, and no more than a very select
company. The place is given up to the aged and the lame.
They move slowly, as one would expect; when a motor-car
turning a sharp bend gives a cautious hoot, one perambulating
old lady turns to another and says "Tch! Tch!"

There are two hotels, each with its own bath-house, and a
separate bath-house for non-residents. The older of the two
hotels, the Park, was reconstructed in 1827, just before Murray
came here, and it is almost exactly as he describes it. The
bath-house is a handsome semi-circular building, its outside
wall prettily diversified in summer with petunias and geran-
iums and yellow marigolds.

The other hotel has nothing particularly interesting about
it save its name: the Habsburg Hotel. At first you might think
that name was no more than a futile, pathetic gesture in the
direction of a world that fell to pieces in 1918. But no. There
is a real connection with the Habsburgs—the most intimate
there could be: for it was here that they emerged into history.
A little way above in the trees, over towards Brugg, lies the
Habsburg, the Hawks' Castle, the cradle of the greatest of all
European royal houses. There, intact, is the original watch-
tower, built about 1020. Murray did not miss its significance,
which he expounds with an admirably succinct clarity.

He has indeed just the combination of qualities one values
most highly in the author of a guidebook. As a writer he is
economical, wasting none of his readers' time in flummery,
accurate and unambiguous. Humorous too, in a dry way: as
when he speaks of the nuns at Solothurn, and the little articles
they offer for sale (p. 10)—"their pincushions are clumsy,
and themselves not very interesting." His information is
sound, within the limits of the knowledge of his time. For
history and antiquities he had to depend mainly on J. G.
Ebel's remarkable gazetteer:[1] a major pioneer work in the

---

[1] *Anleitung, auf die nützlichste und genussvollste Art der Schweitz zur
bereisen.* The edition Murray used was published at Zürich in four
volumes in 1809–10.

literature of European topography, to which he pays just and generous tribute in the opening words of his preface.

The events in recent history that stirred him most, like the majority of the men of his generation, were those of the great French wars. In Switzerland that meant above all the amazing campaign of 1799, when the Austrians and the Russians tried to drive the French out of the country, descending upon them from the Alps and retreating again, when the French were victorious, over the mountains with incredible hardship and loss. Again and again we meet echoes of that sublime contest: on the Albis, not far from Zürich (p. 35), up the valley of the Reuss and the St Gotthard Pass (pp. 93–100), in the remote canton of Glarus (pp. 184, 191–4). From the following year, too, Brockedon picks up in Piedmont memories of the campaign that culminated so marvellously at Marengo (p. 251).

For the rest, Murray published what he had seen and learnt for himself. He never thought it worth while for a traveller to visit a country merely to look at it, however spectacular its landscape might be, or to study its past. The present, the modern world, was the basis of what he set out to describe, and he was determined to have his say about it. That is what led him into the interesting, and highly critical, account of the country in his introduction.

He did not print the whole of what he had originally written. His notebooks, compiled in the course of the four journeys he made to Switzerland in the cause of the *Handbook*, seem unfortunately to have been lost. But a surviving manuscript, apparently a fair copy prepared for the printer, shows some passages that do not appear in the published version. His rejected account of the city of Geneva, for example, is fuller than the one he prints, and scarcely flattering. He characterizes the place as poky and dull: "Mr Bakewell has calculated that the whole town stands upon an area four times as large as Russell Square in London. Like most fortified towns, its ramparts prevented its streets spreading outwards for many centuries and caused the houses to be raised to a considerable height. They are principally built of stone from Meillerie. Many families live under one roof, a single storey or flat usually suffices, as is the case in Edinburgh, for a household." In the published text (p. 131) nothing whatever survives of all this save a generalized reference to the similarity in appearance between Geneva and Edinburgh.

Murray's observation is acute, and constantly on the stretch. He foresees the development of Olten at the expense of Solothurn (p. 12). He fascinates us with his account of the fossilized social distinctions of the "paltry town" of Locarno (p. 219). He looks in at all the resorts: not only at the stately Schintznach Bad and at Pfäfers, whose oddities were famous (p. 171); but at Leukerbad, where the cure was uniquely strange (p. 106); at Heinrichsbad, which accommodated consumptive patients in a cowhouse (p. 180); at St Moritz, in its early infancy as a resort (p. 199); at Interlaken, which he found "a sort of Swiss Margate" (p. 72).

The things that moved Murray most were the triumphs that had been won by man over nature. In the subsequent century Switzerland has given us so much more of this kind to admire, above all perhaps in the construction of its astounding railway system, that it is useful to look at the country before a single mile of railway had been built there and to appreciate some of its earlier achievements: the Linth Canal, for example (p. 30), the draining of the Lake of Lungern (pp. 59–61), the first suspension bridge at Fribourg (p. 114); to which Brockedon adds the no less remarkable story of the tunnelling beneath the dike of the Dranse (pp. 265–8). These wonders have almost wholly disappeared from the modern guidebooks. They deserve to be remembered, and here they have a fine memorial.

Switzerland has changed profoundly since 1838. Not all the changes have been for the better. The particular course that industrial and social development has taken in Switzerland has resulted in the suburbanization of much of the lower-lying countryside;[1] and, for many people, the new motorways sit particularly ill in the Swiss pastoral landscape. They are in part, of course, a by-product of tourism, and it would be idle and ungrateful to complain of that since it has enabled the Swiss to make their chief contribution to the pleasure of our

1 This process was well under way within Murray's own life-time.
　　White houses prank where once were huts.
　　Glion, but not the same!
wrote Matthew Arnold in the 1860s in "Obermann Once More". What would he say now of the spread of Montreux directly below?

own time. But this too has opened up the country, to the destruction of the peace described here. To read the account given in this book of the remoter recesses of Switzerland brings back for us something of

The freshness of the early world.

Yet equally there are new things to admire—that Murray and Brockedon would also have admired, if they had seen them. The wonderful new roads constructed to the orders of Napoleon, on which they both comment with thorough-going enthusiasm (see, for example, pp. 157–8, 329), have their counterpart in the twentieth century in the no less wonderful concrete engineering of Maillart and such works as the new road now under construction with so much difficulty along the mountain-side from Villeneuve to Vevey. Again, when Murray described museums and picture-galleries it was never in very respectful terms, save at Basle (p. 2). Today we too salute the outstanding gallery at Basle, but not that alone. Zürich and Berne, Geneva and many smaller towns can delight us with their treasures, admirably displayed. There are some things, too, that Murray could never have imagined. A single example: the exquisitely-contrived floodlighting of the great church at Berne and, far below, divided from it by a pool of darkness, of the falls of the Aare. Here the use of a modern technique has engendered a memorable work of art.

There are, then, losses and gains. Every traveller who is interested will make his own list of them and strike a balance at the end. Murray's *Handbook*, when it first appeared, depicted Switzerland at what was for her decisively the beginning of the modern age. It is still a valuable companion to the country today, as a varied and shrewd account of a world that has in part vanished, and in part endures.

IV

The *Handbook*, in its original form, was a highly personal production: not because the authors obtruded their opinions, or attempted a tiresome originality, but through the sincere effort they made to present knowledge and advice at first hand, in the clearest, the most direct and unaffected way. The book was as successful as it deserved to be. It quickly became, for English-speaking travellers, a sort of bible, an indication of what was and was not worth seeing in Switzerland. In 1866, the *Handbook* being then in its eleventh edition, Murray received a letter from Morat, which evidently interested him, for he had it bound into the manuscript copy of the original book that he had carefully preserved. The letter is as follows:

Morat, 26 November 1866

Sir,

I take the liberty to intrude upon you, to ask if you could not be so kind as to alter a *severe* paragraph on our dear little town in your world-famous "Handbook for Switzerland"? I am sure the gentleman who wrote it must have arrived here on a very gloomy day, or have had a very bad dinner, or met with some other misfortune, to speak of Morat in that disparaging way. Anyhow, he has not only wounded our sensitive feelings, but he has undoubtedly done us a great deal of harm, commercially. If on investigation you should find our complaint to be a well-founded one, I feel certain you will do us the justice of placing us in a better light with the travelling public. To save you trouble, I send you by the post a No. of "Once a Week" (Dec. 9, 1865), which contains a very nice article on Morat by a gentleman entirely unknown to me or any of us; do please compare *his* impressions with those of your contributor; the one calls us "one of the most picturesque towns in Switzerland", etc., the other a "dismal place", etc. I also enclose a photograph of Morat, which will speak for itself, though it does not render *the colour* of the lake. I shall be very happy to supply you with further particulars if you will be so kind as to enter into the matter at all. In conclusion, I beg to say that my motives for writing are perfectly disinterested. As to my veracity, either with respect to present or any future communication, I beg to refer you to a gentleman in one sense your neighbour, Dr John Tyndall, F.R.S., Royal Institution, Albemarle Street.

I remain, Sir,
Your obedt. Servt.,
John Haas
Directeur du Collège de Morat

This courteous and touching letter gives a clear indication of the repute that the book had attained, and of the dawning

importance of the modern tourist industry: a slighting reference to a place could be thought to do it "a great deal of harm,
commercially", if it occurred in one of the famous *Handbooks*
published by Murray in London.[1]

In subsequent editions the Swiss *Handbook* grew, passing
out of the control of the first authors into those of later editors,
whose task was to keep pace with the rapid changes, especially
in communications, that occurred later in the nineteenth
century. Inevitably it became something of a hotchpotch—
more and more useful as a compilation, as it was extended to
include matter relating to districts and subjects never previously touched on, but with its original personality gone.
In 1891 it was recast entirely, for the eighteenth edition, by
a notable Alpinist, W. A. B. Coolidge. Then in 1904 the book
reached its final form: a volume of 600 pages, not counting a
meticulous index-directory running to sixty more, with thirty-
three folding coloured maps. (How can it have been sold, even
then, for no more than ten shillings?) This nineteenth edition
is a treasure-house: the fullest account of the land of Switzerland that has ever been published in English, a valuable
quarry for any traveller or student still. A few sentences from
the first edition of the *Handbook* survive in it: Murray's
accounts of the end of Toussaint l'Ouverture in the Fort de
Joux (p. 126; 19th ed., p. 62) and of Louis Philippe's sojourn
as a schoolmaster at Reichenau (p. 204; 19th ed., p. 210);
Brockedon's tribute to the canons of the Great St Bernard
(p. 257; 19th ed., p. 116). But these are small things. The book
has been transformed. It is still described on its cover as
Murray's Handbook (though now published not by Murray
but by Stanford). It is the lineal descendant of the book of
1838, but very unlike its progenitor.

Even that nineteenth edition came out over sixty years
ago. What should the modern traveller take about with him
in Switzerland today? The *Blue Guide* is, in its turn, out of
print, apart from a brief excerpt devoted to the Bernese
Oberland. There is a general Swiss guidebook,[2] well above the

1 Murray made a change, in the sense of this letter, in the next edition of
   the *Handbook*. The streets of Morat remained "narrow and dismal" until
   the 12th edition of 1867, when they became (p. 148) "picturesque and
   arcaded".
2 *Switzerland: the Traveller's Illustrated Guide* (4th ed., 1966).

average of such productions but making no pretension to
many of the qualities displayed by Murray. There are admirable guides to historic towns and buildings—the latest successors of Ebel: Jenny's classic *Kunstführer der Schweiz*, the
Schweiz und Liechtenstein in the series published by Reclam
at Stuttgart. But if the English visitor wants a sound companion, which will show him the structure of the country, its
history, and—valley by valley, peak by peak—its topography,
he will if he is wise turn again to Murray: to the nineteenth
edition, and to this one.

V

The book is important to us, and still worth our attention,
for another reason, however: as one of the first, and one of the
very best, volumes in a distinguished and extensive series,
famous in Victorian England. Murray regarded it, as we have
seen, as the third volume of a trilogy that formed the basis
of an ambitious publishing project. Unlike many other such
projects, this one was fulfilled, in a greater amplitude than
Murray himself can have foreseen. It came to comprise, over
the years 1836 to 1895, some thirty volumes, dealing with
every country in Europe; with the Mediterranean and North
Africa, with Egypt and the Near East; with India, New
Zealand, and Japan. It was complemented by a parallel series
of about thirty more *Handbooks* for the British Isles, covering
England county by county, with separate volumes for Wales,
Scotland, and Ireland. The first of these was the *Devon and
Cornwall*, published in 1851, the last the *Warwickshire* of 1899.

These sixty volumes formed, collectively or individually,
the standard equipment of the intelligent English traveller
during the reigns of Queen Victoria and her son. John Murray
III, who wrote the first of them and retained throughout his
life more than the usual publisher's interest in the series he
was sponsoring, was very much a man of his time, and he saw
them as an instrument of education, in a wide sense of the
word. He was interested in something besides the collection
and arrangement of fact, though he never forgot, or allowed
his authors to forget, that that is the first humble business of
a guidebook. He saw his *Handbooks* also as a means of

elevating the standards of conduct and the taste of his countrymen. All contain good advice to tourists on their behaviour: not moral lectures, but sensible hints on the best way of conducting oneself in foreign countries, whether as a traveller or as a sojourner. The advice was sorely needed. The vulgarity, the crude, ignorant *naïveté* of the English tourists who flooded out on to the Continent on the steam packets and the early railways shocked many people, their own more sensitive countrymen above all. The literary men made fun of them: Thackeray, for example, several times, notably in "The Kickleburys on the Rhine". Richard Doyle sketched them neatly and with no more than good-humoured caricature in *The Foreign Tour of Messrs Brown, Jones and Robinson*. Murray held strong views on these matters, and from hints thrown out in the earliest volumes in the series he advanced to an open statement in the *Handbook for France* of 1843. There he included a section (pp. xxxvii–xxxviii) entitled "The English Abroad", which begins with these words: "It may not be amiss here briefly to consider the causes which render the English so unpopular on the Continent; as to the fact of their being so, it is to be feared there can be no doubt." He attributes their unpopularity largely to ignorance and insensitiveness, but to three more specific causes too: the inability of Englishmen to speak foreign languages (he himself having been well schooled in this respect by his father), their boorish behaviour as Protestants in Roman Catholic churches, and their disposition to make too ready use of their fists when annoyed. Did this little homily have any effect on those it was aimed at? There is no way of telling. It kept its place in the French *Handbook* for very many years, through a series of drastic revisions: an indication that, in Murray's eyes at least, the warning was salutary and continued to be useful. It may have done some good, at least to the more teachable of his countrymen.

The educational effect of the *Handbooks* cannot be demonstrated in any precise terms. They quickly became, in Samuel Smiles's phrase, "the badge of the British traveller",[1] a necessary part of his luggage on any foreign journey.[2] One

1 *A Publisher and his Friends* (1891), ii, 463.
2 They had their imitators, the most famous being Karl Baedeker. Though

may cite the way Thackeray treats them in a *Cornhill* paper of 1860.[1] His curiosity is directed to the means by which the inns in Continental towns are graded in the *Handbooks*— "good and clean", "so so", "bad, dirty, and dear"; to the "three inn-inspectors", whom he conceives as being "sent forth by Mr Murray on a great commission, and who stop at every inn in the world". He makes play with the horrible fate of the third of them, "the poor fag, doubtless, and boots of the party", whose assignment it is to stay at the bad inns. The fun would lose its point if Thackeray's attitude were not one of respect for the value of what Murray has to tell him, his assumption that his readers who travel will all use the *Handbooks* too.

The *Handbooks* were highly successful. No publisher could hope to do much better than Murray did with this *Switzerland*, finding a market for twenty-six impressions, totalling well over 50,000 copies, in seventy years;[2] but its success was hardly greater than that of the German volumes or the *France*. Even the *Algeria and Tunis* went through five editions; there were nine of the *Japan*. As for the *India*, that enjoys the unique distinction of being still in print today, in a stout volume of over 700 pages. It is now in its nineteenth edition, having evolved out of the original four volumes of 1859–83.[3]

Murray was unquestionably the pioneer, as sensible German scholars agree (cf. for example *Allgemeine Deutsche Biographie*, xlvi, 1902, 181), some attempts have been made to suggest that Baedeker was the true inventor of the modern guidebook (e.g. in *Neue Deutsche Biographie*, i, 1953, 516). Baedeker himself knew better. His first *Handbook*, to Holland and Belgium, appeared in 1839. Its preface contained the statement that Murray's *Handbook for Travellers on the Continent* had formed its basis. Similar acknowledgments appear in Baedeker's *Germany* (1842) and *Switzerland* (1851). Baedeker silently lifted some of Murray's own words, and occasionally they were ludicrously mistranslated: see *Murray's Magazine*, vi, 628–9. On these matters see also the interesting correspondence in *The Times Literary Supplement*, from 14 May 1931 onwards, especially the letter from Hans Baedeker (11 June). Of course Baedeker's guidebooks ultimately came to have a larger scope than Murray's, being published in three languages, dealing more fully with art and architecture, covering more of the world, and enjoying a longer life. No comparison of quality is intended here; merely a note to keep the record straight in the matter of the origin of books of this kind.

1 *Cornhill Magazine*, ii (1860), 634–5, reprinted with some changes in *Roundabout Papers* (1863).
2 See p. ⟨ 31⟩ below.
3 See the interesting bibliographical particulars given in the preface to the nineteenth edition, pp. v–vi.

The *Handbooks*, then, sold in large numbers, continuing in steady demand during their eighty years' supremacy in Britain. Though one cannot quantify the influence they exercised over those who read and used them, as one can quantify their sale, it was unquestionably powerful. As we read them now, at home or when travelling through the countries they describe, they seem to exemplify many of the best standards of excellence of their time: reliability, derived from their thorough preparation; a solicitous concern for the reader; curiosity, constantly alert; sound judgment, resting on robust common sense. If we look back to the opening years of Queen Victoria's reign, which gave us this book and its early companions, we can see in a true perspective their great importance. For it was then that Englishmen—not merely the wealthy few, but middle-class people in increasing numbers—began to become directly and continuously aware of what lay beyond the English Channel and the North Sea. As the red *Handbooks* appeared one by one, they came to provide the Victorians with a vast panorama—liberally conceived, clear, sharp, and accurate—of their own country and of a large part of the civilized world.

Jack Simmons

BIBLIOGRAPHICAL NOTE

The present volume reprints the first edition of the *Handbook for Travellers in Switzerland*, published in 1838. The *Handbook* appeared in nineteen editions altogether. These are listed below, with a note of the number of copies printed, where known.

1st ed., 1838 (3500).
2nd ed., 1842 (4000); reprinted 1843.
3rd ed., 1846 (5000).
4th ed., 1851 (1000).
5th ed., 1852 (3000).
6th ed., 1854 (2500).
7th ed., 1855 (1500); reprinted 1856 (3250), 1857 (1000).
8th ed., 1858 (3500).
9th ed., 1861 (3500).
10th ed., 1863 (2500).
11th ed., 1865 (2000).
12th ed., 1867 (2000).
13th ed., 1868 (1000); reprinted 1869 (750).
14th ed., 1871 (2000); reprinted 1872 (1000).
15th ed., 1874 (2500).
16th ed., 1879 (2500).
17th ed., 1886 (1500).
18th ed., 1891 (2000); reprinted in two parts 1894.
19th ed., 1904.

All these editions except the last were published by Murray. The 19th edition was published by Stanford. There was also a separate edition, printed in France and published in Paris by Galignani in 1839, described as "a new edition enlarged, with Keller's map corrected". In 1844 Charles Jugel of

Frankfurt published a supplementary volume of *Illustrations to the Hand-book for Travellers on the Continent; comprising a Series of Maps of the most frequented Roads through Switzerland, Savoy and Piedmont . . . accompanied by Plans of the principal Towns . . . engraved . . . by J. Lehnhardt.* The town plans in this volume are particularly interesting.

During the 1860s Murray published a number of *Knapsack Guides*, which were cheaper, shorter and more popular than the *Handbooks*. The *Knapsack Guide for Travellers in Switzerland*, which claimed to be "a condensed and corrected version" of the *Handbook*, was published in 1864 and reprinted in 1867.

A

HAND-BOOK

FOR

TRAVELLERS IN SWITZERLAND,

SAVOY AND PIEDMONT.

The Editor of the HAND-BOOK for SWITZERLAND, PIEDMONT, and SAVOY, is very solicitous to be favoured with corrections of any mistakes and omissions which may be discovered by persons who have made use of the book. Those communications especially will be welcomed which are founded upon personal knowledge, and accompanied by the name of the writer, to authenticate them. Travellers willing to make such communications are requested to have the kindness to address them to the Editor of the HAND-BOOK, care of Mr. Murray, Albemarle-street.

A

HAND-BOOK

FOR

TRAVELLERS IN SWITZERLAND

AND THE

ALPS OF SAVOY AND PIEDMONT,

INCLUDING THE

PROTESTANT VALLEYS OF THE WALDENSES.

————————

LONDON:

JOHN MURRAY & SON, ALBEMARLE-STREET;

BLACK AND ARMSTRONG, LEIPSIG;

GALIGNANI, FRERES, PARIS.

———

MDCCCXXXVIII.

The Hand-Book for Travellers is published in Switzerland at—

AARAU	. . BY	SAUERLAENDER.
BASLE	. . .	SCHREIBER & WATZ.
BERN .	. . .	HUBER & CO.
BREGENZ .	. .	TEUTSCH.
CONSTANCE	. .	GLÜCKER.
CHUR .	. . .	GRUBENMANN.
FREIBURG	. .	HERDER.
ST. GALLEN	. .	HUBER.
GENEVA .	. .	KESSMANN.

LAUSANNE	. BY	GERS.
LUCERNE .	. .	MEYER.
MÜHLHAUSEN	.	ENGELMANN.
ROTWEIL.	. .	HERDER.
SCHAFFHAUSEN	.	HURTER.
SOLEURE	. .	REUTER.
STRASBURG	. .	LEVRAULT.
WINTERTHUR	.	STEINER.
ZÜRICH .	. .	H. FÜSSLI & CO.

In Germany, France, Holland, and Belgium, at—

AIX-LA-CHAPELLE }	BY	MAYER.
AMSTERDAM	.	NAYLER & CO.
AUGSBURG	.	KOLLMAN & CO.
BERLIN	.	DUNCKER.
BRUSSELS	.	PRATT & BARRY.
CARLSRUHE	.	CREUZBAUER & CO.
COBLENTZ	.	BAEDEKER.
COLOGNE	.	DUMONT SCHAUBERG.
DRESDEN	.	ARNOLD.
FRANKFURT	.	C. JÜGEL, F. WILMANS.
GRÄTZ	.	DAMIAN & SORGE.
HAMBURG	.	PERTHES, BESSER, & MAUKE.

LEIPZIG	BY	BROCKHAUS & AVENARIUS.
MANNHEIM	.	ARTARIA & FONTAINE.
MUNICH	.	LITERARISCH-ARTISTISCHE ANSTALT.
NÜRNBERG	.	RIEGEL & WIESSNER.
PESTH	.	HARTLEBEN.
PRAGUE	.	CALVE.
ROTTERDAM	.	A. BAEDEKER.
VIENNA	.	ROHRMANN & SCHWEIGERD, GEROLD, SCHAUMBURG.

PREFACE.

For a very long time Switzerland was the only country in Europe which possessed a *Guide-book*, worthy of the name. The excellent work of Ebel, here alluded to, indeed deserves the highest praise; and it is upon the foundation of the materials collected by him that every succeeding work of the same kind, on that country, has been laid. It is, however, voluminous, extending to four volumes: its arrangement and bulk fit it more for the library than the pocket, or even the travelling-carriage; and the abridged French translation is unskilfully made, inconvenient to consult, and full of gross errors. In addition to this, the original work was written more than forty years ago, and was not corrected at the time of the author's death. In consequence of this, and owing to the great changes which have been made in every part of Switzerland since its publication, a portion of the information is necessarily antiquated. The improvements of roads, the opening of new passes over the Alps, the establishment of steam-boats, and the increased facilities of locomotion, have given rise to a thoroughly different system of travelling. Most valuable contributions to our stock of knowledge, respecting the natural history, resources, &c., of Switzerland, have been made since his time; the geology of the country has assumed a totally different aspect; and the ancient political forms are now scarcely recognised since the recent revolutions.

The Editor of the present work has great pleasure in acknowledging his obligations to Ebel, as well as to the later writers on the country, especially to the scientific researches of Agassiz, Hugi, and Studer, to the compilations of Glutz Blotzheim and Bollman, and to the recent publication entitled " Gemälde der Schweitz." Nor is he less indebted to his own countrymen, having found the greatest assistance from the accurate and interesting works of Brockedon* and Latrobe†. For his own part, he has brought to the task the

---

* The Passes of the Alps, 2 vols. 4to.; and Excursions among the Alps.
† The Alpenstock and The Pedestrian.

experience gained in four different visits to the country, in the course of which he left but a small portion of it unexplored. Notwithstanding this, he cannot speak of the Hand-book for Switzerland with less diffidence than he did of the volumes relating to Germany which have preceded it ; and he must equally trust in the indulgence of his readers to excuse numerous inaccuracies which no doubt pervade it.

He has, however, no hesitation in speaking of the merits of the second section of this volume, relating to Savoy and Piedmont, which has been prepared by a friend and fellow-traveller, most intimately acquainted with those countries, which he has explored in almost every direction, and on many different occasions. The routes contained in it possess great interest, from the total want of any other information respecting the country they traverse, from the extreme accuracy with which they are described, and from their being derived, not from books, but from personal knowledge. They will probably be the means of throwing open to English travellers a region little visited hitherto, but possessing, from its romantic beauties, the highest claim to attention.

SWITZERLAND.

CONTENTS.

INTRODUCTORY INFORMATION.

CONTENTS OF SECTION I.

SWITZERLAND.

LIST OF ROUTES.

•₊• The names of many places are necessarily repeated in several Routes; but, to facilitate reference, they are printed in *Italics* only in those Routes under which they are fully described.

SECTION II.

THE ALPS OF SAVOY AND PIEDMONT.

Preliminary Information—Page 226.
Skeleton Tours—Page 228.

INTRODUCTORY INFORMATION.

§ 1. PASSPORTS.

A TRAVELLER cannot reach Switzerland without a passport from a minister of one or other of the states of Europe ; and, though it is seldom called for while he is in the country, yet he must be prepared to produce it whenever it is required. At the gates of Geneva, and perhaps in one or two other capitals of the cantons, passports are demanded on entering. Persons proceeding from Switzerland to the Austrian states, or Bavaria, must have the signature of the ministers of those countries attached to their passports ; or they will not be allowed to pass across the frontier. The ministers accredited to the Swiss Confederation reside at Bern, or at least have their passport-offices there; even when they themselves follow the Diet either to Zurich or Lucerne. Strangers, therefore, should take care to secure their *visé* as they pass through Bern. See Route 24, p. 67, for further particulars.

In going from Geneva to Chamouny, the signature of the Sardinian Consul is made a *sine quâ non*, in order to secure to that official a fee of four francs.

§ 2. MONEY.

There is hardly a country in Europe which has so complicated a Currency as Switzerland ; almost every canton has a Coinage of its own, and those coins that are current in one canton will not pass in the next. Let the traveller, therefore, be cautious how he overloads himself with more small change than he is sure of requiring.

Detailed tables of Swiss coins are given below, but it is scarcely worth the traveller's while to perplex himself with their intricacies ; since he will find French Napoleons and francs current nearly all over Switzerland. They are indeed, on the whole, the best coins he can take with him ; and, except in some very remote situations, on the east side of the country, in the cantons of St. Gall, Appenzell, and Grisons, which border on Germany, and where Bavarian florins (= 20 pence) and kreutzers are in common circulation, the innkeepeers always make out their bills in Fr. francs, or will do so if required.

It is necessary, however, to prevent being cheated, that the traveller should know the value of one or two Swiss coins.

1 Swiss franc, containing 10 batz = 1½ French franc (1 franc 48 cents.), = (nearly) 1*s.* 2*d.* English.

N.B. This distinction between the value of French and Swiss francs should be particularly attended to.

1 batz contains 10 rappen, and = 1½*d.* (nearly) English.

The Swiss coins most frequently met with are pieces of 5 batzen, or ½ a Swiss franc ; 1 batz, ½ batz, and rappen. Pieces are also coined of 1, 2, 3, and 4 Swiss francs.

Value of some Foreign Coins in Swiss Currency.

1 French Napoleon = 14 Swiss francs.
1   „   5 franc-piece = from 33¾ to 35 batzen.

1 French franc = (commonly) 7 batzen or exactly 6 batzen 8 rapps.
1 English shilling = 9 batzen.
1   ,,   sovereign = 17 Swiss francs 4 batzen 6 rapps.
1 Brabant dollar = 4 Swiss francs, or 40 batzen.
[The Brabant dollar (kronthaler,' or grosse thaler) is an advantageous coin to take into the German cantons, since, although it is worth only 5 Fr. fr. 80 cents., it passes throughout for 6 francs.]

SWISS FRANCS AND BATZEN,—*Reduced to their Value in the Money of*

Swiss Francs of 10 Batzen.		Prussia. Dollar of 30 Silver Gros.		Saxony. Dollars of 24 Groschen.		Bavaria. Florins of 60 Kreutzers = 20d.		France. Francs of 100 Centimes.		England. Pound Sterling of 20 Shillings.		
Fr.	B.	D.	Gr.	D.	Gr.	F.	Kr.	Fr.	C.	£.	s.	d.
—	1	—	1,2	—	—,9	—	4,1	—	15	—	—	1,4
—	2	—	2,4	—	1,8	—	8,3	—	30	—	—	2,8
—	3	—	3,6	—	2,8	—	12,4	—	44	—	—	4,1
—	4	—	4,8	—	3,7	—	16,5	—	59	—	—	5,5
—	5	—	6,—	—	4,6	—	20,6	—	74	—	—	6,9
—	6	—	7,2	—	5,5.	—	24,8	—	89	—	—	8,2
—	7	—	8,4	—	6,4	—	28,9	1	4	—	—	9,6
—	8	—	9,6	—	7,3	—	33,—	1	19	—	—	11,—
—	9	—	10,8	—	8,3	—	37,1	1	33	—	1	—,4
1	—	—	12,—	—	9,2	—	41,3	1	48	—	1	1,8
2	—	—	24,1	—	18,3	1	22,5	2	96	—	2	3,5
3	—	1	6,1	1	3,5	2	3,8	4	44	—	3	5,3
4	—	1	18,1	1	12,7	2	45,—	5	93	—	4	7,—
5	—	2	—,2	1	21,8	3	26,3	7	41	—	5	8,8
6	—	2	12,2	2	7,—	4	7,5	8	89	—	6	10,5
7	—	2	24,2	2	16,2	4	48,8	10	37	—	8	—,3
8	—	3	6,3	3	1,3	5	30,—	11	85	—	9	2,—
9	—	3	18,3	3	10,5	6	11,3	13	33	—	10	3,8
10	—	4	—,3	3	19,7	6	52,5	14	82	—	11	5,5
20	—	8	—,6	7	15,3	13	45,—	29	63	1	2	11,—
30	—.	12	—,9	11	11,—	20	37,5	44	45	1	14	4,5
40	—	16	1,2	15	6,6	27	30,—	59	26	2	5	10,—
50	—	20	1,6	19	2,3	34	22,5	74	7	2	17	3,5
60	—	24	1,9	22	22,—	41	15,—	88	89	3	8	9,—
70	—	28	2,2	26	17,6	48	7,5	103	70	4	—	2,5
80	—	32	2,5	30	13,3	55	—,—	118	52	4	11	8,—
90	—	36	2,8	34	8,9	61	52,5	133	33	5	3	1,5
100	—	40	3,1	38	4,7	68	45,—	148	15	5	14	7,—

FRENCH FRANCS AND CENTIMES COMPARED WITH SWISS FRANCS
AND BATZEN.

French Francs.		Swiss Francs. 1 Fr. of 10 Btz. 1 Btz. of 10 Rapps.			French Francs.		Swiss Francs. 1 Fr. of 10 Btz. 1 Btz. of 10 Rapps.		
Fr.	C.	Fr.	Bz.	R.	Fr.	C.	Fr.	Bz.	R.
—	5	—	0	3	14	—	9	5	2
—	10	—	0	7	15	—	10	2	0
—	15	—	1	0	16	—	10	8	8
—	20	—	1	3	17	—	11	5	6
—	25	—	1	7	18	—	12	2	4
—	30	—	2	0	19	—	12	9	2
—	35	—	2	3	20	—	13	6	0
—	40	—	2	6					
—	45	—	3	0	21	—	14	2	8
					22	—	14	9	6
—	50	—	3	3	23	—	15	6	4
—	55	—	3	7	24	—	16	3	2
—	60	—	4	0	25	—	17	0	0
—	65	—	4	3	26	—	17	6	8
—	70	—	4	7	27	—	18	3	6
—	75	—	5	0	28	—	19	0	4
—	80	—	5	4	29	—	19	7	2
—	85	—	5	7	30	—	20	4	0
—	90	—	6	1					
—	95	—	6	5	35	—	23	8	0
					40	—	27	2	0
1	—	—	6	8	45	—	30	6	0
2	—	1	3	6	50	—	34	0	0
3	—	2	0	4	55	—	37	4	0
4	—	2	7	2	60	—	40	8	0
5	—	3	4	0	65	—	44	2	0
6	—	4	0	8	70	—	47	6	0
7	—	4	7	6	75	—	51	0	0
8	—	5	4	4	80	—	54	4	0
9	—	6	1	2					
10	—	6	8	0	85	—	57	8	0
					90	—	61	2	0
11	—	7	4	8	95	—	64	6	0
12	—	8	1	6	100	—	68	0	0
13	—	8	8	4					

₊ In many instances, the coins in the following tables are
almost obsolete; and, where they still exist, French francs and Swiss
batzen are also current, so that the traveller need rarely have recourse to them.

Aarau, Bern, Basle, Freyburg, Soleure, Vaud, and *Vallais.*

These cantons combined together in 1825 to adopt an uniform currency.

Swiss franc = 10 batzen.
„   batz. = 10 rapps.
„   Gulden = 15 batzen = 60 kreutzers.

Appenzell, St. Gall, Schaffhausen, and Thurgovie.

Accounts are kept in florins (24 gulden foot, as in Frankfort, Baden, &c.).

1 florin, of 60 kreutzers = 20*d.* English.

1 Napoleon	=	9 florins	21 kreutzers.
1 Brabant dollar	=	2 fl.	42 kr.
1 Ducat	=	5 fl.	30 kr.
1 Convention dollar	=	2 fl.	24 kr.

Geneva.

a Florins (petite monnaie) containing 12 sols = 12 deniers.
b Livres, courants of   20 sols = 42 deniers.
c French francs and centimes
d Swiss francs, and batzen

		Genevese Currency.			
		Liv.	Sol.	Den.	Fl.	Den.
1 French 5-franc piece	=	3	1	9 or	10	10
1 French franc	=	26 Genevese Sols.				
1 Brabant dollar	=	3	10	9 or	12	4

(The Pound sterling is usually worth 25 fr. 50 c.)

Glarus.

1 Florin or Gulden = 40 schillings.

Grisons.

Florin contains 15 (light) batzen, 60 kreutzers, or 70 blutzgers = 1 French franc 76 centimes = 16*d.* English.

Brabant dollar	= 3 Gr. florins	20 kreutzers.
French Napoleon	= 11 fl.	36 kr.
„ 5-franc piece	= 2 fl.	53 kr.
„ 1 franc	=	34 kr.
Swiss franc	=	51 kr.
„ piece of 5 batzen	= one fl.	30 blutzgers.
„ „ 1 batz	=	6 blutzgers.
1 Bavarian florin	=	1 Grison florin 14 kreutzers.
2 Zwanzigers	=	1 Grison florin „

Lucerne and Unterwalden.

Florin of 15 (light) batzen, or 40 schillings, or 60 kreutzers.

1 Louis d'or   = 12 florins of Lucerne.
1 5-franc piece = 2 florins of Lucerne. 22 schillings.

Neuchâtel.

Livres of Neuchâtel of 20 sols and 12 deniers.

Louis d'or = 16⅙ Neuchâtel livres.

Schwytz and Uri.

Florin of 15 (light) batzen, or 40 schillings, or 60 kreutzers.

Louis d'or ⚌ 13 florins of Schwytz.

Ticino (*Tessin*).

The lira contains 20 soldi, each of 4 quatrini.

Louis d'or = from 34 to $37\frac{1}{2}$ lire.

Zurich.

Florin = 16 (good) batzen = 60 kreutzers = 2 French francs 35 cents. =
1 Bavarian florin 6 kreutzers.

Brabant dollar	= 2 Zurich florins 27 kreutzers.
French 5-franc piece	= $2\frac{1}{8}$ Zurich florins
„ 20-franc „	= $8\frac{1}{2}$ Zurich florins.

The Zurich florin is also divided into 16 (good) batzen and 40 rapps, and
again into 40 schillings of 4 rapps each.

In August, 1834, twelve of the cantons* agreed to appoint a commission to examine into the present complicated currency, and to
devise a new and uniform system of coinage. They have already
altered and corrected the weights and measures of Switzerland, but
the result of their labours regarding the currency has not yet
appeared.

§ 3. DISTANCES.

There is not less perplexity and variation in the measurement of
distances, than in the calculation of money, in Switzerland.

Distances are reckoned throughout Switzerland not by miles, but
by *stunden* (hours, *i. e.* hours' walking) or leagues. The measures
of length given in the following routes have been taken from the
most perfect tables that could be procured; but the Editor is aware
that there must be many errors, and that an *approach* to *accuracy*
is all that can be expected from them. The length of the stunde
has been calculated at 5278 mètres, or 2708 toises=1800 Bernese
feet; 21,137 of such stunden go to a degree of the equator. To make
this measurement agree with the actual pace of walking, it is necessary to advance 271 Paris feet in a minute.

It is a reproach to the Swiss Government that no authorised measurement of the roads throughout the country should have been undertaken by them at the public expense. Since the correction of
weights and measures in 1833-34, 3-10ths of a mètre (= 3 decimètres,
or 132,988 Paris lines) has been constituted the legal Swiss foot, and
16,000 Swiss feet=1 stunde.

§ 5. MODES OF TRAVELLING IN SWITZERLAND.—POSTING.

The means of travelling in Switzerland have been greatly improved and increased within the last fifteen or twenty years. The

---

* Zurich, Bern, Lucerne, Zug, Glarus, Freyburg, Soleure, Basle, Schaffhausen, St. Gall,
Aargovie, and Thurgovie.

great roads are excellent, and those over the Alps stupendous in addition ; upon almost all of them diligences run; and since 1823, when the first experiment with steam was made on the Lake of Geneva, every one of the large lakes is navigated by steam-boats.

Posting is unknown in most of the cantons of Switzerland, and is confined to the following routes near the frontier:—From Constance to St. Gall and through the Grisons to Coire; over the Splügen to Chiavenna and Milan; over the Bernardin to Bellinzona, Lugano, and Milan ; from Geneva to Milan over the Simplon, along both shores of the Lake Leman, by Lausanne or by Thonon; from Airolo at the south base of the St. Gothard to Bellinzona. The traveller may likewise post from Basle to Schaffhausen, and from Schaffhausen to Constance, if he choose the routes through Baden on the right bank of the Rhine. It is stated that post-horses are kept in Canton Argovie, between Basle and Schaffhausen, and in Neuchâtel, but on this point the writer cannot speak with certainty. The tariff and charges for horses and postilions vary in the different cantons, but the regulations of the adjoining states are for the most part followed. For instance, in Thurgovie and St. Gall the charges are according to the Baden tariff; in Geneva, Vaud, and the Vallais, according to the French ; and in the Grisons, according to the Austrian. Further particulars are given in the respective routes upon which post-horses are maintained.

At Coire, and other post stations on the great road through the Grisons, the post-masters give the traveller a printed ticket, containing the details of all charges according to the distance and number of horses.

₊ It is very generally asserted that the Diet is about to authorise the establishment of post-horses throughout Switzerland, and that this new enactment may be expected to come into force next year.

§ 6. DILIGENCES.—LUGGAGE.

Diligences now run *daily* between most of the large towns of Switzerland, and there are few carriage-roads in the country not traversed by them twice or thrice a week at least.

They generally belong to the government of the different cantons, and are attached to the post-office, as in Germany. The places are numbered, and all baggage exceeding a certain fixed weight is charged extra, and often greatly increases the expense of this mode of conveyance, which is one reason among many why travellers should reduce their baggage to the smallest possible compass. The public conveyances are by no means so well organised as in Germany. On some routes, particularly in going from one canton into another, passengers are sometimes transferred into another coach, and run the chance of waiting several hours for it, being set down in a remote spot to pass the interval as they may, and this not unfrequently in the middle of the night.

The conducteur's fee is included in the fare, but the postilion's trinkgeld is paid separately by the passengers in some parts of the country ; in St. Gall, for instance, they expect from 6 to 9 kr. per stage.

Travellers in Switzerland will frequently be glad to avail themselves of the public conveyances to forward their *luggage* from one place to another, while they are making pedestrian excursions among the mountains. In such cases, they have only to book their packages at the coach-office, after carefully addressing them, and, in some cases, entering a specification of their value in a printed form. They will then receive a receipt, and the article will be forwarded and taken care of until reclaimed.

In making application for packages so consigned, as well as for letters at the post-office, the Englishman should present his name in writing, as our pronunciation is frequently unintelligible to foreigners, and without this precaution the applicant may be told that his luggage has not arrived, when in reality it is all the while lying in the depôt. The traveller may also request to look over the packages in search of his own.

§ 7. VOITURIER.—LOHNKUTSCHER.

Posting, except along the few routes mentioned already in p. 111, ceases at the Swiss frontier, and those who have been travelling post must therefore engage a voiturier at the first Swiss town, with a suitable number of horses to draw their carriage. If it be light, and the party small, two horses will suffice ; but the coachman must then drive from the box ; with a heavy carriage, three or four horses must be taken, and the driver will ride as postilion. The towns of Basle, Schaffhausen, Zurich, Bern, Thun, Lausanne, and Geneva, are the head-quarters of the voituriers; at all of them there are many persons who keep job-horses for hire, and will either conduct the traveller themselves, or send coachmen in their employ. At most of the frontier towns *return* horses are to be met with, and the traveller may save some days of back fare by availing himself of them.

Before making an engagement, it is prudent to consult the landlord of the inn or some other respectable inhabitant—(N.B. not the waiter)—to recommend a person of approved character to be employed. As there are many very roguish voituriers, ready to take advantage of the traveller on all occasions, such a recommendation will be a guarantee, to a certain extent, for good behaviour. The landlord should be referred to apart, not in the presence of the coachman, nor, indeed, with his cognizance. It is a bad plan to intrust a waiter or inferior person with the negociation ; he will most probably sell the traveller to the voiturier, and make a job for his own advantage. The most judicious mode of proceeding is, to discard all go-betweens and subordinates, to insist on seeing the principal, the owner of the horses, and to make the bargain at once with him. Besides ascertaining that the voiturier is a respectable man, that his horses are good, and his carriage (when it also is required) be clean and stout, it is desirable in many cases that he should speak French as well as German, and, in all, that he be acquainted with the roads to be traversed. The engagement should, in the first instance, not be made for any specific time, at least not for a long period, until man and horses have been tried and have given satisfaction. It is better to take him on from day to day, holding out the prospect of his being continued if he behaves well.

Some persons engage a voiturier for a certain sum, to perform a stated journey in a fixed number of days; a bad plan, since it ties down the traveller to a prescribed route, without the power of diverging, if he choose to alter his plans, or of tarrying by the way. The employer should reserve to himself the power of dismissing his voiturier as soon as he reaches a post-road (see the map).

The *established charge* throughout Switzerland, *per diem*, is 9 Fr. francs for each horse, and 1 Fr. franc per horse *trinkgeld* for the driver. This includes the hire of a carriage when wanted.

For this consideration the coachman keeps himself and his horses, supplying fresh ones if his own fall ill or lame : he ought also to pay all tolls, and the charge for leaders (vorspann) to drag the carriage up steep ascents. These two last conditions, however, are not always acceded to, and these charges often fall upon the master.

When the traveller has no servant of his own, the voiturier cleans the carriage, greases the wheels, and assists in packing and unpacking the baggage.

The usual rate of travelling is from ten to fourteen stunden, thirty-two to forty-six miles a-day, proceeding at the rate of about five miles an-hour—ten stunden a-day should be guaranteed by the driver. It is necessary to halt in the middle of the day, about two hours, to rest the horses. On the days during which a halt is made in a town or elsewhere, the charge is reduced one-half; and, should the traveller require the horses for a short drive of an hour or two through the town, this should make no difference.

Back-Fare.—In addition to the daily charges while employed, the voiturier requires, if dismissed at a distance from his own home, to be paid back-fare for the number of days necessary to take him thither. This payment should be calculated at the rate of the longest day's journey, say twelve stunden (nearly forty miles), which is not too much with an empty carriage. At this rate, the back-fare to be paid between some of the principal places in Switzerland would be nearly according to the number of days set down in the following table :—

	Stunden.	Days of Back-Fare.
Basle to Bern	18½	1½
„ Coire	41	3½
„ Geneva	44	3½
„ Lausanne	33½	2⅔
„ Lucerne	19	1½
„ Neuchâtel	22	2
„ Zurich	16⅓	1½

		Stunden.	Days of Back-Fare.
Geneva to	Berne	28½	2
,,	Coire	76	6
,,	Neuchâtel	22⅔	2
,,	Schaffhausen	54	4
,,	Soleure	33	2½
,,	Zurich	51½	4
,,	Lucerne	46	3½

It is more for the traveller's advantage to take one set of horses through the journey than to trust to the chance of engaging them from one town to another—a method, subject to delay and vexation from the uncertainty of finding them at all times, and from the manœuvres of petty inn-keepers, who will often pretend that none are to be had, and will throw every impediment in the way of his departure. Besides which, by such an arrangement, the employer must inevitably pay back-fare for every day, whereas, if he engage the same voiturier for a length of time, he may so arrange his tour, in a circle as it were, as to discharge him within one or two days' journey from his home, and thus considerably reduce the amount of the back-fare.

It is advisable before setting out to have an agreement drawn up in writing, including the stipulations which have been recounted above. A piece of money, called in German *daraufgeld*, in Italian *la caparra*, is then given by one of the contracting parties to the other, after which the bargain is held to be concluded.

There are many excursions in Switzerland that are not to be made in a travelling-carriage : in such cases it must either wait for the traveller, or be sent round to meet him at an appointed spot.

The system of vetturino travelling, with all its advantages and disadvantages, has been so fully explained in the Handbook for North Germany, that it is unnecessary to enter again into fuller details here than have been given above.

§ 8. CHARS-A-BANC.

The char-à-banc, the national carriage of Switzerland, may be described as the body of a gig, or a bench, as its name implies, placed sideways upon four wheels, at a very little distance from the ground. It is surrounded by leather curtains made to draw, whence it has been compared to a four-post bedstead on wheels. There is a larger kind of char, in which the benches are suspended by thongs, not springs, across a kind of long waggon, and are arranged one behind the other. The char-à-banc is a very strong and light vehicle, capable of carrying two persons, or three at a pinch, and will go on roads where no other species of carriage could venture. It is convenient, from being so low that one can jump in, or alight without stopping the horse, while it is going on ; but it is a very jolting conveyance. Such a carriage is to be hired even in the smallest Swiss villages, and the usual *charge*, including the driver, is twelve French francs a-day ;

but the charge will be doubled by back-fare if the driver cannot reach home the same night, after the time when he is dismissed.

§ 9. GUIDES—PORTERS.—CHAISES-A-PORTEURS.

The services of a Guide are needful when the traveller is about to plunge into the recesses of the mountains on foot. He makes himself useful, not only in pointing out the way, but in acting as interpreter to those unacquainted with the language of the country, and also in relieving the traveller of the weight of his knapsack or travelling-bag. He may be said to be indispensable in ascending very lofty mountains, in exploring glaciers, and in crossing the minor passes of the Alps, not traversed by high roads, but by mere bridle or foot-paths, which, being rarely traversed, and in many places not distinctly marked, or confounded with innumerable tracks of cattle, will often bewilder the inexperienced traveller not acquainted with the mountains. When snow is threatening to fall, or after a snow-storm has covered the path and obliterated the footsteps of preceding travellers, a guide may be required in situations where, under ordinary circumstances, his presence might be dispensed with.

Guides by profession are to be met with in most parts of Switzerland; those of Chamouni (in Savoy) are deservedly renowned, being regularly bred to their profession, and subjected to examination as to character and fitness before they are admitted into the fraternity. They are enrolled in a corps, placed under the control of a syndic appointed by the Sardinian Government. (Route 115.) In Switzerland they abound at Interlachen and Thun, Lucerne, and all the other starting-points from which pedestrian excursions are begun. Here, again, the traveller had better trust to the innkeeper to recommend a fit person ; but it is advisable not to hire one for a length of time beforehand. He ought not to be too far advanced in years.

The established rate of hire is six French francs a-day ; but, in addition to this, there will be a claim for money to return, if dismissed at a distance from home, unless the employer find him a fresh master to take back. For this sum the guide provides for himself, and is expected to discharge all the duties of a domestic towards his employer.

For the most part, the guides may be said to be obliging, intelligent, and hard-working men. Few who have employed them but can bear testimony to their coolness, intrepidity, and tact, in moments of danger—in the difficult pass, in the midst of the snow-storm, or among the gaping clefts of the glaciers. It is in such situations that their knowledge of the mountains, their experience of the weather, their strong arm and steady foot, are fully appreciated. The traveller should always follow the guide in crossing glaciers, and, in going over tracts covered with snow, should allow him to choose what his experience teaches to be the safest path. In dangerous situations the guide advances a-head, with cautious step, sounding with his pole beforehand as in a sea beset with shoals.

A little civility and familiarity on the part of the employer—the offer of a cigar from the traveller's own case, or a glass of brandy from his private flask—will rarely be thrown away; on the contrary, it is likely to produce assiduity and communicativeness on the part of the guide. Many of them are fine athletic men, and to carry for 8 or 10 hours a-day, and for a distance of 25 or 30 miles, a load of 30 or 40 lbs. weight is made light of by them.

Some travellers content themselves with Keller's excellent map to guide them, and employ a mere porter to carry their baggage for them. Such a man is paid less than the professional guides; 3 or 4 fr. a-day will suffice for them; others are satisfied with taking a guide only to cross the mountains, from one valley into another, where, as before observed, they are really indispensable. Those who travel in chars or on horseback will find that the driver, or the man who accompanies the horse, will usually serve as guide, and render unnecessary the employment of any other person in that capacity. At Chamouni, however, the guides must be hired distinct from the mules. Let it be observed that, when the travelling party includes ladies, a guide is required to attend on each, during a mountain excursion, to lead down the horses, where the path is steep, and to lend their arms to the fair travellers, when the exigences of the way require them to dismount, and proceed on foot.

Even the aged or invalid female is by no means debarred the pleasure of taking a part in difficult mountain expeditions. Those who are too infirm either to walk or ride, may be carried over the mountains in a " *chaise-à-porteurs* " (Germ. Tragsessel), which is nothing more than a chair, carried in the manner of a sedan, upon poles, by two bearers; two extra bearers must be taken to relieve in turn, and every man expects 6 fr. per diem, and 3 fr. return-money for the days required to reach home.

§ 10. HORSES AND MULES.

Previous to 1800, or even later, until Napoleon commenced the magnificent carriage-roads over the Alps, which will assist in immortalising his name, the only mode of conveying either passengers or goods across them was on the back of horses or mules. Even now, upon all the minor passes, almost the entire traffic is carried on by means of them. In other instances, where the beauties of scenery attract an influx of strangers, mules are kept for their conveyance, even where they are not required for the transport of merchandise.

The customary hire of a horse or mule throughout Switzerland, generally fixed by a printed tariff, amounts to 9 fr. a-day, including the man who takes care of it; at Chamouni it is 6 fr., but there a guide must also be taken. Back-fare must be paid if the animals are dismissed at a distance from home, and at so late an hour of the day that they cannot return before night.

The ponies that are used in the Bernese Oberland, on the Righi, and in other parts of Switzerland, are clever animals, that will carry you up and down ascents perfectly impracticable to horses unused to the mountains; but they are far distanced by the mules of Chamouni and other parts of Savoy. Their sagacity, strength, and sureness of foot, are really wonderful. The paths which they ascend or descend with ease are steeper than any staircase, with ledges of rock, 2 or 3 ft. high, instead of steps. Sometimes they are covered with broken fragments, between which they must pick their way, at the risk of breaking their legs; at others, they traverse a narrow ledge of the mountain, with an abyss on one side and a wall of rock on the other; and here the mule invariably walks on the very verge of the precipice—a habit derived from the animal's being accustomed to carry large packages of merchandise, which, if allowed to strike against the rock on one side, would destroy the mule's balance, and jostle him overboard. In such dangerous passes, the caution of the animal is very remarkable: he needs no rein to guide him, but will pick his own way, and find out the best path, far better than his rider can direct him; and, in such circumstances, it is safer to let the reins hang loose, and trust entirely to his sagacity, than to perplex him by checking him with the curb, at a moment when, by confusing the animal, there will be risk of his losing his footing, and perhaps tumbling headlong.

It is interesting to observe the patient animal, on reaching dangerous ground, smelling with his nose down like a dog, and trying the surface with his foot, before he will advance a step, as the poet has accurately described him:—

"Shunning the loose stone on the precipice—
Snorting suspicion—while with sight, smell, touch,
Trying, detecting, where the surface smiled;
And, with deliberate courage, sliding down,
Where, in his sledge, the Laplander had turn'd
With looks aghast."—*Rogers.*

§ 11. SWISS INNS.

Switzerland is well provided with inns; and those of the large towns, such as the Faucon, at Berne, the Bergues and Couronne, at Geneva, the Bellevue, at Thun, the Three Kings, at Basle, yield, in extent and good management, to few hotels in either France or Germany. The great annual influx of strangers into the country is of the same importance to Switzerland that some additional branch of industry or commerce would be, and renders the profession of host most lucrative. Many of the Swiss innkeepers are very wealthy, and it is not uncommon to find an individual in this capacity who is landamman or chief magistrate of the canton.

The approach to one of the first-rate hotels in the large towns, in the height of summer, exhibits rather a characteristic spectacle. The street before it is usually filled with several rows of vehicles of all sorts, from the dirty and rickety calèche of the German voiturier, to the neat chariot of the English peer, and the less elegant, but equally imposing, equipage of the Russian prince. Before the doorway is invariably grouped a crowd of loitering servants and couriers, of all nations and languages, and two or three knots of postilions and coachmen on the look-out for employment. During the height of the season, should the traveller arrive late in the evening, the chances are against his being admitted, unless he have sent or written beforehand to secure rooms. This object may sometimes be effected by the means of the courier of another party about to set out at an earlier hour.

Couriers, voituriers, guides, and boatmen, are apt sometimes to sell their employers to the innkeepers for a gratuity, so that travellers should not always implicitly follow the recommendations of such persons regarding inns; and it is hoped that the list of inns, drawn up with much care, and given in this book, will render the traveller in future more independent of their recommendations. The innkeepers hitherto have been very much at the mercy of this class of persons, who invariably fare sumptuously, and certainly not at their own expense. It not unfrequently happens that the attendance which ought to be bestowed on the master is lavished upon his menials. Whenever a new inn is started, it is almost invariably by the lavish distribution of high gratuities to coachmen, couriers, and the like, and by pampering them with the best fare, that the landlord endeavours to fill his house, to the prejudice both of the comfort and the purse of their masters. With few exceptions, therefore (which are specified in the following pages), the writer has generally found himself best off in the old-established houses.

It may be laid down as a general rule, that the wants, tastes, and habits of the English are more carefully and successfully studied in the Swiss inns than even in those of Germany. Thus, at most of the large inns, there is a late table-d'hôte dinner at 4 or 5 o'clock, expressly for the English; and the luxury of tea may always be had in perfection. Cleanliness is to be met with almost everywhere, until you reach the S. slopes of the Alps and the approach to Italy. In canton Bern, in particular, the inns, even in the small and remote villages, are patterns of neatness, such as even fastidious travellers may be contented with.

The usual charges are, for dinner at the early table-d'hôte— 3 Fr. fr.=20 batz. Later ditto, 4 or 5 Fr. fr.

Dinner, in private, 6 fr. per head for 1 or 2 persons, at the more expensive inns; and from 3 to 5 fr. per head for a party at smaller inns.

Beds, 1½ to 2 fr.=10 to 13½ batz.

Breakfast, 1½ to 2 fr.=10 to 14 batz.

Tea, 1½ fr.

To this is added, in most of the larger inns, a charge of 1 fr. for a wax candle, to swell the bill.

The charges for rooms vary according to their situation on the lower floors and the views they command; but the best suite of apartments, in first-rate inns, ought not to exceed 4 fr. a-day, for a sitting-room or salon, and 3 fr. for each bed.

It must be remembered that there are generally two sets of charges, one for natives, or Germans, and another for the English, on the principle, that the latter have both longer purses, and also more numerous wants, and are more difficult to serve.

The servants are remunerated nearly as in Germany—1 fr. a-day is ample from each person for the whole household, including the cleaning of clothes, boots, and shoes.

It is often remarked by the English that the Germans pay very little to the servants at inns; but they should bear in mind how much less trouble the Germans give, and how slight the attendance which they require generally speaking.

French is almost invariably spoken at the inns, even in the German cantons, except in remote parts, as in the side valleys of the Grisons. Nevertheless, the German language is a very valuable acquisition to the traveller.

Swiss inns have, in general, the reputation of being expensive, and the innkeepers of being extortionate. A recent journey through the greater part of the country has scarcely afforded an instance of either; but, where such cases have occurred, notice has been taken of them in the following pages. At minor and remote inns manœuvres are sometimes resorted to for the purpose of detaining the guests.

Among the mountains the traveller may obtain, in perfection, the small alpine trout, which are of great excellence; sometimes, also, chamois venison, which, by the way, is far inferior to park venison; wild strawberries are very abundant, and, with a copious admixture of delicious cream, the staple commodity of the Alps,—are by no means to be despised.

Those who enter a Swiss inn, tired, hot, and thirsty, after a long walk or dusty ride, may ask for a bottle of " limonade gazeuse," under which name they will recognise a drink nearly resembling ginger beer, but with more acidity, and, when good, very refreshing. It supplies here the place of hock and Seltzer-water on the Rhine.

The best Swiss wines are those of Neuchâtel and Vaud; such as they are procured at inns, they merit no great praise. An effervescing sweet Sardinian wine (vin d'Asti) is common, and may be resorted to for a change.

§ 12.—DIRECTIONS FOR TRAVELLERS, AND REQUISITES FOR A JOURNEY IN SWITZERLAND.

The *best season* for travelling among the Alps is the months of July, August, and September, in which may, perhaps, be included the last half of June. The higher Alpine passes are scarcely clear of snow before the second week of June; and before the middle of October, though the weather is often still serene, the nights draw in so fast as to curtail, inconveniently, the day's journey. During the long days, one may get over a great deal of ground. The judicious traveller will economize the daylight by rising, and setting forth as soon after sun-rise as possible.

The *average daily expense* of living at the best inns in Switzer-

land will vary between 8 Fr. fr. and 10 fr. a-day, excluding all charge
for conveyances, horses, and guides. The pedestrian who, with Keller
in his pocket, can dispense with a guide, may travel in the remoter
valleys of Switzerland at the rate of 5 to 7 fr. a-day, provided he
knows German and French. The German students, who understand the art of travelling economically, always proceed in a party,
and usually send on one of their number a-head, to their intended
night-quarters, to make terms with the innkeeper. There is this
advantage in travelling with a party, that numbers are more welcomed
at an inn and better attended than a solitary individual ; on the
other hand, when inns are full, few stand a better chance than many.
All arrangements for the hire of carriages, horses, or guides, should be
concluded over-night: he that waits till the morning will generally
find either the conveyances engaged by others, or the price demanded
for them increased, and, at all events, his departure delayed.

Saussure recommends those who are inexperienced in Alpine
travelling to accustom themselves for some time before they set
out to look down from heights and over precipices, so that, when
they really enter upon a dangerous path, the eye may be fami-
liarized with the depths of the abyss, and the aspect of danger, and
the head relieved from the vertigo which the sudden sight of a precipice is otherwise apt to produce.

It is scarcely necessary to repeat the caution against " drinking
cold water" or cold milk, when heated ; but the guides, and natives
accustomed to mountain travelling, never drink before resting ;
exercise afterwards will render the draught harmless.

It is tiresome and unprofitable in the extreme to walk along a level
road at the bottom of a valley, where conveyances are to be had,
and there is a carriage-road : here it is best to ride ; the expense in
money is counterbalanced by the economy of time.

In crossing one of the minor passes of the Alps — those not
traversed by carriage-roads, but merely by foot or bridle-paths—a
guide should always be taken, as, in the upper part of the valleys,
such paths almost invariably disappear, and become confounded
with the foot-tracks of the cattle. This rule should especially be
observed when the pass terminates in snow or glacier. It is also
advisable to eschew short cuts, remembering the old proverb of
" the longest way round."

After the middle of June, the season for travelling in Switzerland,
there is little danger to be feared from *avalanches,* except immediately after snow-storms, which constantly occur among the high
Alps, even in the height of summer. The precautions to be adopted
in crossing spots exposed to avalanches are stated in § 18.

It is rash to attempt to cross a *glacier* without a guide, and he
should always be allowed to take the lead, and the traveller follow
his footsteps. The few instances of fatal accidents occurring to
strangers among the Alps arise from their either not taking a guide
with them, or neglecting to follow his advice. In the same way, in
traversing *Swiss lakes,* notorious for their sudden storms, implicit
reliance should be placed on the advice of the boatmen, and no

attempt should be made to induce them to launch their boats when they foresee danger.

Avoid, sedulously, stopping for the night near the embouchure of a river, where it empties itself into a lake. The morasses and flat land, created by the deposits of the river, are the hotbeds of malaria, and inevitably teem with disease. To stop in such situations for the night will probably be followed by a fever; and it is even dangerous to sleep in a boat or carriage in crossing such districts. Should, however, any accident compel the traveller to take up his night-quarters in such a spot, let him choose the highest house in the village, and the loftiest room in the house: the malaria does not rise above a certain height; and let him close carefully the windows. It is, however, far better to walk on all night, should there be no other means of advancing or avoiding a spot so situated, than to run the risk. Such morasses are most dangerous in spring and autumn.

Signs of the Weather among the Mountains.—When, in the evening, the wind descends the valley, it is usually a sign of fine weather; the contrary when it ascends. The same may be said of the march of the clouds at all times of the day.

When the roar of the torrent and the knell of the church-bell reach the ear, at one time loud and clear, at another, indistinct and apparently distant, it is a warning of rain.

If, when the clouds clear off, after several days of rain, the mountain-tops appear white with fresh snow, steady, fine weather will almost invariably follow.

It is a bad sign when the outline of the distant mountain-peaks appears particularly sharp and defined—cut out, as it were, against the horizon.

To cure blistered Feet.—Rub the feet at going to bed with spirits, mixed with tallow dropped from a candle into the palm of the hand; on the following morning no blister will exist. The spirits seem to possess the healing power, the tallow serving only to keep the skin soft and pliant. This is Captain Cochrane's advice, and this remedy was used by him on his " Pedestrian Tour." To *prevent* the feet blistering, it is a good plan to soap the inside of the stocking before setting out.

At the head of the list of *requisites for travelling in Switzerland* may properly be placed *Keller's admirable map* of that country, which indicates, not only every place and every road, but distinguishes each kind of road, whether carriage, char, bridle-road, or foot-path; marking at the same time the heights of the mountains, the depths of the lakes, the waterfalls, points of view, and other remarkable objects. It almost enables the traveller to dispense with a guide. Of course, it cannot be faultless, but its errors are remarkably few.

Travellers should provide themselves with the Swiss edition of this map, published by Keller himself, at Zurich, 1833. Both the English and French copies of it are very inferior both in clearness and accuracy.

The little map published by the Useful Knowledge Society (London, 1838), under the able superintendence of Captain Beaufort, is remarkably correct and distinct for its size.

"The *shoes* ought to be double-soled, provided with iron heels and hob-hails, such as are worn in shooting in England : the weight of a shoe of this kind is counterbalanced by the effectual protection afforded to the feet against sharp rocks and loose stones, which cause contusions, and are a great source of fatigue and pain. They should be so large as not to pinch any part of the foot. The experienced pedestrian never commences a journey with new shoes, but with a pair that have already conformed to the shape of the feet. Cotton stockings cut the feet to pieces on a long walk ; in their place, thick knit worsted socks ought invariably to be worn. Gaiters are useful in wet weather to keep the socks clean ; at other times to prevent small stones from falling into the shoes ; but they are liable to heat the ankles. It is advisable to travel in cloth trousers, not in linen, which afford no protection against rain or changes of temperature in mountain regions. A frock-coat is better than a shooting-jacket, which, though well enough in remote places, is strange, and will attract notice in the streets of a foreign town. A straw hat is the most pleasant covering for the head, from its lightness and the protection afforded to the face by a broad brim."

" A very serviceable article in a traveller's wardrobe is a *blouse* (Kittel, or Staub-hemde, in German), somewhat resembling a ploughman's *smock-frock* in England, but by no means confined to the lower orders abroad, as it is a common travelling costume of nobles, gentles, and peasants. It may be worn either over the usual dress, to keep it clean and free from dust, or it may be substituted for the coat in hot weather. This kind of garment may be purchased ready-made in any German town. A *knapsack* (Germ. Tornister) may be purchased at a much cheaper rate abroad (10 fr.), and on a much better plan than those made in England, where they are scarcely to be got under 20*s*. or 30*s*. Portmanteaus are better in England than anywhere else. A Mackintosh cloak is almost indispensable, and it is difficult to procure one abroad."

" A *flask*, to hold brandy and kirschenwasser, is necessary on mountain excursions ; and very convenient cups of patent leather, capable of being folded, and so carried in the pocket, may be got at Paris and Geneva. It should be remembered, however, that spirits ought to be resorted to less as a restorative than as a protection against cold and wet, and to mix with water, which ought not to be drunk cold or unmixed after walking. The best restorative is tea ; and, as there are some parts of the Continent in which this luxury cannot be procured, it is advisable to take a small quantity from England. Good tea, however, may be bought in all the large towns of Switzerland."

" Carey, optician, 181, Strand, makes excellent pocket *telescopes*, about four inches long, combining, with a small size, considerable power and an extensive range. A compass for the pocket is useful on Alpine journeys."—(*From Hand-book N. Germany.*)

Paper, pen and ink, and soap, should by all means be deposited in the knapsack, being articles difficult to meet with at every place. Berry's patent inkstands and fire-boxes are much to be recommended for their portability.

The pedestrian, in packing his knapsack, if he intend to carry it on his own back, should not allow its weight to exceed 20 lbs., even if he be strong. The most part of travellers, however zealous at first in bearing their own pack, grow tired of it after a day or two, transferring it to a guide, who, if young and stout, will carry with the greatest ease a weight of 35 or 40 lbs.

The *alpenstock* is an almost indispensable companion upon mountain journeys, and may be procured everywhere in Switzerland for 2 fr. It is a stout pole, about 6 ft. long, with an iron spike at one end for use, and a chamois' horn for show at the other. The pedestrian who has once tried it will fully appreciate its uses as a staff and leaping-pole, but chiefly as a support in *descending* the mountains; it then becomes, as it were, a third leg. It enables one to transfer a part of the weight of the body from the legs to the arms, which is a great relief in descending long and steep hills. By the aid of it, the chamois-hunters glide down snow-covered slopes, almost perpendicular, checking the velocity of their course, when it becomes too great, by leaning back, and driving the point deeper into the snow. In crossing glaciers, it is indispensable, to feel the strength of the ice, and ascertain whether it be free from crevices and able to bear the weight.

When about to traverse the glaciers for any distance, the traveller should provide himself with a green gauze veil, and with coloured spectacles to protect his eyes from the glare of the snow, which is very painful, and often produces temporary blindness. Lip-salve, or some kind of grease, to anoint the skin of the face, and prevent it from blistering and peeling off, should also be taken. Further requisites for such an expedition are—ropes to attach the travellers and their guides together, so that, in case one fall or slip into a crevice, his descent may be arrested by the others; iron crampons for the feet—the surface of the glacier, though soft in the middle of the day, becomes hard and very slippery as soon as the sun begins to decline; a ladder, to cross those crevices which are too broad to leap over; and a hatchet, to cut steps, or resting-places for the feet, in the ice.

These preparations are quite unnecessary for a mere visit to the glaciers of Chamouni or Grindelwald, and are required only when a journey over them of many hours', or of one or two days' duration, is meditated.

§ 13. OBJECTS MOST DESERVING OF NOTICE IN SWITZERLAND—THE COUNTRY AND PEOPLE.

In order to travel with advantage in a country previously unknown, something more seems necessary than a mere detail of certain lines of road, and an enumeration of towns, villages, mountains, &c. The following section has been prepared with a view to furnish such preliminary information as may enable the tourist to turn his time to the best account; to decide where to dwell, and where to pass quickly. The task is difficult: let this serve as an excuse for its imperfect execution.

Switzerland owes the sublimity and diversified beauty of its scenery, which it possesses in a greater degree, perhaps, than any other country of the globe, to the presence of the Alps—the loftiest mountains of Europe, the dorsal ridge or back-bone, as it were, of the Continent. These run through the land, and occupy, with their main trunk, or minor spurs and offsets, nearly its whole surface. They attain the greatest height along the S. and E. frontier line of Switzerland; but, as they extend N., subsiding and gradually opening out to allow a passage to the Rhine and its tributaries, they are met by the minor chain of the *Jura*, which forms the N.W. boundary of Switzerland. It is from the apex of this advanced guard, as it were, of the Alps, or from one of the intermediate outlying hills, that the traveller, on entering the country, obtains the first view of the great central chain. From the brow of the hill, at the further extremity of a landscape, composed of undulating country —woods, hills, villages, lakes, and silvery, winding rivers—sufficient of itself to rivet the attention, he will discover what, if he has not before enjoyed the glorious spectacle of a snowy mountain, he will probably take for a border of fleecy cloud floating along the horizon. The eye, unaccustomed to objects of such magnitude, fails at first to convey to the mind the notion that these clearly defined white masses are mountains, 60 or 70 miles off. Distance and the intervening atmosphere have no effect in diminishing the intense white of the snow; it glitters as pure and unsullied as if it had just fallen close at hand.

There are many points of view whence the semicircular array of Alpine peaks, presented at once to the eye, extends for more than 120 miles, from the Mont Blanc to the Titlis, and comprises between 200 and 300 distinct summits, capped with snow, or bristling with bare rocks, having their interstices filled with towering glaciers:—

> " Who first beholds those everlasting clouds—
> Those mighty hills, so shadowy, so sublime,
> As rather to belong to heaven than earth—
> But instantly receives into his soul
> A sense, a feeling, that he loses not—
> A something that informs him 'tis an hour
> Whence he may date henceforward and for ever."—*Rogers.*

It was such a prospect that inspired those remarkable lines of Byron:—

> " Above me are the Alps,
> The palaces of Nature, whose vast walls
> Have pinnacled in clouds their snowy scalps,
> And throned Eternity in icy halls
> Of cold sublimity, where forms and falls
> The Avalanche—the thunderbolt of snow !
> All that expands the spirit, yet appals,
> Gather around these summits, as to show
> How earth may soar to heaven, yet leave vain man below."

The points from which such an *Alpine panorama* may be enjoyed to the greatest advantage are—

The Dôle, above St. Cergues, on the road from Dijon to Geneva ;

The Chaumont, above Neuchâtel ;

The Weissenstein, above Soleure ;

The Upper and Lower Hauenstein, on the road from Basle to Soleure and Lucerne ;

The Albis, between Zurich and Zug ;

Monte Salvadore, rising amid the intricacies of the Lago Lugano ;

The Kamor, near Gais, in St. Gall ;

The Righi, between the Lakes of Zug and Lucerne ;

The Faulhorn, adjoining the Bernese Alps.

Of these the Righi is probably the finest, as it is certainly one of the most accessible ; some give the preference to the Faulhorn, from its proximity to the great chain. The passion for climbing mountains so ardent in a young traveller, soon cools ; and they who have surmounted the Righi, the Faulhorn, and the Dôle, may fairly consider any further ascents a waste of time and labour. For a *near view* of alpine scenery, amidst the recesses of the mountains, the spots which afford a concentration of the most grand and sublime objects are the valleys of the Bernese Oberland, and those around the base of Mont Blanc, including, of course, Chamouni. It is in these two districts that the combination of fine forms, and great elevation in the mountains ; of vast extent of glaciers and snow fields, with the accompaniments of the roar of the avalanche and the rush of the falling torrent—are most remarkable. Here, in particular, the glaciers, the most characteristic feature of this country, are seen to greatest advantage—not only those fantastically fractured masses of iceberg which descend into the low grounds, but those vast fields of ice, called Mers de Glace. To Chamouni, and the neighbourhood of Mont Blanc, of the two, must be given the preference, in point of sublimity ; and the traveller will, for this reason, do well in reserving, for the termination of his tour, and the crowning act of his journey—Mont Blanc, with its attendant aiguilles and circumambient leagues of ice.

The glaciers of the Aar, near the Grimsel (which may be comprised in the Bernese Oberland) ; that of the Rhone, near the Furca ; those of the Rhine, above Splügen ; and of the Bernina, in the Engadine — are likewise deserving of mention from their extent. That of Rosenlaui is celebrated for its extreme purity, and the dark blue colour of its chasms.

Lakes. — Madame de Staël has somewhere remarked, on the proximity of lakes to mountains, that nature seems to have placed them in the midst of her grandest scenes, at the foot of the Alps, in order to serve as mirrors, and multiply their enchanting forms. The lakes of Switzerland are very numerous, and they certainly add a principal charm to its scenery. It is difficult to classify them according to their respective merits, as almost every one has some peculiarity which characterises it and renders it worthy of attention. The most remarkable are, the Lake of Lucerne, which exhibits, in perfection, savage grandeur and sublimity ; Wallenstadt, Thun, and Brienz, all thoroughly Swiss ; the Lake of Geneva, or Lac Leman, distinguished for its great extent, and for the diversified character it presents, being, at one end, rugged and sublime, at the other, soft and smiling —it occupies an intermediate rank between the Swiss and Italian lakes. These last, that is to say, Maggiore, Lugano, and Como, may be included in the tour of Switzerland, either from portions of them being actually situated within its territory, or from their vicinity to it. Their character is rather smiling than frowning ; they are blessed with a southern climate, in addition to their own attractions; their thickets are groves of orange, olive, myrtle, and pomegranate ; and their habitations are villas and palaces. Along with the lakes named above must be mentioned the little Lake of Orta, which, though situated in Piedmont, lies so close to the Simplon, and possesses such high claims to notice from its surpassing beauty, that no traveller, approaching that corner of Switzerland to which it is a neighbour, should omit to visit it.

The attempt to fix an order of precedence for the *Swiss Waterfalls* is not likely to meet with general approval, because so much depends on the seasons and the weather, as well as on the taste and temper of the spectator. A fine waterfall is, indeed, a magnificent spectacle ; but it will be appreciated, not merely by its own merits, but, to use a mercantile phrase, according to the abundance of the supply. Now, in Switzerland, waterfalls are as numerous as blackberries. The traveller, after a week or fortnight's journey, is *pestered* by them, and will hardly turn his head aside to look at a fall which, if it were in Great Britain, would make the fortune of an English watering-place, and attract visitors half-way across our island to behold it. The fact seems to be that there is a certain monotony and similarity in all falls of water; and, after the curiosity has once been satiated by the sight of three or four, it is tiresome to go out of one's way to visit another, unless it be much finer, and have a distinctive character from any seen before. Thus, then, there is utility even in an attempt to classify these natural objects.

1. The Fall of the Rhine, at Schaffhausen, deserves the first rank, from the volume of water ; but it is rather a cataract than a cascade—it wants height.

2. Fall of the Aar, at Handek, combines a graceful shoot with great elevation ; an abounding river and a grand situation. It may be said to attain almost to perfection—(Terni being a perfect waterfall).

3. Fall of the Tosa, in the Val Formazza : remarkable less for its form than for the vast volume of water, but in this respect very fine.

4. The Staubbach, or Dust Fall : a thread or scarf of water, so thin that it is dispersed into spray before it reaches the ground ; beautiful, however, from its height and graceful wavings.

5. The Giesbach.

6. The Fall of the Sallenche, near Martigny, sometimes called Pissevache.

7. Reichenbach Fall.

8. The Fall of Pianazzo, or of the Medessimo, on the Splügen.

9. Turtmagne Fall, near the Simplon road.

Other falls, too numerous to mention, are not placed (to use the language of the race-course) ; though, in any other country but Switzerland or Norway, they would deserve especial notice.

The design of this enumeration is to spare the traveller a long walk, or a day's journey, to see a fall, probably inferior to others which he has already seen.

The principal and most interesting of the *Swiss Alpine Passes* (see § 15) are the Simplon, the St. Gothard, the Splügen, and the Bernardin, regarding at once their scenery, and the magnificent and skilfully constructed carriage-roads which have been made over them. Of passes not traversed by carriage-roads, the most striking, in point of scenery, are those of the Monte Moro and Cervin, between the Vallais and Piedmont ; the Tête Noire and Col de Balme, leading to Chamouni ; the Grimsel, Furca, and the Gries, branching off at the head of the valley of the Rhone ; the Gemmi, one of the most singular of all the passes ; and the Great St. Bernard, chiefly visited on account of its celebrated Hospice.

Alpine Gorges.—Especially deserving of notice are some of the avenues leading up to these passes ; in many instances mere cracks, or fissures, cleaving the mountains to the depth of several thousand feet.

None of these defiles at all approach the *Ravine of the Via Mala,* one of the most sublime and terrific scenes anywhere among the Alps—unless, perhaps, it be equalled by another magnificent but little-visited gorge on the way to the Monte Moro. The gorge of the Schöllenen, on the St. Gothard ; that of Gondo, on the Simplon ; and that extraordinary glen, in whose depths the *Baths of Pfeffers* are sunk—one of the most wonderful scenes in Switzerland —also deserve mention.

The most beautiful *Swiss Valleys* are those of Hasli, near Meyringen ; the Simmenthal ; the Vale of Sarnen ; the Kanderthal ; and the Emmenthal—all distinguished for their quiet pastoral character, and the softness and luxuriance of their verdure. And here it may be remarked that the traveller in Switzerland must not suppose that beauty of scenery is confined to the High Alps : the Jura, and the intermediate undulating country, which, though still greatly elevated above the sea, may be called the Lowlands, in reference to the Highlands of Switzerland, abound in peculiar and unobtrusive beauties—hills tufted with woods, among which picturesque masses of bare rock project at intervals, slopes bursting with rills, and meadows which, by the aid of copious irrigation, yield three crops of grass a-year, presenting at all seasons a carpet of the liveliest verdure, and of a texture like velvet, equal to that of the best-kept English lawns;—such are the beauties of these lowland scenes. The frequent hedgerows, the gardens before the cottages, and the neatness of the dwellings—the irregular, winding roads, free from the straight monotony and everlasting avenues of France and Germany—remind one frequently of England. There are, besides, among the Jura, many scenes of great grandeur; such, especially, is presented by the Val Moutiers, or Münster Thal, between Basle and Bienne; the pass of Klus, at the foot of the Ober-Hauenstein, &c.

With regard to the natural beauties of Switzerland, there can be but one sentiment of admiration. On the subject of the *moral condition of the Swiss*, and of their character as a nation, there is much greater variety of opinion, though the larger portion of impartial witnesses will concur in a low and unfavourable estimate of them.

The favourable anticipations awakened by historical associations in the mind of the traveller, as he approaches the land of Tell and Winkelried, are wofully falsified, for the most part, on arriving upon the spot. If he take the trouble to inquire into the political state of the country, he will find a Government almost powerless, a confederacy without unity, split into parties by dissentient religions and opposing interests, and nearly every canton either torn by contending factions, or actually split into two, and as much dissevered as though it consisted of two separate states. Patriots are scarce in the land of Tell; and that combination of petty republics which, while firmly united, not only withstood the shocks of foreign invasion, secure in its mountain-fastnesses, but shattered and annihilated the apparently overwhelming armaments of Austria and Burgundy, not in one battle, but on almost every occasion when opposed to them, must now submit to be propped up by its neighbours, and, as a necessary consequence, must endure and stomach the diplomatic insults which are constantly heaped upon it.

The poverty of the land, its slight capabilities for improvements, its deficiency of resources in proportion to the extent of its population, have given rise to that venality of character which has passed into a proverb; a reproach by no means removed, even in the present day. Notwithstanding their long enjoyment of liberty and free institutions, in spite of the glorious examples of their history, we do not find the nation actuated by that independence and nobleness of sentiment which might be expected. On the contrary, a spirit of time-serving and a love of money appear the influencing motives in the national character, and the people who have enjoyed freedom longer than any other in Europe, are principally distinguished for fighting the battles of any master, however tyrannical, who will buy their services; for sending forth the most obsequious and drudging of valets; for extortionate innkeepers, and among the lower class of Swiss for almost universal mendicity; for to beg appears to be regarded as no degradation, and is taught by parents to their children less from necessity than as a sort of speculation. The Tyrolese, the neighbours of the Swiss, and their partners in the same cold climate and unproductive Alpine region, exhibit a remarkable contrast to them in this and other respects.

It is more pleasing to dwell on another result of Swiss poverty, viz., the impulse it has given to commercial industry and manufactures. The natural disadvantages of an inland country, into which the raw material must be conveyed almost exclusively on the axle over snowy passes, and by long journeys, have been overcome, and in the excellence of her manufactured articles Switzerland competes with England, while she often surpasses her in cheapness.

The demoralizing effect produced upon the Swiss by the great influx of travellers into their country, is explained in the following temperate and judicious remarks from Latrobe's 'Alpenstock':—

" It cannot be denied that the character of the majority of the Swiss peasantry, whose habitations are unfortunately in the neighbourhood of the main routes of travellers, or of the particular points of interest to which they lead, is most contemptible; that in such parts it is not only vain to expect to find those simple and guileless manners which in time past were associated with the name of the inhabitants of these mountains, but that even common morality is out of the question. There is a disposition in the majority of those who have been at all exposed to temptation to take advantage of the ignorance of travellers, to make the most exorbitant demands, and to go to the greatest possible length in the system of extortion and deception. Even in those parts of the country where the open profligacy of the cases brought before them has excited the attention and provoked the surveillance of the magistrates, and where, in consequence, a kind of just price has been set upon various articles, opportunities are always greedily seized upon to turn a dishonest penny, when it can be done without serious risk.

" This the writer knows to be unquestionably the fact; yet he must candidly add, what he also knows from observation, that the absurd conduct and unreasonable folly of travellers have strengthened the spring of this dishonest propensity in a very great degree: and while many a *just* complaint has been made against the extortion of those with whom the traveller must come in contact, many an *unreasonable* accusation has also been preferred under circumstances which would not allow the plaintiff to make his case good. An individual who is satisfied, while travelling in a country like this, to identify himself as much as possible with the people among whom he is thrown—who is contented with the general style of living, with the produce of the country, and, more especially, with the customary hours of eating and sleeping, has certainly reason to complain, if the mere circumstance of his being a stranger is deemed a sufficient apology for making him the object of unprincipled spoliation and imposition.

" But if the travellers be of another mind and order—if they pass through the country, as hundreds do, with their eyes shut to the style and manners of the people and difference of their habits from our own, and intent upon keeping up their usual style of corporeal indulgence as much as possible—such have not the same reason in their complaints; which is a lesson many have had to learn, by the refusal of the magistrate to interfere in the quarrel, or by having a verdict given against them.

" I have seen a party of English arrive at a mountain cabaret at nightfall, when the host and his family would, in the usual course of things, have been thinking of their beds ; they order dinner, and insist upon having flesh, fish, or fowl, foreign wines and liqueurs, just as though they were at the Star and Garter at Richmond ; abuse the master and the domestics, dine at eight or nine, and sit over their cheer till past midnight. Mine host can put up with a good deal of extra trouble, with no small quantity of abuse, and will stay up all night with considerable temper, because he knows he can make them pay for it in hard money.

" The next morning, as might be anticipated, he hands in a bill of nearly as many dollars as they had expected francs, without doubt exorbitant and overcharged, but at any rate there are plausible excuses for this exorbitancy.

" The host will shrug his shoulders, in answer to their ill-expressed and angry expostulation, and merely say, that the gentlemen must not expect to have articles which, however plentiful in towns, are luxuries on the mountains, without paying well for them.

" The worst is that, little by little, the show of justice that there once existed, and the distinction which was made between the individual who gave no trouble, and was contented with what entertainment was easily provided, and those last described, is fast waning away ; and to be a foreigner is sufficient to excite the plundering propensities of mine host and his coadjutors. He has frequently a regular system to pursue, according as the visitor announced is an Englishman, a Frenchman, or a German. The latter obtains the most grace in his eyes, and pays perhaps only ten or twenty per cent ; the Frenchman must expocket something more in consideration of his polish and politeness, and the old grudge borne him for past events ; and the poor Englishman may esteem himself very happy if, after partaking of the same fare, he finds himself desired to lay down a sum which only excites his surprise and keeps him on the grumble for the next three miles, and does not at once make him fly into a passion and get a prejudice for life against everything Swiss.

" And it is not only those parts of the country through which the great stream of travellers sets that have by this means become degraded: the fame of these doings has gone abroad throughout the greater part of the whole community, and very few are the retired corners where you do not detect more or less of this dishonourable bent in the lower orders, if any way exposed to temptation.

" But it is not only in this point that the moral character of the common people is debased. It will not be a matter of wonder that the present Swiss peasantry as a nation cannot longer be supposed to be the simple, virtuous, patriarchal race, that their forefathers were. It is evident, from the perusal of their history, that the deterioration had been steady and gradual for some time previous to the close of the last century ; and that nothing contributed more to it than that system of foreign military service which, it would appear, had become necessary to the existence of the community.

" Then the overpowering deluge of the French Revolution swept over the Jura, and gave accelerated impulse to the downward current of moral feeling in every rank of society in this unhappy country.

" What evil influence this had at the time upon the principles of the people in general, as well as the virtue of families and individuals, it would now be a difficult and ungrateful task to decide. Much of that evil may at this time be supposed to have been already obviated ; yet, now that the waters of that fearful political phenomenon have retired, we may still see left behind the scum and the mud with which their polluted stream was heavily charged.

. . . . . .

" ' I have not been in the Oberland for years,' is an expression I have heard time after time from worthy natives ; and the reason is perfectly comprehensible. A true lover of his country may well grieve over the dishonour and the loss of moral feeling in Switzerland, and avoid going where he must be constantly reminded of its downfall."—p. 324-328.

Another point to be considered in reference to the condition of the people, is the influence of the Roman Catholic religion in those cantons where it prevails. And here it may be observed, that the least enlightened portions of the country at present are the Vallais, Uri, Unterwalden, Schwytz, Tessin, a large part of the Bernese Oberland, and the Grisons. In passing from a Catholic to a Protestant canton, the traveller will scarcely fail to remark a striking change. Yet, in his comments thereon, let him bear in mind the benevolent precept so beautifully conveyed in the following verses, composed in one of the Catholic cantons of Switzerland :—

> Doom'd, as we are, our native dust
> To wet with many a bitter shower,
> It ill befits us to disdain
> The Altar, to deride the Fane
> Where patient sufferers bend, in trust
> To win a happier hour.

I love, where spreads the village lawn,
  Upon some knee-worn cell to gaze;
    Hail to the firm, unmoving cross,
    Aloft, where pines their branches toss,
And to the chapel far withdrawn,
  That lurks by lonely ways.

Where'er we roam, along the brink
  Of Rhine, or by the sweeping Po,
    Through Alpine vale, or Champaign wide—
    Whate'er we look on, at our side
Be Charity—to bid us think
  And feel, if we would know.

Wordsworth.

We are so accustomed to look upon Switzerland as " the land of liberty," that the generality of travellers will take the thing for granted; and it is only after diving to a certain depth in Swiss annals, that the question arises, what was the nature of this freedom, and how far was it calculated to foster nobility of sentiment and public spirit among the people? Was the abolition of the Austrian dominion succeeded by a more equitable government, extending to all the same privileges, and dividing among all alike the public burthen? Was political equality accompanied by religious tolerance and harmony? Did the democratic principle produce fruit in the disinterestedness and patriotism of the children of the land? To all these inquiries there remains but one answer—a negative. The cowherds of Uri, Schwytz, and Unterwalden, who had so nobly, and with so much moderation, emancipated themselves from a foreign yoke, in process of time became themselves the rulers of subject states, and, so far from extending to them the liberty they had so dearly purchased, and which they so highly valued, that they kept their subjects in the most abject state of villenage ; so that, down to the end of the last century, the vassals of no despotic monarch in Europe exhibited a picture of equal political debasement. The effects of this tyrannical rule were equally injurious to the governors and the governed, and the marks of it may be traced in many parts of Switzerland, even down to the present day, in the degraded condition of the people, morally as well as physically. It will be discovered from Swiss history that ambition, and a thirst for territorial rule, is inherent in republics as well as in monarchies, as we may learn from the encroachments and aggrandizing spirit of Canton Berne. She retained, as tributary to her, for two centuries and a half, the district called Pays de Vaud, deriving from it an annual revenue of 1,200,000 francs, and yet denying to the inhabitants all share of political rights. Geneva, a weaker state, after throwing off the yoke of the Dukes of Savoy, with difficulty escaped the wiles of the Bernese Government, which would have plunged them in a slavery not more tolerable than that from which they had just escaped.

Religious dissensions were a source of a long series of troubles to the Confederation, dividing it into two opposite parties, which not only were arrayed against each other in the field of battle, but also interfered with the internal peace of the individual cantons. Although by the laws the two parties in religion were allowed equal freedom of worship, the enjoyment of this privilege was embittered to either party, in the state where the other faith was predominant: it was, in fact, but a nominal tolerance. It is curious to observe, that even in these days of liberal ideas and Catholic emancipation, a citizen of Lucerne is deprived of all political privileges, if he be a Protestant.

Until the two French revolutions, the common people of Switzerland, except in one or two of the cantons, had no more share in the constitutional privileges, which all Swiss were supposed to possess as their birthright, than the subjects of the despotic monarchies of Austria or Prussia. The government was vested in the hands of aristocratic oligarchies, as exclusive, and as proud of birth, blood, and descent, as the most ancient nobility in Europe. The burgher patricians of the great towns managed, by gradual encroachments, to deprive the lower orders of the exercise of their rights, and gradually monopolized all places and offices for themselves and their children.

The *Towns* of Switzerland exhibit many interesting marks of antiquity; their buildings are frequently found unchanged since a very early period, and in Lucerne, Freyburg, Basle, Bellinzona and in several other instances, the feudal fortifications, with battlements and watch-towers, remain perfectly preserved. One characteristic and very pleasant feature are the *Fountains,* the never-failing ornament of every Swiss town and village. They usually consist of a Gothic ornamented pillar, surmounted by the figure of a man, usually some hero of Swiss history, either Tell, the dauntless crossbowman, or Winkelried, with his " sheaf of spears." Sometimes the figures of animals are substituted for the human form.

A singular custom, connected with education, prevails in Switzerland, which deserves notice here from the influence which it exercises over society. In most of the large towns, children of the same age and sex are associated together by their parents in little knots and clubs—called *Sociétés de Dimanche.* The parents seek out for their children an eligible set of companions when they are still quite young. The parties so formed amount to 12 or 15 in number, and the variation of age between them is not more than 2 or 3 years. All the members meet in turn on Sunday evenings at the houses of their parents, while children, to play together and partake of tea, cakes, and sweetmeats, attended by their bonnes or nurses; when grown up, to pass the evening in other occupations and amusements suited to their age. At these meetings not even brothers or sisters are present, except they be members of the society. From thus being constantly thrown together on all occasions, a strict friendship grows up among the members of each brotherhood or sisterhood, which generally lasts through life, even after the parties are settled and dispersed about the world. The females, even when grown up, distinguish their companions by such endearing terms as "ma mignonne," "mon cœur," "mon ange," &c. This practice renders Swiss society very exclusive, and few strangers, however well introduced, penetrate below the surface.

When a young woman marries, her husband is admitted into the society to which she belongs, and thus the wife determines the caste of the husband.

Ranz de Vaches.—It is not uncommon to find the Ranz de Vaches spoken of, by persons unacquainted with Switzerland and the Alps as a single air, whereas they are a class of melodies prevailing among and peculiar to the Alpine valleys. Almost every valley has an air of its own, but the original air is said to be that of Appenzell. Their effect in producing home sickness in the heart of the Swiss mountaineer, when heard in a distant land, and the prohibition of this music in the Swiss regiments in the service of France, on account of the number of desertions occasioned by it, are stories often repeated, and probably founded on fact.

These national melodies are particularly wild in their character, yet full of melody; the choruses consist of a few remarkably shrill notes, uttered with a peculiar falsetto intonation in the throat. They originate in the practice of the shepherds on the Alps of communicating with one another at the distance of a mile or more, by pitching the voice high. The name Ranz de Vaches (Germ. Kuh-reihen), literally *cow-rows*, is obviously derived from the order in which the cows march home at milking-time, in obedience to the shepherd's call, communicated by the voice, or through the *Alp-horn*, a simple tube of wood, wound round with bark 5 or 6 feet long, admitting of but slight modulation, yet very melodious when caught up and prolonged by the mountain echoes. In some of the remoter pastoral districts of Switzerland, from which the ancient simplicity of manners is not altogether banished, the Alp-horn supplies, on the higher pastures, where no church is near, the place of the vesper-bell. The cow-herd, posted on the highest peak, as soon as the sun has set, pours forth the 4 or 5 first notes of the Psalm "Praise God the Lord;" the same notes are repeated from distant Alps, and all within hearing, uncovering their heads and bending their knees, repeat their evening orison, after which the cattle are penned in their stalls, and the shepherds betake themselves to rest.

The traveller among the Alps will have frequent opportunities of hearing both the music of the horn and the songs of the cow-herds and dairy-maids; the latter have been thus described by Mr. Southey:—" Surely the wildest chorus that ever was heard by human ears: a song, not of articulate sounds, but in which the voice is used as a mere instrument of music, more flexible than any which art could produce, sweet, powerful, and thrilling beyond description."

A word may be said on *Swiss Husbandry* to draw the attention of such persons as take an interest in the subject to one or two practices peculiar to the country. The system of irrigating the meadows is carried to a very great extent, the mountain-torrents are turned over the fields by means of trenches and sluices, and not unfrequently, when the ground is much inclined, the stream is conducted to the spot where it is required, through troughs hollowed out of the stem of a fir-tree.

The drainings of dunghills, cow-houses, and pigsties, are not allowed to run to waste, but are carefully collected in a vat by the farmer, and at the fit moment carried out in carts to the fields, and ladled over them, very much to their benefit, and to the equal disgust of the olfactory nerves of all who pass; the air, far and near, being filled with this truly Swiss fragrance.

The Swiss mountaineers are skilful marksmen with the rifle, and, like their neighbours, the Tyrolese, meet constantly to practise and engage in trials of skill. There are clubs or societies in most of the cantons, and every year a *grand federal rifle-match* is held in one or other of the large towns, at which all the best shots from the whole of Switzerland meet to contend for a prize.

Annual *contests in wrestling* (called *Zwing-Feste*) are also held in different parts of Switzerland. The cantons which distinguish themselves for skill in this and other athletic exercises are Bern, Appenzell, and Unterwalden.

§ 14. SKELETON TOURS THROUGH SWITZERLAND AND PART OF SAVOY.

N.B. It is advisable to enter Switzerland from the side of Germany rather than by that of France, as the scenery of Chamouni, the grandest among the Alps, ought to be reserved for the conclusion of the tour.

There are parts of Switzerland which cannot be reached in a travelling-carriage, and those who can neither ride nor walk, and will not submit to be carried in a chair, must forego them.

The pedestrian tours in this list are laid down with the understanding that only the more interesting scenes, and such as are impracticable by other conveyances, are to be travelled on foot, and that on high roads the pedestrian will ride, otherwise he will waste much time unprofitably.

A.—CARRIAGE TOUR OF ABOUT TWO MONTHS, beginning at Basle and ending at Schaffhausen, performed in 1837.

The portion of this tour within brackets would extend it beyond the two months, and must be omitted if the traveller be pressed for time.

Basle.
Münsterthal.

Bienne.
{ St. Peter's Island.
{ Neuchâtel.
Soleure.
Weissenstein.
Lucerne.
Arth and the Righi.
Weggis.
Lake Lucerne to Altorf.
Entlibuch.
Thun. (Leave the carriage.)
Interlachen.

Lauterbrunnen.
Grindelwald.
[Faulhorn.]
Meyringen.
⎧ Grimsel.
| Furca.
| St. Gothard.
⎨ Altorf.
| Lake of Lucerne.
| Stanz.
| Brunig.
⎩ Meyringen.

This part of the tour, except the road of the St Gotthard, can only be performed in chars, on horseback, and across the lake in a boat.

Thun.
Berne.
Freyburg.
Lausanne.
Vevay and Chillon.
Geneva.

Send round the carriage to Martigny, which it may reach in 2 days from Geneva.

Infirm persons, not able to ride or walk over an Alpine pass, may retain their carriage as far as Sallenche, proceed in a char-à-banc to Chamouni, rejoin their carriage at Sallenche, and then proceed by Thonon and St. Maurice to Martigny.
Sallenche, in a hired carriage.
Chamouni, in a char-à-banc.
Moutanvert.
Flegère.
Tête Noire, to
Martigny,
[Great St. Bernard, and back, on mules.]
Baths of Leuk. ⎱ Leave carriage at
Gemmi. ⎰ Sierre or Leuk.
Brieg.
Simplon.
Domo d' Ossola.
Baveno.
[Lago d'Orta.]
Borromean Islands.
Milan. (Rest a week.)
Monza.
Lecco.
[Como.]
Chiavenna.
Splügen.
Via Mala.
Coire.
Pfeffers' Baths.

Lake of Wallenstadt.
[Glarus, Stachelberg, and back.]
Rapperschwyl.
Zurich.
[Baden and Schintznach.]
Schaffhausen.

B.—TOUR OF A FORTNIGHT.

Carriage-roads — * char-roads —
† bridle or foot-paths.

Days.
1 ⎧ Schaffhausen.
⎨ Rhine Fall.
⎩ Zurich.
2† Righi.
3 ⎧ Altorf—St. Gothard.
⎩ Andermatt.
† ⎧ Furca.
4†⎨ Grimsel.
5† Meyringen.
6† Grindelwald.
7 Lauterbrunnen and Thun.
† ⎧ Gemmi Pass.
8 ⎩ Leuk.
9 Martigny.
† ⎧ Tête Noire.
10 ⎩ Chamouni.
12 Geneva—home through France, or by
13 Bern.
14 Basle.

C.—TOUR OF THREE WEEKS ON FOOT.

3 ⎧ Basle.—Münster Thal.
⎨ Weissenstein.
⎩ Soleure.
4 Schintznach.
5 Schaffhausen.
6 Zurich.
7 ⎧ Wesen, and Lake of Wallenstadt.
⎨
⎩ Pfeffers.
8 Kalfeuser Thal to Glarus.
9 ⎧ Muotta.
⎩ Klonthal.
Schwytz.
10 Righi.
11 ⎧ Altorf.
⎩ Andermatt.

Days.

12 { Furca.
     Grimsel.
13 Meyringen.
14 Grindelwald.
15 { Wengern Alp.
     Lauterbrunnen and Interlachen.
16 Gemmi—Baths of Leuk.
17 Martigny.
19 { Tête Noire.
     Chamouni.
20 Geneva.
21 Bern.

D.—Tour of a Month or Five
Weeks.

1 { Schaffhausen and Rhinefall.
    Zurich.
2 Righi.
3 Lake of Lucerne.
4 Lucerne.
5 { Brunig.
    Meyringen.
6 Susten Pass.
7 St. Gothard.
8 { Furca.
    Grimsel.
9 Brienz.
10 Lauterbrunnen.
11 Grindelwald.
13 { Thun.
     Bern.
14 Freiburg.
15 Simmenthal.
16 { Spietz.
     Kandersteg.
17 Gemmi.
18 Martigny.
19 Great St. Bernard.
20 { Aosta.
     Cormayeur.
21 Allée Blanche—Col de Seigne.
22 Col de Bonhomme.
23 24 Chamouni.
25 Martigny, by Col de Balme and
     Tête Noire.
26 { Bex.
     Chillon—Vevay.
28 { Lake of Geneva—Lausanne.
     Geneva—home through France,
     or by

Days.

30 Orbe, the Dôle, and Lac de
     Joux.
31 Neuchâtel.
32 Bienne.
33 Münster Thal.
34 Basle.

E.—Tour of Thirty-two Days,
performed in the Autumn of 1837
by W. and R. H., chiefly on foot.

"Our longest walks never exceeded
10 or 12 leagues; but on turnpike-
roads, such as the Simplon, we always
rode. For some of the passes, such
as the Col de Bonhomme, the Cervin,
and the Rawyl, guides are always
necessary, but wherever there is a
'chemin tracé' guides are a nui-
sance, except after a snow-storm."

*London to Geneva in fourteen days,
including two days at Paris.*

Aug. 26. Geneva.
27. By eight o'clock steamer to
Lausanne; see the town; by another
steamer to Villeneuve; by diligence
to Bex.
27. To Martigny (short day).
28. Walked to Hospice of the
Great St. Bernard.
29. Back to Martigny (an improvement to go by the Col de Ferret,
Orsières, and along the Dranse).
30. Tête Noire to Chamouni (a
new way, first explored this summer,
is to ascend from Val Orsine to the
summit of the Col de Balme, on account of its magnificent view; thus
including the finest part of both
passes. It is not quite two hours
longer than the straight road).
31. Ascended the Flegère; then
crossed the valley to the Montanvert to the Mer de Glace—Chamouni.
Sept. 1. Walked across the Col de
Vosa to Contamines. The journey
would have been divided better by
going on to the Chalets of Nant
Bourant.

2. Crossed the Col de Bonhomme by Chapiu, to Motet—(walked).

3. Walked over Col de la Seigne, through Allée Blanche to Cormayeur.

4. To Aosta, in car. } Might be done
5. Chatillon, ditto } easily in 1 day.

6. On mules to Tournanche—on foot thence to Breuil.

7. Crossed the Cervin (Matterhorn) on foot to Zermatt (fatiguing). [Pierre Meynet, mentioned by Brockedon, is the best guide in the Alps.]

8. Descended on Mules to Visp; walked thence to Brieg.

9. By char, across the Simplon, to Domo d' Ossola; 10 hours.

10. Off at 3 A.M., by courier, to Baveno; arrived 7 A.M.; by sailing-boat, up the Lago Maggiore, to Locarno; by car to Bellinzona (arrived late).

11. By hired carriage to Airolo.

12. Walked over the St. Gothard to Hospital.

13. By carriage to Fluellen, on the Lake of Uri.

14. Crossed lake to Brunnen, by Schwytz and Arth, to the summit of the Righi.

15. On foot to Weggis; by boat to Lucerne; on foot to Winkel; crossed the lake to Alpnach; walked to Sarnen.

16. Crossed the Brunig, on foot, to Brienz; by boat to the Giesbach; by char to Meyringen.

17. Rested at Meyringen; Falls of Reichenbach.

18. Walked to the Hospice of the Grimsel; thence to the glacier of the Rhone; and back to the Hospice to sleep.

19. Returned to Meyringen; taking a three hours' walk up the Susten Pass.

20. Walked over the Scheideck to Grindelwald; thence over the Wengern Alp; slept at the "Jungfrau Gasthof," exactly opposite the Jungfrau Mountain, to see and hear the avalanches.

21. By Lauterbrunnen to Interlachen, on foot; in char to Neuhaus; in steamer to Thun; in diligence to Bern.

22. Returned to Thun, by char, to Frutigen, on foot to Kandersteg.

23. Across the Gemmi to Leuk Baths, on foot; thence direct to Sion.

24. Walked over the Rawyl to An-der-Leuk.

25. On foot, down the Simmenthal to Thun; char thence to Bern. (It would have been better to have gone by Gruyères to Freyburg, Bern, Soleure, and over the Hauenstein to Basle.)

26. By diligence to Basle.

Basle to London by Rotterdam in seven days.

F.—TOUR OF ABOUT TEN WEEKS.

Schaffhausen.
Constance.
St. Gall.
Sentis.
Wesen.
Lake of Wallenstadt.
Pfeffers.
Kalfeuser Thal.
Glarus.
Stachelberg and Linth Thal.
Klön and Muotta Thal.
Einsiedeln.
Rapperschwyl.
Zurich.
Zug.
Lucerne.
Weggis.
Righi.
Schwytz.
Brunnen.
Fluellen.
Altorf.
Andermatt.
Airolo.
Val Formazza; Falls of Tosa.
Gries Glacier.
Rhone Glacier.
Grimsel.
Meyringen.
Up the Brunig for the view, and to Brienz for the Giesbach Fall.
Meyringen.
Scheideck—Rosenlaui.

Faulhorn.
Grindelwald.
Wengern Alp.
Lauterbrunnen.
Thun.
Spiez.
Kandersteg.
Gemmi.
Leuk.
Sion.
Martigny.
St. Bernard.
Aosta.
Cormayeur, or Pré St. Didier.
Up the Mount Cramont and back.
Allée Blanche.
Nant Bourant, or Contamines.
Chamouni.
Flegère; Montanvert.
Jardin, &c.
Col de Balme, and Tête Noire.
Martigny.
Bex.
Vevay.
Lausanne.
Freyberg.
Bern.
Bienne.
Neuchâtel.
Yverdun.
Orbe and the Dôle.
Geneva.

G.—A SUMMER'S TOUR OF THREE
  MONTHS, to include all the spots
  best worth notice in Switzerland,
  passing as little as possible twice
  over the same ground.

*** The figures are the numbers of
  the Routes in which each place is
  described.

Basle, 1.
Münster Thal, 1.
Bienne, 1 (Isle St. Pierre, 45).
Neuchâtel, 44.
[Chaux de Fonds ? 48].
Yverdun, 45.
Orbe, 50.
Lac de Joux, 50.
Morat, 43.
Freyburg, 42.
Bern, 24.
Soleure, 3.

Weissenstein, 3.
Schintznach, 6.
Schaffhausen, 7.
Rhine Fall, 7.
Constance, 7.
St. Gall, 66.
Gais and Appenzell, 68; Weisbad,68.
Sentis; Wildkirchlein, 68.
Rapperschwyl, 14.
Zurich, 8.
Zug, by the Albis, 15 and 16.
Arth and Goldau, 17.
Righi, 17.
Weggis; Bay of Uri, 18.
Brunnen (Schwytz), 17.
Altorf, 34.
Surenen Pass, 31.
Engelberg, 31.
Stanz, 31.
Lucerne, 16.
Brunig, 19.
Meyringen, 27.
Brienz and Giesbach, 27.
Interlachen, 27.
Thun, 27.
Simmenthal, 41.
Sanetsch Pass, 40.
Sion, 59.
Rawyl Pass, 39.

Spiez,
Unterseen,
Lauterbrunnen,
Wengern Alp,   } 27.
Grindelwald,
Faulhorn,
Scheideck,
Meyringen,

Grimsel, 28.
Rhone Glacier, 30.
Gries Pass, 29.
Val Formazza; Tosa Fall, 29.
Airolo, 34.
St. Gothard; Devil's Bridge, 34.
Altorf, 34.

Schachen Thal,
Klausen,   } 72.
Stachelberg,
Glarus,

Klon Thal, } 75.
Muotta,

Schwytz, 17.
Morgarten, } 74.
Einsiedeln,
Wesen, 14.

§ 15. ALPINE PASSES.

No part of the Alps are more interesting, either in a picturesque or in an historical point of view, than the passable gaps or notches in the ridge of the great chain, whereby alone this colossal wall of mountains may be scaled, and a direct passage and communication maintained between northern and southern Europe. It has been through these depressions that the great tide of population has poured since the earliest times; from these outlets have issued the barbarian swarms which so often desolated, and at last annihilated, the Roman empire.

There are more than 50 passes over the Swiss portion of the Alpine chain alone, or immediately communicating with the Swiss frontier. The following are the most remarkable:*—The Simplon, St. Gothard, Bernardine, Splügen, Saanen-moser, Bramegg, am Stoss, Wildhaus, all traversed by excellent high-roads, most skilfully constructed, and passable for heavy carriages. To these may probably soon be added the Julier and Maloya. The Maloya, Julier, Albula, Septimer, Bernina, Buffalora, Schallenberg, Sattel, practicable for light chars:—and the Col de Trient, Col de Ferret, Grand St. Bernard, Col de Fenêtre, Cervin (Matterhorn), Moro, Gries Nüfanen, Furca, Grimsel, Great and Little Scheideck, Gemmi, Rawyl, Sanetsch, Cheville, Susten, Surenen, Brunig Engstelen,

* Mr. Brockedon has admirably illustrated them both with his pencil and pen in his beautiful work entitled " The Passes of the Alps," 2 vols. 4to.

Jochli, Klausen, Oberalp, Lukmanier, Kistengrat, Panix, Segnes, La Foppa, Lenzerheide, Stutz, Greina, Vago, Casanna, Monte del Oro, Druser and Schweitzer-Thor, Schlapiner Joch, &c. &c., which are either bridle-paths or mere foot-paths, and more or less difficult and dangerous.

In seeking a passage over the Alps, the most obvious course was to find out the valleys which penetrate farthest into the great chain, following the course of the rivers to their sources, and then to take the lowest traversable part in order to descend to the opposite side. The variety and sudden transitions presented by such a route are highly interesting. In the course of one day's journey the traveller passes from the climate of summer to winter, through spring. The alteration in the productions keeps pace with that of the temperature. Leaving behind him stubble-fields, whence the corn has been removed and housed, he comes to fields yet yellow and waving in the ear; a few miles farther and the crop is still green; yet higher and corn refuses to grow. Before quitting the region of corn he enters one of dark, apparently interminable forests of pine and larch, clothing the mountain-sides in a sober vestment. Above this the haymakers are collecting the short grass, the only produce which the ground will yield. Yet the stranger must not suppose that all is barrenness even at this elevation. It seems as though nature were determined to make one last effort at the confines of the region of vegetation. From beneath the snow-bed, and on the very verge of the glacier, the profusion of flowers, their great variety, and surpassing beauty, are exceedingly surprising. Some of the greatest ornaments of our gardens, here born to blush unseen,—gentians and lilies, hyacinths and blue bells, intermixed with bushes of the red rhododendron, the loveliest production of the Alps, scattered over the velvet turf, give it the appearance of a carpet of richest pattern. The insect world is not less abundant and varied,—thousands of winged creatures are seen hovering over the flowers, enjoying their short existence, for the summer at these elevations lasts but for 3 or 4 weeks: the rapid progress of vegetation to maturity is equalled by the rapidity of its decay, and in 8 or 10 days flowers and butterflies have passed away. Above this region of spring, with its gush of springs, its young herbage and vivid greensward, its hum of insects just burst forth, and its natural flower-beds glittering with rain-drops, that of winter in Lapland or Siberia succeeds. All around the summit of a pass over the high Alps, is either snow, glacier, or bare rock. The only plants that grow are dry lichens, which seem intended but to keep up the semblance of vegetation, and to perpetuate nature's cheerful hues of green. The rarefied air is icy cold, and exercise and quick motion are necessary to keep up the circulation of the blood. The agreeable murmur of falling water, which has accompanied the traveller hitherto incessantly, here ceases,—all is solitude and silence, interrupted only by the shrill whistle of the marmot, or the hoarse cawing of an ill-omened raven. The ptarmigan starts up from among heaps of unmelted snow at the traveller's approach, and the lammergeyer (the condor of the Alps), disturbed in his repast on the carcass of a sheep or cow, is seen soaring upwards in a succession of corkscrew sweeps till he gains the ridge of the Alps, and then disappears.

Such are the remarkable gradations which the stranger encounters in the course of a few hours, on a single Pass of the Alps ; but the most striking change of all is that from the region of snow and ice on the top of the mountain, to the sunny clime and rich vegetation of Italy which awaits the traveller at the S. foot of the Alps.

The works of nature, however, will not entirely occupy the attention and wonder of the wanderer in such a pass ; at least a share will be demanded for admiration of the works of man. The great highways, passable for carriages, over the high Alps, are, indeed, most surprising monuments of human skill and enterprise in surmounting, what would appear, at first sight, to be intended by nature as insurmountable. These proud constructions of art thread the valleys, cross the debris of rivers on long causeways, skirt the edge of the precipice, with walls of rock tottering over them, and torrents thundering below. Where the steep and hard surface of the cliff has left not an inch of space for a goat to climb along, they are conducted upon high terraces of solid masonry, or through a notch blasted by gunpowder in the wall of rock. In many instances a projecting buttress of the mountain has blocked up all passage for ages, saying "thus far and no farther :" the skill of the modern engineer has pierced through this a tunnel or gallery ; and the difficulty is vanquished, without the least change in the level of the road.

Sometimes an impediment of this nature is eluded by throwing bridges over the dizzy gorge, and shifting the road from side to side, frequently 2 or 3 times within the space of half a mile. Often the road reaches a spot down which the winter avalanches take their habitual course every year, sweeping every thing before them, and which, even in summer, appears reeking and dripping with the lingering fragments of snow which it has left behind. Will not so irresistible an antagonist arrest the course of this frail undertaking of man ?   Not even the avalanche ;—in such a situation the road either buries itself in subterranean galleries, driven through the mountain, or is sheltered by massive arcades of masonry, sometimes half a mile or three-quarters of a mile long. Over these the avalanche glides harmlessly and is turned into the depths below.

Every opportunity is seized of gaining, by easy ascents, a higher level for the road ; at length comes the main ascent, the central ridge, to be surmounted only by hard climbing. This is overcome by a succession of zigzag terraces, called *tourniquets*, or *giravolte*, connected together by wide curves, to allow carriages to turn easily and rapidly.   So skilful is their construction, with such easy bends and so gradual a slope, that in many alpine roads the postilions, *with horses accustomed to the road*, trot down at a rapid pace. Sometimes as many as 50 of these zigzags succeed one another without interruption, and the traveller, as he passes backwards and forwards, hovering over the valley, is, as though suspended to a pendulum, and swinging to and fro. The road itself has a most singular appearance, twisted about like an uncoiled rope or a ribbon unwound.

> " O'er the Simplon, o'er the Splügen winds]
> A path of pleasure. Like a silver zone,
> Flung about carelessly, it shines afar,
> Catching the eye in many a broken link,
> In many a turn and traverse as it glides ;
> And oft above and oft below appears,
> Seen o'er the wall by one who journeys up
> As though it were another, through the wild,
> Leading along, he knows not whence or whither.
> Yet through its fairy course, go where it will,
> The torrent stops it not, the rugged rock
> Opens and lets it in, and on it runs,
> Winning its easy way from clime to clime,
> Through glens lock'd up before."—*Rogers.*

The travelling-carriage descends sometimes rapidly and without interruption for an hour. A drag of tempered iron is quickly worn down, in that time, as thin as the blade of a knife, so great is the friction. It is advisable to substitute for the iron drag a wooden sabot, formed of the section of a fir-tree, with a groove cut in the centre to admit the wheel.

The winter's snow usually falls upon the Alpine passes more than 5000 ft. high, about the second week in October (sometimes earlier), and continues till the first or second week in June. Yet even after this, the passage across the neck or Col, as it is called, is not stopped, except for a few days, until the snow can be cleared away. In some of the minor passes, indeed, traversed by a mere rough footpath, or bridle-path, the traffic is much increased after the fall of the snow, which, by filling up depressions and smoothing the way, permits the transport of heavy merchandize on sledges, which move easily over the surface as soon as it has hardened.

Along the lines of the great carriage-roads strong houses are erected at intervals, called *Maisons de Refuge, Case di Ricovero,* occupied by persons called Cantonniers, who are employed in mending the road and keeping it free from snow in winter, and are also paid to assist travellers in danger during snow-storms.

As near as possible to the summit of the pass a *Hospice* is generally erected, usually occupied by a band of charitable monks, as in the case of the Great St. Bernard, the Simplon, Cenis, St. Gothard, &c. The direction of the road across the summit of the ridge is marked by a line of tall poles, which project above the snow, and, from being painted black, are easily recognised. Patrols are sent out from the hospice in tempestuous weather, when the tourmente is raging, and the mist and falling snow hide the land-marks, to guide the travellers on their way and rescue those in danger. Bells are also rung at such times that the sound may aid when the sight fails.

The morning after a fall of snow labourers and peasants are assembled from all sides to shovel it off from the road. Where it is not very deep it is cleared away by a snow-plough drawn by 6 or 8 oxen. As the winter advances and fresh falls occur, the snow accumulates, and the road near the summit of a pass presents the singular aspect of a path or lane, cut between walls of snow, sometimes 10 or 20 ft. high. Carriages are taken off their wheels and fastened upon sledges; ropes are attached to the roof, which are held by 6 or 8 sturdy guides running along on each side, to prevent the vehicle upsetting and rolling over the slippery ice down a precipice. In this manner very high passes are crossed in the depth of winter with very little risk. The spring is a season during which far greater danger is to be apprehended from the avalanches which then fall.

§ 16. CHALETS AND PASTURAGES.

From the mountainous nature of Switzerland and its high elevation, the greater part of the surface, more than 1800 feet above the sea, which is not bare rock, is pasture-land. The wealth of the people, like that of the patriarchs of old, in a great measure, lies in cattle and their produce, on which account the pastoral life of the Swiss deserves some attention. The bright verdure of the meadows which clothe the valleys of Switzerland is one of the distinguishing features of the country; and the music of the cow-bells, borne along by the evening breeze, is one of the sweetest sounds that greets the traveller's ear.

The Alps, or mountain-pasturages, for that is the meaning of the word Alp in Switzerland and Tyrol, are either the property of individuals or of the commune; to a certain extent common-land, in which the inhabitants of the neighbouring town or village have the right of pasturing a certain number of head of cattle.

" In the spring, as soon as the snow has disappeared, and the young grass sprouts up, the cattle are sent from the villages up to the first and lower pastures. Should a certain portion of these be exhausted, they change their quarters to another part of the mountain: Here they stay till about the 10th or 12th of June, when the cattle are driven to the middle ranges of pastures. That portion of the herds intended for a summer campaign on the highest Alps, remain here till the beginning of July, and, on the 4th of that month, generally ascend to them; return to the middle range of pastures, about 7 or 8 weeks afterwards, spend there about 14 days, or 3 weeks, to eat the aftergrass; and finally return into the valleys about the 10th or 11th of October; where they remain in the vicinity of the villages, till driven by the snow and tempests of winter into the stables.

" That portion of the cattle, on the other hand, which is not destined to pass the summer on the higher Alps, and are necessary for the supply of the village with milk and butter, descend from the middle pastures on the 4th of July, into the valley, and consume the grass upon the pasturage belonging to the commune, till the winter drives them under shelter. The very highest Alpine pasturages are never occupied more than 3 or 4 weeks at the furthest."—*Latrobe.*

Sometimes the owners of the cattle repair in person to the Alps, and pass the summer among them, along with their families, superintending the herdsmen, and assisting in the manufacture of butter and cheese. The best cheeses are made upon pastures 3000 ft. above the sea level, in the vales of Simmen and Saanen (Gruyère) and in the Emmenthal. The best cows there yield, in summer, between 20 lbs. and 40 lbs. of milk daily, and each cow produces, by the end of the season of 4 months, on an average, 2 cwt. of cheese.

The life of the cow-herd (*Vacheror Senner*) is by no means such an existence of pleasure as romances in general, and that of Rousseau in particular, have represented it. His labours are arduous and constant; he has to collect 80 or 90 cows twice a-day, to be milked, to look after stragglers, to make the cheese and keep all the utensils employed in the process in the most perfect state of cleanliness.

The *Chalet* (Germ. Sennhutte) in which he resides, is literally a log-hut, formed of trunks of pines, notched at the extremities so as to fit into one another at the angles of the building, where they cross: it has a low flat roof, weighted with stones to keep fast the shingle-roof and prevent its being blown away by the wind. A building of this kind is rarely air-tight or water-tight. The interior is usually blackened with smoke and very dirty, boasting of scarcely any furniture, except, perhaps, a table and rude bench, and the apparatus of the dairy, including a huge kettle for heating the milk. A truss of straw, in the loft above, serves the inmates for a bed. The ground around the hut on the outside is usually poached by the feet of the cattle, and the heaps of mud and dung render it difficult to approach the door. This description applies to the commoner sort of chalets; those in which the owners themselves reside are generally better, but they are also less numerous. There is another kind of chalet, a mere shed or barn, in which the hay is housed until the winter, when it is conveyed over the snow in sledges down to the villages below. A pastoral Swiss valley is usually speckled over with huts of this kind, giving it the appearance, to a stranger, of being much more populous than it is in reality: in the Simmenthal alone there are, it is said, 10,000 chalets.

The herdsmen shift their habitations from the lower to the upper pasturages, as their cattle ascend and descend the Alps, at different seasons, and they sometimes have 2 or 3 places of temporary abode. The weary traveller in search of repose and refreshment, after a long day's journey, is often disappointed, on approaching what he conceives to be a human habitation, to find either that it is a mere hay-barn, or else a deserted chalet ; and thereby learns, with much mortification, that he has still some tedious miles to trudge before he can reach the first permanently-occupied dwelling. What an agreeable contrast to reach a well-appointed chalet of the better sort, where delicious milk, cooled in the mountain stream, fresh butter, bread, and cheese, are spread out on a clean napkin before the hungry and tired stranger !

The cattle are frequently enticed home, at milking-time, by the offer of salt, which they relish highly, and which is, besides, considered wholesome. The allowance for a cow, in some parts of Switzerland, is 4lbs. or 5lbs. of salt in a quarter of a year.

§ 17. GLACIERS.

The glaciers, one of the most sublime features of the Alps, and one of the most wonderful phenomena of nature, are composed of those vast accumulations of the snow which falls during nine months of the year on the higher summits and valleys, remaining for several months a dry and loose powder, until the heat of the summer sun begins to melt and consolidate it. Under the influence of its warmth, the snow assumes first a granular form ; and to pass over it in that state is like walking among rice or peas, in which the foot sinks up to the knees. Lower down, or as the heat increases, so as to melt a considerable portion, and cause the water to percolate it, it becomes a compact mass. The frosty temperature of the night hardens that which has been dissolved in the day, and thus, after repeated thawings and freezings, the whole undergoes a fresh crystallization, being converted into ice of a coarser grain and less compact substance than common ice. Thus there appears to be a regular transition or passage from the loose powdery snow, to the more dense ice of the glacier. The Swiss, indeed, have two distinct terms for these modifications of the snowy covering of the high Alps. The upper granular and scarcely consolidated part they call *Firn*, (which for want of any corresponding English word we may represent by *Snow-field*,) and apply the term *glacier* (gletscher) to the lower limbs of more solid ice, which stretch down into the valleys. Hugi, a naturalist of Soleure, who, after Saussure, has made the most laborious and curious researches into the nature and formation of the glaciers, maintains, that the point at which firn changes to glacier is unvariable among the Alps ; and his investigations fix it at an elevation of about 7800 feet above the sea-level.[*]

[*] A very serious error is conveyed by the common expression "the line of perpetual snow," or "where snow never melts." There is no spot on the Alps, nor on any other snow-clad mountains, where snow does not melt under the influence of a summer sun at mid-day. It melts even on the top of Mont Blanc, but there, and on the summits of the other high Alps, the accumulation of snow is so great, and the duration of the sun's heat so short, that in the end there is far more snow than the sun can dissolve. What is

Ebel has computed the number of glaciers among the Swiss Alps at 400, and the extent of surface occupied by them at 130 square leagues; this, however, must be but a vague estimate. They vary from a few square yards to acres and miles in extent, covering, in some instances, whole districts, filling up entirely the elevated hollows, and basins between the peaks and ridges of the Alps, and sending forth arms and branches into the inhabited valleys, below the region of forests, and as far down as the level at which corn will grow.

It is such offsets of the glacier as these that are presented to the view of the traveller from the villages of Chamouni and Grindelwald. These, however, are, as it were, but the skirts and fringes of that vast, everlasting drapery of ice which clothes all the upper region of the Alps. These fields or tracts of uninterrupted glacier have been called " Seas of ice"(Mers de glace, Eismeeren), and there are three such among the Swiss and Savoyard Alps which merit especial mention; that around Mont Blanc, that around the Cervin, and that of the Bernese Oberland, around the Finster-Aar-horn. The last sends out no less than thirteen branches, and its extent has been estimated at 125 square miles.

The greatest thickness of the glaciers has been commonly estimated at between 600 and 800 feet. This is probably an exaggeration. Hugi rarely met with any thicker than 150 feet; he estimates the average depth at between 60 and 100 feet, and the greatest thickness of the Mer de glace near Chamouni at 180 feet. Saussure had calculated it at 600 feet.

Notwithstanding their great extent and solidity, the glaciers are by no means stationary, even in the winter. Although the movement is slight, they do not remain quite still. They are undergoing a perpetual process of renovation and destruction. The arms or skirts descending into the lower valleys are gradually dissolved by the increased temperature which prevails at so low a level. The summer sun, aided by particular winds, acts upon the surface, so that, in the middle of the day, it abounds in pools, and is traversed by rills of water. The constant evaporation from every part exposed to the air produces great diminution in the upper beds; but, above all, the temperature of the earth, which is at all seasons greater than that of ice, is constantly melting away its lower surface. The vacancy thus caused from below is partially or entirely filled up from above by the winter's snow falling upon the mountain-tops, and on the whole upper region, which is drifted into the higher valleys, and pressed down by its own weight. After

called " *the snow-line*," does not depend on elevation alone, and can be taken only as a very general test of it. Independently of its variation, according to the degree of latitude in which the mountain is situated, it varies on the two sides of the same mountain, being higher on the S. side than the N. The snow will likewise rest longer and extend lower down upon a mountain of granite, than upon one of limestone, in proportion as the two rocks are good or bad conductors of heat, and this is the case even in contiguous mountains, members of the same chain.

it has concreted into ice, the slope of the mountain-sides, and the descent of the valleys in which the glaciers lie, serve as inclined planes, down which the ice slides by the force of gravity, assisted by the melting on its under surface, which prevents any adhesion to the rock below it. Indeed the German word Gletscher comes from glitschen, to glide. Hugi, in one of his journeys, found his way under a glacier, by following the bed of a dried-up torrent which passed below it. He wandered about beneath the ice for the distance of a mile. The ice was everywhere eaten away into dome-shaped hollows, varying from 2 to 12 feet in height, so that the whole mass of the glacier rested at intervals on pillars or feet of ice, irregular in size and shape, which had been left standing. As soon as any of these props gave way a portion of the glacier would of course fall in and move on. A dim twilight prevailed in these caverns of ice, not sufficient to allow one to read, except close to the fissures which admitted the day-light from above. The intense blue of the mass of the ice contrasted remarkably with the pure white of the icy stalactytes, or pendents descending from the roof. The water streamed down upon him from all sides, so that after wandering about for 2 hours, at times bending and creeping to get along under the low vaults, he returned to the open air, quite drenched and half frozen.

The nature of the upper surface of the ice depends upon that of the ground on which it rests; where it is even or nearly so, the ice is smooth and level; but whenever the supporting surface becomes slanting or uneven, the glacier begins to split and gape in all directions. As it approaches a steeper declivity or precipice the layers of ice are displaced, up-heaved, and squeezed one above another; they rise in toppling crags, obelisks, and towers of the most fantastic shapes, varying in height from 20 to 80 feet Being unequally melted by the wind and sun, they are continually tottering to their fall, either by their own weight or the pressure of other masses, and tumbling headlong, are shivered to atoms with a roar like thunder.

The glaciers assume this fractured character only when the foundation on which they rest is very uneven, generally near their lower extremity, when they begin to bend down towards the valley.

The crevices, or fissures, which traverse the upper portion of the glacier, before it becomes entirely fractured and disruptured, run in a transverse direction, never extending quite across the ice-field, but narrowing out at the extremities, so that when they gape too wide to leap across they may generally be turned by following them to their termination. These rents and fissures are the chief source of danger to those who cross the glaciers, being often concealed by a treacherous coating of snow, and many a bold chamois-hunter has found a grave in their recesses. Ebel mentions an instance of a shepherd who, in driving his flock over the ice to a high pasturage, had the misfortune to tumble into one of these clefts. He fell in the vicinity of a torrent which flowed under the glacier, and, by following its bed under the vault of ice, succeeded in reaching the foot of the glacier with a broken arm. More melancholy was the fate of M. Mouron, a clergyman of Grindelwald : he was engaged in making some scientific researches upon the glacier, and was in the act of leaning over to examine a singular well-shaped aperture in the ice, when the staff, on which he rested, gave way ; he was precipitated to the bottom, and his lifeless and mangled body was recovered from the depths of the glacier a few days after.

These crevices, though chiefly formed mechanically by the movement of the glacier to fill up vacancies, and the unequal pressure of different parts, are greatly assisted by the action of the sun and wind. The S.E. wind, in Uri and among the Bernese Alps, is very instrumental in causing the glacier to split, and the loud reports thus occasioned, called by the herdsmen the growlings (brullen) of the glacier, are regarded as a sign of bad weather. The traveller who ventures to cross the Mer de Glace of Chamouni or Bern may, at times, both hear and see the fissures widening around him. The crevices exhibit in perfection the beautiful *azure blue* colour of the glacier ; the cause of which has not been satisfactorily accounted for. It is the same tint of ultramarine which the Rhone exhibits at Geneva, after leaving all its impurities behind it in the lake ; and the writer has even observed the same beautiful tint in footmarks and holes made in fresh-fallen snow, not more than a foot deep, among the high Alps on the borders of Tyrol.

The traveller who has only *read* of glaciers is often disappointed at the first sight of them, by the appearance of their surface, which, except when covered with fresh-fallen snow, or at very great heights, has none of the purity which might be expected from fields of ice. On the contrary it exhibits a surface of dirty white, soiled with mud and often covered with stones and gravel. Such beds of dirt and rubbish are common to most glaciers, and are called, in German, Guffer. They are supposed to be formed in the following manner :—the edge of the glacier receives the masses of stone and sand falling from the mountains above, produced by the disintegrations of moisture and frost. During the summer heat the glacier shrinks away from the rocks that bound it, and carries away the rubbish lying upon it. The intervening space between the foot of the mountains and the ice is filled up by the snow of winter, which is gradually changed into ice, and receives a fresh heap of gravel from above. This again is carried forward by the shrinking of the glacier. Thus these lines of loose stones are constantly advancing, one behind another, like waves ; and where the glacier from one valley joins that out of another, the heaps are often confounded and intermixed.

A singular circumstance occurs when a boulder, or large mass of rock, has fallen upon the glacier ; the shade and protection from the sun's rays afforded by the stone prevents the ice on which it rests from melting, and, while the surface around is gradually diminished, it remains supported on a pedestal or table, often attaining a height of several feet. When a leaf, insect, or such light body falls upon the ice, it gradually sinks, and at length disappears.

Another circumstance peculiar to the surface of the snow-field or upper glacier (firn) is the occurrence of Red Snow. This phenomenon, which at one time was treated with incredulity, is of common occurrence among the high Alps, and is produced by a species of fungus, called Palmella Nivalis, or Protococcus, a true vegetable, which plants itself on the surface of the snow, takes root, germinates, produces seed, and dies. In the state of germination it imparts a pale carmine tint to the snow ; this increases, as the plant comes to maturity, to a deep crimson blush, which gradually fades, and, as the plant decays, becomes a black dust or mould. By collecting some of the coloured snow in a bottle, and pouring it on a sheet of paper, the form of the plant may be discovered with a microscope, as soon as the water has evaporated.

Increase and Diminution, Advance and Retreat of the Glaciers.

It has been already observed that the vacancy caused by the melting of the lower portion of the glacier is filled up by the winter snow from above. But, as may be supposed, it often happens, after mild winters and warm summers, that the supply is not equal to the void, and, *vice versâ*, after severe winters and rainy summers, the glacier is overloaded, as it were ; indeed, it is scarcely possible that an exact equilibrium of supply and consumption should be preserved. Yet it seems probable, after all that has been said on the subject, that there is no material variation either in the extent or position of the glaciers among the Alps. Instances have occurred of the sudden advance of a glacier, as in the Gadmenthal (Route 32), where a road has been destroyed by this cause, and even of the formation of new glaciers within the memory of man, as in the Upper Engadine (?), and at the base of the Titlis ; but these have been followed by a similar retrocession, and the newly-formed ice-fields are rarely permanent. It is certain that, at present, both the Mer de Glace, under Mont Blanc, and the Grindelwald Glacier, appear to have shrunk, and sunk considerably below the level they once attained ; but this may be merely temporary, or even only their dimensions in summer, when most reduced. Another circumstance has been lost sight of in the consideration of this subject, viz., that the erosive powers of the ice may have, in many instances, considerably enlarged the bed of the glacier.

Professor Hugi has recently made some interesting experiments and observations upon the movement and rate of progress of the glaciers. In 1829 he noted the position of numerous loose blocks lying on the surface of the lower glacier of the Aar, relative to the fixed rocks at its sides. He also measured the glacier and erected signal-posts on it. In 1836 he found everything altered ; many of the loose blocks had moved off and entirely disappeared, along with the ice that supported them. A hut, which he had hastily erected, to shelter himself and his companions, had advanced 2184 feet; two blocks of granite, between which it stood, then eight feet apart, had been separated to a distance of 18 feet, the beams and timbers had fallen in between them, and the nails and pieces of iron used in fastening them exhibited not the slightest trace of rust. A mass of granite, containing 26,000 cubic feet, originally buried under the snow of the firn, which was now converted into glacier, had not only been raised to the surface, but was elevated above it, in the air, upon two pedestals, or pillars, of ice; so that a large body of men might have found shelter under it. A signal-post, stuck into a mass of granite, had not only made as great an advance as the hut, but the distance between the two had been increased 760 feet by the expansion of the glacier. The mass of the glacier had grown or increased near the point where it begins to descend 200 feet; lower down there was less augmentation perceptible. The advance of the ice-field of the Mer de Glace is calculated at between 400 and 500 feet yearly, and for 8 or 10 years past, the mass of the glacier has been shrinking and retiring gradually.

At the extremity of almost all glaciers a high transverse ridge of rubbish, called *The Moraine*, exists; it consists of fragments of rock which have fallen from the surrounding mountains, the transported debris of the Guffer, and of masses detached by the glacier itself. These are heaped up sometimes to a height of 80 or 100 feet. Not unfrequently there are 3 or 4 such ridges, one behind another, like so many lines of intrenchment. The broken stones, mud, and sand, mixed with shattered fragments of ice, of which they are composed, have an unsightly and shabby appearance, being perfectly barren of vegetation; but each heap is, as it were, a geological cabinet, containing specimens of all the neighbouring mountains. The glacier, indeed, seems to have a natural tendency to purge itself from impurities, and whatever happens to fall upon it is gradually discharged in this manner. It likewise exerts great mechanical force, and, like a vast millstone, grinds down, not only the rock which composes its channel, but all the fragments interposed between it and the rock; forming, in the end, a sort of stone-meal. The extent of the moraine depends on the character of the strata of the mountains around the glacier: where they are of granite, or other hard rock, not easily decomposed by the weather, the moraine is of small extent; and it is largest where the boundary rocks are of brittle limestone and fissile slate. Recent researches of Swiss naturalists (Agassiz and Charpentier) have discovered extensive moraines, not only in the lower part of the Vallais, but even on the shores of the Lake Leman, at a height of not more than 200 or 300 feet above it; clearly proving that, during some anterior condition of our planet, the valley of the Rhone was occupied by glaciers, in situations at present 40 or 50 miles distant from the nearest existing ice-field, and 3000 or 4000 feet below it.

It is highly interesting to consider how important a service the glaciers perform in the economy of nature. These dead and chilly fields of ice, which prolong the reign of winter throughout the year, are, in reality, the source of life and the springs of vegetation. They are the locked-up reservoirs, the sealed fountains, from which the vast rivers traversing the great continents of our globe are sustained. The summer heat, which dries up other sources of water, first opens out their bountiful supplies. When the rivers of the plain begin to shrink and dwindle within their parched beds, the torrents of the Alps, fed by melting snow and glaciers, rush down from the mountains and supply the deficiency; and, at this season (July and August), the rivers and lakes of Switzerland are fullest.

During the whole summer, the traveller who crosses the glaciers hears the torrents rustling and running below him at the bottom of the azure clefts. These plenteous rills gushing forth in their sub-glacial beds, are generally all collected in one stream, at the foot of the glacier, which, in consequence, is eaten away into a vast dome-shaped arch, sometimes 100 feet high, which gradually increases, until the constant thawing weakens its support, and it gives way and falls in with a crash. Such caverns of ice are seen in great perfection in some years, at the source of the Arveyron, in the valley of Chamouni, and in the glaciers of Grindelwald. The streams issuing from glaciers are distinguished by their turbid, dirty-white, or milky colour.

§ 18. AVALANCHES AND SNOW-STORMS.

" The avalanche,—the thunderbolt of snow."—*Byron.*

Avalanches (Germ. Lawinen) are those accumulations of snow which precipitate themselves from the mountains, either by their own weight or by the loosening effects of the sun's heat, into the valleys below, sweeping everything before them, and causing, at times, great destruction of life and property. The fearful crash which accompanies their descent is often heard at a distance of several leagues.

The natives of the Alps distinguish between several different kinds of avalanches. The *staub-lawinen* (dust avalanches) are formed of loose fresh-fallen snow, heaped up by the wind early in the winter, before it has begun to melt or combine together. Such a mass, when it reaches the edge of a cliff or declivity, tumbles from point to point, increasing in quantity as well as in impetus every instant, and spreading itself over a wide extent of surface. It descends with the rapidity of lightning, and has been known to rush down a distance of 10 miles from the point whence it was first detached; not only descending one side of a valley, but also ascending the opposite hill, by the velocity acquired in its fall, overwhelming and laying prostrate a whole forest of firs in its descent, and breaking down another forest, up the opposite side, so as to lay the heads of the trees up the hill in its ascent.

Another kind of avalanche, the *grund lawinen*, occurs in spring,

luring the months of April and May, when the sun becomes power-
ʾul and the snow thaws rapidly under its influence. They fall constantly from different parts of the mountains, at different hours
of the day, according as each part is reached by the sun : from the
E. side between 10 and 12, from the S. side between 12 and 2,
and latei in the day from the W. and N. This species is more
dangerous in its effects, from the snow being clammy and adhe-
sive, and also hard and compact. Any object buried by it can
only be dug out by the most arduous labour. Men ôr cattle overwhelmed by the staub-lawine can sometimes extricate themselves
by their own exertions; or, at any rate, from the snow being less
compact, may breathe for some hours through the interstices.
In the case of the grund-lawine, the sufferers are usually either
crushed or suffocated, and are, at any rate, so entangled that
they can only be rescued by the aid of others. Such avalanches
falling upon a mountain-stream, in a narrow gorge, have sometimes been hollowed out from beneath by the action of the water,
until it has forced a passage under them ; and they have then been
left standing for the whole summer, serving as a bridge over which
men and cattle might pass.

The avalanches have usually a fixed time for descending, and an
habitual channel down which they slide, which may be known by
its being worn perfectly smooth—sometimes even appearing polished, by the heap of debris at its base. The peasants, in some
situations, await with impatience the fall of the regular avalanches,
as a symptom of the spring having fairly set in.

Danger arises from avalanches either by their falling unexpectedly, while persons are traversing spots known to be exposed to
them, or else (and this is the more fearful cause of catastrophes)
from an unusual accumulation of snow formed by the wind, or, in
consequence of the severity of the season, causing the avalanche to
desert its usual bed, and to descend upon cultivated spots, houses, or
even villages. There are certain valleys among the Alps in which
scarcely any spot is totally exempt from the possible occurrence of
such a calamity, though some are naturally more exposed than
others. The Val Bedretto, in Canton Tessin, the Meyenthal, in
Canton Uri, and many others, are thus dreadfully exposed. To
guard as much as possible against accidents, very large and massive
dykes of masonry, like the projecting bastions of a fortification, are,
in such situations, built against the hill-side, behind churches,
houses, and other buildings, with an angle pointing upwards, in
order to break and turn aside the snow. In some valleys, great
care is bestowed on the preservation of the forests clothing their
sides, as the best protection of the district below them from such
calamities. These may truly be regarded as sacred groves; and no
one is allowed to cut down timber within them, under pain of a
legal penalty. Yet they not unfrequently show the inefficiency
even of such protection against so fearful an engine of destruction. Whole forests are at times cut over and laid prostrate by the
avalanche. The tallest stems, fit to make masts for a first-rate man-

of-war, are snapped asunder like a bit of wax, and the barkless and branchless stumps and relics of the forest remain for years like a stubble-field to tell of what has happened.

A mournful catalogue of catastrophes, which have occurred in Switzerland, since the records of history, from avalanches, might be made out if necessary; but it will suffice to mention one or two instances.

In 1720 an avalanche killed, in Ober-Gestelen (Vallais), 84 men and 400 head of cattle, and destroyed 120 houses. The same year, 40 individuals perished at Brieg, and 23 on the Great St. Bernard, from a similar cause.

In 1749 the village of Ruaras, in the Tavetsch Thal, was carried away by an avalanche; 100 men were overwhelmed by it, 60 of whom were dug out alive; and some of the houses, though removed to some distance from their original site, were so little shaken that persons sleeping within them were not awakened.

In 1800, after a snow-storm of three days' continuance, an enormous avalanche detached itself from the top of the precipice of Klucas above Trons, in the valley of the Vorder Rhein; it crossed the valley and destroyed a wood and some chalets on the opposite pasture of Zenin; recoiling, with the force it had acquired, to the side from which it had come, it did fresh mischief there, and so revolving to and fro, at the fourth rush reached Trons, and buried many of its houses to the roof in snow.

In 1827 the greater part of the village of Biel, in the Upper Vallais, was crushed beneath a tremendous avalanche, which ran down a ravine, nearly two leagues long, before it reached the village.

One of the most remarkable phenomena attending the avalanche is the blast of air which accompanies it, and which, like what is called the wind of a cannon-ball, extends its destructive influence to a considerable distance on each side of the actual line taken by the falling mass. It has all the effect of a blast of gunpowder: sometimes forest-trees, growing near the sides of the channel down which the snow passes, are uprooted and laid prostrate, without having been touched by it In this way, the village of Randa, in the Visp-Thal, lost many of its houses by the current of an avalanche which fell in 1720, blowing them to atoms, and scattering the materials like chaff. The E. spire of the convent of Dissentis was thrown down by the gust of an avalanche, which fell more than a quarter of a mile off.

Travellers visiting the Alps between the months of June and October are little exposed to danger from avalanches, except immediately after a snow-storm; and, when compelled to start at such times, they should pay implicit obedience to the advice of the guides. It is a common saying, that there is risk of avalanches as long as the burthen of snow continues on the boughs of the fir-trees, and while the naturally sharp angles of the distant mountains continue to look rounded.

It is different with those who travel from necessity in the spring, and before the annual avalanches have fallen. Muleteers, carriers, and such persons, use great caution in traversing exposed parts of the road, and with these they are well acquainted. They proceed, in parties, in single file, at a little distance from one another, in order that, if the snow should sweep one off, the others may be ready to render assistance. They proceed as fast as possible, carefully avoiding any noise, even speaking, and, it is said, will sometimes muffle the mules' bells, lest the slightest vibration communicated to the air should disengage the nicely-poised mass of snow above their heads.

The avalanches, seen and heard by summer tourists on the sides of Mont Blanc and the Jungfrau, are of a different kind from those described above, being caused only by the rupture of a portion of the glaciers, which give way under the influence of the mid-day sun and of certain winds, during the summer and autumn, when other avalanches, generally speaking, have ceased to fall. They differ, also, in this respect, that, for the most part, they do no harm, since they fall on uncultivable and uninhabited spots. It is more by the roar which accompanies them, which, awakening the echoes of the Alps, sounds very like thunder, than by the appearance which they present, that they realize what is usually expected of avalanches. Still they are worth seeing, and will much enhance the interest of a visit to the Wengern Alp, the Cramont (on the S. side of Mont Blanc), or the borders of the Mer de Glace; especially if the spectator will bear in mind the immense distance at which he is placed from the objects which he sees and hears, and will consider that, at each roar, whole tons of solid ice are broken off from the parent glacier, and, in tumbling, many hundred feet perhaps, are shattered to atoms and ground to powder.

The *Snow-storms, Tourmentes,* or *Guxen,* which occur on the Alps, are much dreaded by the chamois-hunter, the shepherd, and those most accustomed to traverse the High Alps; how much more formidable must they be to the inexperienced traveller! They consist of furious and tempestuous winds, somewhat of the nature of a whirlwind, which occur on the summit-ridges and elevated gorges of the Alps, either accompanied by snow, or filling the air with that recently fallen, while the flakes are still dry, tossing them about like powder or dust. In an instant the atmosphere is filled with snow; earth, sky, mountain, abyss, and landmark of every kind, are obliterated from view, as though a curtain were let down on all sides of the wanderer. All trace of path, or of the footsteps of preceding travellers, are at once effaced, and the poles planted to mark the direction of the road are frequently overturned. In some places the gusts sweep the rock bare of snow, heaping it up in others, perhaps across the path, to a height of 20 feet or more, barring all passage, and driving the wayfarer to despair. At every step he fears to plunge into an abyss, or sink overhead in the snow. Large parties of men and animals have been overwhelmed by the snow-wreaths on the St. Gothard, where they sometimes attain a height of 40 or 50 feet. These tempests are accompanied almost every year by loss of life;

and, though of less frequent occurrence in summer than in winter and spring, are a chief reason why it is dangerous for inexperienced travellers to attempt to cross remote and elevated passes without a guide.

The guides and persons residing on the mountain-passes, from the appearance of the sky, and other weather-signs known to them, can generally foresee the occurrence of tourmentes, and can tell when the fall of avalanches is to be apprehended.

§ 19. GOITRE AND CRETINISM.

"Quis tumidum guttur miratur in Alpibus?"—*Juv.*

It is a remarkable fact that, amidst some of the most magnificent scenery of the globe, where Nature seems to have put forth all her powers in exciting emotions of wonder and elevation in the mind, man appears, from a mysterious visitation of disease, in his most degraded and pitiable condition. Such, however, is the fact. It is in the grandest and most beautiful valleys of the Alps that the maladies of *goitre* and *cretinism* prevail.

Goitre is a swelling in the front of the neck (of the thyroid gland, or the parts adjoining), which increases with the growth of the individual, until, in some cases, it attains an enormous size, and becomes "a hideous wallet of flesh," to use the words of Shakspeare, hanging pendulous down to the breast. It is not, however, attended with pain, and generally seems to be more unsightly to the spectator than inconvenient or hateful to the bearer.

Cretinism, which occurs in the same localities as goitre, and evidently arises from the same cause, whatever it may be, is a more serious malady, inasmuch as it affects the mind. The cretin is an idiot—a melancholy spectacle—a creature who may almost be said to rank a step below a human being. There is vacancy in his countenance; his head is disproportionately large; his limbs are stunted or crippled; he cannot articulate his words with distinctness; and there is scarcely any work which he is capable of executing. He spends his days basking in the sun, and, from its warmth, appears to derive great gratification. When a stranger appears, he becomes a clamorous and importunate beggar, assailing him with a ceaseless chattering; and the traveller is commonly glad to be rid of his hideous presence at the expense of a batz.

Various theories have been resorted to, to account for this complaint: some have attributed it to the use of water derived from melting snow; others, to the habit of carrying heavy weights on the head; others, again, to filthy habits; while a fourth theory derives it from the nature of the soil, or the use of spring water impregnated with calcareous matter; and a recent author has published the following statement regarding it:—

"The proportion of the inhabitants of each rock, who are affected with goitre and cretinism will stand to the healthy in the following order:—

" Granite and gneiss—goitre, $\frac{1}{500}$; cretins, none.
" Mica-slate and hornblende slate—goitre, none; cretins, none.
" Clay-slate—goitre, $\frac{1}{166}$; cretins, none.
" Transition-slate—goitre, $\frac{1}{149}$; cretins, none.
" Steatitic sandstone—goitre, none; cretins, none.
" Calcareous rocks—goitre, $\frac{1}{3}$; cretins, $\frac{1}{32}$.

" Are we to suppose that these interesting results are the effects of chance, or of an accidental association of circumstances confined to a particular spot? When we recollect that a space of upwards of a thousand square miles has been made subject to the inquiry, and that, in every portion of this space, the same invariable circumstances attended the presence of the disease, and that its absence was invariably distinguished by the absence of those circumstances, it is more philosophic to view them in the light of cause and effect."—*Dr. M'Clelland.*

As the goitre occurs in Derbyshire, Notts, Hants, &c., where no permanent snow exists—and no rivers spring from glaciers—also in Sumatra and in parts of South America, where snow is unknown, it is evident that the first cause assigned is not the true one; as for the second and third, they would equally tend to produce goitre in the London porters, and in the inhabitants of the purlieus of St. Giles's. If the limestone theory be true, all other rocks should be exempt from it, which is not the case, as far as our experience goes. Goitre is found only in certain valleys; nor, when it does occur, does it exist throughout the valley. It appears in one spot; higher up it is unknown, and in another situation, a mile or two distant, perhaps, it is again prevalent.

A careful attention to the circumstances accompanying its appearance will show that it is connected with the condition of the atmosphere, and is found in low, warm, and moist situations, at the bottom of valleys, where a stagnation of water occurs, and where the summer exhalations and autumnal fogs arising from it are not carried off by a free circulation of air. It is found in places where the valley is confined, and shut in, as it were—where a free draft is checked by its sides being clothed with wood, or by a sudden bend occurring in its direction—where, at the same time, the bottom is subject to the overflowings of a river, or to extensive artificial irrigation. The conjecture which derives the disease from breathing an atmosphere of this kind, not liable to be purified by fresh currents of air to carry off the vapours, is, perhaps, the one most deserving of consideration.

The disease is much more common in females than in males, and usually occurs about the age of puberty. It becomes hereditary in a family, but children born and educated on spots distant from home and in elevated situations are often exempt from it. Iodine has been applied with success as a remedy in some cases; but, as it is a dangerous remedy, the administration of it must be resorted to with the greatest caution.

PLAN OF THE HAND-BOOK.

ABBREVIATIONS, &c.

The points of the Compass are often marked simply by the letters N. S. E. W.

(*rt.*) right, (*l.*) left,—applied to the banks of a river. The right bank is that which lies on the right hand of a person whose back is turned towards the source, or the quarter from which the current descends.

Miles.—Distances are always reduced to English miles, except when foreign miles are expressly mentioned.

The names of Inns precede the description of every place, (often in a parenthesis,) because the first information needed by a traveller is where to lodge.

Instead of designating a town by the vague words "large" or "small," the amount of the population, according to the latest census, is almost invariably stated, as presenting a more exact scale of the importance and size of the place.

In order to avoid repetition, the Routes are preceded by a chapter of preliminary information; and, to facilitate reference to it, each division or paragraph is separately numbered.

Each Route is numbered with Arabic figures, corresponding with the figures attached to the Route on the Map, which thus serves as an Index to the Book; at the same time that it presents a *tolerably* exact view of the great high-roads of Europe, and of the course of public conveyances.

The Map is to be placed at the end of the Book.

The View of the Bernese Alps to face page 1.

⁎⁎ The Coats of Arms on the cover are those of the 22 Cantons forming the Swiss Confederation.

In preparation,

A HAND-BOOK FOR TRAVELLERS IN FRANCE;
Post 8vo.

A HAND-BOOK FOR TRAVELLERS IN NORTHERN ITALY;
Post 8vo.

A HAND-BOOK FOR TRAVELLERS IN DENMARK, NORWAY, SWEDEN, AND RUSSIA;
Post 8vo.

SECTION I.

SWITZERLAND.

ROUTE 1.

BASLE TO BIENNE AND BERN BY THE
VAL MOUTIERS (MÜNSTER THAL),
WITH EXCURSION TO THE WEISSEN-
STEIN.

BASLE, or Bâle. (Germ. Basel,
Ital. Basilea.)—*Inns:* Drei Könige
(Three Kings), well situated, overlooking the Rhine, which washes its
walls—a good inn, but expensive;
dinner at the table d'hôte, 3 fr. at 1
o'clock—4 fr. at 5 o'clock—in private, 6 fr.;—the Stork (Cigogne),
good;—Krone (Crown); Kopf (Tête
d'Or).

Basle, capital of the now subdi-
vided canton called Basle-town, is
situated on the Rhine, and the larger
portion lies on the l. bank, which is
connected with the rt. by a bridge of
wood, partly supported on stone piers.
The territory of the town extends for
about 4 miles on the rt. side of the
river. It has 21,240 inhab., and it
enjoys considerable prosperity from
the residence of many rich merchants,
bankers, and families of ancient descent, and from its position in an
angle on the frontiers of France,
Germany, and Switzerland, about a
mile below the spot where the Rhine
first becomes navigable. It has some
manufactures, of which the most
important are those of ribands and
paper. English travellers have
hitherto been too much in the habit
of considering Basle merely as a
halting-place for the night, which

they quit as soon as they are furnished with horses; yet its situation
on high, sloping banks, overlooking
the Rhine, which rushes past in a
full broad flood of a clear, light green,
bounded by the hills of the Black
Forest on the one side, of the Jura
on the other—but, above all, its
Minster, and its Gallery of the Works
of Holbein, deserve some attention.
It must be remembered that Basle,
though *politically* a portion of the
Swiss Confederation, is yet, *historically,* a part of Suabia, and that it
retains many of the characteristics of
an imperial free town more distinctly
than many of those which have continued German, and have become incorporated in modern sovereignties.

The *Cathedral,* or Münster, on the
high bank on the l. of the Rhine,
above the bridge, distinguished by
its two spires, and the deep-red
colour of the sandstone of which it is
built, is an interesting and picturesque
edifice, though not of beautiful architecture. It was begun by the emperor
Henry II. in 1010, and consecrated
1019: the choir, the lower part of
the E. end, and the crypt beneath,
are of this period, and exhibit a style
of ornament widely different from
what is usually termed Saxon or
Norman. The 4 columns, formed
of groups of detached pillars, with
singular and grotesque capitals; the
tomb of the empress Anne, wife of
Rudolph of Habsburg, and mother
of the line of Austrian princes, whose
body was removed to St. Blaize in

1770 ; a stone font, date 1465; are worth notice in this part of the building. So likewise is the portal of St. Gallus, leading into the N. transept, and decorated with statues of Christ and St. Peter, and of the wise and foolish virgins. In the W. front are groups of statues: St. George and the Dragon, and St. Martin and the Beggar, stand forth with great boldness. The church is used now for the Protestant service, and the altar stands between the choir and nave, nearly underneath a rich Gothic gallery or rood-loft (date 1381). On the l. of the altar, against a pillar, is the red marble tombstone of Erasmus, who died here in 1536. A staircase, leading out of the choir, conducts into a small apartment— the Chapter House, or *Conciliums Saal*—in which some of the meetings of the Council of Basle, or rather of its committees, were held between 1436 and 1444. It is a low room, with four Gothic windows—distinguished not only in an historical point of view, but also as being quite unaltered since the day of the Council. On the S. side of the choir are situated the very extensive and picturesque *Cloisters*—a succession of quadrangles and open halls— which, with the space they inclose, still serve, as they have done for centuries, as a burial-place, and are filled with tombs. Within them are the monuments of the 3 Reformers, Œcolampadius, Grynæus, and Meyer. They were constructed in the 14th century, and extend to the verge of the hill overlooking the river. It is not unlikely they may have been the favourite resort of Erasmus.

Behind the Minster is a *Terrace*, called *Die Pfalz*, nearly 60 ft. above the river, planted with 10 chesnut trees, and commanding a beautiful view over the Rhine, the town, and the Black Forest hills. Close to it is the Club called *Cassino*, containing a reading-room, &c.

The Minster is situated in a square of considerable size—in one corner

of which, in a recess, stands the *Public Library*, containing 50,000 volumes—among them, the Acts of the Council of Bâle, 3 vols., with chains attached to the binding, many very important MSS., of which there is a good catalogue, and a few of the books of Erasmus ; also, a copy of his " Praise of Folly," with marginal illustrations by the pen of *Holbein*. There are autographs of Luther, Melancthon, Erasmus, and Zuinglius. On the ground-floor is the *Gallery of Paintings and Drawings by the younger Holbein*—a highly interesting collection of the works of that master, including the Passion of Christ, in 8 compartments ; a dead Christ—both formerly in the Minster ; Holbein's Wife and Children, with countenances full of grief and misery ; portraits of Erasmus, of Froben the printer—excellent; of a Mlle. von Offenburg—twice repeated; two representations of a School, painted by the artist at the age of 14, and hung up as a sign over a schoolmaster's door in the town of Basle. Among the drawings are Holbein's own portrait—a work of the highest excellence ; heads of the family Meyer, sketched for the celebrated picture now in the Dresden Gallery ; original sketch for the famous picture of the family of Sir Thomas More—the names of the different personages are written on their dresses ; 5 sketches for the frescoes which formerly decorated the Rathhaus in Basle, with one or two fragments of the frescoes themselves ; sketches in ink for glass windows, for the sheaths of daggers, for the organ in the Minster; the Costumes of Basle, &c. &c. Here are also preserved some fresco fragments of the original Dance of Death, which once adorned the walls of the Dominican Church in Basle, and a set of coloured drawings of the whole series of figures. The Dance of Death has been attributed without cause to Holbein, since it existed at the time of the Council of Basle, at east 50 years before his birth. Holbein was born at Basle in 1489: his circumstances were by no means prosperous; he was even reduced to work as a day-labourer and house-painter, and painted the outer walls of the houses of the town. It is related of him that, being employed to decorate the shop of an apothecary, who was intent on keeping the young artist close to his work, and being disposed to repair to a neighbouring wineshop, he painted a pair of legs so exactly like his own on the underside of the scaffolding, that the apothecary, seated below, believed him to be constantly present and diligently employed. Erasmus, writing from Bâle a letter of introduction for the painter to one of his friends, complains that " hic frigent artes," and the want of encouragement, drove Holbein to seek his fortune in England, where he met with high patronage, as is well known.

In the lower story of the Library are also deposited a number of antiquities, bronzes, fragments of pottery, coins, &c., from Augst, the site] of the Roman *Augusta Rauracorum,* 7 miles from Basle.

The *University* of Basle, founded 1460, was the first great seminary for the advancement of learning established in Switzerland : it once enjoyed a high reputation, and numbered among the lists of its professors the names of Erasmus, Euler, and Bernouilli—the two last, mathematicians and natives of Basle. The University has been greatly injured by the recent and unjust seizure of part of its funds by the country division of the canton. Besides the Library mentioned above, there is a small and not very important *Museum of Natural History,* placed in a building near the Minster.

The *Rathhaus,* in the Market-place, is a building of pleasing Burgundian Gothic architecture, founded 1508, and recently repaired without changing its character. The frescoes, however, said to be designed by Holbein,

previously partly obliterated, are now removed. The frieze contains the emblazoned shields of the original Swiss cantons; the armorial bearing of canton Basle is said to be meant to represent the case of a cross-bow. At the foot of the stairs is placed a statue of Munatius Plancus, the founder, according to tradition, of Bâle and of the Roman colony of Augst.

The greater and lesser councils of the canton hold their sittings in the apartments above.

The *Arsenal* contains a limited collection of ancient armour, of which the only curiosities are a suit of chain mail, once gilt, with plate mail beneath it, worn by Charles the Bold at the battle of Nancy; two Burgundian cannon, of iron bars bound round with hoops ; and several suits of Burgundian and Armagnac armour.

The terraced *Garden of M. Vischer,* an eminent banker, overlooking the Rhine, is a very pretty spot.

The gateways, battlemented works, watch-towers, and ditch, which formed the ancient defences of the town, remain in a good state of preservation. The *Paulusthor* retains its advanced work or *Barbican,* similar to those which formerly existed at York, and, with its double portcullis and two flanking towers, is particularly picturesque. The machicolations are supported by strange but clever figures approaching to the grotesque.

Basle is scarcely surpassed in cleanliness even by the towns of Holland : its streets are plentifully supplied with fountains ; and it would indeed be a reproach to the inhabitants, if, with the rapid and abundant current of the Rhine to cleanse them from all filth, they were allowed to remain dirty.

Down to the end of the last century (1795), the clocks of Basle went an hour in advance of those in other places of Europe—a singular custom, the origin of which is not precisely known. According to tradition, it arose from the circumstance of a conspiracy to deliver the town to an enemy at midnight having been defeated by the clock striking 1 instead of 12.

Attached to the clock-tower on the bridge is a grotesque head, called Lallenkönig, which, by the movement of the pendulum, is constantly protruding its long tongue and rolling its goggle eyes—making faces, it is said, at Little Basle, on the opposite side of the river.

The ancient sumptuary laws of Basle were singular and severe. On Sunday all must dress in black to go to church; females could not have their hair dressed by men; carriages were not permitted in the town after 10 at night, and it was forbidden to place a footman behind a carriage. The official censors, called Unzichterherrn, had the control of the number of dishes and wines to be allowed at a dinner party, and their authority was supreme on all that related to the cut and quality of clothes. At one time they waged desperate war against slashed doublets and hose.

Since the Reformation, Basle has been regarded as the stronghold of Methodism in Switzerland. The pious turn of its citizens was remarkably exhibited in the mottoes and signs placed over their doors. These have now disappeared; but two very singular ones have been recorded—

> Auf Gott ich meine hoffnung bau,
> Und Wohne in der *Alten Sau.*

> In God my hopes of grace I big,
> And dwell within the Ancient Pig.

> Wacht auf ihr menschen und that Buss,
> Ich heiss *zum goldenen Rinderfuss.*

> Wake, and repent your sins with grief;
> I'm call'd the Golden Shin of Beef.

Even now, should the traveller arrive at the gates of the town on Sunday during church-time, he will find them closed, and his carriage will be detained outside till the service is over. The spirit of trade, however, went hand in hand with that of religion— and Basle has been called a city of usurers; 5 per cent. was styled a " Christian usance " (einen Christ-

lichen zins), and a proclamation of the magistrates (1682–84) denounced those who lent money at a discount of 4 or 3½ per cent. as " selfish, avaricious, and dangerous persons;" those who lent their capital at a lower rate were liable to have it confiscated, because, forsooth, such persons, " by their avarice, did irremediable injury to churches, hospitals, church property, &c., and are the ruin of poor widows and orphans."

The dissensions which broke out soon after the Revolution of 1830 between the inhabitants of the town of Basle, and those of the country, led to a civil war between the parties, and a bloody contest near Liesthal occasioned, in 1832, the Swiss Diet to pass an act for the formal separation of the canton into two parts, called Basle Ville and Basle Campagne. The latter consists of two-thirds of the territory of the whole canton, and has for its capital Liesthal. Each sends a deputy to the Diet; but the two divisions enjoy only half a vote each, and when the deputies of the two parts take opposite sides (which hitherto has been invariably the case), their vote does not count. This Revolution has left the town of Bâle saddled with a debt of two millions of francs.

About two miles out of the town, just within the French frontier, is the ruined fortress of *Hüningen,* erected by Louis XV. to overawe his Swiss neighbours, and dismantled in 1815.

A good representation of the Dance of Death, in burnt clay, may be purchased of Maehly and Schablitz, who have a manufactory peculiar (it is believed) to the spot of " figures plastique en terre cuite."

The traveller, entering Switzerland by Basle, is particularly recommended to take the following route by the Val Moutier, or Münster Thal on his way either to Berne or Geneva.

Posting ceases at Basle, and travellers should therefore engage voiurier's horses to carry them on their journey. Return-coachmen are generally to be found at all the inns, and there are persons in the town who keep horses and carriages for hire.

Public Conveyances.

A *Diligence* goes daily, in two days and three nights, to Paris.

Postwaggons daily to Berne and Neuchâtel, by Moutiers and Bienne ; to Chaux de Fonds and Geneva.

Mond., Wed., Sat., to Olten, So-eure, and Lucerne.

Daily, to Aarau, Zurich.

———— Baden, Strasburg, Frank-urt a M.

———— Mühlhausen and Colmar.

Mond., Thursd., Sat., Schaffhau-en.

Bâle to Bienne.

16½ Swiss stunden = 54 Eng. miles. Thence to Berne by Aarberg, 6 tunde = 20 Eng. miles.

A diligence runs daily to Berne and Neuchâtel.

The valley of the Birs, commonly called the Val Moutiers (Münster Thal, in Germ.), through which this xcellent road passes, is the most nteresting and romantic in the whole ange of the Jura. It consists of a eries of narrow and rocky defiles, lternating with open basins, co-ered with black forests above, and erdant meadows below, enlivened by villages, mills, and forges. A oad was originally carried through he Val Moutiers by the Romans, to keep up the communication between Aventicum, the Helvetian capital, and Augst, their great fortified out-post on the Rhine.

At St. Jacob, about a quarter of a nile beyond the gates of Bâle, in the angle between two roads, a small Gothic cross has been erected, to commemorate the *battle of St. Jacob*, fought in 1444, when 1600 Swiss had the boldness to attack, and the courage to withstand for 10 hours, a French army tenfold more numerous, commanded by the Dauphin, after-wards Louis XI. Only 10 of the

Swiss escaped alive, the rest were left dead on the field, along with thrice their own number of foes, whom they had slain. This almost incredible exploit first spread abroad through Europe the fame of Swiss valour; and Louis, the Dauphin, wisely seeing that it was better to gain them as friends than to oppose them as enemies, courted their al-liance, and first enrolled them as a permanent body-guard about his person—a practice continued by the French monarchs down to Charles X. The Swiss themselves refer to the battle of St. Jacob as the Thermo-pylæ of their history. The vineyards near the field produce a red wine, called Schweitzer Blut (Swiss blood).

A few miles farther, near Reinach, on the opposite bank of the Birs, is another battle-field—that of *Dorn-ach*—where the Swiss gained a victory over a much larger Austrian force in 1499, during the Suabian war. The bone-house, in which the remains of the slain were collected, still exists near the Capuchin Convent, and is filled with skulls gathered from the field. In the church of the village Maupertuis is buried. A monument, set up to his memory by his friend Bernouilli, was destroyed by the curé of the village, who was in the habit of repairing his hearthstone when broken, with slabs taken from the churchyard. It has been replaced by a fresh monument set up at the expense of canton Soleure.

Beyond Oesch the road enters that part of the Canton Bern which an-ciently belonged to the Archbishop of Basle; the valley contracts, in-creasing in picturesque beauty as you advance. The castles of Angerstein and Zwingen are passed before reach-ing

4¼ Lauffen,—a walled village.

2½ Soyhière, — a village prettily situated, with a small country inn, tolerably good. A contracted pass, the rocks of which on the rt. are sur-mounted by a convent, leads into the open basin of Délémont (Delsberg) ;

but it is unnecessary to pass through that little town (situated on the way to Portentruy), as our road turns to the l., and, continuing by the side of the Birs, enters a defile higher, grander, and more wild than any that have preceded it. This is, properly speaking, the commencement of the Val Moutiers. Rocky precipices overhang the road, and black forests of fir cover the mountains above. In the midst of it are the iron furnaces and forges of

1¼ Courrendelin, supplied with ore in the shape of small granulated red masses, varying from the size of a pea to that of a cherry, from the neighbouring mines. The remarkable rent by which the Jura has been cleft from top to bottom, so as to allow a passage for the Birs, exhibits marks of some great convulsion of the earth, by which the strata of limestone (Jura-kalk) have been thrown into a nearly vertical position, and appear like a succession of gigantic walls on each side of the road. The gorge terminates in another open basin, in the midst of which lies

1¼ Moutiers Grandval, or Münster—(*Inn:* Krone, good)—a village of 1250 inhabitants, named from a very ancient *Minster* of St. Germanus on the height, founded in the 7th century, and now fast falling to ruin. There is a car road from Moutiers to the *summit of the Weissenstein,* a distance of about 10 miles, up-hill nearly the whole way, and the latter part very rough and bad; fit only for the cars of the country, one of which, drawn by two horses, may be hired here to go and return for 20fr. It passes through the villages of Grandval (Grossau) and Ganzbrunnen; the ascent occupies 3½ hours, and the jolting is very severe. The Weissenstein is described in Route 3.

At the upper end of the basin of Moutiers the road is conducted through another defile, equally grand, at the bottom of which the Birs foams and rushes, overhung

by perpendicular cliffs and funerea firs. To this succeeds the littl plain of Tavannes, in which ar situated the villages of Court, Mal leray, and Dachsfelden, or

3½ Tavannes (where the Couronn and the Croix are good inns, bette than that at Moutiers). There ar foot-paths over the mountains from Court and Bévilard to Reuchenette by which some distance is saved on th way to Bienne, but the Pierre Pertui is thus missed. The valley to the E of Court, called Chaluat (Tschaywo) is inhabited by the descendants o the Anabaptists, expelled from Bern in 1708-11. They are distinguishe by their industry and simple man ners: the young men wear beards A few miles above Tavannes is th source of the Birs; before reachin it our road quits the valley, moun ing up a steep ascent, in the midd of which it passes under the singula and picturesque archway formed i the solid rock, called

¼ *Pierre Pertuis.* It is probabl a natural opening, enlarged by ar It existed in the time of the R mans, as is proved by a deface inscription on the N. side.

```
·NUMINI AUG———
———VM —
VIA    CTA    PERT —
DV —— VM PATER —
IL VIR — COL HELV—
```

It stood on the boundary-line, s parating the people of the Raurac who extended to Bâle, from th Sequani. The archway is abou 40 ft. high and 10 or 12 thick. Th pass was fortified by the Austrians i 1813.

½ Sonceboz—(inn not very good —a village in the Val St. Imie (Germ. Erguel), up which runs good road to Chaux de Fonds, an out of which another branches S. t Neuchâtel from Villaret. The roa to Bienne descends the valley alon the l. bank of the Süze, which form several small cascades. The pr jecting rock of Rond Châtel wa occupied in feudal times by a for

nd held by the powerful Bishops of
Bâle, to whom it gave the command
f this pass. The view from the last
lope of the Jura, over Bienne, and
ts lake, backed in clear weather by
he snowy range of the Alps, is ex-
eedingly beautiful.

3 Bienne (Germ. Biel) — *Inns :*
H. du Jura, outside the town, re-
ently established, and good ;—Cou-
onne, within the town. — Bienne
s prettily situated at the mouth of
he valley of the Suze, at the foot of
he Jura ; here mantled with vines,
nd about a mile from the head of
he lake of Bienne (Route 45). It is
till surrounded by its ancient walls
and watch-towers, and is approached
y several shady avenues. The number of inhabitants, chiefly Protest-
nts, amounts to 3000. The town
anciently belonged to the Bishop of
Bâle, but the citizens, early imbued
with the spirit of freedom, formed a
perpetual alliance with Berne in
1352, for the defence of their liber-
ies, in revenge for which the town
was burnt by their liege lord. The
Reformation further weakened the
connexion between the town and its
ecclesiastical ruler, and at the beginning of the 17th century his
authority became nominal. Bienne
s an industrious town, situated at
the junction of the high-roads from
Berne, Bâle, Soleure, and Neuchâtel,
between all which places there are
public conveyances daily. The new
road, recently completed, along the
W. shore of the lake, shortens the
distance to Neuchâtel by nearly 8
miles : it passes near the *Isle St.
Pierre*, celebrated as the residence of
Rousseau, and is described in Route
45.

Those who have a taste for climbing may gratify it by ascending
from hence the *Chasseral*, one of the
highest mountains of the Jura,
3616 ft. above the lake, and 4936 ft.
above the sea, with the certainty of
being rewarded with a magnificent
view if the weather be clear, but the
ascent will occupy 5 hours.

Quitting Bienne the high-road first
crosses the Suze, on its way into the
lake, and a quarter of a mile farther
on, the Thiele (Zihl), on its way out
of the lake. The last is a navigable
river which drains the three lakes of
Bienne, Neuchâtel, and Morat, and
joins the river Aar about four miles
lower down. On the margin of the
lake, at the outlet of the Thiele,
stand Nydau—(*Inn :* Bear)—and its
castle, flanked by round towers and
surmounted by a tall square keep.
The lords of Nydau, an extinct family, to whom it once belonged, were
foes of Berne ; their stronghold now
bears on its front the Bernese bear,
painted of colossal dimensions, and
is converted into the Cantonal salt-
warehouse. From the slope of the
hill, near Belmont, a good view is
obtained of the lake and of St. Peter's Isle.

2¼ Aarberg is a town of 700 inhabitants, on a rocky promontory, nearly
surrounded by the Aar, which, indeed, at high water, actually converts it into an island. The road
enters and quits the town by two
covered bridges.

3¼ BERN—in Route 24.

ROUTE 2.

BASLE TO SCHAFFHAUSEN.

17½ Stunden = 56½ Eng. miles.

There are two roads of nearly equal
length, one on the l. bank of the
Rhine, which is traversed by the daily
diligence (13 hours is the time occupied in the journey); and the
other on the rt. bank, through the
territory of Baden, which is provided
with post horses at the following stations :—Warmbach, 2 Germ. miles,
—Säkingen, 2⅛,—Waldshut, 3½,—
Ober Lauchingen, 1½. — Schaffhausen 3.

The road on the Swiss side of the
Rhine passes through the two villages of

2 Augst, which stand on each

side of the river Ergolz, on the site of
the Roman city *Augusta Rauracorum*,
founded by Munatius Plancus, in the
reign of Augustus. Its existence on
this spot is sufficiently proved by
the quantity of Roman remains that
have been, and still are, discovered
wherever the ground is turned up.
There are indications of an amphitheatre, now converted into pleasure
grounds; but the remains of buildings are very slight.

1¼ Rheinfelden—(*Inn :* Drei Könige)—a town of 1500 inhabitants,
on the l. bank of the Rhine, here
crossed by a wooden bridge, above
and below which the rocks in the
river bed form considerable rapids
and falls. On an island in the middle of the river, above the bridge,
rise the ruins of the feudal *Castle of
Stein*, which was destroyed by the
army of the Swiss Confederacy in
1445.

4¼ Lauffenburg—a town of 900
inhabitants, connected by a wooden
bridge with Klein Lauffenburg, on the
rt. bank of the Rhine. The river is
here interrupted by more rapids and
falls, in German called *Lauffen*,
whence the name of the place. Small
boats descending the stream can only
pass them by unloading their car-
goes above, and being let down gradually by stout ropes, held by men
stationed on the bank.

The road here, crossing the Rhine,
enters Baden and proceeds along the
rt. bank to

2¾ Waldshut, a walled town of
1000 inhabitants, on the skirts of the
Black Forest.

A mile above this, near a small
village called Coblenz (Confluentia),
the Rhine is joined by the Aar. At
Waldshut our road turns away from
the Rhine, and proceeds by Thien-
gen and Erzingen to

5¼ Neunkirch, a Swiss village, in
the canton of Schaffhausen.

2½ SCHAFFHAUSEN.   Route 7.

ROUTE 3.

To Soleure 12 stunden=39¼ Englis
miles ; thence to Bienne 3¾ stunde.

The road, on quitting Bâle, crosse
the river Birs, and proceeds along th
l. bank of the Rhine till within
short distance of Augst (p. 7)
where it turns S. to

3 *Liesthal*—*Inns :* Schlüssel (l
Clé) ;—Baselstab.

Chief town of the division of th
canton distinguished as Bâle Cam
pagne (Basel Landschaft), which
having revolted from the town o
Bâle after the July revolution, wa
separated from it by an act of th
Diet in 1832, though the two divi
sions are still regarded in the Diet bu
as one estate. Bâle Campagne in
cludes 53 parishes, with about 36,00
inhabitants, or about four-fifths of th
canton. Liesthal contains 2170 in
habitants, and since the Revolutio
has been hurriedly fitted up with th
apparatus of government, a "kanz
ley," or chancery, an arsenal, a pri
son, two gens d'armes, and three sen
try-boxes. The pretty and smilin
valley of the Ergolz, in which it i
situated, was the scene of a shockin
massacre in 1833 (August 3). In con
sequence of the aggressions of th
country people the inhabitants of Bâl
town were compelled to march agains
them a force of about 1500 men
chiefly citizens, merchants, and shop
keepers, little skilled in the arts o
war. The countrymen, having gaine
intelligence of the movement, a
the instigation of a number of foreig
refugees, placed themselves in am
bush along the sides of a narrow
defile overlooking the high road
No sooner were the incautious towns
men completely enclosed within th
snare, than a merciless fire was opene
upon them by their enemies from
behind rocks and bushes. They were
instantly seized with a panic, becam

totally disorganised, and, throwing away their arms, attempted to save themselves by flight. Hemmed in, however, on all sides, they were completely exposed to the deadly aim of the rifles of their opponents, who picked off the officers and butchered indiscriminately many of the wounded and prisoners. While of the Bâle countrymen scarcely a man was touched, 70 of the townsmen, including some members of the first families of Bâle, were killed, and 200 wounded, in an affair which, from the advantages, both of numbers and position on the side of the countrymen, deserves the name of a wholesale murder rather than of a battle.

Beyond Liesthal the valley contracts and assumes a very romantic character on approaching

2⅜ Waldenburg—a small village of 600 inhabitants, at the S. base of the Jura, and at the commencement of the ascent of the Ober-Hauenstein. On the height to the E. may be seen the ruins of the castle, destroyed in 1798.

The road over the Ober-Hauenstein, once formidable from the abruptness of the ascent, has been greatly improved, and the steepness of the slope so much diminished, that extra horses are unnecessary except for very heavily laden carriages. A gradual ascent, easily surmounted in an hour, leads to the summit. A heavy toll, amounting to 21 batz for a carriage with two horses, is paid on crossing it. On this account the Swiss voituriers generally avoid this road. The correction which the road has undergone carries it through the village of Holderbank, lower down than the ancient route, which passed over the crest of the mountain. Down to the end of the last century so steep was the old road that loaded waggons were drawn up on one side and let down the other with a rope and windlass.

2 Ballsthal—(*Inns:* Rössli (horse); Löwe;)—a village at the S. foot of the Hauenstein. Above it, and over the road, tower the imposing ruins of the *Castle of Falkenstein ;* it rises midway between the two roads to Bâle, by the Hauenstein and Passwang, which both unite here. This position gave to its ancient owners the power of levying black-mail upon each of these passes. It belonged at one time to Rudolph von Wart, who was broken on the wheel for his share in the murder of the Emperor Albert, and was consoled in his agony by the presence and fortitude of his wife. (See Route 6.) The castle was destroyed by the men of Basle, because a waggon, laden with saffron, belonging to their merchants, had been pillaged by the lords of Falkenstein.

Below Ballsthal the road traverses the singular and romantic defile of Klus, a rent which severs the Jura chain from top to bottom. It derives its name from having been closed (clausus) in ancient times by gate and wall. It is of much importance, in a military point of view, as one of the main portals into Switzerland. In the middle ages it was commanded by 3 castles; that of Neu Falkenstein at its N. entrance, on the E. by the Bechburg, and on the S. by the Blauenstein, whose owners constituted themselves into toll-gatherers, levying taxes on their own behalf from all who passed. At the N. of the pass stands the village of Klus, with its iron furnaces, in which the pea-like iron ore (bohnerz), so common in the Jura, is smelted. Near Klus the traveller is greeted by a fine view of the snowy chain of the Alps. The Castle of Blauenstein was built in the 12th century, by the Counts of Falkenstein, a powerful family, from which many Swiss abbots and other ecclesiastical dignitaries proceeded, while the main branch followed the profession of robber-knights. It was one of these Falkensteins who burnt the town of Brugg. The pass terminates below the small village of Aussere Klus, and the road descends into the valley of the Aar.

2¼ Wiedlisbach.

2 SOLEURE.—(Germ. Solothurn).
—*Inn:* Couronne: the best, but not
very clean.

The capital of the canton is prettily situated on the Aar, at the foot
of the Jura range, and has 4250 inhabitants. In the middle of the
17th century it was surrounded by
fortifications of great extent, which
took 60 years to complete, and consumed vast sums of money. In 1835
the removal of these costly and useless works was decreed by the Great
Council of the canton, and they have
already, in part, been levelled. It is
on the whole a dull town, with little
trade and few manufactures. The
following objects are most worth
notice.

At the end of the principal street,
approached by a flight of steps,
flanked by fountains, stands the *Cathedral of St. Ursus* (a soldier of the
Theban legion), a modern building
of Italian architecture, finished 1773;
distinguished by its size, and on the
whole handsome.

The *clock tower* (Zeitglocken-
thurm), in the market-place (a continuation of the same street), is
stated by the guide books to be a
Roman work, while a German inscription upon it attributes its foundation to a period 500 years earlier
than the birth of Christ; but it owes
its origin in reality to the Burgundian
kings. It is square in form, and
constructed of the most solid masonry,
rough outside, without window or
other opening, for 80 feet. If we
are to believe the two Latin verses
on the front of this building, Soleure
is the most ancient city in N.W.
Europe except Treves.

In Celtis nihil est Solodoro antiquius, unis,
Exceptis Treviris, quorum ego dicta soror.

The *Arsenal* (Zeughaus), not far
from the Cathedral, contains the most
extensive and curious collection of
ancient armour in Switzerland. Here
are shown several standards, said to
have been taken by the Swiss in their

victories over the Burgundians and
Austrians. Those, however, attributed to Morat and Sempach prove
on examination, to be nothing but
pieces of coarse canvass, painted on
one side; the yellow flag with the
Austrian eagle, said to have been
brought from Dornach, is probably
genuine. Among 600 or 800 suits o
armour are many said to be French
and Burgundian. Several specimens
of wall pieces, or long swivels, for
the defence of a fortress, are curious
Some of the armour is for sale.

The *Museum*, close to the bridge
over the Aar, contains a collection o
Jura fossils, chiefly from quarries
near Soleure, which will be viewed
with great interest by the geologist
There are nearly 30 specimens o
fossil turtle, rarely found elsewhere
together with teeth and palates o
fish, and numerous fragments o
saurians. A suite of specimens of the
rocks of the Alps were collected in numerous journeys by Professor Hugi
to whom belongs the merit of forming
and arranging this cabinet.

The Ambassador of France to the
Swiss Confederation resided here
until the French Revolution: his
hotel is converted into a barrack
The Catholic Bishop of Bâle lives
here. The clergy are numerous and
powerful, both in the town and canton. There are several convents at
Soleure. The sisters of *St. Joseph's
Nunnery*, outside the Berne gate,
make artificial flowers, sweetmeats,
and other articles, which they sell at
the grating. Their pincushions are
clumsy, and themselves not very interesting.

Thaddeus Kosciusko, the Pole, spent
the last years of his life here; his
house, in which he died, is next door
to the Post-office, No. 5, Gurzelen-
gasse. His entrails are interred in
the church-yard of Zuchwyl, a mile
distant on the opposite side of the
Aar, under a stone inscribed "Viscera
Thaddei Kosiuszko."

About two miles N. of Soleure, beyond the village of St. Nicholas, lies

the chapel and *Hermitage of St. Verena*, at the extremity of a pretty valley, hemmed in by rocks, embowered in trees, and traversed by a sparkling rivulet. It is rendered accessible by paths, originally formed by the French emigrés, who, at the outbreak of the French Revolution, sought an asylum here, to the number of many hundred, under the guidance of M. de Breteuil. The valley abounds in caves and grottoes, partly natural, partly artificial, and at its further extremity, within a natural shelf of over-arching cliff, stands the little *Chapel of St. Verena;* behind the altar a small cave has been cut in the rock, and now contains a representation of the holy sepulchre. This saint, a pious maiden who accompanied the Theban legion, suffered severe temptation in this solitude, according to the legend, from the devil, who, on one occasion, was on the point of carrying her off, when she saved herself by clinging fast to a small hole in the rock, which still remains. On the way to the hermitage, near the church of St. Nicholas, the *Château of Waldegy* is passed; its old-fashioned gardens, laid out in terraces, are worth notice.

The Weissenstein.—The most interesting excursion, however, in the neighbourhood of Soleure, is that to the summit of the Weissenstein (Whiterock, probably named from its white cliffs of limestone), the mountain immediately behind the town. The distance is about 8 miles, and the time occupied in the ascent 3 hours. The mountain is made accessible for chars-à-banc, by a road somewhat steep, passing through the villages Langendorf and Oberdorf, behind which it is carried up the face of the mountain in a series of zigzags.

A char-à-banc, drawn by 2 horses, may be hired at the Couronne, in Soleure, for 10 or 12 Swiss francs, to go and return. If it be detained on the mountain for the night, 2 francs

extra are paid. Pedestrians may find a short cut, and reach the top easily in 2½ hours; they may visit the Hermitage of St. Verena in their way to or fro.

A *Hotel and Bath-house* has been built at the expense of the town on the brow of the mountain, 3950 feet above the sea level, and 2640 above the Aar, at Soleure. It furnishes about 30 beds, and the accommodation, though homely, is good. The charges are—for dinner at table d'hôte, without wine, 1 fr. 20 rap.; supper 1 fr. bs.; breakfast of tea or coffee alone, 50 rp.; beds from 8 to 10 batz.

The dairy of the establishment is supplied by 60 cows, fed on the pasture on the summit of the mountain, so that milk and cream may be had here in perfection.

Many invalids take up their residence here during the summer months on account of the fresh air, or for the " cure de petit lait" (goat's whey), &c., which is recommended in certain complaints. The daily charge for those who remain here more than a week " en pension," is 6 F. francs.

The greater portion of visitors, however, resort hither merely on account of the view, remaining on the summit one night to enjoy the sunset and sunrise.

The Inn of the Weissenstein, and the still more elevated summit of the mountain, called Rothi-flue, 2 miles to the E. of it, command one of the finest *distant* prospects of the Alps which can be named. The great chain of snowy peaks, &c., here seen, spread out along the horizon, extends for a distance of nearly 200 miles, from the Sentis on the E., to the Mont Blanc in the W. Immediately in front rise the Jungfrau, Schreckhorn, and other giants of the Bernese chain. In the foreground, amidst a varied expanse of wooded hill and verdant vale are seen the lakes of Morat, Neuchâtel, and Bienne, while the silvery Aar, on which stands the town of Soleure, winds like a snake at the foot of the mountain.

Keller has engraved a Panorama of the Weissenstein, in which every mountain, town, village, and other object of interest visible from the top, is marked. One or two copies of it are hung up at the inn for the convenience of visitors.

Another road practicable for a char-à-banc, but very rough, descends the opposite side of the Weissenstein, into the Val Moutiers (described in p. 6).

From Soleure to Bienne is a distance of 3¾ stunde = 12 Eng. miles.—The road runs along the S. base of the Jura. A new line of road now (1837) in progress, will curtail the distance by more than 2 miles. The inn on the Weissenstein continues long a conspicuous object.

1¼ Selzach.

On the rt. of the road lie the Baths of Grange (Grenchen), a large building. At Boujean (Botzingen) almost a suburb of Bienne, our road falls in with that from the Münster Thal (Route 1).

2½ *Bienne,* (p. 7).

ROUTE 4.

BASLE TO LUCERNE, BY THE UNTER HAUENSTEIN, OLTEN, AARBURG, AND SEMPACH.

19½ stunden = 64 Eng miles.

A diligence goes daily.

The road throughout is good.— As far as

3 Liesthal, it is the same as Route 3: here, instead of turning S., it ascends the vale of the Ergolz, as far as

1¼ Sissach, a village of 1100 inhabitants, and

2 Läufelfingen. The pass of the Unter-Hauenstein (the hewn rock), which now commences, is of great importance as an outlet for the merchandise of Switzerland, and as the most direct line of communication from W. Germany to Italy by the St. Gotthard. The improvements completed between 1827 and 1830, at an expense of 260,289 fr., have rendered the slope on both sides so gradual, that extra horses are rarely required for carriages. A toll of 5 batz per horse is paid, but nothing is charged for Vorspann horses. From the summit of the pass, after crossing the boundary-line of Bâle and Soleure, a fine view is obtained of the great chain of the Alps.

2½ Olten—(*Inns:* Krone;—Halber Mond—Half Moon)—though it contains but' 1500 inhabitants, promises to rise into a flourishing town, to the prejudice of Soleure, of which it is becoming the rival. Its prosperity is greatly promoted by its position on the new road of the Unter Hauenstein. It is built on the left bank of the Aar, and is said to be the Roman *Ultinum.* The roads from Bâle to Lucerne, and from Zurich to Soleure and Neuchâtel, cross here. The *old parish church,* converted into a wood warehouse since the new one was built, is of great antiquity: it is mentioned in records as early as 1240.

Our road crosses the Aar by a wooden bridge, and proceeds along its rt. bank, through pleasing scenery, to

¾ Aarburg—(*Inns:* Bär;—Krone), an old town of 1500 inhabitants, distinguished by its extensive *Citadel* on the heights above, constructed in 1660; the only fortress belonging to the Swiss Confederation, but of no use as a fortification, for although it has bomb-proof casemates hewn out of the rock, its works have been allowed to go to decay. It serves as a military storehouse for the Swiss Confederation, and forms a picturesque object in the landscape, such as is met with in the background of old German pictures. Outside the town is an extensive cotton factory.

At Kreutzstrasse, a mile farther, the high road from Zurich to Berne

(Route 13) crosses our route. The Lion is a good inn here.

The road continues along a pretty valley, distinguished by its verdant pasture: its substantial - looking houses, many of them with gardens, whose walls are often covered with thin plates of wood overlapping each other like fishes' scales. It is bordered by a varied outline of wooded heights.

1 Zoffingen. A fragment of the castle of Reiden, and a solitary tree perched on a rock beside it, become conspicuous before reaching the village of Reiden, where a toll of 8 batz, including all the road to and from this to Lucerne, is paid.

A view is obtained of the Lake of Sempach, and of a smaller lake called Mauensee, from the height above.

4 Sursee—(*Inn:* Hirsch; bad and dear)—an old walled town, whose gate-towers still bear the double-headed eagle of Austria carved in stone. " The traveller may well employ a few moments in examining the *Rathhaus,* much dilapidated, but affording a good specimen of the peculiarities of the German-Burgundian style. The general outline resembles the old Tolbooth of Edinburgh."—P. Sursee lies at the distance of about a mile from the N. extremity of the lake of Sempach, which is seen over and among the orchards on the left of the road in going to Lucerne. It has no pretensions to great beauty, but is pleasing, and highly interesting historically from the famous Battle of Sempach (1336)—the second of those great and surprising victories by which Swiss independence was established. It was fought on the E. shore of the lake, behind the little town of Sempach, opposite which the lake comes into full view from our road. In 1805, a portion of the water of the lake was let off, in order to gain land along its banks; thus its extent is diminished, its surface lowered, and its form somewhat altered from

what it was at the time of the battle.

A small chapel, in the form of a portico, is erected to commemorate the victory, on the spot where Leopold of Austria (son of the Duke of the same name who had been defeated 71 years before at Morgarten) lost his life. The names of those who fell, both Austrians and Swiss, were inscribed on the walls, which also bear a rude fresco representation of the noble devotion of *Arnold* of *Winkelried.*

> He of battle-martyrs chief !
> Who, to recall his daunted peers,
> For victory shaped an open space,
> By gath'ring, in a wide embrace,
> Into his single heart, a sheaf
> Of fatal Austrian spears.
> *Wordsworth.*

He was a knight of Unterwalden, who, observing all the efforts of the Swiss to break the ranks of their enemies foiled by their long lances, exclaimed " Protect my wife and children, and I will open a path to freedom." He then rushed forward, and gathering in his arms as many lances as he could grasp, buried them in his bosom. The confederates were enabled to take advantage of the gap thus formed in the mail-clad ranks of the foe, before the Austrian lancers had time to extricate their entangled weapons from his corse. In order to oppose the Swiss, who fought on foot, many of the Austrian nobles had dismounted to form a serried phalanx ; but the armour which rendered them almost invulnerable on horseback, and which, while they remained united and in close column, had formed so impenetrable a barrier to the attack of the Swiss, now that their ranks were broken, disabled them from coping with their light-armed and active foes. 600 nobles were slain, and more than 2000 common soldiers ; while the entire force of the Swiss, who achieved this victory, is said not to have exceeded 1400 men.

At Buttisholz, a village about

3 miles from Sursee, and on the S. of our road, may be seen a mound, called the *English barrow,* because it contains the bones of 3000 of our countrymen, followers of the celebrated Condottiero leader, Ingelram de Coucy, who were defeated here, 1376, by the inhabitants of Entlebuch. This Ingelram de Coucy was son-in-law of Edward III., King of England, and Earl of Bedford. Having a feud against Leopold of Austria, he not only laid waste his territories, but made devastating inroads into the neighbouring Swiss cantons, from the Jura to the gates of Berne and Zurich, until his career was suddenly arrested here by a few hundred Swiss peasants. This action put an end to a struggle known in Swiss history as the English war.

The approach to Lucerne is charming : on the l. rises the Rigi, in shape somewhat resembling a horse's back; on the rt. the Pilatus is distinguished by his serrated ridge. After crossing the small stream of the Emme by a wooden bridge, we reach the banks of the green Reuss, rushing out of the lake of Lucerne. On the rt. the new road to Berne, by the Entlebuch, is passed. Lucerne is surrounded on this side by a battlemented wall, flanked at intervals by a number of tall watch-towers, descending to the margin of the river.

4 Lucerne. Route 16.

ROUTE 5.

BALE TO AARAU, BY THE STAFFELECK.

19 stunden = 62¼ Eng. miles. Diligences daily.

The road is the same as Route 3, as far as

3¼ Rheinfelden. At Stein it quits the side of the Rhine, and ascends the Frickthal to

3¾ Frick, a village of 1800 inhabitants, with a church on a height.

Here our route branches out of the high-road to Zurich. The Frickthal and surrounding district belonged to Austria down to 1801.

1¾ Staffelegg. Above this village is a depression or col in the chain of the Jura, over which an easy carriageroad has been constructed at the expense of the government of the canton. A gradual descent leads down into the valley of the Aar, which is crossed in order to enter

1¼ *Aarau—Inns :* Wilder Mann, (Sauvage) — Ochs (Bœuf) — Cigogne.—The chief town of the canton, Argovie, which was first included in the Confederation 1803, having previously formed a subject province of Canton Bern, contains 4500 inhabitants, and is situated on the rt. bank of the Aar : the bridge over it was swept away by an inundation in 1831. Simond calls it " an odious little place." It lies at the S. base of the Jura, here partly covered with vineyards. There are many extensive cotton-mills here.

The *Rathhaus,* in which the cantonal councils are held, includes within its circuit the tower of a feudal castle of the Counts von Rore, which may be regarded as the nucleus of the town. In the *parish church,* Protestant and Catholic services are performed alternately.

Henry Zschokke, the historian and novel-writer, resides here. When the armies of the French Revolution took possession of Switzerland in 1789, and destroyed its ancient form of Government, Aarau was made capital of the Helvetian Republic, but it was soon transferred to Lucerne.

The *baths of Schintznach* (p. 17) are about 10 miles from this. The road to them runs along the rt. bank of the Aar, passing several castles, the most conspicuous of which is that of Windeck. Close to Schintznach rise the ruins of the *Castle of Habsburg,* the cradle of the House of Austria.

ROUTE 6.

BALE TO ZURICH, BY BRUGG, THE BATHS OF SCHINTZNACH AND BA-DEN.

16⅓ stunden = 53 Eng. miles.
Diligences go daily.

7 Frick. Thus far the road is identical with Routes 3 and 5. Passing through the villages Horn-ussen and Effingen, it crosses the hill of Bötzberg, whose culminating point, 1850 ft. above the sea, com-mands a fine view of the Alps. It was called *Mons Vocetius* by the Romans, who constructed a highway across it; and on this spot, accord-ing to Swiss antiquaries, was fought the battle so fatal to the Helvetians, in which they were defeated by Cœcina, and the Legion called by Tacitus *Rapax*, from its exactions and cruelty, A.D. 69.

A wooden bridge, 70 ft. long, leads across the Aar, which here flows, in a contracted bed, to

3 Brugg, or Bruck—(*Inns:* Stern, Etoile; — Rothes Haus, Maison Rouge)—a walled town of great antiquity, having been an ancient possession of the House of Habsburg, containing 800 inhabitants. It is the birth-place of Zimmerman, physician of Frederick the Great, who wrote on Solitude.

The country around Brugg is interesting, both in a geographical and historical point of view. In the plain, a little below the town, three of the principal rivers of Switzerland which drain the N. slopes of the Alps, from the Grisons to the Jura, the Limmat, the Reuss, and the Aar, form a junction, and, united under the name of the Aar, throw them-selves into the Rhine about 10 miles below Brugg, at a place called Cob-lenz.

Close upon this meeting of the wa-ters, and on the triangular tongue of land between the Aar and Reuss, stood *Vindonissa,* the most important set-tlement of the Romans in Helvetia,

as well as their strongest fortress on this frontier, on which they placed their chief dependence for maintain-ing this portion of their empire. Its works extended 12 miles from N. to S.

Yet scarcely any portion of it now appears above ground; traces of an amphitheatre, a subterranean aque-duct, which conveyed water from Brauneggberg, 3 miles off, founda-tions of walls, broken pottery, in-scriptions, and coins have been turned up by the spade from time to time, and its name is preserved in that of the miserable little village of *Windisch.*

"Within the ancient walls of Vindonissa, the castle of Habsburg, the abbey of Konigsfield, and the town of Bruck, have successively arisen. The philosophic traveller may compare the monuments of Roman conquests, of feudal or Aus-trian tyranny, of monkish supersti-tion, and of industrious freedom. If he be truly a philosopher, he will applaud the merit and happiness of his own time."—*Gibbon.*

Half a mile beyond the walls of Brugg stands the *abbey* of *Königs-felden* (King's field), founded, 1310, by the Empress Elizabeth, and Ag-nes, Queen of Hungary, on the spot where, two years before, their hus-band and father, the Emperor Albert, was assassinated. The convent was suppressed in 1528, and is now con-verted into a lunatic asylum. The *church,* fast falling to decay, con-tains some fine painted glass; and the effigies in stone, as large as life, of a long train of nobles, who fell in the battle of Sempach. The vaults beneath were the burial-place of many members of the Austrian family, including Agnes and Leo-pold, who fell at Sempach, but they were removed hence into the Austrian dominions in 1770. According to tradition, the high altar stands on the spot where Albert fell. He had crossed the ferry of the Reuss in a small boat, leaving his suite on the opposite bank, and attended only by the four conspirators. The chief of them, John of Suabia, nephew of Albert—who had been instigated to the design by the wrong he endured in being kept out of his paternal inheritance by his uncle—first struck him in the throat with his lance. Balm ran him through with his sword, and Walter von Eschenbach cleft his skull with a felling-stroke. Wart, the fourth, took no share in the murder. Although the deed was so openly done in broad day, almost under the walls of the Imperial Castle of Habsburg, and in sight of a large retinue of armed attendants, the murderers were able to escape in different directions; and the imperial retainers took to flight, leaving their dying master to breathe his last in the arms of a poor peasant who happened to pass.

A peasant-girl that royal head upon her
    bosom laid,
And, shrinking not for woman's dread, the
    face of death survey'd:
Alone she sate. From hill and wood low
    sunk the mournful sun;
Fast gushed the fount of noble blood. Trea-
    son his worst had done.
With her long hair she vainly pressed the
    wounds to staunch their tide;
Unknown, on that meek, humble breast,
    imperial Albert died.

                                Mrs. Hemans.

A direful vengeance was wrecked by the children of the murdered monarch; not, however, upon the murderers—for, with the exception of Wart, the only one who did not raise his hand against him, they all escaped—but upon their families, relations, and friends; and 1000 victims are believed to have expiated, with their lives, a crime of which they were totally innocent. Queen Agnes gratified her spirit of vengeance with the sight of these horrid executions, exclaiming, while 63 unfortunate men were butchered before her, " Now I bathe in May-dew !" She ended her days in the convent of Königsfelden, which she had founded and endowed with the con-fiscated property of those whom she had slaughtered. Penance, prayer, and alms-giving would avail but little to stifle the qualms of a guilty conscience for the bloody deeds which she had committed; and it is recorded that a holy hermit, to whom she had applied for absolution, replied to her—" Woman ! God is not to be served with bloody hands, nor by the slaughter of innocent persons, nor by convents built with the plunder of orphans and widows—but by mercy and forgiveness of injuries." The building in which she passed 50 years of her life is destroyed—that which is shown as her cell is not so in reality.

About two miles above Brugg, on a wooded height called Wülpelsberg, stand the remains of the *Castle of Habsburg*, or Habichtsburg (Hawk's Castle), the cradle of the House of Austria, built in the 11th century by Bishop Werner, of Strassburg, an ancestor of the family. A mere fragment of the original building now exists. The tall, square keep of rough stones has walls 8 ft. thick; and beneath it a dungeon, to be entered only by a trap-door in the floor above. The view from it is picturesque and interesting; the eye ranges along the course of the three rivers, over the site of the Roman Vindonissa, and Königsfelden, the sepulchre of imperial Albert : on the S. rises the ruined castle of Braunegg, which belonged to the sons of the tyrant Gessler ; and below it Birr, where Pestalozzi, the teacher, died, and is buried. It takes in at a single glance the whole Swiss patrimony of the Habsburgs—an estate far more limited than that of many a British peer—from which Rudolph was called to wield the sceptre of Charlemagne. The House of Austria were deprived of their Swiss territories by papal ban, 150 years after Rudolph's elevation; but it is believed that the ruin has again become the property of the Austrian Emperor by purchase.

Below the castle, at the foot of the Wülpelsberg, and about 3 miles from Brugg, lie the *Baths of Schintznach*, also called Habsburger Bad, the most frequented watering-place in Switzerland. The principal buildings are the Great Inn, Grosser Gasthof, and the Bath-house, erected within a few years, in a semicircular form. In May and June, 300 people often dine here in the splendid saloon. The house contains sleeping accommodation for 200, and 50 baths. The waters are of the saline sulphureous kind, and have a temperature of 60° Fahr. They are efficacious in cutaneous disorders, in rheumatism, and for wounds. Schintznach owes little to nature, except its waters. Some pretty walks have been made near the houses, and winding paths, under the shade of trees, lead up the hill to Habsburg.

BALE TO ZURICH—(*continued*).

On quitting Brugg, the road passes the convent of Königsfelden, traversing Oberdorf (near which are scanty remains of a Roman amphitheatre), and skirts on the l. the village of Windisch (p. 15), before it crosses the river Reuss. It then proceeds up the l. bank of the Limmat, to

2 **Baden**—(*Inns:* Löwe, Lion;—Engel, Ange). These inns in the town are inferior to those at the baths.—This ancient walled town, of 1800 inhabitants, is squeezed within a narrow defile on the l. bank of the Limmat, here crossed by a wooden bridge. The ruins of the *Castle,* nearly as large as the place itself, overlook it from a rocky eminence. It was anciently the stronghold of the Austrian princes, and their residence while Switzerland belonged to them. Here were planned the expeditions against the Swiss, which were frustrated at Morgarten and Sempach. At length when the Pope, in 1415, excommunicated the Archduke Frederick, the Swiss took it and burnt it. In *the Rathhaus* of Baden the preliminaries preceding the treaty of peace which terminated the war of Succession were arranged by Prince Eugene, on the part of Austria and by Marshal Villars, for France, in 1712.

Baden, like its namesakes in Baden and Austria, was frequented on account of its mineral waters by the Romans, who called it *Thermæ Helvetiæ.* It was sacked and destroyed by Cœcina.

The *Baths*—(*Inns:* Stadthof, best; —Hinterhof; — Raabe) — are situated on the borders of the Limmat, a quarter of a mile below or N. of the town. They are resorted to between the months of June and September by numerous visitors, chiefly natives of Switzerland. The waters are warm and sulphureous, having a temperature of 38 Reaum., and are good for rheumatism, &c.

The *Great Baths,* on the l. bank of the river, are frequented by the upper classes—those on the opposite side by the lower orders.

The Swiss Baden, though not equal in beauty to some of its namesakes in other parts of Europe, has considerable attractions in the country around it, which is particularly interesting to the geologist, as affording proofs of some great convulsion of nature, by which the Limmat and other rivers descending from the Alps forced their way through the opposing barrier of the Jura, to join the Rhine and the sea. The rocky heights on each side of the river—the one surmounted by the ruined castle, the other partly covered by vineyards—form the portal through which this great eruption of waters was poured out. Before this gorge was formed, Baden and the country above it must have been a vast lake.

Agreeable walks are formed for invalids by the side of the Limmat, and many pleasant excursions may be made in the country around—the most interesting being that described above, to Schintznach (8 miles), by Windisch, Königsfelden, and Habsburg.

Roman relics are constantly discovered in this district. Gambling appears to have been a prevailing vice among the visitors to the baths, and the Roman Legions stationed here, since a neighbouring field has obtained the name of *Dice Meadow* (Wurfel Wiese), from the quantity of dice dug up in it.

The pleasantest road to Zurich from Baden is said to be that along the rt. bank of the Limmat. It passes at the distance of about two miles the convent of Wettingen, situated in an angle formed by a bend of the river. Its *church*, founded in 1227, contains tombs of some early Counts of Habsburg and Kyburg, painted glass, carved stalls, &c.

The route taken by the diligence follows the l. bank of the Limmat to 2¼ Dietikon. Near this village the French, under Massena, crossed the river, Sept. 24, 1799—a masterly movement, which led to the defeat of the Russians and the capture of Zurich.

1¾ Zurich. In Route 8.

ROUTE 7.

SCHAFFHAUSEN TO CONSTANCE.

Schaffhausen.—(*Inns:* Faucon, best; Couronne, not recommended. There is a good inn close to the Rhine fall, about 2 miles out of the town.) The Baden post-house is near the Faucon, but the innkeepers will do their utmost to prevent the traveller availing himself of this mode of travelling.

Schaffhausen, a town of 7500 inhabitants, stands on the rt. bank of the Rhine, just above the spot where the rapids and falls commence, which render that river unnavigable as far as Basle. It was originally a landing-place and magazine, at which the portage of goods began and ended,

and owes its origin and name to the boat or *skiff houses*, here erected. It is distinguished above almost every other town in Switzerland by the antique architecture of its houses, whose fronts and projecting oriel windows are decorated with carvings and stucco work. Many of them were originally entirely covered externally with fresco paintings, but of these there are now few examples; the house called Zum Ritter, nearly opposite the Couronne, is one of the most remarkable of those that remain. The houses or *halls* of the ancient *Guilds*, or *Zünfts*, are worthy of attention on account of their quaint inscriptions and allusive ornaments. The wall and turreted gateways of the town have been preserved, and furnish very picturesque subjects for the pencil.

It is almost exclusively on account of its vicinity to the celebrated Falls of the Rhine that Schaffhausen is visited. It has little resort, except from the influx of travellers, it being one of the portals of Switzerland, and there is little within the town to deserve notice. On the height above it rises the curious and perfect feudal *castle* called *Unnoth*, or *Munnoth*. Its towers have walls of great thicknees (18 feet), said to be of Roman (?) construction; the building, however, was not finished in its present state till 1564. It is provided with bomb-proof casemates, capable of sheltering many hundred persons. Many subterranean passages lead from it.

The Minster—originally the Abbey of All Saints—was founded 1052. It is a building in the Romanesque, or round arched style, remarkable for its antiquity, the solidity of its construction, and as exhibiting an unaltered specimen of that style. The arches of the nave are supported by single circular columns, and those in the centre of the transept by square piers of the most massive kind. The cloister attached to the church contains a profusion of monuments of the magistrates and patrician families.

The celebrated wooden bridge over the Rhine, of a single arch, 365 feet in span, was burnt by the French in 1799, and is replaced by one of the most ordinary construction. A model of the original may be seen in the town library; the architect was a carpenter from Appenzell, named Grubenman.

The Town Library contains the collection of books of the celebrated Swiss historian Müller, who was born here.

Diligences go daily from hence to Zurich and Offenburg (on the road to Strasburg and Frankfort), three times a-week to Constance.

A *steamer* runs twice a week between Schaffhausen and Constance.

THE FALLS OF THE RHINE.

The Falls are about 3 miles below Schaffhausen; the road to Zurich passes within a quarter of a mile of them. At the village of Neuhausen, 10 minutes' walk from the fall, there is a clean and moderate small inn, Zum Rheinfall: charges—beds 2 fr.; dinners 3 fr.; breakfast 1½ f.

These quarters are convenient for those who would enjoy the aspect of the cataract at various hours, at sunrise and by moonlight. It will take at least 2 hours to see the falls thoroughly and return to Neuhausen, including the time occupied in crossing and re-crossing the river. Close to the fall is an iron furnace; the wheels of the hammers are turned by the fall, and the draught caused by the rush of the water supplies the place of bellows.

The best mode of visiting the falls from Schaffhausen is to hire a boat from thence (costs 48 fr.), and descend the river, which already forms a succession of rapids, by no means dangerous under the guidance of a boatman accustomed to the river. When the increased celerity of the current and the audible roar announce that the skiff is approaching the falls, the steersman makes for the l. bank,

and lands his passengers under the picturesque castle of *Lauffen*, situated on a high rock overlooking the fall, within the Canton of Zurich. It is occupied and rented by an artist who speaks English, and charges 1 franc admission for each person.

The advantage of approaching the fall on this side is, that nothing is seen of it until it is at once presented in its most magnificent point of view, from the little pavilion perched on the edge of the cliff immediately above it. Its appearance from the opposite side of the river is tame in comparison, and the first impression from thence, made by the finest cataract in Europe, will most probably prove disappointing. Several flights of very rude and slippery wooden steps conduct from this pavilion to a projecting stage, or rude balcony, of stout timbers, thrown out, like the bowsprit of a ship, from the vertical cliff to within a few feet of the fall. It actually overhangs the roaring shoot, and, though perfectly secure, seems to tremble under the impulse of the water. Here, covered with the spray, the traveller may enjoy the full grandeur of this *hell of waters;* and it is only by this close proximity, amidst the tremendous roar and the uninterrupted rush of the river, passing with the swiftness of an arrow above his head and beneath his feet, that a true notion can be formed of the stupendous nature of this cataract. The best time for seeing the fall is about 8 in the morning, when the Iris floats within the spray (provided the sun shines), and by moon-light. The river is usually most full in the month of July. The Rhine, above the fall, is about 300 feet broad; the height of the fall is reduced to 70 feet. Two isolated pillars of rock standing in the middle of the stream divide the fall into 3 shoots. Seen from behind, these pinnacles seem eaten away by the constant friction of the water, and tottering to their fall; indeed, as the rock is soft, the waste of it within the memory of man must be considerable.

The river, after its leap, forms a large semicircular bay, as it were to rest itself; the sides of which are perpetually chafed by the heaving billows. Here, in front of the fall, on the rt. bank, stands the *Castle of Wörth*, a square tower, containing a camera obscura, which shows the fall in another and a very singular point of view. From this tower to the foot of the rock on which the castle of Lauffen stands, several ferry-boats ply, to convey visitors across; charging 4 batz each. The boats are much tossed about in their passage, but sometimes approach the base of the pinnacles above-mentioned without risk, provided they keep clear of the eddies.

The walk from the Falls to Schaffhausen is very pleasant, and commands (as you approach) several pleasant landscapes, of which the town is the principal object.

Schaffhausen to Constance.
9 stunde = 29½ English miles.

A diligence goes 3 times a-week in 5 hours.

A steamer goes twice a-week, but, in ascending the Rhine to Constance, it is necessarily a tedious conveyance, owing to the force of the current against which it has to contend.

The journey may be made more expeditiously by following the road through Baden, on the N. of the Rhine, than along the Swiss side of the river, because it is provided with post-horses. The cost of posting is not so great as that of Vetturin horses.

The relays are—

2½ *Singen.* Near this place you pass at the foot of *Hohentwiel.* The castle is now dismantled. The lofty rock upon which it stands gives it the appearance of an Indian hill fort.

1½ *Rudolfszell.* A desolate town, with a fine church, in the true German-Gothic style.

The scenery throughout the whole of this road is exceedingly agreeable, often striking. The woods abound in most splendid butterflies. Collections of these insects may be bought at Singen, and also at Rudolfszell.

The inn at Rudolfszell, the " *Posthaus*," is very good; that at Singen poor and extortionate.

The Rhine here, suddenly contracted from a lake to a river, is crossed by a wooden bridge, in order to reach Constance.

The Swiss road runs along the l. bank of the Rhine past the Nunneries of Paradies and Katherinethal, the former belonging to the order of St. Clara, the latter of St. Dominic; but the revenues and the number of sisters in both are now much reduced. The Austrian army under the Archduke Charles crossed the Rhine at Paradies 1799.

1¾ Diessenhofen.

2 Stein—(*Inns:* Schwan; Krone) —a town of 1270 inhabitants, on the rt. bank of the Rhine, belonging to Schaffhausen, united by a wooden bridge with a suburb on the l. bank. The *Abbey of St. George* is a very ancient ecclesiastical foundation. The owners of the ruined castle of Hohenklingen, situated on the rocky height, were originally the feudal seigneurs of the town, but the citizens obtained independence from their masters by purchase.

Three miles E. of Stein, at a height of between 500 and 600 feet above the Rhine, are situated the *Quarries of Œhningen*, remarkable for the vast abundance of fossil remains of terrestrial and fresh-water animals found in them, including mammalia, birds, reptiles, fishes, shells, insects, and plants, some of them identical with species now living. The most curious discovery is that of the perfect skeleton of a fossil fox, made by Mr. Murchison; a very large tortoise had previously been brought to light. The beds of rock in which the quarries are worked consist of marls, limestones, shales, and building-stone; they lie immediately above the formation called Molasse, and differ in their organic contents from all other fresh-water formations hitherto discovered.

Above Stein the Rhine expands into a lake called Untersee (lower lake), connected again by the Rhine at its upper extremity with the larger Lake of Constance. In the midst of it is the pretty island *Reichenau;* near Stein a smaller island (Werd) is passed. Feldbach, also a nunnery, belonging to sisters of the Cistercian order, is passed before reaching

2 Steckborn.

Itznang, a small village on the opposite shore of the lake, within the territory of Baden, is the birth-place of Mesmer, the *inventor* of animal magnetism.

Near the village of Berlingen the pretty *château* of the Duchess of Dino appears, and a little further that of *Arenaberg,* the residence of the late Duchess of St. Leu (Hortense, ex-Queen of Holland), and of her son, who foolishly attempted a revolution at Strassburg in 1836. The death of the one, and the foolish exploits of the other, will probably cause the mansion to change owners. Previously it was the centre of a little colony of Napoleonists;—Salenstein, Eugensberg (from its owner Eugene Beauharnois), Wolfsberg, all belonged to friends of Napoleon.

A road turns off from the lake at 1¾ Ermatingen to the *château of Wolfsberg,* formerly celebrated as a pension, but as its owner, an old officer of Napoleon, was involved in the mad enterprise of Strassburg with the son of Hortense, it is believed that the establishment will be given up, at least by him. The following description of Wolfsberg is by a lady who resided in the house in 1835.

" Wolfsberg is a chateau 2 leagues from Constance, well situated on a height above the Untersee. The view from the house and sloping lawn of the lake, and the Isle of Reichenau, is very pleasing, though it cannot boast the grandeur of Swiss scenery in general. Col. and Mad. Parquin are its proprietors, but devolve on Madame Bénézil, a very active good-humoured person, all the details of the establishment. The price is 10 francs a-day, and 4 for servants. The accommodation is so superior to that of Interlachen, that it cannot be considered dear. There is one private sitting-room. The salon is very large, and the society generally a mixture of French, Germans, Russians, Italians, and English, who meet in the evenings, when dancing, music, and charades amuse the younger, and chess and cards the elder part of the company. As M. and Madame Parquin are very well-educated and agreeable people, the tone of the society is particularly good, and there is very little risk of meeting objectionable persons.

" If travellers stay less than a week they pay 12 fr. a-day. Rides in the woods on donkeys, boating-parties, and excursions to the chateaux and points-de-vue in the neighbourhood, occupy the morning.

* * * * * *

" To tourists who wish to enjoy comparative rest in cheerful society and a pleasant country, the advantages of Wolfsberg are great, and, for those who wish to leave children in a safe and healthy spot while they are making mountain excursions, no situation can be superior.—L."

The island of Reichenau formerly belonged to the rich Benedictine Abbey situated on it, founded 724, and sequestrated 1799. The estates belonging to it were so numerous and extensive, that it is said the Abbot, on his way to Rome, need not sleep a night out of his own domains. Within the *Minster Church* (founded 806) Charles the Fat is buried; he died here in want 888. The church possesses, among its treasures, one of the waterpots used at the marriage of Cana! an emerald, weighing

28lb., presented by Charlemagne, now ascertained to be glass, &c.

The Castle of *Gottlieben,* on the l. of the road, built by the Bishops of Constance 1250, on the Rhine, at the point where it enters the Untersee, is remarkable for having been the prison of John Huss and Jerome of Prague, who were confined within its dungeons by order of the Emperor Sigismund and Pope John XXIII. The latter was himself transferred a few months later to the same prison, by order of the Council of Constance. In 1454 Felix Hämmerlin (Malleolus), the most learned and enlightened man of his time in Switzerland, was also confined here. The building is now private property.

2½ CONSTANCE.—(*Inns :* " The *Hecht,* or Brocket, and the Couronne Imperiale, both good; but the latter is to be preferred as the posting-house. The other is in the voiturier connexion; and they do all they can to advise travellers to adopt that mode of transport, saying that you cannot rely upon finding horses, and the like."—P.)

Constance, a decayed city, of 4500 inhabitants, instead of 40,000, which it once possessed, is remarkable for its antiquity, since its streets and many of its buildings remain unaltered since the 15th century. Although situated on the l. or Swiss bank of the Rhine, it belongs to Baden. It is connected with the opposite shore by a long wooden covered bridge, and occupies a projecting angle of ground at the W. extremity of the Bodensee or lake of Constance; its agreeable position and interesting historical associations make amends for the want of life perceptible within its venerable walls.

The *Minster* is a handsome Gothic structure, begun in 1052 : the doors of the main portal, between the two towers, are of oak, curiously carved with a representation of the Passion of our Lord, executed in 1470 by one Simon Bainder. The choir is supported by 16 pillars, each of a single block, and dates from the 13th century. The pulpit is supported b a statue of the " Arch-hereti Huss ;" and the spot where h stood, as sentence of death by burn ing was pronounced on him by hi unrighteous judges, is still pointe out. Robert Hallam, Bishop o Salisbury, who presided over th English deputation to the coun cil, is buried here, in front of th high altar, " under a tomb, which i very remarkable, as being of Englis *brass ;* which is fully proved by th workmanship. It was probably sen over from England by his executors Two sides of the ancient cloisters whose arches are filled in with ex quisitely beautiful tracery, are ye standing. The other sides were no long since destroyed by fire. B the side of the cathedral is a curiou circular chapel, perhaps a baptistry in the centre of which is a Gothi model of the Holy Sepulchre. Th chambers on the cloister portion o the ancient Episcopal palace contai many curious vestments and dusty re lics of the past grandeur of the see."— P.

" The *Dominican Convent,* now cotton factory, is very interesting The church forms a most picturesqu ruin, in the earliest style of Germar Gothic. The cloisters are perfect The little island upon which thi building stands was fortified by th Romans, and a portion of the wall towards the lake, can yet be dis cerned."—P.

In a *Hall of the Kaufhaus* (a ancient edifice, dating from 1388) looking towards the lake, the *Grea Council of Constance* held its sittings 1414—18, in a large room sup ported by wooden pillars. Tha famous assembly, composed, not o bishops alone, like the ancient coun cils, but of deputies, civil and eccle siastical, from the whole of Christen dom, including princes, cardinals (30) patriarchs (4), archbishops (20,) bi shops (150), professors of univer sities and doctors of theology (200) besides a host of ambassadors, inferior prelates, abbots, priors, &c., was convened for the purpose of remedying the abuses of the church; and as those abuses began with its head, the proceedings were prefaced by a declaration, that a council of the church has received, by Divine right, an authority in religious matters, even over that of the Pope. It exerted its influence in curbing the Papal power, by deposing the infamous John XXIII. and Benedict XIII., and by electing in their place Martin V. But there is one act of this council which fixes more lasting and odious celebrity than all the rest—the treacherous seizure and cruel murder of John Huss and Jerome of Prague, in spite of the safe-conduct granted to the former by the Emperor Sigismund, the president of the assembly.

The chairs occupied by the emperor and pope, the Bible of Huss, the door of the dungeon, now destroyed, in which he was confined, the hurdle on which he was dragged to execution, and some other relics of the council, still remain in the hall, besides a collection of Roman and German antiquities, dug up in the neighbourhood.

The *house* in which *Huss* lodged, bearing a rude likeness of him, is pointed out in the Paul's strasse, near the Schnetzthor. He was thrown into prison soon after his arrival, in the *Franciscan Convent,* now a ruin, whence he was removed to a more irksome dungeon below ground, affording scarcely room to move, in the before-mentioned *Dominican Convent.*

The field—outside of the town, in the suburb of Brühl, in which he suffered martyrdom, with a fortitude which moved even his judges and executioners to admiration—nay, even the place where the stake was planted, are still pointed out; and rude images of Huss and Jerome, formed of clay taken from the spot, are offered for sale to the stranger.

In 1474 a perpetual treaty of peace was concluded at Constance, between Sigismund of Austria and the Swiss Confederation, which put an end to the contests which had endured for more than a century and a half, beginning with the fights of Morgarten and Sempach. Constance belonged to the crown of Austria from 1549 to 1805, when, by the treaty of Presburg, it was transferred to Baden. Since 1802 it has ceased to be a bishopric.

Petershausen, on the opposite bank of the Rhine, was until 1803 a Benedictine monastery: it is now a château of the Grand Duke. It is still surrounded by its ancient fosse and ramparts. An excursion to the little *island* of *Meinau,* about 4 miles N. of Constance, will well repay the trouble: it is decidedly one of the prettiest spots on the borders of the Bodensee.

The lake of Constance is described in Route 66. Two steamers run regularly, 5 times a-week, between Constance and the different ports of the lake.

ROUTE 8.

SCHAFFHAUSEN TO ZURICH, BY EGLISAU.

9 stunden = 29½ Eng. miles.

A diligence runs daily, in about five hours.

There is another road, somewhat longer and more hilly, on the l. side of the Rhine, by Andelfingen— (*Inn:* Bär)—a village of 2000 inhabitants, and the large manufacturing town of Winterthur (5 stunde), described in Route 9.

The route by Eglisau passes within a short distance of the Rhine-fall. The roar of the cataract is audible 4 or 5 miles off in a calm night, and the column of vapour from it— " rising like incense from the altar of nature "—is visible at a considerable distance. A corner of the territory of Baden, including the villages of Jestetten and Lostetten, is traversed before reaching

4 Eglisau–(The Lion d'Or is a clean little inn by the river side; Hirsch, Stag).—A little town of 1600 inhabitants, in a contracted valley on the rt. bank of the Rhine, which here flows in a dark green stream, between wooded hills. At the end of the wooden bridge which traverses it rises a tall, square watch-tower of massive masonry: it belonged to a castle now removed. Close to it is a toll-house. This road is much traversed by pilgrims to the shrine of our Lady of Einsiedeln (Route 74); and the traveller encounters, at every step, troops of the poor peasantry of the Black Forest, religiously counting their beads, and muttering their aves and paternosters. From the heights above the town of

1⅓ Bülach (4000 inhabitants) the snowy Alps may be discerned in fine weather, with the Righi in the middle distance.

2 Kloten.

The descent upon Zurich, between vineyards and gardens, amidst neat villas and taverns, with the windings of the Limmat, and the lake and town of Zurich in front, is very pleasing. A little to the rt. of the road rises the hill of *Weid*, 3 miles from Zurich, commanding the finest view of the town and neighbourhood. A short distance outside of the town may be seen the junction of the Sihl with the Limmat. Since 1833, Zurich has ceased to be a fortress; a large portion of the ramparts are already swept away, and the stranger finds himself within its walls without encountering drawbridges and bastions as heretofore.

1⅔ Zurich–*Inns:* Schwerdt (Epée) —overlooking the Limmat, close to the broad wooden bridge which serves as a market-place;—expensive, and neither very good nor clean. Beds, 3 fr.; dinner, table d'hôte, 3 fr.—in private, 4 fr.; tea and breakfast, 2 fr. —Raabe (Corbeau) ;—Storch (Cycogne), table d'hôte, with wine, 2 fr.

8 sous; bed, 2 fr.; breakfast, 1 fr. 4 sous.

The inns at Zurich are notoriously dirty, high priced and ill attended: they have hitherto enjoyed a monopoly, and there has been no inducement to improve. But at this time (1837) two large new inns are building—one near the outlet of the Limmat from the lake, on the rt. bank of the river; the other near the new post-office.

Zurich, the most important manufacturing town of Switzerland, and the capital of a canton distinguished above all others for prosperous industry, has 14,500 inhabitants, and lies at the N. end of the lake of Zurich, and on the banks of the Limmat, just where it issues out of the lake in a rapid and healthful stream, clear as crystal. A Roman station, *Thuricum,* fixed on this spot, probably gave rise both to the town and its name. Zurich is the seat of the Swiss Diet (Vorort) alternately with Berne and Lucerne, for a period of two years together. The flourishing condition of the town is visible in the improvements going forward in it, in the number of the new buildings rising in and around it. The banks of the lake and Limmat, and all the neighbouring hills, are thickly dotted over with houses, which, by the removal of the useless and inconvenient ramparts, will soon be united with the town itself, forming a wide circle of suburbs.

Apart from its agreeable situation and thriving manufactures, there is not much to be seen in Zurich. There are no fine buildings here: that of the most consequence is the *Cathedral,* or *Gross Münster,* on the rt. bank of the Limmat. It is venerable from its age, having been built in the 10th or 11th century, and worthy of respect from having been the scene of Zwingli's bold preachings of reformation in the church, and amendment of morals. It is a heavy, massive building, in a style of architecture resembling that called

Norman in England; very plain within and without, but interesting in the eye of the architect and antiquary. Its nave is supported on square pillars and round arches; beneath it is a very perfect crypt. Its circular portal, and the adjoining *cloisters* raised upon small low triple arches, with slender columns and capitals of various patterns, fantastically carved, are very curious.

The house in which the reformer *Zwingli* passed the last six years of his life is still standing: it is No. 185 in the Grosse Stadt.

The *Church of St. Peter* (with the large clock), on the l. bank of the Limmat, had for its minister, for 23 years, *Lavater*, the author of the renowned work on physiognomy, who was born at Zurich. On the capture of the town by the French army, September 26, 1799, he was shot, within a few steps of his own door, by a brutal French soldier, to whom, but two minutes before, he had given wine and offered money, and while he was in the act of assisting another soldier who had been wounded. A high reward was offered by Massena, the French commander, for the discovery of the murderer; but, though known to Lavater and his family, he refrained from informing against him. After lingering through three months of excruciating agony, he expired, Jan. 2, 1801, at the parsonage: his grave is marked by a simple stone in the *churchyard of St. Anne;* where Ebel, author of the Swiss Guide, and Escher von der Linth (p. 30), are also buried.

The *Rathhaus*, a massive square building close to the lower bridge, and opposite the Sword, is the place of meeting of the *Diet*, when it assembles at Zurich. In the council-chamber is an extravagant painting of the Oath at Grutli, by *Henry Fuseli* (properly Füssli), who was born here.

The *Town Library*, close to the New stone bridge, in a building formerly a church (Wasserkirche), contains, in addition to 45,000 printed volumes and MSS., three autograph Latin letters of *Lady Jane Grey*, addressed to her preceptor, Bullinger, in a beautifully clear and regular hand—a few grammatical errors have been remarked in them; a bust of Lavater, by *Dannecker;* a portrait of Zwingli and his daughter, by *Hans Asper;* a model in relief of a large part of Switzerland; some very curious fossils from Œhningen, including one described by Scheuchzer as a human skull, though in reality a portion of a lizard—fossils of the Glarus slate, chiefly fishes, from the Plattenberg.

The *Old Arsenal* (Alt-Zeughaus) contains some ancient armour; also a cross-bow, said to be (?) that with which William Tell shot the apple from his son's head; and several tattered standards, taken by the Swiss from their enemies, including one of Charles the Bold of Burgundy. This collection is inferior to those in several other Swiss cantons.

The tall and picturesque *Tower of Wellenburg,* rising out of the water at the outlet of the Limmat from the lake, is used as a prison. State-criminals were formerly confined in it: Count Hans of Hapsburg passed more than two years in it. The *Heretics' Tower* (Ketzer *Thurm*) receives its name from the unfortunate Reformers confined in it during the religious troubles of Switzerland.

In 1832-3 a *University* was established at Zurich, and many professors, expelled from other countries for their political opinions, have repaired hither as teachers. The most eminent among them is Oken. As yet the number of students is not great. The building of the suppressed Augustine Convent has been appropriated to its use, and considerable additions to it are contemplated. The *Library* contains many original MSS. of the early reformers, and the *Museum* of *Natural History* some good specimens of Swiss minerals and fossils, together with the Herbarium of John Gessner.

One of the most pleasing features about Zurich is its promenades and points of view. The best of them is decidedly the *Cats' Bastion* (Katzen Bastei), an elevated mound commanding a delightful view of the town, lake, and distant Alps, which originally formed a part of the fortification, and it has been deservedly preserved, though the adjoining ramparts are cut away. It has now assumed the peaceful shape of a garden and shrubbery.

Nothing can be more delightful than the view at sunset from this point, extending over the smiling and populous shores of the beautiful lake to the distant peaks and glaciers of the Alps of Glarus, Uri, and Schwytz, tinged with the most delicate pink by the sinking rays.

The *Hohe Promenade*, another rampart on the rt. bank of the Limmat, also commands a good view, but more confined than the former. Those who desire a complete panorama should ascend the *Weid*, a hill about 3 miles N. of the town, where an inn has recently been built. The triangular piece of ground at the junction of the Limmat and Sihl, below the town, is also a public walk: it is planted with shady avenues, but commands no view. Here is a simple monument to the memory of Solomon Gessner, author of "The Death of Abel," who was a native of Zurich.

Zurich is historically remarkable as the place where the Reformation first commenced in Switzerland, under the guidance and preaching of Ulric Zwingli, in 1519. It was the asylum of many eminent English Protestants banished by the persecutions of the reign of Queen Mary: they met with a friendly reception from its inhabitants during their exile. The first *entire English version* of the Bible, by Miles Coverdale, was printed here in 1535.

Zurich is the native place of Hammerlin, the reformer; of Gessner, the poet, and Gessner, the naturalist; of Lavater; and of Pestalozzi, the teacher.

The principal manufactures are those of silk, the weaving of which occupies many thousands in the town and along the shores of the lake. There are one or two large cotton-factories. The cotton and silk goods made in the neighbourhood, and in other parts of the canton, are the object of an extensive commerce with Germany and Italy. Many of the manufacturers of Zurich have the reputation of great wealth, without much polish; hence the expression, "Grossier comme un Zurichois."

The *Museum* Club contains a capital reading-room, where Galignani, The Times, John Bull, Examiner, Athenæum, and Literary Gazette, Quarterly and Edinburgh Reviews are taken in; besides all the best Continental journals. Travellers can be introduced for a few days by a member.

At the shop of Henry Füssli and Co., near the stone bridge, will be found the best collection of maps, views, &c., such as travellers often require to supply themselves with.

The *New Post and Diligence Office* is built near the Liebfrauen Kirche. A letter reaches England in six days.

Diligences go daily to Schaffhausen, Constance, Basle, Bern, Neuchâtel, Lucerne, Schwytz, Winterthur, and St. Gall, Rapperschwyl, and Coire; four times a-week to Glarus.

A *Steam-boat* goes twice a-day from Zurich to the other end of the lake (Rapperschwyl) and back. Diligences convey passengers thence to Wesen, where another steamer is prepared to carry them across the lake to Wallenstadt. (Route 14.) Travellers proceeding to the Righi may take the boat as far as Horgen.

The *voituriers* (Lohnkutschers) of Zurich have the reputation of being extortioners and uncivil. The writer can, from experience, recommend as an exception to this rule (if rule it be) one Jacob Aberli, living in the Hirschgasse, as having served him with honesty, punctuality, and civility, for more than four weeks.

ROUTE 9.

ZURICH TO CONSTANCE, BY WINTERTHUR.

12 stunden = 39¼ Eng. miles.
A diligence daily in 9 hours.
The road passes through Schwammendingen and Bassersdorf.

On the banks of the Töss, about 3 miles on the rt. of the road, and nearly 4 miles from Winterthur, rise the ruins of the *Castle of Kyburg*, memorable in history as the seat of a powerful family of counts, who, between the 9th and 13th centuries, gained possession of the N. of Switzerland, as far as the Rhine and lake of Constance, and numbered as their dependents and vassals 100 lords of minor castles, now for the most part in ruins. The line becoming extinct in 1264, their domains fell to the share of Rudolph of Habsburg, and the Austrian family, though long since deprived of them, still retain among their titles that of Count of Kyburg. The ruins now belong to a citizen of Winterthur.

The ancient Dominican Convent of Töss, on the road, now converted into a factory, was the chosen retreat of the Empress Agnes after the murder of her father, Albert of Austria. Here her daughter-in-law, St. Elizabeth of Hungary, took the veil, and died in the odour of sanctity: her monument, with the arms of Hungary, is visible in the existing church. The cloisters, built with the church in 1469, are ornamented with fresco paintings from the Old and New Testaments.

4½ Winterthur — (*Inns :* Wilder Mann, good ;—Sonne) — an industrious manufacturing town, of nearly 3500 inhabitants ; consisting of two long parallel streets, crossed by eight smaller ones at right angles.

The weaving of muslin and the printing of cotton are the most thriving branches of industry here.

2¼ Frauenfeld — (*Inns :* Krone, best and clean ; Hirsch)—the chief town of the Canton Thurgovie (Germ. Thurgau), has 1200 inhabitants, and is situated on the river Murg, which sets in motion the wheels of numerous cotton, dyeing, and printing mills.

The stately *Castle*, on the summit of a rock, was built in the 11th century by one of the vassals of the Counts of Kyburg.

On a hill to the S. of the town stands the Capuchin Convent, founded in 1595, now occupied by only seven or eight brothers.

1 Pfyn, a village on the Thur, was, in Roman times, a frontier fort, called *Ad Fines ;* whence its modern name.

¾ Mühlheim.

1¼ Wäldi. A wooden tower has been erected on the summit of a hill near this, called Hohenrain, on account of the extensive view it commands.

2¼ Constance, in Route 7.

ROUTE 10.

ZURICH TO ST. GALL.

14¾ stunden = 48 English miles.
A diligence goes daily.
The road is the same as Route 9 as far as

4½ *Winterthur.* Hence by Elgg and Dutwyl, crossing the Murg to

3¾ Münchwyl,

1 Wyl,

2 Flahwyl, station of post-horses, by the Kratzeen bridge (Route 69), to

3½ *St. Gall.* Route 66.

ROUTE 13.

ZURICH TO BERNE, BY BADEN AND LENZBURG.

23 Stunden = 75½ English miles. A malleposte goes daily in 14, and a diligence in 17 hours. As far as

4⅓ Baden the road is the same as Route 6. This route is very circuitous. There is another direct road to Lenzburg by Bremgarten, but it is a mere cross road, not practicable for heavy carriages.

At Mellingen, the river Reuss is crossed by a wooden bridge. Some have supposed that the battle in which the Roman general Cæcina beat the Helvetians, A.D. 70, was fought here.

3 Lenzburg—(*Inns:* Löwe, good; Krone;)—a manufacturing town of 2000 inhabitants, on the Aa, a stream which drains the lake of Halwyl. The old gothic *castle* on the summit of a sandstone cliff, is now converted into a school, on the plan of that at Hofwyl.

At a village called Hunzenschwyl, the road to Aarau turns off to the right, and that from Schintznach and Brugg joins our route.

1¾ Suhr. On the right rises the ancient fortress of Aarburg (p. 12).

2¾ Kreutzstrasse—(*Inn:* Löwe.)— The high road from Bâle to Lucerne here crosses our route. At Rothrist, 1½ farther on, there is a good inn (Cheval Blanc—Rössli), kept by a civil landlady. The road runs along the rt. bank of the Aar to

1½ Morgenthal — (*Inn:* Löwe, good.)

2½ Herzogenbuchsee — (*Inn:* Sonne;)—a village of 4500 inhabitants.

1½ Hochstetten.

1½ Alchenfluh.

1¼ Hindelbank.

In the village church is the celebrated *Monument* of *Madame Langhans*, wife of the Minister, who died in child-birth. It is by a sculptor, named Nahl, and represents her with her child in her arms, bursting through the tomb at the sound of the last trumpet. Its merit, as a work of art, has been much exaggerated. Its chief excellence seems to be the natural manner in which the crack in the stone is represented. The epitaph was written by Haller. This tomb is formed of sandstone, and is let into the pavement of the church. The chief figure is injured by the loss of the nose, which Glütz Blotzheim asserts (it is to be hoped unfoundedly) was the wanton act of an Englishman.

The *Castle* on the neighbouring height, belongs to the Erlach family.

2¾ BERNE, (in Route 24.)

ROUTE 14.

ZURICH TO COIRE, BY THE LAKES OF ZURICH AND WALLENSTADT.

25 Stunden = 82 Eng. miles.

A diligence goes daily; but it is a tedious conveyance. Down to 1837 it took 23 hours to perform the journey.

A steam-boat traverses the Lake of Zurich, to and fro, twice a day, in 2½ or 3 hours, starting from Rapperschwyl, at 5 A.M., and 2 P.M.; and from Zurich at 8 A.M. and 5 P.M. It is not a quick conveyance, as it zigzags from one side of the lake to the other, to take in and let out passengers at the different towns. Nor is it cheap, the price of a place from Rapperschwyl to Zurich being 32 batz (=4 fr. 60 c.); and the charge for a 4-wheeled carriage, with 4 persons, amounts to 33 fr. Those who have a carriage of their own may proceed as speedily, and at a less cost by land. There is a threat of starting an opposition steamer, in which case all this may be altered.

Diligences are in readiness on the arrival of the steamer at Rapperschwyl and Wallenstadt, to carry on the passengers.

Good carriage-roads run along both sides of the lake, and are traversed daily by diligences. The road to Wallenstadt and Coire runs along the t. or N. bank.

The *Lake of Zurich* has no pretensions to grandeur of scenery; that must be sought for on the silent and savage shores of the lakes of Lucerne, Geneva, and Wallenstadt; but it has a charm peculiarly its own—that of life and rich cultivation. Its borders are as a bee-hive, teeming with population, and are embellished and enlivened at every step by the work of man. Its character is smiling and cheerful. The hills around it are less than 3000 feet high above the sea, and descend in gentle slopes down to the water's edge: wooded on their tops, clad with vineyards, orchards, and gardens on their slopes, and carpeted with verdant pastures, or luxuriantly waving crops of grain at their feet. But the principal feature in this landscape is the number of human habitations: the hills from one extremity to the other are dotted with white houses, villas of citizens, cottages, and farms, while along the margin of the lake, and on the high road, they gather into frequent clusters around a church, forming villages and towns almost without number. Every little stream descending from the hills is compelled to do duty by turning some mill; at the mouths of the valleys enormous factories are erected, and thus the shores of the lake, on either side, have the appearance of one vast uninterrupted village.

The effect of this lively foreground is heightened by the appearance of the snowy peaks of the Sentis, Dödi, and Glärnisch, which are seen at different points peering above the nearer hills. The charms of the Lake of Zurich inspired the Idylls of Gessner: they are celebrated in an ode of Klopstock, and in the prose of Zimmerman. The lake is a long and narrow strip of water, about 26 miles in length from Zurich to Schmerikon, and not more than three broad at the widest part, between Stäfa and Wädensweil. The principal river falling into it is the Linth, which issues out at Zurich, under the name of Limmat.

Scarcely any of the villages or towns on the lake are at all remarkable except as the seats of flourishing industry. A few only of the principal places are enumerated below, with their distance by land from Zurich; the banks are distinguished as rt. and l., in reference to the course of the Limmat.

(l.) The high ridge rising on the W. of Zurich, and bordering the lake for more than 12 miles, is the Albis.

(rt.) 1¾ Kussnacht—(*Inn*: Sonne)—a village of 2114 inhabitants; not to be confounded with its namesake on the Lake of Lucerne, famous in the history of Tell.

(l.) Rüschlikon; behind this are the baths of Nydelbad, with a bathhouse.

2¼ Thalwyl—(*Inn*: Adler.)

Lavater is said to have written a portion of his work on physiognomy at the parsonage of the village of Ober-Rieden, about 3½ miles farther on.

(l.) 1 Horgen—(*Inn*: Schwan; Löwe.)—Here passengers, bound for the Righi, by way of Zug, disembark and cross the hills. (Route 15.)

(rt.) 1¾ Meilen—*Inns*: Löwe; Sonne;)—a very considerable village of 3036 inhabitants, with a gothic church, built 1490-9. Its poorer inhabitants are chiefly silk-weavers.

(l.) 1 Wädenschwyl;—a pretty village of 4357 inhabitants, containing silk factories. Above it stands the castle, formerly residence of the bailiff (ober-amtman), now private property.

(l.) ¾ Richtensweil,—here is one of the largest cotton factories on the borders of the lake. The village is built on the boundary line of Cantons Zurich and Schwytz; behind it the road to Einsiedeln ascends the hills. The pilgrims bound to that celebrated shrine usually disembark here. (See Route 74.) Zimmerman resided here as physician, and in his work on " Solitude" praises the beauty of this spot.

(l.) 1¾ Stäfa — (*Inns:* Krone ; Stern ;)—an industrious village of 3026 inhabitants, by whom much silk and cotton is woven. The extremity of the lake beyond this lies out of the limits of the Canton Zurich. It has been calculated that the number of inhabitants on each of its banks, hence to the town of Zurich, a distance of 16 miles, is not less than 12,000.

On approaching Rapperschwyl and its long bridge, the pretty little isle of *Aufnau* becomes a conspicuous feature and ornament to the landscape. It has some celebrity as the retreat and burial place of Ulric Von Hutten, a Franconian knight, the friend of Luther and Franz of Sickingen, distinguished equally for his talents and chivalrous bravery, but withal a bit of a rouè. His satirical writings contributed not a little to the spread of the Reformation, but raised up against him such a host of enemies, that he was forced to fly from the court of Charles V., and take refuge from their persecution, first, with Franz of Sickingen, and, after his death, in this little island. Zwingli had procured for him an asylum here, in the house of the curate, where he died a fortnight after his arrival (1523), at the age of 36. He was buried by a faithful friend, but all record of the spot in which he lies has long since disappeared.

The *Bridge of Rapperschwyl* is probably the longest in the world; it extends from the town to a tongue of land on the opposite side, completely across the lake, a distance of 4800 feet, or more than ¾ of a mile. It is only 12 feet broad, is formed of loose planks laid (not nailed) upon piers, and is unprovided with railing at the sides, so that only one carriage can safely pass at a time. The toll is heavy—24 batz for a char-à-banc. It was originally constructed by Leopold of Austria, 1358: the existing bridge dates from 1819.

A small stone pier has recently been thrown out into the lake, a little below the bridge, outside the gate of the town, to receive passengers from the steam-boat.

(rt.) 1½. Rapperschwyl — (*Inns* Pfau (Paon d'Or), outside the town best, but dear; Freienhof.)—This is a very picturesque old town, in Canton St. Gall, still partly surrounded by walls, and surmounted by an *old Castle* and a *Church*, near which, from the terrace called Lindenhof, a fine view is obtained.

Rapperschwyl is about 18 miles from Zurich, and the same distance from Wesen. The diligence takes about 3½ hours either way. A char costs 12 f.; and a calèche, with two horses, 20 to 24 f. Roads run from hence to St. Gall, and across the bridge to Einsiedeln.—(Route 74, and Glarus, by Lachen, R. 72.)

At Schmerikon, the road quits the lake of Zurich ; the castle of Grynau, on the rt., stands on the Linth, a little above its entrance into the lake. Pedestrians will find the towing-path along the Linth canal shorter than the carriage-road from Schmerikon to Wesen.

2¾ Uznach,—a small town of 900 inhabitants, on an eminence, the summit of which is occupied by a small square tower of the ancient castle and by that of the church. The road to St. Gall (Route 69) turns off here. There are mines of brown coal at Oberkirch about a mile from Uznach, in a hill 1500 feet high.

Soon after leaving Uznach the valley of Glarus opens out into view with the snowy mountains near its head ; a very beautiful prospect. Out of this valley issues the river Linth, an impetuous torrent, fed by glaciers, and carrying down with it vast quantities of debris, which had accumulated to such an extent 20 years ago, that its channel was obstructed, and its bed raised many feet above the level of the lower part of the valley. From this cause arose repeated and most

angerous inundations, which cover-
d the fertile district on its banks
ith stone and rubbish, and converted
he meadows into a stagnant marsh.
early the entire valley between the
kes of Zurich and Wallenstadt was
educed to a desert, and its inhabit-
nts, thinned in numbers by annual
evers, arising from the pestilential
xhalations, abandoned the spot.
he valley of the Linth was relieved
om this dire calamity by Mr.
onrad Escher, who suggested to the
iet, in 1807, the ingenious plan of
igging a new bed for the waters of
he Linth, and turning it into the
ake of Wallenstadt, in whose depths
: might deposit the sand and gravel
hich it brought down, without
oing any damage. He at the same
me proposed to improve the issues
f the lake of Wallenstadt by digging
navigable canal from it to the
ke of Zurich, so as to carry off the
aters of the Linth and the other
treams falling into it, so that it
ight drain the intervening valley,
istead of inundating it. This im-
ortant and useful public work was
ompleted by Escher in 1822, and
as been attended with perfect suc-
ess. In consequence of it the valley
s no longer steril and unwholesome,
nd the high road to Wesen, which
as often cut off and broken up by
iroads of the river, is now carried
n a straight line along its rt. bank.
mmediately opposite the opening
f the valley of the Linth, at
hose extremity the mountains of
larus now appear in all their
randeur, a simple monumental ta-
let of black marble has been let into
he face of the rock by the road-
ide, to the memory of the public-
pirited citizen who conferred this
reat benefit on the surrounding
ountry. He earned from it, in ad-
ition to his name, the title *Von der
inth*, the only title which a republic
ould properly confer, and which his
escendants may be more proud than
f that of count or baron. The Linth
here crossed by a bridge, called

Ziegelbrucke, over which runs the
road to Glarus. (Route 72.) Near
it are a cotton manufactory and an
establishment for the education of
the poor of the canton Glarus. It is
called the *Linth Colony*, because it
owes its origin to a colony of 40
poor persons, afterwards increased to
180, who were brought hither by
charitable individuals from the over-
peopled villages of the canton, and settled on this spot, which was the bed
of the Linth previous to Escher's improvements, in order to reclaim it by
removing the stones and rubbish, and
rendering it fit for cultivation. They
were lodged, fed, and allowed a small
sum for wages, the expense being de-
frayed by subscription. After having,
in combination with the correction of
the Linth, described above, restored
the valley to a state fit for agriculture, and having, above all, been
saved themselves from starvation, in
a season of scarcity, they were dismissed to seek their fortunes with
some few savings to begin the world;
and, what was of more importance,
with industrious habits, which they
had learned while settled here. In
the school which now replaces the
colony children from 6 to 12 are
taught, and teachers are also in-
structed.

3¼ Wesen.—(*Inn:* L'Epée, well
situated, but not very good fare; had
once the reputation of being dear. The
following are the charges at present,
—for the best bed-room, with two
beds, 3 fr.; dinner 3 fr.; breakfast 2 fr.)

Wesen is a village of about 500
inhabitants, at the W. extremity of
the lake of Wallenstadt, and in the
midst of scenery of great magnificence.

Glarus is six miles from Wesen
(Route 72).

LAKE OF WALLENSTADT.

A steam-boat was established on
this lake, between Wesen and Wallenstadt, in 1837. It made 3 voyages
to and fro *daily* in summer, 2 in au-

tumn, and 1 in winter. The voyage takes up about 1 hour and 10 minutes ; by the common boats it occupied between 2 and 3 hours. Fares —1st place 1 florin (= 1 Fr. fr. 35 cents.); carriages, with 2 horses, 4 florins (= 9 fr. 41 cents.); with 3, 7 florins (= 16 Fr. fr. 47 c.) ; with 4, 10 florins (= 23 F. fr. 53 cent.)

A diligence is provided at either end of the lake to carry on passengers as soon as landed.

Previous to the construction of the Linth canal, the only outlet for the lake of Wallenstadt was a small stream called the Magg, which encountered the Linth, after a course of about 2 miles, and was arrested by the debris and stones, brought down by that river, so that not only were its waters often dammed up behind, but the surface of the lake was raised several feet above its ordinary level, in consequence of which, they overflowed the valley both above and below it, and laid the villages of Wallenstadt, at the one end, and Wesen, at the other, under water for many months during the spring. By Escher's correction of the course of the Linth, its waters are now carried into the Lake, where they have already formed, by their deposit of mud and gravel, a delta nearly half a mile long. Another canal, deep and protected at the side with strong dykes, now supplies the place of the Maag, and drains the lake of Wallenstadt into that of Zurich.

The lake of Wallenstadt is about 12 miles long by 3 broad ; its scenery is grand, but not first-rate ; far inferior to that of the lake of Lucerne. Its N. shore consists of colossal cliffs of lime and sand-stone, regularly stratified, and so nearly precipitous that there is room for no road, and only for a very few cottages at their base, while their steep surface, almost destitute of verdure, give to this lake a savage and arid character. The S. side consists of more gradually sloping hills, covered with verdure and overtopped by the tall bare peaks

of more distant mountains. On th side there are several villages, and very rough and irregular road run along it. The lake had once th reputation of being dangerous t navigate, on account of sudden ten pests; but in this respect it does no differ from other mountain-lakes and there can be little risk in in trusting oneself to experienced boat men. The courier who has passe it 3 times a-week for many yea remembers no instance of an acc dent.

The precipices along the N. ban vary between 2000 and 3000 feet i height, and the stranger is usuall surprised to learn that above ther are situated populous villages an extensive pastures crowded with cat tle. Such a one is the village c Ammon, containing 3000 inhabit ants, nearly 2500 feet above the lak with a church, gardens, and orchard It is approached by one narrow an steep path, which may be trace sloping upwards from Wesen alon the face of the mountain. Severa waterfalls precipitate themselves ove this wall of rock, or descend, b gashes or rents in its sides, into th lake ; but they dwindle into insignifi cance by the end of summer, and ad no beauty to the scene. The princi pal ones are the Beyerbach, 1200 fee high (above which lies Ammon), an the Serenbach, 1600 feet high.

The hamlet of St. Quentin i the only one on this side of th lake. On the opposite (S.) sid there are numerous villages at th mouths of the streams and gul lies. The principal of them i Murg, near which a large cotton factory has been recently built. Be hind it rises the mountain Murtsch enstock. Its summit, 7270 fee high, and almost inaccessible, i traversed through and through by a cavern, which, though of large size looks from the lake like the eye o a bodkin. The hole is best seer when abreast of the village of Mühle horn ; by those not aware of the fact might be mistaken for a patch of snow. This peak is the favourite resort of chamois.

The N.E. extremity of the lake is bounded by the seven picturesque peaks of the Sieben Kurfursten (7 Electors; some say Kuhfirsten). At their feet lies the village of

4 Wallenstadt.— (*Inns:* Rössli (Cheval); Hirsch (Cerf, or Poste); not good. A new inn, called the Aigle d'Or, has been built at the side of the lake, close to the landing-place of the steamer. It is far better situated than the others, and is probably as good as they are in other respects.)

Wallenstadt is a scattered township of 800 inhabitants; nearly half a mile from the lake, of which it commands no view. The flats of the valley around and above it are marshy, and the neighbourhood was formerly very unhealthy, so long as the irregularities of the Linth obstructed the passage of the waters of the lake. The evil might be entirely cured were similar measures adopted to confine and regulate the course of the Scez, which still overflows the valley at times. Wallenstadt is a dull place, and travellers had better avoid stopping here.

There is considerable beauty in the scenery of the valley of the Scez, between Wallenstadt and

2½ Sargans—(*Inns:* Kreutz (Croix Blanc); Löwe;)—a town of 723 inhabitants, on an eminence surmounted by a *castle*, near the junction of the roads from St. Gall and Zurich to Coire. It stands upon the watershed, dividing the streams which feed the Rhine from those which fall into the lake of Wallenstadt; and this natural embankment is so slight (about 200 paces across and less than 20 feet high) that, as the deposits brought down by the Rhine are constantly raising its bed, it is not impossible, though scarcely probable, that the river may change its course, relinquish its present route by the lake of Constance, and take a shorter cut by

the lakes of Wallenstadt and Zurich. It was calculated by Escher von der Linth, from actual measurements, that the waters of the Rhine need but rise but 19½ feet to pass into the lake of Wallenstadt; and it is, indeed, recorded that the river, swollen by long rains in 1618, was only prevented taking this direction by the construction of dams along its banks. Geologists argue, from the identity of the deposits of gravel in the valley of the Upper Rhine with those in the Vale of Scez, that the river actually did pass out this way at one time.

The remainder of this route of the valley of the Rhine by

1½ Ragatz to

(4) 1½ *Coire*, together with the excursion to Pfeffers, which no one who passes this way should omit, is described in Route 67.

ROUTE 15.

ZURICH TO ZUG AND LUCERNE, BY HORGEN AND THE RIGHI.

13 stunden = 42¾ Eng. miles.

This is the most direct road to Zug and the Righi, but it is practicable for heavy carriages no farther than Horgen; they must therefore be sent round by way of Knonau (Route 16) to meet their owners at Zug or Lucerne. As far as

3 Horgen the road runs along the W. shore of the lake of Zurich, described at p. 29. The best mode of proceeding thus far is in the steam-boat (p. 28). At Horgen —(*Inns:* Schwan, rather dear;— Löwe) — a char-à-banc, with one horse, may be hired for 12 or 14 francs to Zug, a drive of about 2¾ hours. The ascent of the Albis ridge behind Horgen is very steep, but commands a fine view of the lake as far as Rapperschwyl and its long bridge. The steep descent which follows leads down to the village of

1¾ Sihlbrücke, so called from a bridge over the Sihl, which conducts the traveller from Canton Zurich into Canton Zug. From the ridge which succeeds, the Righi and Pilatus are first seen, and soon after the borders of the lake of Zug are reached.

1½ *Zug*—(*Inn:* Hirsch, Cerf, good;)—capital of Canton Zug, the smallest state of the Confederation, has 3200 inhabitants, and is prettily situated at the N.E. corner of the lake. It has an antiquated look, surrounded by its old walls, and, being without trade, has a silent and deserted air. Its inhabitants, exclusively Roman Catholics, are chiefly occupied with agricultural pursuits. The rich crops, vineyards, orchards, and gardens, on the borders of the lake, proclaim a soil not ungrateful to the cultivator.

There is a *Capuchin Convent* and a *Nunnery* here. The picture by Caracci in the former, mentioned by the guide-books, is none of his, but is by an inferior artist, Fiamingo, and of no great merit.

The *Church of St. Michael*, a little way outside of the town, has a curious *bone-house* attached to it, containing many hundred skulls, each inscribed with the name of its owner. The church-yard in which it stands is filled with quaint gilt crosses by way of monuments, and the graves are planted with flowers.

In the year 1435 it is recorded that a part of the foundations of the town, weakened probably by an attempt to draw off part of the water of the lake, gave way, whereby two streets, built on the ground nearest the water, were broken off and submerged; 26 houses were destroyed, and 45 human beings perished; among them the chief magistrate of the town. His child, an infant, was found floating in his cradle on the surface of the lake; he was rescued, and afterwards became landammann of the canton.

Diligences go daily from Zug to Lucerne and Zurich.

The Lake of Zug, whose surface is 1340 feet above the sea, is 8 miles long, and about ¾ broad. Its banks are low, or gently-sloping hills, except on the S. side, where the Righi rising abruptly from the water's edge, presents its precipices towards it, forming a feature of considerable grandeur, in conjunction with the Pilatus rising behind it. The *Rufi* or *Ross-berg*, rising in the S. W. corner, is also lofty and steep; the lake, at its base, is not less than 1200 ft. deep. A capital carriage road has been formed along the water-side from Zug to Arth and Immensee. Boats are to be found at all these places, and the fare across, with two rowers, is 20 batz. It takes about 2 hours to go by water to Arth. The road to Arth winds round the base of the Rossberg, which has obtained a melancholy celebrity from the catastrophe caused by the fall of a portion of it. (See Route 17.) Near the chapel of St. Adrian a small monument has been erected on the spot where the arrow is supposed to have fallen which Henry Von Hunenberg shot out of the Austrian lines into the Swiss camp, before the battle of Morgarten, bearing the warning words, " Beware of Morgarten." It was in consequence of this that the confederates occupied the position indicated, and it contributed mainly to their victory on that memorable field. Morgarten (R. 74) lies within this canton, about 14 miles W. of Zug, on the Lake of Egeri.

3 Arth—(*Inn:* Schwarzer Adler, Aigle Noir ;—good) is the best point from which to ascend the Righi ; but Arth—the Righi—and the rest of the road to

4 LUCERNE, are most conveniently described in Route 17.

ROUTE 16.

ZURICH TO LUCERNE, OVER THE
ALBIS.

10 stunden = 32¾ Eng. miles.
A diligence daily in 7 hours.

The high chain of the Albis intervenes between Zurich and Lucerne,
running nearly parallel with the
lake of Zurich. Two roads are carried across it—1. The most northern,
which, though somewhat longer, occupies less time than the southern
road, because it crosses the mountain where it is lower, as it were
turning the flank of the chain, and
going round its N. extremity. This
is the road taken by the diligence,
and the *only one practicable for heavy
carriages* at present (1837). An
improved line is in progress, but
it does not redound to the credit
of the canton that it is not further
advanced, and a year or two will
probably elapse before it is finished.

The northern road commences the
ascent of the Albis at the village of
Albisrieden, about 3 miles from Zurich, passing under the highest summit of the chain, called Hütliberg,
2792 ft. above the sea-level, and
commanding from its top—which
may be reached by a foot-path in
1½ hour from Zurich—an extensive
view. On the opposite descent the
road reaches

2½ Bonstetten (*Inn:* Löwe).
2¾ Knonau. There is an inn at
the castle. At this place the two
roads unite.

---

2 The second route crosses the
High Albis, and in its present (1837)
state is dangerous for a heavy carriage, and not fit for any vehicle but
a char of the country. It is exceedingly steep, and resembles the bed
of a torrent rather than a road. This
line of route, however, is remarkable
for the very beautiful view of the
chain of the Alps, and a large part
of Switzerland, which is seen from
its summit. It skirts the shore of

the lake as far as Adliswyl, where it
crosses the river Sihl, and ascends
to the

2½ Albis Wirthshaus, or Inn of
the Albis, which affords only moderate fare or accommodation, but a
magnificent prospect. The best
point, however, for seeing the view
is the *Signal* (Hochwach, called also
Schnabel), a height off the road,
about a mile above the inn: it takes
in nearly the whole of the Zurichsee;
while, at the foot of the mountain,
between it and the lake, the vale of
the Sihl intervenes. Its wooded slopes
were the favourite retreat of the pastoral poet Gessner: they were occupied
in 1799 by two hostile armies—that
of the French under Massena, who
encamped on the slope of the Albis;
and of the Russians, who occupied
the right bank of the Sihl. They
watched each other from hence for
more than three months; until
Massena, by a masterly movement,
crossed the Limmat, cut off part of
the Russian force, and compelled
the rest to a hasty retreat. On the
S. are seen the little lake of Turl
(Turler See), at the foot of the
mountain; not far off the church of
Cappel, where Zwingli died; farther
off the lake of Zug, and behind it
tower the Righi and Pilatus mountains, between which appears a little
bit of the lake of Lucerne. The
grandest feature, however, of the view
is the snowy chain of the Alps, from
the Sentis to the Jungfrau, which
fills up the horizon. The panoramic
view from the Albis has been engraved by Keller.

The greatest height which the
road attains is 2404 ft., after which
it descends, passing on the rt. the
little lake of Turl, by Rifferschwyl
to

2¼ Knonau. Persons bound to
the Righi, and travelling on foot, or
in a light char, may proceed at once
from the summit of the Albis to Zug
by Hausen, and *Cappel* (5 miles from
the Albis inn), a village of 600 inhabitants, which has obtained a woeful

celebrity in Swiss history as the spot where the Confederates, embittered against each other by religious discord, dyed their hands in the blood of one another, and where Zwingli the reformer fell in the midst of his flock on the 11th of October, 1531. Many of the best and bravest of the citizens of Zurich perished on that day of civil broil, overpowered by the numbers of their opponents, the men of the 4 inner cantons. Zwingli, who, in accordance with the custom of the time and country, attended his flock to the field of battle, to afford them spiritual aid and consolation, was struck down in the fight, and found by a soldier of Unterwalden, who did not know him, but who, finding that he refused to call on the Virgin and saints, despatched him with his sword as a dog and a heretic. His body, when recognised by his foes, was burnt by the common hangman, and even his ashes subjected to the vilest indignities that malice could suggest. The spot where he fell is marked by a tree, about 5 minutes' walk from the church. The *Gothic church* of Cappel, anciently attached to a convent suppressed soon after the commencement of the Reformation, was built in 1280.

The road from Knonau to Lucerne proceeds by Rümeltiken and

1½ St. Wolfgang—where a good carriage-road turns off on the left to Zug and the Righi—Thence it proceeds along the banks of the Reuss to

2 Gysliker-Brücke, Dierikon, Ebikon, and, passing near the monument of the Swiss Guards (p. 37), enters

2¼ LUCERNE. *Inns :* Schwan—a new house, in the best situation, and good ; in 1837, complaints were made that it was dear;—Balances (Waage)—an old-established house, good, clean, and moderate charges. The four daughters of the late host take the management of the establishment, and the traveller will find in it extreme civility and most excellent attendance. Rössli (Cheval). There is a good pension, overlooking the lake close to the Kapel Brücke.

Lucerne, chief town of the canton, and one of the three Vororter, or alternate seats of the Diet, lies at the N.W. extremity of the Lake of Lucerne, and is divided into two parts by the river Reuss, which here issues out of it. Its population is about 7500, all Catholics, except about 180 Protestants. Lucerne is the residence of the Papal Nuncio.

It is not a place of any considerable trade or manufactures, but their absence is more than compensated by the beautiful scenery in which it is situated on the borders of the finest and most interesting of the Swiss lakes, between the giant Pilatus and Righi, and in sight of the snowy Alps of Schwytz and Engelberg. The town is still surrounded by a very picturesque circle of feudal watch-towers, and is walled in on the land side ; but its chief peculiarity is the number and length of its *bridges.* The lowest, or *Millbridge,* is hung with paintings of the Dance of Death ; the second, or *Reussbrücke,* is the only one uncovered and passable for carriages ; the upper, or *Capel-brücke* runs in a slanting direction across the mouth of the Reuss, whose clear and pellucid sea-green waters may here be surveyed to great advantage, as they rush beneath it with the swiftness of a mountain-torrent. Against the timbers supporting the roof of this bridge are suspended 77 pictures ; those seen in crossing from the rt. to the l. bank represent the life and acts of St. Leger and St. Maurice, Lucerne's patron saints. The subjects of those seen in the opposite direction are taken from Swiss history, and are not without some merits. Near the middle of the Capel-brücke, rising out of the water, stands a very picturesque watch-tower, called *Wasserthurm,* forming a link of the feudal fortifications of the town. It is said to have once served as a light-house (*Lucerna*) to boats entering the Reuss, and hence some have derived the present name of Lucerne. The *Hofbrücke*, the longest of all the bridges, was originally 1380 feet long, but has lost 300 feet since 1835. It extends across the lake, within a few feet of the shore to the church of St. Leodegar, and the Convent and Court (Hof) of its former abbots. The paintings in its roof illustrate the Scripture.

" Lessons for every heart; a Bible for all eyes."

It commands a charming view of the lake, the Alps, the Righi, and the Pilatus. Near the middle of it is an index painted on a board, the diverging lines of which point to the different mountains and peaks visible from hence, each of which is named for the convenience of strangers. A considerable portion of ground has been gained from the lake by curtailing this bridge, and throwing out a sort of quay; the new inn of the Swan stands on this space. This is also the landing-place of the steamboat.

In churches and other public buildings Lucerne has no very prominent objects, though several which are highly pleasing as monuments of the progress of the nation, and of its manners and customs, exist. The *church of St. Leger*, Hof- or Stifts-kirche, is a modern building, except the two towers, which date from 1506. The adjoining churchyard is filled with quaint old monuments, and the view from the cloister windows is fine, but similar to that from the bridge.

The *Arsenal*, near the gate leading to Berne, is one of those venerable repositories common to the chief towns of all the cantons, in which are deposited the muskets, artillery, &c., for arming their contingent of troops. It contains some rusty suits of ancient armour and several historical relics and trophies of Swiss valour, such as the yellow Austrian banner, and many pennons of knights and nobles taken at the battle of Sem-

pach; the coat of mail stripped from the body of Duke Leopold of Austria, who fell there; the iron cravat, lined with sharp spikes, destined for the neck of Gundeldingen, the Schultheiss and general of the men of Lucerne, who died in the hour of victory. A sword of William Tell, and a battle-axe, borne by Ulric Zwingli, at the battle of Cappel (p. 35), are of very doubtful authenticity: though the malice of the enemies of Zwingli may have led to the assertion that he took active part in the fight, it is believed that he assisted his countrymen merely with exhortations and consolations of religion. Several Turkish standards deposited here were captured at the battle of Lepanto, by a knight of Malta, who was a native of Lucerne.

The *Stadthaus*, on the rt. bank of the Reuss, a little below the Cappelbrücke, is the place of meeting of the Diet, whose sittings are open to the public. The Council of the canton also assembles in it.

General Pfyffer's model (in relief) of a part of Switzerland may interest those who desire to trace on it their past or future wanderings; but it is not so extensive nor so well made as that at Zurich; besides which 1 fr. 50 c. is demanded for admission—decidedly more than it is worth. The *Gothic Fountains* which are to be observed in all parts of Switzerland are here of singular beauty and originality.

At *Meyer's* shop, near the Swan, books, prints, panoramas, and maps, relating to Switzerland, may be had in great profusion.

One of the most interesting of the *sights* of Lucerne is, without doubt, the *Monument to the memory of the Swiss Guards*, who fell while defending the Royal Family of France in the bloody massacre of the French Revolution, August 10, 1792. It is situated in the garden of Gen. Pfyffer, about half a mile outside the Weggis gate. The design is by Thorwaldsen, executed by Ahorn, a sculptor of Constance. It represents a lion, of colossal size, wounded to death, with a spear sticking in his side, yet endeavouring in his last gasp to protect from injury a shield bearing the fleur-de-lis of the Bourbons, which he holds in his paws. The figure, hewn out of the living sand-stone rock, is 28 feet long, and 18 high, and its execution merits very great praise. Beneath it are carved the names of the soldiers and officers who fell in defending the Tuileries Aug. 10, 1792. The loyalty and fidelity of this brave band, who thus sacrificed their lives for their adopted sovereign, almost make us forget that they were mercenaries, especially standing forward, as they did, as the protectors of Louis and his family, at a moment when deserted, or attacked, by his own natural subjects. There is a quiet solitude and shade about the spot which is particularly pleasing and refreshing. The rocks around are mantled with fern and creepers, forming a natural frame-work to the monument; and a streamlet of clear water, trickling down from the top of the rock, is received into a basin-shaped hollow below it, forming a mirror in which the sculpture is reflected. One of the very few survivors of the Swiss Guard, dressed in its red uniform, now rusty and patched, resides in a cottage hard by, as guardian of the monument and cicerone to the stranger. The cloth for the altar of the little chapel adjoining was embroidered expressly for it by the Duchess d'Angoulême.

There are many pretty *walks* and *points of view* near Lucerne; one of the best is the villa called *Allenwinden,* perched on the top of a hill outside the Weggis gate, from which it may be reached in a walk of 15 minutes, by a path winding up the hill outside the town walls.

Gibraltar,— a height on the opposite side of the Reuss, outside the Basle gate, also commands a fine prospect.

Mount Righi, so celebrated for it panoramic view, is about 10 mile from Lucerne (*i. e.* the base of the mountain). To reach the summi will occupy at least 6* hours, exclusive of stoppages, from Lucerne so that travellers will regulate their departure accordingly, remembering that it is of much consequence to arrive at the top before sunset. There are several ways to it, *by land,* to Kussnacht and Arth; or *by water* to Kussnacht and Weggis. (See Route 17.)

No one should leave Lucerne without exploring the beauties of its lake —called in German Vierwaldstädter See—the grandest in Europe, in point of scenery, particularly the farther end of it, called the bay of Uri; and much additional pleasure will be derived if the traveller who understands German will take Schiller's " Wilhelm Tell " as a pocket companion in which admirable poem so many of the scenes are localized. (Route 18.)

Those who intend to explore the lake, and visit the Righi, and to return afterwards to Lucerne, should combine the two expeditions, which may be effected in two days, *thus—* go by land to Arth, or by water to Weggis, descending next day on the opposite side, and embarking on the lake, either at Weggis or Brunnen Sail up the bay of Uri, at least as far as Tell's Chapel, and return by water to Lucerne the 2nd evening.

A *Steamer* was launched upon the lake of Lucerne in 1837. It plies regularly between Lucerne and Fluellen, calling at the intermediate places. Further particulars respecting it, and the hire of boats, which may be found in abundance on the shore

---

* N.B. The number of hours will be lessened by taking advantage of the new steamer to Weggis.

opposite the Swan inn, are given in Route 18.

DILIGENCES go *daily* from Lucerne to Aarau; Bâle; Berne, by Summis- wald; Berne, by Entlibuch; So- leure; Zug and Zurich; 4 *times a- week* to Schwytz, by Kussnacht and Arth.

Mount Pilate is sometimes ascend- ed from Lucerne, but the journey is difficult, occupying 6½ hours; the greater part must be performed on foot, and the view from the top is decidedly inferior to that from the Righi. The road up it from Lu- cerne proceeds in a S.W. direc- tion, by the side of a wild torrent, which, when swollen by rain, is very injurious to the habitations on its banks; and, in the last century, destroyed many houses in the town. Skirting the base of the mountain it passes through the ham- lets of Krienz, Obernau, and Herr- gotteswald; then, crossing a ridge covered with pasturages, descends into the Alpine valley of Eigenthal. Beyond this the path becomes steeper, and is only practicable on foot. It takes nearly 5 hours to reach the Chalets on the Bründlis Alp,—the highest human habitation, occupied by shepherds only in the summer months. The traveller may here obtain shelter for the night, but no- thing deserving the name of accom- modation. There is a very remark- able echo near the Bründlis Alp. Above this vegetation ceases and naked rock succeeds. A cave in the face of the precipice, near this, is called St. Dominick's Hole, from a fancied resemblance in a stone, stand- ing near its mouth, to a monk. The cavern was reached in 1814 by a chamois hunter, Ignacius Matt, at the risk of his life.

The Tomlishorn, the highest peak of the mountain, is 5766 feet above the lake, and 7116 feet above the sea level; but the view from it is said to be inferior to that from another peak, the Esel (ass). There is another path from the summit down the oppo-

site side of the mountain, by which Alpnach may be reached in 3 hours.

According to a wild tradition of con- siderable antiquity, this mountain derives its name from Pilate, the wicked governor of Judæa, who, hav- ing been banished to Gaul by Tibe- rius, wandered about among the mountains, stricken by conscience, until he ended his miserable existence by throwing himself into a lake on the top of the Pilatus. The mountain, in consequence, labours under a very bad reputation. From its position as an outlier, or advanced guard of the chain of the Alps, it collects all the clouds which float over the plains from the W. and N.; and it is re- marked, that almost all the storms which burst upon the lake of Lucerne gather and brew on its summit. This almost perpetual assembling of clouds was long attributed by the superstitious to the unquiet spirit still hovering round the sunken body, which, when disturbed by any in- truder, especially by the casting of stones into the lake, revenged itself by sending storms, and darkness, and hail on the surrounding district. So prevalent was the belief in this super- stition, even down to times compara- tively recent, that the government of Lucerne forbade the ascent of the mountain, and the naturalist Conrad Gessner, in 1555, was obliged to provide himself with a special order removing the interdict in his case, to enable him to carry on his re- searches upon the mountain.

The lake, the source of all this terror, turns out, from recent investi- gation, to be beyond the limits of canton Lucerne, and on the opposite or the E. side of the Tomlishorn; so that the Town Council had no jurisdiction over that part of the mountain, which belongs to Alpnach. It is rather a pond than a lake, is dried up the greater part of the year, and reduced to a heap of snow, which, being melted in the height of sum- mer, furnishes water to the herds upon the mountain, which resort to it to slake their thirst. There is no other lake upon the mountain.

According to some the name Pilatus is only a corruption of *Pileatus* (capped), arising from the cap of clouds which rarely quits its barren brow, and which is sometimes seen rising from it like steam from a cauldron. The mountain consists, from its base to its summit, of nummulite limestone and sandstone; the strata incline to the S., and abound in fossil remains, especially near the summit, around the Bründlis Alp and the Castelen Alp. Nummulites, as large as a crown-piece, are found near the top.

ROUTE 17.

LUCERNE TO SCHWYTZ AND BRUNNEN, INCLUDING THE FALL OF THE ROSSBERG, AND THE ASCENT OF THE RIGHI.

To Schwytz 6¾ stunden = 22 Eng. miles.

To Arth, at the N. base of the Righi, 4¾ stunden = 15½ Eng. miles.

There is a good carriage-road all the way to Schwytz, traversed by a diligence 4 times a-week.

The *shortest way* from Lucerne to the top of the Righi is to go by water to Weggis, and there commence the ascent. In this way the summit may be reached in 4½ or 5 hours from Lucerne, and even less by the aid of the steamer. The best point of ascent, however, is Arth, which may be reached as follows,—returning by Weggis.

The road to Küssnacht runs nearly all the way in sight of the lake of Lucerne, and of the Alps of Engelberg and Berne beyond. On a headland, at the angle of the green bay of Küssnacht, stands the ruined castle of New Habsburg.

2½ Küssnacht—*Inns:* Adler (Aigle-Noir) ;—Rössli (Cheval)—lies at the bottom of this bay, at the foot of the Righi, whose top may be reached from hence by a steep path in 3½ hours (see p. 46). Mules, guides, chars, and boats may be hired here.

On the slope of the Righi, above the village, a ruined wall may be seen, which goes by the name of *Gessler's Castle*, and is believed to be the one to which he was repairing when shot by Tell. This event occurred in the celebrated *Hollow Way* (Chemin creux — Hohle Gasse), through which the road to Arth passes, about a mile out of Küssnacht. It is a narrow green lane, overhung with trees growing from the high banks on each side. Here Tell, after escaping from Gessler's boat on the lake of Lucerne, lay in wait for his enemy, and shot him as he passed from behind a tree, with his unerring arrow. It is somewhat remarkable that recent researches into the archives of Küssnacht have clearly proved that the ruin, called Gessler's Castle, never belonged to him. At the end of the lane, by the road-side, stands *Tell's Chapel*. By a singular anomaly, a place of worship originally dedicated to "The Fourteen Helpers in Need" (Our Saviour, the Virgin, and Apostles), now commemorates a deed of blood, which tradition, and its supposed connexion with the origin of Swiss liberty, appear to have sanctified in the eyes of the people, so that mass is periodically said in it, while it is kept in constant repair, and adorned with rude fresco, representing Gessler's death and other historical events.

A little way past the chapel the lake of Zug appears in sight, and the road continues by its margin round the hem of the Righi, through Immensee to

1¾ Arth—*Inn:* Schwartzer Adler (Black Eagle), tolerably good; travellers usually halt here while the horses are getting ready to carry them up the mountain. Arth, a village of 2129 inhabitants, occupies a charming position on the lake of Zug, between the base of the Righi and the Rossberg. There is a Capuhin convent here. The Rossberg, a angerous neighbour, threatens no anger to Arth, because its strata lope away from the village. The Lighi is a source of considerable gain) Arth, from the number of guides nd mules furnished by the villagers) travellers to ascend the mountain. 'he ascent properly begins at Goldau, bout 2 miles farther on the road, ince few persons are willing to vail themselves of the shorter but ery difficult and fatiguing footpath irect from Arth. Travellers, how- ver, usually leave their carriages ere.

FALL OF THE ROSSBERG.

" Mountains have fallen, eaving a gap in the clouds, and with the shock locking their Alpine brethren; filling up 'he ripe green valleys with destruction's splinters, lamming the rivers with a sudden dash, Vhich crush'd the waters into mist, and made 'heir fountains find another channel— thus, hus, in its old age, did Mount Rosenberg." — Byron.

On approaching Goldau the tra- eller soon perceives traces of the lreadful catastrophe which buried he original and much larger village f that name, and inundated the val- ey for a considerable distance with . deluge of stones and rubbish. The nountain which caused this calamity till remains scarred from top to ottom : nothing grows upon its arren surface, and ages must elapse efore the aspect of ruin can be re- noved.

The Rossberg, or Rufiberg, is a nountain 4958 ft. high; the upper part of it consists of a conglomerate r pudding-stone, formed of rounded nasses of other rocks cemented to- ether, and called by the Germans Nageiflue, or Nail-head, from the cnobs and protuberances which its urface presents. From the nature f the structure of this kind of rock t is very liable to become cracked, ind if rain-water or springs pene- rate these fissures they will not fail

to dissolve the beds of clay which separate the nagelflue from the strata below it, and cause large portions of it to detach themselves from the mass. The strata of the Rossberg are tilted up from the side of the lake of Zug, and slope down towards Goldau like the roof of a house. The slanting direction of the seams which part the strata is well seen on the road from Arth. If, therefore, the clay which fills these seams be washed out by rains, or reduced to the state of a viscous or slimy mud, it is evident that such portions of the rock as have been detached from the rest by fissures above alluded to, must slip down, like the masses of snow which fall from the roof of a house as soon as the lower side is thawed, or as a vessel when launched slides down the inclined plane pur- posely greased to hasten its descent. Within the period of human records destructive landslips had repeatedly fallen from the Rossberg, and a great part of the piles of earth, rock, and stones, which deform the face of the valley, derive their origin from such catastrophes of ancient date; but the most destructive of all appears to have been the last. The vacant space along the top of the mountain caused by the descent of a portion of it, calculated to have been a league long, 1000 ft. broad, and 100 ft. thick, and a small fragment at its farther extremity, which remained when the rest broke off, are also very apparent, and assist in telling the story. The long and wide inclined plane forming the side of the mountain, now ploughed up and scarified as it were, was previously covered with fields, woods, and houses. Some of the buildings are still standing within a few yards of the precipice which marks the line of the fracture.

The catastrophe is thus described in the narrative published at the time by Dr. Zay, of Arth, an eye- witness:—

" The summer of 1806 had been very rainy, and on the 1st and 2nd

September it rained incessantly. New crevices were observed in the flank of the mountain, a sort of cracking noise was heard internally, stones started out of the ground, detached fragments of rocks rolled down the mountain; at two o'clock in the afternoon on the 2nd of September, a large rock became loose, and in falling raised a cloud of black dust. Toward the lower part of the mountain, the ground seemed pressed down from above; and when a stick or a spade was driven in, it moved of itself. A man, who had been digging in his garden, ran away from fright at these extraordinary appearances; soon a fissure, larger than all the others, was observed; insensibly it increased; springs of water ceased all at once to flow; the pine-trees of the forest absolutely reeled; birds flew away screaming. A few minutes before five o'clock, the symptoms of some mighty catastrophe became still stronger; the whole surface of the mountain seemed to glide down, but so slowly, as to afford time to the inhabitants to go away. An old man, who had often predicted some such disaster, was quietly smoking his pipe, when told by a young man, running by, that the mountain was in the act of falling; he rose and looked out, but came into his house again, saying he had time to fill another pipe. The young man, continuing to fly, was thrown down several times, and escaped with difficulty; looking back, he saw the house carried off all at once.

"Another inhabitant, being alarmed, took two of his children and ran away with them, calling to his wife to follow with the third; but she went in for another, who still remained (Marianne, aged five); just then Francisca Ulrich, their servant, was crossing the room, with this Marianne, whom she held by the hand, and saw her mistress; at that instant, as Francisca afterwards said, 'The house appeared to be torn from its foundation (it was of wood and spun round and round like tetotum; I was sometimes on m head, sometimes on my feet, in tot darkness, and violently separate from the child.' When the motio stopped, she found herself jamme in on all sides, with her head dow wards, much bruised, and in extrem pain. She supposed she was burie alive at a great depth; with muc difficulty she disengaged her righ hand, and wiped the blood from h eyes. Presently she heard the fair moans of Marianne, and called her by her name; the child answere that she was on her back amon stones and bushes, which held he fast, but that her hands were free and that she saw the light, and eve something green. She asked whe ther people would not soon come take them out. Francisca answere that it was the day of judgment, an that no one was left to help them but that they would be released b death, and be happy in heaver They prayed together. At las Francisca's ear was struck by th sound of a bell, which she knew t be that of Stenenberg: then sever o'clock struck in another village, an she began to hope there were sti living beings, and endeavoured t comfort the child. The poor littl girl was at first clamorous for he supper, but her cries soon becam fainter, and at last quite died away Francisca, still with her head down wards, and surrounded with dam earth, experienced a sense of col in her feet almost insupportable After prodigious efforts, she suc ceeded in disengaging her legs, an thinks this saved her life. Man hours had passed in this situation when she again heard the voice o Marianne, who had been asleep, an now renewed her lamentations. I the mean time, the unfortunate fa ther, who, with much difficulty, hac saved himself and two children wandered about till daylight, wher he came among the ruins to look fo he rest of his family. He soon discovered his wife, by a foot which appeared above ground: she was dead, with a child in her arms. His cries, and the noise he made in digging, were heard by Marianne, who called out. She was extricated with a broken thigh, and, saying that Francisca was not far off, a farther search led to her release also, but in such a state that her life was despaired of: she was blind for some days, and remained subject to convulsive fits of terror. It appeared that the house, or themselves at least, had been carried down about one thousand five hundred feet from where it stood before.

" In another place, a child two years old was found unhurt, lying on its straw mattress upon the mud, without any vestige of the house from which he had been separated. Such a mass of earth and stones rushed at once into the lake of Lowertz, although five miles distant, that one end of it was filled up, and a prodigious wave passing completely over the island of Schwanau, 70 feet above the usual level of the water, overwhelmed the opposite shore, and, as it returned, swept away into the lake many houses with their inhabitants. The village of Seewen, situated at the farther end, was inundated, and some houses washed away, and the flood carried live fish into the village of Steinen. The chapel of Olten, built of wood, was found half a league from the place it had previously occupied, and many large blocks of stone completely changed their position.

" The most considerable of the villages overwhelmed in the vale of Arth was Goldau, and its name is now affixed to the whole melancholy story and place. I shall relate only one more incident :—A party of eleven travellers from Berne, belonging to the most distinguished families there, arrived at Arth on the 2nd of September, and set off on foot for the Righi a few minutes before the catastrophe. Seven of them had got about 200 yards ahead—the other four saw them entering the village of Goldau, and one of the latter, Mr. R. Jenner, pointing out to the rest the summit of the Rossberg (full four miles off in a straight line), where some strange commotion seemed taking place, which they themselves (the four behind) were observing with a telescope, and had entered into conversation on the subject with some strangers just come up; when, all at once, a flight of stones, like cannon-balls, traversed the air above their heads; a cloud of dust obscured the valley; a frightful noise was heard. They fled! As soon as the obscurity was so far dissipated as to make objects discernible, they sought their friends, but the village of Goldau had disappeared under a heap of stones and rubbish 100 feet in height, and the whole valley presented nothing but a perfect chaos! Of the unfortunate survivors, one lost a wife to whom he was just married, one a son, a third the two pupils under his care; all researches to discover their remains were, and have ever since been, fruitless. Nothing is left of Goldau but the bell which hung in its steeple, and which was found about a mile off. With the rocks torrents of mud came down, acting as rollers; but they took a different direction when in the valley, the mud following the slope of the ground towards the lake of Lowertz, while the rocks, preserving a straight course, glanced across the valley towards the Righi. The rocks above, moving much faster than those near the ground, went farther, and ascended even a great way up the Righi: its base is covered with large blocks carried to an incredible height, and by which trees were mowed down, as they might have been by cannon,

" A long track of ruins, like a scarf, hangs from the shoulder of the Rossberg, in hideous barrenness, over the rich dress of shaggy woods and green pastures, and grows wider and wider down to the lake of Lowertz and to the Righi, a distance of four or five miles. Its greatest breadth may be three miles, and the triangular area of ruins is fully equal to that of Paris, taken at the external boulevards, or about double the real extent of the inhabited city. I notice, however, that the portion of the strata at the top of the Rossberg, which slid down into the valley, is certainly less than the chaotic accumulation below ; and I have no doubt that a considerable part of it comes from the soil of the valley itself, ploughed up and thrown into ridges like the waves of the sea, and hurled to prodigious distances by the impulse of the descending mass, plunging upon it with a force not very inferior to that of a cannon-ball."*

The effects of this terrible convulsion were the entire destruction of the villages Goldau, Bussingen, and Rothen, and a part of Lowertz ; the rich pasturages in the valley and on the slope of the mountain, entirely overwhelmed by it and ruined, were estimated to be worth 150,000*l.* One hundred and eleven houses, and more than 200 stables and chalets, were buried under the debris of rocks, which of themselves form a mountain several hundred feet high ; more than 450 human beings perished by this catastrophe, and whole herds of cattle were swept away. Five minutes sufficed to complete the work of destruction. The inhabitants of the neighbouring towns and villages were first roused by loud and grating sounds like thunder : they looked towards the spot from which it came, and beheld the valley shrouded in a cloud of dust—when it had cleared away they found the face of nature changed. The houses of Goldau were literally crushed beneath the weight of superincumbent masses. Lowertz was overwhelmed by a torrent of mud.

Those who desire a near view of the landslip should ascend the Gnypenstock, whose summit may be reached in three hours from Arth.

Goldau to Brunnen.

At Goldau one of the most frequented bridle-paths up the Righi strikes off to the rt. See p. 46.

The new chapel and one of the inns at Goldau stand on the site of the village overwhelmed by the Rossberg : its inhabitants, thus destroyed in the midst of security, are said to have been remarkable for the purity of their manners and their personal beauty. The high-road traverses the talus or debris, which extends from the top of the Rossberg far up the Righi on the rt., ascending vast hillocks of rubbish, calculated to be 30 ft. deep hereabouts, but near the centre of the valley probably 200 ft., and winds among enormous blocks of stone already beginning to be moss-grown, and with herbage springing up between them. Between these mounds and masses of rock, numerous pools are enclosed, arising from springs dammed up by the fallen earth.

1½ Lowertz, standing on the margin of the lake round which our road is carried on a terraced embankment, lost its church and several of its houses in the same catastrophe. The lake was diminished by one quarter in consequence of the avalanche of mud and rubbish which entered it, and its waters were thrown up in a wave 70 ft. high to the opposite bank, so as to cover the picturesque island, and sweep away a small chapel which stood upon it. The ruined *Castle of Schwanau,* still existing upon it, has an historical interest from having been destroyed at the first rising of the Swiss Confederates in 1308, to avenge an outrage committed by the Seigneur, in carrying off a damsel against her will, and detaining her in confinement.

---

* Simond's Switzerland.

" There is a wild and sombre tradition attached to this island, that once a-year cries are heard to come from it, and suddenly the ghost of the tyrant is seen to pass, chased by the vengeful spirit of a pale girl, bearing a torch, and shrieking wildly. At first he eludes her swiftness, but at length she gains upon him, and forces him into the lake, where he sinks with doleful struggles ; and, as the waves close over the condemned, the shores ring with fearful and unearthly yellings.' " *

Near the village of Lowertz another footpath strikes up the Righi, which is shorter than going round by Goldau for travellers approaching from Schwytz or Brunnen. About 3 miles above Lowertz it falls into the path from Goldau, p. 47.

Sewen—(*Inn:* Zum Kreutz)—a village at the E. extremity of the lake, is resorted to on account of its chalybeate springs. A direct road to Brunnen here turns to the rt. : it is 1½ mile shorter than that by Schwytz, but is not good.

1 *Schwytz*—*Inns:* Hirsch, good ; —Rössli.

Schwytz, a mere village, though the chief place in the canton—" the heart's core of Helvetia " — from which comes the name Switzerland, contains a population of 4878 inhabitants, including the adjoining scattered houses and villages, which all belong to one parish. It lies picturesquely at the foot of the very conspicuous double-peaked mountain, called Mythe (Mitre) and Hacke. (4598 ft.)

Adjoining the *Parish Church* a modern building, finished in 1774, is a small Gothic chapel, called *Kerker*, erected, according to tradition, at a time when admission to the church was denied the people by a ban of excommunication from the Pope. It was built in great haste, half of it within three days, and the mass was secretly administered within it.

In the cemetery of the *Parish Church* is the grave of Aloys Reding, the patriotic leader (Landeshauptman) of the Swiss against the French Republicans, in 1798.

The *Rathhaus*, a building of no great antiquity or beauty, in which the Council of the canton holds its sittings, is decorated with portraits of 43 Landammen, and a painting representing the events of the early Swiss history.

The *Arsenal* contains banners taken by the Schwytzers at Morgarten, and others borne by them in the battles of Laupen, Sempach, Cappel, Morat, &c. ; also a consecrated standard presented by Pope Julius II. to the Schwytzers.

The *Archiv* (record office) is a tower of rough masonry several stories high, and was probably once a castle : its walls are remarkably thick, and beneath it are dungeons.

Schwytz possesses a Capuchin Convent and a Dominican Nunnery, founded in 1272.

A diligence goes once a day to Lucerne and back.

The Schwytzers first became known in Europe about the year 1200, in a dispute which the natives of this district had with the tenants of the monks of Einsiedeln. The holy Fathers concealing from the Emperor the very existence of such a race as the men of Schwytz, had obtained from him a grant of their possessions, as waste and unoccupied land. The Schwytzers, however, were able to maintain their own property by their own swords, until at length the Emperor Frederick II. confirmed to them their rights.

The name Swiss (Schwytzer) was first given to the inhabitants of the three Forest Cantons after the battle of Morgarten, their earliest victory, in which the men of Schwytz had taken the lead, and prominently distinguished themselves above the others.

At Ibach, a village on the Muotta

* Mrs. Boddington.

(through which the road to Brunnen passes), may be seen the place of assemblage where the Cantons Landes-Gemeinde—consisting of all the male citizens of the canton—formerly met in the open air, to choose their magistrates, from the Landammans down to the lowest officer. Here they used to deliberate and vote on the affairs of the state, decide on peace or war, form alliances, or despatch embassies—a singular example of universal suffrage, and the legislation of the masses. The business was opened by prayer, and by the whole assembly kneeling, and taking an oath faithfully to discharge their legislative duties. According to the Constitution of 1833, the General Assemblies of the Canton are now held at Rothenthurn, on the road to Einsiedeln. At present the meeting of the Circle only is held here.

The road up the Muottathal—which opens out here—is described in Route 75.

1 Brunnen. (Route 18.)

ASCENT OF THE RIGHI.

The summit of the Righi may be reached in about 11 hours from Zurich and 7 from Lucerne, exclusive of stoppages. Heavy carriages can approach the foot of the mountain at Arth (Goldau), and Küssnacht; and if the traveller ascend from the one, he may send round his carriage to meet him on his descent at the other place.

The Righi, or *Rigi* (*Regina* Montium is only a fanciful derivation of the name), a mountain, or rather group of mountains, rising between the lakes of Zug and Lucerne, owes its celebrity less to its height, for it is only 5700 ft. above the sea, than to its isolated situation; separated from other mountains, in the midst of some of the most beautiful scenery of Switzerland, which allows an uninterrupted view from it on all sides, and converts it into

a natural observatory, commanding a panorama hardly to be equalled in extent and grandeur among the Alps. It has also the advantage of being very accessible; no less than 3 mule paths lead up to the summit, so that it is daily resorted to in summer by hundreds of travellers of all countries and ages, and of both sexes. The upper part of the mountain is composed, like the Rossberg, of the brecciated rock called Nagelflue. Externally the entire summit is clothed with verdant pastures, which support more than 2000 head of cattle in summer, and the middle and lower region are girt round with forests.

Owing to the uncertainty of the atmosphere, at high elevations, travellers should prepare themselves for disappointment, since the trouble of an ascent is often repaid with clouds and impenetrable mist, instead of a fine sunrise and extensive prospect. He is wise, therefore, who, in fine weather, manages *to reach the summit before the sun goes down:* he, at least, has two chances of a view. It not unfrequently happens, however, that the traveller who has commenced the ascent in sunshine and under a clear sky, is overtaken by clouds and storms before he reaches the top.

Horses and Guides.

The 3 principal bridle-paths to the *Culm,* or top of the Rigi, are those from Goldau, Küssnacht, and Weggis. At each of these places, as well as at Arth, Lowertz, and Brunnen, horses, guides, and porters may be hired at prices regulated by tariff fixed by the Government of the canton, which is always hung up in the inns.

The usual charge for a horse is 9 Fr. francs to the top, and 6 to return next day by the same road; 9 by a different road on the opposite side of the mountain. A porter, to carry baggage, 6 fr. and 3 to return. A horse may be hired for 6 fr. up to the con-

ent of Maria Zum Schnee, below
which is the steepest part of the
scent. *Chaises à porteur* may be
procured for ladies who do not like
to ride or walk, and each bearer receives 9 fr. up and down. In the
weight of summer, when the concourse of visitors is immense, it is a
good plan to send a lad up the
mountain before you to secure beds
at the Rigi-culm inn. The pedestrian,
unless he desire to be relieved of his
baggage, has scarcely any need of a
guide, as the paths are most distinctly
marked, and are traversed by so
many persons that he can scarcely
miss his way. To those who ride on
horseback, the man who leads the
horse will serve as guide, and no extra charge is made.

Ascent from Goldau,—3½ hours ;
descent 2¼. Travellers usually make
Arth (p. 40) their starting-place (¼
of an hour farther off) because the
inn is better there ; but the ascent of
the mountain begins at Goldau. This
is, indeed, the best point to ascend
from, because the path runs along a
deep gulley, in the interior of the
mountain, the sides of which shut out
all view until the summit is reached,
where it bursts at once upon the
sight: the other paths wind round
the exterior of the mountain.

At Goldau a toll of 5 batz, = 15
sous, is paid for each horse, and goes
to keep the path in repair. The
path strikes at once from the inn of
the Cheval Blanc up the side of
the mountain ; at first across fields
strewn with blocks from the Rossberg, which, by the force acquired in
their descent down one side of the
valley, were actually carried up the
opposite slope.

Near a small public-house, called
Unter Dächli, where the guides
usually stop to give breath to their
animals and a glass of schnaps to
themselves, the path is very steep indeed, carried up a rude staircase
formed of trunks of trees fastened
between the rocks.

This is a good point for surveying

the fall of the Rossberg and the vale
of Goldau below, mourning in ruin
and desolation. The long train of
rubbish thrown down by that convulsion is seen stretching across to
the lake of Lowertz, which it partly
filled up (see p. 44). A steep foot-
path from Arth falls into our road
here. Here begin "the Stations," a
series of 13 little chapels, each with
a painting representing an event in
our Lord's Passion, which lead up to
the pilgrimage church of Mary-of-the-
Snow. The steepest part of the road
is over at the 4th station. At the
chapel of Malchus, containing the
bearing of the cross, the path from
Lowertz falls into our route.

Notre Dame des Neiges, or *Maria
Zum Schnee,* is a little church much
frequented by pilgrims, especially on
the 5th of August, on account of the
indulgences granted by the Pope at
the end of the 17th century to all
who make this pious journey. Adjoining it is a small *hospice,* or convent, inhabited all the year by 3 or
4 Capuchin brothers, who do the duty
of the church, being deputed by the
fraternity at Arth on this service.
The church is surrounded by a group
of inns, the best of which (the
Schwerdt and Sonne) are sometimes
resorted to by invalids, who repair
hither to drink goat's whey, and
might even afford a homely lodging
to travellers benighted or unable to
find room in the two inns on the top
of the mountain : the others are
public-houses, chiefly occupied by
pilgrims. Half an hour's walking, up
gently-sloping meadows, brings the
traveller to the inn called Rigi-
Staffel.

Ascent from Küssnacht,—3½ hours
to mount ; 2½ to descend. A mule
path, as long as that from Goldau,
and more steep. Leaving Küssnacht it passes on the l. the ruins of
Gessler's Castle (p. 40) ; is carried
in zigzags up the steepest part of
the mountain, through forests, and
across the pastures called Seeboden.

The lake of Lucerne is in sight almost the whole way. The path emerges on the brow of the hill in front of the Staffel inn.

Ascent from Weggis.—Weggis—*Inn:* Löwe (Lion), — a small village on a little ledge at the foot of the Rigi, on the Lake of the Four Cantons, is the spot where those who approach the Rigi by water land. It supports 12 horses, 15 boatmen, and guides in corresponding numbers. A bad path, winding round the foot of the Rigi, connects it with Küssnacht; but the chief communication is carried on by water.

The mule-path up the Rigi from Weggis is less steep and a little shorter than the two preceding: 3¼ hours up; 2½ down. It winds along the outside of the mountain, in constant view of the lake, passing, first, the little chapel of Heiligenkreutz (Holy Cross), and then stretching up to a singular natural arch (called Hochstein, or Felsenthor), formed by two vast detached blocks of nagelflue (puddingstone), holding suspended a third, beneath which the path is carried. These broken fragments serve to illustrate the tendency which this rock has to cleave and split, and to this cause may be attributed a singular torrent of mud, which, in the year 1795, descended from the flank of the Rigi upon the village of Weggis, destroying 30 houses and burying nearly 60 acres of good land. It advanced slowly, like a lava current, taking a fortnight to reach the lake, so that the inhabitants had time to remove out of its way. It is supposed to have been produced by springs, or rain water percolating the cracks of the nagelflue, and converting the layer of clay, which separates it from the beds beneath it, into soft mud. Had there been any great fracture in the nagelflue, it is probable that a large portion of the mountain would have given way and slipped down into the lake, since the strata of the Rigi slope at a very steep angle. Had

this been the case, a catastrophe similar to that of the Rossberg might have ensued. As it was, the softened clay was squeezed out by the weight of the superincumbent mass of the mountain, and formed this deluge of mud, traces of which are still visible on the side of the mountain.

About half an hour's walk above the arch lies the *Cold Bath* (kalte bad), where a source of very cold water, issuing out of the rock, supplies a small bathing establishment A new inn, of wood, has lately been constructed, containing 26 bed rooms and 6 baths. It was once the custom for patients to lie down in the bath with their clothes on, and afterwards to walk about in the sun until they dried on the back; but this method is no longer regarded as essential to effect a cure. Close to the cold-bath is a little chapel, dedicated to the Virgin, to which pilgrims repair, and in which mass is daily said for the shepherds on the Rigi.

The spring is called the *sisters fountain*, from a tradition that 3 fair sisters sought refuge here from the pursuit of a wicked and tyrannical Austrian bailiff; and spent the remainder of their days amidst the clefts of the rocks in the exercise of piety.

Summit of the Righi.

All the principal paths converge and unite in front of the *Staffelhaus*, a humble inn to which travellers are sometimes driven for a night's lodging, by the crowded state of the inn on the summit. It is half an hour's walk below the Culm, and it is a bad plan to stop short of it, since those who rest here must get up half an hour earlier next morning if they wish to catch the sunrise from the top.

The *Culm*, or culminating point of the Rigi, is an irregular space of ground of some extent, destitute of trees, but covered with turf. On the apex has been planted a kind of scaffolding, about 18 feet high, a puny additional elevation to that of the mountain, though some ascend it to see the view to advantage. A little lower down, built under the shoulder of the Culm, to protect it from the most serious blasts of wind, stands the *Culm Haus*, an inn, somewhat resembling a barrack, containing more than 40 beds, in rooms not unlike cabins, and affording very tolerable accommodation, considering the height, which exceeds that of the most elevated mountain in Britain. Travellers should bring all their cloaks with them, as the cold is often very intense, and the barometer at times varies as much as 20° Reamur, within the 24 hours. The house is warmed with stoves even in summer. The following notice, relative to the counterpanes, is hung up in every room:—" On avertit MM. les étrangers que ceux qui prennent les couvertures de lit pour sortir au sommet paieront dix batz ;" a threat which seems more likely to suggest than prevent the commission of so comfortable an offence.

During the height of summer, when travellers are most numerous, the Culm inn is crammed to overflowing every evening ; numbers are turned away from the doors, and it is difficult to procure beds, food, or even attention. The house presents a scene of the utmost confusion, servant maids hurrying in one direction, couriers and guides in another, while gentlemen with poles and knapsacks block up the passages. Most of the languages of Europe, muttered usually in terms of abuse or complaint, and the all-pervading fumes of tobacco enter largely as ingredients into this Babel of sounds and smells, and add to the discomfort of the fatigued traveller. In the evening the guests are collected at a table d'hôte supper ; after which most persons are glad to repair to rest. It takes some time, however, before the hubbub of voices and the

trampling of feet subside ; and, not unfrequently, a few roystering German students prolong their potations and noise far into the night. The beds, besides, are not very inviting to repose ; but whether the inmate have slept or not, he, together with the whole household, is roused about an hour before sunrise, by the strange sounds of a long wooden horn, which is played until every particle of sleep is dispelled from the household. Then commences a general stir and commotion, and everybody hastens out with shivering limbs and half-open eyes to gaze at the glorious prospect of a sunrise from the Righi. Fortunate are they for whom the view is not marred by clouds and rain, a very common occurrence, as the leaves of the Album kept in the inn will testify. Indeed the following verses describe the fate of a large majority of those who make this expedition :

Seven weary up-hill leagues we sped,
  The setting sun to see ;
Sullen and grim he went to bed,
  Sullen and grim went we.
Nine sleepless hours of night we pass'd
  The rising sun to see ;
Sullen and grim he rose again,
  Sullen and grim rose we.

View from the Righi.

Long before dawn an assemblage of between 200 and 300 persons is often collected on the Righi Culm, awaiting the sunrise to enjoy this magnificent prospect. A glare of light in the E., which gradually dims the flickering of the stars, is the first token of the morning ; it soon becomes a streak of gold along the horizon, and is reflected in a pale pink tint upon the snows of the Bernese Alps. Summit after summit slowly catches the same rosy hue ; the dark space between the horizon and the Righi is next illuminated ; forests, lakes, hills, rivers, towns, and villages, gradually become revealed, but look cold and indistinct until the red orb surmounts the mountain top, and darts his beams across the landscape. The shadows are then rolled back, as it were, and, in a few moments, the whole scene around is glowing in sunshine. The view is best seen during the quarter of an hour preceding and following the first appearance of the sun; after that the mists begin to curl up, and usually shroud parts of it from the eye.

The most striking feature in this wonderful panorama, which is said to extend over a circumference of 300 miles, is undoubtedly the lakes of Lucerne and Zug; the branching arms of the former extend in so many different directions as to bewilder one at first, and both lave the base of the mountain so closely that the spectator might fancy himself suspended in the air above them, as in a balloon, and think, by one step from the brow of the precipice, to plunge into them. The peculiar greenish blue tint which sheets of water assume when seen from a height has also something exceedingly beautiful. It is said that 11 other lakes may be seen from the Righi, but they are so small and distant as to "look like pools; some almost like water spilt upon the earth."

On the *N. side* the eye looks down into the lake of Zug, and the streets of Arth; at the end of the lake is seen the town of Zug, and behind it the spire of the church of Cappel, where Zwingli, the Reformer, fell in battle. This is backed by the chain of the Albis, and through gaps in its ridge may be discerned a few of the houses of the town of Zurich, and two little bits of its lake. Over the l. shoulder of the Rossberg a peep is obtained into the lake of Egeri, on whose shores the Swiss gained the victory of Morgarten. The N. horison is bounded by the range of the Black Forest hills.

The prospect *on the W.* is more open and map-like, and therefore less interesting. Close under the Righi lie Tell's chapel, on the spot where he shot Gessler, and the village and bay of Küssnacht. Farther off, nearly the whole canton of Lucerne expands to view;—the Reuss winding through the midst of it. Above the Reuss is the lake of Sempach, the scene of another triumph of Swiss valour. Lucerne, with its coronet of towers, is distinctly seen at the W. end of the lake, and on the l. of it rises the gloomy Pilatus, cutting the sky with its serrated ridge. The remainder of the W. horizon is occupied by the chain of the Jura.

On the S. the mass of the Righi forms the foreground, and touching the opposite mountains of Unterwalden, allows only here and there a small portion of the lake of Lucerne to be seen. On this side the objects visible in succession, from rt. to l. are, the lakes of Alpnach and Sarnen, buried in woods; by the side of them runs the road to the Brunig; the mountains called Stanzer and Buochserhorn, and behind them the magnificent white chain of the high Alps of Berne, Unterwalden, and Uri, in one unbroken ridge of peaks and glaciers, including the Jungfrau, Eigher, Finster Aarhorn, the Tittlis (the highest peak in Unterwalden), the Engelberger Rothstock, and the Bristenstock, between which and the Seelisberg runs the road of the St. Gotthard.

On the E. the Alpine chain continues to stretch uninterruptedly along the horizon, and includes the pre-eminent peaks of the Dödi, on the borders of the Grisons, of the Glärnisch, in Canton Glarus, and of the Sentis, in Appenzell. In the middle distance, above the lake of Lauertz, lies the town of Schwytz, the cradle of Swiss freedom, backed by the two singular sharp peaks called,from their shape, the Mitres (Mythen). Above them peers the snowy peak of the Glärnisch; and to the rt. of them is the opening of the Muotta Thal, famous for the bloody conflicts between Suwarrow and Massena, where armies manœuvred and fought on spots which before the shepherd and chamois hunter scarcely dared to tread. Farther to the l. rises the mass of the Rossberg,—the nearest mountain neighbour of the

Righi. The whole scene of desolation caused by its fall (see p. 41); the chasm on the top, whence the ruin came; the course of the terrific avalanche of stones, diverging and spreading in their descent; the lake of Lowertz, partly filled up by it, and the pools and puddles caused in the valley by the stoppage of the watercourses, are at once displayed in a bird's-eye view.

The very distant snowy peak seen above the top of the Rossberg is the Sentis.

The Spectre of the Righi is an atmospheric phenomenon not unfrequently observed on the tops of high mountains. It occurs when the cloudy vapours happen to rise perpendicularly from the valley beneath the mountain on the side opposite to the sun, without enveloping the summit of the Righi itself. Under these circumstances the shadows of the Righi Culm and of any persons standing on the top are cast upon the wall of mist, in greatly magnified proportions. The shadow is encircled by a halo, assuming the prismatic colours of the rainbow, and this is sometimes doubled, when the mist is thick.

Two melancholy accidents have occurred on the top of the Righi:—in 1820 a guide, who had attended an English family, was struck dead by lightning as he stood watching the clouds; in 1826, a Prussian officer, who had reached the summit, accompanied by his wife and children, fell from a very dangerous seat which he had selected on the brow of a precipice (the only spot where the summit is really a precipice), and was dashed to pieces at the bottom. According to another account, the miserable man threw himself off, having previously announced his intention of committing suicide to his wife, who summoned the guide to arrest him, but, after a severe struggle her husband got loose, and effected his purpose.

ROUTE 18.

THE LAKE OF LUCERNE. LUCERNE TO FLUELLEN.

" That sacred lake, withdrawn among the
  hills,
Its depth of waters flank'd as with a wall
Built by the giant-race before the flood ;
Where not a cross or chapel but inspires
Holy delight, lifting our thoughts to God
From god-like men. . . .
That in the desert sow'd the seeds of life,
Training a band of small republics there,
Which still exist, the envy of the world !
Who would not land in each, and tread the
  ground—
Land where *Tell* leap'd ashore—and climb
  to drink
Of the three hallow'd fountains ? He that
  does
Comes back the better. . . .
Each cliff and head-land, and green promontory,
Graven with records of the past,
Excites to hero worship." . .

                  Rogers.

The length of the lake between Lucerne and Fluellen is about 7¾ stunden, = 25½ Eng. miles.

The voyage, in a boat with three rowers, will take about six hours.

A *steamer* was launced on the lake in 1837, to ply between Lucerne, Fluellen, and the intermediate ports on the lake. The boatmen on its shores, regarding this as an infringement of their vested rights, exact of the proprietors a large sum to be paid on every voyage, to indemnify them for the loss.

According to the announcement, printed in 1838, the *steam-boat " La Ville de Lucerne"* will run from Lucerne to Fluellen and back eight times a week during the summer (from June 1 to September 30), and five times a week in the spring and autumn. It will touch at Altstadt, Weggis, Vitznau, Bechenried, Gersau, Brunnen, Fluellen, Stanzstadt, and Alpnach. The fare to Fluellen is 3f. 20 raps Swiss, and less in proportion to the intermediate stations. The voyage will take up about three hours.

Boats may be hired at all the ports on the lake. The charges fixed by tariff are as follows, in French francs :—

To Fluellen, a large boat, capable of holding a carriage, 6f., and each boatman, 3f. The total expense of transporting a carriage should not exceed 26f. or 28f.—five or six men will be required; but it is better for those who have a carriage to go by land to Brunnen, and there embark. A smaller boat, 4f. 50c.; the smallest, 3f. 75c.

To Gersau, Brunnen, or Buochs, boat 3f., man 3f.

To Küssnacht, Weggis, or Stanzstadt, boat, 1f. 50c.—each man, 1f. 50c.

In returning, the charge is only half the above; but the boatmen need not wait more than three hours unless paid the full fare back.

In hiring a boat the employer should stipulate to be landed at Gersau, Grutli, and the Tellenplatte, at his discretion, in order that he may visit these spots by the way.

Much has been said of the dangers of the lake of Lucerne, arising from storms: that it is subject to sudden and tempestuous winds admits of no doubt; but the boatmen can always foresee the approach of a storm, and are very careful not to subject themselves to any risk. The clumsy flat-bottomed boats, indeed, have an unsafe look, and, in windy weather, heave and roll about immoderately; yet instances of accidents are hardly known: either the boatmen will not stir out in bad weather, or put into shore on the slightest appearance of danger. Those who trust themselves on the lake should implicitly follow the advice of the boatmen, and not urge them to venture when disinclined.

The winds on the lake are singularly capricious and variable, blowing at the same time from opposite quarters of the compass in different parts of it, so that the boatmen say that there is a new wind behind every promontory. The most violent is the south wind, or Föhn, which often rushes so furiously down the bay of Uri as to prevent the progress of any row-boat, and renders it doubtful whether even a steamer will be able to face it. During fine weather, in summer, the north wind blows along the bay of Uri from ten to three or four, after which it dies away, and is succeeded by the Föhn, blowing from the S. The boatmen, in coming from Lucerne, endeavour to reach Fluellen before the wind turns.

The only resource, when a storm arises, is to run before the wind.

The *Lake of Lucerne*, or *of the Four Forest Cantons* (Vier-Waldstädter-See), so called from the cantons of Uri, Unterwalden, Schwytz, and Lucerne, which exclusively form its shores, is distinguished above every lake in Switzerland, and perhaps in Europe, by the beauty and sublime grandeur of its scenery. It is hardly less interesting from the historical recollections connected with it. Its shores are a classic region—the reputed sanctuary of liberty; on them took place those memorable events which gave freedom to Switzerland—here the first Confederacy was formed; and, above all, its borders were the scene of the heroic deeds and signal vengeance of WILLIAM TELL, on which account they are sometimes called Tell's Country.

The lake lies at a height of 1360 ft. above the sea-level: it is of very irregular shape, assuming, near its W. extremity, the form of a cross. Its various bays, branching in different directions, are each named after the chief town or village situated on them: thus the W. branch is properly the lake of Lucerne; then come the bays of Alpnach on the S., Küssnacht on the N., Buochs, stretching E. and W.; and lastly the bay of Uri, running N. and S., entirely enclosed within the mountains of that canton.

Quitting Lucerne, and passing the long Hof Brücke, the boat will arrive, in about half an hour, a-breast of a promontory on the l., called Meggenhorn, close off which lies a small island, the only one in the lake. A Frenchman, the Abbe Reynal, took upon himself to raise upon it a monument to the founder of Swiss liberty: it consisted of a wooden obelisk, painted to look like granite, with Tell's apple and arrow on the top! This gingerbread memorial of vanity and bad taste was luckily destroyed by lightning. Thus far the shores of the lake are undulating hills, clothed with verdure, and dotted with houses and villas—a smiling scene, to which the dark ridge of Pilatus adds a solitary feature of grandeur. After doubling the cape of the Meggenhorn, the bay of Küssnacht opens out on the l., that of Alpnach on the rt., and the traveller finds himself in the centre of the cross or transept (so to call it) of the lake. From this point Mount Pilate is seen to great advantage—clouds and darkness almost invariably rest upon his head, and his serrated ridge and gloomy sides have a sullen air in the midst of the sunny and cheerful landscape around. The superstitions connected with this mountain are mentioned at p. 39. It is the weather-glass of the boatmen and shepherds, and, according to the common saying,

(Wenn Pilatus trägt sein Hut
Dann wird das Wetter gut)

it is a bad sign when Pilate is free from cloud, or doffs his hat in the morning; but when the clouds rest steadily on his forehead till late in the afternoon, fair weather may be expected.

Looking up the bay of Küssnacht the ruined castle of Neu Habsburg, a fort belonging to the counts of that name, is seen on the l. perched on a cliff; and at the further extremity the village of Küssnacht. The colossal mass of the Righi occupies the other side of the bay. Its flanks are girt with forests, below which runs a fringe of fields and gardens, dotted with cottages; while, above, it is clothed to its very summit with verdant pastures, feeding a hundred flocks;—an agreeable contrast to his neighbour Pilate.

After weathering the promontory

of Tanzenburg a spur or buttress descending from the Righi, the village of Weggis appears in sight at the foot of the mountain: it is the usual port of disembarkation for those who ascend the Righi from the water (see p. 48), and may be reached by rowing in two hours from Lucerne. The high precipices opposite Weggis belong to Canton Unterwalden, but the narrow ledge of meadow at their base is in Canton Lucerne.

Two rocky headlands projecting from the Righi on one side, and the Bürgenburg on the other—significantly called the Noses (Nasen)—now appear to close up the lake; but as the boat advances, a narrow strait, not more than 1½ mile wide, is disclosed between them. Once through these narrows, the Noses seem to have overlapped each other, and the traveller enters, as it were, a new lake, shut out by high mountains from that which he has traversed before. This oval basin is called the Gulf of Buochs, from the little village at the bottom of the bay on its S. shore, behind which rise two grand mountains, the Buochser and Stanzer-Horn.

On the opposite shore, at the foot of the Righi, nestles the little village *Gersau*—(*Inn :* Sonne, small, but clean)—which, with the small strip of cultivated and meadow land behind it, formed, for four centuries, an independent state, undoubtedly the smallest in civilised Europe.

Its entire territory consists of a slope leaning against the side of the mountain, produced probably by the earth and rubbish washed down from above, by two mountain-torrents breaking out of ravines behind it. The whole extent of land cannot measure more than three miles by two, which would make a very small *parish* in England : scarcely an acre of it is level ground, but it is covered with orchards, and supports a population of 1348 souls, dwelling in 174 houses, 82 of which form the village.

It is recorded that the people of

Gersau bought their freedom from a state of villenage in 1390, with a sum of 690 lbs. of pfennings, scraped together after 10 years' of hard toil, to satisfy the Lords of Moos, citizens of Lucerne, whose serfs they had previously been. They maintained their independence apart from any other canton, and governed by a landamman and council, chosen from among themselves, until the French occupied Switzerland in 1798, since which they have been united with the Canton Schwytz. Though Gersau possessed a criminal jurisdiction of its own, together with a gallows still left standing, no instance of a capital execution occurred during the whole of its existence as a separate state.

There is something very pleasing in the aspect of Gersau on the margin of its quiet cove, shrouded in orchards and shut out from the rest of the world by the precipices of the Righi, for although there is a path hence to Brunnen, and another to the top of the mountain, they are difficult and little used. Its picturesque, broad-brimmed cottages are scattered among the fields and chestnut woods nearly to the summit of the slopes; some perched on sloping lawns, so steep that they seem likely to slip into the lake.

Gersau may be reached in $3\frac{1}{2}$ hours from Lucerne. As soon as it is left behind, the singular bare peaks of the Mythen (Mitres) start up into view—at their foot the town of Schwytz is built, and in front of them stands the village of *Brunnen*—(*Inn*: Goldener Adler; best, not very good)—the port of the Canton Schwytz, built at the mouth of the river Muota. Its position in reference to the surrounding scenery is one of the most fortunate on the lake, commanding a view along two of its finest reaches. It is the depôt for goods going to and from Italy, over the Saint Gotthard. The warehouse, called *Sust*, bears on its outer walls a rude painting of the three Confederates, to commemorate the first alliance which was formed on this spot between the **Forest** Cantons in 1315, after the battle of Morgarten. Aloys Reding here raised the standard of revolt against the French in 1798.

Those who intend to ascend the Righi from this, usually take a char to Goldau (charge, 60 batz); for pedestrians there is a shorter footpath from Lowertz. It takes five hours to reach the top (see p. 45). Saddle-horses may be hired here.

Boats swarm upon the shore: the charges are somewhat exorbitant. A large boat to convey a carriage to Fluellen, costs 100 batz (= 14f. Fr.) —a smaller one, 9f. Fr.; time required, 3 hours. Hence to Lucerne, by water, 4 hours. The steamer now touches here twice a-day.

Opposite Brunnen, the lake of the Four Cantons changes at once its direction and its character. Along the bay of Uri, or of Fluellen, as it is sometimes called, it stretches nearly N. and S. Its borders are perpendicular, and almost uninterrupted precipices, the basements and buttresses of colossal mountains, higher than any of those which overlook the other branches of the lake, and their snowy summits peer down from above the clouds, or through the gullies in their sides, upon the dark gulf below. At the point of the promontory, opposite Brunnen, stands a small inn, called Treib, with a little haven in front, in which boats often take shelter. When the violence of the Föhn wind renders the navigation of the lake to Fluellen impracticable, travellers sometimes follow a footpath from Treib over the mountains by Selisberg. Bauen, Isenthal, and Seedorf. There is a similar and equally difficult path from Schwytz by Morsebach, Sisikon, Tellenrüth, to Altorf, which was nevertheless traversed by the French General Lecourbe, with his army, in pursuit of Suwarrow, in the night, by torch-light, in 1799. The want of boats to transport his forces across the lake compelled him to this daring exploit. On turning the corner of the promontory of Treib, a singular rock, called Wytenstein, rising like an obelisk out of the water, is passed, and the bay of Uri, in all its stupendous grandeur, bursts into view.

" It is upon this that its superiority to all other lakes, or, as far as I know, scenes upon earth, depends. The vast mountains rising on every side and closing at the end, with their rich clothing of wood, the sweet soft spots of verdant pasture scattered at their feet, and sometimes on their breast, and the expanse of water, unbroken by islands, and almost undisturbed by any signs of living men, make an impression which it would be foolish to attempt to convey by words."

" The only memorials which would not disgrace such a scene, are those of past ages, renowned for heroism and virtue, and no part of the world is more full of such venerable ones." —*Mackintosh.*

After passing the Wytenstein about a mile, the precipices recede a little, leaving a small ledge, formed by earth, fallen from above, and sloping down to the water's edge. A few walnut and chestnut trees have here taken root, and the small space of level ground is occupied by a meadow conspicuous among the surrounding woods from the brightness of its verdure. This is *Grütli*, or *Rütli*, the spot pointed out by tradition as the rendezvous of the 3 founders of Swiss freedom,—Werner Stauffacher, of Steinen, in Schwytz; Erni (Arnold) an der Halden, of Melchthal, in Unterwalden ; and Walter Fürst, of Attinghausen, in Uri. These "honest conspirators" met in secret in the dead of night, on this secluded spot, at the end of the year 1307, to form the plan for liberating their country from the oppression of their Austrian governors. They here " swore to be faithful to each other, but to do no wrong to the Count of Habsburg, and not to maltreat his governors.'

" These poor mountaineers, in the 14th century, furnish, perhaps, the only example of insurgents, who, at the moment of revolt, bind themselves as sacredly to be just and merciful to their oppressors as to be faithful to each other." The scheme thus concerted was carried into execution on the following New-year's day ; and such was the origin of the Swiss Confederation.

According to popular belief, which everywhere in Switzerland connects political events with religion, the oath of the Grütli was followed by a miracle, and 3 springs gushed forth from the spot upon which the 3 confederates had stood. In token of this every stranger is conducted to a little hut built over the 3 sources of pure water, and is invited to drink out of them to the memory of the 3 founders of Swiss freedom. It is doubtful whether the 3 sources are not merely 1 split into 3 ; but few would search to detect " the pious fraud."

The view from Grütli is delightful. A small scar may be observed from hence on the face of the opposite precipice of the Frohnalpstock, formed by the fall of a piece of rock. " The fragment which has left such a trifling blemish was about 1200 feet wide : when it fell it raised such a wave on the lake as overwhelmed 5 houses of the village of Sissigen, distant 1 mile, and 11 of its inhabitants were drowned. The swell was felt at Lucerne, more than 20 miles off."—*Simond.*

The shores of the bay of Uri are utterly pathless, since, for the most part, its sides are precipices, descending vertically into the water, without an inch of foreground between. Here and there a small sloping ledge intervenes, as at Grütli, and on one or two other spots room has been found for a scanty group of houses, as at Sissikon, Bauen, Isleten, &c.

A little shelf, or platform, at the foot of the Achsenburg, on the E. shore of the lake, called the *Tellen-Platte*, is occupied by TELL's CHAPEL, and may be reached in ¾ of an hour from Grütli. Here, according to the tradition, Tell sprung on shore out of the boat in which Gessler was carrying him a prisoner to the dungeon of Küssnacht (see p. 40), when, as is well known, the sudden storm on the lake compelled him to remove Tell's fetters, in order to avail himself of his skill as steersman; thus affording the captive an opportunity to escape. The chapel, an open arcade, lined with rude and faded paintings, representing the events of the delivery of Switzerland, was erected by Canton Uri in 1388, only 31 years after Tell's death, and in the presence of 114 persons who had known him personally—a strong testimony to prove that the events of his life are not a mere romance. Once a year, on the first Friday after the Ascension, mass is said and a sermon preached in the chapel, which is attended by the inhabitants of the shores of the lake, who repair hither in boats, and form an aquatic procession.

The murder of Gessler by Tell notwithstanding the provocation, was a stain on the Swiss Revolution, marked as it was equally by the just necessity which led to it and the wise moderation which followed it, in preventing the shedding of blood, so that even the tyrannical bailiffs of the Emperor were conducted unharmed, beyond the limits of the confederacy, and there set free: an act of forbearance the more surprising considering that many of the Swiss leaders were smarting under personal wrongs inflicted by these Bailiffs or Zwing-Herrn.

Tell, acting by the impulse of his individual wrongs, had well nigh marred the designs of the confederates by precipitating events before the plan was properly matured. Yet there is something so spirit-stirring in the history of "the mountain Brutus," that there is no doubt the mere narration of it contributed as much towards the success of the insurrection and the separation of Switzerland from Austria, by rousing the minds of a whole people, as the deep and well-concerted scheme of the 3 conspirators of Grütli.

The view from Tell's chapel is exceedingly fine. The following are the remarks of Sir James Mackintosh on this scene:—"The combination of what is grandest in nature, with whatever is pure and sublime in human conduct, affected me in this passage (along the lake), more powerfully than any scene which I had ever seen. Perhaps neither Greece nor Rome would have had such power over me. They are dead. The present inhabitants are a new race, who regard, with little or no feeling, the memorials of former ages. This is, perhaps, the only place in our globe where deeds of pure virtue, ancient enough to be venerable, are consecrated by the religion of the people, and continue to command interest and reverence. No local superstition so beautiful and so moral anywhere exists. The inhabitants of Thermopylæ or Marathon know no more of these famous spots than that they are so many square feet of earth. England is too extensive a country to make Runnymede an object of national affection. In countries of industry and wealth the stream of events sweeps away these old remembrances. The solitude of the Alps is a sanctuary destined for the monuments of ancient virtue; Grütli and Tell's chapel are as much reverenced by the Alpine peasants as Mecca by a devout Mussulman; and the deputies of the 3 ancient cantons met, so late as the year 1715, to renew their allegiance and their oaths of eternal union."

The depth of the lake, opposite Tell's chapel, is 800 feet. After rounding the cape on which it stands, Fluellen appears in view. On the E. shore the valley of Isenthal opens out: the vista up it is terminated by the grand snowy peaks of the Pristenstock and Uri Rothstock.

Fluellen, the port of the Canton Uri, may be reached in half an hour from Tell's chapel. Here begins the new carriage road over the St. Gotthard. (Route 34.)

ROUTE 19.

HE PASS OF THE BRUNIG.—LUCERNE
TO MEYRINGEN AND BRIENZ, BY
ALPNACH AND SARNEN.

10¾ stunden = 35 English miles.

The *steam-boat* runs daily (?) be-
ween Lucerne and Stanzstad.

From Alpnach (Stad) to Lungern
he road is practicable for chars;
hence over the mountain to Mey
ingen is only a bridle path. The
raveller may either take a boat at
once from Lucerne to Alpnach, or go
u a char to Winkel (about an hour's
Irive), and there embark ; by which
he will save some distance. A boat
o Alpnach, with 2 rowers, costs,
rom Lucerne, 20 batz ; from Winkel
8 batz.

From Winkel, where the char road
ceases, the traveller proceeds by
water through a narrow straight between the village of Stanzstadt (R.
31), on the l., and a spire of the Pilatus, called Lopper, on the rt., into
the beautiful and retired gulph of
the lake of the 4 Cantons, called
Lake of Alpnach. The castle of
Rotzberg, on its E. shore, is remarkable as the first stronghold of the
Austrians of which the Swiss confederates gained possession on New-
year's day, 1308. One of the party, the accepted lover of a damsel within the castle, being, according to the practice of Swiss
lovers even at the present time, admitted by a ladder of ropes to a midnight interview with his mistress, succeeded in introducing, in the same
way, 20 of his companions, who found
no difficulty in surprising and overpowering the garrison. The loves
of Jägeli and Anneli have, from
that day forth, been celebrated in
Swiss song. A series of simultane-
ous risings in other parts of the forest
cantons proved equally successful,
and in 24 hours the country was
freed from the Austrian rule.

Gestad, at the S. end of the bay,

1½ hour from Winkel (*Inn*—Weisses
Ross) is the port for all going to or
from the Brunig. Chars may be
hired here.

3¼ Behind it is seen the taper
spire of Alpnach, or Alpnacht, about
1½ mile distant from the water-side.
It is a village of 1400 inhabitants,
situated at the foot of the Pilatus
(p. 39). The extensive forests which
clothe the sides of that mountain belong, for the most part, to Alpnach,
and would be a source of wealth to
its inhabitants if they could be got at
more easily. It was with a view of
turning to account the fine timber
growing on spots barely accessible
by ordinary means, owing to their
height and the ruggedness of the
ground, that the celebrated *Slide of
Alpnach* was constructed. This was
a trough of wood, formed of nearly
30,000 trees, fastened together
lengthwise, 5 or 6 feet wide at the
top, and 3 or 4 feet deep, extending
from a height of 2500 feet down to
the water's edge. It was planned
and executed by a skilful engineer
from Würtemberg, named Rupp.
The course of this vast inclined plane
was in some places circuitous : it was
supported partly on uprights ; and
thus was carried over 3 deep ravines,
and, in two instances, passed under
ground. Its average declivity did
not exceed 1 foot in 17, yet this sufficed to discharge a tree 100 feet
long and four feet in diameter, in the
short space of 6 minutes, from the
upper end of the trough, where it
was launched, into the lake below, a
distance exceeding 8 English miles.
The trees were previously prepared
by being stripped of their branches,
barked, and rudely dressed with the
axe. The bottom of the trough was
kept constantly wet by allowing
a rill of water to trickle down it,
to diminish thereby the friction.
Professor Playfair, who has written a
most interesting account of the slide,
says, that the trees shot downwards
with a noise like the roar of thunder
and with the rapidity of lightning,

seeming to shake the trough as they passed. Though the utmost care was taken to remove every obstacle, it sometimes happened that a tree stuck by the way, or, being arrested suddenly in its progress, leaped or bolted out of the trough with a force capable of cutting over the trees growing at the side, and which often dashed the log itself to atoms. To prevent accidents, watchmen were stationed at regular distances along the sides during the operation of discharging the wood, and a line of telegraphs, similar to those in use on modern railways, were established, showing, by a concerted signal, when anything went wrong. The timber when discharged was collected on the lake and floated down the Reuss into the Rhine, where it was formed into rafts, such as are commonly met with on that river, and sold in Holland for ship-building and other purposes. Napoleon had contracted for the greater part of the timber, to supply his dockyards; but the peace of 1815, by diminishing the demand rendered the speculation unprofitable, and the slide, having been long abandoned, was taken down in 1819. Similar slides, nearly as long, are common throughout the great forests of the Tyrol and Styria. (See Hand-book for S. Germany.) Since 1833 some French speculators have constructed a cart road up the Pilatus into the centre of its forests, and the timber squared or sawn into planks is now brought down on the axle, drawn by 20 or 30 horses and oxen, without sustaining any injury in its descent.

The *Church of Alpnach*, a handsome modern edifice, was built with the timber brought down by the slide. A char may be hired at Alpnach to go to Lungern for 18 Fr. fr.

The Canton Unterwalden, which we are about to traverse, is totally unprovided with milestones; for this reason, that, by an ancient and respected law, every inhabitant is bound to guide the stranger who questions him, on his way, without fee or charge. The road ascends the valley along the left bank of the Aa to

1½ Sarnen.—(*Inn:* Schlüssel (key) not very good or clean). This village, of 1030 inhabitants, is the capital of the division of the canton called Obwalden, and the seat of the Government. It is pleasingly situated at the extremity of the lake of Sarnen, at the foot of an eminence called *Landenberg,* a spot memorable in Swiss history as the residence of the cruel Austrian bailiff of that name who put out the eyes of the aged Henry An der Halden. This act of atrocity made a deep impression on the popular mind, contributing, with other events, to the out-break of the Swiss insurrection. On New-year's morning, 1308, 20 peasants of Obwalden repaired to the castle with the customary presents of game, poultry, &c., for the seigneur, who had gone at that hour to mass. Admitted within the walls, they fixed to their staves the pike-heads which they had concealed beneath their dress, blew a blast as a signal to 30 confederates who lay in ambush, under the alders outside of the gate, and, in conjunction, captured the stronghold almost without resistance. No vestige of the castle now remains: the terrace which occupies its site, and commands a most beautiful view, has since 1646 served for the annual convocations of the citizens of the canton, who meet there to exercise the privilege of electing their magistrates. Adjoining it is the public shooting house, for the practice of rifle shooting.

The *Rathhaus,* a plain edifice, not unlike the court-house of an English county town, contains, in its "business-like council chambers," portraits of the landammen for several ages. "The artists have been particularly successful in delineating their beards." There is one picture, however, better than the rest, of Nicolas von der Flue, one of the worthies of Switzer-

and, more particularly respected in his canton, where effigies of him bound. He enjoys the rare reputation of a patriot, and, at the same time, a peace-maker, having spent his life in allaying the bitterness and dissentions between his country-men, which, at one time, threatened the destruction of the Helvetian Republic. In the vigour of his years he retired from the world into the remote valley of Melchthal, where he passed his time as a hermit in a humble cell, in exercises of piety. His reputation, however, for wisdom as well as virtue, was so high that the counsellors of the confederacy flock-ed to him in his solitude to seek advice. His sudden appearance be-fore the Diet at Stanz, and his con-ciliating counsels prevented the dis-solution of the confederacy. After enjoying the respect of men during his lifetime, he was honoured after his death (1487) as a saint.

The Melchthal, mentioned above, opens out to the E. of Sarnen. At its mouth, close to the chapel of *St. Niklausen*, stands an isolated tower, one of the most ancient buildings in the canton, dating from the earliest Christian times, when it was erected, probably as a belfry. Melchthal was the native place of Arnold An der Halden, one of the conspirators of Grütli (p. 55). While ploughing his field near Schild, he was interrupted by a messenger sent from the bailiff Landenberg to seize his yoke of oxen. Enraged by the insolence of the servant, and the injustice of the demand, Arnold beat the man so as to break his finger; and fearing the tyrant's vengeance, fled over the mountains into Uri, little anticipating that his rash act would be visited by the tyrant upon his father, by depriving him of sight.

The valley of Sarnen, bounded by gently sloping hills, has nothing Alpine in its scenery ; its character is quiet, and pastoral, and pleasing. The successful experiment of letting off the waters of the lake of Lungern

has led to a similar project of reduc-ing that of Sarnen, which will, pro-bably, be carried into effect sooner or later.

The road skirting the E. shore of the lake traverses the pretty village of Sachslen. Within the *Parish Church,* Nicholas von der Flue, the hermit and saint, is interred. His bones lie, but do not repose, in a richly ornamented shrine, under the high altar ; for at stated seasons they are raised in order to be exhibited to the crowds of pilgrims who repair hither to pay their vows to the saint. He is known to the peasants by the name of *Bruder Klaus.* The walls are lined, by devotees, with votive tablets offered to the shrine of St. Nicolas, recording miracles supposed to have been performed by him. The village Gyswyl, on the rt. of the road, was half swept away in 1629 by an inundation of the torrent Lauibach, which brought so much rubbish into the valley as to dam up the waters of the Aa. A lake, thus created, lasted for 130 years, when it was finally let off by an artificial canal into the lake of Sarnen.

The steep ascent of the Kaiserstuhl requires to be surmounted before the road reaches a higher platform in the valley occupied by the *lake of Lun-gern.*

This lake was formerly a beautiful sheet of water, embowered in woods sweeping down to its margin, and partly inclosed by steep banks. The dwellers on its shores, less influenced by admiration of its picturesqueness, than by the prospect of enriching themselves in the acquisition of 500 acres of good land, previously buried under water, have recently tapped it, lowering its surface by about 20 feet, and reducing its dimensions—and thereby its beauty—by nearly one half. The works designed to effect this object were commenced in 1788, but had been repeatedly interrupted by want of funds, and by political commotions. They owe their recent completion to a joint-stock company, consisting of the inhabitants of the district, aided by a skilful engineer, named Sulzberger. The earlier attempts had been limited to the boring of a tunnel through the ridge of the Kaiserstuhl, which, crossing the valley between the lakes of Sarnen and Lungern, forms a natural dam to the waters of the latter. The tunnel begins near Burglen, and is carried in a sloping direction gradually upwards towards the lake. Before Sulzberger took the matter in hand it had made considerable progress; but still the most difficult part of the task remained, viz., to complete it, and break a passage into the lake without injury to the lower valley, or loss of life to those employed. Having with much labour driven the tunnel as near to the bed of the lake as the excavations could with safety be carried, it became necessary to guard against any sudden irruption. With this object in view, he at first proposed to bore a number of small holes with an auger through the intervening rock, and to close them with cocks to open and shut at pleasure. A boring-rod, 12 feet in length, driven through the rock, was followed by a discharge of mud and water, and a blow struck with a hammer by the miner from within was reverberated on the surface of the lake so as to be perceived by persons stationed in a boat above the spot—proving that the basin of the lake had been perforated.

The engineer now, however, discovered that the friable nature of the rock traversed by the rod, and the clay and sand above it, rendered the plan of draining the lake by a number of small perforations impracticable. He was thus compelled to have recourse to a mine, and for this purpose he enlarged the end of the tunnel by driving a shaft or chamber, about 6 ft. square, upwards, so as to reach within 6 ft. of the water. A cask, containing 950 lbs. of powder, was then conveyed to the end of the shaft, and finally hoisted into this vertical chamber, by propping it upon logs of wood; then, a match being attached to it, the end of the tunnel was rammed tight with sand many feet thick, to prevent the mine exploding backwards. Upwards of 500 men, relieving each other day and night, were employed to execute this part of the task, the difficulty of which consisted not merely in the weight to be transported along a passage not more than a foot wider than the cask on any side, but in the foulness of the air inhaled by so many labourers, which soon became so bad as to extinguish all the lights; while the constant influx of water, pouring in through the crannies of the gallery, threw further impediments in the way of the miner. As it was impossible to renew the air by artificial ventilation, it became necessary to withdraw the men for several hours at a time. In addition to all this a great part of the operations were necessarily performed in the dark.

The length of the tunnel was 1305 ft. Strong flood-gates had been erected at its lower extremity, to modify and restrain the issue of the flood. All things being thus prepared, on the morning of January 9, 1836, a cannon-shot, fired from the Kaiserstuhl, answered by another on the Landenberg, gave notice to the whole valley of what was about to happen, and a bold miner, named Spire, was despatched with two companions to fire the train. The length of the match was so regulated as to give them ample time to escape through the tunnel: and their return to daylight was announced by the firing of a pistol. A multitude of spectators had collected on the surrounding hills to witness the result of the experiment which had cost so much time and money to execute, and in which many were so deeply interested —while considerable anxiety prevailed as to its happy result. Expectation was now at the utmost stretch; ten minutes had elapsed beyond the time allotted to the natch, and nothing was heard. Some began to fear;—in a minute two dull explosions were heard; but they neither shook the ground above, nor even broke the ice which at that season covered the lake. No one doubted that the mine had failed, when, on a sudden, a joyful shout from below announced its success, as a black torrent of mud and water intermixed was seen by those stationed near the lower end of the tunnel to issue from its mouth. The winter season had been expressly chosen for the consummation of the undertaking because the waters are then lowest, and many of the tributary torrents are frozen or dried up.

The drainage of the Lake of Lungern was effected gradually and safely. In six days the water fell 4 feet, and in ten days more the lake had sunk to a level with the mouth of the tunnel. The lake of Iyswyl, indeed, was filled again, and lasted for a few days; during which it laid several houses under water, but it was soon drained off. On the shores of the lake of Lungern appearances were at first alarming. The steep banks, derived on a sudden of the support of the water, began to crack; large masses broke off, and a very considerable fissure appeared near the village of Lungern, which threatened injury to it; so that the church and many of the houses were dismantled and abandoned, and the bells removed from the tower. A piece of ground, several acres in extent, did, in fact, separate, and slide into the water, just after a house and shed, which stood on it, had been pulled down and removed. Fortunately this was the extent of the mischief, and church and village are till safe. The uncovered land presented, for some months, only a blank surface of mud and sand, to which the crows resorted in great numbers to feed on the worms and shell fish left dry by the receding waters. By the latter end of the year

a scanty crop of potatoes was raised on part of it, but some time must elapse before it can become valuable for agricultural purposes. The aqueous deposits brought down into the lake by tributary brooks, and laid bare by this drainage, will be remarked with interest by the geologist, as illustrating the progress of the formation of strata, and the variation of their dip. Much float wood was found in the bed of the lake; it had assumed the appearance of brown coal.

The cost of this enterprise was 51,826f. (5000*l.*), and 19,000 days' labour performed by the peasants.

3 Lungern (*Inns:* Sonne, better than that at Sarnen; Löwe), the last village in the valley, situated at the foot of the Brunig, and at the S. end of the lake, now removed by the drainage some distance from it. Here the char-road ceases, and the rest of the way must be travelled on foot, or on horses, which are kept here for hire. (§ 8 and 10.)

From Lungern to Meyringen is a journey of between 3 and 4 hours. A steep path leads up to the summit of the Brunig, 3580 feet above the sea-level, where a

1 Toll-house (furnishing beds in case of need) marks the frontier of Canton Berne, and the culminating point of the pass. From a little chapel near this a charming and first-rate view is obtained along the entire valley of Nidwalden, backed by the Pilatus, with the Lungern See for a foreground, forming altogether " one of the most delicious scenes in Switzerland," to use the words of Latrobe, though destitute of the grandeur presented by snowy peaks. To survey these, however, the traveller has only to proceed a few yards farther, to the brow of the descent, where the valley of Hasli, with the Aar winding through the midst, opens out to view, backed by the gigantic and snow-white crests of the Wetterhorn, Eigher, and others of the Bernese Alps. Here the road separates, one branch leads to the

lake of Brienz, on the rt.; the other to Meyringen, seated in the midst of the rich flat which forms the bottom of the valley. From the opposite precipices, two or three streaks of white may be discerned—these are the falls of the Reichenbach.

1½ *Meyringen.* (Route 27.)

ROUTE 22.

LUCERNE TO BERNE, OR THUN, BY THE ENTLEBUCH.

17⅙ stunden, = 56 Eng. miles.

A diligence goes daily in summer.

This is the best and shortest of the two *carriage*-roads to Berne.

3 At the village of Schachen the ascent of the Bramegg commences, and continues gradually upwards for about 5 miles. An excellent road, passing the baths of Farnbühl (a solitary inn), has been constructed within a few years over this mountain: its top commands a good view of the Pilatus and Righi. The slope of the Bramegg on the opposite side is more rapid, but the descent is rendered easy by zigzags skilfully constructed. Another road has been formed, by the Convent of Werthenstein, to avoid the Bramegg altogether; but it is longer by 1½ hour, and only to be recommended for very heavy vehicles. It takes about 4 hours from Lucerne to reach the village of

2⅓ Entlebuch, at the W. foot of the Bramegg, (*Inn:* Au Borde—tolerable) prettily situated on a slope (Borde), with the torrents Entle and Emme roaring beneath it.

The vale of Entlebuch is about 30 miles long, and is flanked by mountains covered with woods and pastures. The men of the valley are celebrated as the best wrestlers in Switzerland. They hold a great wrestling-match, called Zwing Fest, on the first Sunday in September, when they try their skill against the athletes of the neighbouring valleys. The Bernese highlanders from Hasli are formidable rivals.

2⅔ Escholzmatt (*Inns:* Krone;—Löwe—good) is a scattered villag in a very high situation. A littl way beyond it the road quits th Entlebuch, and descends, by the sic of the Ilfis torrent, into the canton Berne.

3 Langnau (*Inns:* Cerf?—good Löwe) is the principal place in th Emmenthal—an extensive, fertil and industrious valley—famed for it cheeses, made on the high pasture near the tops of the hills, and exporte all over Germany; and for its manu factures of linen. Its meadows are the brightest verdure, and of th texture of the finest velvet, like a English lawn; the cottages neat an substantial, with pretty gardens be fore them. The Emme, which tra verses it, and its tributaries, at time commit fearful devastation, by inun dating their banks and overspreadin them with gravel and debris. Suc an occurrence in August, 1837, oc casioned by a thunder-storm, create serious injury, destroying man houses and almost all the bridges several lives were lost.

It is not necessary to pass throug Langnau, and a mile is saved b leaving it on the rt. The Ilfis i crossed, and afterwards the Emme before reaching

1½ Signau—(*Inn:* Ours, toler able)—a pretty village, with a ruine castle above it.

About 2 miles farther, the road t Thun (4½ stunde) turns off on th l., and shortly falls into the high road from Berne to Thun. (Rout 27.)

The road to Berne proceeds by

1½ Gross Hochstetten, and Worb an industrious village, with a Gothi castle above it.

3⅙ Berne (in Route 24).

ROUTE 23.

LUCERNE TO BERNE, BY SUMMISWALD.

18⅙ stunden = 59¾ English miles.

A diligence goes daily in 12 hours.

This road is less frequented since

at by Entlebuch was macadamised.
he first part of this route, as far
s

4¾ Sursee and the lake of Sem-
ach, is the same as that to Bâle (p.
3). Here our road turns W., pas-
ing on the rt. the little lake Mauen-
e, and traverses the villages Et-
swyl and Zell to

4½ Huttwyl — (*Inns :* Krone;
tadthaus) ; a small walled town in
anton Berne.

3¼ Summiswald—(*Inn :* Bär); a
ourishing village. The poor-house,
a rock above, was the first esta-
ishment of the kind in Switzerland.
he building it occupies was the
stle of the landvoght, or bailiff. On
e Arni Alp, about 10 miles to the
., much cheese is made.

The road now passes across " the
een Emmenthal, one of the richest
d most fertile of the Swiss valleys :
country that would make a grazier's
eart sing with joy — such a prodi-
ality of horned cattle."

4 Engestein.

Near this village are mineral baths,
upplied by a chalybeate spring.

At Worb this route falls into the
receding.

2½ BERNE (in Route 24).

ROUTE 24.

SOLEURE TO BERNE.

6¼ stunde = 21¼ English miles.
A diligence runs daily in 4 hours.
The road crosses the Aar on quit-
ng Soleure, passing near Zuchwyl,
e retreat of the Protestants driven
ut of Soleure by their fanatic fellow-
tizens in 1533. In a grave in the
urchyard are interred " Viscera
haddei Kosciuskzo."

We enter Canton Berne before
aching

Bätterkinden, a large village on
e Emme, here crossed by a
ridge.

1 Fraubrunnen. Not far from
his the Bernese defeated the English

Switz.

mercenary Ingelram de Coucey, in
1375. A stone, by the road side,
commemorates the event (see p. 14).

Jegistorf. At Urtinen, 2 miles
from this, a cross road turns off on
the right to *Hofwyl*, the agricultural
and educational institution of M.
Fellenberg. It consists of

1. A *seminary*, for young gentlemen, about 80 in number, from all
parts of Europe: there are many English. They receive here an education on very moderate terms. Every
summer, during the vacation, they
make a pedestrian tour through
Switzerland, under the guidance of
their tutors. There is a separate
school of instruction for schoolmas-
ters.

2. A *school for the poor* who are
taught according to the system of
M. Fellenberg, on an extensive scale,
having the double object of instruct-
ing farmers and introducing agricultural improvements.

3. An agricultural establishment,
consisting of an academy for practical husbandry ; a model farm ; an
experimental farm ; an extensive
collection of agricultural implements,
and a manufactory for making them.

The surrounding district was little
better than a bog when M. Fellenberg settled here in 1799 : he has
since gradually brought it into cultivation. There is a direct road from
Berne to Hofwyl by the Enghe,
Reichenbach, and Buchsee, about 9
miles.

A little beyond the further extremity of the avenue of the Enghe, lies
the old castle of Reichenbach, which
belonged to Rudolph of Erlach, the
hero of the battle of Laupen, who
was murdered here, in his old age,
by his son-in-law, Jost von Rudenz,
with the very sword which he had
wielded at that glorious victory. The
assassin was pursued, as he fled from
the scene of his crime, by the two
bloodhounds of the aged warrior, who
broke loose at their master's cries.
They tracked his footsteps of their
own accord, and after some hours

returned with gore-stained lips, and nothing more was heard or known of Jost von Rudenz.

3. BERN.—(*Inns:* Falke (Faucon), one of the best inns in Switzerland. Charges—table d'hôte, at one, 3 fr. ; at four, 4 fr. ; breakfast, 1 fr. 10 sous; tea, ditto ; beds, 2 fr. 10 sous.

Families and persons desiring to be quiet, may be accommodated in a separate house, called Petit Faucon, in a back street, from the roof of which there is a fine view ; Couronne, not very clean, but otherwise good ; Cigogne (Storch). The *Abbayes,* or houses of the guilds, also, accommodate travellers : the best is the Distelzwang, or Abbaye aux Gentilshommes.

Berne, capital of the largest of the Swiss cantons, seat of the Swiss Diet (Vorort) alternately with Zurich and Lucerne, and residence of most of the foreign ministers, contained, in 1837, 22,422 inhabitants. It is built on a lofty sandstone promontory, formed by the winding course of the Aar, which nearly surrounds it, flowing at the bottom of a deep gully, with steep and in places precipitous sides (stalden). It is proposed to remedy the inconvenient ascent and descent by which the town can alone be reached from the E., by throwing a lofty bridge of stone or wire over this gully. The distant aspect of the town, planted on this elevated platform, 1600 feet above the sea, is imposing, and there is something striking in its interior, from the houses all being built of massive stone. It has this peculiarity, that almost all the houses rest upon arcades (Lauben), which furnish covered walks on each side of the streets, and are lined with shops and stalls. The lowness of the arches, however, and the solidity of the buttresses supporting them, render these colonnades gloomy and close. Along the brow of the precipice, overhanging the Aar, and removed from the main streets, are the more aristocratic residences of the exclusive patricians.

Rills of water are carried throug the streets to purify them, and the are abundantly furnished with *Fou tains,* each surmounted by some quai effigy. One of these, the *Kinderfre ser-Brunnen* (Ogre's-fountain), on th Corn-house-square, receives its nam from a figure (probably Saturn) de vouring a child, with others stuck i his girdle and pockets ready fo consumption. Some bear the figur of armed warriors, such as Sampso and David ; another is surmounted k a female figure, probably Heb but the favourite device is th *Bear,* the armorial bearings of th canton, which is what the Frenc heralds calls an "armoirie pa lante ; " the word "*Bern*" signif ing a bear, in old German, or rath in the Suabian dialect. Indeed th animal is as great a favourite here in the house of Bradwardine. Thu the upper fountain in the principa street is surmounted by a bear in a mour, with breast-plate, thigh piece and helmet ; a sword at his side and banner in his paw. The *Schütze Brunnen* is the figure of a Swiss cros bowman of former days, attended b a young bear as squire ; and two ston bears, larger than life, stand as ser tinels on either side of the Morat gat

Along the line of the principa street are three antique watch-tower The *Clock tower* (Zeitglochenthurm stands nearly in the centre of th town, though, when originally buil in 1191, by Berchtold V., of Zährin gen, it guarded the outer wall. I droll clock-work puppets are object of wonder to an admiring crowd o gaping idlers. A minute before th hour strikes, first, a wooden cock ap pears, crows twice, and flaps h wings ; and, while a puppet strikes th hour on a bell, a procession of bear issues out, passes in front of a figur on a throne, who marks the hour b gaping and by lowering his sceptre Further on in the street stands th *Käficht Thurm* (cage tower), now used as a prison ; and beyond it *Christo pher's tower,* also called Goliath'

om the figure of a giant upon it.
he great charm of Berne is the
ew of the Bernese Alps, which the
wn and every eminence in its neigh-
ourhood commands in clear weather.
his is excellently seen from the
latform, a lofty terrace, planted
ith shady rows of trees, overlooking
e Aar, behind the Minster.   More
an a dozen snowy peaks of the
eat chain are visible from hence;
ey appear in the following order,
ginning from the E. :—1, Wetter
orn; 2, Schreckhorn; 3, Finster-
arhorn; 4, Eigher; 5, Mönch; 6,
ungfrau; 8, Gletscherhorn; 9, Mit-
ghorn; 10, Blumlis Alp; 11, In
e middle distance, Niesen; 12,
tockhorn.

There cannot be a more sublime
ght than this view at sunset; espe-
ally at times when, from a pecu-
ar state of the atmosphere, the
anting rays are reflected from the
lpine snows in hues of glowing
ink.   It is hardly possible to gaze
n these Alps and glaciers without
esiring to explore their recesses
hich enclose some of the most mag-
ificent scenery in Switzerland. The
latform itself, supported by a mas-
ve wall of masonry, rises 108 feet
bove the Aar; yet an inscription on
e parapet records that a young stu-
ent, mounted on a spirited horse,
hich had been frightened by some
hildren, and leaped the precipice,
eached the bottom with no other
urt than a few broken ribs.   The
orse was killed on the spot.   The
ider became minister of Kerzerz, and
ved to a good old age!

The *Minster*, a very beautiful
othic building, was begun 1421,
nd finished 1457.   One of its archi-
ects was the son of Erwin of Steinach, who built Strasburg; and
many of the ornaments,—such as the
pen parapet running round the roof,
nd varying in pattern between each
uttress, are not inferior in design
r execution to those of Strasburg.
The chief ornament is the great W.
ortal, bearing sculptured reliefs of

the Last Judgment, flanked by figures
of the wise and foolish Virgins, &c.
The interior is not remarkable.   In
the windows are the coats of arms of
the aristocratic burghers of Berne, in
all the pomp of heraldry; along the
walls are tablets, bearing the names
of 18 officers and 683 soldiers, citizens of Berne, who fell fighting
against the French 1798.   There is
also a monument erected by the town,
in 1600, to Berchtold, of Zähringen,
founder of Berne.

The *Museum* contains one of the
best collections of the natural productions of Switzerland to be found
in the country.   It is open to the
public 3 times a-week: strangers
may obtain admittance at all times
by a small fee.

In the zoological department there
are stuffed specimens of the bear at all
ages. Two young cubs, about the size
of kittens, respectively 8 and 21 days
old—hideous and uncouth monsters
—enable one easily to discover the
origin of the vulgar error that the
bear was licked into shape by its
mother.   The lynx of the Alps, and
the Steinbock, both from the Bernese
chain, are interesting from their
rarity; these animals having nearly
disappeared from Europe.

Here is deservedly preserved the
skin of *Barry*, one of the dogs of St.
Bernard, who is recorded to have
saved the lives of 15 human beings
by his sagacity.

A chamois with three horns, one
growing out of the nose; a specimen of a cross breed between the
steinbock and domestic goat, which
lived 7 years; a wild boar, of gigantic size and bristling mien, are also
worth notice.

In the *Ornithological* department
are the lämmergeyer (vulture of
lambs), the feathered monarch of the
Alps, and inferior in size to the condor alone among birds.   It breeds
only on the highest mountains.

In addition to the native birds of
Switzerland, a perfect collection of
which, with very few exceptions, is

to be seen here, together with their
nests and eggs, there are specimens of
several foreign and tropical birds
which have found their way into
Switzerland by accident; viz., a flamingo killed near the lake of Morat,
and a pelican from Constance. "Possibly the flamingo came from the
waters of the district around Nismes
and Avignon, where these birds are
not uncommon." P.

The departments of geology and
mineralogy are very rich. The geology of Switzerland may be well
studied in the very complete series of
fossils collected by *M. Studer*, an
eminent living geologist, and others.

There are a number of beautiful
specimens of all the rarest and finest
minerals from St. Gothard.

Several plans in relief of various
parts of Switzerland will prove equally
instructive to the student of geography and geology.

In a small collection of *Antiquities*
the following objects seem to deserve
mentioning:—Some Roman antiquities dug up in Switzerland; the
Prie Dieu of Charles the Bold, and
part of his tent-hangings, captured
by the Bernese at Grandson; the
pointed shoes worn by the Bernese
nobles in the XVIth century; some
dresses, &c. from the South Sea
islands, and the dagger with which
Captain Cook was slain (?), brought
over by Weber, the artist, who accompanied the expedition, who was
of Swiss origin.

The *Town Library* is a good collection of 40,000 volumes, and is well
stored with Swiss history. Haller,
who was born at Berne, was librarian.
The butter-market is held beneath
this building.

The *Arsenal* has scarcely any
curiosities to show since it was robbed
by the French in 1798; the arms for
the contingent of the canton are kept
in it.

The *Diet* assembles in the Aussere
Standes-Haus (formerly the Marks-
mans Guild); it met here last in
1835 and 36.

Berne is celebrated for the numb
and excellence of its Charitable I
stitutions: they are perhaps mo
carefully attended to than any
Europe. There is a public grana
in case of scarcity, two orpha
houses, an infirmary, and an exte
sive *Hospital*, bearing the inscriptio
"Christo in pauperibus." It w
for a long time the finest, indeed t
only grand building in the town,
just subject of pride; but it has
late been eclipsed by the coloss
dimensions of the new prison ar
penitentiary; a circumstance chara
teristic of the present period, pe
haps, in other countries besides t
Canton Berne.

Since 1834, an *University* or hig
school has been established at Ber

The prevailing reverence for t
Bear at Berne does not confine its
to the multiplying of his effigy c
the coins, sign-posts, fountains, an
public buildings of the canton. F
many hundred years living spec
mens of the favourite have bee
maintained at the public expense
and the ditch outside of the Aarber
Gate, called the *Bärengraben*, is a
lotted to them for a habitation. N
traveller will quit Berne witho
paying them a visit, unless he wishe
to have the omission of so importa
a sight thrown in his teeth every tim
the name Berne is mentioned; an
indeed a vacant half hour may b
worse employed than in watchin
the gambols of Bruin, and supplyin
him with cakes and apples. Th
connexion between the town and t
animal is accounted for by the a
cient tradition, that on the day o
which Berchtold laid the foundatio
of Berne, an enormous bear was sla
by him upon its destined site.

The bears were formerly hand
somely provided for. At the begi
ning of the last century an old lad
dying without near relatives, b
queathed her fortune of 60,000 livr
to them. The will was disputed b
some distant connexion of the d
ceased; but the cause of the brute

vas so ably pleaded by one of the nost distinguished members of the ar of Berne that the plaintiff was onsuited. The bears, declared the ightful heirs, were taken under the guardianship of the supreme council, vho, treating them as wards in hancery, or minors, administered heir property. In order to maintain he succession to the estate, a pair of oung bears was always reared, in ase of the demise of the elders; and o prevent too large an increase of the ace, all that were born beyond this vere fattened to furnish a dainty for he civic feasts of the Berne burgo-masters.

The bears, however, did not long enjoy their fortune. The French Revolution broke out, and its sweeping consequences, not confined to crowns and kingdoms, descended even to bears. The French army having defeated the Swiss in several engagements, entered the town (1798), and immediately took possession of the treasury. Eleven mules were despatched to Paris laden with specie found in it; two of them bore away the birthright of the bears, amounting at the time to 70 millions of francs. The bears themselves were led away captives, and deposited in the Jardin des Plantes, where one of them, the celebrated Martin, soon became the favourite of the French metropolis. When, after a series of years, the ancient order of things was restored at Berne, one of the first cares of the citizens was to replace and provide for their ancient pensioners. A subscription was raised in consequence, and a small estate purchased, the rents of which, though diminished from various causes, are appropriated to their support. The cost of keeping them amounts to between 600 and 700 francs per annum; and well-grounded fears are entertained that modern legislators, forgetful of the service rendered by Bruin for so many centuries, in figuring upon the shield of the canton, may soon strike him off the pension list.

The fortifications of the town, no longer of use as defences, are converted into *Promenades*, and make very agreeable walks. The banks of the Aar, which they overlook, are most picturesque; and the Alps, when visible, form a back-ground of the utmost sublimity.

They, however, as well as the city of Berne itself, are best seen from a terrace walk called the *Enghe*, a little more than a mile outside the Aarberg Gate, the favourite resort of the citizens. On the way to it, immediately beyond the gate, the bears' ditch and den are passed on the l., and the *Shooting*-House,where rifle matches take place, on the rt. hand.

Two other more distant and elevated points, which are most advantageous for commanding the panorama of the Alps, are the hill of *Altenberg*, ½ an hour's walk on the N. of the town, reached by a foot-bridge across the Aar; and the *Gurten*, a height an hour's walk to the S. of the town.

There are *Baths* on the island in the Aar, charge, 1fr., linen included; a flight of steps leads from the Platform down to the river.

The *Cassino*, a handsome building in the Ober-Graben, contains a reading-room, supplied with newspapers; a ball-room, &c. There is also a *Theatre* in the town.

Burgdorfer, opposite the Clock-tower, is the principal bookseller, and keeps a good supply of maps, views, and costumes, &c. of Switzerland.

Passports.—Travellers going from Switzerland into Austria, Italy, France, or Bavaria, must bear in mind that it is *necessary* to have their passports countersigned by the ministers of those powers residing here. The Secretaries of Legation remain on the spot even when the ministers attend the Diet at Lucerne or Zurich.

The English and Austrian ministers sign passports only early in the morning from 10 to 11 or 12. In cases of urgency they would probably not refuse their signature at other hours, but this is liable to uncertainty. The traveller pressed for time, and wishing to avoid delay, may leave his passport with the master of the inn, to be forwarded to him by post. The Austrian signature, if not obtained here, can only be got at Turin or Stuttgard, the nearest capitals where Austrian ministers reside.

Hindelbank, which is sometimes visited from Berne, on account of the tomb of Madame Langhans, is described in Route 13; and Hofwyl, Mr. Fellenberg's establishment, in Route 24, p. 63.

The excursion from hence through the *Bernese Oberland,* Route 27, may be made in 3 days, though it deserves longer time to be devoted to it.

Diligences go from Berne *daily* to Basle by Olten; Basle by Delsberg, to Aarau, Freiburg, Lausanne, Geneva, Lucerne, Neuchatel, Soleure, Zurich, and *twice a-day,* to Thun.

History and Government of Berne.

Berne owes its foundation, in the XIIth century, to Berchtold V., Duke of Zähringen, who held, as his ancestors had done, the office of Warden, or Proprietor of W. Switzerland, from the Emperor. At that period the Faustrecht, or law of the strong hand, was at its height; a great part of the land was still unreclaimed forest, and the only human habitations were the hovel of the defenceless serf or peasant, and the frowning and well-defended castle of the lawless baron, who lived by rapine and pillage. The efforts of the Dukes of Zähringen had long been directed towards the curbing and humbling of this provincial nobility, who, from their number and power, were no less formidable to their liege lord than to the peasant or merchant over whom they tyrannised. To raise up a counterpoise to the overbearing noblesse, and their strongholds or robber-nests, he collected the scattered peasantry into communities, the chief of which he formed in 1191, on a peninsula, protected by the Aar on all sides but one, which he fortified with strong walls. Behind these the craftsman, the merchant, and all others who needed protection for their person and property, found it. Berchtold fostered the infant city by immunities and privileges; and, what was by far more important, he succeeded in having it acknowledged as a free town of the empire, independent of his own house and of all sovereign but the emperor. Invited by these advantages, not only persons of the poorer sort, but many of the inferior nobles, settled here to enjoy the proffered freedom. These, and the more flourishing class of citizens, in a short time engrossed in their own hand the entire administration of government, and their numbers being limited, and the right of citizenship hereditary, they soon formed an aristocracy as powerful in proportion to the extent of the state as that of Venice and Nuremberg, and as proud as any feudal noblesse in Europe. The great council of the canton, which at one time contained some democratic elements, by the admission of members from the lower trades and craftsmen, in process of time was filled solely by the higher burghers, and all elections were renewed from their own body. Thus all public offices were monopolised for ages by certain families. The Erlachs, for instance, held possession of the post office, the eldest sons succeeded to their fathers as matter of course, and the higher commands in the Swiss regiments in foreign service furnished employment for those who could not find place at home. The most ancient families of burghers, *i. e.* those who had been admitted to the privilege of citizens before 1635, were called regiments-fähig (eligible to the magistracy), but of these only a small number were actually the rulers (regierende): in 1785 the number of the latter was only 69 families. Such a state of things naturally gave

se to great discontent among the
wer order of citizens, not so much
om any abuses of their rulers, who
em to have governed with prudence
d honesty, without oppressing or
eavily taxing, but from their over-
earing haughtiness, exclusiveness,
d the secrecy with which all their
oceedings were conducted. By the
rench Revolution this ancient ari-
ocracy lost much of its power; and
e events which followed that of July
830 have stripped them of the re-
ainder. A new constitution, passed
d approved by an assemblage of
ost of the inhabitants of the canton,
ow gives to every citizen equal poli-
cal rights. The hereditary rule and
onopoly of the supreme authority
y the aristocratic families was thus
estroyed, and the people admitted
) a share of the government. A
ewly-appointed supreme council
ntered upon its duties in Oct. 1831;
nd considering its want of experience,
om the previous exclusion *in toto*
f the popular party from all share
n the government, their administra-
on appears to have been respect-
ble. The chief reproach cast upon
hem is their persecution of the oli-
archists, many of whom have since
een imprisoned. The new rulers
ere relieved of much embarrassment
n the department of finance, by the
iscovery, in the exchequer, of the
evenue of seven years hoarded up,
ccording to an ancient practice, by
heir predecessors. Instead of allow-
ng this to lie idle they very wisely
urned it to account, in improving the
oads of the canton, and in other
ublic works.

ROUTE 27.

The Bernese Oberland.

Berne to Thun ;—Interlachen;
—Lauterbrunnen ; over the Wengern Alp to Grindelwald ;—Ascent of the Faulhorn ;—over the
Scheideck to Meyringen ; — and
by Brienz back to Thun.

This agreeable excursion may be

made in 3 days, 1st to Grindelwald,
2nd to Meyringen, and returning to
Berne on the evening of the 3rd day.
Most persons, however, will feel disposed to devote longer time to it.
But it is by no means necessary to
return to Berne : the passes of the
Gemmi (R. 38), of the Brunig (R.
19), and of the Grimsel (R. 28),
connect the Oberland with the general tour of Switzerland.

It was in this magnificent highland
district that Byron " repeopled his
mind from nature," and gathered
many of the ideas and images which
he has so exquisitely interwoven in
his tragedy of Manfred, the scene of
which lies among the Bernese Alps.
He preferred many of the scenes
among these mountains and lakes to
Chamouni, and calls them " some of
the noblest views in the world."

Berne to Thun.

5⅙ stunden = 16¾ English miles.
An easy 3 hours' drive.
A diligence goes twice a-day.
The road is excellent, and in fine
weather the snowy Alps are in sight
nearly the whole way. The scenery
of the valley of the Aar is most
pleasing ; laid out in pasture lands,
with abundance of villages, and substantial farm-houses, with broad
roofs, surrounded by neat gardens. The river itself runs at some
distance on the rt., and is rarely visible. The principal village passed
on the way is
2½ Münsingen, memorable in
recent Swiss annals as the spot
where the great public meeting of
the men of the canton was held in
1831, which adopted the new constitution, and overthrew the rule of
the oligarchy.
The Stockhorn, with its conical
peak, and the Niesen, two limestone
mountains, forming, as it were, the
advanced guard of the high Alps,
posted on the opposite side of the
lake, become conspicuous objects
before reaching
2⅔ Thun—*Inns :* H. de Bellevue.

Outside the town, and beyond it, a new and first-rate hotel, well situated in a garden commanding a view of the Aar. It is however rather dear.

Dinner, table d'hôte, at 2, 3 fr.; at 5, 4 fr.—tea, 1 fr. 10 sous—wax-lights, 1 fr. each, beds, 2 fr.

The Bateau à Vapeur, another inn, a few yards farther, belongs to the same landlord, who is also proprietor of the steam-boat plying on the lake, and is a clever, active, and enterprising person. He is civil withal, and well acquainted with Switzerland, so as to be able to advise travellers on their proposed routes.— Freyenhof, within the town, formerly the chief inn, but now second-rate; —Faucon, said to be good.

The Pension Baumgarten is well spoken of, and is usually so full that it is difficult to obtain rooms without long previous application. "The landlady is extremely respectable and civil; the apartments cheerful and pleasant; living good. Charges 5 fr. a-day for each master, and ½ for a servant, everything included.'"—L.

There is not a more picturesque town in Switzerland than Thun, situated about a mile from the lake, upon the river Aar, which here rushes out of it clear as crystal. Preeminent above the other buildings rise a venerable church, and a picturesque feudal castle 700 years old. Thun contains 4876 inhabitants; but within its walls there is nothing worth notice. It is, however, from its position, and its beautiful environs, one of the most agreeable places of residence in Switzerland, and being the starting place for those who visit the Bernese highlands, it is thronged with a constant succession of travellers through the whole summer.

The view from the *Churchyard terrace* "along the lake, with its girdle of Alps, fine glaciers, and rocks wooded to the top," is mentioned by Byron. A more extensive prospect is gained from the little Pavilion of St. Jacques; but better

than either is the view from t grounds of a pretty country-hou called the *Chartreuse*, about mile below the Hotel Bellevue. T Jungfrau, Mönch, and Eigher a visible from hence. The *Milita School* of the Swiss Confederation at Thun.

Vehicles of various kinds, a guides may be hired at Thun.

A new carriage-road has be constructed up the Simmenth from the lake of Thun to Veva (Route 41.)

Lake of Thun—Thun to Interlache

Since 1835 a small iron *steam-bo* plies on the lake of Thun betwe Thun (the Hotel du Bateau Vapeur) and Neuhaus. The voya takes up about 65 minutes. It sta from Thun at 9 A.M. and 2 P.M. from Neuhaus at 12 and 4.

N.B. These were the hours 1837; but, as they are liable to l altered from year to year, travelle should inquire before hand. *A rou boat* with 3 oars costs 75 batz = 1 fr. 5 sous. The tarif fixed by th authorities being 3 fr. for eac rower, and 2 fr. 5 sous for the boa The voyage takes up about 3 hours

The steamer does not take ca riages; but a good carriage-road ha been made to Interlachen, alon the S. shore of the lake. The di tance is about 4 stunden = 13 Englis miles.

The lake is about 10 miles long.

The banks of the lake near Thu are occupied with neat villas an cheerful gardens: further on, its N shore is precipitous, and not ver interesting. Among its scant villages and hamlets, the most im portant is Oberhof, distinguished b the square tower of its castle.

The S. shore is more strikin Here the two remarkable mountains the Stockhorn, with a sharp peak projecting like a horn, or thorn, an the pyramidal mass of the Niesen with its conical top, stand sentinel. at the entrance of the Kander an immenthal. The river Kander, conducted into the lake by an artificial channel formed for it in 1714, has deposited around its mouth, within less than a century and a half, delta or sand-bank of several hundred acres. The progress and extent of this recent formation, so interesting to geologists, has been ably investigated by Mr. Lyell.

S. At the foot of the Niesen, on a projecting tongue of land, stands the picturesque castle of *Spietz*, founded, according to tradition, by Attila (?), and belonging to the family of Erlach. At Spietzwyler there is a neat inn.

N. When about two-thirds over the lake, a projecting promontory of precipitous rock, called the Nose, is passed, and a fine view is obtained of the Eigher and Mönch, which fill up the extremity of the lake with the white mass of their snow. To the E. of them appear the Jungfrau and Finster Aarhorn.

In front of the Nose the lake is 120 feet deep.

N. Farther on, in the face of the mountain, is the *Cave of St. Beatus*, above a small cascade, which may be seen leaping into the lake. St. Beatus, according to tradition, a native of Britain, converted the inhabitants of this part of Helvetia to Christianity. Being minded to take up his residence on the shores of the lake, he fixed his eyes upon a grot well suited to a hermit's abode, which happened at the time to be occupied by a dragon. The monster, however, was easily ejected, without force, and simply by hearing a notice to quit addressed to him by St. Beatus. Among the miracles performed by the anchorite, in addition to the above, must be mentioned that of his crossing the lake on his cloak, which, when spread out on the water, served him instead of a boat. A rivulet issues out of the cave, and is subject to sudden rises, which fill the cavern to the roof, and are accompanied by a loud report,

like that of a cannon. It may be reached in a quarter of an hour from the shore.

At Neuhaus, a solitary cabaret at the end of the lake, about 10 miles from Thun, and about 2 miles from Unterseen, the passengers are landed. A long array of carriages, porters, guides, and horses, will be found awaiting their disembarkation; also a diligence, which runs to Interlachen; fare, 1fr.

N.B. Travellers bound on the *tour of the Oberland* generally engage an equipage here for the whole journey, and if they find a good stout pair of horses, there is economy in doing so; since, where the carriage-roads cease, the horses are taken out and used for riding. The owner will provide saddles and act as guide. Thus, if the same horses are continued during the whole journey, and brought back to Unterseen, one or even 2 days of back fare are saved.

¾ Unterseen, a thoroughly Swiss village, composed (except the *Castle* on the market-place, and *Rathhaus*) of wooden houses, many of them brown from age, being 2 centuries old, contains about 1000 inhabitants.

It is situated about half-way between the lakes of Thun and Brienz, whence its name, and that of Interlachen, both signifying "between the lakes." "There are several pensions here, where the charge is 3 fr. a-day; but they are not so good as those of Interlachen; in fact, they are altogether inferior establishments, chiefly resorted to by Germans and Swiss, and the hours are more primitive, dinner being served at 1." —L.

N.B. Those who wish to make the most of their time, and intend to return to Thun, will turn off at once from Unterseen to Lauterbrunnen, as they must pass through Interlachen (where there is nothing particular to be seen) on their way from Brienz.

¾ *Interlachen*. Besides the inn, called

Hotel de Interlachen, or Landhaus, and said to be good, there are at least a dozen pensions, or boarding-houses here, where travellers are now received for one day. Formerly no one was taken in for less than a week. The charges for board and lodging vary between 5 and 6 fr. a-day, exclusive of wine. The principal pensions are Müller's; Seilers; the Cassino (6fr.); and Hofstetters; the latter is kept by a very obliging landlord, and affords as good accommodation as any in the place. At most of these houses there is a daily table d'hôte, and during the season balls are constantly given at one or other.

Interlachen has few sights or lions for the tourist or passing traveller, who need not stop here, unless he require to rest himself. Its beautiful position, however, on a little plain between the lakes, in full view of the Jungfrau, whose snowy summit is seen through a gap in the minor chain of Alps, its vicinity to numerous interesting sites, and some of the most pleasing excursions in Switzerland, together with its exceeding cheapness as a place of residence, have spread its reputation through Europe, and have literally converted it into an English colony, two-thirds of the summer visitors, on a moderate computation, being of our nation, who have converted the place into a sort of Swiss Margate. The village itself, a collection of staring, white-washed lodging-houses, has nothing Swiss in its character. Still, however, though no longer a place of retirement, Interlachen must not be disparaged; its almost endless walks and rides, its boating parties on the two lakes, its picnics, and balls, would, in the society of friends, afford amusement for a season. In front of the lodging-houses runs a magnificent avenue of walnut-trees, most inviting from its cool shade. The wooded slopes of the Harder, a hill on the opposite bank of the Aar, rendered accessible by easy paths,

commanding a delightful view, a the old castle of Unspunnen are with the distance of a walk even for I dies; while the Giesbach Falls, La terbrunnen with the Staubach, a Grindelwald with its glaciers, a within a short morning's row or rid They are described in the followin tour of the Oberland. There is Subscription *Reading-room* and L brary here, at which "The Times and "Galignani" are taken in.

The *English Church Service* is pe formed every Sunday in the chur by an English clergyman, for who a small stipend is formed by volu tary contributions among his count men.

Very good saddle-horses may l hired at Interlachen. As far a Lauterbrunnen and Grindelwal there is a good char-road, and th saddle-horses may be used to dra the chars.

From Unterseen, or Interlachen, Lauterbrunnen, is about $3\frac{1}{4}$ stunde = 10 Eng. miles—a drive of near 2 hours. The road is practicable fo the carriages of the country. Aft passing a tract of verdant meadow land, on which great wrestling matches (one of which has been de scribed by Madame de Stael) ar periodically held, the road passes o the rt. the *Castle of Unspunnen:* is in a very dilapidated state, but square tower, with a flanking roun turret rise picturesquely above th brushwood surrounding them. It i the reputed residence of Manfrec and its position in front of the hig Alps renders it not unlikely tha Byron may have had it in his eye The *real* owners of the castle wer the barons of Unspunnen, a nobl and ancient race, who were lords o the whole Oberland, from the Grimse to the Gemmi. Burkard, the las male descendant of this family, ha a beautiful and only daughter, Ida who was beloved by a young knigh attached to the Court of Berchtold of Zähringen, between whom and Burkard a deadly feud had long sub sted. Under such circumstances the youthful Rudolph of Wadenshwyl, despairing of obtaining the ather's consent to their union, scaled the castle-walls by night, carried Ida ff, and made her his bride. Many ears of bloody strife between the two arties followed this event. At length Rudolph, taking his infant son by da along with him, presented himelf, unarmed and without attendants, o Burkard, in the midst of his stronghold. Such an appeal to the old nan's affections and generosity was rresistible; he melted into tears, orgot his wrongs, and, receiving his hildren into his bosom, made Ruolph's son the heir of his vast possesions. At the time of the reconciliaion, the old baron had said, " Let his day be for ever celebrated among is;" and rural games were in consequence, for many years, held on the pot. These were revived in 1805 nd 1808, and consisted of gymnastic xercises, wrestling, pitching the tone, &c., in which the natives of he different cantons contended with ne another, while spectators from ar and near collected on a naural amphitheatre. A huge fragnent of rock, weighing 184lbs., vhich was hurled 10 ft. by an athlete rom Appenzell, may still be seen.

Leaving behind the villages of Wylderschwyl and Mühlinen, whose nhabitants are sadly afflicted with goitre (§ 19), the road plunges into he narrow and savage gorge of the orrent Lutschine, and " we enter apon a range of scenes beyond all lescription or previous conception. Not far up, the road passes a spot of evil repute as the scene of a fratricide—" just the place for such a leed." It was marked by an inscription in the face of a projecting rock, called, from the murder, the Evil Stone (Bösestein), or Brother's Stone. The recent encroachments of the river upon the road have rendered it necessary to blast a portion of the rock in order to widen the carriage-way, in doing which the in-

scription has been displaced. The murderer, according to the story, was lord of the castle of Rothenflue, which stood on the opposite side of the valley. Stung with remorse, he fled away from the sight of man, wandered an outcast among the wilds like Cain, and perished miserably.

2 At the hamlet of Zweilutschinen, about two miles from the entrance of the valley, it divides into two branches; that on the l., from which flows the Black Lutschine, is the valley of Grindelwald, terminated by the gigantic mass and everlasting snows of the Wetterhorn (see p. 77); that of the rt., traversed by the White Lutschine, is the valley of the Lauterbrunnen, and it ought to be visited first.

The valley of Lauterbrunnen is remarkable for its depth, its contracted width, and for the precipices of limestone, nearly vertical, which enclose it like walls. Its name, literally translated, means " nothing but fountains;" and is derived, doubtlessly, from the number of streamlets which cast themselves headlong from the brows of the cliffs into the valley below, looking at a distance like so many pendulous white threads.

The road crosses the Lutschine under the base of a colossal precipice, called Hunnenflue, whose face displays singular contortions in the limestone strata. If the clouds permit, the summit of the Jungfrau now bursts into sight; and soon after, surmounting a steep slope, we reach

1¾ *Lauterbrunnen* (*Inn:* Capricorn, tolerably good).

This village contains about 1350 inhabitants, in rustic houses, scattered widely apart, along both banks of the torrent. It lies 2450 feet above the sea, so sunk between precipices that in summer the sun does not appear till 7 o'clock, and in winter not before 12. Only the hardier species of grain grow here, and the climate is almost too rough for pears and apples. About 30 shoots of water dangle from the edge of the rampart which forms the side of the valley : and, when its top is enveloped in clouds, appear to burst at once from the sky : many of them are dried up in summer. These minor falls, however, are all eclipsed by that of the *Staubbach,* distant about three quarters of a mile from the inn. It is one of the loftiest in Europe, measuring between 800 and 900 feet in height; and from this cause, and from the comparatively small body of water forming it, it is shivered by the wind into spray like dust long before it reaches the bottom (whence its name, literally, *Dust*-fall).

Strangers, who expect in the Staubbach the rushing and roaring rapidity of a cataract, will here be disappointed ; but in the opinion of many, this want is atoned for by other beauties peculiar to this fall. The friction of the rock, and the resistance of the air, retard the descent of the water, giving it, when seen in front, the appearance of a beautiful lace veil suspended from the precipice, and imitating, in its centre, the folds of the drapery. When very full it shoots out from the rock, and is bent by the wind into flickering undulations. Byron has described it admirably, both in prose and verse :—

" The torrent is in shape, curving over the rock, like the *tail* of a white horse streaming in the wind—such as it might be conceived would be that of the ' pale horse ' on which Death is mounted in the Apocalypse. It is neither mist nor water, but a something between both : its immense height gives it a wave or curve—a spreading here or condensation there—wonderful and indescribable."—*Journal.*

" It is not noon — the sunbow's rays still arch
The torrent with the many hues of heaven,
And roll the sheeted silver's waving column
O'er the crag's headlong perpendicular,
And fling its lines of foaming light along,

And to and fro, like the pale courser's tail
The giant steed to be bestrode by Death,
As told in the Apocalypse.''

Manfred

The Staubbach is seen to perfe tion before noon, when the i formed by the sun falling full up it, " like a rainbow come down to p a visit—moving as you move," a the shadow of the water on the fa of the rock, give an additional i terest. At other times it is as we seen from the inn as from the neare point which can be reached witho becoming drenched with spra Wordsworth has called it " a heave born water-fall ;" and when th clouds are low and rest on the side of the valley, it literally appea to leap from the sky. In winte when the torrent is nearly arres ed by the frost, a vast pyrami of ice is formed by the dripping the water from above, increasing gr dually upwards in the manner of stalagmite, until the colossal icic reaches nearly half way up the pr cipice. There is a smaller upper-fa above the one seen from Lauterbrur nen. A foot-path leads up to it i three quarters of an hour, but fe think it worth the trouble of the a cent.

Above Lauterbrunnen vegetatio languishes, and in a few miles i limited to scanty grass. There ar more water-falls in this direction, the traveller be not already weary o them. The *Schmadribach*, about 1 miles beyond the church of Lauter brunnen, is by some esteemed fine than the Staubbach; but it is only t be reached by a difficult foot-path leading past the little cascade of th Trimbelbach, twisting and roarin in a cleft on the l., and over the debri of an avalanche which falls annuall from the Jungfrau, and spreads it ruins of broken rocks, mixed wit fragments of ice, over a surface o many hundred acres. It is calle the Trachsel-Lauine. Near it is group of miserable chalets—farthe on a single chalet, called Steinberg 'rom which the fall is reached. It is a desolate and wild spot, pent in by abrupt rocks and glaciers, and might truly be termed *The World's End.*

Lauterbrunnen to Grindelwald.—
1. By the char road.
2. By the Wengern Alp.

By the high-road the time occupied in going to Grindelwald is about 2½ hours— the distance about 12 miles; but this route should be taken only by those who can neither ride nor walk, or who prefer the ease of a char à banc to avalanches, Alps, and fatigue—or in case of bad or cloudy weather. It is necessary to return down the valley as far as the Zwei-Lutschinen, then, crossing the White, to ascend, by the side of the Black Lutschine—a toilsome steep, through a gloomy valley, closed up by the precipices of the Wetterhorn, and the peaks of the Eigher. Nearer to Grindelwald the two glaciers appear in sight.

The traveller in the Oberland is sadly subjected to the persecution of beggars—some under the pretext of offering him strawberries, or flowers, or crystals,—others with no other excuse but their poverty, not unfrequently united to goitre and cretinism, as an additional recommendation to the compassion of strangers. Every cottage sends forth its ragged crowds of dishevelled and unshod children ; behind every rock is an ambuscade of native minstrels, who, drawn up in line, assail the passers-by with the discordant strains of their shrill voices. " They beset the devious footway leading up the hillside in a long scattered line, to a considerable height, just like a train of gunpowder, which only awaited my approach to explode."—*Latrobe.*

2 In fine weather there is not a more interesting or exciting journey among the Alps than that over the *Wengern Alp,* or *Lesser Scheideck.* Independent of the view of the Jungfrau, and other giants of the Bernese chain (unrivalled, owing to its proximity to these sublime objects), it is from the summit of the Wengern Alp that the avalanches are seen and heard in greatest perfection. and no one should abandon the expedition without an effort. The path is practicable for mules, and is about 18 miles long ; but, from its steepness, its great elevation, and the time spent in enjoying the view from the top, it occupies at least 7 hours. Though fatiguing, it is not dangerous, and is constantly traversed by ladies on horseback, or even in a chaise à porteur (§ 9).

A steep zigzag path leads out of the valley of Lauterbrunnen, in order to surmount the ridge separating it from that of Grindelwald. After nearly an hour of toilsome ascent, passing the houses of a scattered hamlet, it reaches a more gradual slope of meadow land. The valley of Lauterbrun, beneath whose precipices the traveller has previously crept with some little awe, presents from this height the aspect of a mere trench ; the Staubbach is reduced to a thin thread; and its upper fall, and previous winding, before it makes its final leap, are exposed to view.

The path crosses the meadows advancing towards the Jungfrau, which now rises in front of the spectator, with its vast expanse of snow and glacier, in all its magnificence. Not only its summit, but all the mass of the mountain above the level of the spectator, is white with perpetual snow of virgin purity, which breaks off abruptly at the edge of a back precipice, forming one side of a ravine separating the Jungfrau from the Wengern Alp. It appears to be within gun-shot of the spectator—so colossal are its proportions, that the effect of distance is lost.

From a chalet (Sennhutte) planted on the brow of the ravine, 5350 feet above the sea-level, directly facing the Jungfrau, the mountain is best seen, as well as the avalanches descending from it. The precipice before alluded to, which forms the base of the mountain, is channelled with furrows or grooves, down which the avalanches descend. They are most numerous a little after noon, when the sun exercises the greatest influence on the glacier in loosening masses of it, and causing them to break off.

The attention is first arrested by a distant roar, not unlike thunder, and in half a minute a gush of white powder, resembling a small cataract, is perceived issuing out of one of the upper grooves or gullies; it then sinks into a lower fissure, and is lost only to reappear at a lower stage some hundred feet below; soon after another roar, and a fresh gush from a lower gully, till the mass of ice, reaching the lowest step, is precipitated into the gulf below. By watching attentively the sloping white side of the Jungfrau, the mass of glacier which produces this may be seen at the moment when disengaged and before the sound reaches the ear. Sometimes it merely slides down over the surface, at others it turns over in a cake; but in an instant after it disappears, is shattered to atoms, and, in passing through the different gullies, is ground to powder so fine, that, as it issues from the lowest, it looks like a handful of meal; and particles, reduced by friction to the consistence of dust, rise in a cloud of vapour. Independent of the sound, which is an awful interruption of the silence usually prevailing on the high Alps, there is nothing grand or striking in these falling masses; and, indeed, it is difficult, at first, to believe that these echoing thunders arise from so slight a cause in appearance. The spectator must bear in mind that at each discharge whole tons of ice are hurled down the mountain, and apparently that insignificant white dust is made up of blocks capable of sweeping away whole forests, did any occur in its course, and of overwhelming houses and villages. During the early part of summer three or four such discharges may be seen in an hour; in cold weather they are less numerous; in the autumn scarcely any occur. The avalanches finally descend into the valley of Trumlaten, the deep and uninhabited ravine dividing the Jungfrau from the Wengern Alp; and, on melting, send forth a stream which falls into the Lutschine, a little above Lauterbrunnen. A part of Lord Byron's " Manfred " was either written or mentally composed on the Wengern Alp, in full view of the Jungfrau, and (he says in his Journal) within hearing of its avalanches.

" Ascended the Wengern mountain; left the horses, took off my coat, and went to the summit. On one side, our view comprised the Jungfrau, with all her glaciers; then the Dent d'Argent, shining like truth; then the Little Giant, and the Great Giant; and last, not least, the Wetterhorn. The height of the Jungfrau is 13,000 feet above the sea, and 11,000 above the valley. Heard the avalanches falling every five minutes nearly.

" The clouds rose from the opposite valley, curling up perpendicular precipices, like the foam of the ocean of hell during a spring tide— it was white and sulphury, and immeasurably deep in appearance. The side we ascended was not of so precipitous a nature; but, on arriving at the summit, we looked down upon the other side upon a boiling sea of cloud, dashing against the crags on which we stood—these crags on one side quite perpendicular. In passing the masses of snow, I made a snowball and pelted Hobhouse with it."— *Swiss Journal.*

" Ye toppling crags of ice—
Ye *avalanches,* whom a breath draws down
In mountainous o'erwhelming, come and
    crush me !
*I hear ye momently above, beneath,
Crush with a frequent conflict;* but ye pass,
And only fall on things that still would live;
On the young flourishing forest, or the hut
And hamlet of the harmless villager.

he mists boil up around the glaciers;
clouds
rise curling fast beneath me, white and sulphury.
like foam from the roused ocean of deep
hell!"

Manfred.

About 2 miles beyond this chalet
he summit of the pass is attained,
280 feet above the sea-level. Near
t there is another chalet, which, as
well as the former, furnishes beds to
strangers, who sometimes pass the
night here to await the sunrise. The
view from the top is very fine, including, besides the Jungfrau, the
Monch, the two Eighers, and the
Wetterhorn. The *Jungfrau*, or Virgin, received its name either from
the unsullied purity of the snow,
or because (till lately) its crest had
never been reached or trodden by human foot. She has now lost her
claim to the title on the latter score,
the highest peak having been attained
in 1812, by two brothers, named
Meyer, from Aarau; and, in 1828,
by six peasants, from Grindelwald.
It is the fourth in height of all European mountains, rising to an elevation of 13,748 feet above the sea-level. The Silber-hörner are, properly speaking, inferior peaks of the
Jungfrau. Farther on appears the
Monch or Klein Eigher, 13,524 feet,
and the Great Eigher (Giant), 13,050
feet. On approaching Grindelwald,
the Shreckhorn (Peak of Terror),
13,470 feet, comes into sight. The
sharp, needle-formed point of the
Finster-Aarhorn, the highest of the
group, 14,070 feet above the sea-level,
is only visible at intervals peering
above his brethren. The glaciers,
which cling around these peaks, and
fill up the depressions between them,
extend without interruption from the
Jungfrau to the Grimsel, and from
Grindelwald in Canton Berne, nearly
to Brieg in the Vallais. The extent
of this glacier has been calculated at
115 square miles, or about one-sixth
of all the glaciers among the Alps.

Within a few years, a *chalet* has
been erected on the very summit of

the Wengern Alp, to afford refreshment by day to passing travellers,
and shelter by night to those who
wish to enjoy the sunrise from hence.
Both the fare and the beds are of
a very humble description. The descent from this chalet to Grindelwald
takes up about three hours. The
path is steep and difficult, strewn
with fallen rocks. It passes within
sight of a forest mown down by the
fall of avalanches. The trunks,
broken short off close to the ground,
still stand, like stubble left by the
scythe. Byron describes " whole
woods of withered pines—all withered; trunks stripped and barkless,
branches lifeless; done by a single
winter,—their appearance reminded
me of me and my family."

In descending into the valley, the
Wetterhorn is seen in front, and on
the l. the Faulhorn, surmounted by
an inn, like that on the Righi, which
furnishes night-quarters to those who
ascend for the sake of the sunrise, and
the celebrated panoramic view (p. 79).
On the rt., low down, appears the
white glacier of Grindelwald, issuing
out of a gorge, on a level with the
habitations of the valley. Travellers,
instead of proceeding at once to
Grindelwald, usually skirt along the
base of the mountain, in order to visit
this glacier on their way.

Grindelwald (Inns : Adler—Eagle;
Bär—Bear; both tolerable). They
are more than a mile distant from
the lower glacier: in summer they are
often very full, so that it is advisable
to send on beforehand to secure beds.

The village of Grindelwald, consisting of picturesque wooden cottages, widely scattered over the valley, lies at a height of 3250 feet above
the sea, from which cause, and from
its vicinity to the glaciers, the climate of the valley is cold, and unstable even in summer. Its inhabitants are chiefly employed in rearing
cattle, of which 6000 head are fed
on the neighbouring pastures. Some
of the peasants act as guides; the
younger females pick up a few batz

by singing Ranz de Vaches at the inns, and most of the children are beggars—occupations arising from the influx of strangers into the valley, which has exercised an injurious influence upon its morals and ancient simplicity of manners.

Grindelwald owes its celebrity, as a place of resort for travellers, to the grandeur of the mountains which surround it, and to its two *Glaciers* (§ 17), which, as they descend into the very bottom of the valley below the level of the village, and almost within a stone's-throw of human habitations, are more easily accessible here than in other parts of Switzerland. Three gigantic mountains form the S. side of the val'ey—the Eigher, or Giant; the Mettenberg (Middle Mountain), which is, in fact, the base or pedestal of the magnificent peak, called Schreckhorn; and the Wetterhorn (Peak of Tempests), at the upper end. Between these three mountains the two glaciers of Grindelwald issue out. They are branches of that vast field or ocean of ice mentioned above as occupying the tableland, and high valleys amidst the Bernese Alps, and being pushed downwards by the constantly-increasing masses above, descend far below the line of perpetual snow (§ 17).

Their chief beauty arises from their being bordered by forests of fir, which form, as it were, a graceful fringe to the white ice, while the green pastures, with which they are almost in contact near their base, contrast agreeably with their frozen peaks. Though inferior in extent to those of Chamouni, they yield to them alone; and the traveller who has not seen them will do well to explore the Glaciers of Grindelwald. *The Lower Glacier*, also called the smaller, although four times as large as the upper one, forces its way out between the Eigher and Mettenberg, and its solid icebergs descend to a point only 3200 ft. above the level of the sea. A path, practicable for mules, ascends for nearly 2 hours along its

left margin, beneath the precipice of the Mettenberg, commanding a most interesting view of the bristling minarets of ice, rising in the most various and fantastic shapes. The glacier, which is narrow at the bottom, gradually widens, and spreads out into what is called the Sea of Ice (Eismeer), where its surface, though traversed by crevices, is less shattered than below. The best view of it is from the grotto called Nellenbalm. Strangers should not venture upon the ice without a guide. In 1821, M. Mouron, a clergyman of Vevay, was lost in one of the crevices. Suspicions were entertained that the guide who accompanied him had murdered him, and search was immediately commenced for the body. After 12 days of fruitless attempts it was at length drawn out of an abyss in the ice, said to have been 700 feet deep (?), by a guide named Burguenen, who was let down from above, at the peril of his life, by a rope with a lantern tied to his neck. He was twice drawn up without having been able to find it, nearly exhausted for want of air; the third time he returned with it in his arms. It was much bruised, and several limbs were broken; so as to lead to the belief that life, or at least sensation, had departed before it reached the bottom; but both the watch and the purse of the unfortunate man were found upon him, so that the suspicions regarding the guide were proved to be groundless. He was buried in the church of Grindelwald.

On the way up to the Eismeer a singular depression in the rocks, called *Martinsdruck*, is pointed out to the traveller; and opposite to it, in the crest of the Eigher, a small hole, called *Martinsloch*, through which the sun's rays shine twice a-year. Once on a time, according to the tradition, the basin now occupied by the Eismeer was filled with a lake, but the space between the Mettenberg and the Eigher being much narrower than at present, the outlet from it was constantly blocked up, and inundations produced, which ruined the fields of the peasants in the valley below. At length St. Martin, a holy giant, came to their rescue; he seated himself on the Mettenberg, resting his staff on the Eigher, and then with one lusty heave of his brawny back not only burst open the present wide passage between the two mountains, but left the marks of his seat on the one, and drove his walking-stick right through the other.

The *Upper Glacier* may be visited in going over the Scheideck.

Ascent of the Faulhorn.

The Faulhorn is a mountain 8140 feet above the sea-level; situated between the valley of Grindelwald and the lake of Brienz, and commanding from its summit an excellent view, especially over the neighbouring chain of Bernese Alps. On this account it is ascended in the summer-time, like the Righi, by numerous parties of travellers.

"For an excursion up the Faulhorn, the horses that have brought travellers to Grindelwald may be used. For ladies who do not ride, and are yet willing to undergo the fatigue of the ascent, chairs may be hired at the inns, with capital bearers, four to each chair, at 6 francs each; or if the party sleep on the Faulhorn, 9 frs. The inn on the summit, which is only tenanted for 4 months of the year, and is totally abandoned to the wind and rain in October, affords 3 very tolerable apartments, and one or two lofts; still it is but sorry sleeping accommodation, the *désagrémens* of which are hardly compensated to ladies by the *uncertain* beauty of the early view of the glaciers: for gentlemen the quarters are good enough. The ascent from Grindelwald is totally free from danger, and not very difficult. It may be made in less than 5 hours, and the descent in 3½. The larder of mine host is said to be better than heretofore; but every thing is of course very dear."—*L.*

A faggot of firewood costs from 10 to 15 batz. The path leads over the Bachalp, by the side of a small lake, 1000 feet below the summit. The view of the Bernese Alps from the top forms the chief feature of the panorama, which in this respect, and from the proximity of the Faulhorn to those snowy giants, far surpasses the prospect from the Righi. On the other hand, though the lakes of Thun and Brienz are both visible, only a small strip of each appears, which is but a poor equivalent for the wide expanse of blue water which bathes the foot of the Righi.

There is a footpath from the top of the Faulhorn, passing the waterfall of the Giesbach to Brienz; the distance is about 14 miles. A bridle-path leads down to Rosenlaui, on the way to Meyringen, so that travellers about to cross the Scheideck need not return to Grindelwald.

Grindelwald to Meyringen, by the Great Scheideck.

6½ stunden = 20¾ English miles.

Beyond Grindelwald the char road ceases, and those who cannot travel on horseback or on foot can reach Meyringen only by crossing the lake of Brienz, returning first to Interlachen.

An hour's walk up the valley from Grindelwald, and a slight detour to the rt. of the direct path to Meyringen, leads to the *Upper Glacier.* It does not materially differ from the one below, nor is it finer; but it sometimes has a larger vault of ice at its lower extremity. These two glaciers are the chief feeders of the Black Lutschine.

It takes 3 hours to reach the summit of the Scheideck from Grindelwald. The ascent is easy, and during the whole of it the *Wetterhorn* (Peak of Tempests) overhangs the path, an object of stupendous sublimity. It rises in one vast precipice of alpine limestone, apparently close above the traveller's head, though its base is more than a mile off. Four different avalanches descend from it in the spring; some of them reach to the path; and patches of their snow often last through the summer. Upon the slope in front of the Wetterhorn is usually stationed one who blows the *alpine horn*, a rude tube of wood, 6 or 8 feet long. The traveller should on no account omit to stop and listen. A few seconds after the horn has ceased, the few and simple notes of the instrument are caught up and repeated by the echoes of the vast cliff of the Wetterhorn, and return to the ear refined and softened, yet perfectly distinct, as it were an aërial concert warbling among the crags.

The view down the valley of Grindelwald, from the top of the Scheideck, is very striking; its green pastures contrast agreeably with the bare wall of the Wetterhorn. Beyond it on the l. rises the sharp crest of the Eigher, resembling the up-turned edge of a hatchet; and the pointed cone of the Schreckhorn appears above the Mettenberg. On the top of the Scheideck (6711 feet above the sea-level, stands a chalet, weather-tight, affording one or two beds for such travellers as are driven to sleep here; and a cup of coffee or hot milk for those who desire to warm themselves after their cold morning's ride over the mountains.

The prospect in the opposite direction, into the vale of the Reichenbach or of Rosenlaui, is not remarkable. High upon the rt. appears the glacier of Schwarzwald, between the Wetterhorn and Wellhorn; further on, between Wellhorn and Engel-hörner (angels' peaks), the *Glacier of Rosenlaui* lies embedded. An hour and a half's walking from the chalet, partly through a wood of firs, brings the traveller abreast of this glacier, which lies about a mile to the rt. of the path in the midst of a forest of firs. It is smaller than those of Grindelwald, but is celebrated above all others in Switzerland for the untarnished purity of its white surface, and the clear transparent azure of its

icebergs. This peculiarity arises doubtless from the character of the rocks around it; these, in decomposing, do not turn into black gravel or mud, which stains and disfigures the Grindelwald glaciers. A steep path on the l. of the glacier leads in about ½ an hour to the summit of a cliff, which projects midway into the icy sea, and bends its course considerably. It forms a good point of view.

The guides usually halt for an hour to refresh themselves and their beasts at

4 The Baths of Rosenlaui, a homely inn, called the Steinbock, erected over a source of mineral water, which supplies 5 or 6 rude tubs of wood, serving as baths. The number of guests who resort hither for the use of them is very limited. This house is distant about 1½ mile from the glacier. A few yards behind it, the Reichenbach torrent issues out of a cleft in the rock. The path to Meyringen runs by the side of this stream, first crossing a charming little green plain, carpeted with soft turf, like that of an English lawn, and dotted with chalets. The view up the valley from this point deserves particular notice; it is a favourite subject for the pencil of the artist. The Wetterhorn, the Wellhorn, and the craggy peaks called Engelhörner, form a mountain group unrivalled for picturesqueness.

Below this the valley contracts, numerous waterfalls are seen dangling from its sides: one of them, from its height and tenuity, is called the Rope-fall (Seilbach); and now a bird's-eye view opens out into the vale of Hasli, or Meyringen, which in comparison with the narrow glens of Grindelwald and Lauterbrunnen deserves the name of a plain, though bounded by mountains high and steep.

The latter part of the descent leading into it, is both difficult and dangerous, unless the horses are very sure-footed, owing to the steepness and ruggedness of the path and its being paved with smooth and slippery blocks of stone. On this account travellers are usually invited to dismount and descend on foot. The stream of the Reichenbach performs this descent of nearly 2000 feet in a succession of leaps, the longest of which are the celebrated *Falls of the Reichenbach.* The upper fall is situated about 100 yards to the l. of the road near the village called Zwirghi. A small fee is exacted for the liberty to cross the meadow between it and the road, and a hut called Belvedere is built beside it. But it is best seen from a rocky headland shooting out in front of the bare amphitheatre of cliffs over which the cataract dashes, and just above the struggling torrent, hurrying downwards after its fall. A little lower is another, but inferior, fall, and by a third, still lower, the stream gains the level of the valley, and hastens to join its waters to the Aar. The lowest fall is not more than 50 yards from the

Baths of Reichenbach, a new inn, on a very extensive scale, situated directly under the road leading to the Scheideck, beneath a hanging wood and in grounds that remind one of an English park. Though provided with hot and cold baths it is less resorted to by invalids than by passing travellers. It is a good house, not dear; table d'hôte at 1 and 7. It is distant about a mile from the village of

2¼ Meyringen—(*Inns :* Sauvage, good; Bär, Ours).—Of late these houses have been, to a certain extent, deserted for the above-named Baths of Reichenbach, situated on the opposite side of the valley. There is another good inn, the Couronne, on this side.

Meyringen, the chief place in the vale of Hasli, lies on the rt. bank of the Aar, and contains about 700 inhabitants. The picturesqueness of its situation is much praised. Brockedon says, " The vale of Meyringen concentrates as much of what is Alpine in its beauties as any valley in Switzerland." Its precipitous

and wooded sides, streaked with white cascades almost without number, and here and there over-topped by some snow-white peak, are indeed beautiful features. Yet the flat plain, 3 miles broad, half marsh and half dry gravel, from inundations of the river, are unpleasing from many points, and as a dwelling-place it has serious drawbacks from the danger to which it is exposed of being swept away or inundated, if not buried by the neighbouring torrents. It was to guard against such accidents that the stone dyke, 1000 feet long and 8 wide, was constructed; but its protection has not been altogether effectual. The chief cause and instrument of all the mischief is the *Alpbach,* a mountain torrent, pouring down from the height behind the village, out of a narrow gorge. The district in which it rises, and through which it takes its course, is composed of the rock known to geologists as the lias marle. Being very soft it is easily disintegrated and washed away, so that the torrent, when swollen by rain or snow, collects, and bears along with it heaps of black sand and rubbish, intermixed with uprooted fir-trees, and is converted almost into a stream of mud, on which masses of rock float like corks. A torrent of such consistence is easily interrupted in its course through the narrow crevices, which it seems to have sawn for itself by the force of its current; it then gathers into a lake behind the obstacles which impede it, until it is increased to such an extent as to bear everything before it, and to spread desolation over the valley through which its course lies. A catastrophe of this sort, in 1762, buried a large part of the village of Meyringen, in one hour, 20 feet deep in rubbish, from which it has hardly yet emerged. The church was filled with mud and gravel to the height of 18 feet, as is denoted by the black line painted along its walls, and by the debris which still covers many of the fields and gardens around. In 1733 an inundation of the same stream carried away many houses.

The intelligent traveller Hugi, from whom the above particulars are derived, recommends travellers to visit the Fall of the Alpbach about 9 in the morning, on account of the *triple bow,* or iris, formed in its spray, when the sun shines on it. The inner iris forms nearly a complete circle; and the outer ones are more or less circular as the water in the falls is abundant or not. The spot whence it is visible is within the spray, from the cataract, so that those who would enjoy it must prepare for a wetting.

On a rock above the village rise the ruins of the *Castle of Resti :* it belonged to an ancient and noble family, to whom the praise is given of never tyrannizing over their humble dependants. The men of Hasli are celebrated for their athletic forms and strength. They hold Zwingfeste, or wrestling matches every year, on the 10th of August, with their neighbours of Unterwalden ; and on the first Sunday in September with those of Grindelwald. The women, again, enjoy the reputation of being prettier, or rather, less plain than those of most other Swiss valleys. Their holiday costume is peculiar and not ungraceful, consisting of a boddice of black velvet, reaching up to the throat, starched sleeves, a yellow petticoat, and a round black hat, not unlike a soup-plate, and about the same size, stuck on one side of the head, and allowing the hair to fall in long tresses down the back.

Five roads concentrate at Meyringen : 1, to Brienz (a char road); 2, to Lucerne, by the Brunig ; 3, over the Susten to Wasen on the St. Gotthard road (12 stunden) ; 4, to the Grimsel ; 5, to Grindelwald, by the Scheideck. The magnificent fall of the Aar at Handeck on the way to the Grimsel (Route 28), is about 14 miles distant. Travellers, not intending to cross the whole pass, may make an interesting excursion thither from Meyringen ; as they may also to the summit of the Brunig, about 6 miles distant, whence there is a beautiful view of the vale of Hasli on one side, and of Lungern on the other. (Route 19.)

Meyringen to Interlachen by Brienz and the Giesbach Fall.

$3\frac{1}{2}$ stunden to Brienz, and $3\frac{3}{4}$ thence to Interlachen by water = $23\frac{3}{4}$ English miles.

There is an excellent char road down the valley, passing numerous cascades leaping down the wall of rock. After proceeding for about 4 miles along the l. bank of the Aar, it crosses the river by a wooden bridge, just at the point where the branch of the Brunig road, leading to Brienz, descends into the valley. The Aar pursues its course through monotonous marsh and flat meadow land, but near its influx into the lake of Brienz, the forms of the mountains on its l. bank, above which towers the Faulhorn, is grand. In skirting the margin of the lake the road crosses vast heaps of debris, covering acres of land once fertile. A torrent of mud, in 1797, destroyed a considerable part of two villages near Kienholz, and a landslip from the Brienzergrat, the mountain immediately behind Brienz, overwhelmed in November 1824, 40 acres of land, and swept 6 persons into the lake. It is $1\frac{1}{2}$ hours' drive from Meyringen to

$3\frac{1}{2}$ Brienz—(*Inn :* Weisses Kreutz, Croix Blanche, clean)—a small village at the E. end of the lake, on a narrow ledge at the foot of the mountains, remarkable only for its beautiful situation and its vicinity to the Giesbach Fall.

Lake of Brienz.—Giesbach Falls.

A boat, with 3 rowers, from Brienz to Interlachen, stopping at the Giesbach, costs 63 batz = about 9 Fr. fr.

There is a very rough road along the N. shore of the lake; the guides with the horses may be sent round by it, and desired to meet the travellers close to the bridge at Interlachen. It takes 25 minutes to row from Brienz to the landing-place close to the outlet of the Giesbach, where travellers begin to ascend the steep height leading to the Falls. They are a succession of cascades, leaping step by step from the top of the mountain; and, though inferior in height to the Reichenbach, surpass it in beauty, and in the adjuncts of a rich forest of fir, through the midst of which they break their way. The Giesbach is one of the prettiest of waterfalls; there is nothing wild about it, and the immediate contact of green turfy knolls and dark woods, has the effect of a park scene. It is possible to pass behind the middle fall by means of a gallery constructed beneath the shelving rock, from which it casts itself down; and the effect of the landscape seen athwart this curtain of water is singular. The cottage opposite the Falls is inhabited by the schoolmaster of Brienz, whose family and himself are celebrated as the best choristers of native airs in Switzerland. He is now a patriarch of 64, and most of his children are married; but he is training his grand-children to the same profession of songsters. The concert, accompanied by the Alpine horn, with which travellers are saluted on their departure, is very sweet. Good specimens of the Swiss manufacture of carved wood may be purchased at the Giesbach. There is a path from the Giesbach to the top of the Faulhorn, a walk of nearly 5 hours. The lake of Brienz is about 8 miles long, near the mouth of the Giesbach, 500 feet deep; but in the deepest part 2100 feet. Its surface is 10, or according to some statements, 30 feet higher than the lake of Thun.

ROUTE 28.

PASS OF THE GRIMSEL,—MEYRINGEN TO OBER-GESTELEN AND BRIEG.

To the Hospice 6¼ stunden = 20 English miles.

Thence to Ober-Gestelen 9¼ stunden = 30¼ English miles.

Ober-Gestelen to Brieg 10¾ stunden = 35 English miles.

A much frequented, but rather difficult, bridle-path. It is a good day's journey of 8 hours to reach the Hospice from Meyringen, though a stout pedestrian might push on in one day either to Ober-Gestelen, or across the Furca to Hospital.

It is one of the grandest and most interesting passes across the Alps.

Above Meyringen (p. 81) the vale of Hasli contracts, and in about 2 miles is crossed by a mound or hill of considerable height, called the Kirchet, which appears at one time to have dammed up the waters of the Aar. At present they force their way through a singularly narrow rent, which cleaves the eminence from top to bottom. The path, quitting for a short time the side of the river, mounts this steep in zigzags, and then descends through a forest, into the retired green valley of Upper Hasli, which is in the form of a basin, surrounded by hills, and was once probably a lake. Two valleys open out into it; on the W. that of Urbach, on the E. that of Gadmen, up which runs the path leading by the pass of the Susten (Route 32) to Wasen. On the rt. lies the village Im-Grund, and, crossing the Aar, another village, called Im-Hof, situated between it and the Gadmen river, is passed. Another ravine is succeeded by a second enlargement of the valley called Im-Boden. Higher up is " the small and lonely village" of

3 Guttanen, where there is an inn; but the best place for a mid-day halt to rest the mules is the chalet of

1¼ The Handek, about 1½ hour's walk beyond Guttanen. It can furnish a bed upon an emergency, and refreshments only of a very humble kind—such as milk, cheese, kirschwasser, and spirit of gentian. It stands at the distance of a few yards from the *Falls of the Aar*, perhaps the finest cataract in Switzerland, from its height (more than 100 feet), the quantity and rush of water, the gloom of the gorge into which it precipitates itself, and the wild character of the rocky solitude around it. It is also remarkably easy of access, so that the traveller may form a full estimate of its grandeur; surveying it, first, from below, through the vista of black rocks into which it plunges, and afterwards from above, stretching his neck over the brow of the precipice from which the river takes its leap, and watching it (if his nerves be steady) till it is lost in the spray of the dark abyss below.

The view from this point, not more than 5 or 6 feet above the fall, which few will hesitate to call the best, is exceedingly impressive and stimulating. So plentiful is the rush of water that it reaches more than half way down in one unbroken glassy sheet before it is tossed into white foam; and, what adds to its beauty, is, that another stream (the Erlenbach), pouring in from the right at this very spot, takes precisely the same leap, mingling its tributary waters midway with the more powerful column of the Aar.

The dark forest of fir through which the route has wound for a considerable distance, now dwindles away into a few dwarf bushes, and disappears entirely a little above Handek. To them succeed the scanty vegetation of rank grass, rhododendron, and lichen; and even this partial covering disappears prematurely, in some places being abraided and peeled off by the avalanches. There is a spot about 2 miles above Handek, where they descend in winter, directly across the path, and in their course

over the sloping and convex mass of granite, have ground smooth, and polished its surface for a space of nearly a quarter of a mile. It is prudent to dismount here, and cross this bad bit of road (Böseplatte) on foot, since the path runs by the edge of the precipice, and the surface of the rock, though chiselled into grooves, to secure a footing for the horses, is very slippery. A single false step might be fatal to man and beast, precipitating both into the gulph below: the slight wooden rail, which is swept away almost every winter, would afford but little protection. The valley of the Aar, up which the narrow path is carried, looks stern and forbidding from its sterility, and the threatening cliffs of granite which overhang it. The Aar is crossed several times by dizzy bridges of a single arch, formed of granite slabs, without a parapet. There is but one human habitation between Handek and the Hospice, the miserable chalet of the Räterisboden, or Roderichsboden, where the ravine expands once more into a basin-shaped hollow, probably once a lake-bed, with a marshy bottom, affording scanty herbage for a few goats. A little above this the path quits the Aar, which rises in the Aar-glacier, about a mile higher up on the rt., and ascending a glen, strewed with shattered rocks, reaches

2 The *Hospice of the Grimsel*, an inn of the rudest kind, originally designed to shelter travellers from necessity, and afford a gratuitous aid to the poor; but now daily occupied during the summer months by travellers for pleasure, sometimes to the number of 40 or 50 at once, who pay for their accommodation, as in any other inn, and sit down at a table d'hôte usually about 7 o'clock in the evening: the fare is plain, not delicate, but the charges are not high. It is a massy building of rough masonry, designed to resist a weight of snow, and with few windows to admit the cold. It contains

about 20 beds, and affords such homely fare as may reasonably be expected in a spot 6000 feet above the sea, and removed by many miles from any other human dwelling. It is occupied by the innkeeper, who rents it from March to November. One servant passes the winter in the house, with a provision of cheese, to last out the whole time, sufficient to support himself and any chance wanderer who might accidentally pass that way. Its situation is as dreary as can be conceived. It lies in a rocky hollow, about 1000 feet below the summit of the pass, surrounded by soaring peaks and steep precipices. The rocks around are bare and broken, scarcely varied by patches of snow, which never melt, even in summer, and by strips of grass and green moss, which shoot up between the crevices, and are eagerly browsed by a flock of goats. A considerable supply of peat is dug from a bog within a few yards of the door. In the bottom of this naked basin, close to the house, is a black tarn, or lake, in which no fish live. Beyond it lies a small pasturage, capable of supporting, for a month or two, the cows belonging to the hospice, and the servants cross the lake twice a-day, in a boat, to milk them. It is a landscape worthy of Spitzbergen or Nuova Zembla. This wilderness is the haunt of the marmot, whose shrill whistle frequently breaks the solitude; and the chamois, become rare of late, still frequents the neighbouring glaciers; both animals contribute at times to replenish the larder of the Hospice.

On the 22nd March, 1838, the Hospice was overwhelmed and crushed by an avalanche, which broke through the roof and floor, and filled all the rooms but that occupied by the servant, who succeeded with difficulty in working his way out through the snow, along with his dog, and reached Meyringen in safety. The evening before, the man had heard a mysterious sound, known to the peasants of the Alps, and believed by them to be the warn-

ing of some disaster: it appeared so like a human voice that the man supposed it might be some one in distress, and went out with his dog to search, but was stopped by the snow. The next morning the sound was again heard, and then came the crash of the falling avalanche. The Hospice will probably be repaired in the course of the summer (1838), but the traveller should ascertain beforehand in what state it is.

During the campaign of 1799 the Austrians actually encamped for some time upon the top of the Grimsel, and during their stay gutted the Hospice, using every morsel of woodwork for fuel. Every attempt of the French General Lecourbe to dislodge them had failed, when a peasant of Guttanen, named Nägeli, offered to conduct a detachment by a circuitous path, known only to himself, to the rear of the Austrian position, on condition that the mountain he was about to cross should be given to him as his reward. This being agreed to, a party, commanded by General Gudin, led by Nägeli over the Döltihorn and the glaciers of Ghelman, fell upon the Austrians unawares, from a point above that which they occupied. They were seized with a panic and fled at once; many in the direction of the glacier of Aar, where escape was hopeless, and those who were not shot by the French, perished in the rents and chasms, where human bones, rusty arms, and tattered clothes are even now met with, and attest their miserable fate. The guide of the French did not profit by his barren mountain, remaining as poor as before he became possessed of it, but it has since been called after him, Nägeli's Grätli.

The source of the Aar lies in two enormous glaciers, the Ober and Unter-Aar-Gletscher, to the W. of the Hospice. The Unter-Aar glacier is the best worth visiting, and may be reached in 2 hours. It is remarkable for the evenness of the surface of ice and the rareness of cavities on its surface. In places it is covered with accumulated rubbish which has fallen from the granite rocks around. It is about 18 miles long, and from 2 to 4 broad. Out of the midst of it rises the Finster-Aar-horn; the Schreckhorn is also conspicuous. There is no danger and little difficulty in exploring it for 2 or 3 hours, accompanied by a guide; and a path has recently been made by which it is accessible even on horseback. Hugi traversed the whole glacier in this manner on a horse hired from the Hospice.

The best panorama of the Grimsel and the neighbouring peaks and glaciers may be seen from the top of the Seidelhorn, a mountain on the rt. of the path leading to Brieg and the Furca; its summit may be reached in 3 hours from the Hospice: it is 8634 feet above the sea-level.

The summit of the pass of the Grimsel (7016 feet above the sea) is 2 miles from the Hospice—a steep path, marked only by tall poles stuck into the rock to guide the wayfarer, leads up to it. On the crest lies another small lake, called Todten See, or Lake of the Dead, because the bodies of those who perished on the pass were thrown into it by way of burial. Along the crest of the mountain runs the boundary-line between Berne and the Vallais, and here the path divides—that on the l. side of the lake leads by the Meyenwand to the glacier of the Rhone (distant about 5 miles), and to the pass of the Furca (Route 30); that on the rt. of it goes to Ober-Gestelen, but it would be worth the while of the traveller bound thither to make a detour of about 6 miles to visit the glacier and source of the Rhone. By the direct road it is a walk of 6 miles from the summit to

3 Ober-Gestelen (Fr., Haut Cha-tillon). The inn, kept by Bertha, used to be a decent house. This is the highest village but one (Ober-wald being the highest) in the Upper Vallais, and is 4360 feet above the sea-level. It is situated on the rt.

bank of the Rhone, about 8 miles below its source in the glacier. It i the depôt for the cheese transporte out of Canton Berne into Italy, and is a place of some traffic, as it lies a the junction of the three bridle-roads over the Grimsel, the Furca, and the Gries (Route 29).

In 1720, 84 men were killed here by an avalanche.

The descent of the Upper Vallais to Brieg, a distance of 35 miles, is very uninteresting. The road runs along the rt. bank of the Rhone. For a part of the way it is practicable for chars, and will be finished, it is said, *all the way*, in two or three years. (?) Opposite the village of Ulrichen, the valley of Eginen opens out—up it runs the path leading over the Gries and the Nufanen (Route 35).

The Upper Vallais (Ober-Wallis) is very populous, and numerous unimportant villages are passed in rapid succession. One of the largest is Münster, containing about 400 inhabitants. The natives of the Upper Vallais are a distinct and apparently superior race to those of the Lower. The language is German. The Romans never penetrated into the higher part of the Rhone valley.

4 Viesch lies at the entrance of a side-valley, blocked up at its upper extremity by a glacier, above which rise the peaks called Viescher-Hörn-er. There exists a tradition, that a path once led up this valley to Grindelwald: it is now entirely stopped by the glacier, and this circumstance is supposed to prove a great increase of the mass of ice. From Lax to Brieg the char-road is completed.

The stream of the Massa, descending from the W., is supplied by the great glacier of Aletsch, a branch of that vast expanse of ice which extends to Grindelwald in Canton Berne (§ 17).

3¼ Naters, a village of 600 inhabitants, lies in a milder climate, where the chestnut begins to flourish. Above it rises the ruined castle of Fluh, or Saxa (Supersax).

A wooden bridge leads across the Rhone to ½ *Brieg*, at the foot of the Simplon (Route 59).

ROUTE 29.

PASS OF THE GRIES. OBER-GESTELEN TO DOMO D'OSSOLA, BY THE VAL FORMAZZA (POMMAT), AND THE FALLS OF THE TOSA.

About 14 stunden = 46 Eng. miles. A mule-path, not dangerous, though it crosses a glacier, but difficult and very fatiguing. A guide should be taken over the Col.

The inns on the Italian side of the pass are wretched, but the traveller will be rewarded by its scenes of wildness and grandeur, which, according to Brockedon, " are nowhere exceeded among the Alps."

Below Ober-Gestelen (page 86) a bridge leads across the Rhone, and the path follows the l. bank as far as the village Im Loch, where it turns to the l., and begins to ascend the Eginenthal, crossing the stream of the Eginen above a pretty cascade 80 feet high, which it forms. A hard climb of about 2 hours, first through larchwood, then across a steril, stony tract, and finally over a little plain of green meadow, dotted with the chalets of Egina, brings the traveller to the foot of the final and most difficult ascent. Near this point a path, striking off on the l., leads over the pass of the Nüfanen (Route 35) to Airolo. Here vegetation ceases, snow appears first in patches, and at last the glacier blocks up the termination of the valley. It takes about 20 minutes to cross it. The direction of the path over the ice is marked by poles stuck upright in the ice. Along the crest of the mountain runs the frontier-line separating Switzerland from Sardinia. The summit of the pass is 7900 feet above the sea.

" Bare and scathed rocks rose on either side in terrible grandeur out of the glaciers to an immense height. The silence of the place added greatly to its sublimity; and I saw, in this most appropriate spot, one of the large eagles of the Alps, the Lämmergeyer, which was whirling its flight round a mountain-peak, and increased the deep emotion excited by the solitude of the scene."— *Brockedon.*

In clear weather a magnificent view presents itself from this point of the chain of Bernese Alps. The descent on the Sardinian side of the pass (as usual among the Alps) is steeper than that on the N.; it is also more difficult. The upper part of the Piedmontese valley of Formazza, or Frutval, presents four distinct stages or platforms, separated by steep steps or dips from each other. The first is called Bettelmatt; the second, Morast (morass), on which the miserable group of chalets, called Kehrbächi (the highest winter habitations), are situated; the third, is Auf der Frutt, with another hamlet of chalets, and a small chapel. Before reaching it, the traveller falls in with the river Toccia, or Tosa, which rises in the upper extremity of the valley, and terminates in the Lago Maggiore. Beyond the hamlet the path crosses to the l. bank of the stream, and, descending the fourth steep declivity, arrives at the *Falls of the Tosa*, the approach to which has for some time previously been proclaimed by the increasing roar of the water. It is one of the most remarkable cataracts among the Alps, less on account of its form than for its vast volume of water, in which it is surpassed only by that of the Schaffhausen. It does not descend in one leap, but in a succession of steps, forming an uninterrupted mass of white foam for a length of perhaps 1000 feet, while the entire perpendicular descent is not much less than 500. Seen from below, it has a triangular appearance; above, not more than 80 feet wide, and expanding gradually towards the bottom.

2 miles below the Falls is the vil-

lage of Frutval, situated on the 4th plateau, whose inn affords accommodation of the most wretched kind. Two miles farther is the village of Formazza, also called in the Italian Al Ponte, and in German Zumsteg and Pommat. The inhabitants of the upper part of the valley, as far as Foppiano, are of German descent, speaking that language; and, according to tradition (?), descendants of a colony from the Entlebuch. Owing to this intermixture of languages almost all the villages have a German as well as Italian name. Formazza is about 23 miles from Ober-Gestelen. The inn here is called the Cross (Kreutz).

The lower part of the vale of the Tosa abounds in exquisite scenery. The Gorge of Foppiano (Germ. Unter-Stalden), 5 miles below Formazza, is particularly grand. Lower down it expands, and displays all the softer beauties of high cultivation, luxuriant vegetation, and thick population. Below the village called Premia, a stream descending from the W. joins the Tosa, and the valley changes its name into Val Antigorio.

"The savage grandeur of the Val Formazza, down which the river takes its passage, and the delicious region through which it rolls in the Val Antigorio, cannot be painted in too glowing colours. In these high valleys, fully exposed to the power of the summer sun, there is truly a 'blending of all beauties.' The vine, the fig, and the broad-leafed chestnut, and other proofs of the luxuriance of the soil of Italy, present themselves everywhere to the eye, intermixed with the grey blocks resting on the flanks and at the feet of the high granite ridge, out of whose recesses you have not as yet escaped. Instead of the weather-stained and simple habitation of the hardy Vallaisan, sheltered by the bleak belt of forest, upon which alone I had glanced yesterday, I now saw, on the southern declivity of the same range, the substantial Italian structure, with its regular outline and simple yet beautiful proportion, and the villa, the handsome church, or the stone cottage, surrounded by its girdle of vines—the vine, not in its stiff and unpicturesque Swiss or Rhenish dress, but the true vine of Italy and of poetry, flinging its pliant and luxuriant branches over the rustic veranda or twining its long garland from tree to tree."—*Latrobe.*

This charming valley is the chosen retreat of numerous retired citizens, such as bankers, jewellers, &c., who have built themselves villas in it. The mica-slate rocks occurring near Premia and San Michele, are stuck as full of red garnets as a pudding is with plums.

At Credo there is a Sardinian Custom-house. The road then crosses the river twice, before it reaches San Marco, and about two miles farther enters the *Simplon road*, at the lofty and beautiful bridge of Crevola, near the junction of the Vedro with the Tosa (Route 59).

3 miles farther on lies *Domo d'Ossola.*

ROUTE 30.

PASS OF THE FURCA, FROM THE GRIMSEL, TO HOSPITAL ON THE ST. GOTHARD, BY THE GLACIER OF THE RHONE.

About 7 stunden = 23 Eng. miles.

A bridle-path, by no means dangerous, and not very difficult, excepting the part between the summit of the Grimsel and the glacier of the Rhone, which it is better to cross on foot than on horseback. The distance from the Hospice of the Grimsel to the glacier of the Rhone is about 5 miles. On reaching the summit of the pass (p. 86), the path leaves on the rt. hand the gloomy little Lake of the Dead, and, skirting along the brink of a precipitous slope, called the Meyenwand, descends very rapidly. This portion of the road is the worst of the whole, being very steep, slippery, and muddy, in consequence of the melting snow, which generally lies near the summit. However, it soon brings the traveller in sight of the glacier, though at a considerable depth below him. On attaining the bottom of the valley he will find a very rustic cabaret, affording refreshment of some kind, and a bed upon an emergency. N.B. Its character as a house of entertainment is said to have improved of late. About half a mile above it the Rhone issues out to day at the foot of the *Rhone Glacier*, one of the grandest in Switzerland, fit cradle for so mighty a stream. It fills the head of the valley from side to side, and appears piled up against the shoulder of the Gallenstock, whose tall peak overhangs it. The source of the Rhone, in a cavern of ice, is about 5400 ft. above the sea. The path leading to the Furca ascends along the E. side of the valley, having the glacier on the l. for a considerable distance. From this point the best view is obtained of this magnificent sea of ice, and a correct idea may be formed of its extent and thickness as the traveller passes within stone's-throw of its yawning crevices. The path then turns off to the rt., mounting upwards through a valley of green pastures to the summit of the pass, or *Fork*, between two mountain-peaks, from which it receives its name. From this point, 8300 feet above the sea, near the Cross which marks the boundary of the cantons of the Vallais and of Uri, there is a beautiful view of the Bernese Chain, the Finster-Aar-Horn being pre-eminent among its peaks. The top of the Furca is never altogether free from snow: there is no plain or level surface on it. The descent commences, as soon as the crest is crossed, into the valley of the Sidli Alp, which is covered with pastures, but monotonous and uninteresting in its scenery and destitute of trees. The traveller must pick his way as he best may among a multitude of deep ruts, cut by the feet of mules and cattle. Except a few scattered chalets, no human habitation occurs between the Chalet of the Rhone Glacier and the small hamlet of Realp, where refreshments may be obtained from the Capuchin monks, who have a small chapel and convent of ease here, in which they receive strangers. It is about 4 miles from hence to Hospenthal, on the St. Gothard (Route 34).

ROUTE 31.

PASS OF THE SURENEN, FROM STANZ-STADT, AND BUOCHS, TO ALTORF, BY THE CONVENT OF ENGELBERG AND THE BASE OF THE TITLIS.

13¾ stunden = 45 Eng. miles.

There is a good char-road as far as Engelberg ; thence to Altorf, across the pass, a very difficult foot-path.

Stanzstadt, the landing-place for those coming from Lucerne, is a small village on the margin of the lake immediately opposite Winkel (p. 57), under the Rotzberg, whose ruined castle is an historical monument (see p. 57). Stanzstadt is distinguished by its tall watch-towers, 5 centuries old. In 1315, a little before the battle of Morgarten, a vessel laden with Austrian partisans was crushed and swamped by a mill-stone hurled from the top of this tower. An avenue of walnut-trees leads, in 2 miles, to Stanz.

Travellers coming from Brunnen, or from the E. end of the lake of Lucerne, land at Buochs, a village at the foot of the Buochser-Horn. It has no good inn, but can furnish chars or horses. Like Stanzstadt, it was destroyed by the French in 1798. It is 3 miles from

Stanz. *Inns:* Krone (Crown) ; Engel (Angel). Capital of the lower division (Nidwalden) of Canton Unterwalden, contains 1200 inhabitants. It was in the *Rathhaus* of Stanz that the venerable Swiss worthy Nicolas

Von der Flue appeased the burning dissensions of the confederates, in 1481, by his wise and soothing councils. In the existing building there is a picture (? daub) representing him taking leave of his family. In the market-place is a statue of Arnold of Winkelried, a native of Stanz (see page 13), with the " sheaf of spears " in his arms. His house is also shown here, but it seems modern, or at least is modernized. The field on which it stands is called in old records " the meadow of Winkelried's children. On the outer walls of the bone-house, attached to the handsome *Parish-Church,* is a tablet to the memory of the unfortunate people of Nidwalden (386 in number, including 102 women and 25 children) who were massacred in defending their homes by the French in September, 1798. In that year this division of the canton was the only part of Switzerland which refused the new constitution, tyrannically imposed on it by the French republic. The ancient spirit of Swiss independence, fanned and excited by the exhortations of the priests (which in this instance must be termed fanatic,—as all resistance was hopeless and useless), stirred up this ill-fated community to engage an army ten times greater than any force they could oppose to it, and consisting of veteran troops. At a time when the larger and more powerful cantons had yielded, almost without a struggle, the brave but misguided men of Unterwalden and Schwytz afforded the solitary proof that Swiss bravery and love of freedom was not extinct in the land of Tell. Their desperate resistance, however, served only to inflame the fury of their foes.

After a vain attempt made by the French to starve the Unterwaldeners into submission, " on the 3rd of September, 1798, General Schauenberg, the French commander, directed a general attack to be made, by means of boats, from Lucerne, as well as by the Oberland. Repulsed with great

spirit by the inhabitants, only 2000 strong, the attack was renewed every day from the 3rd to the 9th of September. On this last day, towards two in the afternoon, new reinforcements having penetrated by the land-side, with field-pieces, the invaders forced their way into the very heart of the country. In their despair the people rushed on them with very inferior arms. Whole families perished together ; no quarter was given on either side. Eighteen young women were found among the dead, side by side, with their fathers and brothers, near the chapel of Winkelried. Sixty-three persons, who had taken shelter in the church of Stanz, were slaughtered there, with the priest at the altar. Every house in the open country, in all 600, was burnt down; Stanz itself excepted, which was saved by the humanity of a *chef de brigade.* The inhabitants who survived this day, wandering in the mountains without the means of subsistence, would have died during the ensuing winter, if they had not received timely assistance from the other cantons, from Germany and England, and from the French army itself, after its first fury was abated."—*Simond.*

The attack upon Stanztad was conducted by the celebrated General Foy, afterwards so prominent a leader of the liberal party in France. That unfortunate village was totally consumed.

The distance from Stanz to Engelberg is about 13 miles. The road follows the course of the Aa upwards, gradually ascending, and passing Wolfenschiess with its ruined castle, and Gräfenort, where there is a small inn. Beyond this the valley contracts. The road is carried up a steep ascent nearly 6 miles long, traversing thick woods amidst scenery of the highest sublimity. In the midst of it, in the depth of the valley, lies the village and *Abbey of Engelberg*—(*Inns :* Engel; Rössli) —3220 feet above the sea. It is hemmed in on all sides by lofty mountains topped with snow, and based by precipices, from which, in winter time, and in spring, numerous avalanches are precipitated. At their base, upon a verdant slope, contrasting agreeably with rock and snow, the Benedictine Abbey rises conspicuous among the ordinary habitations of the village. It was founded in 1120, and received from Pope Calixtus II. the name of *Mons Angelorum,* from a tradition that the site of the building was fixed by angels—

" Whose authentic lay,
Sung from that heavenly ground, in middle
    air,
Made known the spot where Piety should
    raise
A holy structure to th' Almighty's praise."
                                Wordsworth.

Having been three time destroyed by fire, the existing edifice is not older than the middle of the last century. " The architecture is unimpressive, but the situation is worthy of the honours which the imagination of the mountaineers has conferred upon it." The convent is independent of any bishop or sovereign but the Pope himself, or his legate: its revenues, once more considerable, were seriously diminished by the French, but it still possesses valuable alpine pastures, and the cheeses produced on them are stored in an adjacent warehouse. It contains, at present, only 19 brothers: it has a large Church and a Library of some value; the roof of the apartment in which it is placed has been cracked by an earthquake. Travellers are received and entertained in the convent — those of the poorer classes gratuitously.

The Titlis, the chief of the mountains which overhang this romantic solitude, rises on the S. of the convent to a height of 7530 ft. above the valley, and 10,570 ft. above the sea-level. Its principal peak, the Nollen, composed of limestone, is said to be visible (?) from Strasburg: it is frequently ascended, and without danger.

It is covered with glaciers, 175 feet thick, from which numerous avalanches fall, in spring, with a roar like thunder.

The difficult pass of the Jöchli (6714 ft.) leads directly from Engelberg, W., into the Melchthal.

From Engelberg to Altorf, by the *Pass of the Surenen,* is a fatiguing journey of 9 hours, about 29 miles. The foot-path reaches, after about 3 miles, the dairy belonging to the convent, called Herrenreuti, where good cheese is made: 50 cows are attached to it; the pastures are refreshed by more than 20 springs rising upon them. From the steep sides of the Hahnenberg, on the N.E., a beautiful water-fall bursts forth, called Dätschbach. The path now winds round the base of a projecting mountain, beyond which the valley makes a bend in a N.E. direction, and, following the course of the Aa for about 6 miles, crosses it, and then turns nearly due E. The Stierenbach, the principal feeder of that stream, is now seen descending in a pretty cascade into the deep abyss. Half an hour's walk below the summit stand a few chalets, and beyond them the traveller has to make his way across a field of perpetual snow, to the summit of the pass, or Sureneck, a narrow ridge not more than 5 ft. wide, between the Blakenstock on the l. and the Schlossberg on the rt., 7220 ft. above the sea. During the greater part of the ascent the Titlis shines forth an object of the greatest magnificence, and a long line of peaks and glaciers extend from it uninterruptedly to the Surenen. Another view now opens out on the opposite side into the valleys of Maderan and Schachen, and is bounded in the extreme distance by the snowy top of the Glärnish in Canton Glarus. On the side of the Surenen, lying within the limits of Canton Uri, the surface of snow to be crossed is greater, and the descent is steeper. Traversing the snow, and a desolate tract covered with broken rocks beyond, the chalets of Waldnacht are passed; and then, by the frightful gorge of Boghy, the path is conducted into the valley of the Reuss, forking off on the rt. to Erstfeld, for those who wish to ascend the St. Gothard—and on the l. to Attinghausen, for those who are bound to Altorf.

In 1799, a division of the French army, under Lecourbe, crossed this pass with cannon to attack the Austrians in the valley of the Reuss, but were soon driven back the same way by the impetuous descent of Suwarrow from the St. Gothard.

Altorf. (See Route 34, p. 94.)

ROUTE 32.

PASS OF THE SUSTEN, FROM MEYRINGEN TO WASEN.

12 stunden = 39¼ English miles.

In 1811, when the Vallais was added by Napoleon to the French empire, a char-road was constructed from Meyringen to Stein, and on the side of Canton Uri from Wasen to Ferningen, to enable the inhabitants of Canton Bern to convey their produce into Italy through the Swiss territory; but now that circumstances are altered, it has fallen out of repair in many places, and can only be regarded as a bridle-path. The word Sust means toll or customhouse, whence the name. The route of the Grimsel is followed from Meyringen as far as Im-Hof (p. 83), where, quitting the side of the Aar, the path follows the course of the Gadmen, ascending the valley called, at its lower extremity, Muhli-thal, higher up Nessel-thal; and beyond the village of

4¼ Gadmen, Gadmenthal. This village contains 550 inhabitants. The inn, a very sorry one, is at Obermatt, ¾ of a mile higher up. The charroad was not carried further than the chalets of Stein, and a portion of it was destroyed a few years ago

by the sudden advance of the glacier of Stein, which was originally a mile distant from it, descending from a valley on the S. The appearance of the glacier is remarkable, as it assumes a fan shape at its termination. A steep ascent of 1¾ hour brings the traveller to the top of the Susten Pass, 6980 feet above the level of the Mediterranean. The view is very fine; the serrated ridges and the many-pointed peaks of the mountains bounding the Mayenthal, through which the descent lies, especially arrest the attention. There is always some snow on the east declivity of the pass. The first chalets are met with on the Hundsalp. The stream is crossed several times, until at the Hauserbrücke, a considerable distance below Ferningen, the unfinished char-road again commences. Lower down is the village of Meyen. Most of the houses of this valley, which numbers but 400 inhabitants, are protected from the descending avalanches by a stone dyke, or well-propped palisade of wood raised on the hill side behind them, to turn away the falling snow from their roofs. Near the junction of the valleys of the Mayen and the Reuss are shattered remains of an hexagonal redoubt (schanze), which was fortified by the Austrians in 1799, and stormed and taken from them by the French, under Loison, who forced the enemy back up the vale of the Reuss, and, after five assaults, made himself master of Wasen, an important point. A very steep and rough road leads down from this into the village Wasen, on the St. Gothard (p. 96).

ROUTE 34.

THE PASS OF ST. GOTHARD, FROM FLUELLEN, ON THE LAKE OF LUCERNE, TO BELLINZONA.

23 stunden = 75½ English miles.

A posting establishment, not on a

ry perfect footing, has been set on ot by a number of private indivi- als, chiefly innkeepers, in the Can- n Tessin, or Ticino. Their tariff 3 Fr. francs for each horse per post, d 50 centimes to the postilion; d the distances are laid down as low :—

Fluellen to
Hospital, is calculated as 4 posts.

	Relays are kept only
St. Gothard.	on the Italian side, &
Airolo.	as far as Hospital.
Faido.	N.B. The above ta-
Pollegio.	riff was valid in 1834;
Bellinzona.	since that time it
Lugano.	may possibly have
	been altered.

This was anciently perhaps the ost frequented passage over the lps, as it offered the most direct nd practicable line of communica- on between Basle and Zurich, om Northern Switzerland and W. ermany, to Lombardy, and the im- ortant cities of Milan and Genoa. Tot less than 16,000 travellers and 000 horses crossed it annually on an verage, down to the commencement f the present century; but being nly a bridle-path it was almost en- rely abandoned after the construc- ion of the carriage-roads over the Simplon and Bernardin. Deprived f the traffic across it, the inhabitants f the villages traversed by the road, hiefly innkeepers and muleteers, were reduced to ruin, and the reve- nues of the canton, which before drew 20,000 florins annually from the tolls upon it, were seriously di- minished. The cantons of Uri and Tessin, through which this road runs, at length became sufficiently alive to their own interests to perceive the necessity of converting it into a car- riage-road, and thus rendering it fit to compete with the rival routes as a channel of communication and of transport for merchandise. In con- sequence, in 1820, the work was be- gun, and in 1832 finally completed and opened. The expenses were de- frayed by a joint-stock company,

formed in Uri and the neighbouring cantons. The construction of the road was intrusted to an engineer of Altorf, named Müller.

The poverty-stricken canton of Uri had scraped together, with great difficulty, funds sufficient to exe- cute her portion of the undertaking, but a storm, such as had not been known in the memory of man, burst- ing on the summit of the pass, in August 1834, in the course of a few hours swept away nearly one-third of the road, together with bridges and terraces without number, which had been constructed with so much labour, cost, and difficulty. Consi- dering the previous drain upon the resources of the canton, it is sur- prising how soon the mischief was repaired.

At present the road is excellent, not inferior in its construction to any other of the great Alpine highways, and certainly not surpassed by any in the interest and grandeur of its scenery.

The journey between the lake of Lucerne and the Lago Maggiore may be performed in $1\frac{1}{2}$ or 2 days; a courier makes it 2 or 3 times a-week, and takes 1 or 2 passengers in the post- waggon, which runs between Airolo and Bellinzona. No regular relay of post-horses has yet been established in Canton Uri, but horses and chars may be hired at Altorf, Wasen, Airolo, Faido, and Bellinzona. The passage is usually free from snow for 4 or 5 months of the year; but in the depth of winter carriages are safely transported across on open sledges, except immediately after a snow storm, when the road is some- times blocked up for a week.

The canton of Uri and the valley of the Reuss possess an historical celebrity, as the theatre of the me- morable campaign of 1799, when the armies of the three nations of France, Austria, and Russia, dispossessing each other in turns, marched, fought, and manœuvred on heights where the snow never melts, and which were previously deemed accessible only to goatherds and hunters. In the month of June, in the above-named year, the Austrians, aided by the natives of Uri, had expelled the French from the valley. Satisfied with the possession of it, they passed nearly 2 months in entire inactivity, when, by a combined movement, planned by Massena, they were attacked at all points by French corps, poured in upon them from the lake of Lucerne, which was crossed by a flotilla of boats, and from every western passage leading over the Alps and into the valley of the Reuss. Lecourbe crossed the Surenen, Loison the Susten and Gudin, with a large force, fought his way over the Grimsel and Furca, threatening the Austrians in front, in flank, and in the rear. In an engagement which took place on the 14th of August, and which lasted 5 hours, they were driven step by step up the valley, as far as Andermatt. On the two following days the French pursued them out of the valley of the Reuss into the Grisons by the Oberalp, where a bloody encounter took place. A little more than a month after this, intelligence was brought to Lecourbe, the French commander, that another large army had appeared at the S. foot of the St. Gothard. While still at a loss to imagine to what European power it might belong, fresh tidings arrived that the veteran Suwarrow, at the head of a Russian army of 18,000 foot and 5000 Cossack horse, having broken up from his encampment in the plains of Lombardy, had forced the passage of the St. Gothard. The French retired slowly but steadily before them as far as the lake of Lucerne, where Lecourbe, after removing all the boats from Fluellen, entrenched himself in a strong position at Seedorf, on the l. bank of the Reuss. Suwarrow, whose object was to unite himself with the Russian army before Zurich, of the defeat of which by Massena he

had not yet heard, here found himself without the means of transporting his army, threatened on all sides by enemies. He took little time to consider, but immediately planned and executed his wonderful and almost incredible retreat over the Kinzig Culm and into the valley of Motta; and, though constantly annoyed by the French in his rear, finally conducted his army into the valley of the Rhine, with a loss of 3000 men, of whom more perished from cold, fatigue, and hunger, than from the enemies' bullets. (See Routes 72, 74 and 76.)

Fluellen (in Italian Fiora)—(*Inn* Croix Blanche; good)—the port of the Canton Uri, at the S. extremity of the lake of the Four Cantons, is a small village in a most unhealthy situation, as is proved by the pale faces, crippled limbs, and goitred necks of its inhabitants; and by the number of cretins among them. The malaria, from the marshy ground, produced by the deposits of the Reuss at its entrance into the lake, is the cause of this. Boats may be hired here to convey carriages and passengers to Brunnen or Lucerne. The plan of continuing the road along the margin of the lake to Brunnen has been proposed, but in Switzerland such projects are talked of very long before they are put into execution. In 1838 the *steam-boat* commenced plying on the lake (Route 18, p. 51). Chars are let for hire to convey travellers along the St. Gothard road. About 2 miles off lies

½ *Altdorf*—(*Inns :* Adler, Eagle; Löwe, Lion)—the capital of the canton of Uri, the poorest and least populous in the confederation, numbering altogether only 13,000 souls, is a dull lifeless village of 1664 inhabitants, without trade or manufactures, and still exhibiting signs of the conflagration of 1799, which reduced the larger part of it to ashes. Its only claim to interest the traveller is its connexion with William Tell. If redit is to be given to tradition, it was on the open square in the centre of Altdorf that he shot the apple from off his son's head. The place where e stood to take aim is marked by a stone fountain, surmounted with statues of the dauntless cross-bowman and his child. The lime-tree, upon which Gessler's cap was stuck, for all men to do obeisance to it as they passed, and to which the child was bound, to serve as a mark for his father's bolt, existed, a withered trunk, down to 1567, when it was cut down and replaced by the other fountain.

The tall *Tower*, ornamented with rude frescos, representing Tell and Gessler, has been stated erroneously by some writers to occupy the site of the lime-tree; but it is proved by records, still in existence, to have been built before the time of Tell.

On quitting Altdorf the road crosses the mouth of the vale of Schachen, traversing, by a bridge, the stream in which, according to tradition, William Tell lost his life (1350) in endeavouring to rescue a child from its waters swollen by an inundation. He was a native of the Schachenthal, having been born in the village of Bürglen, a little to the l. of our road. A small *Chapel* still standing, rudely painted with the events of his life, was built in 1522 on the spot where his house stood, near the churchyard. The inhabitants of this valley are considered the finest race of men in Switzerland. A path runs up it, and across the Klausen Pass (Route 72), to the baths of Stachelberg, in Canton Glarus, and another over the Kinzig Culm, into the Muotta Thal.

On the l. bank of the Reuss, opposite its junction with the Schachen, stands Attinghausen, the birth-place of Walter Fürst, one of the three liberators of Switzerland ; his house is still pointed out. Above it rise the ruins of a castle, whose baronial owners became extinct in 1357, when the last of the race was buried in his helmet and hauberk. At Bötzlingen, 3 miles above Altdorf, the parliament (Landesgemeinde) of the canton Uri is held every year, on the first Sunday in May, to settle the affairs of the state. Every male citizen above the age of 20, except a priest, has a vote. The authorities of the canton, on horseback, with the Landammann at their head, preceded by a detachment of militia, with military music, and the standard of the canton, attended by the beadles in their costume of yellow and black, and by two men in the ancient Swiss garb of the same colour, bearing aloft the two celebrated buffalo horns of Uri, march to the spot in procession. From a semicircular hustings, erected for the purpose, the business of the day is proclaimed to the assembled crowd, and the different speakers deliver their harangues, after which the question is put to the vote by show of hands. When all affairs of state are despatched, the Landammann and other public officers resign, and are either re-elected or others are chosen in their place.

"The first part of the way, towards the St. Gothard, lies through agreeable scenery, among rich meadows, shaded by chestnut and walnut trees." —*L.*

At Klus it approaches the margin of the Reuss, and beyond Silinen, where it is partly cut through the rock, passes under the ruins of a tower, by some supposed to be the castle of *Zwing Uri* (Restraint of Uri), the construction of which by the tyrant Gessler, to overawe the peasants, roused the suspicion and indignation of the Swiss ; so that it was demolished by them in 1308, on the first outbreak of the revolt against Austria. Under it, upon the high road, is situated the village of

3 Amsteg—(*Inns:* Hirsch; Stern ;) —on the high road and at the mouth of the *Maderaner Thal,* which

stretches E. as far as the base of Mount Dödi, a valley little visited, but well worth exploring; abounding in waterfalls and glaciers.

The road now first crosses the Reuss and begins to ascend, having on the l. hand the gigantic mass of the Bristenstock; and on the rt. the river below, dashing from rock to rock in an almost uninterrupted cataract. A second bridge carries it back to the rt. bank; and, after traversing a wood, a third, called Pfaffensprung (priest's leap), from a fable of a monk having leaped across it with a maiden in his arms, brings the traveller to

2 Wasen, or Wesen—(*Inn* : Ochs) —a village of 550 inhabitants, on the l. bank of the Reuss, at the mouth of the Mayenthal, up which runs the road to the Susten (Route 32). Near this a toll of ½ a batz for each person, and 5 or 6 batz for every horse, is paid. Winding from side to side the road slowly toils upward to Göschenen, where the valley assumes a more savage character, contracting into the narrow ravine of Schellinen, bounded for nearly 3 miles by impending cliffs of granite. One vast fragment, skirted by the road, was dropped here, according to the popular legend, by the devil, and is thence called *Teufelstein.* "This defile exceeds all that one can imagine of desolation and awful grandeur; the walls of rock seem almost to exclude the light of day, scarce a blade of grass is to be seen, and nothing heard but the wild dashing of the Reuss at the foot of the precipice below the road, from which hoarse sounds this part of the valley gets the name of Krachenthal."—*L.* This part of the road is much exposed in spring to danger from avalanches, on which account galleries have been constructed to cover it in 1 or 2 places. The difficulties of the ascent are here overcome by the skill of the engineer, who constructed a series of complicated zigzag terraces, first on one side of

the Reuss, and then on the othe by means of which, and of numerou bridges, the traveller at lengt reaches

The *Devil's Bridge*, situated i the midst of the most stern bu magnificent scenery of the whol pass. The Reuss leaps down int the head of this savage gorge, i a lofty cataract, and in the ver midst of its din and spray 2 bridge have been thrown across. Vertica rocks hem in the bed of the river o both sides; those on the left ban especially, are perfectly smooth an perpendicular, leaving not an incl of space for the sole of a foot at thei base, except what has been hewn ou of it by human art. For ages thi must have been an impassable den a complete cul-de-sac, until, by hu man ingenuity, the torrent wa bridged and the rock bored through The old bridge, a thin segment of circle, spanning a terrific abyss, ha originally an air at once of bold ness and fragility, much of which i has lost by the contrast with th towering and more solid structur which has now entirely superseded it and seems, as it were, to dominee over it, like the horse over the ass in Æsop's fable. The single arch o slight masonry, suspended in the ai at a height of 70 feet above the Reuss, with scarce a parapet at the side, and with barely breadth to allow two persons to pass, almost seemed to tremble with the rushing of the torrent under the feet of the traveller. Modern improvements have deprived the bridge and its vicinity of much of its terror and sublimity. A commodious and gradually-sloping terrace, hewn out of the solid rock at the foot of the precipice, leads to the broad and massive new bridge of 2 arches, which, though nearer to the fall than the old, may be passed without the slightest emotion of the nerves, thanks to its solidity and high parapets. The construction of this part of the road presented great difculties to the engineer from the hardness and smoothness of the precipitous rocks and the want of easy access to them: indeed, the mines necessary for blasting the granite could only be formed by workmen suspended by ropes from above, and dangling in the air like spiders at the end of their threads. The ancient bridge was first founded by Abbot Gerald, of Einsiedeln, in 1118, so that, in the naming of it, the devil has received more than his due. The existing structure, however (which is allowed to remain, though of no use), is by no means the original one. During the extraordinary campaign of 1799, the Devil's Bridge and the defile of the Schellinen were twice obstinately contested within the space of little more than a month. On the 14th of August the united French column, under Lecourbe and Loison, having surprised the Austrians, drove them up the valley of the Reuss, as far as this bridge, which, having been converted into an entrenched position, was defended by them for some time. At last even this was carried by the French, who, in their impetuous pursuit, followed their enemies across the bridge. In a moment, while a crowd of combatants were upon it, it was blown into the air, and hundreds were precipitated into the abyss below. During the night the Austrians, alarmed by the appearance of another French force in their rear, evacuated altogether the valley of the Reuss. On the 24th of September following the tide of war took an opposite turn; Suwarrow, pouring down from the summit of the St. Gothard, at the head of 5000 horse and 18,000 foot, compelled the French, in their turn, to retire before him. The progress of the Russians was arrested here for a short time, as they found the road broken up, the Urnerloch filled with rocks, and the bridge over the Reuss destroyed. A murderous fire from the French swept away all who approached the edge of the chasm; but the Russian columns, eager for advance, by their pressure, pushed the foremost ranks into the foaming Reuss. The impediments in the road were soon removed; an extemporaneous bridge was constructed, by binding together beams of wood with officers' scarfs; and over this the Russian army passed, pursuing the enemy as far as Altdorf.

Immediately after passing the Devil's Bridge the road is carried through a tunnel, bored for 180 feet through the solid rock, called *Urnerloch*, or *Hole of Uri*. It is 15 feet high and 16 feet broad. Previous to its construction, in 1707, the only mode of passing the buttress of rock which here projects into the river, so as to deny all passage, was, by a bridge, or shelf of boards, suspended on the outside by chains from above. By means of this the traveller doubled, as it were, the shoulder of the mountain, enveloped in the spray of the torrent, within a few feet of which the frail structure was hung. The Gallery of Uri was originally constructed by a Swiss engineer, named Moretini; but was only passable for mules, until, in reconstructing the St. Gothard road, it was enlarged to admit carriages.

Out of this gallery the traveller emerges into the wide basin-shaped pastoral valley of Urseren, which, in contrast with the savage gorge of Schellinen, and from the suddenness of the transition, has obtained from most travellers the praise of beauty and fertility. Taken by itself, however, it has little but its verdure to recommend it; owing to its great height, 4356 feet above the sea, scarcely any trees grow in it, and the inhabitants supply themselves with corn for bread from more fortunate lands. It was probably once a lake, until a passage was opened for the Reuss through the rocks of Schellinen. It was originally colonized, it is supposed, by the Rhætians. The usual entrance to it was

by the pass of the Oberalp. Its inhabitants spoke the language of the
Grisons, and the valley was a dependence of the abbot of Dissentis.
Down to the 14th century it remained closed up at its lower extremity,
and had no direct communication
with the lower valley of the Reuss.
About that time, however, a path
seems to have been opened, and the
men of Urseren, allying themselves
with those of Uri, threw off the yoke
of their former feudal lords. A mile
from the gallery of Uri lies

2½ Andermatt, or Urseren (Ital.
Orsera)—(*Inns :* Drei Königen,Three
Kings, good ; Sonne, Sun). It is a
village of 600 inhabitants, and the
chief place of the valley. The cheese
made on the surrounding pastures is
excellent, and the red trout of the
Oberalp See enjoy the reputation,
with hungry travellers, of being
the finest in the world. They are,
at least, an excellent dish, either at
breakfast or dinner. The *Church* of
St. Columbanus is said to have been
built by the Lombards. On the slope
of the mountain of St. Anne, which
is surmounted by a glacier, above
the village, are the scanty remains
of a forest, the last relic of that
which perhaps at one time clothed
the sides of the valley entirely. " It
is of a triangular form, with one of
its angles pointed upwards, and is
so placed as not only to break the
fall of heavy bodies of snow, but to
divide the masses, throwing them off
on its two sides. It is now a slight
and seemingly a perishable defence."
The improvidence of the inhabitants,
at an early period, had reduced it to
a small grove, which those of later
times had learned to value, for
the protection it afforded to their
dwellings from falling avalanches.
They therefore guarded it with the
utmost care, abstaining from cutting
down a stem of it; but, in 1799,
foreign invaders, reckless of the consequences, felled a great part of it,
and consumed it for fire-wood or to
repair the Devil's Bridge. "Weaken-

ed by this inroad, each successiv
year has seen a decrease of thes
all-important sentinels. A few mor
winters, and those that are left ma
be swept away at a single swoop
when it will become necessary t
abandon the village. Such is a
Alpine existence."—*Cooper.*

This was but one of the evils which
that calamitous year brought upo
this remote and peaceful valley,whe
the armies of three nations chose i
for the arena of their combats, lettin
loose the furies, fire, famine, an
slaughter, upon its unfortunate in
habitants. Suwarrow's hordes ar
rived at Andermatt in that year
famished with hunger. Like raven
ous wolves they seized and consume
everything they could lay hands on
They greedily devoured a store o
soap which they found in the larde
of the inn, and, cutting into pieces
some skins which had been hung
out to dry previous to being tanned,
boiled and ate them also.

A bridle-path stretches up the
side valley behind Andermatt, across
the Oberalp, and past its lake, to Dissentis, in the Grisons (Route 77).

The vale of Urseren is about 9
miles long and nearly 1 broad. It
contains 4 villages and 1360 inhabitants, who gain a subsistence by
rearing cattle and keeping dairies,
and by forwarding the transit of goods
across the St. Gothard, for which
purpose 300 horses are kept in it.
At Andermatt, Hospital, and Airolo,
are many mineral dealers, from whom
specimens may be purchased of the
many rare and valuable minerals
with which the range of the St.
Gothard abounds. The variety of
species is surprising, and the cabinet
of the mineralogist derives some of
the rarest substances from these
Alps.

On the l. of the road, in going to
Hospital, two rude stone pillars may
be seen ; they are the *potence* or
gallows, belonging to Andermatt,
dating from the time when the valley
of Urseren was an independent state,

nd Andermatt the chief place in it, njoying the right of criminal juris-iction, now removed to Altdorf. It s curious to observe to what an xtent the possession of a gallows nd the right of hanging criminals nereon, was an object of pride in ncient times. Such relics as this nay be found throughout Switzer-ind : they seem everywhere to have een preserved almost with venera-ion, and are kept in constant repair nough destined never more to be sed.

¾ Hospital, or Hospenthal—(*Inn :* *oldener Löwe* (Golden Lion), good ; aid to be even better than that at Andermatt. Excellent honey here.

Hospital receives its name from an .ospice which no longer exists here. Above the village rises a venerable ower, said to be, like the church of Andermatt, a work of the Lombards. There is a fine collection of minerals ere for sale, formed by two monks : he prices seem high. The mule ath over the Furca (Route 30) leads ence, in 5 hours, to the glacier of he Rhone, and in 2 more to the hos-ice of the Grimsel. Our high road ow quits the valley of Urseren, and ollowing the course of the Reuss, egins to ascend by numerous zigzags o the summit of the St. Gothard, which may be reached in about 2¼ ours from Hospital.

Under the name of St. Gothard are comprised, not merely the depression, or Col, over which the road passes, out a group or clump of mountains, ill exceeding in elevation the snow line, situated between the cantons of Uri, Vallais, Ticino, and Grisons ; and containing the sources of the Rhine, the Rhone, the Reuss, and the Ticino, all of which, with innu-merable tributaries, rise within a cir-cle of 10 miles, described from the summit of the pass.

The river Reuss may be said to fall, rather than flow, into the lake of the Four Cantons. Between Ur-seren and Fluellen it descends 2500

feet, and between Urseren and the top of the pass 2000 feet, forming a succession of cataracts. Near the summit of the pass the road crosses it for the last time by the bridge of Rodunt, which marks the boundary of the Cantons Uri and Ticino. The source of the Reuss is in the small lake of Lucendro, a short distance on the right of the road, 6808 feet above the sea. The summit of the pass is a valley, or saddle-shaped depression, in the great granite ridge of the central chain, overlooked by snow-clad peaks varying between 8000 and 10,000 feet in height. It is a scene of the most complete sterility and desolation : the road winds among several other small lakes or ponds, some of which flow N., but the greater part are feeders of the Ticino, on the S. side of the pass. They may, indeed, be regarded as the head-waters of that river, which gives its name to the Canton Tessin, or Ticino.

2. The *Hospice,* a massive and roomy building, constructed at the expense of the Canton Ticino, which has also caused several houses of refuge to be built, is designed for the accommodation of travellers, being fitted up as an inn, containing 15 beds, and placed under the ma-nagement of two Capuchin friars. Attached to it are warehouses for goods. A very humble house of re-fuge, and a chapel have existed on this spot ever since the 13th century, owing their origin to the Abbot of Dissentis, who stationed a monk here to attend to the spiritual as well as physical wants of distressed travel-lers. In the 17th century, St. Carlo Borromeo suggested the construc-tion of a hospice on a larger scale, which, after his death, was executed by his brother. This building, how-ever, was swept away in 1775, by an avalanche : another which suc-ceeded it, was gutted by the French, while encamped on this spot in 1799-1800, and every particle of wood

burnt as fuel. It has remained ever since a ruin, and the only house for the reception of travellers on this inhospitable height, was the older hospice, converted into a miserable cabaret fit only for carters and muleteers. The new hospice will prove a convenient substitute for this hovel.

The passage in winter and spring is by no means free from danger: the snow is sometimes heaped up in drifts 40 feet high on the summit, and the descent towards Airolo is much exposed at times to tourmentes and avalanches (§ 18). A year seldom passes without the loss of 3 or 4 lives, and at times melancholy catastrophes have occurred. The spot called Buco dei Calanchetti is so called from a party of glaziers from the Val Calanka, who, persisting in pushing on from the hospice, in spite of the warnings of the inmates, were buried here beneath the snow. In 1478, an avalanche swept away a troop of 60 Swiss soldiers: in 1624 another, which fell from the Cassadra, buried 300 persons; and one in 1814 overwhelmed 40 horses laden with goods. The new line of road is carried as much as possible out of the course of these dangers, and though it is unprotected by any covered galleries, accidents of this kind are more rare.

The descent towards Italy displays much skilful engineering; and the difficulties of a slope, much steeper on this side than on the other, have been overcome by a series of zigzag terraces not exceeded in numbers and tortuous direction on any other Alpine pass. They begin a little beyond the old hospice, and continue nearly all the way to Airolo. The turnings are less sharp than on many other passes; and a carriage drawn by horses accustomed to the work may trot down at a quick pace. Near the uppermost zigzag the words *Suwarrow Victor*, in large letters on the face of the rock, record the success of the Russians in gaining the

pass from the French in 1799. was on this ascent that the Ru. sian grenadiers were for some tim arrested by the fire of the Frenc riflemen posted behind rocks an trees. The aged Suwarrow, indig nant at being foiled for the first tim in his life, caused a grave to be dug and lying down in it, declared hi resolution to be buried on the spe where "his children" had been re pulsed. This appeal was respond ed to by his soldiers with warmth and, no sooner did he put him self at their head, than they drov the republicans from their position The upper part of the gully, dow which the road passes, is called Va Tremola (Germ. Trümmeln Thal Trembling Valley, from its suppose effect on the nerves of those wh passed it. Since the new road ha been made its terrors, whatever the were previously, have been muc softened. It is, however, exposed t some danger from avalanches i spring; and one or two houses c refuge have been built to shelter tra vellers. A very pretty minera named from this locality, where i was first found, Tremolite, abound in the rock of the valley, and speci mens of it occur even in the wall and loose stones at the road-side The old road lay along the l. ban of the Ticino; the new keeps on th rt. side of it, and before reaching Airolo makes many wide sweep along the flank of the mountain, u into the Val Bedretto, traversing th forest of Piotella, where the slate rocks are full of crystals of garnet The view up and down the vale o the Ticino, and over the snowy mountains on the opposite side of it is extremely grand.

2½ Airolo (Germ. Eriels)—*Inns* the best is that called the Post, kept by the brothers Camossi: they are dealers in minerals, and have some choice specimens. Airolo lies on the l. bank of the Tessin, near the junction of the branch flowing out of the al Bedretto with that rising on the t. Gothard. It is 3794 feet above the sea-level, and its inhabitants, both in habit and language, are Italian. It possesses two relics of antiquity: an old house called *Il Castello*, and the stump of a tower (Casa dei Pagani), built, it is said, by Desiderius, king of the Lombards, A.D. 774. The Lombard kings constructed a line of similar forts from this all the way to Como, many of which will be passed by the traveller in descending the valley. The situation of Airolo, at the foot of the St. Gothard, and the consequent transit of travellers and goods, are its chief sources of prosperity. The summit of the pass may be reached by a carriage in 3 hours; by the old road a pedestrian might reach it in less than 2. Several mule paths also concentrate here. 1. That leading up the Val Bedretto to the Jufanen pass (Route 35), and to the Fries (Route 29); 2. Over the Leuk-manier into the Grisons; 3. A sum-mer path, and difficult, up the Val Canaria, past the beautiful waterfall of Calcaccia (?), and over the Sella-drat to Andermatt, in 5 hours.

The Val Bedretto terminates about 2 miles below Airolo, at the mouth of the picturesque glen of Stalvedro, which is guarded on the rt. by an-other of the Lombard towers of King Desiderius, and by a third at its lower extremity, near Quinto. This pass was defended in September, 1799, by a body of 600 French against 3000 grenadiers of Suwar-row's army for 12 hours, after which they effected their retreat over the Gries into the Vallais. The part of the valley of the Ticino traversed by the road from this to Biasca is called Val Levantina,—Livinen Thal in Germ. A few miles lower down the river threads another defile, named, after a toll-house within it,

2½ *Dazio Grande*, one of the most picturesque scenes on the whole route. It is a rent in the Monte Piottino (Platifer), nearly a mile long, and so narrow that in ancient times the path down the valley found no access to it, but was carried over the mountains, high above the river on either side. The existing car-riage-road threads the depths of the gorge, supported for a great part of the way on arches and terraces, and crossing the river thrice on bridges. During the storm of 1834 (before alluded to) the swollen Ticino swept away nearly the whole of these costly constructions; the defile was ren-dered totally impassable, and tra-vellers were compelled to find their way by the long-abandoned footpath over the heights.

Chestnut trees first appear soon after quitting the defile of Dazio, and vines are cultivated at

1 Faido—(*Inns;* Angelo;—Sole)—the principal place in the valley, a village of 615 inhabitants. A revolt of the people of the Val Levantine, in 1755, against their tyrannical lords and masters the cowherds of Uri, to whom they had been subject since the XVth century, was terminated on this spot by the execution of the ringleaders, whose heads were fas-tened to the trunks of the vast chest-nut trees, in the presence of 3000 men of the valley. The troops of the Confederation had previously sur-rounded and disarmed this ill-starred band of rebels, and afterwards com-pelled them, on bended knees, to sue for mercy. The revolt was, perhaps, not to be justified; but one thing at least is certain, that the freedom which had been the boast of the Swiss republicans was, down to the end of the last century, denied by them to the states dependent on them, who groaned under a bondage more intolerable than that of any monarchical despotism! A footpath runs from Faido over the Lukmanier (R. 78) to Dissentio.

Through a wilderness of stones and fallen rocks the road reaches

2 Giornico (Germ. Irnis), a vil-lage of 700 inhabitants, containing the following objects of antiquity:—A high tower; the *Church of Santa*

Maria di Castello, whose substructure is said to exhibit traces of a fort, attributed to the Gauls (?), and the Church of San *Nicholas da Mira*, regarded by the vulgar as originally a heathen temple. Both these churches are certainly examples of the earliest form of Christian buildings, and highly deserve the attention of the architect and antiquary. " Service is not performed in St. Nicholas, though it is kept in repair. The architecture is of the rudest Romanesque style, and the E. end offers, perhaps, the most unaltered specimen of the choir raised upon substructions that can hardly be called a crypt, found in the ancient Lombard churches of Italy, distinguished by staircases, whereas it here subsists in its primitive form. The whole neighbourhood is exceedingly picturesque, and deserving at least of quite as much attention as many places which enjoy much more extended reputation."—P.

Half way to Bodio a heap of large rocks (Sassi Grossi) serves as a monument of the victory gained here in 1478 over the Milanese by the Swiss, who had made a foray across the St. Gothard as far as Bellinzona, under pretext of redressing the injury done by the Milanese, in having felled some trees belonging to Canton Uri. The winter had set in with severity, and the main body of the Swiss had returned across the pass with their plunder, leaving behind only about 600 men under Captains Stanga of Giornico, and Troger of Uri. The Milanese, 15,000 strong, pressed forward to expel the highland invaders, who, resorting to stratagem to counteract the preponderance of numbers, laid the flat land in this part of the valley under water, and placing themselves behind it, awaited their enemies at the foot of some rocks. In the course of the night the water froze hard, and next morning, while the advance of the Italians across the ice was naturally slow and faltering, the Swiss, provided with crampons to cross the native glaciers, rushed down upo them in a furious charge, and at onc put them to the rout. Their co fusion was increased by vast mass of rock hurled from the rocks abov by parties stationed for the purpos and the slaughter was enormou According to some accounts 140 according to others 4000, of th Milanese fell on this occasion.

The Val Levantine terminates a li tle beyond Pollegio, at the junction the Blegno. After crossing that riv the traveller reaches Biasca, whic also contains a very ancient *churc* situated on the slope of the hill. chain of chapels, or Via Crucis, lead from it up to the Chapel of S Petronilla, whence there is a pleasin view.

In 1512, an earthquake shook dow from the mountain of Val Crenon near the entrance of the Val Blegn so vast a mass of earth and roc that it arrested the course of th river, and extended high up on th opposite side of the valley. Fo nearly two years so great was th strength of this dam that the water accumulated behind it into a lak many miles in extent, inundatin numerous villages, and driving ou the inhabitants by the rising flood At length, in 1514, it began t flow over the barrier, which, being thus loosened and weakened, sud denly gave way about Easter. The deluge thus occasioned swept of everything before it,—towns, villages houses, and trees, as far as Bellin zona (a part of which was destroyed) and the Lago Maggiore. The accu mulated debris of rocks and mud which it carried down with it covere the cultivated land with desolation, and traces of the ruin thus caused may be still traced along the valley Various causes, conformable with the superstitious notions of the times were assigned for this catastrophe Some attributed it to the vengeance of God against the sins of the inhabitants of Biasca, called forth by the power of a Papal Brief; others traced it to the influence of "certain magicians from Armenia." It is satisfactorily accounted for by the supposition of an earthquake, since at the same time a similar fall took place from the opposite side of the mountain, which buried the village of Campo Bagnino, in the Val Calanka. About 8 miles below Biasca the Moesa is crossed, and our road falls into that from the Pass of the Bernardin (Route 90), near the battle-field of Arbedo, which was as fatal to the Swiss as that of Giornico was to their opponents. An account of it, as well as a full description of

Bellinzona, is given in the above-mentioned route.

ROUTE 35.

PASS OF THE NUFANEN (NOVENA) FROM OBERGESTELEN TO AIROLO.

9 stunden = 29½ English miles. A footpath. It ascends the Vale of Eginen, as in Route 29, but before reaching the Gries Glacier turns to the left, and crossing the ridge of the Nüfanen, 7260 feet above the sea-level, descends into the Val Bedretto. On the s. slope of the pass one of the branches of the river Ticino takes its rise. The path descends along its l. bank to the

6 Hospice al' Acqua, a house of refuge to accommodate travellers, 5000 feet above the sea. A path crosses the valley from this s. into the Val Formazza. The Val Bedretto, from its elevation, has but an inhospitable climate; long winters, and frosts not uncommonly in the height of summer, morning and evening. It is clothed with forests and pastures, from which its 612 inhabitants derive support in summer; while in winter the males migrate to Italy, to seek employment as servants. It is flanked on either side with glaciers and is dreadfully exposed to avalanches (§ 18). The masses of fallen

snow often remain unmelted on the margin of the Ticino till the end of September. At

½ Bedretto, the principal hamlet, the church-tower, which has been once swept away, along with the parsonage, is now protected by an angular buttress, directed toward the side from which the avalanches fall, so as to break and turn them away. In the lower part of the valley a scanty crop of rye is grown.

2¼ Airolo, in Route 34, p. 100.

ROUTE 38.

PASS OF THE GEMMI, THUN, TO THE BATHS OF LEUK (LOECHE), AND TO LEUK IN THE VALLAIS.

17 stunden = 55 English miles.

The Gemmi (pronounced Ghemmi) is one of the most remarkable passes across the Alps. Its scenery is perhaps extraordinary rather than grand, and to be seen to advantage it ought to be approached from the Vallais. There is a good char road as far as Kandersteg, at the N. foot of the pass: the pass itself can only be surmounted on foot or on horseback. The char road recommences at the Baths of Leuk, connecting them with the Simplon road. There are good inns at Kandersteg, and at the Baths.

The first part of the route lies along the beautiful shores of the lake of Thun. Near the tall tower of Strättlingen it crosses the Kander by a lofty bridge. That river originally avoided the lake altogether, and, flowing for some distance parallel to it, behind the hill of Strättlingen, joined the Aar below Thun. Owing to the quantity of mud and gravel which it brought with it, and the slight inclination of its channel in this part of its course, it converted the surrounding district into an unhealthy marsh, and gave rise to a project, which was executed in 1714 at the expense of the canton, of turning the river into the lake of

Thun. This was effected by cutting a canal, 3000 ft. long and 272 ft. broad, into which the river was turned; and which, seen from the bridge in crossing, has much the appearance of a natural ravine. By this change of course the land on the banks of the Aar has been drained and made profitable, while the deposit of sand and stones brought down by the river into the lake has so accumulated as to form a delta around its mouth, extending already nearly a mile from the shore, and annually increasing.

The road passes the mouth of the Simmenthal (Route 41), guarded on one side by the Stockhorn, and on the l. by the Niesen, two noble mountains, between which the valley opens out, a scene of exceeding beauty, with the castle of Wimmis standing as it were in its jaws. On the margin of the lake rises another picturesque castle, that of Spietz. Skirting the base of the pyramidal Niesen we enter the valley of Frutigen, which is remarkable for its verdure and fertility, and may be said to exhibit Swiss pastoral scenery in perfection. Ascending by the side of the Kander we reach

4¾ Frutigen (*Inns :* Ober, and Unter-Landhaus), a village of 900 inhabitants: its houses are for the most part not older than 1826-7, at which time nearly the whole of the buildings were destroyed in two consecutive conflagrations. Behind it the valley divides into two branches: that on the W. leads to the Adelboden; that on the E. (down which flows the Kander) to the Gemmi.

The road passes under the castle of Tellenburg, the residence of the amtman, or bailiff, of the district, and, crossing the Kander, proceeds up its rt. bank to

2½ Kandersteg (*Inn :* Cheval Blanc ; good, clean, and reasonable ; furnishes excellent trout). Chars may be had here to Frutigen—a ride of about 2 hours, for 7½ fr. ; also good mules to cross the mountain to

the baths of Leuk, at about 8 fr. each and 1½ f. to the driver—a journey of 6 hours. Kandersteg is the last village in the valley : its scattered habitations contain about 700 individuals. It is beautifully situated 3280 ft. above the sea, at the N. base of the Gemmi.

Those who have time to spare may be rewarded by walking about 5 miles into the remote valley of Oeschinen, running directly E. from Kandersteg, where, hemmed in by precipices and glaciers, they will find a beautiful clear lake, which mirrors on its smooth surface the snowy peaks of the Blumlis Alp, at whose base it lies.

Above Kandersteg the char-road ceases, and in about 1½ mile from the inn, the ascent of the Pass of the Gemmi commences in earnest. The path lies at first through forests, soon passing the boundary-line of the Cantons Berne and Wallis, and then emerges upon a tract of open pasture land, rendered desolate by the fall of an avalanche from the Rinder Horn, in 1782. The path winds, for a considerable distance, among the fragments of rocks brought down by it. Farther on stands the

3 Solitary inn of Schwarenbach, a mere chalet, affording no other refreshment than cheese, milk, and brandy ; and containing 6 or 8 miserable beds—accommodations which, however humble, are doubtless often most acceptable in such a situation. A small toll is demanded here for the maintenance of the road. A circumstance which occurred on this spot has furnished the German poet, Werner, with the plot of a tragedy, somewhat extravagant and improbable, called " The 24th of February." In the course of the 17th century, a traveller, having the appearance of a foreigner, in crossing the pass, asked for a night's lodging at this hovel. Its tenant was a peasant, whom misfortune had reduced to the depth of poverty and misery. His daughter had been accidentally killed by her brother, while they were both

hildren, and the boy had in conse-
uence disappeared. The man's cat-
le had died, his land had become
arren, and, at the moment of the
tranger's arrival, his creditors had
hreatened to seize all he possessed
nd eject him. Urged by the sight
f the wealth which the stranger
arried, by the presence of want, and
he prospect of escaping detection in
uch a remote solitude, the peasant
onceived and executed the murder
f his guest—plunging his knife into
is booom while he slept. The dying
man ere he breathed his last, had just
ime to reveal to the assassin that he
vas his long-lost child, returned after
an absence of 20 years, virtuous, and
wealthy enough to have raised his
ather above all future distress. He
had delayed discovering himself until
ne could gain his father's affections.
The murderer of his child, it appears,
had also slain his own father, and the
curse of his dying parent had alight-
ed on himself, pursued him through
life, and blighted his existence.
The moment at which the murder
of the stranger was committed
was midnight, on the 24th of February, the anniversary of the paternal
malediction. The guilty wretch,
overwhelmed with remorse, gave
himself up, of his own accord, to justice, and suffered by the hangman.

About 2 miles above this, the path
reaches and winds along the E. margin of a small lake, called Dauben
See, supplied by snow, not by springs,
which often swell it so as to cover
the path: for 8 months of the year it
is frozen. Nothing can exceed the
dreary aspect of the seared and naked
limestone rocks which form the summit of the pass: they seem too barren for even the hardiest lichens.
The culminating point traversed by
the road is 7160 ft. above the sea-
level. From a rocky eminence on
the l. of the path a superb view is obtained of the Monte Rosa, and the
chain of Alps beyond the Rhone, separating the Vallais from Piedmont,
the Weisshorn (Cervin), and the Arc

de Zan. It is one of the most striking views in Switzerland.

Near the verge of the descent
stands a small shed, capable of
affording only partial shelter in a
storm. A little lower down the tra
veller finds himself on the brink of a
precipice, from which a plumb-line
might be thrown into the valley be
low, nearly 1600 ft., almost without
touching the rock, so vertical are its
sides. It is along the face of this
vast wall, that one of the most extraordinary of all the alpine roads, constructed in 1736-41, by a party of
Tyrolese, has been carried. Its zigzags have been very ingeniously
contrived, for in many places the
rocks overhang the path, and an
upper terrace projects farther out
than the one immediately below it.
It varies in width from 3 ft. to 5 ft.,
is bordered at the side by a dry wall,
and is practicable for mules. There
is no danger in it, but its proximity
to the abyss must be a trial for some
nerves.

The wonders of this pass are increased to those who approach it from
the side of Leuk.

"The upper end of the valley, as
you look towards the Gemmi, has all
the appearance of a cul-de-sac, shut
in by a mountain wall. Up to the
very last moment, and until you reach
the foot of the precipice, it is scarcely
possible to discover the way out, or
to tell whither the road goes, or how
it can be carried up a vertical surface of rock. It is a mere shelf—in
some parts a mere groove cut in the
face of the huge cliff, just wide
enough for a mule to pass; and at
the turns of the zigzags you constantly overhang a depth of nearly
500 ft. We were recommended to
dismount in several places, but I believe that the foot of an alpine mule
is seldom *less* sure than that of the
biped he carries. It is yet down this
difficult road that invalids are carried
to the baths: it is the only way of
approaching them from the N., unless you were to make a *slight* detour

of 200 miles by Berne, Friburg, Vevay, and Martigny. Persons who are very infirm are borne on men's shoulders, in a sort of litter, and it is said, often have their eyes bandaged to prevent the shock which might be given to weak nerves by the sight of the terrors of the pathway.

" While at Leuk I copied the following clause, relative to the transport of invalids, from the printed regulations issued by the director of the baths:—' Pour une personne audessus 10 ans il faudra 4 porteurs, si elle est d'un poids audessus de commun 6 porteurs, si cependant elle est d'un poids extraordinaire et que le commissaire le juge nécessaire il pourra ajouter 2 porteurs, et jamais de plus.' I was amused by this provision for excessive corpulence. The ascent from the baths to the summit takes up nearly 2 hours."

2¾ *Baths of Leuk* (Leukerbad, Fr. —Loèche). *Inns:* Maison Blanche ; the best, and good;—Croix d'Or ; several pensions. The accommodation is as good as can be expected, considering that the houses (except the first) are of wood, not very well built, shut up and abandoned from October to May. The fare is tolerable, everything but milk and cheese being brought from the valley below.

The baths consist of 5 or 6 lodging-houses, attached to a hamlet of about 300 inhabitants, situated more than 4500 ft. above the level of the sea, *i.e.* higher than the highest mountain in Great Britain. Its hot springs annually attract a number of visitors, chiefly Swiss and French, during the season, viz., in the months of July and August, though the inns are open from May to October. From the dreariness of the situation, the coldness of the climate, and the defects of the lodgings, few English would desire to prolong their stay here, after satisfying their curiosity by a sight of the place. The baths and adjacent buildings have been three times swept away by avalanches since their establishment in

the 16th century ; and, to guard against a recurrence of the calamity a very strong dyke is now built behind the village to ward off the snow Such danger, however, is passed before the bathing season begins. One of the first patrons of the baths wa the celebrated Cardinal, and Archbishop of Sion, Matthew Schinner.

The springs, to the number of 1 or 12, rise in and around the village and nine-tenths of them run off int the Dala torrent without being used *The chief spring of St. Lawrence* bursts forth out of the ground between the inn and the bath-house ; a rivulet in volume at its source, with a temperature of 124° Far. It is used for the baths after being slightly cooled. The other springs var somewhat in temperature, but little in contents. They contain only a small portion of saline matter, and seem to owe their beneficial effects less to their mineral qualities than to their temperature and the mode of using them. The patient begins with a bath of an hour's duration, but goes on increasing it daily, until at length he remains in the water 8 hours a day—4 before breakfast and 4 after dinner. The usual *cure time* (kur) is about 3 weeks. The want of the accommodation of private baths, and the necessity of preventing the ennui of such an amphibious existence, if passed in solitude, has led to the practice of bathing in common. The principal bath-house is a large shed divided into 4 compartments or baths, each about 20 ft. square, and capable of holding 15 or 20 persons. To each of these baths there are two entrances, communicating with dressing-rooms, one for the ladies, the other for the gentlemen. Along the partitions dividing the baths runs a slight gallery, into which any one is admitted, either to look on or converse with the bathers below. The stranger will be amazed, on entering, to perceive a group of some 12 or 15 heads emerging from the water, on the surface of which float wooden tables, holding coffee-cups, newspapers, snuff-boxes, books, and other aids, to enable the bathers to pass away their allotted hours with as small a trial to their patience as possible. The patients, a motley company, of all ages, both sexes, and various ranks, delicate young ladies, burly friars, invalid officers, and ancient dames, are ranged around the sides on benches, below the water, all clad in long woollen mantles, with a tippet over their shoulders. It is not a little amusing to a by-stander to see people sipping their breakfasts, or reading the newspapers, up to their chins in water—In one corner a party at chess, in another an apparently interesting *tête-a-tête*, is going on ; while a solitary sitter may be seen reviving in the hot water a nosegay of withered flowers. The temperature of the bath is preserved by a supply of fresh water constantly flowing into it, from which the patients drink at times. Against the walls are hung a set of regulations and sumptuary laws for the preservation of order and decorum in the baths, signed by the burgomaster, who enforces his authority by the threat of a fine of 2fr. for the highest offence against his code.

" Ar. 7. Personne ne peut entrer dans ces bains sans être revetue d'une chemise longue, et ample, d'une étoffe grossiére, sous peine de 2fr. d'amende.

" Ar. 9. La même peine sera encouru par ceux qui n'en entreraient pas, ou n'en sortiraient pas d'une maniére decente."

Four hours of subaqueous penance are, by the doctor's decree, succeeded by one hour in bed ; and many a fair nymph in extreme *négligé*, with stockingless feet, and uncoifed hair, may be encountered crossing the open space between the bath and the hotels. From their condition one might suppose they had been driven out of doors by an alarm of fire, or some such threatening calamity.

The principal curiosity of the neighbourhood is the *Ladders* (Leitern). A rough path through the woods, on the l. or E. side of the Dala, about 1½ mile long, leads to the foot of the precipice, which, as before observed, hems in the valley of Leuk on all sides, as with a colossal wall. Upon the summit of this precipice, however, stands a village, called *Albinen;* and the only mode by which its inhabitants can communicate directly with the baths, is by a series of 8 or 10 ladders placed perpendicularly against the face of the cliff. It can hardly be called difficult to climb to the top, but it would not do for any of weak nerves, and a dizzy head, as many rounds of the ladder are loose, others broken ; and the ladders themselves, which are pinned to the crevices of the rock by hooked sticks, are often awry and very unsteady : yet they are traversed at all seasons, day and night, by the inhabitants of the village above—by men as well as women and children, often with heavy burdens. The use of the ladders, which the nature of the sides of the valley render indispensable, has given rise to a singular modification of the dress of the female peasants, which here includes those nether habiliments confined in other parts of the world to men and shrews. Nor are they ashamed of this portion of their attire, as, in climbing the mountains, the petticoat is tucked up, and the wearers do not differ in appearance from boys.

The rocky pass, called Felsen Gallerie, on the opposite side of the Dala, on the way to Siders, near Inden, is a very striking scene.

Mules are kept at the baths, under the direction of a commissaire, to transport travellers : the prices are fixed by a printed tariff (§ 10).

There are two ways from the baths into the valley of the Rhone and the road of the Simplon—the one follows the course of the Dala torrent through the centre of the valley, and conducts, in about 9 miles, to the village of Leuk: it is just passable for a *char à banc*, but is very rough.

2⅔ Leuk (*Inns:* Kreutz; Stern)— a village of 620 inhabitants, on the rt. bank of the Rhone, near its junction with the Dala. A covered bridge over the Rhone connects it with the Simplon road (Route 59). Above it are ruins of two castles, destroyed by the Vallaisans in 1414.

The other, a mule-path carried along the W. side of the valley of the Dala, but high above that river, conducts at once to the town of Sierre (Siders), 15 miles distant, and is a short cut for those who wish to descend the valley of the Rhone towards Martigny and Geneva. It traverses the high pasturages, and beyond them a forest of larch, and passes, first, the village of Imden, near which a most extensive view is gained over the valley of the Rhone, its towns, villages, farms, and old castles. The unsightly debris brought down by the furious torrents issuing from the opposite valley, and the wide expanse of bare gravel overflowed by the Rhone in spring, and converted into a river-channel— but in summer left bare and arid, —give a desolate character to the scene.

Between Imden and another village, called Varen, the road makes an abrupt turn, and the traveller finds himself beneath the shadow of a most tremendous and overhanging precipice. The effect of approaching it from the side of Sierre is grand in the extreme, and totally unexpected, after turning a corner of the rock. The path is carried along a narrow ledge in front of the cliff; beneath it is a gaping abyss, extending nearly down to the bed of the Dala, and above, the rocks lean so far forward, that stones falling from their tops would descend upon the road, and it is therefore partly protected by a roof. This spot is called the *Gallerie*, and was the scene of a

bloody combat in 1799, when the Vallaisans defended this spot for several weeks against the French, effectually checking all attempts to pass, by rolling down stones and logs from above.

A rough and steep descent leads from this, in about 1½ hour, to Sierre, upon the Simplon road (Route 59).

ROUTE 39.

PASS OF THE RAWYL.   THUN TO SION, CROSSING THE GRIMMI.

22 stunden = 72 Eng. miles.

This pass was once more frequented than at present: it is in places difficult and dangerous. It is only practicable on foot, and should not be attempted except by one of sure foot and steady nerves, nor without the aid of an experienced and stout guide.

An der Lenk, at the N. foot of the pass, is a good halting-place; thence to Sion, over the mountain, forms a day's journey.

It is about 12 miles from Thun, along the margin of the lake (see Route 38, p. 103) to

3½ Erlenbach, at the entrance of the Simmenthal. As that valley (described in Route 41) makes a considerable curve, the shortest way to the Rawyl is to strike up the Diemtigen Thal, running nearly due S. from Erlenbach. The pass crosses the stream of the Chivel, and follows its l. bank through Diemtigen and Narrenbach, then crosses it to

2¾ Thiermatten, where there is an inn. About a mile beyond this it again crosses the stream, and, leaving it on the l., gradually ascends to the pass of the Grimmi (5580 ft.). Descending through the Fermel Thal (a fertile valley, only 6 miles long), it reaches

3½ Matten, in the Upper Simmenthal. About 4 miles above this, on the l. bank of the Simmen, lies the village of

1¼ An der Lenk—(*Inns: Bär ; Kreutz ;*)—beautifully situated, surrounded by high peaks and glaciers. "The Wildstrubel (11,000 feet), with the waste of snowy glaciers beneath it, forms the most striking and prominent feature, rising into the air above an unusually long line of grey precipices, down which 10 or 12 cascades are seen rolling into the country at the base."—*Latrobe.*

The Simmen rises about 6 miles above An der Lenk, at the foot of the glacier of Razliberg, from a source called the Seven Fountains. In the source itself there is little to compensate for the trouble of the ascent to it, but the scenery around it is of great grandeur. Between it and An der Lenk the Simmen forms several cascades.

The direct road from Lenk over the Rawyl to Sion, a distance of 11 leagues, or 30 miles, adheres to the W. side of the valley, and instead of proceeding to the source of the Simmen, ascends by the bank of its tributary, the Iffigenbach, flowing from the S.W. to Iffigen, a group of wretched chalets, at the foot of the Rawyl (Les Ravins). A series of short zigzags lead up the mountain over fallen rocks and detached patches of snow, crossing the channel grooved by the descending avalanches; and then along a ledge, in many places not a foot broad, with a precipice on one side and an abyss on the other. "When about 1500 feet above the Iffigenthal the path becomes more and more hazardous. . . . Here one cascade, from the higher part of the precipice, flies over the head of the passenger as he creeps between it and the rock ; and there, in a black and dismal rift, round which the pathway winds, a second falls upon the very ledge upon which you pass, and sweeps down the precipice below you. To be caught on this passage by a tornado, or violent thundergust, which instantly adds to the volume of these cascades, can hardly fail to entail loss of life, which, in this part particularly, not unfrequently occurs in bad weather and early in spring. After 1½ hour's climb (from Iffigen) I reached the summit of the precipices without accident. The pathway emerged upon a flat, partly loose, wet shale, partly thick grass,"—*Latrobe.*

A bed of snow lying on the W. bank of a small lake, the Rawyl See, must then be crossed ; an acclivity succeeds which brings you to the cross marking the summit of the pass (7450 feet).

4½ The summit of the ridge, or plateau, between the N. and S. declivities, is several miles broad. Another small lake is reached before the traveller gains the brow of the S. declivity of the mountain, consisting of precipices similar to those on the side of Berne. The view hence of the mountains on the S. side of the vale of the Rhone, especially of the Matterhorn and its glaciers, is very sublime. A zigzag path conducts down the cliffs, and then bearing away to the rt., ascends another steep mountain, passing over rough ground, and through fir forests ; a walk of 4 hours from the summit before it reaches the first hamlet

4¼ Ayent—(No *Inn* here)—"Among the many cascades on the S. declivities of the Rawyl I noticed, in particular, one, as I descended the line of precipices, of an uncommonly fine and singular appearance, bursting out of a black cleft in the face of a broad and precipitous rock, in 5 or 6 distinct columns, and afterwards forming a fine wild tumble of foaming water."—*Latrobe.*

2 *Sion* (Route 59).

*** The above route is not described from personal knowledge, but chiefly from Latrobe, and some German authorities. The editor will be thankful for any personal information respecting the passes of the Rawyl and Sanetsch.

ROUTE 40.

10¼ stunden = 34½ English miles.
This is " a walk of 8 hours without interruption ; a long, steep, and tedious pass, but not dangerous, except in very bad weather." The village of Saanen (or Gessonay) and the road between it and Thun is described in Route 41.

At Staad the path turns S. by the valley of the Saane, the upper end of which is called Gsteig-Thal, to

3 Gsteig—(*Inns :* Bar; Rabe)—the highest village in it ; situated close under the lofty and precipitous Mittaghorn, and near the foot of the Sanetsch, the most westerly of the passes over the Bernese chain. The direction of the path from Gsteig is S.E., still by the side of the Saane, through a confined and savage gorge, until its source is passed. The summit may be reached in 1½ hour.

2⅓ The summit is 7500 feet above the sea, and presents a wild rocky solitude, unvaried by vegetation ; but the view from the S. side over the chain of Alps and glaciers, from Mont Blanc to the Cervin, is very noble.

After descending for some time, skirting along under the edge of the great glacier de Champ Fleuri, the path reaches the stream of the Morge, and crosses it to

3⅔ Champignol, thence descending upon

1½ Sion (Route 59).

ROUTE 41.

24½ stunden = 80½ English miles.
The road through the Simmenthal has only recently been made practicable for carriages. It is a little longer than the highway by Berne and Freiburg, Route 42.

The entrance to the Simmenthal lies between the Stockhorn on the rt. and the Niesen on the l., and is approached from Thun by the road along the margin of the lake, and the banks of the Kander, as far as its junction with the Simmen, a little below the picturesque castle of Wimmis, which our road passes on the l.

3½ About two miles farther on, "the house of the pastor of Erlenbach indicates, by its neatness, the extreme comfort of its internal arrangements. Large airy rooms and a capital German library, with the society of the worthy pastor and his wife, offer many inducements to a lover of quiet and romantic scenery. The clergymen in this neighbourhood are all willing to receive boarders at the very moderate rate of 4 or 5 Louis a month. From this parsonage Latrobe started on those alpine expeditions which he has described in so admirable and interesting a manner in his *Alpenstock* (an excellent English guide with a foreign name). The Stockhorn rises almost immediately behind the village of Erlenbach."—(*Inns :* Lowe, and Bär).—*L.*

1¼ Weissenburg " has a good inn, where mules may be hired and chairs, with bearers, to convey persons, who do not choose to walk, to the *Baths of Weissenburg*, distant between 2 and 3 miles from this. There is an ascent immediately on leaving the village, but after that the path winds through the most beautiful and picturesque defile, narrowing at every step into a profound chasm, till suddenly the Bath-house, singularly situated in its recesses, bursts upon the view. This large building is placed in a little nook between the boiling torrent Büntschi and the rocks, barely space sufficient for the house and baths. In this retired spot the traveller is surprised to find himself surrounded by a *crowd of* peasants. In July there were 75 of that class, and 30 of a higher class of visitors: later in the year the latter preponderate. It is difficult to imagine how they pass their time in this solitude. Three weeks is the "cure" or period allotted to the trial of the remedy of the waters, which are sulphureous, and are supposed to be most efficacious in removing all internal obstructions. Great must be their power to induce patients to remain in so melancholy a place; yet the scenery around is highly picturesque, but inaccessible to all but stout climbers, except along the road to Weissenburg. The source is situated about ½ a mile higher up in the gorge, and the water, which has a temperature of above 22° Reaum., is conveyed to the baths in wooden pipes carried along the face of the precipice.

"The bath-house is entirely of wood: the food is said to be coarse but good; table d'hôte at 12; salle a manger large but low; bed-rooms small. The whole expense, baths included, 9 fr. a-day for the superior class, and about half for the peasants."—*L.*

Some way up the ravine the peasants have formed a pathway out of it to the upper pastures, by cutting notches, or rude steps, in the face of the rock, and partly by attaching ladders to it. By this means they scale a dizzy precipice between 200 and 300 feet high. The pedestrian bound for the upper Simmenthal need not retrace his steps to Weissenburg, as there is a short cut direct from the baths to Oberwyl, on the high road.

The Simmenthal is thus described by Inglis:—"I have seen few parts of Switzerland more beautiful than this valley; no part of it so riante. I should think it must be impossible to travel through it without being conscious of an inward cheerfulness; it is fruitful, smiling, abundant, beautiful. There is no sublimity to be seen, scarcely even anything of the

picturesque. The hills, which slope gracefully back, are covered to the summit with a varied carpet of meadow, wood, and corn. Houses, hamlets, and villages, lie thickly along the banks of the river, which flows through a succession of orchards and gardens."

2 Boltingen—(*Inn:* Bär;)—a village situated 2600 feet above the sea, a little to the S. of the old castle of Simmeneck. The river is crossed three times before reaching

2⅛ Zweisimmen—(*Inns:* Löwe; Bär:)—a village situated at the junction of the great and lesser Simmen. The castle of Blankenburg crowns the height about a mile above it. The road now quits the Simmenthal, and, turning to the S.W., crosses an elevated track of marsh land, till it descends upon

2¼ Saanen (Fr. Gessonay)—(*Inns:* Grosses, and Kleines Landhaus;)— the principal place in the pastoral valley of the upper Saane (Sarine), whose inhabitants are almost exclusively cattle-owners, or occupied in their dairies, and in manufacturing most excellent cheese, exported to all parts of the world as Gruyères cheese. A kind peculiar to the valley, and which is too delicate to bear exportation, is called Fötschari-käse. A mile below Saanen the road passes out of Berne into Canton Vaud. German, the language of the upper extremity of the valley, is soon exchanged for a French patois, in the lower portion, which is called Pays d'en haut Romand. The first Vaudois village is Rougemont (Germ. Retchmund). Its château was formerly a convent.

2 Château d'Oex—(*Inns:* L'Ours; Maison de Ville;)—a village of 612 inhabitants, 3030 feet above the sea, lately rebuilt after a conflagration which almost entirely consumed it. The road next crosses the Saane, and traversing the narrow pass of La Tine, reaches

2 Montbovon, which Byron calls "a pretty scraggy village, with a

wild river and a wooden bridge :" it is situated in Canton Freiburg. A path practicable for mules, over the pass of the *Dent de Jaman*, descending upon the lake of Geneva above Montreux, will bring the traveller to Vevay in 6 stunden = 10⅔ miles. Byron, who crossed it, describes the whole route as "beautiful as a dream :"—

"The view from the highest points (we had both sides of the Jura before us in one point of view, with alps in plenty) comprises, on one side, the greatest part of Lake Leman ; on the other, the valleys and mountain of the canton of Fribourg, and an immense plain, with the lakes of Neufchâtel and Morat, and all which the borders of the lake of Geneva inherit.

"The music of the cows' bells (for their wealth, like the patriarch's, is cattle) in the pastures, which reach to a height far above any mountains in Britain, and the shepherds shouting to us from crag to crag, and playing on their reeds where the steeps appeared almost inaccessible, with the surrounding scenery, realised all that I have ever heard or imagined of a pastoral existence :—much more so than Greece or Asia Minor, for there we have a little too much of the sabre and musket order, and if there is a crook in one hand, you are sure to see a gun in the other :—but this was pure and unmixed—solitary, savage, and patriarchal. As we went they played the "Rans de Vaches" and other airs, by way of farewell. I have lately repeopled my mind with nature."—*Byron's Journal.*

The Dent de Jaman is 4500 feet high. The carriage-road to Vevay makes a very long detour from Montbovon, descending the valley of the Saane, and passing at the base of the Moleson (6181 feet), the highest mountain in Canton Fribourg.

2 Gruyères (German, Greyerz)— *Inns :* Stadthaus ; Lilie, said not to be good. This dirty little mouldering town of 375 inhabitants, is built on a hill, the top of which is crowned

by the *Castle,* one of the most extensive and best preserved feudal monuments in Switzerland. Its owners the Counts of Gruyères were sove reigns of the surrounding district down to 1554, when the family became bankrupt, and thus forfeited the lordship, so that their last descendants died in a strange land. It is now occupied by the bailiff of the district. The gloomy antiquity of the interior corresponds with the picturesque character of its watch-towers, battlements, loopholes, from without. The walls are 14 ft. thick, the halls vaulted and dimly lighted by small windows : in one hall is a fire-place at which oxen were roasted whole. The *torture* chamber still contains (or did till within a few years contain) the rack which had been used since the beginning of the present century, to inflict punishment. If tradition be credited, the castle was founded in the 15th century, by the chief of a Vandal horde. The language spoken by the people of the district, a dialect of the Romansch (called, in German, Gruverin-Welsch), is thought to prove their descent from the Burgundians. It is a subject worthy the attention of travellers. The district is also famous for its cheeses, and supplies from its rich pastures a great part of the 40,000 centners (cwt.) of cheese which Canton Fribourg manufactures yearly, and which is chiefly exported under the name of Gruyère. The *church of St. Thomas* is remarkable for its antiquity. The inhabitants of the town are a lazy set, many of them pensioners of a very rich *Hospital* here.

The watch-tower of La Tour de Treme was an outpost of the Counts of Gruyères.

1 Bulle—(*Inns :* Cheval Blanc ; Maison de Ville, said to be good ;)— one of the most industrious towns in the canton. It contains nearly 1500 inhabitants, and is the chief depôt for the Gruyère cheese, made in the valleys of the Saarine and of Charmey. It is distant about 18 miles from Fri-

oourg, and the same from Vevay. Our course now turns S. along the high road between these two places, skirting the W. base of the Moleson, to

4½ Chatel St. Denis—(*Inn:* Maison de Ville;)—a picturesque village, with an elevated castle on the l. bank of the Vevayse. Half a mile S. of it the road enters Canton Vaud.

A gradual descent towards the beautiful lake Leman, conducts the traveller to

1½ *Vevay.*—(Route 56.)

ROUTE 42.

BERNE TO LAUSANNE, BY FREYBURG.

17 stunden = 55¾ Eng. miles.

A diligence runs daily, in about 14 hours. The road is hilly, but an improved line to Freyburg is nearly completed (1838).

Quitting Berne by the gate of Morat, flanked by its two bears, we traverse a fertile, but not very interesting country. At Neueneck, where there is a good inn (the Hirsch), the stream of the Sense, which separates Canton Berne from Freyburg, is crossed. About 4 miles lower down this stream is *Laupen,* famous for the battle in which the Swiss Confederates, under Rudolph of Erlach, defeated the mailed chivalry of Burgundy and Suabia, in 1339.

At Neueneck a steep ascent commences, to surmount which vorspann are required. The gauze wings and dark dress of the female peasantry of Berne is exchanged for broad-brimmed, flapping straw hats and red petticoats; while the numerous crosses at the road-side announce a Catholic canton.

The appearance of Freyburg from the Berne road is singularly striking and picturesque, as the road, winding round the shoulder of the steep hill overlooking the valley of the Saarine, brings the traveller suddenly

in view of its antique battlements and numerous towers, crowning the summit of a precipitous rock on the opposite side of the gorge. Near the top of the hill is seen the Jesuits' Pensionnat, a staring modern building, like a manufactory, with 5 stories and many windows; not far from it the Jesuits' college and convent; next, the Gothic tower and the church of St. Nicholas; beyond appears the suspension-bridge, hung by 4 ropes of iron across the river, and linking together the two sides of the valley. Previous to its construction the only way of reaching the town from Berne was by descending the steep hill on the one side, and following numerous circuitous zigzags which led to the water side. The road then crossed the river 3 times by 3 different low bridges, after which it immediately ascended another slope equally steep. A diligence, or heavy carriage, performing this meandering and difficult route, required not much less than an hour to pass through the town; at present the traveller rolls luxuriously over this beautiful bridge, and, without either ascending or descending, is transported in 2 minutes through a breach formed in the old houses, on the edge of the precipice, into the centre of the town. A moderate toll of half a batz for every person, and one batz for each horse and carriage, is paid on crossing.

5 FREYBURG.—(*Inns:* Zähringer Hof, close to the bridge—new and good; beds, 2f.; breakfast, 2f.; tea, 1f.;—Hotel des Marchands, near the church, also good.)

This town, the capital of Canton Freyburg, is situated on a promontory formed by the windings of the Saarine (Saane). Many of the houses stand on the very edge of the precipice overhanging the river, and their quaint architecture, the long line of embattled walls stretching up hill and down dale, varied by the chain of feudal watch-towers, and gateways of the ancient fortifications which still exist in a perfect state, together with the singular and romantic features of the gorge of the Saarine, give the distant view of the town an aspect different from that of any other in Europe, which is at once imposing and highly picturesque. The narrow dirty streets and mean buildings of the interior do not altogether correspond with these outward promises of interest.

Freyburg was founded in 1175, by Duke Berchthold, of Zähringen. The number of inhabitants at present is about 8484.

The Suspension Bridge, the longest in the world, was completed and thrown open in 1834. The engineer who constructed it is M. Chaley, of Lyons. Its dimensions, compared with those of the Menai bridge, are as follows:—

	Length.	Elevation.	Breadth.
Freyburg	905ft.	174ft.	28ft
Menai	580	130	25

It is supported on 4 cables of iron wire, each containing 1056 wires, the united strength of which is capable of supporting 3 times the weight which the bridge will ever be likely to bear, or 3 times the weight of 2 rows of waggons, extending entirely across it. The cables enter the ground on each side obliquely for a considerable distance, and are then carried down vertical shafts cut in the rock, and filled with masonry, through which they pass, being attached at the extremity to enormous blocks of stone. The materials of which it is composed are almost exclusively Swiss; the iron came from Berne, the limestone masonry from the quarries of the Jura, the woodwork from the forests of Freyburg : the workmen were, with the exception of one man, natives who had never seen such a bridge before. It was completed in 3 years, at an expense of about 600,000f. (25,000*l*. sterling), and in 1834, was subjected to various severe trials to prove its strength. First, 15 pieces of artillery, drawn by 50 horses and accom

panied by 300 people, passed over it at one time, and were collected in as close a body as possible, first on the centre, and then at the two extremities, to try the effect of their concentrated weight. A depression of a metre (39⅜ inches) was thus produced in the part most weighed upon, but no sensible oscillation was produced. A few days after the bridge was opened by the bishop and authorities of the town, accompanied by about 2000 persons, who passed over it twice, in procession, preceded by a military band, and keeping step. On this occasion a slight horizontal vibration was produced, but it is very improbable that the bridge in its ordinary service will ever receive such a multitude at once. The passage of 2 or 3 heavy carriages or carts across it does not cause the slightest perceptible oscillation ; and nothing is more extraordinary in this beautiful structure than the combination of stability with such apparent fragility. The bridge is well seen from the platform of the Hotel de Zähringue, from the old road below it, and from the singular gorge of Gotteron. A similar bridge is now (1837) being built over the same river at Courbiere, on the l. of the road to Vevay.

The principal *Church of St. Nicholas* is rather a handsome Gothic building. The portal under the tower is surmounted by a curious bas-relief, representing the last judgment. In the centre stands St. Nicholas, and above him is seated the Saviour; on the l. an angel is weighing mankind in a huge pair of scales, not singly but by lots, and a pair of imps are maliciously endeavouring to pull down one scale, and make the other kick the beam ; below is St. Peter, ushering the good into Paradise. On the rt. hand is the reverse of this picture—a devil, with a pig's head, is dragging after him, by a chain, a crowd of wicked, and carries a basket on his back, also filled with figures, apparently about to precipi-

te them into a vast caldron sus-
ended over a fire, which several
her imps are stirring. In the corner
Hell, represented by the jaws of a
onster, filled up to the teeth with
vil-doers, and above it is Satan,
ated on his throne.

The *Organ*, built by Mooser, a nave of the town, is one of the finest
struments in Europe. The organ-
t is allowed to play on it for the
ratification of travellers only at
ours when the mass is not going on
-in the morning at half-past nine,
nd in the afternoon. His fee is
1f. for a party, and the valet de
lace will make an appointment with
im. The performance terminates
ith the imitation of a storm, introduc-
g the howling of the wind, and the
aring of the thunder, interspersed
ith a few flashes of lightning, from
Der Freischutz." The instrument
as 64 stops and 7800 pipes, some of
em 32ft. long.

Canton Freyburg presents a re-
arkable instance of a state with a
onstitution purely democratic, in
hich the chief influence is exercised
y the hierarchy. The town of Frey-
urg is a stronghold of the Romish
riesthood : it is the see of a bishop,
ho still styles himself Bishop of
ausanne, although since the Re-
ormation, the Canton Vaud is cut off
rom his diocese : it contains no less
han 9 convents (5 for monks and
for nuns), 12 churches, and 10 cha-
els. The *Jesuits*, still interdicted
rom most other states of Europe, are
ere openly tolerated, having been
ecalled in 1818 by a decree of the
Grand Council of the Canton. The
Jesuits' convent, or college, was
ounded in 1584 by Father Canisius,
vho died in the odour of sanctity at
he age of 77, and is interred in the
Jesuits' church, awaiting the honours
of canonization which have been, it
s said, long promised to his remains. Henry IV. of France sub-
scribed towards the building of the
church, and presented the high
altar, little aware of his coming fate
from the dagger of a Jesuit. The
College supports 60 brothers, chiefly
teachers and professors, who instruct
the pupils of the Pensionnat, and lec-
ture at the *Lyceum*, a college recently
erected. The building of the convent
is of very humble kind, rather mean
than otherwise, and contains nothing
remarkable. Its walls are lined with
bad portraits of the generals of the
order of Jesuits, and of the rectors of
the establishment.

The Pensionnat, or Jesuits' School,
the most conspicuous building in
the town, situated on a spot overlooking the other edifices, is destined
for the reception of about 400 pupils,
many of them children of the Roman
Catholic noblesse of France and Germany, who are sent hither for their
education. The establishment is
said to be very well conducted. In
the summer holidays the boys, in
little troops, headed by a tutor,
make the tour of Switzerland.

Among the curiosities of Freyburg
is the ancient trunk of a *Lime-tree*,
planted, according to tradition, on
the day of the battle of Morat, in
1476. The story relates that a
young Freyburgois, who had fought
in the battle, anxious to bring home
the good news, ran the whole way,
and arrived on this spot, bleeding,
out of breath, and so exhausted by fatigue, that he fell down, and had barely time to cry " Victory !" when he
expired. The branch of lime which
he carried in his hand was immediately planted and grew into the
tree, of which this decayed trunk,
20ft. in circumference, is the remains. Its branches are supported
by stone pillars.

Near to it is the ancient *Rathhaus*, a
building of no consequence, but
standing on the site of the Duke of
Zähringen's castle.

A long flight of steps leads from
this down to the lower town, and river
side: it is called the *Rue Court
Chemin*, and the roofs of some of its

houses serve as pavement for the street above it, called *Rue Grande Fontaine*.

The Canton Freyburg is singularly divided between the German and French languages, and the line of separation, extending from the S.E. corner to the N.W., passes through the town of Freyburg—so that in the upper town French is spoken, and in the lower German. This distinction, however, is wearing out.

The walls and gates of the town are singularly perfect specimens of ancient fortification, and contribute, along with the general air of antiquity, to carry back the spectator to a remote state of society. One tower, near the Préfecture (thrown across the street, and now converted into a prison), has acquired the name of *La Mauvaise Tour,* because it contains the rack. Though the torture had been disused in the canton for many years, it was not legally abolished until 1830!

The singularly romantic character of the winding gorge of the Saarine, on whose margin Freyburg is planted, has been before alluded to. Close to the old bridge of Berne, another gorge, deep sunk between rocks of sandstone, called *Gorge de Gotteron,* opens into the Saarine. It is a singularly wild spot, and the wire bridge, with its web-like filaments, is well seen from it.

About three miles lower down the valley of the Saarine, is the *Grotto of St. Magdalene,* a hermitage and chappel cut out of the sandstone rock, by a native of Gruyères, named Dupré, between 1670 and 1680. Its wonders have been exaggerated by the guide-books, and it is scarce worth a visit.

Morat is about 10 miles from Freyburg (Route 43). Coaches run to and fro in correspondence with the steamer navigating the lake to Neuchâtel. There is a good road from Freyburg to Vevay by Bulle (Route 41, p. 112).

The shortest way to Lausanne by Romont, but the road is so b&
that it is rarely followed. Instead it, the circuitous route by Payern in Canton Vaud, is usually taken it is hilly and not very interesting.

4 Payerne—Germ. Peterlingen—(*Inns:* Bär, is newer, but not bett than the Hotel de Ville). There a two churches in this walled town the one, now turned into a warehous is in the round style, and very a cient. Bertha, Queen of Burgund the founder of it, and of the adjoi ing convent (suppressed since th Reformation, and now a school) w buried in it. The curiosity of th place is Queen Bertha's Saddle, ke in the church, from which it appea that, in her days, it was the fashio for ladies to ride *en cavalier;* b Bertha spun as she rode, having distaff planted on the pummel.

The road ascends the valley of th Broye, past Lucens and its castle, to

4 Moudon—Germ. Milden—(*Inn* Cerf; dirty and dear). This tow was the Roman *Minidunum,* hence it modern name.

At the village of Carouge a roa turns off on the l. to Vevay.

The stage to Lausanne, about 1 miles, consists of nearly 7 of lon and incessant ascent, and 5 of de scent. Extra horses are required fo the first. From the summit and S slope of the Jorat (for that is th name of the hill) a beautiful view expands over the Leman Lake, an in clear weather the snows of Mon Blanc and the high Alps border th horizon.

It is a drive of 3 hours from Mou don to

4 LAUSANNE (Route 56).

ROUTE 43.

BERNE TO LAUSANNE, BY MORAT, AND AVENCHES (AVENTICUM).

16⅔ stunden = 54¾ Eng. miles.
Diligence daily, in 14 hours.

A distant view of the Alps is ob-
ained on the l. The Saarine is crossed

2¾ Allenluften, and a little farther
the road enters Canton Freyburg.
his part of it exhibits a more indus-
ious and thriving aspect than the
st: it is Protestant.

2½ *Morat*—Germ. Murten—(*Inns :*
ouronne ; Croix Blanche)—a thriv-
g town of 1650 inhabitants, situat-
d on the E. shore of the lake of
Morat, on the high road from Berne,
asle, and Soleure, to Lausanne. Its
arrow and somewhat dismal streets
re overlooked by an old *Castle ;* and
is still partly surrounded by feudal
rtifications—the same which, for
0 days, withstood the artillery of
harles the Bold.

> There is a spot should not be pass'd in
> vain—
> Morat ! the proud, the patriot field ! Where
> man
> May gaze on ghastly trophies of the slain,
> Nor blush for those who conquer'd on that
> plain.
> Here Burgundy bequeathed his tombless
> host,
> A bony heap through ages to remain ;
> Themselves their monument."
>
> *Byron.*

The battle of 1476, which has
endered the name of this otherwise
nsignificant town famous all over
he world, was fought under its walls.
The Swiss were drawn up along the
eights a little to the S.W., and no-
hing could resist their impetuous
charge. The loss of the Burgundians was immense : 15,000 dead
bodies were left on the field, and
thousands perished in the lake. The
bodies of the slain were collected by
the Swiss in an Ossuary, which, after
standing 300 years, was destroyed
in 1798 by the soldiers of the Burgundian Legion in the Revolutionary
French army, anxious to efface this
record of their ancestors' disgrace and
defeat. The ringleaders were the
band of the 75th half-brigade.

Byron, who visited the spot in
1816, says—" A few bones still remain, notwithstanding the pains

taken by the Burgundians for ages
(all who passed that way removing a
bone to their own country), and the
less justifiable larcenies of the Swiss
postilions, who carried them off to
sell for knife-handles—a purpose for
which the whiteness, imbibed by the
bleaching of years, had rendered
them in great request. Of those
relics I ventured to bring away as
much as may have made a quarter of
a hero, for which the sole excuse is,
that, if I had not, the next passer-by
might have perverted them to worse
uses than the careful provision for
which I intended for them."—*Byron.*

Since Byron visited the spot the
scattered remains have been collected
and buried, and an obelisk has been
set up over them (in 1822), by the canton, at the road-side, about a quarter
of a mile S. of Morat, on the site of
the bone-house. The inscription belonging to it, and one or two cannon,
made of iron hoops, used in the
battle, are still preserved in the
Town-house of Morat.

The best view of the battle-field
and lake is from the hill of *Münch-
wyler,* near an enormous lime-tree,
36ft. in circumference, and 90ft.
high, still in full vigour and luxuriant
foliage ; it is probably at least 600
years old, since, according to tradition, the Swiss held a council of
war before the battle, under its
shade. According to Ebel, the tree
is 36 feet *in diameter,* and the
American, Cooper, in consequence,
took a long walk up the hill, under a
hot sun, to see it. "There we went,
dragging our weary limbs after us,
to discover that for ' diamètre ' we
ought to have read ' circonférence.'
I wish the erratum had been in his
book instead of mine."

The lake of Morat is about 5 miles
long and 3 broad : it is separated by
a narrow flat tract of land from the
lake of Neuchâtel, but empties itself
into it through the river Broye.

The *steamer* from Neuchâtel proceeds, 3 times a week, to Morat, up
the Broye, returning the same days.

About 5 miles beyond Morat is 1½ Avenches—Germ. Wiflisburg —(*Inns:* Couronne; Hotel de Ville) an ancient walled town of 1050 inhabitants, situated in the S.W. angle of the area once occupied by *Aventicum,* the Roman capital of Helvetia. It appears to have existed before the time of Cæsar: it attained the height of its prosperity, and a population of 60,000 souls, in the reign of Vespasian and Titus; and it was destroyed, first by the Allemanni, and afterwards by Attila. The ancient walls may be traced for nearly 4 miles, in some places 14ft. thick and 15ft. high. The modern town fills but one-tenth of the space they enclosed—the rest is meadow-land or corn-field. About a mile before reaching Avenches the road from Morat is carried through a breach in these ancient fortifications. On the l. is seen a tower, which, though ruined, is the most perfect of the Roman edifices here. They owe their total destruction to their massy masonry having been for ages regarded as a quarry, out of which the neighbouring houses and villages have been built. Close to the modern town, on the l. of the road, a solitary Corinthian column, 37ft. high, is still standing, and has, for a long time, served the storks as a pedestal to build their nests on.

" By a lone wall a lonelier column rears
　A gray and grief-worn aspect of old days:
'Tis the last remnant of the wreck of years,
　And looks as with the wild-bewilder'd gaze
Of one to stone converted by amaze,
　Yet still with consciousness; and there it stands,
Making a marvel that it not decays,
　When the coeval pride of human hands,
Levell'd Aventicum, hath strew'd her subject lands."

Other traces of former splendour, such as broken cornices, inscriptions, the remains of an amphitheatre, and fragments of an aqueduct, exist, and may be discovered by minute search.

Tacitus has recorded the history a young Aventian priestess, nam Julia Alpinula, who, when her ther, the chief man of the city, h been condemned to death for aidi and abetting an insurrection again the Romans (A.D. 69), betook hers to the camp of the Roman Gener and, throwing herself at his feet, b sought him to spare her father's li He proved inexorable to her tear her youth and innocence were ali unavailing; the sentence was f filled, and she died of a broke heart.

". . oh ! sweet and sacred be the name !—
Julia—the daughter, the devoted—gave
Her youth to Heaven; her heart, beneat a claim
Nearest to Heaven's, broke o'er a father grave.
Justice is sworn 'gainst tears, and her would crave
The life she lived in; but the judge wa just,
And then she died on him she could n save.
Their tomb was simple, and without bust,
And held within one urn one mind, on heart, one dust."

1500 years after this event the epi taph of Julia was found among thes ruins:—it run thus :—" Julia Alpi nula: Hic jaceo. Infelicis patris in felix proles. Deæ Aventiæ Sacerdos Exorare patris necem non potui : Mal mori in fatis illi erat. Vixi anno xxiii. (I, Julia Alpinula, lie here— unfortunate child of an unfortunat parent, priestess of the Goddess Aventia. I failed in averting by my prayers, the death of my father the Fates had decreed that he should die ignominiously. I lived to the age of 23.)" Byron says —" I know of no human composition so affecting as this, nor a history of deeper interest. These are the names and actions which ought not to perish, and to which we turn with a true and healthy tenderness, from the wretched and glittering detail of a confused mass of conquests and battles, with which the ıind is roused for a time to a false ınd feverish sympathy, from whence : recurs at length with all the nausea onsequent on such intoxication."— *Byron.*

This inscription has been bought ıy an Englishman and removed from ıhe spot.

The *feudal Castle* was built by a Count Wivilo, in the 7th century, whence the German name of Avenhes.

At Domdidier, 2 miles from Avenhes, a road strikes off on the right ıo Freyburg, described, along with its ıemarkable bridge, in Route 42.

2 Payerne. Here we fall into the Route 42. From Freyburg to

8 LAUSANNE. (Route 56.)

ROUTE 44.

BERNE TO NEUCHÂTEL.

9 stunden = 29½ English miles.
Diligences go daily in 6 hours.

There is another way by Morat, and thence in the steamer to Neuchâtel; but it only goes 3 times a week, and the days and hours must be ascertained before setting out. The following road passes by Seedorf, a village named from a pretty little lake, to

3⅔ Aarberg—(*Inn:* Krone;) —a town of a single street, on a promontory on the Aar, which, when high, sometimes flows entirely around it. Here the roads from Basle, Soleure, Neuchâtel, and Lausanne meet. Travellers desirous of visiting Rousseau's island, on the lake of Bienne (Route 45), may proceed from this by Walperschwyl and Teuffelen to Gerolfingen, on the margin of the lake, about 4 miles from Aarberg. The road to Neuchâtel is carried through Siselen and

2¾ Anet, or Ins, a village on an eminence, from which the Alps are well seen in clear weather, with the lake of Morat and Neuchâtel near at hand. The lake of Bienne lies

about 3 miles to the N. of this place. Skirting the hill of Jolimont we cross the river Thiel, or Zihl, through which the waters of the lake of Neuchâtel are discharged into that of Bienne. It forms the boundary line of Cantons Berne and Neuchâtel. The Castle, close to the bridge, is now a prison; a road runs from this to Erlach (Cerlier), a town of 1000 inhabitants, on a spur of the Jolimont, which projects into the lake like a wall or causeway, nearly as far as Rousseau's Island. The castle of Erlach was the cradle of the noble family of that name: among its members was Rudolph, the hero of Laupen.

Near St. Blaize the road, recently macadamized and improved, reaches the margin of the lake of Neuchâtel, and continues along it at the foot of the Chaumont, as far as

2¾ NEUCHÂTEL, German Neuenburg—(*Inns:* Faucon, good;—H. des Alpes, at the water-side, recently built).

Neuchâtel, the chief town of the canton, is built upon the steep slope of the Jura mountains, and along a narrow shelf of level ground between the hills and the lake, partly gained by embankments from the water. Within a few years several new streets have been built on the land thus acquired. It has nearly 6000 inhabitants. Except as the threshold of Switzerland, it has little to interest the passing traveller: it has but little trade, and not much activity except on market days. Its objects of curiosity are few and unimportant, and the scenery of its lake, though agreeable, is tame, compared with that of other Swiss lakes. On the other hand, to one newly arrived in the country, the first, and under all circumstances glorious, view of the Alps from the heights of the Jura above the town, must appear magnificent; and should the sky be clear, and the traveller's temper even, the objects around will assume a different aspect, and Neuchâtel, with its picturesque old castle, its numerous white country houses, its vine-clad hills, and its blue expanse of lake, will be pronounced beautiful.

The *Old Castle* on the height, now occupied by the Prussian Governor, was originally the residence of the French princes of Neuchâtel of the house of Chalons (Longueville), who were, at least nominally, the sovereigns of this little state : literally a principality, with republican institutions, yet retaining many feudal tenures. The subjects, indeed, of the Prince of Neuchâtel, maintained jealously their privileges and liberties, allowing him but very limited authority over them. When the house of Chalons became extinct in 1707, the King of Prussia was chosen as the nearest descendant by the female line, to be sovereign, or stadtholder. The rule of the house of Brandenburg was interrupted by Napoleon, who made Marshal Berthier Prince of Neuchâtel, but has been resumed since 1815. The king has the right of appointing a governor, the mayor and 45 members out of the 75 who compose the Grand Council. Of these the governor alone is permitted to be a foreigner : 70,000 francs are paid out of the taxes annually to the King. Though long an ally of the Swiss cantons, Neuchâtel was not formally incorporated as a member of the Confederation until 1814.

The *Church*, adjoining the castle, is a Gothic building of the 12th century; but the E. end, in the round style, is older. Within it is a curious monument of the French princes of Neuchâtel, decorated with their effigies. Farel, the reformer, was buried on the terrace, in front of the building, but the situation of his grave is unknown. There is a pleasing view from this terrace.

The *Hotel de Ville*, in the lower town, is a large modern edifice, faced with a Grecian portico. In it the meetings of the Grand Council of the canton are held.

The *Gymnasium*, a handsome new building near the lake, erected by the town, as a kind of public school contains a very interesting *Museum of Natural History*, including good collections in zoology, conchology and geology. The specimens of rock and fossils, illustrating the structure of the Jura mountains, are very complete and instructive. This institution owes much to the zeal and talents of Professor Agassiz, a native of Neuchâtel, whose interesting discoveries in the history of fossil fishes have thrown more light on that branch of the study than any one since Cuvier had done.

The charitable institutions of this town, for which it is indebted to its own citizens, are on a very splendid scale. In 1786 one David Pury left his whole fortune of 4,000,000 of livres (166,000*l.*), to endow an hospital and poor-house, and for other purposes connected with the improvement of his native town. He had quitted it a poor lad, without money or friends, had gradually, by industry and talent for business, increased his means, becoming, in turn, jeweller, owner of mines, banker, and, finally, millionaire, at Lisbon, where he died.

The *Hospital Pourtales* is a similar monument of the benevolence and public spirit of a townsman. It is open to people of all religions and countries alike.

Those who would enjoy one of the finest distant views of the Alps, with the lakes of Neuchâtel, Morat, and Bienne in the foreground, and the long range of the Jura on the N. should ascend to the *summit of the Chaumont*, the hill immediately above Neuchâtel. It is but an hour's walk, and a carriage-road was about to be made thither in 1837. It is 5580 feet above the sea level. The view comprehends the whole array of Alps, from the Titlis to Mont Blanc, and is said to be finer even than that from the Weissenstein. It must, however, be borne in mind, that the atmosphere is seldom perfectly clear;

that this magnificent view is, per-aps, seen to perfection not more an between 10 and 20 times in a mmer.

On the slope of the hill, about a ile above the town, lies the largest oulder-stone known on the Jura; is called "pierre a bot," (toad-tone), and is situated in a wood, ear a farm-house; it is 62 feet long y 48 broad, and is calculated to ontain 14,000 cubic feet. It is of ranite, similar to that of the Great t. Bernard, from which part of the ilps it probably came, as there is no imilar rock nearer at hand; yet it xhibits no symptoms of attrition, all ts angles being perfectly sharp. No atisfactory explanation has yet been iven of the extraordinary multitude f similar detached rocks, which strew he entire N. slope of the Jura, and which, from the nature of the stone, nust have all been derived from the iigh Alps.

The *Gorge of the Seyon* (the stream assing through the town), immedi-tely behind Neuchâtel, is a most ingular scene, and those who find ittle to amuse them in the town will ot repent a walk to explore it, hough its recesses are only to be eached by scrambling and climbing. It is a deep narrow fissure, cleaving he centre of the chain of the Jura, and llowing the river Seyon to escape from the Val de Ruz, into the lake of Neuchâtel. The section it presents of the strata of the Jura limestone will prove particularly instructive to the geologist. In one spot they may be observed curved and fractured, probably by the upheaving force from below, which first broke this cre-vice in the mountain. Outside the town, near a singularly-placed water-mill, the rent, or gorge, makes a sud-den bend at right angles to its former direction, and the rocks nearly close over the stream, which there sweeps round the eminence on which the castle stands, and flows into the lake after passing through the centre of the town. Though in winter a furious torrent sweeping everything before it, it is reduced in summer to a noisome driblet of water, exhaling unwholesome effluvia. A tunnel has, in consequence, been projected through the rock at the bend before alluded to, for the purpose of carry-ing its waters entirely clear of the town into the lake, at a considerable distance S. of its present outlet.

A new road to Vallengin has been traced up this gorge, following nearly the line of the conduit which supplies Neuchâtel with water. It will require to be cut through the limestone rock for nearly 2 miles, but will avoid altogether the painful as-cent and descent which the existing road makes.

The principal produce of the can-ton is wine; the best sorts resemble Burgundy, but are much inferior. The chief manufacture is watches and clocks, of which 130,000 are, it is said, exported annually: the cen-trical seat of it may be said to be the valley of Chaux de Fonds and Locle (Route 48); but much is done in the town of Neuchâtel. The watches of this canton are of an inferior kind to those of Geneva.

The *Steamer* navigating the lake sets out from Neuchâtel at 6 A.M., reaches Yverdun at 9; sets out to return at 10; reaches Neuchâtel at 12 or 1. Three times a-week it leaves for Morat at 2, returns thence at 4, and arrives at Neuchâtel at 7 P.M. By means of this conveyance a traveller, leaving Neuchâtel in the morning may reach Lausanne at 1½; in time for the Geneva steamer, so as to arrive at that place by 6½ P.M.

Coaches run from Morat to Berne and Freyburg, in correspondence with the steam-boat.

The new road to Bienne, along the W. shore of the lake, shortens the journey to that place, to Soleure, and to Bâsle, by 3 hours, and is far pret-tier than the old road (Route 45).

Diligences go daily from Neuchâtel to Pontarlier and Besançon, to Berne and Bâle, to Geneva and Lausanne.

ROUTE 45.

BIENNE TO YVERDUN AND LAUSANNE,
BY THE LAKES OF BIENNE AND
NEUCHÂTEL.

18½ stunden = 60¾ English miles.
Bienne is described in Route 1.

An excellent new road was finished in 1837, along the W. shore of the lake of Bienne, partly by cutting a passage through the rock. It is about 8 miles shorter than the old road by Siselen, and perfectly level, while the other is very hilly.

The *Lake of Bienne* (German *Bieler See*) is about 10 miles long and nearly 3 broad. It is 8 feet lower than the lake of Neuchâtel, and receives its waters at the S. extremity by the Thiel, discharging them again at the N.E. corner, through a continuation of the same river. Its banks are neither bold nor striking, and it owes its celebrity to Rousseau's residence on it, and to his somewhat extravagant praises, rather than to any pre-eminent beauty of its scenery. The *Isle St. Pierre*, on which he took refuge for 2 months, in 1765, after his proscription at Paris, and his pretended stoning at Motiers (Route 49), is situated about 6 miles from Bienne. Boats may be hired at almost all the villages on the lake to row to it.

The island, a pretty object, is a ridge of sandstone, rising 12 feet above the lake, and prolonged southwards, under water, to the hill called Jolimont. It is crowned by a beautiful grove of magnificent old oaks, the shade of which in summer is most refreshing. The following description is given of it by Rousseau in his Reveries :—

" De toutes les habitations, où j'ai demeuré (et j'en ai eu de charmantes), aucune ne m'a rendu si véritablement heureux, et ne m'a laissé de si tendres regrets que l'île de

St. Pierre au milieu du lac de Bienne. Cette petite île qu'on appelle à Neuchâtel *l'île de la motte*, est bien peu connue, même en Suisse. Cependant elle est très-agréable et singulièrement située pour le bonheur d'un homme qui aime à se circonscrire car quoique je sois peut-être le seul au monde à qui sa destinée en ait fait une loi, je ne puis croire être le seul qui ait un goût si naturel, quoi que je ne l'aie trouvé jusqu'ici chez nul autre.

" Les rives du lac de Bienne sont plus sauvages et plus romantiques que celles du lac de Genève, parce que les rochers et les bois y bordent l'eau de plus près ; mais elles ne sont pas moins riantes : il y a moins de culture de champs et de vignes moins de villes et de maisons ; il y a aussi plus de verdure naturelle, plus de prairies, d'asiles ombragés de bocages, des contrastes plus fréquents et des accidens plus rapprochés. Comme il n'y a pas sur ces heureux bords de grandes routes commodes pour les voitures, le pays est peu fréquenté par les voyageurs* ;) mais il est intéressant pour des contemplatifs solitaires, qui aiment à s'énivrer des charmes de la nature et à se recueillir dans un silence que ne trouble aucun bruit que le cri des aigles, le ramage entrecoupé de quelques oiseaux, et le roulement des torrents qui tombent de la montagne. Ce beau bassin d'une forme presque ronde, renferme dans son milieu deux petites îles, l'une habitée et cultivée, d'environ demi-lieue de tour ; l'autre, plus petite, déserte et en friche, et qui sera détruite à la fin par les transports de la terre qu'on en ôte sans cesse pour réparer les dégats que les vagues et les orages font à la grande. C'est ainsi que la substance du faible est toujours employée au profit du puissant.

" Il n'y a dans l île qu'une seule maison, mais grande, agréable et commode, qui appartient à l'hôpital

---

* Steam boats and new roads, especially that just completed along the W. shore of the lake, within a musket-shot of the island, have produced a great change on this head since Rousseau wrote.

e Berne, ainsi que l'île, et où loge le
eceveur avec sa famille et ses domes-
iques. Il y entretient une nombreuse
.asse-cour, une volière et des réser-
'oirs pour les poissons. L'île dans
a petitesse est tellement variée dans
.es terrains et dans ses aspects,
qu'elle offre toutes sortes de sites, et
.ouffre toutes sortes de culture: on y
.rouve des champs, des vignes, des
.ois, des vergers, des gras pâturages
.mbragés de bosquets et bordés d'ar-
.risseaux de toute espèce, dont le
.ord des eaux entretient la fraîcheur;
.ne haute terrasse plantée de deux
.angs d'arbres enlace l'île dans toute
.o longueur, et dans le milieu de cette
.errasse on a bâti un joli salon, où les
.habitants des rives voisines se rassem-
.blent et viennent danser les di-
.manches durant les vendanges. Une
.de mes navigations les plus fréquentes
.était d'aller de la grande à la petite
.île, d'y débarquer et d'y passer l'après-
.dinée, tantôt à des promenades très-
.circonscrites au milieu des marceaux,
.des bourdaines, des persicaires, et des
.arbrisseaux de toute espèce; et tan-
.tôt m'établissant au sommet d'un
.tertre sablonneux, couvert de gazon,
.de serpolet, de fleurs, même d'espar-
.cettes et de trèfles qu'on avait vrai-
.semblablement semés autrefois.

" Quand le lac agité ne me per-
mettait pas la navigation, je passais
mon après-midi à parcourir l'île,
m'asseyant tantôt dans les réduits les
plus raints et les plus solitaires pour
y rêver à mon aise, tantôt sur les ter-
rasses et les tertres pour parcourir des
yeux le superbe et ravissant coup
d'œil du lac et de ses rivages, cou-
ronné d'un côté par des montagnes
prochaines, et de l'autre élargi en
riches et fertiles plaines dans lesquelles la vue s'étendait jusqu'aux
montagnes bleuâtres plus éloignées
qui la bornaient. En sortant d'une
longue et douce rêverie, me voyant
entouré de verdure, de fleurs, d'oiseaux, et laissant errer mes yeux au
loin sur les romanesques rivages qui
bordaient une vaste étendue d'une eau
claire et cristalline, j'assimilais à mes
fictions tous ces aimables objets; et
me trouvant enfin ramené par degrés
à moi-même, et à tout ce qui m'en-
tourait, je ne pouvais marquer le
point de séparation des fictions aux
réalités, tant tout concourait égale-
ment à me rendre chère la vie re-
cueillie et solitaire que je menais
dans ce beau séjour. Que ne peut-
elle renaître encore! Que ne puis-je
aller finir mes jours dans cette île
chérie, sans en ressortir jamais, ni
jamais y revoir aucun habitant du
continent qui me rappelât le souvenir
des calamités de toute espèce qu'ils
se plaisent à rassembler sur moi de-
puis tant d'années!"

He has further recorded the mode
of passing his time on the island, in
botanizing, in music, in climbing the
trees, with a bag tied round him to
gather the fruit, in carrying over a
colony of rabbits, to stock the neighbouring islet, and in allowing himself to drift for hours across the lake,
stretched on his back in a little boat.
The farm-house in which he dwelt
now serves as an inn, but Rousseau's
room is preserved nearly in the state
in which he left it, except that its
walls, doors, shutters, and windows
are scribbled over with names of
visitors of all nations. For some
time after his arrival he remained
almost unknown; but as soon as the
presence of the author of the " Con-
trat Social" on the island became
noised abroad, it was inundated with
shoals of curious visitors. To escape
their importunities he used to climb
up by a stove, through a trap-door
into the garret, and frequently, when
informed by his host that a party
had come expressly to see him, refused to appear—"Je ne suis pas ici
dans une ménagerie."

After having, by his own account,
made up his mind to end his days on
his beloved island, he was at length
expelled the canton of Berne, by a
decree of the Grand Council, after in
vain begging them, in preference, to

commute his sentence into perpetual imprisonment, and to lock him up for life in some old castle.

3 Neuveville (Germ. Neustadt), a little town of 1200 inhabitants, on the edge of the lake at the foot of the Chasseral, and a little to the S.W. of the two islands.

On the opposite side of the lake, near its S. extremity, stands Erlach (Cerlier), at the foot of the Jolimont, a hill of sandstone, which sends out the spur prolonged into the Isle St. Pierre, producing shallows covered with reeds stretching into the lake.

The borders of the lake of Neuchâtel are reached at

1½ St. Blaize, and an improved road, skirting the edge of the vineyards, conducts thence to

1 NEUCHÂTEL (see Route 44, p. 120).

A steam-boat (see p. 121) and diligence run daily between Neuchâtel and Yverdun.

A little more than a mile from the gates of Neuchâtel the road crosses the glen of Serrières by a handsome stone bridge, built by Marshal Berthier. The bottom of it is occupied by a little hamlet, composed of a group of water-mills, turned by a remarkable stream, rising in the head of the dell and falling into the lake, after a course of not more than half a mile. Though it remains, as it were, but a few minutes above ground, it rises in sufficient force and volume to turn a wheel within 200 yards of its source, and subsequently sets in motion several others, both above and below the bridge. It is fed from secret reservoirs within the mountain, and is probably to be identified with some of those singular streams which bury themselves in various places among the cavernous range of the Jura.

About 3 miles farther is Columbier, once the seat of the Scotch Marshal Keith, the friend and general of Frederick the Great: he was governor of Neuchâtel. Cortaillod, by the water-side, produces one of the best wines in the canton.

3¾ St. Aubin—(*Inn:* Couronne; —a village half-way to Yverdun. Near it are the castles of Gorgier and Vaumarcus. An excursion may be made from this over the hills to the Creux de Vent (Route 49).

It was with the view of relieving the unimportant fort of Vaumarcus in which some of his councillors and friends were besieged by the Swiss, that Charles the Bold of Burgundy abandoned his strongly fortified camp behind Grandson, and marched his forces down to the narrow strip between the lake and the mountains, where there was not space to deploy a third part of them, and where his cavalry and artillery were useless. The advanced guard of the Swiss, who came from Neuchâtel, was posted near Concise (a village in Canton Vaud), and their batteries on the heights did great execution upon the Burgundians. Here, falling on their knees in prayer, as was the custom of the Swiss at the opening of a battle, they received on their lances the charge of the Burgundian horse, who mistook their attitude for one of submission. From the hills above, later in the day, echoed the war-horns of Uri and Unterwalden, announcing the arrival of reinforcements from those cantons, and spreading dismay in the hearts of Charles and his forces. The scene of the battle lies between Concise—(*Inn:* L'Ecu de France, comfortable)—and

2¼ *Grandson*—(*Inns:* Lion d'Or; Croix Rouge, not good ;)—a town of 890 inhabitants, with a venerable castle, now converted into a snuff-manufactory, on an eminence above the lake. It is historically remarkable because before the battle of Grandson it resisted for 10 days the assaults and artillery of the Burgundian army. When at length the garrison, reduced by famine and invited by the offer of free pardon, by a spy or deserter who had entered the castle by stealth, surrendered it, Charles, with a ferocity peculiar to his character, caused them to be stripped and hung by undreds on the surrounding trees, nd as many more to be drowned in ne lake. But two days after, on ne 3rd of March, 1476, he expiated nis atrocious crime, and experienced ne vengeance of the Swiss in the me-norable defeat of his host 50,000 trong, by the army of the confede-ates, amounting to not much more han ⅓ of that number; and was nimself compelled to fly for his life cross the mountains, with but five ollowers. The spoil of his camp, vhich fell into the hands of the vic-ors, included 120 pieces of cannon, ‘00 standards, all his jewels and egalia, costly hangings, and military chest; on that day gold and dia-nonds were dealt out to the Swiss by nandfuls.

The *Church* of Grandson is very ancient; Farel preached the reform-ed doctrines from its pulpit. There is a path over the hills from Grand-son to Motiers Travers.

1 *Yverdun* (German Ifferten)— *(Inns :* H. de Londres, good but dear ; Maison Rouge, also good, and said to be more reasonable)—a town of 3248 inhabitants, at the S. extremity of the lake Neuchâtel, at the spot where the Orbe (thenceforth called Thiele) falls into it. It is built upon the site of the Roman *Ebrodunum,* whose name, with a little change, it still inherits.

The *Castle,* built in the 12th cen-tury by Conrad of Zähringen, became the school-house and residence of Pestalozzi, from 1805 to 1825. Al-though the founder of a system of education, and of many schools both in Europe and America, he was a very bad practical schoolmaster himself; and this establishment, the head-quarters as it were of his system, turned out a signal failure.

A very delightful excursion may be made from this up the Val Orbe to the Lac de Joux (Route 50). The road hence to Geneva passes through Val Orbe.

Diligences go to Lausanne, and a steam-boat to Neuchâtel from Yver-dun daily.

About a mile S. of the town, at the extremity of an avenue of poplars, a mineral bath is passed : the water is warm and sulphureous.

1⅗ Essertines.

1⅘ Echallens, a village on the river Talent, with 714 inhabitants.

2¾ LAUSANNE (in Route 56).

ROUTE 48.

NEUCHÂTEL TO LA CHAUX DE FONDS AND LOCLE,

6 stunden = 19¾ Eng. miles. Diligences daily.

The high road to Vallengin is at present carried over the steep hill at the back of Neuchâtel; a new line is proposed, which will conduct it di-rectly through the profound chasm of the Seyon (see p. 121).

1¼ Vallengin—(*Inn :* Couronne)— is the principal place in the fertile Val de Ruz. Its *Castle* (now a pri-son) is in part as old as the 12th century: its base is washed by the Seyon.

A steep and long ascent up the Tête de Rang leads, through unin-teresting country, to

3 La Chaux de Fonds—(*Inn :* Lilie)—a scattered village, of 6550 inhabitants, in a bleak, upland, and desolate valley, bare of wood, and, from its great elevation of 3070ft. above the sea, capable of producing only a scanty crop of oats. After Locle, it is the chief seat of the ma-nufacture of clocks and watches. This is not carried on in large facto-ries, but in the separate dwellings of the workmen. Each man usually makes only one particular piece of machinery, leaving even the finishing of it to others. An expert workman can easily earn 8f. a day, and the youngest apprentice 8 sous. There are two *subterranean mills* here, turned by the stream of the valley previous to its sinking underground; the rocks have been blasted to afford space for the mills; but those at Locle are even more curious.

Instead of following the high-road to Locle, the pedestrian may take a foot-path (a walk of six hours) across the hills to the *Saut du Doubs,* or waterfalls of the Doubs—the river which separates Switzerland from France. It here traverses one of those singular gaps or rents in the rock, between 300ft. and 400ft. deep, which are common in the Jura. Numerous mills are turned by the force of the stream. Some large fragments of rock, which have fallen into the bed of the river, dam it up partly, and form what is called the Lac des Brennets. The scene is wild, and has been compared to a Welsh landscape, but its beauty has been exaggerated. Brennets is about 3 miles from Locle.

There is a carriage-road direct from Chaux de Fonds to

1¾ Locle—(*Inn :* Trois Rois)— another scattered village, occupied by an industrious population of 5886 souls—the men chiefly watch-makers, the women lace-makers.

The little stream of the Bied, which traverses the valley, loses itself, at a short distance from Locle, in a chasm in the rock. This outlet, however, proved insufficient to drain the valley; and the district around the town was, in consequence, inundated at the season of the melting of the snows—and not much better than a morass at any time. To remedy this evil, a tunnel, 950ft long, was pierced through the screen of solid limestone-rock which encompasses the valley, and this now effectually carries off into the Doubs the previously stagnant waters. At a short distance from this artificial drain or emissary, and about a mile from Locle, the river disappears in a natural opening, sinking into the heart of the mountain, through a vertical abyss, more than 100ft. deep. This water-power, or privilege, as an American would call it, is not lost ; but, in order to render it available, 3 or 4 mills have been constructed, one below the other, in

the cavernous cleft—each receiving in turn, the stream which puts it wheels in motion. " You go dow flights of broken and slippery stairs cut in the rock, to these mills, place one under another, in very frightfu situations undoubtedly, but rendere more so to the imagination of th beholder from the circumstances o darkness and ignorance of the mean by which the works are secured, by the noise, the unfathomable depth below," &c.—*Simond.*

There is another road from Locle to Neuchâtel by Chaux de Milieu Les Ponts, the heights of La Tourne and Courcelle.

ROUTE 49.

PONTARLIER (IN FRANCE), TO NEUCHÂTEL, BY MOTIERS TRAVERS.

10¾ stunden = 35 Eng. miles.
A diligence daily.

At Pontarlier — (*Inns :* La Poste good — Lion d'Or)—the last town in France : an arrangement may be made with the postmaster to convey a carriage as far as Motiers, more than half way to Neuchâtel. The road first ascends by the side of the river Doubs, and through the pass of La Cluse, which may be called a mountain-gateway between France and Switzerland, to St. Pierre de Joux. The defile is commanded by the *Château de Joux,* situated on the summit of a precipice, at the foot of which the roads from Pontarlier and Salins, and those from Neuchâtel and Geneva, by Jougne, unite. This frontier-fort was the prison of the unfortunate Toussaint l'Ouverture, when treacherously carried off from St. Domingo by command of Napoleon. He ended his days here, some say by violent means ; but the sudden transition from the climate of the tropics to that of the Jura sufficiently explains the cause of his death, without the need of violence.

Between the villages of Verriéres de Joux and

3¼ Verriéres de Suisse, the French
ntier is crossed. The Custom-
use regulations on this part of the
ench frontier are more than usually
orous. In some places, there is a
ble line of douaniers, which makes
advisable to have the luggage
ombè at the first station. In some
ces the douaniers attend only dur-
g certain hours of the day, and
rsons arriving in their absence must
ait their return. Travellers should
certain by previous inquiry what
ese hours are.

The country now becomes exceed-
gly romantic—the hills clothed with
rests, the valleys carpeted with the
hest verdure, and sprinkled with
at cottages in the picturesque style
architecture peculiar to the chain
the Jura and Alps. Cheese, nearly
good as that of Gruyeres, and sold
der that name, is made on the
land pastures of the Jura.

The descent from the summit of
e ridge into the Val Travers is
rough another narrow gorge, called
a Chaine, because the passage was
t one time stopped by a massy
ain drawn across the road, and
stened to staples in the rock. This
imitive fortification is said to be a
lic of the Burgundian wars, in-
nded to arrest the artillery of
harles the Bold.

At the village of St. Sulpice the
ver Reuse, which waters the Val
ravers, rises out of the rock. This
undant source is said to be the out-
t of the Lac d'Etalieres, situated
bout 10 miles off, among the hills.

3 Motiers Travers—(*Inn:* Maison
e Commune)—is a village inhabited
y watch and lace-makers, on the rt.
ank of the Reuse, which has ob-
ained some notoriety as the place of
esidence of Jean Jacques Rousseau
fter his banishment from Geneva.
n the house occupied by him, his
esk is shown, at which he wrote his
elebrated "Lettres de la Montagne;"
nd up-stairs, in a wooden gallery,
wo peeping-holes, through which he
ould observe people out of doors

without being seen himself. He quitted the place under the pretence of
having been persecuted, and because
the boys threw stones at his windows.
During his residence here, Voltaire
vented his bile against him in a sa-
tire, of which the following verses
are a sample:—

" Dans un vallon fort bien nommé *Travers*
S'élève un mont vrai séjour des hivers,
Son front altier se perd dans les nuages,
Ses fondemens sont au creux des enfers.
Au pied du mont sont des antres sau-
        vagoo,
Du Dieu du jour ignorés à jamais.
C'est de Rousseau le digne et noir pa-
        lais;
Là se tapit, ce sombre énergumène
Cet ennemi de la nature humaine;
Petri d'orgueil et dévoré de fiel
Il fuit le monde et craint de voir le ciel."

The Val Travers is highly picturesque. A few miles lower down
it is bounded on the rt. by a remarkable mountain, called *Creux de Vent*,
4800ft. above the sea. " Its summit
is hollowed out into a vast and profound cavity, 500ft. deep, surrounded
by an amphitheatre of limestone
rock from the top to the bottom." It
is more than 2 miles in diameter.
" At times when a change of weather is impending, the crater of the
mountain is seen to become suddenly
filled with a cloud of white vapour,
working, and rising and falling with
an easy but perceptible motion, until
the whole hollow presents the appearance of an immense caldron of boiling
vapour, which seldom rises above the
edge. If any escape, it is by the
opening towards the defile; and I
have seen it repeatedly issue in a
thin white line, and float gradually
down the centre of the valley till im-
perceptibly diminished and dissipated."—*Latrobe.*

The echo produced by firing a
gun within the Creux de Vent, is
like a scattered fire of musketry,
or a succession of discharges from
a battery; and the hollow may be
called the very cradle of the winds,
which appear to be perpetually blowing from it.

La Clusette, near Brod, is a very

picturesque defile—the road hanging over the precipice. A steep ascent carries the road out of the Val Travers; and at the top of the ridge, nearly under the castle of

2¾ Rochefort, a beautiful view opens through the gap of the defile, over the lake of Neuchâtel, and the Alps along the horizon.

1¾ NEUCHÂTEL (Route 44).

ROUTE 50.

YVERDUN TO GENEVA, BY ORBE, WITH EXCURSION TO THE LAC DE JOUX.

15⅔ stunden = 51¾ Eng. miles.

The daily diligence performs the journey from Neuchâtel to Geneva in 16 hours.

2 Orbe—(*Inn:* La Maison de Ville)—a picturesque and ancient town of 1927 inhabitants, built on a hill nearly insulated by the Orbe, which is crossed by a bold arch. It was the Roman station *Urbigenum*, and a place of importance in the middle ages, under the Burgundian Kings, who had a *Royal Castle* here. The fair but cruel Brunehilde, Queen of the Franks, took refuge here, with her grand-daughter, but was soon put to death. The 3 sons of Lothaire I. met here, in 855, to divide his kingdom. In 1475 the Swiss took Orbe by assault; but the *Castle,* whose venerable and extensive ruins, especially the solitary towers of antique structure, are still a conspicuous object in the view of the town, made a lengthened resistance. The garrison yielding step by step, disputed the possession of each chamber, stair, and passage. The last remnant were pursued into a tower, which the Swiss set fire to, and the few who fell into their hands alive were thrown over the battlements. "The *circular tower* of the Castle, not unlike the celebrated Irish towers in *construction,* though of very different proportions, should be attentively examined."

There is a high-road into France from Orbe, along the l. bank of t Orbe, by Jougne and Salins.

About 2 miles above the town, ne Mont Charand, is a cavern, w stalactites, called Grotte aux Fée not far from it is a cascade of t Orbe.

An interesting excursion may made from Orbe to the *Lac de Jou.*

The carriage-road thither tur away from the river at once, and pr ceeds through Romainmotier, und the singular mountain called Dent Vaulion, to Le Pont, on the Lac Joux. The vale of the Orbe is o of the most beautiful in the Jura, a the pedestrian may find a foot-pa along its banks, up to its source, the cliff below Pont.

Pont, a little village, named fro a bridge across the channel whi connects the Lac de Joux with t small Lac des Brennet, is the be head-quarters, as it has a tolerab inn. It is prettily situated, at the base of the *Dent de Vaulion,* one si of which is a sheer precipice of ba limestone 2000ft. high—the other steep slope, or inclined plane, cover with verdant turf. It requires a stea head to look from the top over t verge of the precipice.

About 3 miles N. of Pont, and th same distance above Vallorbe, is t source of the Orbe, which rises once a copious stream, supplied, it supposed, by subterranean condui from the Lac de Joux.

The valley in which the *Lac* Joux is situated contains two oth lakes, Le Ter and Brennet, and entirely shut in by high hills; so tha although these sheets of water are fe by all the streams of the valley, the have no visible outlet above groun There are, however, large cavities an orifices in the beds of these lake called *entonnoirs,* through which th waters escape. These fissures ar sometimes rendered incapable of car rying off the waters from interna obstructions, and thus inundation are caused in the valley. A tunne of no very great extent, might drai ne lake entirely. The source of the Orbe is about 700ft. lower than the surface of the lake. The scenery of the Valley de Joux is most romantic, and will alone compensate for a visit. Along the S.E. side of the lake rises the imposing mass of the Mont Tendre, 5730ft. high: its lower slopes are well wooded. The view from its summit, extending to Mont Blanc on the one side, and to Soleure on the other, will repay the trouble of the ascent. There is a path down the opposite side of the mountain, leading, in 2 hours, to the village of Mont Richer. An unfortunate English gentleman, named Herbert, who was drowned in a well near the chalets of the Mont Tendre, in 1837, is buried at Mont Richer. Henri Chenu, cruitier, is said to be a good guide for the Mont Tendre. There is a cross-road along the N.W. shore of the Lac de Joux from Pont to Les Rousses, on the great post road from Dijon to Geneva. Another road, winding round the shoulder of the Mont Tendre, runs direct from Pont to Aubonne, on the way to Geneva, rendering it unnecessary to return to Orbe.

———

The lake of Geneva is only about 190ft. lower than that of Neuchâtel. The road from Orbe traverses the high ground, or water-shed separating the two basins. An attempt was made, in 1639, to connect the two lakes, and through them unite the Rhine with the Rhone, by means of a canal cut between the rivers Orbe and Venoge. It was finished as far as Entre Roche, a distance of about 12 miles; but difficulties, either in the levelling, or occasioned by the interference of private interests, prevented its being carried farther. The plan of completing it has been revived in 1838. It lies about a mile and a half to the E. of the road.

1½ La Sarraz is an ancient town, romantically situated on the Venoge. About 4 miles farther is Cossonez,

from which town roads branch off to Lausanne and Morges.

4½ Aubonne—(*Inn*: Couronne)—an ancient town of 1667 inhabitants, with an Eastern-looking *castle*. Byron says of it—" The entrance and bridge, something like that of Durham: it commands by far the fairest view of the lake of Geneva (and of Mont Blanc behind it); a grove, on the height, of very noble trees. Here Tavernier, the Eastern traveller, bought (or built) the château, because the site resembled and equalled that of Erivan, a frontier city of Persia. Here he finished his voyages." Aubonne is less than 3 miles distant from the lake.

1 Rolle, on the high-road from Geneva to Lausanne (Route 56).

6¾ Geneva (See Route 53).

ROUTE 53.

DIJON TO GENEVA.

25 French posts = 110 Eng. miles. Diligences run daily.

Dijon. *Inns*: Hotel du Parc, in a sort of park outside the town;— H. de Cloche in the midst of the town.

Dijon, the ancient capital of the Dukedom of Burgundy, owes its origin and name to the Roman town *Dibio*: it is now chief town of the department of Côte d'Or, and contains 26,000 inhabitants.

The *Church of St. Benigne* merits notice, but, like the other ecclesiastical edifices in the town, it has not recovered the injuries it sustained in the Revolution. " The *Church of Notre Dame* is a very fine specimen of the purest and earliest Gothic, and very interesting for the boldness of its construction. It was much studied for this reason by the celebrated Vauban. The façade of the building exhibits a remarkable effect of light and shade. On this façade still stand the clock and striking figures brought by Philip le Bon from Courtray."—P.

The *Museum* contains a collection of second-rate pictures, and some very interesting relics of the middle ages. In it are also placed two very curious monuments of Jean Sans Peur and Philip le Hardi, Dukes of Burgundy, formerly in the Carthusian Church. They were taken down and pulled to pieces at the Revolution, but have been repaired "and restored with great skill. The alabaster figures of mourners by which they are surrounded are, perhaps, the finest specimens of sculpture of the sort now existing.

" There are some valuable private collections here, particularly one formed by the late M. Baudot, where, amongst other objects, may be seen the Bauble of the celebrated fraternity called ' La Mère Folle.'

"A day may be well and agreeably spent in this fine city.' —*P.*

2 Genlis. This village is often mistaken for the residence of the celebrated Madame de Genlis;—she, however, lived at another Genlis, in Picardy.

1¾ Auxonne—(*Inn :* Hotel du Grand Cerf)—a fortress on the Sôane.

2 Dôle (*Inn :* Hotel de la Ville de Paris). In clear weather Mont Blanc may be seen from this neighbourhood.

2½ Mont Sous Vaudrey. A delightful road leads from this to Neuchâtel, by Salins and the Val Travers (Route 49).

2¼ Poligni (*Inn :* Hotel de Genève). The road hence over the Jura was constructed by Napoleon.

1½ Montrond.

1½ Champagnole has two small inns, Hotel de Genève and de Lyon.

1½ Maisonneuve.

1½ St. Laurent (*Inn:* La Poste).

1½ Morey (*Inn :* La Poste).

1½ Les Rousses. Here is the frontier Custom-house of France. Travellers arriving from Geneva undergo strict search. Trinkets, musical boxes, and watches (more than one) are prohibited, and, if declared, are confis-

cated; if discovered concealed, the are confiscated with a fine. Fro recent information (1838), it a pears that watches may now b introduced by paying a duty of 4 f apiece.

1¾ La Vattay. In descending th mountain a sublime view is disclose of the Alps, Mont Blanc, the lake Geneva, and the intervening plai There is another road to Geneva b St. Cergues (instead of Gex), " branches off a little beyond Les Rous ses, and is very preferable in ever respect. This road has been mad at a great expense by the Canton d Vaud within the last 10 years, and i is one of the finest works of the kind In going *from* Geneva to Paris, it i particularly to be recommended, a the ascent is much less severe.

" Les Rousses to St. Cergues, 1 post; St. Cergues to Nyon.

"The traveller is recommended t mount the steep and picturesqu streets of Nyon up to the fine ol Château, once the seat of the Bailli de Nyon, in order to see the view from the Terrasse des Marroniers."

" St. Cergues is the spot from which the Dôle, the highest summi of this part of the chain of the Jura can be most easily ascended. Mule and guides can be procured at the small inn of St. Cergues, which af fords tolerable accommodation for a night. The ascent of the Dôle from St. Cergues requires about three hours' march; but it is neithe fatiguing nor dangerous. Perhaps there is no mountain in Switzerland which better repays the traveller for his fatigue ; and no view more wonderfully extensive, and admirably diversified, than that which it commands."—*R.*

2 Gex. Ferney, Voltaire's residence (described in page 139), is passed 5 miles before reaching

2 GENEVA.—(*Inns :* Hotel des Bergues, a grand establishment, recently built, facing the lake—expensive. *Charges*—Table d'hote at 1, 3f.; at 5, 4f., including wine; dinner

private, 6f., without wine; break-st, 2f.; tea, 1½f. For 4 beds and sitting-room overlooking the lake, f. a-day were charged in 1837; rvants' board, 4f. a-day;—Cou-nne, a very good house, recently re-ilt, and also facing the lake, capital isine, and more moderate charges; room on the 2nd floor, fronting e lake, cost only 3f. a-day;—'Ecu de Genève;—La Balance. t Sècheron, about 1½ mile from eneva, on the road to Lausanne, the Hotel d'Angleterre, kept by ejean, and nearer to the town on e same side the Hotel des Etran-ers, which is well spoken of.)

Geneva, though capital of the nallest of the Swiss Cantons, except ug, is the most populous town in ae Confederation, since it contains),960 inhabitants. It is well situ-ed, at the W. extremity of the lake ' Geneva, at the point where "the tue waters of the arrowy Rhone" sue out of it. The river divides the wn into two parts, and the intensely lue colour of its waters, alluded to y Byron, is certainly very remark ble, and resembles nothing so much s the discharge of indigo from a yer's vat. The cause of it has not een satisfactorily explained. Sir Iumphry Davy attributed it to the resence of iodine. The extreme urity lasts but for a short space, ince a mile below the town it is pol-uted by the admixture of the waters f the turbid Arve, and retains the ame dingy hue all the way to the sea.

Geneva, if approached from the ake, now presents a very imposing ppearance, in consequence of im-rovements recently completed, for vhich it is indebted, in no slight de-gree, to the circulation of the gold f English travellers among its inha-itants. An entirely new quarter as started up on the rt. bank of the Rhone, called Quartier des Bergues, nd displays a handsome front of tall uouses, among which is the Hotel les Bergues, lined with a broad quay, owards the lake. A spirit of emu-lation has been excited on the oppo-site bank by the sight of this modern rival. The unsightly houses which lined the margin of the lake have been refaced and beautified, while a broad belt of land has been gained from the water to form a Quai. This is connected with the Quai des Bergues by two handsome bridges, thrown across the lake, and united with a small island, formerly a part of the fortifications, now occupied by a very inferior statue of Rousseau. Geneva is still surrounded with ram-parts and bastions, erected in the middle of the last century by the aristocratic magistracy of that period. It is divided into the upper and lower town; and this distinction, arising from the uneven nature of the ground, is perpetuated in the rank and con-dition of the inhabitants of the two divisions. The upper town consists almost entirely of the large and handsome hotels of the burgher aristocracy, heretofore the senators and magistrates of the republic. The lower town is the seat of trade and of democracy: its streets are narrow, its houses lofty, and it has something of the air of the old town of Edinburgh. A few of the older buildings are furnished with a shed or pent-house, called here, " *Dome,*" projecting from the roof over the street, and supported by wooden props, and reaching from the pave-ment to the roof. About 25 years ago they were almost universal, but their number, of late, has diminished, and the whole row which lined the houses in the Rue Basse has been taken down by order of the govern-ment.

The feuds arising between the high and low town were not few, nor void of interest; indeed, they would fill a long and amusing historical chapter: they often led to bloodshed, but the democrats below generally brought their exalted neighbours to reason by the simple expedient of cutting off the water-pipes, taking especial care to guard the hydraulic machine which furnished the supply to the upper town, and which is situated in their quarter.

Although Geneva is a great focus of attraction for travellers of all nations, 30,000 being the number which is calculated to pass through the town annually, it possesses few objects of interest to the passing stranger. As a town it is not very prepossessing; it has no fine public buildings, and scarcely any *sights*. It is owing to its beautiful environs, to its vicinity to Chamouni, to the charming scenery of its lake, and to its position on the high road from Paris to Italy, that it has become a place of so much resort.

The *Cathedral*, or *Church of St. Pierre*, is of an extreme simplicity of architecture. The Corinthian portico added on the outside is a blemish where it is placed, but its interior possesses interest as a very early and uncorrupted specimen of the Gothic of the eleventh century. It contains the tombs of Agrippa d'Aubigny, the friend of Henry IV., and grandfather of Mad. de Maintenon, and that of the Comte de Rohan, a leader of the French Protestants in the reign of Louis XIII.

The *Musée Rath*, so named after its founder, General Rath, who left the reversion of his fortune to it, is a neat building, close to the Porte Neuve; it contains a collection of pictures and other works of art, of no very great merit, the greater part by native artists. Among the Genevese painters, Töpfer, Guignon, Hornung, and Calame, deserve to be mentioned.

The *Musée d'Histoire Naturelle*, in the Grande-Rue, is chiefly interesting to the student as containing the geological collections of Saussure; the fossil plants of M.M. Brogniart and Decandolle, and the collections of M. Necker. It is principally filled with the native productions of Switzerland, and contains specimens of the chamois, of the Bouquetin, the dog of St. Bernard, of all the fishes of the rivers and

lakes of this country; among the the *ferra*, the lotte, and a trout weighing 43lbs. from the lake of Geneva.

There is the skin of an elephant which lived a long time in a menagerie in the town, but at length becoming unruly was shot.

There is also a cabinet of *antiquities*; some of them found in the neighbourhood, such as a silver buckler, discovered in the bed of the Arve, inscribed "Largitus Valentniani Augusti;" some instruments of sacrifice found near the rocks Neptune in the lake, &c. &c. Also the lantern carried by the sentinel who, in going his rounds, discovered the Savoyards scaling the walls 1602 (see p. 134).

The *Reading-room*, in the upper story of the museum, is well supplied with the best European journals, including the Times, John Bull, Athenæum, &c. Strangers receiving " carte d'entrée" from a member are liberally admitted for a month.

The best and most fashionable club in Geneva is that called the *Cercle* de la Rive.

The *Public Library* attached to the *College*, a scholastic-looking building, of no architectural pretensions, behind the cathedral, founded by Calvin, contains 40,000 volumes, and the following curiosities :—3 folio volumes of autograph letters of Calvin (there is one addressed to Lady Jane Grey while a prisoner in the Tower); many of Calvin's manuscript sermons; several volumes of letters of Theodore Beza; the manuscript of the " Noble Leçon," a work of the ancient Waldenses. The account-book of the household of Philip le Bel, written with a style upon waxed tablets, but now almost effaced; a translation of Quintu Curtius, taken along with the baggage of Charles the Bold, at Morat The discourses of St. Augustine, a MS. on papyrus of the 7th century The library is opened only 3 times a-week—Monday,Tuesday, and Wednesday, from 1 to 4.

Geneva, if looked at in an historical int of view, may be said to possess a interest for the intelligent travel- r far greater than that to be de- ved from the individual objects of riosity contained within its walls. ne influence which she has ex- cised, not only over Europe but er the world, by means of her chil- en, or those whom she has adopt- d as her citizens, is quite out of oportion to the limited extent of territory which one may traverse om end to end in a morning's ride. oltaire ridiculed its diminutiveness saying, " Quand je secoue ma rruque je poudre toute la repub- que ;" and the Emperor Paul called e disputes of its citizens a tem- st in a tumbler of water; yet om Geneva emanated those reli- ous doctrines whence Scotland, olland, and a large part of France, ermany, and Switzerland derive eir form of faith, and which was ansported by the pilgrim fathers to e opposite shores of the Atlantic. ere also were sown those political pinions which bore fruit in the Eng- sh revolution under Charles I., in e American and the French revo- tions.

Some few memorials still exist in e town serving to recall the events hich have occurred in it, and the reat names connected with it.

On the island, in the middle of the hone, not far from the Hydraulic achine, traces may, it is said, be dis- vered of a Roman structure, sup- osed to be the foundations of one the towers erected by Julius æsar, to prevent the Helvetians ossing the river. The earliest ention of Geneva occurs in his ommentaries, where it is described s " the last fortress of the Allo- roges, and nearest to the Helvetian ontier." " Near the ' Bourg du our ' is a very ancient arch, possi- ly Roman, but which some anti- uaries have considered a portion of e Palace of Clotilda, queen of lovis; others attribute it to Beitha,

queen of Burgundy. It is, at all events, of very early date. Near it is the town residence of the cele- brated M. Sismondi."—*P.*

The building of the *Old Prison*, still called the Evêché, near St. Peter's church, was originally the palace of the bishops, who governed the city as temporal rulers, elected by the citizens, for many ages ; but at length became almost nominees of the Duke of Savoy. The citizens, from the very first, enjoyed a liberty above other great towns of the empire, and showed a bold and steady resistance to the encroachments of their rulers, main- taining, against force and persuasion, the municipal prerogatives derived from their ancestors and from the Golden Bull of the Emperor Charles IV. Thus, by a cautious and well- conducted policy, they avoided being swallowed up by their powerful neigh- bours, Savoy and France, or by their friends the Swiss Cantons, who, though called in as allies to protect them, were equally ambitious of in- corporating Geneva in their own territory as a subject state.

John Calvin, the reformer, is sup- posed to have lived in the house now occupied by the Evangelical Society, No. 116, in the rue des Chanoines, and he probably died there. It was in the year 1536 that he passed through the town a fugitive, on his way from Italy to Basle. Two years had not elapsed since the Genevese had abolished Roman Catholicism, expelled their bishop, and adopted the Reformation. Farel, who was the means of introducing it, was then preaching at Geneva, and, aware of Calvin's talents and powerful elo- quence, entreated him to remain. Calvin obeyed the call, and, in a short space, the itinerant preacher and foreigner was raised to be the dictator of the republic, ruling its turbulent democracy with a sway not more mild than that of the dukes of Savoy and bishops of Ge- neva, under which the citizens had groaned for ages, and from which the reformation had at length released them. From the pulpit of St. Peter's church, which became at once the tribune and judgment-seat of the reformer, he denounced the prevailing immorality of the town with such eloquence and force that profligacy was obliged to hide its head. His hearers, running into an opposite extreme, adopted a rigorous and puritanical austerity of manners, and every transgression of Calvin's code of morals was visited with punishment of the utmost severity.

But Calvin's influence was not confined to the pulpit; he was elected president of the Consistory, of which one-third of the permanent members were ministers, and the remainder laymen holding office for a year only. This counsel assumed an authority far more despotic than that of the bishops: it exercised the power of an inquisition, to examine into men's private lives, and into the affairs of families of whatever rank.

The sumptuary laws enacted by Calvin were severe, but were rigidly enforced by the Consistory. They contained such enactments as the following: a dinner for ten persons was limited to five dishes; plush breeches were laid under interdict; violations of the sabbath were followed by a public admonition from the pulpit; adultery was punished with death; and the gamester was exposed in the pillory, with a pack of cards tied round his neck.

Calvin was equally rigorous in the maintenance of orthodoxy. Servetus, condemned by him for holding anti-trinitarian doctrines which, however, he did not attempt to disseminate in Geneva, was burnt at the stake in the *Champ de Bourreau,* the ancient place of execution outside the walls. The hole in which it was planted is now filled up, and the destination of the spot is changed. This act of the stern lawgiver admits of no palliation, as his victim was not a subject of Geneva, and therefore not amenable to its laws. The execution Servetus casts a stain upon Gene and the cause of the Reformation great as that with which the murd of Huss taints the Papist Council Constance.

Geneva, thus become the metr polis of Calvinism, and " the Ron of Protestantism," was resorted by many foreigners, who soug refuge here from religious persec tions in their own country. Amor a number of English and Scot exiled by the atrocities of the rei of Bloody Mary, was John Kno He was made a citizen of Geneva 1558, and did not finally quit it t 1560. Calvin died in 1564, at t age of 55, after 23 years of uninte rupted power: he was buried in t old *cemetery of the Plain Palais,* no abandoned; but he forbade the G nevese to mark the spot where h remains were laid with a monumen and the very site of his grave is n known with certainty. A Geneve law now limits the period of propert in a grave to 15 years, after which may be opened for a fresh occupant.

The Duke of Savoy, whose auth rity within the town had been d stroyed by the expulsion of the bisho was unwilling, notwithstanding, abandon his claim to the possessio of it. For many years after th event he was engaged in repeate open contests with the citizens; nc did he omit to maintain within th walls, spies and secret partisans, i the hopes of gaining possession of by surprise. The street called *Co raterie,* at the time of the town ditcl was the scene of the most memorab of these attempts, known in Swis history as *the Escalade.* In 1602 th inhabitants, lulled to security by display of pacific intentions on th part of the reigning Duke Charle Emanuel, had neglected all precau tions to guard against an attack, eve though warnings had been give them of approaching danger. O the night of Dec. 20th, the town wa aroused from sleep by the firing o

usketry, and an alarm that the
nemy was already in possession. It
ppeared that a sentinel, in going
s rounds with a lantern, had fallen
mong a party of armed men, who
ad quickly despatched him, but not
efore his cries and the report of his
atchlock had alarmed the rest of
ne guard. It was quickly disco-
ered that a party of Savoyards, 200
trong, detached from a still larger
rce of 2000 men, who had approach-
d the city in the darkness, and were
osted on the Plain Palais, a little
istance beyond the walls, had de-
cended into the fosse of Corraterie,
nd by the aid of scaling-ladders,
ainted black in order that they
night not be seen, had surmounted
ne ramparts, were proceeding in
mall parties to burst open the Porte
Neuve, and thus admit their asso-
iates on the outside. The Savoyards
ad already despatched a messenger
nnouncing to their commander the
apture of the town ; but the citizens,
hough completely taken by surprise,
vere by no means seized with the
anic which such an occurrence was
ikely to produce. Every man, arm-
d as he might be, issued out into
he streets; the small body of Savoyards who had gained the ramparts
were quickly overpowered ; the first
gun fired from the walls, by a chance
shot, swept away three of the scaling-
ladders ; and the enemy on the outside, on approaching the Porte Neuve,
found that, instead of being blown
up, it was strongly guarded, with the
portcullis down. Many anecdotes
are told of the prowess of the town's-
people on that night, and an iron
saucepan, with which an old woman
knocked down a soldier, is still preserved in the arsenal along with a
piece of the scaling-ladders. The
storming party thus unexpectedly
attacked, and at the same time cut
off from their friends, were quickly
killed or made prisoners. Those who
fell alive into the hands of the Genevese were hung next day as house-
breakers : 67 heads were planted

along the ramparts ; but many more
than these fell in the ditch and outside the town. In the *cemetery of
St. Gervais*, on the right bank of the
Rhone, a monument epitaph was set
up to commemorate the names of
17 Genevese who were killed on the
occasion ; and the venerable Theodore Beza, at that time 80 years old,
gave out from the pulpit next day the
124th Psalm, which has been sung
ever since on the anniversary of the
Escalade.

Jean Jacques Rousseau, son of a
watchmaker of Geneva, first saw the
light in a street of the Quartier St.
Gervais, since named after him (Rue
de Rousseau), and in the house No.
69. It is no longer in its original
condition, having been altered and
partly rebuilt. His book, the *Emile*,
was burnt, in conformity with an
order of the Council of Geneva, by
the common hangman, in front of
the Hôtel de Ville in 1762. The in-
stigators of this act were Voltaire and
the Council of the Sorbonne, who,
by a singular coincidence, in this
instance, acted in unison. The
Council at the same time issued a
warrant for the arrest of the author.

The *Botanic Garden* behind the
theatre and near the Porte Neuve
deserves mention, as having been
laid out under the direction of the
eminent botanist Decandolle; but the
funds are so limited that the collection
of plants is of no great importance.
The ground it occupies has also painful historical associations. Geneva, for
ages the nursery of republicanism
and democratic opinions, became "a
principle of explosion to revolutionary France, placed at its extremity,
as the *fuse* is on the surface of the
bomb," but she likewise reaped the
fruits of the seed sown by her in the
establishment of a tribunal of blood
and the enactment of a reign of terror in 1794; a humble imitation
of that of Paris. On this spot
took place fusillades and but-
cheries, too horrible to be detailed,
in which the blood of the most

respectable citizens of the town was shed, condemned to execution by a band of wretches, most of whom were their fellow-citizens, though directed by a deputy from the Comité de Salut Public, at Paris. Here, as in other places, subjected to the madness of the reign of terror, the atrocities were committed by a mere handful of assassins, while thousands looked on, disapproving, but yet not raising a voice to condemn, nor an arm to resist. Another result of the connexion of Switzerland with France was the forfeiture of its independence. After resisting, for ages, the encroachments and attacks of the Dukes of Savoy, and the intrigues of despotic France, even when under the rule of the all-powerful Louis XIV., the republic was destined to fall by the treachery of fellow-republicans, with whom she had so recently fraternized. Geneva was taken by surprise April 15, 1798, and arbitrarily annexed to France, forming a part of the department of the Leman.

Besides the names of Calvin and Rousseau, which are connected with Geneva—the one by adoption, the other by birth—it is the birth-place of many illustrious men, whose reputation may be styled European. The list includes those of Abauzit and Casaubon; of Lefort, the friend and councillor of Peter the Great; of Necker, the weak and ill-starred minister of Louis XVI., and father of Madame de Stael; of the naturalists Saussure, who first ascended Mont Blanc, Bonnet, and De Luc; and Huber, the biographer of the bee and ant; and of Dumont, the friend and adviser of Mirabeau and Jeremy Bentham. Among the living there are Sismondi, the historian; Decandolle, the botanist; Neckar, the geologist; De la Rive, the chemist; and Marmoir, the oculist.

Geneva may be regarded as the intellectual metropolis of Switzerland, and strangers who choose it as their residence, if provided with good

introductions, will find among th upper classes a very agreeable societ including many individuals disti guished for their literary and scie tific acquirements.

The staple manufacture of Geneva from which it derives its chief com mercial prosperity, is-that of *watche musical boxes*, and *jewellery*. Th first watch was brought to Genev in 1587, and at the end of the las century 4000 persons were employ ed within the town, and 2000 wit out the walls, on this manufactur At present the number is diminishe to less than 3000, though, from im provements in the mechanical pro cesses and increased skill of th workmen, the number of watche made is much greater than before more than 20,000 being now manu factured annually. Upwards of 5 watchmakers' and 70 jewellers' work shops are kept in constant employ ment in the town, and it has bee calculated that in good years 75,00 ounces of gold, 5000 marks of silver and precious stones to the value o a million of francs, are used in them A committee of master workmen wit a syndic at their head, called *com mission de surveillance*, are appointe by the Government to inspect ever workshop and the articles made i it, to guard against fraud in the sub stitution of metals not of legal alloy and thus to prevent any deterioratio in a branch of industry productive o so great an advantage to Geneva Lecoultre et François are recom mended as respectable watchmakers their shop is in the Rue de la Corrat terie. Capt Aubert, Place du Rhone opposite the bridge, seems to have a good assortment of jewellery. As a working jeweller Schatz-Viguier, a the corner of the Cité, is very good and more moderate in his prices.

The French Custom-house is very severe in prohibiting the entrance o Genevese manufactures into France musical snuff-boxes, and more than one watch are contraband, and l iable to seizure. (It is possible that these estrictions may have been recently ...odified.) The jewellers of Geneva, owever, will guarantee the safe delivery of any articles purchased from them either in Paris or London, upon payment of a small per centage on their value by way of insurance. Smuggling is carried on to an enormous extent between the Swiss and French frontiers.

Theatrical performances, for centuries interdicted in Geneva by one of the austere laws of Calvin, are now tolerated, and a *Salle de Spectacle* has been built close to the Porte Neuve. Voltaire greatly shocked the prejudices of the citizens by acting plays, as it were under their very nose, at Les Délices and Ferney. Rousseau writes to him, " Je ne vous aime pas, vous avez corrompue ma république en lui donnant des spectacles."

Passports are demanded at the gates with as much strictness and formality as in the dominions of a despotic monarch. Before going to Chamouni (Route 115) (an excursion which no traveller should omit, as it includes the sublimest Alpine scenery in Europe), the signature of the *Sardinian consul* is necessary, and for it 4 francs are charged. His house is in Rue Verdine, not far from the Porte de Rive.

The *gates of Geneva* are shut at 10 in the evening, and a small toll is exacted up to midnight, after which it is doubled. In former times they finally closed before midnight, and it will be remembered that it was the accident of being shut out one evening, on his return from a walk in the country, that induced Rousseau to fly from his native town and a tyrannical master, whom he, as a truant apprentice, feared to face.

On the grand Quai, close to the port where the steamers land, a *limnimetre* (lake measure) has been erected to mark the rise and fall of the waters of the lake.

Near the *Boucheries,* on the same quai, the town maintains, at the pub-

lic expense, a brace of eagles. These birds are the armorial bearings of Geneva, as the bear is of Berne.

The *English church service* is performed in the church of the hospital every Sunday at half-past 11.

The *Post-office* is in the Rue du Rhone: a letter reaches England in 6 days.

Diligences go *daily* to Paris in 72 hours, to Lyons in 24 hours, to Berne in 22 hours, to Zurich and Basle in 44; to Lausanne, Vevey, and St. Maurice; to Neuchâtel in 16 hours ; to Sallenche, on the way to Chamouni, *daily ;* to Chamberry and Turin, by way of Annecy, 3 or 4 times a-week; 3 *times* a-week over the Simplon to Milan, in 67 hours.

De Jean, a celebrated master voiturier ($ 7), has an office in the Place du Rhone.

" Placed as Geneva is on the furthest range of those states, in which freedom of trade is allowed, it may be useful to add, that the English traveller, especially if he be proceeding to the French or Austrian dominions, will do well to provide himself here with those little English comforts which he will not find beyond the next custom-house. At the shop of Archinard and Bordier, in the Rue Basse, all kinds of English cutlery and household goods may be had genuine. The Demoiselles Lacour, in the Grande Rue, are celebrated for gloves and ladies' shoes ; and the tourist will not disdain to be told that Wistag, at the Château Royal, near the Porte de Cornavin, has the best supply of cigars, tobacco, and snuff, which is to be met with on the continent. Wesel, in the Grande Rue, has a complete assortment of English stationery."—*R.*

Steam-boats traverse the lake daily, and two of them make the voyage to Villeneuve and back in 8½ hours (see p. 142).

Environs of Geneva.

It has been already observed, that

Geneva is chiefly distinguished for its beautiful situation, on the margin of an enchanting lake, whose gently-sloping banks are scattered over with villas, surrounded by gardens, and looking more like English country-houses than any to be found in other parts of the Continent.

The rides, walks, and views in the vicinity are delightful, and almost endless; but the great charm of every prospect is the *Mont Blanc*, and the range of Alps of Savoy, when they deign to show themselves, which they do not, in perfect distinctness, more than 60 times a-year, on an average. There cannot be a more lovely sight than that of Mont Blanc, and the surrounding Aiguilles, tinged with the pink hue which the departing sun sheds upon them, in certain states of the atmosphere.

The *Ramparts*, no longer of much use as fortifications, serve as promenades. Three suspension bridges of iron wire have been thrown over them, to facilitate ingress and egress between the town and surrounding country. The *Bastion de Chante-poulet* is a good point of view to see the lake and Mont Blanc. In the *Cemetery* of *Plain Palais*, a little way beyond the Porte Neuve, Sir Humphry Davy, who died here in 1829, is buried.

In the bed of the lake lie many granitic boulders, transported from the high Alps. Two of these, a short distance beyond the port of Geneva, and a little to the S.E. of the town, are so large as to project above the water. They are called *Pierres de Niton*, from a tradition that sacrifices were offered upon them to the god *Neptune* by the Romans. Indeed instruments of sacrifice have been found near them.

The *junction of the Arve with the Rhone* is worth visiting, and is best seen from the grounds of a country-house, called Chatellainie, or Campagne Matthieu, on the rt. bank of the road, about 1½ mile beyond the Porte de Cornavin. On the way to

it, Les Delices, a country-house c Voltaire, is passed.

The Arve, a furious torrent, fed b the snows and glaciers of Mon Blanc, looks like a river of muc The pellucid blue waters of th Rhone, though driven on one side b the furious entrance of its new all for a long time refuse to mix wit it, and the line of separation betwee the blue and white water is most dis tinctly marked. At length the Arv gains the mastery, and the Rhone once polluted, does not recover it purity before reaching the sea.

On the S.E. side of Geneva rise the *Mont Salève*, a long line of lime stone precipices, seeming to impen over the town, though it is in realit 5 miles off, and within the Sardinia territory. Those who are acquainte with Edinburgh may be reminded o Salisbury Crags in looking at it The S. side of this mountain is gentle slope, covered with verdan pasture, and sprinkled with houses The whole of this vast inclined plan facing the Alps is strewn over wit fragments of rock (protogîne), iden tical with that of which Mont Blan is composed. By what agency the have been transported hither—a dis tance of 50 miles, as the crow flies— let the geologist explain. The larges of these masses is 7 ft. long.

The summit of the Salève, more thar 3100 ft. above the lake, is frequentl scaled by the inhabitants of Geneva who make picnic parties to enjoy th view from its summit. The shortes road to it is by Carouge and Veyrier 3 miles; whence a very steep path practicable only on foot, leads up a gap in the mountain, partly formed by steps cut in the rock, and called *Pas de l'Echelle*, to the village o Monetier (pronounced Monte) 2 miles. Those who cannot walk may reach Monetier by a carriage-road which makes a detour of 8 miles from Geneva, through the beautiful village of Mornex, at the back of the moun tain. The pleasantest way is to be driven to Monetier, thence to ascend the Petit, or the Grand Salève, on foot, and to descend the Pas de l'Echelle on foot to Veyrier, whither the carriage may be sent round to wait for the party."—*R.*

From Monetier to the top is about two miles. The view extends S. up the valley of the Arve over the Mole to Mont Blanc; E. over a vast expanse of the lake; N. to the town of Geneva, the Rhone, and the Jura behind; W. the eye follows the valley of the Rhone as far as the gap in the Jura Mountain, through which the river forces its way into France.

On the S. shore of the lake, about 2 miles from Geneva, and a little to the l. of the high-road to Thonon, is the *Campagne Diodati*, Lord Byron's residence in 1816 ; where he wrote the greater part of his " Manfred," and the 3rd canto of " Childe Harold."

The object of the greatest attraction to travellers, however, near Geneva, is, commonly, *Ferney*, the residence of Voltaire. It is situated within the French territory, about 5 miles N. of Geneva, on the road to Paris by Gex. On the way thither, near Grand Saconnex, an eminence presents one of the best points of view of Mont Blanc.

Voltaire resided for nearly 20 years at Ferney, from 1759 to 1777. He may be said to be the founder of the village, which, before his time, consisted of but 6 or 8 hovels. He collected industrious colonists, introduced useful manufactures among them, and improved his estate of about 900 acres by draining, &c., besides building on it the *Château* which still exists. On the l. hand, as you enter the gates, stands the *Church*, originally inscribed with the words " Deo erexit Voltaire ;" the *Theatre* stood opposite, in which his own tragedies were acted by amateurs, but it no longer exists. The Château was never handsome, and is now somewhat dilapidated. Two rooms are still preserved, nearly in the state in which Voltaire left them. The furniture is faded by time, and decayed principally from the depredations of mischievous, relic-hunting visitors. The curtains of his bed are reduced to one-third of their original length by such thefts, and, if the practice be not arrested, will soon disappear altogether. On the walls of his bed-room hang some bad prints, but selected and placed there by himself; and worse paintings of his friends, Frederick the Great (a present from himself), Le Kain the actor, Catherine II. of Russia (executed in needle-work by her own hand), and Madame de Châstelet. The Russian Empress, it will be remembered, sent an embassy from St. Petersburg to Ferney to compliment the Nestor of poets. On one side of the room is a monument, intended to hold his heart, inscribed, " Mes manes son consolés puisque mon cœur est au milieu de vous :" it was set up by his adopted daughter, the Marquise de Vilette, and bears a strong resemblance to a German stove. By the side of it hang portraits of his seamstress, of the Savoyard boy, his servant, and of Pope Ganganelli. In the ante-room is a singular picture, painted by some artist of sign-post calibre, but designed by Voltaire himself. On the l. hand he appears in the act of being introduced to Apollo by Henry IV., who holds in his hand a copy of the " Henriade." On the opposite side, the same Voltaire is seen conducted in triumph by the Muses to the Temple of Memory, while his enemies and detractors, prostrated before him, writhe in torments beneath his feet.

The situation of Ferney is most charming, in full view of the lake and of Mont Blanc; but of its beauty Voltaire seems to have had no idea, or at least no taste for it, as the windows of the house are turned directly away from the landscape. In the garden is a long berceau walk closely arched over with clipped horn beam—a verdant cloister, with gaps cut in it, here and there, to admit a glimpse of the prospect. Here he used to walk up and down, and dictate to his secretary. Among the trees of the grove round the house is an elm, planted by his own hand in 1763 : it was struck by lightning in 1824. The old gardener of Voltaire, who was living within a few years, related some curious particulars of his master. He was always addressed by the people of the village as " Monseigneur :" he drove out every day in a gilt coach, drawn by 4 horses, and he was a terror to all the little boys he met in his walks. Ferney, at present, belongs to the family of M. Budé de Boissy.

Perte du Rhone.

For travellers who are unacquainted with the route from Lyons to Geneva, the excursion to the Perte du Rhone at Bellegarde on the French frontier, may be recommended. The distance is about 16 miles, and by starting early it may easily be accomplished in a day. The road lies through St. Genix, where it turns off to the W., and skirts the base of the Jura to Collonges. A little beyond this village you enter

———— " where the swift Rhone cleaves his way between
Heights which appear as lovers who have parted."

The lofty Vuache on the side of Savoy, and the huge mass of the highest part of the Jura chain, slope precipitously down to the torrent of the Rhone. The road hangs midway in this prodigious passage, and the celebrated *Fort de l'Ecluse,* the fortress which gives its name to the pass, commands this entrance of France. Infinite labour and expense have been used by the French Government to strengthen this position ; additional batteries have been hewn in

the rock above the lower fortress, and these communicate with the guard-rooms below by a broad staircase, more than 100 feet in height, hewn inside the solid mountain. Leave may sometimes be obtained from the governor to view the fortress ; but at any rate the road passes through it, and enables the traveller to see something of its remarkable defences. From Collonges to Belle-garde (*Hotel de la Poste*) the road sweeps along the wild gorge through which the Rhone pours. At Belle-garde it crosses the narrow and rocky bed of the Valseline. The traveller will walk from the inn to the Perte du Rhone ($\frac{1}{4}$ of a mile) ; he will find plenty of squalid guides to show him the spot where the river, which he has accompanied from the clear cistern of its waters through the rough mountain pass, plunges at once into the earth. When the waters are tolerably low, as in the spring or winter, the whole river is absorbed for a distance of 120 yards. No bottom has ever been found to the huge cavern which engorges the Rhone ; nor has any substance or living thing thrown into it been known to come out again. The bed of the Valseline is more picturesque and scarcely less curious than the Perte. It is worth while to descend from the garden of the inn into the worn channel of this little river, which is almost dry in summer time, except where a runlet of its water burrows into the clefts and fantastic bends of the calcareous rock.

Another pleasant excursion may be made to D'Ivoune where the river Versoix takes its rise in a pretty grotto at the foot of the Jura ; and people go to eat the small delicate trout which are taken in it. The view from the terrace of the Château D'Ivoune is very fine. The best road to go is by Coppet and Celigny (where the water-falls should also be visited), and to return by Ferney. The distance from Geneva to D'Ivoune is about 8 miles.

ROUTE 55.

THE LAKE OF GENEVA.

Lake Leman, in a Calm.

" Clear, placid Leman! thy contrasted
    lake,
With the wild world I dwell in, is a thing
Which warns me, with its stillness, to
    forsake
Earth's troubled waters for a purer
    spring.
This quiet sail is as a noiseless wing
To waft me from destruction; once I
    loved
Torn ocean's roar, but thy soft murmur-
    ing
Sounds sweet as if a Sister's voice re-
    proved,
That I with stern delights should e'er have
    been so moved.

It is the hush of night, and all between
Thy margin and the mountains, dusk,
    yet clear,
Mellow'd and mingled, yet distinctly
    seen,
Save darken'd Jura, whose capt heights
    appear
Precipitously steep; and drawing near,
There breathes a living fragrance from
    the shore,
Of flowers yet fresh with childhood; on
    the ear
Drops the light drip of the suspended
    oar,
Or chirps the grasshopper one good-night
    carol more.

At intervals, some bird from out the
    brakes
Starts into voice a moment, then is still.
There seems a floating whisper on the
    hill,
But that is fancy,—for the starlight dews
All silently their tears of love instil,
Weeping themselves away."

Lake Leman, in a Storm.

" Thy sky is changed! — and such a
    change! Oh night,
And storm, and darkness, ye are wondrous
    strong,
Yet lovely in your strength, as is the
    light
Of a dark eye in woman! Far along,
From peak to peak, the rattling crags
    among
Leaps the live thunder! Not from one
    lone cloud,
But every mountain now hath found a
    tongue,
And Jura answers, through her misty
    shroud,
Back to the joyous Alps, who call to her
    aloud!

Now, where the swift Rhone cleaves his
    way between
Heights which appear as lovers who have
    parted
In hate, whose mining depths so inter-
    vene,
That they can meet no more, though
    broken hearted!
Though in their souls, which thus each
    other thwarted,
Love was the very root of the fond rage
Which blighted their life's bloom, and
    then departed:
Itself expired, but leaving them an age
Of years all winters,—war within them-
    selves to wage.

Now, where the quick Rhone thus hath
    cleft his way,
The mightiest of the storms hath ta'en
    his stand:
For here, not one, but many, make their
    play,
And fling their thunder-bolts from hand
    to hand,
Flashing and cast around: of all the
    band,
The brightest through these parted hills
    hath fork'd
His lightnings,—as if he did understand,
That in such gaps as desolation work'd,
There the hot shaft should blast whatever
    therein lurk'd.

And this is in the night:—Most glorious
    night!
Thou wert not sent for slumber! let me
    be
A sharer in thy fierce and far delight,—
A portion of the tempest and of thee!
How the lit lake shines. a phosphoric sea,
And the big rain comes dancing to the
    earth!
And now again 'tis black,—and now, the
    glee
Of the loud hills shakes with its moun-
    tain-mirth,
As if they did rejoice o'er a 'young earth-
    quake's birth.

Sky, mountains, river, winds, lake, light-
    nings! ye!
With night, and clouds, and thunder, and
    a soul
To make these felt and feelings, well may
    be
Things that have made me watchful; the
    far roll
Of your departing voices, is the knoll
Of what in me is sleepless,—if I rest.
But where of ye, oh tempests! is the
    goal?
Are ye like those within the human
    breast?
Or do ye find, at length, like eagles, some
    high nest?"

Byron.

The Lake of Geneva, called by the
Romans Lacus Lemanus, has nearly

the shape of a half-moon, its horns being turned towards the S. It is the largest lake in Switzerland, being 55 miles long, measured close to its N. shore, and about 40 miles along its S. bank ; it is 6 miles wide at the broadest part (between Rolle and Thonon), and its greatest depth (between Evian and Ouchy) is 900 ft. Its waters often vary in one year more than 50 inches, being usually lowest in the winter, between January and April, and highest in August and part of July and September, owing to the supplies then derived from the melting snows and glaciers. Besides these periodical variations, the lake is subject to other more arbitrary changes of level, called *seiches.* This phenomenon consists of a sudden rise and fall of the water in particular parts of the lake, independently of the agency of the wind or of any other apparent cause. It is most common in the vicinity of Geneva. During these oscillations the waters sometimes rise 5 ft., though the usual increase is not more than 2 ; it never lasts longer than 25 minutes, but is generally less. The cause of these seiches has not been explained with certainty, but it is believed to depend upon the unequal pressure of the atmosphere upon different parts of the surface of the lake ; and they are observed to occur most commonly when the clouds are heavy and low. The lake never freezes entirely, owing to its great depth ; but in severe winters the lower extremity is covered with ice. The sand and mud brought down by the Rhone and deposited around its mouth have caused considerable encroachments upon its upper extremity: even within the records of history Porte Vallais stood on its margin, and its basin is reported to have originally extended upwards as far as Bex.

" Mon lac est le premier" are the words in which Voltaire has vaunted the beauties of the Lake of Geneva ; and it must be confessed that, though it wants the gloomy sublimity of the

Bay of Uri and the sunny softness of the Italian lakes, with their olive and citron groves, it has high claims to admiration. It also possesses great variety of scenery. The vine-covered slopes of Vaud contrast well with the abrupt, rocky precipices of Savoy. Near Geneva the hills subside, admitting an exquisite view of Mont Blanc, whose snowy summit, though 60 miles distant, is often reflected in its waters.

" Lake Leman woos me with its crystal face,
    The mirror where the stars and mountains
        view
    The stillness of their aspect in each trace
    Its clear depth yields of their far height
        and hue."

At its eastern or upper extremity it extends to the very base of the high Alps, which by their close vicinity give its scenery a character of increased magnificence.

The boats on the lake are very picturesque, having latine sails like the craft of the Mediterranean.

Steam-boats, 1838.—There are 4 steamers on the Lake of Geneva. The best and swiftest of these, the *Aigle* and *Vaudoise,* run from Geneva to Villeneuve and back [in 8½ hours, almost as quickly as the other two perform the voyage from one end to the other. The *Leman* and *Winhelried* (the first is the best) set out from either end of the lake daily, and reach the opposite extremity in 7 or 8 hours. The fare is 50 batz. They stop to land and receive passengers at Coppet, Nyon, Rolle, Morges, Ouchy (the port of Lausanne), Vevay, and Villeneuve—all situated on the N. shore of the lake, and described in the next route. The S. or Savoyard shore is described in Route 57.

ROUTE 56.

GENEVA TO MARTIGNY, BY LAUSANNE, VEVAY, CHILLON, BEX, AND ST. MAURICE.

17¼ posts = 71 Eng. miles.

This is a post-road, tolerably supplied with post-horses, the charges being the same as in France, viz. 1 fr. 50 c. for each horse per post, and 75 c. to the postilion, except that for every person in the carriage above the number of horses 1 fr. 50 c. is charged instead of 1 fr. (as in France). The postboys expect 40 sous a post.

Diligences go twice a-day to Lausanne, and four times a-week to Martigny. A voiturier will take about 6½ hours to Lausanne, exclusive of stoppages. The tolls at each post are heavy.

N.B. The road by the S. shore of the lake (Route 57) to St. Maurice is 2½ posts shorter than this by Lausanne.

The greater part of the first stage out of Geneva lies among villas and pleasure-grounds not unlike English country-seats. Few spots in Europe present so many admirable sites for a dwelling as the shores of Lake Leman in full view of Mont Blanc. About a mile from Geneva the Hotel of Sécheron is passed. After a mile or two Mont Blanc is hid behind the intervening mountains of Voirons, and does not reappear until near Nyon.

The parish of Versoix, through which the road passes, formerly belonged to France. The Duke de Choiseul, minister of Louis XV., irritated with some proceedings of the inhabitants of Geneva, proposed to raise a rival city at Versoix which should deprive Geneva of its trade. A pier was projected into the lake, to form a port, a grand place was laid down, and streets running at right angles were marked out; but beyond this the plan was never carried into execution. Hence the verses of Voltaire:—

" A Versoix nous avons des rues,
  Mais nous n'avons point de maisons."

A little beyond Versoix (now an inconsiderable village) we pass out of the Canton of Geneva into that of Vaud.

1¾ Coppet, a small village of 600 inhabitants, only remarkable for the

Château, which belonged to Madame de Staël, immediately behind it. It is now the property of the Duc de Broglie, her son-in-law. It is a plain edifice, forming three sides of a square, the front towards the lake being flanked with a tower at each end. It was the residence of Madame de Staël as well as of her father, the French minister Necker. There is a portrait of her by *David,* and a bust of Necker. One room is pointed out as the study in which the author of *Corinne* composed many of her works. Her inkstand and desk are still preserved. The grounds are traversed by shady walks; and a clump of trees surrounded by a wall, in a field a little to the W. of the house, shrouds from view a sort of chapel in which Necker and his daughter are buried.

1½ Nyon—(*Inn:* Soleil)—a town of 2682 inhabitants, stands on a height; but its suburb, through which the high road runs, extends down to the lake. It was the Roman Novidunum.

An excellent carriage-road ascends the Jura from this in zigzags to St. Cergues (Route 53). From the top of the Dôle, on the left of this road, and 15 miles from Nyon, there is an exquisite view (see p. 130).

1½ Rolle. (*Inn:* Tête Noir, small and not first rate.) The hills around this village are covered with vineyards, producing a tolerable wine. One of the best Vaudois wines is grown on the slope between Rolle and Aubonne, called La Cote. On the opposite shore of the lake is discerned the Gulf of Thonon, and the snowy head of Mont Blanc peering over the mountains of the Chablais. A little further on the rocks of Meillerie and the entrance of the Valais appear.

1¾ Morges. (*Inn:* La Couronne.) Behind this little town of 2800 inhabitants rises the old castle of Wufflens, distinguished by its tall square donjon and group of minor turrets, built of brick, with deep machicolations. It is said to have been built by Queen Bertha in the tenth century. It is well preserved and highly picturesque. On the next stage the river Venoge is crossed.

The distant view of Lausanne, seated on sloping hills and surmounted by its cathedral and castle, is pleasing. Between it and the lake, at the distance of ¾ of a mile, stands the suburb or village of Ouchy (*Inn :* Ancre, at the water-side), which may be termed the port of Lausanne. Lord Byron wrote the Prisoner of Chillon in this little inn, in the short space of *two days,* during which he was detained here by bad weather, June, 1816 : " thus adding one more deathless association to the already immortalised localities of the lake."

Traversing the shady promenade of Montbenon we enter

1½ LAUSANNE. (*Inns :* Faucon, excellent, but rather expensive ; — a new house, to be called Hotel de Gibbon, is in progress (1838) ; Lion d'Or, a comfortable and not expensive house.) Lausanne, capital of the Canton Vaud, contains 14,120 inhabitants. The Pays de Vaud (Germ. Waadtland), was originally subject to the Dukes of Savoy, but having been conquered by the Bernese, remained tributary to the republic for 2½ centuries, until 1798, when it purchased its own independence. The town stands on the lower slope of the Mont Jorat, which sinks gradually down to the lake, but is intersected by several ravines, giving it the form of distinct eminences. From this cause the streets ranging over broken ground are a series of ups and downs ; many are very steep, and run in a direction parallel to the lake, so as to exclude all view of it. They are mostly narrow and not very clean, and few of the houses stand on the same level. If the stranger would emerge from this labyrinth of dusky buildings to look about him, he must climb up the steep ascent behind. A very good point of view is the

Terrace of the Cathedral. At the foot of the flight of steps leading to it from the market-place ask for the keys of the door, kept at the sexton's house, No. 6. The *Cathedral,* a very extensive building, and internally the finest Gothic church in Switzerland, was founded A.D 1000, and some traces of the original edifice may perhaps be traced in the round arches behind the high altar. With this exception the existing building dates from the 13th century, 1275. Some of the pillars supporting the nave are detached. The circular window in the N. transept, 30 ft. in diameter, is remarkable. Among the monuments within the church are a mailed effigy of Otho of Gransom, whose ancestor, Otto de Grandeson, held several important offices in England, under Henry III. and Edward I ; the monument of Victor Amadeus VIII. (Voltaire's " Bizarre Amadée"), who was duke of Savoy, Bishop of Geneva, and pope under the title of Felix V., but resigned in succession all these dignities, preferring to end his days as a monk in the convent of Ripaille, on the opposite shore of the lake. His tomb is much mutilated. The monument of Mrs. Stratford Canning, a vase with a bas-relief, by *Bartolini* (not by Canova, as most guide-books have it), is not very remarkable. Here also is interred the venerated Bernard de Menthon, founder of the Hospice of the Great St. Bernard, which is named after him.

On another platform, a little way behind the Terrace of the Cathedral, stands *the Castle,* a picturesque, massive square tower with four turrets at the angles. It was originally the residence of the Bishops of Lausanne, but is now the council-house of the canton.

Lausanne possesses a *College,* founded 1587, and a *Cantonal Museum,* in which are some objects of interest—such as a collection of minerals from Bex and a model of the salt-mines there. It is not deficient in the other branches of natural history. A specimen of the silurus glanis, one of the largest fresh-water fishes, came from the Lake of Morat. Many *antiquities* discovered within the canton, at Aventicum and on the borders of the Lake Leman, are preserved here.

The house of Gibbon the historian is in the lower part of the town, behind the church of St. Francis, and on the right of the road leading down to Ouchy. It is said not to be changed. It has a garden, a terrace overlooking the lake, a summer-house, and a few acacias; but another summer-house, in which he is said to have finished his history, and his berceau-walk, have been removed. He alludes to them in the following remarkable passage:—

" It was on the day or rather the night of the 27th of June, 1787, between the hours of eleven and twelve, that I wrote the last line of the last page in a summer-house in my garden. After laying down my pen I took several turns in a berceau, or covered walk of acacias, which commands a prospect of the country, the lake, and the mountains. The air was temperate, the sky was serene, the silver orb of the moon was reflected from the waves, and all nature was silent."

" Much has been done of late years by the Canton of Vaud to improve the institutions of this little state. The *Penitentiary*, *Prison*, and *Normal School*, may interest some travellers, and may bear witness to all of the munificent and enlightened spirit of the councils of one of the smallest and most democratic communities in Europe."—*H. R.*

There is an excellent *reading-room* here (? Cassino), to which strangers are admitted by a member's introduction.

The *English church service* is performed every Sunday in the Chapelle du Culte. The Lutheran service is also performed in the same building in the course of the day.

The *Post* and *Diligence-office* is in the Place St. François, near the church. The office for *post-horses* is in the Rue Martheray, No. 57.

Steam-boats touch at Ouchy, the suburb of Lausanne, at the water-side, twice a-day, on their way to either extremity of the lake.

The neighbourhood of Lausanne is unrivalled for the number and beauty of the walks which it presents. Partial and pleasing glimpses of the lake are obtained from the *terraces* within the town, and from that of Montbenon, just outside the walls, on the way to Geneva; but far more extensive and beautiful prospects are presented from the heights above it. The best spot for an extensive survey is the elevated platform called the *Signal*, but the ascent to it is very fatiguing. Near it is the extensive forest of Sauvabellin (Silva Belini), in which it is said the Druids once worshipped the god Bel, and thence its name. There are a great number of country-seats in the vicinity; that of *Vernens* is highly praised; its grounds have the character of an English park, with the Alps and the lake in addition. Cooper, the American novelist, thus describes the view from the heights above Lausanne:—

" The form of the lake prevents an entire view of it from any single spot. One is as well placed at Lausanne as at any other spot perhaps for such a purpose; but even there the W. end of the sheet is quite concealed by the curvature. If the foot of the lake is hid from the eye, its head, on the contrary, lies open before the spectator, and it offers one of the grandest landscapes of this the noblest of all earthly regions. In that direction the mountains of Savoy rise like ramparts, and the valley of the Rhone retires in the distance, until it is lost in the sublimity of mystery (?). Whichever way the eye wanders over the wide range of hill-sides, villages, vineyards, mountains, and blue water, it never fails to return to this one spot, which on the whole offers one of the nicest combinations of the great and the enchanting in scenery of any place within my knowledge." Mont Blanc is not visible from the Signal, but may be seen from the top of the Jorat, on the road to Berne.

About 2 miles out of Lausanne, beyond the Calvaire, on the Berne road, is the *Cemetery of Pierre de Plain.* John Philip Kemble, the tragedian. is buried within it.

N.B. *Posting* (§ 5) begins at Lausanne, and continues over the Simplon into Italy, and by Geneva into France. *Diligences* run *daily* in summer from Lausanne to Vevay and Bex, to Berne, to Geneva, to Neuchâtel. and to Bâle.

The road to Vevay is very narrow, and partly enclosed between the high walls of vineyards, rendering it very tiresome, and in summer dreadfully hot, being unsheltered by trees. (? A new road has, it is said, been lately made.) It improves near Vevay, as the gorge of the Rhone appears in sight, overlooked by the snowy peaks of the Dent de Midi.

2½ *Vevay.* (*Inns :* Trois Couronnes, the best, and good ; Ville de Londres.)

Vevay (Germ. Vivis, the Roman Vibiscum) is the second town in Canton Vaud, and has 4486 inhabitants. It is principally distinguished for the exceeding beauty of its situation, on the margin of the Lake Leman, at a point where the scenery of its banks is perhaps most beautiful. The writings of Rousseau have contributed not a little to its celebrity in this respect. He says in his Confessions—" J'allai à Vevay loger à la clef, et pendant deux jours que j'y restai sans voir personne, je pris pour cette ville un amour qui m'a suivi dans tous mes voyages. et qui m'y a fait établir enfin les héros de mon roman. Je dirai volontiers à ceux qui ont du gout et qui sont sensibles, Allez à Vevay, visitez le pays, examinez les sites, promenez vous sur le lac, et dites si la nature n'a pas fait ce beau pays pour une Julie, pour une Claire, et pour un Saint Preux ; mais ne les y cherchez pas."

From the little terrace at the end of the market-place the eye surveys the scenery of the Nouvelle Heloise. On the E. the village of Clarens, Montreux, Chillon ; beyond it Villeneuve and the gorge of the Rhone, backed by the gigantic Alps of the Vallais, the Dent de Midi, and Pain de Sucre (neighbours of the Great St. Bernard) ; while on the opposite shore of the lake rise the rocks of Meillerie, surmounted by the peaks of the Dent d'Oche, and the village of St. Gingough, at the foot of the mountains.

In the *Church of St. Martin,* a little above the town, Ludlow the regicide is buried, as well as Broughton, who read the sentence of death to Charles I. They died here in exile, a price having been set upon their heads ; and repeated applications were made to the canton of Berne to deliver them up, which the government very properly refused to accede to. *Ludlow's house* still exists ; he placed over his doorway this inscription—" Omne solum forti patria."

The *wines* of the neighbourhood of Vevay. especially of the sunny district extending hence to Lausanne, and called La Vaux, enjoy a considerable reputation. The Romans are believed to have first planted the vine on these hills ; and the discovery of a stone inscribed " Libero Patri Colliensi" proves that they had erected a temple to Father Bacchus at Collium, a little village now called Cully, on the margin of the lake, between Vevay and Lausanne.

A society or guild of very high antiquity, called *l'Abbaye des Vignerons,* having for its motto the words " Ora et labora," exists at Vevay. Its object is to promote the cultivation of the vine ; and for this purpose it despatches every spring and autumn " experts," qualified persons, to sur-by all the vineyards of the district, and upon their report and testimony rewards the most skilful and industrious vinedressers with medals and pruning-hooks (serpes d'honneur) as prizes.

In accordance with a custom handed down from very ancient times, which is possibly a relic of Pagan superstition, this society celebrates once in 15 or 20 years a festival called *la Fête des Vignerons.* It commences with the ceremony of crowning the most successful cultivator of the vine, which is followed and accompanied by dances and processions formed of the lads and lasses of the neighbourhood attired as Fauns bearing the thyrsus, and nymphs. Father Bacchus in his car, and Ceres throned on a waggon filled with wheatsheaves, appear in the most classical costume in the midst of their followers. But the procession includes a singular mixture of scriptural characters along with these heathen Bacchanals. Thus Silenus riding on his ass is followed by Noah in his ark, and Pomona is succeeded by the spies from Canaan bearing between them the bunch of grapes. A vine-press and a forge at work are also exhibited, drawn by fine horses. On other days of the fête (for it lasts for several) the spectators are entertained with the native dances and songs of Switzerland, performed by the herdsmen and shepherdesses of the neighbouring Alps; and the concluding and perhaps the most interesting part of the festivities consists in the bestowing upon a young maiden, the fairest in fame and form in the vicinity, a dower, and in the celebration of her marriage with a partner of her choice. As many as 700 persons took part in the last festival, and one of the ballet-masters of the French opera repaired hither from Paris, several weeks beforehand, to drill and instruct the rustics in dancing. The ground was kept by 100 young men in the picturesque ancient Swiss costume, which has

been delineated by Holbein. The 2 last anniversaries were in 1819 and 1833, and multitudes of spectators flocked from all parts to witness them.

The road from Vevay to Freyburg by Bulle is described Route 41.

The path from Vevay over the Dent de Jaman, and the road thence to Thun, form Route 41.

" The gardens of M. de Hauteville are situated about 1 mile from Vevay, and deserve to be visited as much for their fine horticulture as for the superb view they command."—*B.*

About 2 miles off, on a swelling eminence overlooking the lake, stands the ancient *Castle of Blonay*, built in the 10th century, which belonged to the same family for 700 years. Further on, by the lake-side, is *Chatelard*, another castle.

About a mile out of Vevay the hamlet of La Tour de Peil, with a castle built at the water-side in the 13th century, is passed. A mile further lies

Clarens, so sentimentally described by Rousseau in the Nouvelle Héloise. It is a poor, dirty village, far less attractive than many of its neighbours, and it probably owes its celebrity to a well-sounding name, which fitted it for the pages of a romance. Rousseau's admirers have puzzled themselves with endeavouring to identify the localities, though he has himself stated that they are " grossièrement altérées." The spot on which the beautiful " bosquet de Julie" is sought for is now a potato-field. Byron says that the trees were cut down by the monks of St. Bernard, and lavishes some unworthy and undeserved abuse upon those hospitable ecclesiastics ; but he has forgotten to ask whether the bosquet really ever had any existence except in Rousseau's imagination. Byron indeed viewed the spot with a poet's eye, and the exquisite beauty of the surrounding scenery, which has been accurately described by Rousseau, called up all the poet's enthusiasm and inspiration.

Clarens! sweet Clarens, birthplace of
deep Love !
Thine air is the young breath of passion-
ate thought ;
Thy trees take root in Love ; the snows
above
The very glaciers have his colours caught,
And sunset into rose-hues sees them
wrought
By rays which sleep there lovingly : the
rocks,
The permanent crags, tell here of Love,
who sought
In them a refuge from the worldly shocks
Which stir and sting the soul with hope that
woos, then mocks.

Clarens! by heavenly feet thy paths are
trod—
Undying Love's, who here ascends a
throne
To which the steps are mountains; where
the god
Is a pervading life and light,—so shown
Not on those summits solely, nor alone
In the still cave and forest; o'er the flower
His eye is sparkling, and his breath hath
blown,
His soft and summer breath, whose ten-
der power
Passes the strength of storms in their most
desolate hour.

All things are here of *him*; from the black
pines,
Which are his shade on high, and the
loud roar
Of torrents, where he listeneth, to the vines
Which slope his green path downward to
the shore,
Where the bow'd waters meet him, and
adore,
Kissing his feet with murmurs; and the
wood,
The covert of old trees, with trunks all
hoar,
But light leaves, young as joy, stands
where it stood,
Offering to him and his a populous solitude.

A populous solitude of bees and birds,
And fairy-form'd and many-colour'd
things,
Who worship him with notes more sweet
than words,
And innocently open their glad wings,
Fearless and full of life: the gush of
springs,
And fall of lofty fountains, and the bend
Of stirring branches, and the bud which
brings
The swiftest thought of beauty, here ex-
tend,
Mingling, and made by Love, unto one
mighty end.

'Twas not for fiction chose Rousseau this
spot,
Peopling it with affections; but he found

It was the scene which passion must all
To the mind's purified beings; 'twas t
ground
Where early Love his Psyche's zone u
bound,
And hallow'd it with loveliness : 'tis lor
And wonderful, and deep, and hath
sound,
And sense, and sight of sweetness; he
the Rhone
Hath spread himself a couch, the Alps ha
rear'd a throne."

" In July, 1816, I made a voyag
round the Lake of Geneva ; and, a
far as my own observations have le
me in a not uninterested nor inat
tentive survey of all the scenes mos
celebrated by Rousseau in his ' H
loïse,' I can safely say that in thi
there is no exaggeration. It woul
be difficult to see Clarens (with th
scenes around it—Vevay, Chillor
Bôveret, St. Gingo, Meillerie, Evian
and the entrances of the Rhone
without being forcibly struck wit
its peculiar adaptation to the person
and events with which it has bee
peopled. But this is not all ; th
feeling with which all around Cla
rens, and the opposite rocks of Meil
lerie, is invested, is of a still highe
and more comprehensive order thar
the mere sympathy with individua
passion ; it is a sense of the exist
ence of love in its most extended an
sublime capacity, and of our own
participation of its good and of it
glory ; it is the great principle of the
universe, which is there more condensed, but not less manifested, and
of which, though knowing ourselve
a part, we lose our individuality, and
mingle in the beauty of the whole.
If Rousseau had never written no
lived, the same associations would
not less have belonged to such
scenes. He has added to the interest of his works by their adoption;
he has shown his sense of their
beauty by the selection ; but they
have done that for him which no
human being could do for them. I
had the fortune (good or evil as it
might be) to sail from Meillerie
(where we landed for some time) to
St. Gingo during a lake storm, which

lded to the magnificence of all round, although occasionally accompanied by danger to the boat, which was small and overloaded. : was over this very part of the lake aat Rousseau has driven the boat of t. Preux and Madame Wolmar to Meillerie for shelter during a tempest. On gaining the shore at St. #ingo I found that the wind had een sufficiently strong to blow down ome fine old chestnut-trees on the ower part of the mountains."—*Byron.*

Chailly, the residence of Rousseau's friend Madame de Warens, es above Clarens, at some distance rom the road. The house still exists.

The swelling hills and vine-clad lopes which form the banks of the ake nearly all the way from Geneva, aere give place to beetling crags and ofty precipices rising abruptly from he water's edge. The road sweeps u curves round the retired bays at heir feet.

The village of *Montreux* is prettier n itself and in its situation than even Clarens. It lies at the foot of the Dent de Jaman, across which runs a path into the Simmenthal (Route 41).

" It is celebrated as the most sheltered spot on the banks of the Lake of Geneva, and the remarkable salubrity of its climate renders it desirable winter-quarters for invalids who cannot cross the Alps. Very good accommodation may be had in the village inn. Boarding and lodging houses are also to be met with there. The traveller who turns aside from the high-road to the church-yard of Montreux will carry away from that enchanting spot one of the sweetest impressions of his life. The statistical researches of Sir F. d'Ivernois have shown that Montreux is the place in the world where there is the smallest proportion of deaths and of imprudent marriages. The old pastor Bridel, the head of this happy community, is a hale mountaineer, full of the legends and beauties of the country he has wandered over for

nearly 80 years, and will give a hearty welcome to the traveller."–*R.*

About 2 miles from Montreux stands the picturesque and renowned *Castle of Chillon,* on an isolated rock surrounded by deep water, but within a stone's throw of the shore and of the road, with which it communicates by a wooden bridge. It was built in 1238 by Amadeus IV. of Savoy, and was long used as a state prison, where, among other victims, many of the early reformers were immured. When Byron, in the Prisoner of Chillon, described the sufferings of an imaginary captive, he was not acquainted with the history of the *real* prisoner, Bonnivard, prior of St. Victor, who, having rendered himself obnoxious to the Duke of Savoy by his exertions to free the Genevese from the Savoyard yoke, was seized by the duke's emissaries, and secretly carried off to this castle. For 6 long years he was buried in its deepest dungeon, on a level with the surface of the lake. The ring by which he was attached to one of the pillars still remains, and the stone floor at its base is worn by his constant pacing to and fro. Byron afterwards wrote the sonnet on Bonnivard, from which the following lines are taken :

" Chillon ! thy prison is a holy place,
  And thy sad floor an altar; for 'twas
  trod
Until his very steps have left a trace
Worn, as if thy cold pavement were a
  sod,
By Bonnivard ! May none those marks
  efface !
For they appeal from tyranny to God."

At length, in 1536, the Swiss wrested the Pays de Vaud from the hands of Charles V. of Savoy. Chillon was the last place which held out for him; but an army of 7000 Bernese besieging it by land, while the gallies of the Genevese assaulted it by water, soon compelled it to surrender, and Bonnivard, with other captives, was set free. The changes which had occurred during the years of his imprisonment almost realised the legend of the Seven Sleepers. He had left Geneva a Catholic state, and dependent on the Duke of Savoy; he found her free, and a republic, publicly professing the reformed faith.

The castle is now converted into a magazine for military stores. A curious old chapel serves as a powder-magazine, and is not shown. Strangers are readily conducted over other parts of it, and (independent of the associations connected with the building) may find something to interest them in its " potence et cachots." The former is a beam, black with age, extended across one of the vaults, to which the condemned were formerly hung. The cachot is an oubliette, whose only entrance was by a trap-door in the floor above. The dungeon of Bonnivard is airy and spacious, consisting of two aisles, almost like a church; its floor and one side are formed by the living rock, and it is lighted by a solitary window. Byron inscribed his name on one of the pillars, but it is far more lastingly associated with the spot.

" Lake Leman lies by Chillon's walls;
A thousand feet in depth below
Its massy waters meet and flow;
Thus much the fathom-line was sent
From Chillon's snow-white battlement (? ?),
Which round about the wave enthrals:
A double dungeon-wall and wave
Have made—and like a living grave.
Below the surface of the lake
The dark vault lies wherein we lay,
We heard it ripple night and day.
In Chillon's dungeons deep and old
There are seven columns massy and grey,
Dim with a dull, imprison'd ray,
A sunbeam which hath lost its way,
And through the crevice and the cleft
Of the thick wall is fallen and left,
Creeping o'er the floor so damp,
Like a marsh's meteor lamp."

Byron has exaggerated the depth of the lake, which near the castle does not exceed 280 ft. " It is by this castle that Rousseau has fixed the catastrophe of his Héloïse, in the rescue of one of her children by Julie from the water; the shock of which, and the illness produced by the immersion, is the cause of her death."

Villeneuve—(*Inns:* Croix Blanche, Lion d'Or, both indifferent)—is small and ancient walled town of 148 inhabitants (*Pennilucus* of the R. mans), situated at the E. extremity of the lake, where the road quits is borders to enter the valley of the Rhone. A diligence awaits the ar rival of the steamers to convey pa sengers on to Bex, where there ar good sleeping-quarters.

About a mile from Villeneuve lie a small island, the only one in the lake: it is thus mentioned by Byro in the Prisoner of Chillon:—

" And then there was a little isle,
Which in my very face did smile,
    The only one in view ;
A small green isle, it seem'd no more,
Scarce broader than my dungeon-floor,
But in it there were three tall trees,
And o'er it blew the mountain-breeze,
And by it there were waters flowing,
And on it there were young flowers growing
    Of gentle breath and hue."

The commencement of the valley of the Rhone is dreary and uninte resting. The low ground is a flat alluvial deposit, formed by mu brought down by the river, and stil remaining in the state of a barren and unwholesome morass. The en croachments of the land upon the lake even within the period of his torical record have been very great. Port Vallais, Portus Vallesiæ of the Romans, in their time stood on the margin of the lake, but is now more than a mile and a half inland; the intervening tract has been gained since. The Rhone itself creeps slowly along, impeded by its windings, and as it were burdened with mud, very unlike the torrent of azure and crystal which bursts out of the lake at Geneva. Upon this plain, at the mouth of the valley of the Rhone, Divico, the first Helvetian chief mentioned in history, defeated, B.C. 107 (the 646th year of Rome), the Roman forces under Lucius Cassius, slaying their general and compelling his army to pass under the yoke.

The top of the mountain above Yvorne was thrown down by an

earthquake, 1584. A good wine now grows on the slope.

2¾ L'Aigle — (*Inn:* La Croix Blanche)—a village of 1650 inhabitants (*Aquileia*). Black marble is quarried near this.

1 *Bex*—(*Inns:* L'Union, good. It comprises a boarding-house and an establishment of baths, supplied from a sulphureous spring rising in the vicinity, which causes Bex to be resorted to as a watering-place in summer. Guides, horses, and chars-à-banc for excursions among the mountains may be hired here.—L'Ours.)

Bex, a village of 3000 inhabitants, situated on the high road to the Simplon, is chiefly remarkable for its *Salt-Mines* and *Salt-Works.* Salt has been obtained from brine-springs here since the middle of the 16th century. For a long time they belonged to a merchant family of Augsburg named Zobel, but they are now property of the government of the canton. Down to 1823 the brine-springs alone furnished the salt, and they were gradually failing, when M. Charpentier suggested the plan of driving shafts and galleries into the mountain in search of rock-salt. The result was the discovery of a large and rich vein of the mineral, which has been traced for a distance of 4000 ft. and for a height of 600 ft., varying in thickness from 2 ft. to 50 ft.; and the annual produce of salt is now augmented to 20,000 or 30,000 quintals. Strangers visiting Bex commonly pay a visit to the mines, which are situated about 2 miles off, in the valley of La Gryonne. A steep road, but practicable for chars-à-banc, leads through most beautiful scenery to the entrance of the mines. The salt is obtained either from the brine-springs, six or seven of which, of various degrees of strength, burst forth in different parts of the interior of the mountain, or from the rock-salt, which, after being extracted by the help of gunpowder, is broken into pieces, thrown into large reservoirs, called dessaloirs, cut in the anhydrite rock (sulphate of lime without water) in the interior of the mountain, and there dissolved in water. Each reservoir is usually filled with water 3 times. The 2 first solutions (lessivages) furnish a liquor with 25 or 26 per cent. of salt; the 3rd is much weaker, having only 5 or 6 per cent. The brine, either from the sources or from these reservoirs, containing above 20 per cent. of salt, is conveyed in pipes made of fir-wood at once to the boiling-house (maison de cuite); that which is less strong must be subjected to the process of graduation in the long buildings or sheds, open at the sides, which are passed at Bexvieux and Devins, between Bex and the mines. These evaporating-houses, or *maisons de graduation*, are filled up to the roof with stacks of fagots of thorn-wood, over which the salt water, after being raised to the roof by pumps, is allowed to trickle drop by drop. The separation of the water in passing through colanders, and its exposure to the atmosphere as it falls, produce rapid and considerable evaporation of the watery particles, while the gypsum dissolved in it adheres, in passing, to the twigs, and crystalizes around them. The water is thus made to ascend and descend several times; it becomes stronger each time, and at length is brought to the condition of saturated brine, fit for boiling in the salt-pans. It will easily be perceived how much fuel is thus spared by not subjecting the weak solution to the fire at first.

This short explanation may enable the visitor to understand the process pursued in the mines. The principal mines are those called *Du Fondement* and *Du Bouillet;* the latter contains a gallery driven horizontally into the bowels of the mountain for a distance of 6636 ft., 7½ ft. high and 5 ft. wide. At 400 ft. from its entrance is the round *reservoir*, 80 ft. in diameter and 10 ft. deep, excavated in the rock, without any support to its roof. In it the weak water is collected, which requires to undergo the pro cess of graduation. A little farther on is another irregular reservoir, 7933 ft. in extent, supported by pillars, and destined to hold the stronger brine fit for the salt-pans without undergoing any intermediate process.

Many beautiful minerals are obtained from the salt-mines of Bex—such as very clear crystals of selenite, muriacite, anhydrite, &c.

There is a short but difficult path (Route 58) from Bex to Sion by the Bergfall of Les Diablerets. A guide would be required for this journey.

A little way above Bex a curious discovery was made, a few years ago, of a warm sulphureous spring in the very bed of the Rhone. It has been enclosed, and employed in supplying medicinal baths, the healing properties of which are attributed to the quantity of azote gas contained in the water.

" Journeying upward by the Rhone,
　That there came down a torrent from the
　　Alps,
　I enter'd where a key unlocks a kingdom:
　The mountains closing, and the road, the
　　river
Filling the narrow space."—*Rogers.*

Such is the scene presented to the traveller at the *Bridge of St. Maurice,* which spans the rapid river with one bold arch, 70 ft. wide, leaning for support (appuyé) on the rt. side upon the Dent de Morcles and on the l. upon the Dent de Midi, whose bases are pushed so far forward as barely to leave room for the river.

The bridge, erroneously attributed to the Romans, is not older than the 15th century, but may possibly rest on Roman foundations. It unites the canton Vaud with the canton Vallais; and a gate at one end, now removed, formerly served to close the passage up and down: a circumstance alluded to in the lines of Rogers. A small fort was erected by the Swiss in 1832, above the road, to defend the pass. Here our route is joined by the road from Geneva along the S. shore of the lake, through St. Gingough. (Route 57.)

No one can cross the bridge of St Maurice without being struck with the change in the condition of the inhabitants of the two cantons. The neatness and industry of the Vaudois are exchanged within the space of a few hundred yards for filth and beggary, equally apparent in the persons and habitations of the Vallaisans. Their physical condition is lamentable ; no part of Switzerland is afflicted to a greater extent with the maladies of goître and cretinism (§ 19), and the victims of them shock the traveller's sight at every step.

Immediately beyond the bridge, squeezed in between the mountain and the l. bank of the Rhone, stands ¾ St. Maurice — (*Inn:* L'Union, tolerably good)—a town of 1050 inhabitants, occupying the site of the Roman Agaunum. It owes its present name to the tradition that the Theban Legion, under the command of St. Maurice, suffered martyrdom here by order of Maximian, A.D. 302, because they refused to abjure Christianity.

The *Abbey,* founded in honour of *St. Maurice* by Sigismond King of Burgundy, contains in its *Treasury* a museum of ancient art. Here are preserved a vase of Saracenic workmanship, presented by Charlemagne ; a crozier of gold, in the shape of a spire, the niches of it filled with figures an inch high, most elaborately worked ; a chalice of agate, presented by Charlemagne ; another, given by Bertha Queen of Burgundy, and several besides, of a very early date.

" The *Church* was much damaged by fire in the 17th century, but the tower is unaltered, and several Roman inscriptions are built into its walls."—*P.*

On quitting the town we perceive on the right, upon a projecting platform of rock considerably above the road, the Hermitage of Nôtre Dame des Sex. Lower down on the road is the chapel of Veriolez, raised on the precise spot of the Theban massacre (!), and covered with rude frescoes. In the autumn of 1835 a torrent of mud descended from the summit of the Dent de Midi into the Vallais near Evionaz. It covered the high road for a length of 900 ft., and overwhelmed many fields, and orchards, and some few houses; but no lives were lost, as the slow progress of the current allowed every one time to remove out of its way. It is conjectured to have been caused by a glacier bursting and sweeping along with it the debris of the Moraine, which it converted into mud. Blocks of stone, many tons in weight, were carried down with it, and floated like corks on the surface.

This part of the valley has a dreary and barren aspect from the quantity of bare gravel and broken rock strewed over it.

About 6½ miles from St. Maurice, 4 from Martigny, is the famous *Waterfall of the Sallenche,* which here descends into the valley of the Rhone out of a narrow ravine, apparently excavated by its waters. The perpendicular descent of the stream is about 280 feet, but the final leap of the cascade not more than 120 feet. It is a fine object, both from its volume and height, visible from a considerable distance up and down. It is best seen in a sunny morning before 12 o'clock, when the iris, formed in the cloud of spray, hovers over it. The neighbouring village of Mieville sends forth an importunate crowd of beggars and self-appointed guides to conduct travellers from the road to the fall, a distance of a few hundred yards. Before reaching Martigny we cross another stream, the Trient, descending from the celebrated pass of the Tête Noire. On the outskirts of Martigny, upon a commanding rock, rises the castle of La Batie, formerly a stronghold of the archbishops of Sion. The deep dungeon beneath its tall tower is only accessible by a trap-door in the floor of the chamber above. The river

Dranse passes out into the Rhone, between La Batie and

2¼ *Martigny* (Route 59).

ROUTE 57.

GENEVA TO MARTIGNY, BY THONON AND MEILLERIE, ALONG THE SOUTH SHORE OF THE LAKE OF GENEVA.

14¾ posts = 68 English miles.

The greater part of this road lies through the Sardinian territory, but for the convenience of reference it is placed here.

After quitting Geneva by the Porte de Rive, a fine view opens out on the right; beyond the Saléve rises the Môle, and the vista of the valley of the Arve is terminated by the Buet, by Mont Blanc and its glaciers. The shore of the lake is dotted over with villas of the Genevese. One of these, near the village of Cologny, the *Campagna Diodati,* is interesting as having been the residence of Lord Byron in 1816. He wrote here a great part of the 3rd canto of Childe Harold and the tragedy of Manfred.

Beyond the village of Corsier the Genevan territory is left, and we enter the kingdom of Sardinia and the ancient province of Chablais, which extends along the lake as far as St. Gingough. A monotonous plain is traversed in order to reach

2½ Douvaine, the first Sardinian post-station, where passports and baggage are examined.

2 Thonon—(*Inn:* Les Balances, improved of late)—an ancient town of 3740 inhabitants, originally capital of the Chablais.

On quitting Thonon we pass on the left, between the road and the lake, *Ripaille,* anciently an Augustine convent, founded by Amadeus VIII. of Savoy, in which he ended his days, having assumed the cowl of an Augustine monk. He abdicated, in succession, the dukedom of Savoy, the Papacy (into which he had been installed with the title of Felix V.)

and the bishop's see of Geneva. He resided here after his second abdication, passing his time, not in the austere penance of an anchorite, but in weaving political intrigues and laying schemes for future aggrandisement. Hence the French proverb—" Aller à Ripaille." The castle, with 7 towers, built by Amadeus for himself and the six knights whom he chose as companions, has nearly disappeared. The relic of the convent is converted into a farmhouse. A long bridge of 24 arches carries the road over the Dranse, a torrent descending from the Buet.

Through groves of most magnificent chesnut-trees we pass Amphion, where are baths supplied by a chalybeate spring, and reach

1½ Evian—(_Inn:_ H. du Nord; Poste)—a town of 1670 inhabitants, at the water-side.

The _Rocks of Meillerie,_ celebrated by Rousseau and Byron, were, under the orders of Napoleon, and with the help of gunpowder, blasted to form a passage for the magnificent road of the Simplon, which is here carried partly through them, partly on a terrace 30 or 40 feet above the lake. The little village of Meillerie was, previous to its construction, barely accessible, except by boats. About a mile off the shore, at Meillerie, the lake attains its greatest depth, 920 Fr. ft. Here Byron was nearly lost in a storm. Rousseau, in the N. Héloïse, has conducted St. Preux and Mad. Wolmar also to this port for shelter from a tempest. On the opposite shore is seen Clarens, and the white wall of the castle of Chillon (p. 149).

2½ St. Gingough—(_Inn:_ Poste, comfortable). A deep ravine here divides Savoy from the Swiss territory of the Vallais; travellers entering from the Vallais are subjected to custom-house regulations here.

Bovaret, the next village, lies within the valley of the Rhone, here a broad, flat, and unwholesome swamp. Port Vallais, in the days of the Romans, stood on the water-side; all the ground between it and the lake has been produced since the records of history, by the deposits of the river. At Port du Sex the rocks on the rt. encroach so far upon the Rhone as barely to leave a passage for the road at their base. This defile was originally guarded by an old castle; and, by raising a drawbridge, the passage up or down was cut off. There is a ferry over the Rhone near this, but the cross-roads leading to the opposite side of the valley among the morasses are very bad.

The canal of Stockalper, running nearly parallel with the road, was cut about a century ago, to drain this portion of the valley.

2 Vionnaz.

2 St. Maurice, (Route 56).

2¼ _Martigny_ (Route 59).

ROUTE 58.

BEX TO SION, BY LES DIABLERETS AND COL DE CHEVILLE.

11½ stunden = 37 English miles.

Bex is described in Route 56. A difficult, and in parts dangerous, path; at times painfully steep and hardly to be followed without a guide. It is a very long day's journey, and there is no inn (worthy the name) by the way. After snow it is almost impracticable. It ascends the valley of the Avençon, running in a direction nearly due E. from Bex, passing Bexvieux to the Chalets of Charnemey (2 hours), and the Chalets of Anzeinde (2 hours). Here the path begins rapidly to ascend in a tortuous course (4¾) to the summit of the Col de Chéville. The valley into which it descends on the E. side of the pass is nearly occupied by the wreck of the fall of the _Mont Diablerets,_ a name given to the spot by the peasantry. it is said, because they regard it as the vestibule of hell. This mountain is composed of limestone strata, much deranged and steeply inclined. The lower beds, being soft and shaley, are disintegrated by the infiltration of water from the vast glaciers on the N.E.; and, after the supports and foundation are thus removed, large masses are detached from the mountain into the valley below, forming éboulemens of the most tremendous kind. During the last century two catastrophes of this kind occurred, in 1714 and 1749. By the former many persons and cattle were buried alive. One man succeeded in working his way out, after 3 months had elapsed. He had been overwhelmed in his cottage, but escaped being crushed to death, and managed to support life upon a store of cheese laid up for the winter, and with water from a brook which found its way through the fallen rocks. The fall of 1749 arrested the course of the Liserne, forming two small lakes, called Derborenze, which still exist. Along the W. side of these the path runs, crossing, for the space of two leagues, heaps of rubbish and fallen rocks. The scene is one of the utmost desolation; overhead towers the ridge of the Diablerets, 9862 ft. above the sea-level. Three of its five peaks have already fallen, and the two which remain threaten, sooner or later, to follow. The accumulated debris of the mountain is said to cover a space of 8 miles. At one point, on reaching the borders of the Liserne, a narrow and dangerous path has been formed across the talus, at the edge of a precipice overhanging the stream: it is called *Le Saut du Chien.*

Thenceforth the path follows the l. bank of the Liserne as far as the chapel of St. Bernard, where it bears away to the E., descending upon St. Severin and Haut Couthey, and thence enters the valley of the Rhone and the high road of the Simplon, within 2½ miles of

6¾ *Sion* (Route 59).

ROUTE 59.

THE PASSAGE OF THE SIMPLON; MARTIGNY TO MILAN, BY SION, BRIEG, AND DOMO D'OSSOLA.

36½ posts = 176 English miles.

This grand and excellent road is tolerably well supplied with post-horses, but travellers who require more than two to their carriage must bespeak them by avant-courier, if they wish to avoid delays. With post-horses the journey may barely be accomplished in 3, or easily in 3½ days, resting 1st night at Brieg, 2d at Baveno, 3rd at Milan; or, 1st at Turtman, 2nd at Domo d'Ossola, 3rd at Arona. There is a tolerably comfortable inn at Simplon, near the summit of the pass.

Diligences go 4 times a-week from Milan, making numerous halts, and performing the distance to Milan in not less than 3 days and nights.

The picturesque round tower of the castle of La Batie, rising on a rock, with a village at its foot, is seen some time before the town of Martigny is reached. It was destroyed by George Superax in 1518.

Martigny (German Martinach).— *Inns:* Post, good, the best; Cygne, tolerably good and moderate; daily table d'hôte, 3 fr., wine included.— La Tour.

Martigny (Octodurus of the Romans) consists of two parts—the one situated on the Simplon road, the other, Bourg de Martigny, more than a mile distant up the valley of the Dranse. Its position on the high road of the Simplon, at the termination of the char-road from the St. Bernard, and the mule-path from Chamouni, renders it the constant resort of travellers. It is a small town of no prepossessing appearance, 1480 Fr. ft. above the sea, placed near the spot where the Rhone receives the Dranse, a torrent by which Martigny itself and the village of Bourg de Martigny have been twice nearly destroyed, in 1545 and in 1818. Marks of the last inundation (described in Route 109) are still visible on the walls of many of the houses, and the massive construction of the lower walls of the post-house is designed to protect it from the effects of similar catastrophes. The monks of St. Bernard have their head-quarters in a *Convent* within the town, from which the members stationed on the Great St. Bernard are relieved at intervals. The Monastery of the Great St. Bernard is a journey of 10 hours from hence. (See Route 108.)

The valley of Chamouni may be reached in 5 hours by the passes of the Tête Noire (R 116), or Col de Balme (Route 117).

The Waterfall of the Sallenche is 4 miles from Martigny, lower down the valley. (See p. 153.)

At Martigny the Rhone makes an abrupt bend, forming nearly a right angle. For many miles above the town the bottom of the valley through which it flows is a flat swamp, rendered desolate and unwholesome by the overflowings of the Rhine and its tributaries, which, not being carried off by a sufficient declivity in their beds, stagnate, and exhale a most injurious malaria under the rays of a burning sun. From this cause and the absence of pure drinking-water, the valley is a hot-bed of disease; its inhabitants are dreadfully afflicted with goître (§ 19), cretinism, and agues; and the appearance of decrepitude, deformity, and misery, arrests the traveller's attention at every step. A tolerable wine, called Coquempin, is grown upon the hills; the low flats produce little except rushes, rank grass, and alders. The mountains which here bound the valley have a bare and desolate aspect.

2¼ Riddes. After crossing the Rhone the road passes the foot-path leading to the Diablerets (Route 58), and soon after the twin castles of Sion appear in sight.

2¼ *Sion* (German Sitten).—*Inns:* Poste; Croix Blanche, dirty. This town, anciently the capital of the Seduni, is the see of a bishop, whose predecessors were at one time among the most powerful and wealthy seigneurs in Switzerland, and who still convoke and preside over the General Assemblies of this democratic canton. It is the chief town of the Vallais, and has 2450 inhabitants. It has no less than 3 extensive castles, which give the town a picturesque and feudal aspect from a distance. *Tourbillon*, the castle seen on the l. in advancing from Martigny, built 1492, and long the bishop's residence, is now a complete ruin. That on the left, or S. peak, called *Valeria*, contains a very ancient church; and serves now as a Catholic seminary. Beneath there is a third castle, called *Majoria*, from the majors, or ancient governors of the Vallais, its first occupants; it was burnt in 1788 by a conflagration which destroyed the greater part of the town. The *Jesuits* have a *Convent* in the town; they have formed a collection of the natural history of the Vallais.

The *Hospital*, under the care of the Sœurs de la Charité, contains many victims of goître and cretinism, the prevailing maladies of the district.

There is a mule-path from this over the mountains to Bex, passing the Diablerets (Route 58).

Above Sion German is the prevailing language of the Vallais.

2¼ Sierre (Germ. Siders)—*Inn:* Soleil, a humble one.

Mules may be hired here for the ascent of the remarkable Pass of the Gemmi (Route 38). The path leading to it by the Baths of Loèche turns out of the post-road a little way beyond the town, before reaching the bridge. It is steep but highly romantic.

The post-road, after crossing the Rhone, and winding for some distance among irregular hillocks, passes, on the rt. bank of the river, at the mouth of the gorge of the Dala, the picturesque village of Loèche. The Baths are situated about 9 miles above the village; a char-road leads to them. Travellers coming from the Simplon turn aside here to visit them, and ascend the Gemmi. (Route 38.)

2¼ Tourtemagne (Germ. Turtman) —(*Inn:* Poste, Lion or Sun (?) tolerably good, but dear). 20 minutes' walk behind the inn is a *Cascade* of some repute among tourists. The volume of water is considerable. It is on the whole inferior to the fall of the Sallenche near Martigny, but the scene is interesting on account of its entire seclusion. The neighbourhood is overspread with marshes and stagnant pools.

2¼ Visp (Viège), a miserable village, with no *good* inn, but finely situated at the junction of the Visp with the Rhone. The valley divides at some distance above Visp into two branches; the l. leads to the foot of Monte Rosa by the pass of the Moro, one of the finest in Switzerland (Route 105); that on the rt. ascends the vale of St. Nicholas to the Mont Cervin (Route 106).

The Gamsen and other torrents which fall into the upper end of the Vallais are most dangerous neighbours to the villages and cottages on their banks. The bed of the torrent Visp is 4 metres above a part of the village, and the Saltine is 3 metres higher than Brieg. The miserable and poverty-stricken inhabitants are in consequence obliged to construct very considerable dykes to restrain them, but even these defences are liable to destruction every 2 or 3 years.

The desolation which the torrents spread over the fields, by their debris, will attract the remark of every traveller; and the evil is constantly increasing, as the beds of the torrents rise as fast as the dykes are raised to restrain them, till they flow along the top of a colossal aqueduct or wall of loose rocks, which the road ascends and descends like a hill.

The ascent of the Simplon properly begins at Glys, a village distinguished by its large church; but, as the post-house and inn are both situated at Brieg, a detour of about 2 miles is made to pass through it.

1½ *Brieg.* (The *Inn*, Hôtel d'Angleterre (post), is the usual halting-place of travellers before or after crossing the Simplon: it contains 50 beds, but is not very comfortable.) Brieg is a small town of 650 inhabitants, situated on a sunny slope by the side of the Saltine, and overlooking the course of the Rhone, which here makes a sharp bend. The most conspicuous building is the *Jesuits' College.* The number of brothers at present (1837) does not exceed 10, and their pupils amount to only 30. There is also an *Ursuline Convent.*

The upper valley of the Rhone above Brieg, and the route to the Grimsel and Gries, are described in Routes 28 and 29.

At Brieg the Simplon road quits the vale of the Rhone, beginning to ascend immediately from the post-house. The distance from Brieg to Domo d'Ossola is 15 leagues = about 40 English miles; and the journey usually occupies 10 hours—7 to reach Simplon, and 3½ thence to Domo d'Ossola. On foot it will take full 10 hours' good walking to go from Brieg to Domo d'Ossola.

The construction of a route over the Simplon was decided upon by Napoleon immediately after the battle of Marengo, while the recollection of his own difficult passage of the Alps by the Great St. Bernard (at that time one of the easiest Alpine passes) was fresh in his memory. The plans and surveys by which the direction of the road was determined, were made by M. Céard, and a large portion of the works was executed under the superintendence of that able engineer. It was commenced on the Italian side in 1800 and on the Swiss in 1801. It took 6 years to complete, though it was barely passable in 1805, and more than 30,000 men were employed on it at one time. To give a notion of the colossal nature of the undertaking, it may be mentioned that the number of bridges, great and small, constructed for the passage of the road between Brieg and Sesto amounts to 611, in addition to the far more vast and costly constructions, such as terraces of massive masonry miles in length; of 10 galleries, either cut out of the living rock or built of solid stone; and of 20 houses of refuge to shelter travellers, and lodge the labourers constantly employed in taking care of the road. Its breadth is throughout at least 25 ft., in some places 30 ft., and the average slope nowhere exceeds 6 inches in 6½ feet.

To use the eloquent words of Sir James Mackintosh, "the Simplon may be safely said to be the most wonderful of useful works, because our canals and docks surpass it in utility, science, and magnitude, but they have no grandeur to the eye. Its peculiar character is, to be the greatest of all those monuments that at once dazzle the imagination by their splendour and are subservient to general convenience." It may be observed in addition that (except the Cenis) the Simplon was the first of the great carriage-roads opened across the W. Alps; and, though others since constructed surpass it in some respects, especially in the elevation attained (*e. g.* the Stelvio), yet this has the merit of originality, and the others are mere copies. This is the first example of the triumph of human power and intellect over nature, apparently invincible.

The cost of this road averaged about 16,000*l.* per league (*i. e.* 400,000 fr.) The object of Napoleon in its formation is well marked by the question which, on two different occasions, he first asked of the engineer sent to him to report progress —" Le canon quand pourra-t-il passer au Simplon?"

The postmasters on both sides of the mountain have the right to attach one extra horse to light carriages and 2 or more to heavy ones

in ascending the mountain: indeed, as many as eight horses are sometimes required to drag up a heavy landau. Berisol, the first posthouse above Brieg, is sometimes without horses, in which case those from Brieg are taken on for two stages. By following the old char-road the pedestrian may abridge the distance to the summit by several miles; but it is rough, and more fatiguing than the carriage-road.

The ascent of the Simplon begins at once from the posthouse in Brieg. About ½ a mile above the town the road passes, on the rt., the lofty covered bridge over the Saltine, now little used, since most vehicles make the detour by Brieg instead of going direct to or from Glys, whither this bridge conducts. The road then makes a wide sweep, turning away from the Glytzhorn, the mountain which bounds the valley on the rt., towards the Breithorn, on the opposite side, skirting a little hill dotted with white chapels and crowned by a calvary. It then again approaches the gorge of the Saltine, skirting the verge of a precipice, at the bottom of which the torrent is seen at a vast depth, forcing its way among black and bristling slate-rocks, which seem still shattered by the convulsion which first gave a passage to its waters. It is a scene of grandeur, almost of terror. At the upper end of the ravine, high above his head, the traveller may discern the glaciers under which the road is carried, but which he will require at least 3 good hours to reach, on account of the sinuosities of the route. Looking back, he will perceive the valley of the Rhone, as far as Tourtmagne, spread out as a map at his feet; Brieg and Naters remain long in sight. It is a constant pull against the collar from Brieg to the second refuge. Here the road, carried for some distance nearly on a level, is compelled to bend round the valley of the Ganther until it can cross the torrent which traverses it by another lofty bridge, called *Pont*

Ganther. The upper end of this old ravine is subject to avalanches most every winter, the snow of which early fills it up, and reaches sometimes to the crown of the arch. This ridge is left uncovered, from the fear justly entertained by the engineers that the terrific gusts or currents of air which accompany the fall of an avalanche might blow the arch entirely off, were much resistance to it presented to it. The road originally traversed a gallery cut in the rock near this, but it has been removed. After crossing the bridge the road turns down the opposite side, and then ascends by several zigzags to the third refuge, called

2½ Béresal, or Persal, a homely tavern, consisting of 2 buildings connected by a roof across the road, where a few posthorses are kept, and brandy, cheese, milk, and such-like refreshments may be procured. It may be reached in 2½ hours from Brieg.

The first gallery which the road traverses is that of Schalbet, 95 feet long—1195 metres above Glys. Near this, and hence to the summit, should the sky be clear, the traveller's attention will be riveted by the glorious view of *the Bernese Alps,* which bound the Vallais and form the rt.-hand wall of the valley of the Rhone. The glittering white peaks of the Breithorn, Jungfrau, and Mönch are magnificent objects in this scene, while below them is spread out the glacier of Aletsch, one of the most extensive in the Alps.

Fifth Refuge, called Schalbet. " Here a picture of desolation surrounds the traveller. The pine has no longer the scanty pittance of soil which it requires for nourishment; the hardy but beautiful Alpine flower ceases to embellish the sterile solitude; and the eye wanders over snow and glacier, fractured rock and roaring cataract, relieved only by that stupendous monument of human labour the *road itself,* winding along the edges of precipices, penetrating the primeval granite, striding over the furious torrent, and burrowing through dark and dripping grottoes beneath accumulated masses of ice and snow."—Johnson.

The portion of the road between the fifth refuge and the summit is the most dangerous of all, at the season when avalanches fall, and tourmentes arise, on which account it is provided with 6 places of shelter, viz. 3 galleries, 2 refuges, and a hospice, within a distance of not more than 3000 metres. The head of the gorge of Schalbet, a wild recess in the flanks of the Mount Simplon, or Monte Leone, is filled up with glaciers, beneath which, along the edge of a yawning abyss, the road is necessarily conducted. These fields of everlasting ice, forming the Kaltwasser glacier, in the heat of summer feed 5 or 6 furious torrents, the sources of the Saltine, and in winter discharge frequent avalanches into the gulf below. To protect this portion of the road 3 galleries, called, from their vicinity to the glaciers, *Glacier Galleries,* partly excavated, partly built of masonry strongly arched, have been constructed. By an ingenious contrivance of the engineer they serve in places as bridges and aqueducts at the same time, the torrents being conducted over and beneath them; and the traveller is surprised to find his carriage suddenly driven in perfect safety underneath a considerable waterfall. These galleries have been recently extended far beyond their original length, for greater security. In the spring the avalanches slide over their roofs.

The Sixth Refuge is also a barrier, at which a toll of 2 fr. is paid for each horse, to defray the cost of keeping the road in repair. A simple cross of wood, a few yards further, marks the highest summit or culminating point of the road, 2018 metres, or about 6562 ft., above the level of the sea. About ½ a mile beyond it stands the *New Hospice,* founded by Napoleon for the reception of travellers, but long left unfinished for want of funds, and even now not entirely furnished within. Externally it is a plain, solid edifice, containing several very neat bedrooms for masters, a drawing-room provided with a piano, a refectory, a chapel, and about 30 beds for travellers of the common sort. It is much more comfortable than the hospice on the Great St. Bernard, and is even warmed with a heating-apparatus. It is occupied by 3 or 4 brothers of the Augustine order, members of the same community as those on the Great St. Bernard. The prior is the amiable Father Barras, whose civility must be remembered by all who have visited the Great St. Bernard within the last 25 years, during which he resided there. Several of the celebrated dogs of St. Bernard are kept here, but they are rarely employed in active service. The monks are very happy to show the mansion to travellers, and to receive, lodge, and entertain them in stormy weather and during winter; but at other times strangers have no excuse for availing themselves of the hospitality of the house, since the inn at Simplon is good, and not far distant. The establishment is similar to that on the Great St. Bernard, except that it is more limited in extent and funds. (For further particulars see Route 108.)

A large open valley of considerable extent, bounded by snow-clad heights, having the appearance of a drained lake, occupies the summit of the Simplon. It is devoid of picturesque interest, all around is barrenness, and nothing but lichens and coarse herbage grow on the bare rocks. Below the road, on the rt., stands a tall tower, the original hospice before the new one was built. A gradual but continued descent leads past the Seventh Refuge (ruined), in about 3 miles, to the village of

3½ Simplon (Ital. Sempione). (*Inn:* Poste; affords clean beds, and a good dinner at 3 fr.) The belated traveller may easily content himse with such quarters—indeed, no oth are to be found nearer than Dom d'Ossola, a drive of 3½ hours at th least. The traveller should he supply himself with a wooden sab to save the iron drag of his carriag as the descent now becomes rapi in spite of the wide circuit whic the road makes in order to diminis the steepness.

By a well-constructed bend th traveller reaches the *Gallerie d'A gaby,* the first excavation on th Italian side, about 9 leagues fro Brieg and 5 from Domo d'Ossol on the banks of the torrent Doveri: The lower orifice of this tunnel : half blocked up by a wall with loop holes, constructed, 1814, to defen the passage and convert it into a mili tary post. The road dives int this gallery, and then, by a mor gradual slope, enters the *Gorge Gondo,* one of the grandest and mos savage in the Alps, which narrow and deepens at every step, until it precipices in some places actuall overhang the road, which is squeeze in between them on one side an the fretting torrent on the other. It i bounded by slate rocks, whose smoot vertical sides deny support to an vegetation; only now and then : tuft of grass lodged in a cleft, or a fringe of fir-trees growing above th gorge, and visible at a great heigh on the verge of the precipice, contrast agreeably with the unvaried surface of black rock. The base of these cliffs and the bed of the stream are in places heaped up with vast shattered fragments, ruins of the mountains above; while loosened masses still hanging on the slope seem to threaten the passenger below.

The Doveria is now crossed by a wooden bridge called Ponte Alto, an approach to which has been formed by scarping the rock with gunpowder. Some way further a vast projecting buttress of rock juts out from the mountain on the l., and seems to block up all further passage. It in-

eed formed a serious impediment
o the construction of the road, over-
ome, however, by the skill of the
ngineer, who has bored it through,
with another of those artificial ca-
erns. This *Gallery of Gondo* is the
ongest cut through solid rock in the
whole line of the Simplon, as it mea-
ures 596 ft.; it was also the most
difficult and costly to make, on ac-
ount of the extreme hardness of
he rock (granite?): for it required
he incessant labour of more than
100 workmen, in gangs of 8, relieving
ach other day and night, to pierce
a passage in 18 months. The progress of the work would have been
still more tedious had the labourers
confined themselves to the two ends;
but the engineer caused two lateral
openings to be made, by which means
the rock was attacked in 4 places at
once. The miners were suspended
by ropes to the face of the rock until
a lodgement was effected, to commence these side openings, which
now serve as windows to light the
interior. Opposite one of them is
seen the inscription " *Ære Italo,*
1805."

Close to the very mouth of this
remarkable gallery the roaring waterfall of the Frascinodi leaps down
from the rocks, close to the road,
which is carried over it on a beautiful bridge. Mr. Brockedon, an artist
of skill, as well as a traveller of experience, remarks, in his Excursions
among the Alps, that the scenery of
this portion of the Val Doveria, in
coming from Switzerland, bursting
suddenly upon the traveller as he
issues from the gallery, " offers perhaps the finest assemblage of objects
to excite an emotion of the sublime,
that is to be found in the Alps." The
traveller should pause and look back
after proceeding about 40 yards. The
rocks rise on both sides as straight
as walls, attaining the summit of wild
sublimity. The little strip of sky
above, the torrent roaring in the dark
gulf below, the white foam of the
waterfall, the graceful arch, and the

black mouth of the cavern, form a
picture which has been spread over
the world by the pencils of all our
first landscape-painters. A number
of zigzags now conduct to a bridge
which was carried away by an avalanche during a dreadful storm which
ruined a great part of the Simplon
road, on the 24th of August, 1834,
and has only recently been replaced.

Gondo, the last village in the Vallais, consists of a few miserable huts,
grouped round a singular, tall building, 7 stories high. An hour's walk
by the side of the torrent, which falls
in a cascade down the rt.-hand wall
of the valley, leads to a gold-mine,
which, though it barely produces a
few particles of the precious metal,
is still worked in the hope of gain.
The traveller enters Italy a short
while before reaching the Sardinian
village of

2½ Isella, where the custom-house
and passport-office are situated.

The tempest of 1834 fell with all
its violence upon this part of the
road, which it destroyed for a space
of nearly 8 miles; that is to say,
for this distance the portion which it
carried off was greater than that
which it left. Every bridge of stone
was swept away; in some instances,
even the materials of which the bridge
was built disappeared, and the very
place where it stood was not to be
recognised. Every torrent falling
into this part of the valley brought
down with it an avalanche of stones;
the damage done to the road is even
now (1837) scarcely repaired, but the
air of desolation caused by it will
never be effaced. The Gallery of
Isella, a narrow arch of rock a little
below the village, was flooded by the
torrent pouring through it, so high
were the waters swollen. At the
mouth of the Val Dovedro, a handsome new bridge supplies the place
of the one demolished by the torrent
over which it passes.

Hereabouts a change comes over
the valley, from nakedness to the
rich green foliage of the chestnut,

which shades the road, and to that of the dark fir which clothes the summits of the hitherto bare mountains above. The last gallery is traversed a little before reaching Crevola, where the Doveria is crossed for the last time by a fine lofty bridge of 2 arches, nearly 90 ft. high, previous to its flowing into the river Toccia, or Tosa, which here issues out of the Val Formazza, and the Val Vedro terminates in the Val d' Ossola. The mule-roads from the Gries and Grimsel, passing the falls of the Tosa (Route 29), fall into the Simplon route at Crevola.

It is now that the traveller really finds himself in a different region and in an altered climate: the softer hues of earth and sky, the balmy air, the trellised vines, the rich, juicy stalks of the maize, the almost deafening chirp of the grasshoppers, and, at night, the equally loud croakings of the frogs—the white villages, with their tall, square bell towers, also white, not only scattered thickly along the valley, but perched on every little jutting platform on the hill-sides—all these proclaim the entrance to *Italy.* Eustace has remarked that " the valley which now opens out to view is one of the most delightful that Alpine solitudes enclose, or the foot of the wanderer ever traversed;" a remark which, though true, will bear much modification, in the opinion of those who quit Italy by this route instead of entering it. It is only by those who approach it from the north that its charms can be fully appreciated.

2¼ Domo d' Ossola — (*Inn :* La Posta—tolerably good, and as clean as Italian inns usually are). This is a small and unimportant town, with few objects of interest, save that it is Italian—in very stone. Houses with colonnades, streets with awnings, shops teeming with sausages, macaroni, and garlic, lazy-looking, loitering lazzaroni, in red nightcaps, and bare, mahogany-coloured legs, inter-

mixed with mules, burley priests, and females veiled with the mantilla, fill up the picture of an Italian town.

The ascent from this to Simplon occupies 7 hours. From Domo to Milan takes up 12 hours' posting exclusive of stoppages. The bridge over the Tosa, about 6 miles below Domo, was carried off by the tempest of 1834, and has not yet been replaced (1837). Carriages are ferried across to

2 Vogogna—The Tosa, in spite of its rapidity, is navigable a short distance above this place; the barges are towed up by double teems of 6 or 8 horses on each bank. The interesting valley of Anzasca (Route 105), leading up to Monte Rosa, opens out opposite Vogogna. Near Ornavasca are the marble quarries (of magnesian limestone) which have supplied the stone for Milan Cathedral.

At Gravellona a small stream is crossed which drains the Lago d' Orta, and a road, running up its l. bank, leads, in ¾ of an hour, to the lake of Orta, *one of the most picturesque on the Italian border.* (See Routes 101,102.) At Fariolo the Lago Maggiore bursts into view, with the Isola Madre, the northernmost of the Borromean Islands, in the distance. A little further are quarries of a beautiful pink granite, which derives its colour from the prevalence of pink felspar in it. That mineral is obtained here in beautiful flesh-coloured crystals.

3 Baveno—(*Inn:* La Posta, near the lake, but the road runs between it and the water; tolerably good cuisine, but want of cleanliness).

The *Monte Monterone*, rising behind the village, commands one of the finest panoramic views of the Alps—having at its feet the Lago d' Orta on one side, and Lago Maggiore on the other. It takes 3 hours to reach the top. Its slopes are said to be infested with snakes.

The W. shore of the lake, as far as Sesto, being the Sardinian fronier, is lined with custom-house officers, who search all who land from the states of Austria or Switzerland.

The *Borromean Islands* may be conveniently visited from Baveno; and the traveller on his way to Milan may send round his carriage to meet him at the Count's Stables (l'Escuderia), the nearest point, or at Stresa. A boat from Baveno, with 2 rowers, to go and return, costs 5 fr. if not kept more than 2 hours; beyond that, 10 sous per rower is charged for every hour. The steam-boat which navigates the Lago Maggiore passes near the islands every morning, about 9, on its way to Sesto, and again, on its way back, at 3; so that, by setting off early from Baveno, a traveller (having no carriage) might see them, and avail himself of this rapid conveyance to reach Sesto.

It takes 25 minutes to row from Baveno to the Isola Bella, passing, on the way, the Isola Pescatori, so called because its inhabitants are poor fishermen, whose rude semi-plastered hovels contrast abruptly with the stately structures on the neighbouring island. The *Isola Bella* belongs to the Count Borromeo, who resides a part of the year in the vast, unfinished Palace which occupies one end of it. An ancestor of the family, in 1671, converted this mass of bare and barren slate-rock, which lifted itself a few feet above the surface of the lake, into a beautiful garden, teeming with the vegetation of the tropics. It consists of 10 terraces, the lowest founded on piers thrown into the lake, rising in a pyramidal form one above another, and lined with statues, vases, obelisks, and black cypresses. Upon these, as upon the hanging gardens of Babylon, flourish in the open air, not merely the orange, citron, myrtle, and pomegranate, but aloes, cactuses, the camphor-tree (of which there is a specimen 20 ft. high), sugar-cane, and coffee-plant—all inhabitants of tropical countries—and this within a day's journey of the Lapland cli-

mate of the Simplon, and within view of the Alpine snows.

The proverbial disagreement of doctors is nothing in comparison with the discord of travellers on the merits of this island. To *Simond* the sight of the island at a distance suggests the idea of "a huge Perigord pie," stuck round with the heads of woodcocks and partridges;" *Matthews* extols it as "the magic creation of labour and taste . . . a fairy-land, which might serve as a model for the gardens of Calypso;" *Saussure* calls it "une magnifique caprice, une pensée grandiose, une espèce de création;" while *Brockedon* sternly pronounces it as "worthy only of a rich man's misplaced extravagance, and of the taste of a confectioner." To taste, it may have little pretension; but, for a traveller fresh from the rigid climate of the north, this singular creation of art, with its aromatic groves, its aloes and cactuses starting out of the rocks—and, above all, its glorious situation, bathed by the dark-blue waters of the lake, reflecting the sparkling white villages on its banks, and the distant snows of the Alps, cannot fail to afford pleasure, and a visit to the Isola Bella will certainly not be repented of.

Every handful of mould on the island was originally brought from a distance, and requires to be constantly renewed. It is probable that its foundation of slate-rock favours the growth of tender plants by long retaining the heat of a noon-day sun; but few persons are aware that, in addition to this, the terraces are boarded over during winter, and the plants protected from the frost by stoves heated beneath: thus converting the terraces into a sort of hothouse. The garden is let out to a nurseryman from Genoa, who keeps it in order, shows it to strangers, and receives their douceurs.

A laurel (bay) of gigantic size is pointed out, as well for its remarkable growth as for a scar on its bark, where Napoleon, it is said, cut with a knife the word "battaglia," a short while before the battle of Marengo. Rousseau once thought of making the Isola Bella the residence of his Julie, but changed his mind on reflecting that so artificial an abode would not be consistent with the simplicity of her character.

The *Palace*, standing cheek-by-jowl with a group of ruinous and very humble cottages, is shown to strangers, but is, on the whole, scarcely worth entering, unless the visitor has plenty of time on his hands. The most remarkable among the pictures it contains are those by *Tempesta*—an artist who murdered his wife to marry another, and took refuge here after the deed, being sheltered by the owner of the mansion. The lower story is a suite of grottoes, intended as a cool retreat from the heat of summer.

The *Isola Madre*, the largest of the islands, also contains a beautiful garden, and has more natural beauty than the *Isola Bella*. The upper end of the Lago Maggiore is described in Route 91.

The Simplon road, where it skirts the lake, is an almost uninterrupted terrace of masonry, studded with granite posts at intervals of a few feet. Travellers coming from Milan may embark on the lake to visit the Borromean islands at Stresa, where boats are kept.

Beyond Belgirate, a pretty village, remarkable for the number of villas with terraces and gardens in front: the colossal statue of *St. Carlo Borromeo* appears on the hill above the road.

2½ Arona—(*Inn:* Posta, close to the water; tolerably good).

An ancient town, of 4000 inhab., with a small castellated harbour. It is built on the very margin of the lake; the principal street, in which the inn is situated, is so narrow that only one carriage can pass. The Simplon road runs through the upper part of the town. The steamer touches here twice a-day; carriages can be embarked here.

The principal *Ch.* (*Santa Maria*) contains a beautiful picture by *Gaudenzio Ferrari*—a Holy Family, with shutters, bearing figures of saints, and the portrait of a Countess Borromeo, by whom it was presented to the church. St. Carlo Borromeo was born at Arona, 1538, in the old castle, now nearly destroyed.

On the summit of a hill, about half an hour's walk from the town, stands the *Colossal Statue* of *St. Charles Borromeo*, 66 ft. high, and placed on a pedestal 40 ft. high. The head, hands, and feet, alone, are cast in bronze, the rest of the figure is formed of sheets of beaten copper, arranged round a pillar of rough masonry which forms the support of it. The saint is represented extending his hand towards the lake, and over his birth-place, Arona, bestowing on them his benediction. There is grace in the attitude, in spite of the gigantic proportions of the figure, and benevolence beams from the countenance;—altogether the effect of it is good and very impressive. It was erected, 1697, by subscriptions, principally contributed by the Borromean family. It is possible to enter the statue and to mount up into the head, but the ascent is difficult and fatiguing, and not to be attempted by the nervous. It is effected by means of two ladders, tied together (provided by a man who lives hard by), resting on the pedestal, and reaching up to the skirt of the saint's robe. Between the folds of the upper and lower drapery the adventurous climber squeezes himself through—a task of some difficulty, if he be of corpulent dimensions; and he then clambers up the stone pillar which supports the head, by placing his feet upon the iron bars or cramps by which the copper drapery is attached to it. To effect this, he must assume a straddling attitude, and proceed in the dark till he reaches the head, which he will find capable of holding 3 persons at once. Here he may rest himself by sitting down in the recess of the nose, which forms no bad substitute for an arm-chair. In the neighbouring church several relics of St. Carlo are preserved.

The view of the peaked snowy ridge of the Monte Rosa, from the lower part of the Lago Maggiore, is magnificent. A ferry-boat conveys the traveller across the Ticino, which forms the outlet of the lake, into the territory of Austrian Lombardy, and the small town of

1½ Sesto Calende.—No good inn. Passports are strictly examined, and *no traveller is allowed to pass the frontier unless he be provided with the signature of an Austrian minister*— in default of which he is sent back to Turin or Berne to procure it. Sesto is said to have been a Roman station, and to have received its name from a market held here on the 1st of the month—*Sexto Calendarum.* It stands upon the left bank of the Ticino, just below the spot where it quits the Lago Maggiore. The *Ch. of St. Donato* is a structure of the middle ages.

A *Steamer* starts at one o'clock every day, but Sunday, for the head of the lake, stopping at Arona and calling off the Borromean Islands. It corresponds with the velocifera (omnibus) to Milan, which sets out within half an hour of the arrival of the steamer. For fares, and other particulars respecting the Lago Maggiore, see Route 91.

The road to Milan lies over a monotonous flat, the beginning of the great plain of Lombardy, between avenues of cabbage-headed mulberry-trees, hedges of acacia, and rows of vines trained between fruit-trees, so as completely to hide all view on either side. The country is excessively fertile, but void of interest, and the road usually most disagreeable from the dust. The posting is not on a good footing, and the rate of driving is very slow—even the prospect of double buono-mano has little effect in accelerating the postilions.

The name of every village is written on the wall at the entrance. The first which we pass is Soma, containing an ancient castle of the Visconti, fringed with swallow-tailed battlements, and a remarkable cypress-tree of great age, one of the largest known. It is stated to have been a tree in the days of Julius Cæsar; it is 121 ft. high and 23 ft. in girth. Napoleon respected it at the time of the construction of the route of the Simplon, causing the road to diverge from the straight line on account of it.

Near this was fought the first great battle between Scipio and Hannibal, commonly called the Battle of the Ticinus, in which Scipio was worsted.

1¼ Gallerati.—Beyond this is Cascina delle Corde (of the ropes), also called Cascina del bon Jesu. At Busto, a mile to the W. of this, is a church designed by Bramante, and containing frescoes by *Gaudenzio Ferrari.*

1 Legnanello.

1 Rho.—Outside the town is a very handsome church, designed by Pellegrini ; the façade, recently finished, is by Pollack. Near this are extensive rice-grounds, the vicinity of which is very unhealthy.

The road terminates and enters Milan by the *Arco del Sempione* (della Pace), commenced by Napoleon, and finished by the Austrian government 1838.

1¼ MILAN — (*Inns:* Gran Bretagna ; Albergo Reale; Croce di Malta — good and quiet.) For a description of Milan, see Starke's Travels, or THE HAND-BOOK FOR TRAVELLERS IN NORTHERN ITALY.

ROUTE 66.

CONSTANCE TO ST. GALL, BY THE LAKE OF CONSTANCE.

8½ stunden $=$ 27¾ Eng. miles. Constance is fully described in Route 7.

The Lake of Constance.

Three steam-boats navigate the lake of Constance, making voyages 2 or 3 times a-week between Constance and Schaffhausen; Constance and Ueberlingen; Ludwigshafen, Friedrichshafen, Rorschach, Lindau, and Bregenz. The time and place of starting are promulgated in a printed tarif, which will be found hung up in all the inns near the lake. It takes 5 hours to go from Constance to Bregenz, and 3 to Rorschach or Friedrichshafen.

The lake of Constance, called by the Germans *Boden See*, and anciently known to the Romans under the name *Lacus Brigantinus* (from Brigantia, the modern Bregenz), is bordered by the territories of 5 different states—Baden, Würtemberg, Bavaria, Austria, and Switzerland, and a portion of its coasts belongs to each of them. It is about 44 miles long, from Bregenz to Ueberlingen, and 30 from Bregenz to Constance; about 9 miles wide in the broadest part; 964 ft. is its greatest depth; and it lies 1255 feet above the sea.

Its main tributary is the Rhine, which enters at its E. extremity, and flows out under the walls of Constance. Its accumulated deposits have formed an extensive delta at the upper end of the lake, and are annually encroaching further.

Its banks, either flat or gently undulating, present little beauty of scenery compared with other Swiss lakes; but they are eminently distinguished for their fertility, and its S. shore is studded with a picturesque line of ruined castles or hill-forts of the middle ages.

It is only at its E. extremity, in distant glimpses of the snow-topped mountains of Vorarlberg, that it displays any alpine features.

Its waters, on an average, are lowest in the month of February, and highest in July, when the snows are melting: it sometimes swells a foot in 24 hours at that season.[1]

Post-horses may be obtained on the route from Constance to St. Gall, nearly on the same terms as in Baden. From Constance to Hub is reckoned as 1 post.

Diligences go daily in 5 hours from Constance to St. Gall.

On quitting Constance the road passes the Augustine convent of Kreuzlingen, which still maintains 10 brothers of the order. Though the foundation is very ancient, the existing edifice dates from the end of the 30 years' war, in the course of which the preceding building was destroyed.

The canton of Thurgovia, which occupies the S. shore of the lake from Constance to Arbon, is distinguished for its surpassing fertility. Instead of rocks and mountains, and alpine pastures, the characteristics of other parts of Switzerland, this canton presents richly-cultivated arable land, waving with corn and hemp; the place of forests is supplied by orchards: it is indeed the garden and granary of Helvetia. The country is at the same time thickly peopled, abounding in villages and cheerful cottages.

1¼ The nunnery of Münsterlingen, about 4 miles on the road, was suppressed in 1838, and converted into an hospital. The surviving sisters are allowed to occupy one wing of the building during their life-time.

2 Uttwyl.

After passing Romanshorn, a village built on the point of a tongue of land, the E. end of the lake, with the distant Alps towering above it, comes into view. On the opposite shore of the lake is Friedrichshafen and the *Villa* of the King of Würtemberg, in which he usually passes a part of the summer. See HAND-BOOK FOR SOUTHERN GERMANY.

At Hub relays of post-horses may be obtained. Hence to St. Gall the distance is reckoned 1½ post, and the charge for two horses is 4 fr. 3 kr. From Hub to Constance is 1 post, and to Rorschach 1¼ post.

2 Arbon, a walled town of 660 inhabitants, close upon the lake. The Romans, under Augustus, built a fort here, upon the high road from Augst and Windisch to Bregenz, which they called *Arbor Felix*. It was abandoned by them to the Allemanni in the 5th century. The *Castle*, on an eminence overlooking the lake, was built 1510, but its tower is said to rest on Roman foundations. The *belfry*, detached from the church, is boarded, not walled, on the side nearest the castle, in order that no force hostile to the lords of the castle should be enabled to shelter themselves in it, or annoy the castle from thence. The monk St. Gall is said to have died at Arbon (640), and the place was a favourite residence of Conradin of Hohenstauffen.

Travellers bound direct for Coire will proceed at once on to Rorschach, 1¼ post from Hub (Route 67), while the road to St. Gall turns S.

A gradual but long ascent leads up-hill the whole way from the borders of the lake along a pleasing valley, near the upper end of which, 1060 feet above the lake of Constance, is situated

2¾ *St. Gall—Inns:* Hecht (Brochet), very good ; Rössli (Cheval).

St. Gall, capital of the canton, is situated in an elevated valley on the banks of a small stream called the Steinach, and has a population of 10,333 souls. It is one of the principal seats of manufacturing industry in Switzerland. The manufacture of muslins, known as Swiss muslins all over Europe, is the most flourishing ; but the spinning of cotton is also rapidly increasing. There are extensive bleacheries in the town, and the neighbouring slopes are white with linen.

The antique walls, however, which still surround the town, and the ditch, now converted into gardens, tell of a totally different period and state of society, and recall to mind the ancient history of St. Gall. If

we may believe the legend, it was in the early part of the 7th century that St. Gallus, a Scotch monk (? Irish), left his convent in the island of Iona, one of the Hebrides, and, after travelling over a large part of Europe converting the heathens, finally settled on the banks of the Steinach, then a wilderness buried in primæval woods, of which bears and wolves seemed the rightful tenants rather than men. He taught the wild people around the arts of agriculture, as well as the doctrines of true religion. The humble cell which the Scotch missionary had founded became the nucleus of civilization ; and 50 years after his death, when the fame of his sanctity, and the miracles reported to have been wrought at his tomb, drew thousands of pilgrims to the spot, it was replaced by a more magnificent edifice, founded under the auspices of Pepin l'Heristal. This Abbey was one of the oldest ecclesiastical establishments in Germany. It became the asylum of learning during the dark ages, and was the most celebrated school in Europe between the 8th and 10th centuries. Here the works of the authors of Rome and Greece were not only read but copied, and we owe to the labour of these obscure monks many of the most valuable classical authors, which have been preserved to modern times in MSS., treasured up in the Abbey of St. Gall ; among them Quintilian, Silius Italicus, Ammian Marcellinus, and part of Cicero, may be mentioned.

About the beginning of the 13th century St. Gall lost its reputation for learning, as its abbots exchanged a love of piety and knowledge for worldly ambition, and the thirst for political influence and territorial rule. The desire of security, in those insecure times, first induced the abbot to surround his convent and the adjoining building with a wall and ditch, with 13 towers at intervals ; and from that moment (the end of the 10th century) may be dated the foundation of the town. He and his 100 monks of the Benedictine order thought it no disgrace to sally forth, sword in hand and helmet on head, backed by their 200 serfs, in the hour of danger, when the convent was threatened by ungodly laymen. The donations of pious pilgrims from all parts of Europe soon augmented enormously the revenues of the abbots. They became the most considerable territorial sovereigns in N. Switzerland; their influence was increased by their elevation to the rank of princes of the empire; they were engaged in constant wars with their neighbours, and were latterly entangled in perpetual feuds with their subjects at home. These bold burghers, who, in the first instance, owed their existence and prosperity to the convent, became, in the end, restive under its rule. In the beginning of the 15th century the land of Appenzell threw off the yoke of the abbot; at the Reformation St. Gall itself became independent of him; and in 1712 the ecclesiastical prince was obliged to place the convent under the protection of those very citizens whose ancestors had been his serfs.

The French revolution caused the secularization of the abbey, and the sequestration of its revenues followed in 1805. The last abbot, Pancratius Forster, died in 1829, a pensioner on the bounty of others, in the convent of Muri.

The *Abbey Church*, now cathedral, was so completely modernized in the last century, that it possesses little to interest the stranger.

The deserted *Monastery* is now converted into a public school, and the part of it which formed the abbot's *Palace* (*Die Pfalz*) now serves for the public offices of the Government of the canton.

The *Convent Library* (Stifts Bibliothek) still exists in the town, and contains many curiosities, such as various ancient MSS. either from Ireland, or transcribed by Iris monks; also a MS. of the Niebelun zen Lied.

At the *Cassino Club* will be foun an excellent *reading-room*.

The *Freudenberg*, the neighbou ing mountain on the W. of the town commands from its summit, about miles off, a fine panorama, includin the lake of Constance and the moun tains of St. Gall and Appenzell, wit the Sentis at their head. A carriage road leads up to the top, where an inn is built.

Diligences go from St. Gall *daily* to Constance, Winterthur, and Zurich; 4 *times a-week* to Wesen and Rapperschwyl; *twice a-week* to Lindau; *once a-week* to Bregenz and Innsbruck; 3 *times a-week* to Donaueschingen and Carlsruhe; 3 *times a-week* to Coire, by Rorschach, Altstetten, and thence to Milan by the Splugen and Bernardin.

Extra Post in Canton St. Gall.

Tax per Post, two Horses.

Posts		Fl.	kr.
1	St. Gall to Rorschach	2	42
1¼	——— Rheineck	4	3
1½	——— Hub	4	3
1¼	——— Flawyl	3	22
1¼	Flawyl—Munichweiler	3	22
½	Rorschach—Rheineck	1	40
1¼	——— Hub	3	22
1⅛	Rheineck—Bregenz	3	2
1⅛	——— Hohenems	3	2
1¼	——— Allstadten	3	22
1¼	Sennwald	3	22
1¼	Sevelen	3	22
1¼	Ragatz	3	22
1½	Chur	4	3
	3 horses per post	4	3
	4 ———	5	24
	Postillion's Trinkgeld, 2 horses	0	32
	——— 4 do.	0	40

ROUTE 67.

ST. GALL TO COIRE, BY RORSCHACH, RHEINECK, ALSTETTEN, THE VALLEY OF THE RHINE, AND THE BATHS OF PFEFFERS.

8 Swiss posts = 61½ Eng. miles.

This road is supplied with post horses (see above, and § 5). It is traersed by diligences 3 times a-week. Travellers should endeavour to reach Pfeffers in one day, as the intermediate stations are not good sleeping-places. There is a direct road from St. Gall to Altstetten, avoiding the detour by Rorschach and the Lake of Constance; but it is very steep and bad, not fit for a heavy carriage. The pedestrian, with the aid of a guide, may reach Coire by Appenzell, crossing the mountains to Wildhaus (Routes 68 and 71).

1 Rorschach—(*Inn :* Post ; Krone, dear and uncivil ; Löwe). This little lake-port and town of 1650 inhabitants is the principal corn-market in Switzerland. The grain required to supply the greater part of the Alpine districts of N. Switzerland is imported from Suabia, in boats, across the lake, and is deposited temporarily in large warehouses here. Much muslin is made at Rorschach.

A *steam-boat* goes 5 times a-week between it and Friedrichshafen, in Würtemburg, and the steamers from Constance and Lindau also touch here regularly. The deposits of the Rhine are, it is said, forming themselves into shallows between Rorschach and Lindau, which may soon impede the direct navigation of the lake between these two places. On the slope a little above the town is the large dilapidated building, called *Statthallery*, or Marienberg, a palace once of the proud abbots of St. Gall, now a farm-house. It commands a fine view from its terrace. Near it, perched on a projecting sandstone rock, is the desolate *Castle of St. Anne*, with its square keep.

Skirting the foot of low hills clad with vineyards, beneath which the yellow-bellied pumpkins may be seen basking in the sun, the road passes along under the shade of fruit-trees, but soon quits the margin of the lake to cross the flat delta of the Rhine. The district around the mouth of the river abounds in marsh and is by no means healthy.

1½ Rheinegg—(*Inn :* Krone)—a village of 1370 inhabitants, on the l. bank of the Rhine, about 4 miles above its embouchure, situated under vine-clad hills, surmounted by a ruined castle, which was destroyed 1445 by the Appenzellers. There are several other castles on the neighbouring heights.

St. Margarethen, a pretty village completely embowered in a grove of walnut and fruit trees, is situated near the Austrian ferry, over the Rhine, which must be crossed in going to Bregenz or Lindau (see Hand-book for S. Germany), but which our road leaves on the l. It turns soon afterwards due S. up the valley of the Rhine, through an uninteresting district of flat and unhealthy marsh, interspersed with gravel-beds, which the traveller should get over as fast as possible, on account of malaria. The Rhine here is a wide, shallow, muddy, and unsteady stream, constantly changing its channel and overflowing its banks: it is not navigated except by wood rafts, which float down it.

1¼ Altstetten—(*Inn :* Rabe, Corbeau ; just tolerable)—a village of 1815 inhabitants, in a fruitful neighbourhood. There is a road from this over the hill of Stoss to St. Gall, by Gais (Route 68) ; but it is very steep, only to be surmounted by the aid of extra horses, and barely practicable for English carriages. It takes two hours to reach the top. The view from it over the Alps of the Voralberg is fine.

1¼ Sennwald—(*Inn :* Post, by no means first-rate, but tolerable). Down to the 17th century, the district which we now traverse belonged to the powerful barons of Hohen Sax, many of whose castles, reduced to ruins by the Appenzellers, may still be discerned upon the heights on the W. of the Rhine valley. One of this family, a brave and noble soldier and a Protestant, escaped with difficulty from the massacre of St. Bartholomew at Paris, and on his return home was murdered by his nephew. After this foul deed, it is the popular belief, that the blessing of God was withdrawn from the race: it is certain they never prospered. In 1616 their vast domains were sold to Zurich, and the family became extinct soon after. The body of the murdered man is still preserved in a perfect condition, in a coffin with a glass lid, dried like a mummy, under the church-tower of Sennwald. This circumstance, and the story connected with it, have given to the remains a reputation for sanctity; so that, though a Protestant, the Catholics have stolen some of the limbs as relics, and once actually carried off the body across the Rhine: it was, however, speedily reclaimed.

Werdenberg—(*Inn:* Post)—was the seat of a noble family of that name, who played an important part in early Swiss history. The *Stammschloss*, the cradle of the race, still stands in good preservation above the town. A cross road runs hence through the vale of Toggenburg, and past Wildhaus, to Schaffhausen (Route 71).

1¼ Sewelen.

Below Sargans (described in Route 14), which we pass a little on the rt., the roads from the Grisons, and from Zurich, meet that from St. Gall.

1½ Ragatz—(*Inn:* Poste; Hotel of the Tamina; not very good)—a village situated at the mouth of the gorge (tobel) through which the torrent Tamina issues out into the Rhine. Mules and guides may be hired here (for 6 fr.) to go to Pfeffers. The authorised charges may be seen in the tarif hung up, both at the inns here and at the baths.

The BATHS OF PFEFFERS, which no one should omit to visit from Ragatz, are situated about 6½ miles off, up the valley of the Tamina. The excursion to the baths and back need not occupy more than 6 or 8 hours, which will be well spent in exploring one of the most extraordinary spots in *Switzerland.* There are two path leading to them, practicable only on foot or on horseback—one, on the rt. bank of the Tamina, leads pas the Convent of Pfeffers; beyond which a horse cannot go, and is 1½ mile longer than that on the l. bank the one commonly chosen, which is practicable for horses as far as the baths. The pedestrian may take one in going, the other in returning.

The bridle-path on the l. bank of the Tamina, is carried at first up a very steep and fatiguing ascent which it requires an hour to surmount, through beech-woods, and at times along the edge of the precipice, at whose foot the Tamina is heard, chafing and roaring. After surmounting this portion the traveller emerges from the wood and crosses the sloping pastures which clothe the upper part of the valley. On the opposite side the Convent of Pfeffers is seen. At the hamlet of Valens the path begins to descend by zigzags into the gloomy gorge of the Tamina, which is just like a crack traversing the valley longitudinally, and at the bottom of this the traveller finds himself arrived at the *Baths.*

The path along the right bank crosses the Tamina at Ragatz, and surmounts an equally steep ascent, on the top of which it reaches the *Convent of Pfeffers,* finely placed on an elevated mountain-platform, commanding, on one side, the valley of the Rhine, backed by the majestic Falkniss; on the other, opening out towards the Lake of Wallenstadt and the peaks of the Sieben Kurfürsten. The Benedictine monastery of Pfeffers, founded 713, was suppressed, after an existence of 10 centuries, in 1838, by a decree of the Government of the canton of St. Gall. "This suppression was effected by the Radical party, in opposition to the Conservatives; and, being contrary to the act of Confederation and the guarantees of the Congress of Vienna, will probably, in due time, be assigned as a reason for military interference."—*P.* The Convent once possessed a very extensive territory; its abbots were princes, but the French, as usual, appropriated their revenues ; and the little property that was restored to them at the termination of the French rule, including the baths, of which they were proprietors, is now to be appropriated to pious works, the education of the people, &c. The revenues of the convent were valued at 216,365 Swiss florins. The members of the fraternity are to be pensioned for their lives. The convent, a vast edifice, but not otherwise remarkable, was built 1665, in place of one destroyed by fire. It encloses a church in the centre, like all the convents of the Benedictine order. Near the convent stands the ruined castle of Wartenstein.

After leaving behind the convent and hamlet, the path lies over the pastures of the upland valley, here carpeted with bright green, while its sides are clothed in woods, out of which rise bare limestone peaks and cliffs. The river Tamina flows, concealed from view, at the bottom of the deep gash, or gorge, in the centre, which is so narrow that in places, the two sides appear united. The path, gradually descending, approaches this gorge near a small wooden shed projecting over it, and containing a sort of *crane* or *pulley*, intended to lower down provisions and other things to the baths. This is, perhaps, the best point for viewing this singular spot. On looking over the verge of the precipice you perceive, at the bottom of the ravine, at the vast depth of 600 ft. below, the roofs of two large buildings, like cotton factories, in size and structure. So completely vertical are the walls of rock, that the rope from the pulley descends nearly straight into the roof of the bath-house.

The only mode of reaching the baths from this side is by a staircase (stiege) formed partly of trunks of trees, attached to the face of the cliff, and partly of steps cut in the rock, and situated about 100 yards higher up than the crane. At the bottom of the ladder the Tamina is crossed by a natural bridge of rock, beneath which the river forces its way out of sight and hearing. Ten minutes' walk below this point lie

The Baths; two large piles of building connected together by a chapel. They are built on a narrow ledge of rock, a few feet above the roaring Tamina, and so deeply sunken between the rocks that they may be said to be half buried ; so that in the height of summer, the sun appears above them only from 10 to 4. They are large gloomy buildings, damp and not over clean. There are rooms enough to receive between 200 and 300 persons, and, in the season, they are almost all occupied ; but they are ill-furnished, and not comfortable. The houses are traversed by vaulted corridors, 400 ft. long. At one end is the pump-room, and on the ground-floor the baths, 12 or 14 shallow wooden pans, designed for the reception of several persons at once, in chambers so filled with vapour that the patient is half blinded on entering them. There are also private baths ; both are supplied with a current of hot water, constantly running through them. Since the dissolution of the convent it is probable that the baths may fall under new and better management.

As the accommodation for strangers is homely, so is the fare simple. There is a daily table d'hôte, at 12, for 2nd class guests, and at 1 for 1st class ; at which 200 persons sometimes assemble : the price, including a bottle of wine, is 1 fl. 6 kr. The physician exercises an equally powerful sway over the dinner with the cook, since his fiat banishes all unwholesome viands and limits the number of dishes.

The hot springs of Pfeffers were not known to the Romans. There is a story that they were discovered by a hunter who, having ventured into the abyss of the Tamina, in the pursuit of game, remarked the column of vapour arising from them. For many years nothing was done to facilitate access to them, and patients desirous of profiting by their healing virtues were let down to the source from the cliffs above, by ropes, and, in order to reap as much benefit as possible, were accustomed to pass a week together, both day and night, in them, not only eating and drinking but sleeping, under hot water, instead of under blankets. The sources of the virtue of the water is not very evident, as a pint contains scarcely 3 grains of saline particles; it has a temperature of about 98° Fahrenheit.

The situation of the baths is both gloomy and monotonous, hemmed in between dripping walls of rock, and shaded by dank foliage, with only a narrow strip of sky overhead, and without even space or facilities for locomotion and exercise, unless the patient will scale the sides of the valley above him. To one fresh arrived from the upper world, its meadows and sunshine, a visit to Pfeffers has all the effect of being at the bottom of a well or a mine. The atmosphere is kept at one regular temperature of chilliness by the perpetual draft brought down by the torrent, and the solitary and imprisoned ray of sunshine which about noon, and for an hour or two afterwards, finds its way into these recesses, is insufficient to impart warmth or cheerfulness. A small terrace, 6 or 8 feet wide, close to the baths, is the only level space near them, if the sojourner wishes to walk he has no choice, but must begin to ascend. It is to be presumed, that few English travellers would be disposed to make any stay here. A passing visit of a few hours, or at most, a single night spent here, will satisfy the curiosity of most persons. No one, however, should depart without visiting the

Source of the hot spring.

Most of the guide-books describe this as a service of danger: the writer of this cannot help thinking that its terrors have been exaggerated. The spring is constantly visited even by ladies. At the same time persons of weak nerves and subject to giddiness in the head, should on no account attempt it. If the stranger have any fears, they will be considerably allayed by the sight of the guide who shows the way, and whose qualifications for this task of danger appear to consist in his having a wooden leg! A few yards above the spot where the bath-house stands, the sides of the ravine of the Tamina contract in an extraordinary manner, so as to approach within a few feet of each other; a little farther they even close over and cover up the river, which is seen issuing out of a cavernous chasm. A bridge of planks across the Tamina, leads to the entrance, which is closed by a door. The bridge is prolonged into the gorge, in the shape of a scaffolding or shelf, suspended by iron stanchions to the rocks, and partly laid in a niche cut out of the side. It is never more than 3, but generally is only 1 plank, wide; and is carried all along the chasm as far as the hot spring, affording the only means of approach to it, as the sides of the rent are quite vertical, and there is not an inch of room between them and the torrent, for the sole of a foot to rest. A few yards from the entrance the passage is darkened by the overhanging rock. The sudden chill of an atmosphere never visited by the sun's rays, the fearful rushing and roaring of the torrent, 30 or 40 feet below, the threatening position of the rocks above, and the trembling and quivering of the narrow planks on which you tread, protected by no railing, or balustrade, are enough to cause a slight shudder, even to one possessed of strong nerves. In parts, it is almost dark, where the sides of the ravine overlap one another, and actually meet over-head, so as to form a natural arch. The rocks in many places show evident marks of having been ground away, and scooped out by the rushing river, and by the stones brought down with it. For several hundred yards the river pursues an almost subterranean course, the roof of the chasm being the floor, as it were, of the valley. In some places the roots of the trees are seen dangling through the crevice above your head, and at one particular spot you find yourself under the arch of the natural bridge leading to the staircase mentioned before (p. 171). Had Virgil or Dante been aware of this spot, they would certainly have conducted their heroes through it to the jaws of the infernal regions.

The shelf of planks extends nearly a quarter of a mile from the baths. At its extremity, at the bottom of a cavern in the rocks, rises the hot spring; its temperature being about 100° Fahrenheit; it is received into a reservoir nearly 15 feet deep, from which it is conducted in pipes to the baths. The first baths were miserable hovels, built over the spring, and suspended, like swallows' nests, to the face of the rock: the only entrance to them was by the roof, and the sick were let down into them by ropes and pulleys. The springs generally cease to flow in winter, but burst forth again in spring; they are most copious when the snow has fallen in abundance, and continue till autumn, after which their fountains are again sealed. The water has little taste or smell; it bears some resemblance, in its mineral contents, to that of Ems; and is used both for bathing and drinking.

Mr. Brockedon observes of the walk up to the springs, " It is one of the very few spots that I have seen where no disappointment can arise from previous description."

Those who have arrived at the baths by way of Valens should not quit the spot (if they intend return-

ing by the same road) without ascending the staircase and looking down upon the baths from the shed which contains the crat.e and pulley (p. 171).

The Kalanda, or Galandaberg (the mountain on the rt. bank of the Tamina, above the baths, which separates the valley from that of the Rhine), is sometimes ascended on account of the view from its top—a 5-hours' walk.

There is a path from Pfeffers direct to Reichenau up the valley of the Tamina, crossing at its head the pass La Foppa am Kunkels, a walk of about 24 miles. Another foot-path leads up the Kalfauer-Thal to Glarus. (Route 76, p. 193.)

The pedestrian traveller, going from the baths to Coire, need not return to Ragatz, but may proceed by the Convent of Pfeffers, whence a path strikes down directly to the bridge over the Rhine, called Untere Zoll Brücke, a walk of about 2 hours.

A char-à-bane, with 1 horse, may be hired from Ragatz to Coire for 10 zwanzigers.

The high road from Ragatz runs along the l. bank of the Rhine as far as the Untere Zollbrücke (Lower Toll-bridge), the only bridge on the Rhine between the Lake of Constance and Reichenau. It was entirely swept away by the tremendous flood in the autumn of 1834, which did immense injury to the valley. In crossing this bridge, the traveller passes out of Canton St. Gall into the Grisons. The valley of the Rhine has a grand appearance from this point. The peak of the Falknisberg is a conspicuous and striking object in the view to the N.E. The Rhine alone is unpicturesque, from the width of its bed and the large space of unsightly sand and gravel left bare in summer. Its bed is constantly rising, so as to threaten more fearful inundations; and a plan has been proposed of cutting a new channel for its unruly stream, from this point as far as the Lake of Constance. A short way above the bridge, the Landquart, an impetuous torrent, descending from the valley of Prettigau, enters the Rhine. The road up it is described in Route 81.

Beyond this, the Convent of Pfeffers is visible from the road; the snowy heights of the Galanda rise into sight on the opposite bank of the Rhine; and the ruins of feudal castles, perched upon rocky knolls, overlooking the valley, give a highly picturesque character to the scene. One of the most conspicuous is Haldenstein, nearly opposite Coire.

1¼ *Coire*, Germ. Chur — (*Inns:* Weisses Kreutz (White Cross), good and cheap, the best; Post, or Freyeck, tolerable ; Capricorn, outside the town, very civil people, and a moderate and good house). The wine of the Valteline is generally consumed in the Grisons, and may be had tolerably good here.

The capital of the Grisons, the *Curia Rhætorum* of the Romans, is an ancient walled town, of 4786 inhab., about a mile from the Rhine. Its prosperity arises almost entirely from the high roads upon which it stands, which form the channel of communication from Italy into Switzerland and Western Germany, and unite the great commercial towns of Milan and Genoa, south of the Alps, with Zurich and St. Gall on the north. Coire is the staple place of the goods transported over the two great Alpine carriage roads of the Splügen and Bernardin. It is the place of meeting of the Council of the Grisons ; a member of which claims the title of "Your Wisdom" ("Euer Weisheit").

The town has narrow streets, and stands on uneven ground ; much curious domestic architecture will be found in it. The *Bishop's Palace*, and the quarter around it, inhabited by Catholics, occupy the summit of an eminence, and are separated from the rest by walls and battlements, closed by two fortified gates. Here is situated the *Church of St. Lucius*, or the *Dom*—the oldest parts of which, in the circular or Romanesque style, date from the eighth century. The detached portal, its sculptures, and the monsters which support its pillars and form the capitals, are very curious—" they are the prototypes of those existing in the Lombard churches." Within, there are one or two singular old paintings — one attributed to *A. Durer* (?). In the sacristy are preserved the bones of St. Lucius, " a British king, according to the ' English Martyrologie,' and the founder of St. Peter's Ch., Cornhill,"—P., and one or two specimens of church plate. The crypt is supported by a single pillar, the base being a monster.

The *Episcopal Palace*, near the church, is an antique building ; the staircase and halls are singularly decorated with stucco-work ; and the chapel, within a tower, is said to be one of the earliest specimens of Christian architecture. Coire is the oldest bishopric in Switzerland. Behind the Palace is a kind of ravine, lined with vineyards, across which a path leads to the *Catholic Seminary*, from which is a remarkably picturesque view of the town.

Besides the roads from Coire to Italy by the Splügen (Route 88) and Bernardin (Route 90), and those to Zurich and St. Gall, and along the rt. bank of the Rhine to Feldkirch and Bregenz, several new lines are in progress, leading in different directions through the Grisons. A carriage road, commenced some years ago, between Coire and the Engadine, over the Julier Pass, is already finished as far as Tiefenkasten, and will probably be completed the whole way in 1838. See Route 82.

Diligences go 4 times a-week to Zurich (Route 14), communicating with steamers on the Lakes of Wallenstadt and Zurich ; 4 times a-week to St. Gall ; 4 times to Milan ; once a-week to Lindau.

Post horses are kept on all the great high-roads leading from Coire through the Grisons and canton of St. Gall. The postmaster at Coire will furnish travellers with a printed tariff of the charges and distances. (See also p. 168.)

Money.—The canton of the Grisons has a coinage of its own; though, since napoleons and francs, Austrian florins, and Brabant dollars, are current on all the high roads, the traveller need not perplex himself with the intricacies of this currency, but may desire his bills to be made out in francs or florins. It will probably suffice to remember that 1 Grison flor.—2 zwanzigers, or 1 French fr. 74 centimes.

1 Fr. fr.=3½ Grison kreutzers.

1 Brabant dollar=3 Gris. flor. 20 kr.

The Grison florin, or gulden, is composed of 60 kr., or 70 blützgers.

1 batz.=5 blützgers.

The Romansch Language.

A newspaper is printed at Coire in the Lingua Romanscha, a dialect peculiar to the Grisons and neighbouring alpine country of Tyrol, derived, like the Italian, Spanish, and French, from the Latin, but corrupted by the admixture of other languages. In this remote part of Europe it has kept its ground since the destruction of the Roman empire. It is said, however, to be gradually disappearing before the German language.

It may be divided into at least three distinct dialects :—1. The Ladin, spoken in the Lower Engadine, and vale of Münster: it comes nearest to the Latin, and is, perhaps, not very dissimilar from the vulgar tongue, spoken by the Roman peasantry, as described by Livy. 2. The Romansch of the Upper Engadine, the valleys of Bregaglia, Oberhalbstein, Schams, &c. 3. The patois of the Grison highlanders in the vale of the Vorder and Hinter Rhine.

The difference between the three may be shown in the following translation of the first sentence in the Lord's Prayer:—

Pater noster qui es in cœlis.

1. Bab noss, qual ca ti eis entschiel, &c.

2. Pap noss, quel tii est en cêl, &c.

3. Pap noss, quel chi esch in'ls cêls, &c.

According to a very obscure tradition, the inhabitants of this part of the chain of Rhætian Alps are the descendants of some Tuscan fugitives, driven out of Etruria by inroads of the Gauls. Many curious resemblances have been traced between the existing names of obscure villages of these remote valleys and those of places in ancient Etruria and Latium—as Lavin, *Lavinium;* Thusis, *Tuscia;* Ardez, *Ardea;* Ro mein, *Roma;* Falisc, or Fläsch, *Falisci;* Madullein, *Medullinum;* Peist, *Pœstum;* Umbrien and Mount Umbrail, *Umbria.*

Owing to the scanty literature, there being but few printed books, except a translation of the Bible, one or two of the New Testament, and a few other books, the Romansch language is not rich in words. From the circumstance, however, of its having been made the language of the pulpit at the Reformation, when the greater part of the population of the Grisons became Protestant, it has kept its ground till the present day.

The whole of Romansch literature may be comprised in about 30 books, mostly religious works, including the Bible, liturgy, and catechisms. The first grammar and dictionary of the Romansch language was published by a clergyman named Conradi at Zurich, in 1820 and 1823. In 1836 a newspaper, called Il Grischun Romansch, was printed in the Romansch dialect at Coire.

History and Government of the Grisons.

The government of the Grisons deserves some consideration from the traveller.

It must not be supposed that the conspiracy on the Grütli, in 1307, and the exploits of Tell, gave freedom to the whole country now called Switzerland, or even influenced more than a very small part of it—the forest cantons—except in as far as such a spirit-stirring example is capable of influencing the minds of a neighbouring people. For more than a century after the first Swiss union, the country of Rhætia, now called Grisons, groaned under the tyranny of almost numberless petty lords, who, though they possessed but a few acres of land, or even no more than the number of square feet on which their castle stood, yet assumed the rights of independent sovereignty, waging perpetual petty war with their neighbours—oppressing their own subjects, and pillaging all travellers—the ancient form of levying duties and customs. The best notion of the state of society which existed during this period of the Faustrecht (club law), may be formed from the quantity of feudal ruins which stud not only the main valleys of the Rhine, but even the lateral valleys and gorges of the Rhætian Alps. At last a day of retribution came. The peasants rose in revolt, and threw off the yoke of the nobles—with less violence than might be expected, chiefly because the great ecclesiastical potentates, the Bishop of Coire, the Abbots of St. Gall and Dissentis, and some of the more influential barons sided with the peasants, directing, instead of opposing, the popular feeling.

The result of this was a Rhætian Confederacy, quite distinct from the Swiss Confederacy, composed of *Three Leagues* (Bünden)—the Upper, or Grey League (Ober, or Graue Bund), 1424 (named from the simple grey home-spun coats of those by whom it was formed) ; the League of God's House (Caddè in Romansch, in Germ. Gotteshaus Bund), so called from the church of Coire, the head of this league, and its capital, 1396 ; and the League of the Ten Jurisdictions (Zehn-Gerichte), of which Mayenfeld is chief town (1428).

The government produced by this revolution presents, perhaps, the most remarkable example the world has yet seen of the sovereignty of the people and of universal suffrage. Not only every valley, but, in some cases, every parish, or even hamlet, in a valley, became an independent commonwealth, with a government of its own, with peculiar local administrative rights and privileges, in many instances existing at the present day. Sometimes one of these free states, sometimes several together, form a commune or schnitze, literally slice (gemeinde or gericht); each commune has its own general assembly, in which every citizen of the age of 18, sometimes younger, has a vote, and by which the magistrates and authorities, down to the parson and schoolmaster, are elected. A number of communes forms a Hoch-Gericht, under a magistrate, styled Landamman, Podesta, or Landvoght. Above this comes the Diet of the League ; and, above all, the Diet of the Three Leagues. There still are 26 Hoch-Gerichts ; the number of communes was 49 ; that of the smaller communities is not known. Amidst such a labyrinth of government—a complication of machinery, wheel within wheel—it is difficult to understand how any government could have been carried on; and we accordingly find the history of the Grisons little better than a long series of bickerings, feuds, revolts, conspiracies, massacres, intrigues, and peculations. The wisest decisions of the diet of the canton were annulled or frustrated by the votes of the general assemblies, according as the interest or caprice of the most influential popular leader might sway these meetings at the moment. Two great families, those of Planta and De Salis, in the end, long monopolised the chief influence, as well as the patronage and offices of the federal government.

Such, then, was the *practical* result of this democracy of the purest form *in theory*.

The Grisons were united with the Swiss Confederation in 1803, and are represented by a deputy in the diet. The Three Leagues are still composed of 26 high jurisdictions (Hoch-Gerichte), each possessing its own constitution, which often differ entirely from one another. The supreme federal government of the canton is vested in the great council of 15 members, which meets at Coire.

ROUTE 68.

CANTON APPENZELL. — ST. GALL TO THE BATHS OF GAIS AND APPENZELL, WITH EXCURSIONS TO THE STOSS, TO THE WEISSBAD, THE WILDKIRCHLEIN, AND THE HOCH SENTIS.

The canton Appenzell lies out of the beat of travellers, completely surrounded (enclavé) by the territory of canton St. Gall, and shut in, at its south extremity, by the Alps; no great high-roads pass through it; and Appenzell itself lies in a cul de sac of the mountains, except for such as will take the difficult paths over the high Alps and glaciers. On this account, it is but little visited by English travellers. The canton is divided into 2 parts or districts, called *Rhoden,* quite independent of each other, but enjoying only one vote at the diet. Outer Rhoden is a very thickly peopled district, having 8781 inhabitants to the German sq. mile. These are almost exclusively engaged in manufactures, chiefly of cotton, muslin, tambouring, &c. Inner Rhoden, on the contrary, is a land of herdsmen: its high and bleak mountains produce nothing but rich pasturage and sweet grass, upon which vast herds of cattle are fed. The government, in both states, is a pure democracy—the General Assembly, or Landesgemeinde, is composed of every male born in the canton.

To Appenzell, 3½ stunden = 11¾ English miles.

To Gais, 2⅝ stunden = 8 English miles.

Travellers going from St. Gall to Coire may, instead of following the beaten track by Rorschach (Route 67), proceed to Altstetten by way of Gais, and make an excursion thence to Appenzell.

The road quits the canton of St. Gall and enters that of Appenzell (Ausser-Rhoden) a little before reaching

1⅙ Teuffen—(*Inns:* Hecht; Bär). The inhabitants of this village are chiefly engaged in the manufacture of muslin. Grubenman, the carpenter, who built the celebrated bridge of one arch at Schaffhausen, was born here.

1⅙ Gais — (*Inns:* Ochs (Bœuf); Krone (Couronne) ; the two best, and both said to be good. Rooms cost from 4 fl. to 10 fl. weekly; table d'hôte, 1 fl. ; whey, 20 kr. daily—it is brought from the high Alps every morning. The bread is very good here. This little village of 42 houses, mostly converted into lodging-houses by the peasants their owners, irregularly scattered over lawn-like meadows, is situated in a bare, bleak country, with scarce a tree or shrub; nothing but pastures around, at an elevation of 2900 ft. above the sea level. Yet the reputation of its pure and bracing air, and of its cure of goat's whey (molken-kur; cure de petit lait), annually attract hither many hundred invalids from all parts of Europe; and during the season, in July and August, the principal inns are generally crammed full.

The peasants' houses are particularly neat and clean, trimly painted outside, as though they had just issued from a bandbox.

Gais lies at the S. side of the Gäbris, and the view from the top of that mountain is said to be very fine.

The native songs of the cow-herds and dairy-maids of Appenzell are highly melodious.

It is a walk of about five hours

from Gais to Herisau (see Route 69).

2 miles to the E. of Gais, on the road to Altstetten, is the *Chapel of Stoss*, erected on the summit of the steep pass leading down to the Rhine Thal, to commemorate the almost incredible victory gained by 400 men of Appenzell over 3000 Austrians in 1405. The Archduke of Austria and the Abbot of St. Gall had hoped to take the Swiss by surprise with this preponderating force. But a handful of the mountaineers, under the conduct of Count Rudolph of Werdenberg, assembled in haste, gave them battle, and defeated the invaders, with a loss of 900 men, losing only 20 of their own party. The blood of the slain discoloured the mountain torrent which flowed past the battle-field as far as its influx into the Rhine. The view from the Stoss over the valley of the Rhine, 2000 ft. below, and of the snowy mountains of Tyrol and Vorarberg beyond, is of great beauty.

A very steep descent leads from the Stoss to Altstetten in the valley of the Rhine (Route 67), a distance of 6½ miles.

It is a distance of nearly 6½ miles S.W. from Gais to

2 Appenzell—(*Inns:* Hecht (Pike); Weisses Kreutz; respectable alehouses).

Though the chief place of the district of Inner-Rhoden, this is but a dull and dirty village of 1400 inhabitants, consisting of old and ill-built houses, with two convents, and a modern Church, hung with several flags; and contains nothing remarkable in it.

The *Landesgemeinde,* or Assembly of the canton, meets on a square, near a lime-tree, every year. In the Record Office, *Archiv,* are preserved a number of banners, conquered by the Appenzellers of old, and the only surviving trophies of their valour. Here are the flags of Constance, Winterthur, Feldkirch ; the Tyrolese banner and free ensign, with the motto

" Hundert Teufel," conquered at Landek, 1407 ; the Genoese banner of St. George, and two captured from the Venetians, 1516, in the battle of Agnadel.

It is stated on all hands that a remarkable change greets the traveller, on entering Catholic Inner-Rhoden, from Protestant Outer-Rhoden. He exchanges cleanliness and industry for filth and beggary. What may be the cause of this, is not a subject suitable for discussion here. The Appenzellers are passionately fond of gymnastic exercises ; and a part of every holiday is devoted to wrestling and boxing matches. Hurling the stone is another frequent exercise. A mass of rock, varying in weight from a half to a whole cwt., is poised on the shoulder, and then cast forward a distance of several feet. In 1805 a man of Urnäsch hurled a stone, weighing 184 lbs., 10 ft. The Appenzellers are also capital shots : rifle-matches are held almost every summer on the Sundays, and the cracking reports resound on all sides. The laws of the canton (especially of Outer-Rhoden) restrict dancing to 3 or 4 days of the year; but, as the people are much addicted to this amusement, the law is frequently infringed, and the peasants will often cross the frontier of the canton in order to enjoy unmolested their favourite amusement.

There is a road from Appenzell to Herisau. (See Route 69.)

About 2½ miles S. E. of Appenzell is *Weissbad,* " an excellent boarding house and bathing establishment, situated in a beautiful and retired spot, at the foot of the Sentis, surrounded by pleasure-grounds, from which run walks leading up the mountains. The house is capable of accommodating 200 visitors. I have seen few places in the course of my travels where a person fond of exploring and desirous of tranquillity, combined with accommodation on a superior scale (to be procured without trouble or effort on his part), could spend a

ew days in greater enjoyment."—
Dates and Distances.

In addition to the cure of goats' whey, there are also mineral springs at Weissbad, and the bath-houses contain 80 baths.

Three small torrents, issuing out of 3 Alpine valleys deeply furrowed in the sides of the Sentis, in whose glaciers they take their rise, unite at Weissbad, and form the river Sitter. About 5 miles up the middle valley is the singular hermitage and chapel of the *Wildkirchlein.* It is reached by crossing the Alpine pasture of the Ebenalp, which, in spite of its elevation of 5094 ft. above the sea, is in summer a perfect garden, unfolding a treasure to the botanist, and affording the sweetest herbage to the cows.

In a recess scooped out of the face of a precipice, 170 ft. above these pastures, a little chapel has been perched. It was built 1756 by a pious inhabitant of Appenzell, and dedicated to St. Michael, and on that saint's day mass is celebrated here annually. A bearded Capuchin occupies the hermitage adjoining, and will conduct strangers through the long caverns hung with stalactites, which perforate the mountain behind his dwelling. The pilgrimage will be repaid by the charming prospect from the window which he opens.

The *Sentis* (from Latin Sentis, a thorn ?), the highest mountain in Appenzell, 7700 ft. above the sea level, may be ascended from Weissbad. The view from the top is much extolled, and a panorama of it has been engraved. Various paths lead up to it; the best and easiest, which is also perfectly safe in the company of a guide, leads by way of the Meggisalp (3 stunden); Wagenlucke, (2 stunden); to the summit, (1 stunden), a walk of nearly 20 miles.

In 1832, an engineer named Buchmuller, while making trigonometrical observations on the summit, accompanied by a servant, was struck by lightning. The shock took away

his senses, and he remained in that state nearly an hour ; when he came to himself he found his servant dead beside him, and himself so severely injured in one of his legs, that it was with the utmost difficulty and danger that he could crawl down to the nearest human habitation.

A steep and difficult path leads S. over the ridge of the Sentis from Weissbad to Wildhaus, the birthplace of Zwingli, in Toggenburg (Route 71), a distance of 20 miles.

Another path leads in about 4 hours from Weissbad to Sennewald in the valley on the Rhine. It passes over the shoulder of the *Kamor*, on the right hand of that mountain, whose top commands a remarkable panorama. Even from the road to Sennewald, the traveller has a delightful prospect over the Sentis and Canton Appenzell, on one side, and over the lake of Constance, Tyrol, and the Rhine on the other.

ROUTE 69.

ST. GALL TO RAPPERSCHWYL ON THE LAKE OF ZURICH, BY HERISAU AND THE HEINRICHSBAD.

13 Stunden = 42½ Eng. miles.

About 4 miles from St. Gall, a little beyond the village of Bruggen, the road crosses the Gorge of the Sitter, by the magnificent Krätzeren Brücke, a bridge 590 ft. long, and 85 ft. above the stream. A little after we enter Canton Appenzell.

2. *Herisau.—Inns:* Löwe (Lion) the best ;—Hecht (Brochet).

Herisau, the flourishing and industrious chief village of the Protestant district of Appenzell, called Ausser-Rhoden, contains 2200 inhabitants, and is advantageously situated at the junction of two streams, the Glatt and Brühlbach, which turn the wheels of its numerous manufactories. " It is a very singular place from its extraordinary irregularity of construction, and is quite unlike any other town in Switzerland." There are beautiful walks on the surrounding heights ; two of them are topped by ruined castles, the Rosenberg and Rosenburg, which, according to the story, were once connected together by a leathern bridge The lower part of the *Church Tower*, in which the Archives are deposited, is the oldest building in the Canton, dating probably from the 7th century.

The articles chiefly manufactured here are muslins, cottons and silk, the last, a recent introduction: 10,200 persons are employed in Ausser-Rhoden, in weaving muslins, and a very large number in embroidering them.

There is a direct road from Herisau to Appenzell (Route 68), by Waldstadt, (1¾ stunden) ; Urnäsch, (1¼), and Gonten (1), in all 5 stunden = 16¼ miles.

About a mile to the E. of Herisau is the watering-place called *Heinrichsbad*. The *Badhaus* is the most elegant establishment of the sort in Switzerland, after Schintznach, surrounded by agreeable pleasuregrounds, the creation of one Heinrich Steiger, a rich manufacturer. Two springs rising out of gravel, and variously impregnated with iron, carbonic acid, &c., are used for drinking, and to supply the baths. Goats' whey and asses' milk are also furnished to those invalids for whom they are prescribed. Accommodation in a cowhouse is provided for invalids suffering from diseases of the chest. The neighbourhood is exceedingly picturesque.

Through an undulating country, we reach the frontier of Appenzell, and re-enter that of its grasping neighbour, St. Gall, before arriving at

2 Peterzell : 3 miles beyond the ruined Castle of Neu-Toggenburg, lies

2 Lichtensteig, (*Inn :* Krone,) a town of 700 inhabitants on the right

bank of the Thur, in the ancient county of Toggenburg.

Opposite Wattweil, a pretty manufacturing village about 1½ mile farther, stand the convent of Santa Maria and the Castle of Iberg.— (*Inns ;* Rössli ; Löwe.)

The road soon after surmounts the steep ascent of the ridge of Himmelwald. From its top a beautiful prospect expands to view ; in front the lake of Zurich, with the castle, town, and bridge of Rapperschwyl, in full relief on its margin ; behind it the pine-clad and snow-topped Alps of Schwytz and Glarus ; on the E. the remarkable peaks of the Sieben Kuhfirsten, and behind the fertile vale of Toggenburg. The road divides on the opposite side of the hill ; those bound for Glarus or Wallenstadt, take its l. branch, leading to Utznach :— we follow the rt. to Eschenbach, and

.7 Rapperschwyl. Route 14.

ROUTE 71.

SCHAFFHAUSEN TO COIRE BY TOGGENBURG AND WILDHAUS.

A good carriage-road leads through Schlatt and Neusom to

5 Frauenfeld, in Route 9.

3½ Wyl, a little town of 1064 inhabitants in the valley of the Thur, distant about a mile from its l. bank. We here leave on the l. the road to St. Gall, and continue up the l. bank of the Thur, as far as Dietfurth, where we cross to

3¾ Lichtensteig (in Route 69).

1½ Ebnat.—Toggenburg, as the long and fertile valley of the Thur is called, extends for nearly 40 miles, from Wyl up to the source of that river. It is bounded by high mountains ; on the N. by the Sentis, and on the S. by the peaks of the Kühfirsten. It was anciently governed by counts of its own. When their line became extinct, 1436, the district was claimed by canton Zurich. In the feud which ensued, the Zurichers vere worsted; it fell to the Abbot of St. Gall; and, since 1805, forms part of canton St. Gall. It is thickly peopled; its inhabitants, an industrious race, are chiefly occupied with the manufacture of muslin and cotton.

3½ Alt. St. Johann.—The inn is said to be good here.

Upon the high ground, dividing the valley of the Thur from that of the Rhine, stands the remote village, *Wildhaus*, 3450 ft. above the level of the sea, and at the S. base of the Sentis. It is remarkable as the birth-place of the Swiss reformer, Ulrich Zwingli. The house in which he first saw the light (Jan. 1, 1484) still exists: it is a humble cottage of wood; its walls formed of the stems of trees—its roof weighed down by stones to protect it from the wind. It has resisted the inroads of time for more than 350 years; and the beams and trunks which compose it are black with age. Zwingli's family were humble peasants; he quitted home when 10 years old, to go to school at Bâle.

The road descends into the Valley of the Rhine, near Grabs, and soon after reaches

3½ Werdenberg, which, with the following stations, is described in Route 67.

Sevelen.
1½ Ragatz.
1¼ *Coire*, in page 174.

ROUTE 72.

WESEN TO GLARUS, THE BATHS OF STACHELBERG, AND THE PANTEN-BRÜCKE.—PASS OF THE KLAUSEN TO ALTORF.

A diligence goes 4 times a-week from Zurich to Glarus. It is a drive of 2 hours from Wesen thither—2 hours more to Linthal—and again 2 hours on foot to the Pantenbrücke.

The canton of Glarus consists of one great Alpine valley, and of several secondary or tributary valleys,

branching off from it, and penetrating deep into the high Alps. There is but one carriage road into it, which terminates, after a distance of 26 miles, at the baths of Stachelberg; and, except for pedestrians, there is no egress save the portal which has admitted the traveller. It is a truly Alpine district, abounding in very wild scenery.

The road from Wesen crosses the Linth canal (Route 14, p. 31) by the Ziegelbrucke, and passes the jaws of the valley of Glarus, flanked by precipices almost perpendicular, and backed by the vast mass and snowy head of the Glärnisch Mountain.

The road from Zurich and Rap-perschwyl to Glarus passes through Lachen on the S. side of the Lake of Zurich, and along the l. bank of the Linth canal to Nieder-Urnen, where that from Wesen joins it.

1½ *Näfels*, in the gorge of the valley, a village of 1700 inhabitants, and the chief place in the Catholic division of the canton, is a Swiss *battle-field* of some celebrity. 11 simple stones, set up on the meadow of Reuti, hard by, mark the spot where, in 1388, 1300 men of Glarus met a force of 6000 Austrians, who, having taken Wesen by treachery, had burst into the canton, ravaging and plundering the country as they advanced. When tidings of this reached the ears of Matthias am Buhl, the lands-captain, he hastily collected a handful of shepherds, and not only checked the career of the forayers, in spite of the disproportion of numbers, but, after 11 distinct charges, aided by volleys of stones and rocks discharged from the precipices above, which threw the Austrian cavalry into confusion, finally repulsed the invaders, with a loss of 2500 of their number left dead on the field.

The anniversary of the fight of Näfels is still celebrated through the canton by an annual festival. An engagement took place at Näfels, in 1799, between the Austrians and French.

From Mollis, the village opposite Näfels, the river Linth is conducted into the lake of Wallenstadt by the artificial canal constructed by Escher (see p. 31). In the churchyard of Mollis the heroes of Näfels are buried.

The valley of the Linth is subject to much danger and injury from its sudden rises, and the swelling of its tributary torrents. The broad fringe of unsightly sand and gravel visible on both sides of the Linth, the common drain of the district, will show what mischief it occasions after storms of rain, and during the melting of the snows. The whole of the lower part of the valley is at times converted into a lake; and the little patches of ground, which have cost the peasant much hard labour and care to cultivate, are at once overwhelmed and ruined. The limestone mountains of this district abound in caverns, which serve as reservoirs for the melting glaciers. In the spring and early summer, the rocks appear to stream from every pore, while every gorge and hollow sends forth a raging torrent.

1½ *Glarus*, or Glaris—(*Inn*: Aigle d'Or, not large, but comfortable; Rabe). This little village, the capital of the canton, is chiefly remarkable for its secluded situation at the base of the Glärnisch and Schilt, encompassed by the Alps, whose bare and bleak precipices and tops contrast remarkably with the milder verdure about their base. The inhabitants, 4320 in number, are distinguished by their industry and enterprise, which has converted Glarus into a place of manufactures, especially of cotton, printing of muslins, &c. They are reported to retain that simplicity of manners which their seclusion from the rest of the world would lead one to expect.

They possess a *Club* (Cassino), and a *Free School* for 700 children, erected by private subscriptions, and reflecting much credit on the public spirit of the citizens. The houses, chiefly of stone, and many of them ancient, are frequently ornamented outside with fresco paintings; one o them bears the figure of a knight in armour and a Turk fighting, the ori gin of which is not satisfactorily ac counted for. The Gothic church i open to Protestant and Catholic alike The Linth is crossed by two bridges

The name *Glarus* is said to be a corruption of *Hilarius*, a saint to whom a shrine was built among these mountains at a very early period.

There is one manufacture peculiar to the canton Glarus, that of the *green cheese*, called *Schabzieger*. It owes its peculiar appearance, smell, and flavour, to an herb (Trifolium melilotus cæruleum; blue pansy; Germ. kle), which is partly cultivated for this purpose in gardens within the canton, and partly imported from others. To fit it for use, it is dried, ground to powder, and, in that state, mixed with the curds, in the proportion of 3 lbs. of the herb to 100 lbs. of curds. The cheese is said to be made of cows' milk, like any common cheese, and not of goats'. The curds are brought down from the high pastures into the valley in sacks, and, after having a due proportion of herb incorporated with them, are ground in a mill resembling that used for making cyder. After being thoroughly kneaded by this process for an hour or two, it is fit for pressing. The cheese is ripe for use after a twelvemonth's keeping. A large quantity of it is exported to America; and the manufacture of it is considered a lucrative trade. The natives attribute its peculiar character to some virtue in the pastures on which the cows are fed.

Many mountain paths, practicable only on foot, ramify in various directions from Glarus—

1. The pass of the Pragel to Schwytz, by the Muotta-thal and the Klon-thal; the latter, a most beautiful pastoral valley, a tributary of the Linth; the finest part of it is not

iore than 8 miles from Glarus.—
Route 75.

2. The pass of the Klausen to
Altorf.—(Described below.)

4 Passes into the Valley of the
Vorder Rhine :—

a To Dissentis, over the Sandfirn
8999 ft.), 13 stunden.

b To Brigels, by the Kistengrat
8650 ft.), 8 st.

c To Panix, by the Panixer pass,
9 st.

d To Flims, by the Segnes pass,
3½ st.

The most interesting excursion is
that up the valley of the Linth. A
good road leads along the rt. bank
of the river, about 13 miles, to the
village of

4 Lintthal, where, in a remote
spot, surrounded by torrents, rocks,
and glaciers, a handsome hotel and
bathing establishment, called the
Baths of Stachelberg, have been built.
It has greatly risen in repute as a
watering-place within a few years,
and on account of the exquisite
beauty of its situation, and the virtues of its concentrated alkaline
sulphureous spring, which distils,
drop by drop, from a fissure in the
Braunberg, is much resorted to. The
period of the " cure" is fixed at between 20 and 24 days. The hotel
stands on the l. bank of the Linth,
here crossed by a wooden bridge,
and is surrounded by walks and
pleasure-grounds.

Above the baths the vale of the
Linth becomes wilder and more savage, and at length contracts into a
chasm, low in the depths of which
the river worms its way, while a narrow and steep path alone leads along
the edge of the precipice. 5 miles
up, at a spot where the gorge is
deepest, a singularly bold bridge of
a single arch of stone, 20 ft. long,
and 200 ft. above the torrent, has
been thrown across it. This is the
Pantenbrücke, an object of considerable romantic beauty, from the
boldness of this work of man in such
a scene of wild nature, and from the

depth of the gulf below. It is often
visited by ladies ; but the excursion,
though not dangerous, is fatiguing.

A waterfall considerably higher
up on the Linth, above the bridge, is
said to be peculiarly grand, and superior to the fall of the Fätsch, yet
but little visited.

The valley of the Linth terminates
in a group of magnificent mountains,
whose tops are occupied by vast fields
of never-trodden glaciers. The Dödi,
or Todiberg (12,800) is the giant of
this portion of the chain of Alps. A
difficult and dangerous path, practicable only in the height of summer,
leads across these glaciers to Dissentis.

The *Klausen pass—Stachelberg to
Altorf.*—The distance is about 26
miles ; the path is practicable for
horses. It turns out of the valley of
the Linth to the W., about a mile
above the baths, and ascends the
valley of the Fätsch, or Urner Boden,
keeping along its l. bank. Within a
mile above the junction of the Fätsch
and Linth the valley belongs to canton Uri. It abounds in fine mountain pastures, and many of the inhabitants of the Schachen-thal pass
their summer here among their cows.
About 8 miles up, the culminating
point, or Klausen pass, is reached.
It is a ridge 6150 ft. high, connecting the snowy chain of the Clariden
Alps on the N. with the shattered
Zingel, Glatten, and Kamli. On the
top stands a little chapel.

The path descends by long and
steep zigzags into the *Schachen thal ;*
on the l. hand is seen the very pretty
cascade of the Stäubi. Opposite the
chapel of St. Anne a bergfall occurred
in 1833, which arrested for some
time the course of the Schachen, and
produced a small lake. At the village
of Unter Schachen another branch of
the valley opens S., and sends forth
the main stream of the Schachen.
The Spitze, the mountain on the l.
bank of the torrent, discharges dangerous avalanches in spring. At Spi-
ringen and a little lower down, near

the chapel of St. Anthony, there are inns, tolerably good for this country.

It was over the steep and barely accessible ridge of the *Kinzig Culm*, which walls in this portion of the valley to the N., that Suwarrow's memorable retreat was conducted, 1799. Having pounced down, as it were, upon the French from the heights of the St. Gothard, and driven them before him to Altorf, he there found his progress barred by the lake of Lucerne, without a boat to cross it, his troops exhausted by fatigue and famine, and the country so completely drained by war as to be quite incapable of supporting them. The only alternative that remained to him, was to attempt to join the forces of the allies, through the horrible defile of the Schachen; and to cross the rarely-trodden summit of the high Alps. The only passage up this valley was by a mere path; so that his army was obliged to advance in single file, abandoning much of their artillery and baggage. Their march lasted 14 hours; and before the rear-guard had left Altorf the van had reached Muotta. Many of the Russians sank from fatigue by the wayside, and perished; others fell into the hands of the French, who hovered in their rear; the valley was strewn with dead bodies of men and horses, with arms and equipments. The remainder of this memorable march is described in Route 75.

Burglen, the birthplace of Tell, stands at the mouth of the Schachen thal. Route 34.

Altorf, p. 95.

ROUTE 74.

RAPPERSCHWYL TO EINSIEDELN AND SCHWYTZ, WITH EXCURSION TO MORGARTEN.

8¼ stunden = 27 Eng. miles.

The road is practicable for carriages of the country, but it is by no means good.

The Abbey of Einsiedeln, though one of the finest buildings in Switzerland, will bear no comparison wit the churches of Italy, and, except o account of the pilgrims and durin the season of the pilgrimage, is no worth going out of one's way to visit

After crossing the long bridge o Rapperschwyl (Route 14) the roa enters canton Schwytz, and soo commences the steep ascent of Moun Etzel, which commands from its to a delightful view over the lake o Zurich, and a glimpse of the Mythen mountains in the S. The holy hermit Meinrad, the founder of Einsiedeln, originally fixed himself on the top of the Etzel, but the concourse of people attracted to the spot by his reputation for holiness drove him in search of solitude deeper into the wilderness. A little *chapel* stands on the spot supposed to have been occupied by his cell. Near it is an inn.

The road is studded at intervals with chapels called *stations*, each containing a representation of some event in the Passion of our Lord, according to the Romish tradition, at which the pilgrims may stop and tell their beads.

The river Sihl is crossed by a covered bridge, called (Teufels brucke) the Devil's bridge, before reaching

3¾ EINSIEDELN (French Notre Dame des Erèmites ; Lat. Monasterium Eremitarum). *Inns :* there are 55 inns and 20 alehouses here, mostly designed for the reception of poor pilgrims, and distinguished by a singular variety of signs. The best is the Ox, celebrated for its extortionate charges, especially during the pilgrimage; Pfau (Paon); Adam and Eve.

The Abbey of Einsiedeln, which forms the nucleus of a village of a few hundred inhabitants, is situated on a naked undulating plain 3000 ft. above the sea, producing little but pasture. It is partly sheltered by a range of wooded hills on the S.E.

The *Monastery* itself, an extensive building in the modern Italian style, is imposing, less from its architecture han its size and its situation in so remote and naked a solitude. The existing edifice dates from the 18th century (1719), and is the 6th or 7th raised on this spot since the first foundation of the abbey, the others having been destroyed by fire. It occupies a stately site upon the hill-side, separated from the humbler buildings of the village by a wide square.

The origin of the abbey is thus accounted for in the histories published under the authority of the monks.— In the days of Charlemagne a holy anchorite named Meinrad, of the noble house of Hohenzollern, repaired to this remote wilderness (then called the Finsterwald) to end his days in solitude and prayer, devoting himself to tend a little black image of the Virgin which had been given to him by St. Hildegarde, abbess of Zurich. This holy man was murdered by two robbers in 861; but their foul deed, which they had hoped would escape detection on a spot so remote from the haunts of men, was brought to light by two pet ravens reared by Meinrad, which pursued the murderers with croaking cries, and flapping wings, over hill and dale, as far as Zurich, where their guilt was detected, and they suffered for it on the place now occupied by the Raven inn. The reputation of sanctity, however, surrounding the spot where the saint had lived, increased so much after his death, that his cell was rebuilt, and a church founded by a community of Benedictine hermits (Einsiedlern). The first abbot was Eberard; and it is affirmed by the monkish legend, and perpetuated in the bull of Pope Pius VIII., that when the Bishop of Constance was about to consecrate the church on the 14th of September, 948, he was aroused at midnight by the sounds of angelic minstrelsy, and was informed next day, by a voice from heaven, that there was no need for him to proceed with the sacred rite, as the church had been already consecrated by the

powers of heaven and by the presence of the Saviour! The pope pronounced this a true miracle, and, in consideration of it, granted plenary indulgence to all pilgrims who should repair to the shrine of Our Lady of the Hermits, in the words inscribed upon the church, " Hic est plena remissio peccatorum a culpâ et à pœnâ." The consequence of this has been that during 9 centuries there has been an almost uninterrupted influx of pilgrims from the surrounding countries to this shrine, and of wealth to the monastery. In process of time these pious benefactions increased its revenues and domains to an enormous extent; it ranked second to St. Gall alone of all the monasteries in Switzerland. Its abbot became a prince of the holy Roman empire, with a seat in the diet. He had his hereditary officers, his chamberlain, marshal, and cupbearer; and these posts were filled by personages of noble or princely rank. He also enjoyed the right of criminal jurisdiction and the power of life and death in several parishes and circles. Down to the 16th century the abbots themselves were of noble families.

The French revolutionary invaders of 1798 stripped Einsiedeln of its resources and treasures, and carried off the figure of the Virgin to Paris; but the monks, on abandoning the convent, transported with them into Tyrol a duplicate figure, which they assert to be the authentic original. Notwithstanding these untoward circumstances, the abbey remains at the present day the richest in Switzerland, and the Black Virgin, whether an original or a copy, has lost none of her reputation. The average annual number of pilgrims who receive the sacrament in the church is 150,000. In the course of the year 1700 there were 202,000; in 1834, 36,000 pilgrims repaired to the shrine within a fortnight. Every parish of Canton Schwytz, and most of the other Roman Catholic Cantons, send an annual deputation hither, headed by the Landamman and the authorities. The Roman Catholics of Switzerland, indeed, make 2 or 3 journeys hither, in the course of their lives. Many of the pilgrims are deputies paid by others, wealthier sinners, to do penance for their principals, who remain at home, and a pilgrimage thus performed by proxy is rendered equally efficacious with one made in person.

In 1835, the convent contained 77 monks of the Benedictine order, including lay-brothers, novices, &c.

In the square in front of the convent stands a fountain, with 14 jets of water, from all of which the pilgrims drink, as it is traditionally reported, that our Saviour drank from one, but from which of them is not known. In the centre of the pile of conventual buildings stands, as is usual in Benedictine monasteries, the *Church*, which has been compared with that of St. John Lateran at Rome. The interior is somewhat gaudily ornamented with inferior paintings, marble and gilding. A few feet from the entrance stands the *Shrine* or *Chapel of the Virgin*, of black marble, with a grating in front, through which, by the glare of an ever-burning lamp, the spectator perceives the palladium of the temple, a little black figure of the Virgin and Child, attired in gold brocade, glittering with jewels, and bearing crowns of gold on their heads. The space in front of the shrine is rarely free of worshippers, and commonly hundreds, nay, at times, thousands of devotees may be seen prostrate before it. The walls of this part of the church are literally covered with votive tablets, rude paintings in oil, on which no kind of accident or misfortune is omitted, though they are chiefly devoted to representations of escapes from fire and water, all effected by the supposed miraculous interference of the image. Its influence, however, is not limited to incidents of private life; many of the great events of history, such as the victory of the

Roman Catholic cantons at Kappe are classed among the triumphant in terpositions of our Lady of th Hermits. 250 new votive tablets wer hung up in 1835, older ones bein removed to make way for them.

In the *Chapel of the Magdalen* a church of itself in size, on th l. of the choir, are 28 confessional over each of which is written th language in which confessions wi be received in it, either German Italian, French, or Romansch.

The *Treasury*, once so rich in churc plate, was plundered by the Frenc in 1798, and one splendid monstrance alone remains, but it is not readily shown. The monastery includes, be sides the lodgings for the Abbot, an the brethren, a handsome refectory a kitchen, an hospital, a *library*, containing 26,000 vols., a museum, containing some fossils and minerals, a free school, and boarding-school, the pupils of which are taught by the monks, and a large cellar running under the greater part of the edifice. During meals, passages of some approved author, such as Lingard's History of England, Cobbett's History of the Reformation, &c., are read aloud to the assembled brotherhood, and even at times portions of newspapers.

Zuingli, the reformer, was curate of Einsiedeln from 1516 to 1519. Theophrastus Paraselsus von Hohenheim was born here, or in the neighbourhood, in 1498.

The following description relates to the last jubilee celebrated at Einsiedeln, in September 1834.

"This place is annually visited by many thousand pilgrims, especially on the 14th September, and whenever the 14th falls on a Sunday, the festivities are greater than usual.

"For the last ten days, even before we left Baden, and while in the French territory, we have met at almost every step troops of pilgrims plodding on their way to this Swiss Loretto. The parties seemed generally members of one family, or of one village, from the similarity of their

ess, and they were invariably re-
ating their aves and pater-nosters
oud as they passed along, or uniting
gether in singing a hymn. They
nsisted almost entirely of the lower
ass of peasants, who repair to this
ot from far and wide. Alsatia
id Lorraine, the Black Forest, Sua-
a, the Grisons, Bavaria, —and the
hole of Switzerland, all contri-
ite their quota to augment the
rong; thousands usually issue out
f Tyrol, but the Austrians this year
ave refused to let any persons go
ito Switzerland without passports,
hich has served as a complete pre-
entive to their undertaking the
urney.

" It was growing dusk as we
ntered the valley in which Einsiedeln
es. Just as we began to descend our
ttention was roused by the repeat-
d reports of cannon, which, though
oud in themselves, awakened echoes
n the adjacent hills, which made it
ppear as though a whole broadside
ad been fired. Soon after, the deep-
oned bells of the convent began to
ound, the firing ceased, and the
ong and loudly-repeated prayers of
he pilgrims whom we passed on the
oad, proclaimed that it was the hour
f vespers.

" As we drew nearer the bells had
ceased, and we heard the sound of a
drum and band of music. This odd
umble of noises, profane intermixed
with sacred, which gave me no very
distinct idea of what was going forward, was afterwards explained by
the intelligence that the pilgrimage
is not considered a religious matter
only, but is mixed up with somewhat
of festivity—which induces the brotherhood of the convent to pay for
salvos and *feux de joie*, while they
encourage the forming of a band of
music composed of the towns-people.
Their performance is pretty much on
a par with that which is found in the
booths of a fair in England, — but
under its escort we entered the town.
The musicians had just paraded to

the end of the street of which Einsiedeln consists, and were returning,
followed by a crowd large enough to
stop our progress till it had passed.
The one street which I have mentioned is, with scarcely an exception,
composed entirely of inns and pothouses, principally for the reception
of the poorer pilgrims. As the band
passed by, every window was crowded
with projecting heads, which had a
curious effect, lighted up by the solitary lantern which dangles in front
of each house.

" The inn where I was lucky enough
to find lodging (with the threat of
having two other persons put into
the same room, in case more visitors
should arrive), is directly in front of
the convent and church, and as soon
as I had finished my supper I issued
out to explore it. I found it already
crowded with pilgrims, partly met to
keep the eve of the festival, partly to
take up their night's lodging in the
church. For though a bed may be
had in the town for the value of a
halfpenny, and a supper for as little,
many of these people are so poor that
they cannot afford to pay for a bed ;
their only food is a crust of bread and
a bit of cheese, which they bring with
them, and they must pass the vigil in
the open air if the church be not
opened to receive them.

" As I elbowed my way into the
church I found it dark except one
solitary lamp before the altar, and a
few candles, brought in by the people
themselves and laid on the pavement,
or placed on their laps to enable them
to read their prayer-books. The
crowd was very great, for, though the
gloom prevented my seeing the extent of it, the sounds which burst on
my ears as I entered the door were
such as could only arise from thousands. It was a confused mixture
of sounds, singing in all tones and
tunes, many very shrill, and as a bass
to this, a low long-continued murmur or buzzing. I found that the
singing proceeded from many distinct

parties in different parts of the church, each composed of the members of one family or parish, who were now practising here the hymns they were accustomed to sing together in concert at home, but without any attention to the tune which their next neighbours were chanting. The partial but vivid light thrown upon visages hard and soft, though mostly of the former character, and the total blackness of the back-ground, would have furnished a painter with many a novel effect. The low and uninterrupted buzzing came I found from a vast and dense crowd stationed near the entrance of the church, in front of the chapel which contains the miraculous black image of the Virgin, the ostensible object of this pilgrimage, which shines in silk and jewels, lighted up by a great number of lamps. The little chapel stands in the middle of the church, and is open only on one side, on which the image can be seen through an iron *grille*. Fortunate were those among the crowd of devotees who could manage to place themselves in a position where a view was to be obtained of it. By far the greater part were quite out of sight of it, but still all persevered with the same devout mumbling of prayers, with expressions of extreme devotion, intent upon their books or rosaries.

*   *   *

"Next morning I was suddenly awakened by a great concussion which shook the house and made me start. It was again the discharge of cannon and rockets to open the festival. Daylight had not yet dawned, but I heard the sound of numerous footsteps pacing across the square to the church. About half past nine I repaired again to the church. I knew how thronged it would be, and therefore took the precaution of securing admission to the gallery, from which I looked down upon a sea of heads, into which the bases of the pillars of the church appeare to be sunk. Every aisle and ang was crammed, and whenever movement was made by those e deavouring to enter or depar the space was instantly filled up though a drop of water had bee displaced. I know no mode of gi ing an idea of the numbers; the e act number cannot be ascertaine till to-morrow, when a census is mad of the persons to whom wafers hav been distributed by the priests in th communion. I placed myself im mediately above the high altar, so a to see the whole ceremony of hig mass performed in its greatest pomp The legate sent by the Pope as res dent in Switzerland, who officiated was an archbishop; he was attende by two bishops. The splendour o his robes, which he put on one afte the other—the mitre and crosier assumed or laid down from time t time, as different parts of the cere mony were performed—the satin shoes—the purple train, borne up b attendants as he moved to and fro be tween his throne and the altar—had a very imposing effect.

"To have an idea of the great solemnity of the whole ceremony, you must take into consideration the host of fervent worshippers assembled before the altar, filling the whole body of the church as far as the eye could reach, aided by the effect of the most solemn music performed by a full band and two organs. The whole was worked up to a height at the moment when the legate finally receives the cup, and afterwards bestows his benediction and absolution upon the congregated pilgrims. The thunder of drums, trumpets, and diapasons of the organs, was, as it appeared to me, assisted by some machinery by which the roof of the church was struck, in order to produce the effect of the building having been shaken: at the same moment a signal is given on the outside, the bells begin to toll, and the cannons fired off from the neighbouring ls. This over, the organs commence some popular overture, from ozart or Rossini, and the people rush t to bargain for relics, at the booths ected round the church, which ve the square in front the appearance of a fair. The commodities for le were limited to the wants of the grims, temporal and spiritual, and peared to be confined to umbrellas, ly tapers to burn in the churches, saries, little medals with a figure of e Virgin of the Hermits, and bread d cheese.

" The ceremonies of this festival d not terminate until the evening. s it began to grow dusk the long and ately façade of the building was luminated by rows of lamps; nd a temporary altar, erected on ne side of the square opposite the ain entrance was entirely studded ith lamps, till it became one blaze f light. While this was preparing, he vast square gradually filled with eople, until the assembled multitude mounted to not less than 30,000 ersons, chiefly pilgrims. When ll was ready the great doors of the hurch were thrown open, and out narched a venerable procession of cclesiastics, their abbot at their head, receded by banners and crucifixes, nd followed by a long train of orch-bearers. Lifting up their melodious voices in a solemn chant, they conveyed the sacred elements towards the altar, as is usual, under a canopy, escorted by soldiers, and accompanied by a band of music and a moveable organ on wheels. While the mass was being performed in the open air I sallied out among the throng: the view looking towards the altar was as singular as that in the opposite direction. The blazing altar, the long line of torches and tapers flaring and glittering in the night, had a most singular effect, increased by the illuminations of the town behind; every house was lighted up, and, as they are all built in the Swiss fashion, with gables outward, they looked

like so many fiery pyramids. No sooner was mass finished than the procession retired again into the church, the crowd disappeared also into it, the exterior lights were extinguished —in half an hour the whole square was dark and empty: it seemed like a dream. The interior of the church, however, was still filled with people; the whole being studded with lamps, especially the chapel of the Virgin: the throng of worshippers before it seemed undiminished, and many lingered in front of it, on bended knees and with eyes fixed on the image, till late in the night.

" Next morning I left Einsiedeln on my way out of Switzerland: I set out about 6, and all the way passed through one continued line of dirty, ragged, and brown-visaged pilgrims, on their way home, chanting, without cessation, their paters and aves, &c., which their confessors had prescribed for them to repeat between the time of their departure from and return to their homes. I passed across the Lake of Zurich by the long bridge of Rapperschwyl; and in the evening crossed the Lake of Wallenstadt. Still I had not got out of the line of pilgrims; 2 boats' full set sail along with that which conveyed me; and the wind which filled our broad and unwieldy sail, and carried us quickly along, wafted with it the same responses and chants which I had heard from the pilgrims on the road.

" We Protestants, of course, would condemn, or possibly laugh at all this; still, I cannot help thinking, from the fervid earnestness of the poor pilgrims, that their journey, notwithstanding superstition was its object, might still be productive of good; and I remembered how the humble publican went home justified, rather than the self-satisfied and uncharitable Pharisee."—*MS. Journal of a Traveller.*

There is a path over the Mythenberg, from Einsiedeln to Schwytz, shorter than the carriage-road.

The carriage-road to Schwytz makes, at first, a considerable detour : the foot-path is shorter, crossing the Katzenstrick, a considerable track of upland meadow or common, direct to Altmatt.

2¼ Rothenthurm, a village of nearly 800 inhabitants, is the place of meeting of the general assembly of the canton Schwytz, convened here every two years, in the open air, on the first Sunday in May, or, if the weather be bad on that day, on the first fine Sunday after. The landamman is president, and every citizen above the age of 18 has a vote. These meetings afford no favourable specimen of the working of universal suffrage, as they frequently terminate in rioting and violence. For example, in May, 1838, 9000 voters collected here; the show of hands was declared to be in favour of the government; but the Liberal party being dissatisfied with the result, a battle ensued, in which the hustings were broken and many persons much injured. The democrats, enraged at their defeat, published a manifesto, calling on the " Liberals to meet in their districts, and expel the rich from their assemblies as their ancestors expelled Gessler, since the government of the rich has become a government of murderers." Rothenthurm receives its name from a Red Tower still standing and forming part of the defences of a long wall or rampart (letze), erected by the Schwytzers along their W. frontier, to ward off the inroads of their lordly and lawless neighbours. It extended hence as far as Arth.

About 2 miles W. of Rothenthurm, on the confines of the canton of Zug, and on the margin of the small lake of Egeri, is MORGARTEN, memorable in Swiss annals as the scene of their first struggle for independence, as the spot where the chivalry of Austria was worsted, and their leader, Duke Leopold, compelled to fly with disgrace, on the 15th of November, 1315, 8 years after the expulsion of the Austrian bailiffs. Fired with the hope of revenge and with fe[e]ings of hereditary hatred, the du[ke?] led on his mail-clad cavalry alo[ng] the narrow strand between the la[ke] and the hills. Just where the asce[nt] into the upland country of Schwy[tz] commences, running up a narr[ow] defile, the Austrians were met [by] the confederates, a mere handful [of] men in comparison with their ho[st,] but of hardy frame and resolute spiri[t,] posted on the ridge of the Sattel, nea[r] Haselmatt. The first bold charg[e] of the Swiss, rushing on wit[h] swords and clubs, was aided by [a] discharge of rocks from the height[s] above, which quickly threw into co[n]fusion the ranks of heavy-arme[d] knights. They attempted to fa[ll] back, but their evolutions were pre[-] vented by the infantry pressing o[n] in their rear. Without room to ma[-] nœuvre, or even to turn (for the natu[-] rally confined margin of the lake wa[s] at that time diminished by an unusua[l] increase of its waters), the prou[d] knights were totally at the mercy o[f] their light-armed foes. Many, i[n] order to escape the sword, perishe[d] by plunging into the lake ; the rush of the cavalry overwhelmed the in[-] fantry behind, and in a short while the whole army was thrown into panic and disorder. The Austrians lost the flower of their nobility, and Leopold with difficulty escaped. This astounding victory, the Marathon of Swiss history, was gained in an hour and a half, over a force of 20,000 well-armed men, by 1300 mountaineers, who now for the first time met an army in the field.

The appropriate memorial of their success erected by the Swiss was, according to custom, a *Chapel*, dedicated to St. James ; and service is performed in it annually on the anniversary of the fight. It is still standing on an eminence above the lake, at the foot of the hill of Morgarten, close to the village of Schorno, by the road-side as you descend from Rothenthurm.

The little village of Biberegg, on

e opposite (E.) side of Rothen-
urm, was the cradle of the family
Reding, one of the oldest and no-
est in the canton, and whose name
pears oftener with credit than any
her. There is scarcely a battle in
nich they are not mentioned, and
ey have 45 times filled the office
landamman, the highest in the
ate. In 1798 Aloys Reding, a hero
orthy of such an ancestry, led on
e brave inhabitants of these moun-
ins to oppose, in defence of their
berties and constitution, a far out-
umbering force of French under
eneral Schauenberg. The Swiss
et the invaders in the valley of
othenthurm, and drove them back
s far as the lake of Egeri and the
eld of their ancient victory of Mor-
arten. This proved but a tempo-
ary gleam of success. Their victory
ad cost them so large a number of
en, that they were unable to renew
ne contest; and an overwhelming
orce of French marching into the
anton rendered all further resistance
opeless.

A long descent, commanding a
ine view of Schwytz, of the singular
nd picturesque Mythen and Hacken
Mountains behind it, and of the lake
f Lowertz, with part of the fall of the
Rossberg (p. 41-45), leads through
Sattel, past the chapel of Ecce Homo,
o Steinen, a small village, memorable
as the birthplace of Werner Stauffacher, one of the three conspirators
of the Grutli (p. 55). A small *chapel*, adorned with rude fresco of scenes
from his life, and the battle of Morgarten, is dedicated to his memory.
It was built in 1400. The *Bonehouse*
is as old as 1111.

3 *Schwytz.* (Route 17, p. 45.)

ROUTE 75.

SCHWYTZ TO GLARUS, BY THE MUOTTA
THAL, THE PASS OF THE PRAGEL,
AND THE KLÖNTHAL.

10 stunden = 32¾ Eng. miles.

A very rough char-road ascends

the valley as far as Muotta. Some
distance may be saved to the pedestrian by keeping to foot-paths known
to the guides. The road crosses the
plain to Ibach, a village of scattered
houses at the mouth of the Muotta
thal, which here assumes the character of a contracted gorge; higher
up it opens out, and exhibits considerable capabilities for cultivation;
it abounds with exquisite scenery.
The road ascends the l. bank of the
stream, traversing Ober Schönen-
bach, down to which point the Russians, under Suwarrow, drove the
French, commanded by Massena,
Mortier, and Soult, in his desperate
attempt to force his way through
them to join the Russian army at
Zurich, in 1799. " The bridge near
this, which carries the road over to
the rt. bank, was taken and retaken
many times; the mingled blood of the
2 nations crimsoned the stream which
carried down their floating bodies."

Beyond Ried there is another
bridge, and a third brings the traveller to

2¾ Muotta, or Mutten, the principal village of the valley, on the rt.
bank of the stream. The parish
contains 1480 inhabitants. In the
neighbourhood is the *Nunnery of St.
Joseph*, a very ancient and primitive
convent, founded 1280. The sisters
are poor, and their mode of living
homely; they make their own clothes
and their own hay; the superior is
called Frau Mutter. They receive
visits from strangers without the
intervention of a grating, and will
even give a lodging to a respectable
traveller. Whoever avails himself
of this must remember that the convent is too poor to afford gratuitous
hospitality.

On the night of the 27th and 28th
of September, 1799, the inhabitants
of the remote and peaceful valley of
Muotta were surprised by the arrival
of an army of an unknown nation
and tongue, whose very name many
of them had never heard, which
came pouring down upon their cot-

tages and green fields from the heights of the Kinzig Culm, by pathless abysses and precipices which the very shepherds cross with difficulty and dread. These were the 24,000 Russians under Suwarrow, whose previous march out of Italy has already been detailed in Routes 34 and 72. Here the general first heard the news of the defeat of Korsakow and the main Russian army at Zurich. He at first gave no credence to the report, and would have hung the peasant who communicated it as a spy and traitor, but for the intercession of the lady mother of St. Joseph's nunnery. He was now beset on all sides; part of Lecourbe's division followed his rear, Molitor occupied the summit of the Muotta thal, and Mortier and Massena blocked up its mouth. The bold attempt to cut his way out, through the forces of the latter general, was defeated, as already mentioned, chiefly by the unexpected arrival of a fresh reinforcement under Lecourbe in person, though with vast loss to the French. The veteran conqueror was compelled for the first time in his career, to order a retreat, and to adopt the only alternative of ascending the valley and crossing the Pragel into Glarus. The detachments of Molitor's advanced guard were quickly driven in before him, and the greater portion made prisoners. Suwarrow's rear-guard, however, encumbered with sick and wounded, was greatly harassed by Massena; but the republicans were again repulsed with loss, and driven back nearly to Schwytz. Suwarrow expected to be able to reach Zurich from Glarus, there to join and rally the broken forces of Korsakow; but Molitor in person, warned of his approach, took possession of the position of Näfels, blocking up the outlet of the Linth thal as Massena had intercepted his passage down the Muotta thal, and the Russian once more found his plans foiled and baffled. Fearing to be hemmed in on all sides by the

French, he gave his troops a fe days of rest at Glarus, rendered a solutely indispensable by the fatigu they had undergone, after which once more took to the mountains, a cending the Sernft thal (Route 7 to the Grisons.

The path from Muotta to the pa of the Pragel (Suwarrow's line march) is rather steep and stony, b is practicable for horses. The di tance from Muotta to the lake Klön is calculated at about 20 mile about 3¼ to the foot of the ascent, to the cross, nearly 3 to the summ of the pass, 1¾ to Klön, and 6 t Auen, on the lake.

3¼ The summit of the pass, 5200 f above the sea, is the boundary-lin of cantons Schwytz and Glarus. is rarely free from snow before th month of June.

The Klönthal, into which the tra veller now descends, is exceedingl beautiful. On the rt. hand it i walled in by the Glärnisch rising i an abrupt and sheer precipice, termi nated by a sharp edge of ice, and o the l. by the Wiggis, scarcely les abrupt. Deep in the recesses of thi charming valley lies a beautiful lak about 2 miles long, embedded deepl at the foot of the Glärnisch, whose vast grey precipices descend at thi point almost perpendicularly into th water. "It is surrounded by mea dows of the most verdant green covered until the end of autumn with flowers. The precipitous tracks along the side of the valley, along which some adventurous French pushed forward in pursuit of the Russians, are pointed out. Ebel deservedly calls the Klönthal "une des vallées les plus gracieuses qu'il y ait dans les Alpes." Two Swiss have inscribed on a rock at the foot of the Glärnisch, by the side of a waterfall, an epitaph in memory of Soloman Gessner, the pastoral poet, author of the Death of Abel, who used to repair hither from Zurich, and spend the summer in a chalets. This spot is about 8 miles from Glarus. After

ssing through Riedern the traveller
on reaches the high road, and turn-
g to the rt. ascends the Lintthal
bout a mile to

4 *Glarus*, in Route 72.

ROUTE 76.

GLARUS TO COIRE, UP THE SERNFT THAL.

13¼ stunden = 43½ Eng. miles. A
har-road as far as Elm; beyond that
footpath, difficult and fatiguing.

About 3 miles above Glarus the
alley of the Linth divides into two
ranches. Out of the l. or E. branch
ssues the Sernft: it is sometimes
alled Kleinthal, to distinguish it from
he larger W. branch, or Linththal.

At Enghi, the first village, there
s no inn. Matt, another village,
tands on the rt. bank of the Sernft
and at the mouth of the minor vale
of the Krauchthal, up which runs a
path to Sargans, over the Reiseten
bass, 7 stunden.

The quarries in the Plattenberg, a
mountain of grauwacke and clay-
slate on the l. side of the valley, opposite Matt, furnish excellent slates
for roofing or for writing. Most of the
schools in Switzerland are supplied
from hence; and the slate was formerly exported down the Rhine to
Holland and the Indies. This slate
is well known to geologists for the
beautiful and perfect casts of fossil
fish in which it abounds. The lower
portion of the valley is unhealthy, as
may be learned from the occurrence
of goître and cretinism (those afflicted
with the latter are here called Töl-
pel, § 19); but the inhabitants of the
upper extremity are a fine and hardy
race.

4½ Elm (where the inn is better
than lower down) is the highest
village in the valley.

There is a way from Elm to the
Baths of Pfeffers—a fatiguing walk
of 13 hours. The path ascends the
Unter-thal, crosses the ridge of the
Ramin into the Weistannen Thal.
There is a tolerable path as far as a

chalet on the E. slope of the pass;
beyond this there is scarcely any trace
of one, and the passage is not practicable for mules. From this chalet
you turn to the S. of E., and cross 2
ravines into the Kalfeuser Thal, a
mile or two below the source of the
Tamina, which rises at the head of
that valley, in the glacier of Sardona.
The scenery of the Gorge of the Tamina is magnificently grand. The
Kalfeuser Thal terminates at Vättis,
at the foot of the Calanda-berg, where
the river suddenly alters its course,
and bends to the N. There is no village where refreshment or accommodation can be obtained between Elm
and Vättis.

At Elm the valley of the Sernft
divides again, and minor paths ramify
hence—1. Up to the head of the valley and over the pass of Panix, called
in the language of the Grisons *ai
quolm de Pejnu*. I.; 2. The pass of
the Segnes, which we propose to follow. Near the Tschingel is the Martinsloch, a singular hole or gap in
the precipice, through which the sun
shines 2 or 3 times in the year upon
the village of Elm.

Suwarrow, after the almost incredible march detailed in the preceding
route, remained like a stag at bay for
3 or 4 days at Glarus for the purpose
of resting his wearied troops, though
not a day was passed without skir-
mishes more or less severe with the
enemy. At length, finding it hopeless to attack a French force now so
greatly superior in numbers to his
own, he adopted the tremendous, but
only remaining, alternative of again
leading his exhausted and diminished
followers over the highest crest of the
Alps, in order to rescue them from
annihilation and enable him to unite
himself with the scattered fragments
of the Russian army in the Grisons.
He broke up from his quarters on the
5th of October. The lateness of the
season, the difficulties of the passage,
and the vastly superior force pressing
on the heels of his dispirited soldiers,
rendered this a far more hazardous

enterprise than that which he had previously accomplished. The miserable path up the valley would barely admit 2 men abreast: along this the army painfully wound its way in single file. The difficulty of the ascent was greatly increased by a fall of snow 2 ft. deep; but, as though the hardships of the way were not enough, the indefatigable French, ascending the opposite bank of the Sernft, allowed the Russians no respite from their harassing assaults. Numbers lay down, exhausted from fatigue, to perish on the snow; many, slipping down the insecure fragments of slate, and along the rocks, polished by the frost, were hurled over the precipices and crushed in the abyss below, while the enemy's bullets were not slow in further thinning their ranks. After 5 days of toil and 4 nights of little repose, since they were spent on the bare surface of the snow and the glaciers, where many men were frozen to death, Suwarrow crossed the ridge of Panix, between 7000 and 8000 ft. above the sea, and on the 10th of October reached the valley of the Rhine at Ilanz. Even on reaching the descent into the Grisons many perished in attempting to cross the fearful chasm of the Araschka Alp. For months and months the foul birds and beasts of prey were gorged with their bodies, and the bones of many a warrior are still blanching in the crevices and ravines of the Jätzer. Thus terminated a march of 18 days' duration, perhaps the most extraordinary ever performed by an army incessantly engaged, fighting a battle almost every day, and obliged to traverse a country totally unknown and completely destitute of resources. This remarkable retreat was accomplished with the loss of all his artillery, the greater part of the beasts of burden, and ⅓ of his men.

The Segnes pass, the best way from Glarus to Coire, ascends a minor valley running in a S.E. direction behind the village of Elm. The height of the pass above the sea is 7500 ft. It

is about 15½ miles from this to the first village in the Grisons valley of Segnes.

4¾ Flims ⎫
1¼ Trins ⎬ described in Route 77
2¾ Coire, in Route 67.

ROUTE 77.

COIRE TO ANDERMATT ON THE ST GOTHARD, UP THE VALLEY OF THE VORDER RHEIN, TO DISSENTIS, AND ACROSS THE OBERALP.

20 stunden = 65½ English miles.

The great post-road from Coire (Route 67), up the valley of the Rhine, is followed as far as

1¾ Reichenau (described in Route 87), where the waters of the Vorder and Hinter-Rhein unite. Thenceforward a cart-road, of the very worst kind, is the only mode of communication up the valley of the Vorder-Rhein, and will be, most probably, for some time to come, though a new carriage-road to Dissentis is promised in 3 years. The want of roads and of inns, the pothouses which supply their place being of the most inferior kind, has hitherto prevented this beautiful district being visited by travellers as much as it deserves. Quitting the highway, our cart-track strikes up the side of the hills on the l. bank of the Rhine, to the village of Tamins, directly over Reichenau. For some distance the traveller enjoys a beautiful view up both valleys of the Rhine. The entrance of that of Hinter-Rhein, up which runs the road to the Splügen, is guarded by the castle of Rhætzuns, backed by villages and church-towers without number. Beyond Trins the road turns aside from the Rhine, and bends round a little monticule rising in the midst of the valley into a small sequestered basin, in the midst of which lies

2¾ Flims, a village 3360 ft. above the sea, named from the number of sources around it *ad flumina*. Here the path to Glarus, by the Segnes

ass (Route 76), strikes off. After
ontinuing some time out of sight of
he Rhine, we join it again, after
a steep descent, about 3 miles beyond
Ilax.

3¾ Ilanz (in Romansch, Glion or
lon).—(*Inn* : Löwe, near the bridge.
Latrobe calls it the cleanest, prettiest,
and most unassuming inn he had
een since he left England.)—Ilanz
s the only place in the valley deserv-
ng the name of town, and is the
capital of the Graue Bund, or Grey
League, p. 176. Its 568 inhabitants
speak the Romansch tongue, and
this dialect prevails in a large portion
of the valley. This place, situated
on the rt. bank of the river, exhibits
marks of poverty, though the country
around is fertile ; its walls are in a
state of dilapidation.

Ober Saxen, a village on the same
side of the Rhine as Ilanz, and about
4 miles higher up, is German, while
all the villages around it are Romansch. In its vicinity stand 4
ancient castles, now picturesque ruins,
about 1½ mile apart from one another.
Their names are Mooreck, Schwartz-
enstein, Riedburg, and Axenstein.
Before reaching Ober Sax the road
crosses the river, but again crosses to
the l. bank before arriving at

Trons (in Rhœtian, Tron)—(*Inn :*
Casa Nuova ?)—a village in a singu-
larly-beautiful situation, at a little
distance from the Rhine. Its 800
inhabitants are Catholics and speak
Romansch. There are iron-works
in the vicinity. Trons is chiefly remarkable, however, as the cradle of
liberty among the Rhœtian Alps, the
Grütli of Grison history. Beneath
the shade of the neighbouring forest
the peasants met at the beginning of
the fifteenth century to concert the
plans of liberating themselves and
their children from the oppression
and slavery of their feudal lords, 3
or 4 of whose castles, now in ruins,
may still be seen frowning down from
the neighbouring crags.

Near the entrance of the village
stands the decayed but venerated

trunk of a *Sycamore* (Acer Pseudopla-
tanus : German, ahorn), now probably
6 or 7 centuries old, a mere trunk,
cloven and hollow, beneath whose once
spreading branches the deputies of
the peasants met the nobles who were
favourable to their cause, in March,
1424, and took the oath of fidelity to
one another, and to their free constitution then established. Such is the origin of the GREY LEAGUE, *Graue Bund,*
so called from the grey beards, or
the grey homespun garb of the venerable assembly. Close to the syca-
more-tree stands the little *Chapel of
St. Anne,* whose portico is adorned
with the mottoes " In libertatem vo-
cati estis "—" Ubi Spiritus Domini,
ibi Libertas "—" In te speraverunt
Patres"—and with two fresco paintings. One represents the first formation of the League, the principal
figures being the Abbot of Dissentis,
in the robes of his order ; the Count
of Sax, with a white flowing beard ;
and the Lord of Rhœtzuns. The
other picture shows the renewal of
the oath in 1778 : the deputies here
appear with starched frills, and hair
powdered and frizzled ; in silk stockings and walking-sticks. It is recorded that the deputies on the
former occasion brought their dinners
in sacks on their backs, which they
hung up by nails to the rocks, while
they quenched their thirst in the
brook which traverses the meadow
of Tavanosa. The more courtier-like
deputies of the second meeting were
more sumptuously feasted in the
mansion of the Abbot.

The inhabitants of the upper part
of the valley, about Dissentis, are
Catholics, as will become apparent
from the increased number of churches
and crosses. The mountains which
bound it change from limestone to
primitive rocks, and give a different
character to its scenery.

Opposite Sumvix the valley of
that name opens out ; it stretches
many miles S., far into the Alps.
Beyond it the eye is arrested by the
view of the abbey and village of

2¼ *Dissentis—(Inn:* Rathhaus, bad)—The *Benedictine Abbey* of Dissentis (in Romansch Mustär, or Monster, from Lat. Monasterium) is venerable as one of the oldest ecclesiastical establishments in Switzerland, founded, it is said, by the Scotch Monk Siegbert, a companion of St. Gall, and as the nucleus of early civilization in this wild and remote country. It stands on the slope of a hill, protected by a forest above it from falling avalanches, on the l. bank of the Vorder-Rhine, at the junction of the two Alpine torrents which unite in forming that branch of the river. The word venerable will not apply to the actual building, for, though dilapidated, it is modern, having been built since 1799, when the ruthless French invaders burnt it, and along with it the library formed in the seventh and eighth centuries. It must be allowed that provocation was given for this act of vengeance, by the barbarous and cruel murder of a party of French soldiers, who had been disarmed and taken prisoners by the Swiss Landsturm, and who were here set upon by the infuriated inhabitants of this part of the valley, and literally cut or torn to pieces. The abbey has, however, an imposing appearance from its size and position, towering above the humble hovels of the village below, as its rich and powerful abbots, in the middle ages, lorded it above their vassals. They were at one time firm allies of the House of Habsburg, and the abbot and his banner occupied the van at the battle of Morgarten. At a later period however, 1424, Abbot Peter of Pontaningen was one of the founders of Grison liberty who met under the sycamore at Trons. Dissentis is situated at a height of 3700 ft. above the sea-level.

There is a steep and difficult foot-path hence over the Lukmanier to Bellinzona (Route 78), another up the Medelser-Thal, and thence down the Val Piora to Airolo, 10¼ stunden; a third, difficult and dangerous,

runs N. over the Dödi-Grat, by the Sandalp, to the Baths of Stachelberg Route 72.

The path from Dissentis up to the Oberalp leaves the Medelser-Thal on the l. and ascends the vale of Tavetsch by the l. bank of the Vorder-Rhein now reduced in breadth and volume to a mountain-torrent. The path passes the villages Mompetavetsch, Sedrun, or Tavetsch, the chief place in the valley, and Ruaras. A narrow gorge now leads out of the lower into an upper valley. This part of it is dreadfully exposed to avalanches. In 1808 one fell from the Ruenatsch upon the village of Selva, and killed 42 human beings and 237 head of cattle. Here begins the last and most difficult part of the ascent; all regular track disappears, and the numerous furrows worn by the feet of the cattle perplex the traveller, who will hardly be able to find his way without a guide.

4 Ciamot is the last village in the valley deserving that name, and provided with a church; it is 5000 ft. above the sea. The valley of Tavetsch is the cradle of the Vorder-Rhine; it is supplied from 3 branches, having their sources in the vast mountains which wall in its upper extremity. The l.-hand branch flows from the foot of the Crispalt, on the S. side of the valley, the middle from the glaciers of the Sexmadau (Cima de Badus), the third comes from the Val Cornära on the S. At Ciamot the l.-hand branch is crossed and the middle branch followed for about a mile, after which adieu to the Rhine; a constant ascent leads the traveller to the summit of the pass of the Oberalp, 6174 ft. above the sea, by the cross between the Calmot and the Neugallas.

On reaching the opposite declivity, a small lake, famed for its trout, lies at the foot of the traveller. This is the Oberalp-See, one of the head-waters of the Reuss, it is beset with bogs, across which the traveller must pick his way cautiously. This spot

vas the scene of a hard struggle
between the French and Austrians,
in 1799. The path winds along the
N. or rt. side of the lake. The vale
of Urseren, with Hospital in the distance, now opens out to view, and a
long and wearisome descent, through
a naked valley of pastures, brings
the traveller to

3¼ Andermatt, on the St. Gothard,
Route 34, p. 97.

ROUTE 78.

PASS OF THE LUKMANIER—DISSENTIS
TO OLIVONE IN THE VAL BLEGNO.

10 stunden = 32¾ English miles.
A foot-path, much frequented in
summer. The valley of Medels, up
which it lies, runs in a direction
nearly due S. from Dissentis, and is
traversed through its whole length
by the Middle Rhine. The entrance
to it is by a rocky and wooded gorge,
about 2 miles from Dissentis, in the
midst of which the Rhine forms two
cascades, and beyond which the valley opens out into a wide basin, lined
with pastures and forests, in the
remoter parts of which the bear is still
found, while the chamois abounds
on the granite peaks forming the
highest summits of the surrounding
Alps. The path runs through Cu-
raglia, or Kuragla. Plutta is the
principal place in the Medelser
Thal. Perdatsch is situated at the
opening of the Val Cristallina, which
runs in a S.E. direction, and sends
forth one branch of the Middle Rhine.
Another branch comes from the W.
out of the Lake Dim, at the end of
the Val Cadelina; and a third, between these two, issues from the foot
of the Monte Scuro.

5 Sta. Maria, a hospice, kept up
for the benefit of poor travellers,
nearly on the culminating point of
the Pass of the Lukmanier (in Latin,
Mons Lucumonius; in Romansch,
Lukmajn, or Quolm Sta. Maria), 5740
it. above the sea. It is said that the

army of Pepin passed this way A.D.
754. Poles, stuck into the rocks,
mark the direction of the path across
the Col. Paths branch off from the
hospice to Airolo, through the Val
Termini, or Val Forno, the Val
Piora, by Altanca, Brugnasco, and
Madrano: 5½ stunden.

The path to Olivone and the Val
Blegno descends the Alpine Val Casaccia, to

2 The Hospice of Casaccia; and,
a few miles lower, to that of

2 Camperio, both founded, it is
said, by St. Carlo Borromeo, for the
reception of travellers.

1 Olivone is the highest village in
the Val Blegno, and stands at the
point where the lateral valley of
Casaccia joins it; it has about 740
inhabitants.

The Val Blegno (Germ. Polenzer-
thal) is traversed by the stream of
the Brenno; and a tolerable char-
road has recently been formed along
the l. bank of the stream, from Olivone to Biasca, on the route of the
St. Gothard (Route 34, p. 102), a
distance of 4 stunden.

Many of the chocolate-sellers and
chestnut-roasters, who swarm in the
streets of the cities of Italy, come
from the Val Blegno.

ROUTE 81.

THE PRETTIGAU.—MAYENFELD TO
FIDERIS AND DAVOS.

Mayenfeld is an ancient walled
town of 1200 inhabitants, on the rt.
bank of the Rhine, but at a little
distance from the river. It stands
on the high-road from Bregenz to
Coire, about 12 miles N. of the latter
place. It is the chief town of the
League of the 10 Jurisdictions
(Zehngerichten-Bund). There is a
cross-road direct from Mayenfeld to
Malans, but it is better to follow the
high-road as far as the Zollbrücke,
and there to turn off on the l. to
Malans, a village of 1054 inhabitants,

overlooked by several ruined castles, and situated near the mouth of the *Prettigau* (? Rhæti-gau). The entrance of that valley is through a narrow gorge or defile, called Klus, a mile long, broken through by some geological phenomena, so as to give passage to the waters of the Landquart, a furious torrent. The valley abounds in fine scenery, is shut in by high mountains and glaciers, and is famed for its large breed of cattle. The rt., or N. side of the valley, is occupied by the Alpine chain of the *Rhætikon,* which separates it from the Vorarlberg and from the vale of Montafun. Its most remarkable summits are the Falknis, overlooking the Rhine, the Scesa Plana, and the Fermund (*Ferreus Mons*), on the borders of the Engadine. It is crossed by several passes—one is called Druser-Thor. The road ascends on the rt. bank of the Landquart by Grüsch and Schiersch to Rütinen, where it crosses the stream to

Fideris. About 2 miles S. of the village, in the wild, romantic vale of the Raschitsch, a tributary of the Landquart, stand the Baths of Fideris, considered efficacious in cases of intermittent fevers, supplied by several alkaline acidulous springs, the strongest of their class in Switzerland. Visiters are accommodated in two *Bath Houses,* capable of lodging 100 persons. The visiters are almost exclusively Swiss.

Above the village of Fideris rises the ruined Castle of Strahleck; and, on the rt. bank of the Landquart, opposite, that of Castels, which was stormed and taken, in 1622, by the peasants, armed with sticks alone, from the soldiers of the Emperor Ferdinand, who at that period wanted to make himself master of the passes of the Grisons, to extinguish the Protestant religion in this country, and to seize and banish its ministers. A path leads S., in 3½ hours, over the mountains, into the Schalfik-thal.

About 13 miles above Fideris, on the rt. bank of the Landquart, lies

Klosters (*Inn,* near the bridge), a village, named after a convent suppressed 1528.

Paths go from hence S. over the Stutz into the Davos-thal, and E. over the Selvretta into the Engadine. The latter runs up the valley of Vareina, and down the valley of Süss. Süss is 9 stunden from Klosters.

ROUTE 82.

PASS OF THE JULIER, FROM COIRE UP THE VALLEY OF OBERHALBSTEIN, TO THE BATHS OF ST. MAURITZ, IN THE ENGADINE.

16¾ stunden = 52½ English miles.

The long-projected carriage road up the valley of the Oberhalbstein, and across the Julier, has at length been undertaken by the canton of the Grisons, and was so far advanced, in September, 1837, that carriages, with 2 or 4 horses, could drive as far as Tiefenkasten. The rest of the journey may be performed in a char. But the entire road may possibly be completed in 1838. There is as yet great want of inns between Coire and St. Mauritz. Lenz is a tolerable dining-place; but the traveller will do well in stowing away some eatables in his wallet, in case of accidents. He will everywhere be able to procure the tolerable wine of the Valteline.

On quitting Coire, the traveller leaves, on the l., the entrance to the Schalfik-thal, and passes through the villages of Malix, Churwalden, and Parpan; then, over a barren heath, to

4¾ Lenz—(*Inn:* Krone; not very good). Here the road divides; one branch, a path, runs to the Albula (Route 83); the other is the carriage-road to the Julier. Beyond Lenz, the Romansch tongue (p. 175) is almost exclusively spoken; even German is rarely understood, except in the inns.

The river Albula is crossed, in order to reach Tiefenkasten (Rom. Casté), a village, situated, as its

ame implies, in a deep hollow, at
ne entrance of the Oberhalbstein.
This valley runs up to the foot
f the Julier and Septimer, a dis-
ance of about 20 miles. It is scat-
ered over with ruins of castles ; no
ess than 10 of which may still be
ounted. Immediately above Tiefen-
asten, the road is carried through a
emarkable gorge, called the *Stein*,
vhich has been compared, in the
grandeur of its scenery, with the Via
Mala (Route 87).

2 Conters. Above this lies Sa-
ognin, or Schweiningen. At

1 Tinzen—*Inn*—travellers are re
eived at the house of the magistrate
Landvoght), Dosch ; it is but hum-
ıle quarters. This part of the valley
s very bleak and bare ; its inhabitants, the women especially, have
ı most squalid aspect. A constant
and steep ascent through the villages
of Rofna, Molins (Muhlen), to reach
which the road crosses the stream,
re-crossing it to the next village of
Saur and Marmels, brings you at
length to

3½ Bivio Stalla (the Capucin, who
acts as parish priest, would possibly
accommodate a traveller). This village lies at the foot of two passes,
the Septimer, on the rt., leading into
the Val Bregaglia and the Julier, in
a direction nearly due E. It is placed
in a secluded basin, shut in by high
mountains, in a climate so severe
that all vegetation is stunted. Not
a tree can grow in the neighbourhood,
and the people are reduced to burn
sheep dung for fuel. Potatoes rarely
ripen at this height—5630 ft. above
the sea.

It takes about two hours to ascend
from Stalla to the summit of the
Julier Pass, 6830 ft. above the sea
level. The ascent is not difficult,
and the pass is remarkably safe from
avalanches. Its scenery is not particularly grand, the outline of the
mountains being round. On the top,
the road passes between two rudely-
hewn pillars of granite (derived from
the neighbouring mountains), be-

lieved to be Roman, called *Julius's
Columns*. They are about 4 ft. high,
destitute of inscription, but may have
been set up as mile-stones in the time
of Augustus, who caused a Roman
highway to be carried from Chiavenna over the passes of the Malöja
and Julier. A carriage road was
formed across this pass to St. Mauritz in 1823 ; but, as no attempt was
made, till very lately, to improve the
approach to it through the Oberhalbstein, little advantage was gained
by it. Flocks of Bergamesque sheep
are often found on the highest pastures, near the summit of the pass, in
summer. A still more easy descent
leads into the Engadine, to the village of

3½ Silva Plana, situated between
two small lakes, which are feeders
and reservoirs of the river Inn, at the
junction of the roads from the two
passes of the Julier and Malöja,
5560 ft. above the sea.

About 4 miles lower down, on the
l. bank of the Inn, stands

1¼ *St. Mauritz.*—There are three
Inns here, the Upper (Obere), best ;
Mittlere and Untere Gasthof: the
accommodation in all is of the home-
liest kind. This little village is rising
into repute in Switzerland as a watering-place, upon the strength of its
very powerful chalybeate waters, first
described, 1539, by Paracelsus. The
spring rises at the foot of Mount
Rosegg, on the rt. bank of the Inn.
A *Kurhaus* has been built over it.
The water is heated to supply the
baths.

The village contains but 160 inhabitants. Its situation is really delightful, overlooking the Inn, and several
beautiful green lakes which that river
forms in this part of its course. The
climate is too cold to allow even
barley to flourish ; the surrounding
land is chiefly laid out in pastures,
which are let to Bergamasque shepherds ; and there are some forests of
larch on the neighbouring mountains. The little lake, close to the
village which is generally frozen

over from St. Andrew's-day (the end of November) to the beginning of May, furnishes capital trout.

In one of the most recent descriptions of the Engadine, the author mentions that, on repairing to church on a Sunday, at St. Mauritz, he found the parish fire-engine drawn up by the side of the pulpit—the church, in this and other villages, being somewhat profanely used as an engine-house. He found the office of watchman filled, and its duties discharged, by a woman, and a female also occupied the situation of baker, the bakehouse being the property of the parish.

The principal *Excursions* to be made from St. Mauritz are up the valley to the Lugni See, the source of the Inn (Route 89); to the great Bernina glacier (Route 85); and, down the valley, to the pass of Finstermünz (Route 84).

ROUTE 83.

COIRE TO PONTE IN THE ENGADINE, BY WEISSENSTEIN, AND THE ALBULA PASS.

14½ stunden = 47½ Eng. miles.

A bridle-path, barely practicable for light carts. As far as

4½ Lenz, it is identical with the preceding route, but at Lenz it turns round the shoulder of the mountain to the E., leaving Tiefenkasten on the right, and, passing the village of Brienz, ascends the vale of Albula. On the left towers the Castle of Belfort, on an almost inaccessible rock. In about 3 miles more we reach the Baths of Alveneu, on the rt. bank of the Albula, and, crossing the mouth of the Davos Thal and the stream running out of it, follow the Albula, ascending, in a S.E. direction, to

2¾ Filisur, a village on its rt. bank. Near it stand the ruins of Schloss-Greifenstein. The inhabitants of this and the adjoining valley emi-

grate from home to various parts of Europe, where they exercise the craft of pastry-cooks, frequently returning hither to end their days in opulence earned by industry. Two miles above Filisur are the abandoned silver mines of Bonacelsa, and 4 miles from hence the path enters the narrow ravine called Berguner Stein, which, like that near Tiefenkasten (p. 199), has been compared with the Via Mala. For a distance of more than 1000 ft. the path is hewn, or blasted, out of the face of the rock, and the Albula roars at a depth of 500 or 600 ft. below.

2 Bergün (Rom. Bergogn), a village of about 600 inhabitants, chiefly Protestants, speaking Romansch, and muleteers or carters by profession. A Protestant synod was held here 1617.

A steep ascent leads to the inn, or chalet, of

2 Weissenstein, 4900 ft. above the sea, in the vicinity of a small lake, the fountain head of the Albula. "A few stunted firs are scattered about the lower end, where the water is shallow; on all other sides the lake lies dark and treeless, beneath the frightful precipices that tower above." The ascent from this point is very rapid, the path lies along the N. side of the lake; traces of the Roman road may be discovered near this. A savage ravine, called Trümmer-thal, because filled with fragments of broken rocks, hurled down from the heights above, along with the avalanches, which render this part of the pass dangerous in spring, brings the traveller to

1¼ the summit of the pass of the Albula. The culminating point, marked by a cross, is 6980 feet above the sea level: near it is another small lake. It is a scene of complete desolation. On the N. of the path rise the two peaks of the Albula—Crap Alv, or White Rock, 7560 ft.; and on the S.E. that of Piz Err, 8770 ft. high.

The descent into the Ober-Enga-

line is also at times exposed to avalanches.

2 Pont, or Punt, in Route 84.

ROUTE 84.

THE ENGADINE; ST. MAURITZ TO NAUDERS, AND THE PASS OF FINSTERMÜNZ.

15 stunden = 49 Eng. miles.

A tolerable chai-road, traverses the Engadine.

The Engadine, or Valley of the Upper Inn, is nearly 60 miles long, and is one of the highest inhabited valleys among the Alps, varying between an elevation of 5600 ft. above the sea, at Sils, the highest village, and 3234 ft. at Martinsbruck, the lowest. It has at least 20 tributary valleys. Owing to this high elevation, and the icy barrier of enormous glaciers which separates it from Italy on the S., it possesses a most ungenial, nay, severe climate. In the language of its inhabitants it has 9 months of winter and 3 of cold weather. The only grain grown in it is rye and barley, a stunted crop; and, in the upper portion, potatoes rarely come to maturity; yet it is one of the most opulent valleys among the Alps, though the source of its wealth must be sought for in another theatre than the valley itself. Its inhabitants, aware of the inclemency of their climate and of the barrenness of its soil, are but little addicted to agriculture. The surface, where not actually bare rock, is either covered with forests or converted to pasture, with the exception of small patches on the lower grounds, set apart for the plough or spade. Yet even of this the natives appear to take small account; they let their pastures annually to the Bergamasque shepherds, and intrust the mowing of their meadows and the gathering of the hay harvest to Tyrolese haymakers, who resort to the valley at the season when their labour is required. The sons of the valley, for the most part, emigrate at an early age, scatter themselves over all parts of the Continent, and may be found in most of the great capitals exercising the professions of pastry-cooks, confectioners, distillers of liqueurs, keepers of cafés, and sellers of chocolate. Many of them in the exercise of their calling acquire considerable wealth, and become millionnaires in florins, with which they retire to end their days by the side of the stream of their native valley. They display their wealth especially in the architecture of their houses, which are distinguished by their large dimensions, by their decorations of whitewash and fresh paint. They are usually decked out with fresco frieses, and pillars, reminding one of the pretension to taste of a cockney citizen's box near London, combined with the studied neatness of a Dutchman's country house, both equally unexpected and out of place, amidst the savage landscape of a Grison valley. Some of the buildings really may be called splendid, though few are in good taste. The windows are few and small, to guard against admitting the cold. Poverty is rare, beggary almost unknown, and the people, who are, with the exception of one or two parishes, Protestants, are creditably distinguished for their morality, and are exempt from the vices common in other parts of Switzerland. Their pastors are held in great respect, but their pay is miserable, affording a striking proof of the working of a *voluntary system.* The sabbath is strictly observed; strangers only are allowed on that day to ride or drive until after church-time.

The accommodation of travellers is not, as yet, much studied in the Engadine. The *Inns* (except at St. Mauritz) are very inferior, and the traveller who resorts to them must be prepared often to content himself with hard rye bread, baked only once a-quarter; eggs, cheese, and perhaps coffee. The universal language is the *Ladin* (see p. 175); but among the return- ed emigrants, in almost every village, may be found individuals speaking French, Italian, or even English. Many of the retired patissiers are otherwise well-informed men ; so that it is seldom that the stranger will not find an interpreter. The wine of the Valteline may be had good and cheap, and pastry (made with flour imported from St. Gall) is set before the traveller in spots where wheaten bread is not to be had; indeed, some villages, which cannot boast a shoemaker or tailor, possess 10 or 15 pastry-cooks.

The higher Alpine pastures of the Engadine are let out every summer to Bergamasque shepherds, from the valleys Seriana and Brembana, on the Italian side of the Alps—a wild, dark, and scowling class of men, but hardy and honest, clad in homespun brown and white blankets, and feed- ing frugally on water pollenta of maize-meal, and a little cheese. They arrive about the beginning of July, with their flocks lean and meagre, after their long march, performed generally in the cool of the night. After a solitary sojourn of nearly 3 months, spending often the night as well as day in the open air among their flocks, they return home with fattened kine and long fleeces, which are sold to the wool manufacturers of Bergamo.

―――

Just below St. Mauritz, the Inn, on quitting the small lake, forms a pretty fall. The first villages passed are Celerina and Samadan (Sommo d'On, Romansch ; summum Œni), the principal and wealthiest village in the Upper Engadine, with 500 inha- bitants. Opposite to it, the valley of Pontresina opens out, up which runs the road to the Bernina (Route 85).

Beyond Bevers the path from the Albula (Route 83) descends into the valley.

At the foot of the Albula li Ponte, and Madulein, and ove the latter village towers the ruinec Castle of *Gardoval*, connected wit which the following story is told:— In the days of the Faustrecht, befor Switzerland was free, this castle wa held by a tyrannical and licentiou Seigneur or Bailiff, who greatly op- pressed the peasantry around, retain ing in his pay a body of lawless sol- diers for the purpose of overawing his neighbours. This libertine lord in an evil hour cast his eyes on the fair daughter of Adam, a farmer of the opposite village of Camogask The maiden was still of a tender age, but of surpassing beauty, like an opening rosebud. One morning, her father, who doated fondly on her, was surprised by a summons brought by two of the bailiff's servants, to convey his daughter to the castle. The father stifled his indignation, promised obedience, and next morn- ing set out, conducting his daugh- ter attired as a bride, and accompa- nied by a number of his friends in festive garments as to a wedding, but with mournful mien. The lord of the castle watched the approach of his victim with impatience, and rushing down to meet her was about to clasp her, when, ere his polluting lips could touch her fair cheek, her father's dagger was buried deep in his breast, and his companions throw- ing off their peaceful garb, and bran- dishing their concealed weapons, fell upon the guards, and made them- selves masters of the tyrant's strong- hold. It was immediately burnt, and from that day freedom dawned upon the serfs of the Engadine.

3 Zutz, or Suoz, is a village of 550 inhabitants. An old tower still re- mains of the Stammhaùs, or original castle of the family of Planta, who, as far back as 1139, held the Enga- dine in feof. The climate here first becomes a little milder, Zutz being sheltered from the cold blasts de- scending from the Maloya. There is a path from Scanfs to Davos, over

:he Scaletta pass, 7820 ft., a distance of about 20 miles.

At the Ponte Alto, under the Casannaberg, is the division between Upper and Lower Engadine; the country now assumes a more romantic character, but the road is rougher and more hilly.

4 Cernetz, or Zernets, is a considerable village with a handsome church, and two feudal towers, one of which anciently belonged to a branch of the Planta family, and is called Wildenberg. Up the opposite valley of Forno runs a path into the Münster Thal, by the Buffalora Pass. 6 stunden. By the Val Forno you may reach Bormio, at the foot of the grand Pass of the Stelvio.

The names Lavin, Zutz, and Ardetz, three villages in this part of the Engadine, are said to be a Romansch corruption of the Latin Lavinium, Tutium, and Ardea.

The road winds much up and down to reach the villages, which are often perched on the top of steep heights, as in the case of Guarda. Between Ardetz and Fettan, it also makes a wide sweep, away from the river Inn. Tarasp, on the rt. bank of the Inn, opposite Fettan, is the only Catholic village in the Engadine; its inhabitants differ from their neighbours in another respect, that they do not emigrate. Though less enlightened perhaps, they devote themselves to tilling their own land.

4 Schuols or Schulz, the most populous place in the valley, contains 1143 inhabitants, and is prettily situated. There is much corn-land near this. Avalanches sometimes fall from the hill of Balluns behind. At Schuols, the first Romansch translation of the Bible was printed 1679. See p. 175. Perhaps the most picturesque scene in the Engadine is near Remus, where a wooden bridge, 60 feet span, is thrown over the deep gorge called Wraunka Tobel, through which a torrent issues out of the vale of Ramosch. Above the bridge,

which is called Ponte Piedra, rises the ruined castle Chiamuff, burnt by the Austrians in 1475.

The scenery of the valley of the Inn is very grand on approaching

3 Martinsbruck (Pomartino). Here the traveller, after crossing the river, leaves the Inn to find its way at once through the pass of Finstermünz; the path takes a more circuitous route, and ascends a considerable wooded eminence, forming the boundary between Switzerland and Tyrol, and enters the Austrian dominions a short while before reaching Nauders, where there is a tolerable inn, about a mile distant from the remarkable defile of Finstermünz. (See Handbook for South Germany.)

ROUTE 85.

PASS OF THE BERNINA, FROM SAMADAN IN THE ENGADINE TO TIRANO IN THE VALTELINE, BY PONTRESINA, AND PUSCHIAVO.

10 stunden = 32¾ Eng. miles.

The Bernina is a very lofty chain of mountains, separating the valleys of the Engadine and of Bregaglia on the N., from the Valteline on the S. They vary in height between 8000 and 12,000 ft., the highest summits being the Ligoncio, the Monte del Oro, the Rosegg (Rosatch, and in Romansch, Ruseig), the Monte della Disgrazia, and the Pizzo Scalino. Several arduous paths cross it, but the most frequented is that called, *par excellence,* the *Bernina Pass,* a bridle-path, practicable at its two extremities for chars, and traversed annually by 700 or 800 mules.

From Samadan the road turns S. ascending the Val Pontresina, by the rt. bank of the torrent Flatz, to

1¼ Pontresina, a village having an inn. From this place, an excursion may be made in a S.W. direction to the glacier of Bernina, one of the largest in the Alps, filling the upper extremity of the Val Rusegg. The Flatz issues out of a cave of ice called Sboccadura, at its base. This glacier is stated to extend without interruption a distance of 50 miles. Several other arms or branches of this vast sea of ice descend the side valleys on the W. of our route, and appear from time to time in view.

1¾ Near the summit of the pass are 3 inns; the middle one is said to be the best.

1⅓ By the culminating point, 7180 ft. above the sea, are several lakes. A branch path passes them, and descends at once to the village of Puschiavo (Germ. Puschlaf). The other branch, usually taken, turns off to the E., near the extremity of the Lago Biancho, and crosses the ridge called Camino, to

1⅓ Piscadella, the first village in the valley of Puschiavo.

2⅓ Puschiavo, a village of 1015 inhabitants, the principal place in the valley, is mainly supported by the considerable traffic of goods through it. Above it, on a height, stand the ruins of the Castle of Oligati.

Nearly one-third of the inhabitants of this populous valley are Protestants, the language spoken is a corrupt Italian.

About three miles lower down, the road skirts along the W. margin of the charming little lake of Puschiavo, famed for its trout.

2 Brusio is the last Swiss village. On quitting the lake, the river passes through a very narrow defile, barely allowing room for the road and the stream. It is a raging torrent, and as it approaches the Adda, requires to be restrained within stone dykes of solid masonry, which have, nevertheless, proved insufficient to protect its banks from inundation. Beyond this, the Valteline, or Vale of the Adda, opens out at

1 Tirano. See Handbook for South Germany.

ROUTE 87.

COIRE TO SPLÜGEN, BY THE VIA MALA.

3¾ posts = 32 Eng. miles.

A diligence or malle poste goes 4 times a week : twice over the Splügen and twice over the Bernardin. The road is excellent all the way. It is a drive of about 6 hours, posting, from Coire to Splügen, and about 4½ hours from Splügen to Coire. Excellent inns at Andeer and Splügen.

From Coire (Route 67) to Reichenau there is not much deserving notice in the scenery of the valley of the Rhine ; but the mountain Galanda, on its l. bank, is a conspicuous object. The road runs along a nearly level bottom as far as

Reichenau, which is a group of houses situated at the junction of the 2 Rhines. Its chief buildings are the Toll-house (16 kr. paid for 2 horses); the inn zum Adler (Aigle); and the *Château*, a handsome whitewashed country-seat of the Planta family. At the end of the last century it was converted into a school by the burgomaster Tscharner. In 1793, a young man calling himself Chabot, arrived here on foot with a stick in his hand, and a bundle on his back. He presented a letter of introduction to M. Jost, the head master; in consequence of which he was appointed usher, and for 8 months gave lessons in French, mathematics, and history. This forlorn stranger was no other than Louis Philippe, now King of the French, then Duke de Chartres, who had been forced by the march of the French army to quit Bremgarten and seek concealment here in the performance of the humble duties of a schoolmaster, and in that capacity made himself equally beloved by masters and pupils. His secret was known only to M. Jost. During his residence here he must have heard the news of his father's death on the scaffold, and his mother's transportation to Madagascar.

At Reichenau the road is carried over the two arms of the Rhine by two covered wooden bridges, each of one elegant arch. The lower bridge is 237 ft. long and 80 ft. above the river. The junction of the rivers is well seen from the castle garden. The more abundant waters of the Hinter Rhein, coming from the Bernardin and the foot of Mount Adula, are of an ash colour or dirty blue; while those of the Vorder Rhein, rising in the glaciers of the Crispalt and Lukmanier, are observed to be of a greenish hue. The road up the Vorder Rhein to its source, and to Andermatt, on the St. Gothard, is described in Route 77.

The road to the Splügen follows the course of the Hinter-Rhein. On the rt. of it, as you ascend the hill beyond Reichenau, the *Gallows* may be seen standing in a field. A little further, on the top of a commanding rock on the l. bank of the Rhine, and approached by a long bridge, rises the Castle of Rhœtzuns (Rhœtia ima): it is still inhabited.

This part of the Rheinthal, called the valley of Domleschg (Vallis Domestica), is particularly remarkable for the vast number of *castles* (21) which crown almost every rock or knoll on either side of the river, mostly in ruins, sometimes standing out boldly from a dark background of forest, at others so identified by decay, by the weather tints, and by the lichen growth, with the apparently inaccessible rocks on which they stand, as barely to be distinguished. Their picturesque donjons and battlements contribute not a little to enhance the charms of the landscape ; they serve at the same time as historical monuments to commemorate the revolution by which the power of a tyrannical feudal aristocracy, the lords of these fastnesses, was broken and their strongholds burnt by the peasants of this valley, whom they had long oppressed.

Another peculiarity of this district is the intricate intermixture of language and religion. There are scarcely two adjoining parishes, or even hamlets, speaking the same tongue and professing the same faith. Thus at Coire German is the prevailing language, and Protestant the religion of the majority ; at Ems, the first village on the road, Romansch (p. 175) is spoken. Tamins and Reichenau are Catholic and German; Bonaduz, divided from them only by the Rhine, is reformed, and speaks Romansch. Rhœtzuns and Katzis are two Romish villages; but in the first the language is German, in the second Romansch. The inhabitants of Heinzenberg are Protestant and German; at Thusis they are reformed and German; at Zillis and Schams reformed and Romansch. Splügen and Hinter Rhein form the boundary at once of the Romansch language and Protestant religion.

The castle of Ortenstein, on the rt. bank of the Rhine, is one of the finest and best-preserved in the valley: it is still inhabited by the Travers family.

Near the village of Kätzis a beautiful view opens out, on the opposite side of the Rhine, up the valley of Oberhalbstein, with the snows of Mount Albula (Route 83) at the termination of the vista. The river Albula enters the Rhine between Kätzis and Thusis.

This part of the Rhine valley exhibits dismal traces of the ravages produced by the torrent Nolla, which, rising at the base of the Piz Beveren, on the W. of our route, joins the Rhine nearly at right angles to the direction of the course of that river. It is subject to very sudden swells after rain, when it rushes down, tearing up the rocks and carrying along with it heaps of stone, mud, and gravel, which not only overspread its own banks, but frequently block up the bed of the Rhine and cause desolating inundations. Thus a district, previously fertile and beautiful, has been in the course of a few years (since 1807) converted into a desert, and its fields either buried under stony rubbish or converted into marsh. The evil has been annually increasing for several years past, but hopes are entertained of arresting it and recovering the land. With this view extensive dykes are being constructed along the banks of the Rhine.

1¾ Thusis—(*Inn:* Aigle d'Or, tolerable)—a village of 670 inhabitants, finely situated on a terrace under the Heinzenberg. Thusis, according to some, is only the word *Tuscia*, the country of the Tuscans, who first colonised these valleys, changed in the Romansch dialect.

Immediately on the outside of Thusis the Nolla is crossed by a handsome bridge. On the rt., at the end of the valley, appears the peak of the Piz Beveren.

Above Thusis the valley of the Rhine seems closed up by the mountains; it is only on a nearer approach that the eye discovers the opening of that singular chasm which has cleft them through, affording a passage for the river, and in modern times, by artificial means, for the road. The rt. side of this colossal portal is guarded by the castle of *Realt* (Rhœtia Alta), standing in the fork between the Albula and the Rhine, and from its lofty platform, 400 ft. high, looking down upon both valleys. It is accessible only from the east: on all other sides the rock is a precipice. These mouldering ruins are traditionally reported to owe their origin to Rhœtus, chief of the Etruscans, who, driven out of Italy by an invasion of the Gauls, established his stronghold on this spot B.C. 287, and transplanted into the Alps the people and language of Etruria. The ruined chapel of St. John, on a neighbouring height, is stated to have been the earliest, and for a long time the only Christian temple in the valley, where heathenism prevailed to a comparatively late period.

The VIA MALA, which commences bout a mile above Thusis, and extends for a distance of more than 4 miles, is, without doubt or exaggeration, the most sublime and tremendous defile in Switzerland. It is difficult to give, with any precision, the dimensions of this gorge, which has cleft the mountains through the chine. The precipices, which often rise perpendicularly on both sides of it, are certainly in some places 1600 ft. high, and, in many places, not more than 10 yards apart. The Rhine, compressed within this narrow, stony bed to the width of a pigmy rivulet, is barely audible as it rushes through the depths below the road.

The rocks of slate and limestone, composing the walls of the ravine, are so hard that they appear to have suffered no disintegration from the weather; the fracture is so fresh and sharp that, were the convulsive force from below, which divided them, again called forth to unite them, it seems as though the gulf would close, and leave no aperture behind.

When the traveller enters the mouth of the defile, the sudden transition from the glare of sunshine to the gloom of a chasm, so narrow that it leaves but a strip of sky visible overhead, is exceedingly striking. The walls of rock, on both sides, afford naturally not an inch of space along which a goat's foot could clamber; and, in ancient times, this part of the pass was deemed quite inaccessible. The peasants gave it the name of the Lost Gulf (Trou perdu, Verlohrnes Loch); and, when they wanted to go from Thusis to the higher valley of Schams, they ascended the vale of the Nolla for some distance, clambering over the tops of high mountains, round the shoulder of the Piz Beveren, and descended on the opposite side at Suvers. A second road, formed in 1470, crossed the mountains as before, but dipped down, from the village of Rongella, into the depths of the Via Mala, near the first bridge; still avoiding altogether the Trou perdu. This inconvenient path, after being used for more than 300 years, was superseded by the present magnificent highway, constructed by the engineer Pocobelli. Avoiding the useless detour, and the fatiguing ascent and descent, he at once plunged into the defile, and pierced the projecting buttress of rock, which had previously denied all access to it, by the gallery or tunnel of the Verlohrne Loch, 216 ft. long, through which the road now passes. The view, looking back from this, through the dark vista of black rock, and the fringe of firs, upon the ruined tower of Realt, and the sun-lit valley of Domleschg, is very pleasing. The grooves of the boring-rod, by which the very hard slate rock is everywhere streaked, indicate how arduous was the labour of constructing this part of the road. It was literally forcing a passage through the bowels of the earth; and the whole width of the carriage-way has been gained by blasting a notch, as it were, in the side of the mountain. For more than 1000 ft. it is carried along beneath a stone canopy, thus artificially hollowed out. The road is protected by a parapet wall, below which, at a depth of many hundred feet, the contracted Rhine frets the foot of the precipice. The road is in places steep, and fit for only one carriage to pass. A little higher up, the gorge bulges out into a sort of basin, in the midst of which stands a solitary house; but it soon contracts again, and the scenery of the pass may be said to attain the height of grandeur beyond the first of the three bridges, by means of which the road is conveyed from side to side of the Rhine.

This portion of the pass at least, should be traversed on foot; the traveller, hurrying through in his carriage, is quite incapable of appreciating its awful magnificence.

The *Middle Bridge*, a most striking object, from its graceful proportions, and the boldness with which its light arch spans the dark and deep gulf below, is approached by a second small gallery, protected by a wooden roof to ward off falling stones. Hereabouts, the lofty precipices on the one side actually overhang those on the other, the direction of the chasm being oblique, and the smooth wall of rock on either side being nearly parallel, and scarcely wider apart above than below. Looking over the parapet of this bridge, the Rhine, reduced to a thread of water, is barely visible, boiling and foaming, in the depths below. Indeed, in one place, it is entirely lost to view—jammed in, as it were, between the rocks, here so slightly separated that small stones and trunks of fir-trees, falling from above, have been caught in the chink, and remain suspended above the water. The ordinary height of the bridge above the river is 400 ft.; and the water, as mentioned above, is in one place invisible at ordinary times, yet, at the commencement of the fearful inundation of 1834 (already alluded to in several routes), the postmaster of Thusis, who drove up the Via Mala during the storm, found that the water had risen to within a few feet of the bridge; the roar was terrific; and, as he drew up a little further on, in consequence of the road being destroyed, two mangled human bodies were swept past him by the flood.

The road, again, is no more than a shelf hewn out of the face of the precipice overhung by the rock, so as to be almost a subterranean passage, and the width of the defile is, in places, not more than 24 ft. Near the third, or Upper Bridge, however, a fine new structure—built to replace the one swept off in 1834—it widens out, and the road emerges into the open valley of Schams (Sexamniensis, from six brooks, which fall into the Rhine from its sides), whose green meadows and neat white cottages have a pleasing effect when contrasted with the gloomy scene behind. It has, however, suffered much from the inundation of 1834, which converted the valley into a lake, destroyed a great part of the road, and rendered a new line necessary. The first village is Zillis;

between it and Andeer, a stone, bearing the following inscription, was set up, by the road-side, on a bridge, after the completion of the great highways over the Splügen and Bernardine:—" *Jam via patet hostibus et amicis. Cavete, Rhœti! Simplicitas morum et Unio servabunt avitam libertatem.*"

1 Andeer—*Inn:* Post; good and cheap—bed, tea, and breakfast, cost 1½ fr. each. It contains mineral baths, but they are not much used. This is the chief village in Schams, and has 400 inhabitants, who, like their neighbours, are Protestants, and speak Romansch (p. 175). Over the doors of many of the cottages, quaint verses and mottoes in that language are inscribed.

Above Andeer a very large landslip or bergfall occurred in 1835, by the giving way of a mountain, which buried the road, and, for 16 days, cut off all communication up and down the valley. Luckily it happened in the night, so that no one was hurt.

The ruined castles, visible in the valley of Schams, have an historical interest, from being monuments of the dawn of Grison liberty. In the last half of the fourteenth century they served as the residence of bailiffs, zwingherrn, or landvoghts, dependents of the Counts of Vatz or of the Bishop of Coire, petty tyrants and oppressors of the poor—akin in character to Gessler, the victim of Tell's vengeance. At length, a peasant, of the Schamser Thal, named Jean Chaldar, exasperated at the sight of two horses which the chatelain of Fardun had turned out to graze in his field of green corn, gave vent to his anger by killing the animals. He suffered punishment for this act by being long detained prisoner in a dark dungeon. One day, after his release, the chatelain of Fardun, in passing his cottage, entered as the family were at dinner, and, when invited to partake of their humble meal, evinced his contempt by spitting in the dish. Chaldar, roused by this filthy insult, seized the oppressor by the throat, and thrusting his head into the smoking dish, compelled him to partake of it, saying, " Malgia sez la pult cha ti has condüt"—" Eat the soup thou hast thus seasoned." This bold deed served as a signal for a general rising; the peasants flew to arms—and the castles were stormed and burnt.

One of the first that fell was Bärenburg, which is passed on the l. of the road after quitting Andeer. As soon as the road has crossed the mouth of the Val Ferrera and the stream of the Aversa, it begins to mount in zigzags into the gorge of the Rofla, which closes up the S. end of the oval vale of Schams, as the Via Mala does the N. Its scenery, though fine, is vastly inferior to the lower pass. The Rhine here descends in a cataract, called the fall of the Rofla. It does not rank as a first-rate waterfall, but the scenery around is picturesque—the sides of the valley being thickly wooded, and the river studded by saw-mills, where the timber of the neighbouring forests is sawn into planks. A timber-slide, similar to that of Alpnach (Route 19), was constructed to convey the trees to the borders of the Rhine.

The oldest mule-path, which traversed this valley to Coire, crossed the river by a wooden bridge, still standing, to Suvers, where it began painfully to ascend the mountains, and proceeded along the high ground to descend again at Thusis.

The new road leaves the bridge on one side, traverses a small gallery cut in the rock, then crosses to the l. bank of the Rhine, and soon reaches

1 Splügen (Ital. Spluga)—(*Inn:* Post; very good, and not dear: the landlady is French, and prides herself on her cuisine). This little village is situated on the Rhine, at the point of departure of the two alpine passes of the Splügen and Bernardin, at a height of 4430 ft. above the sea. It suffered most severely from the flood of 1834, which swept away more than a dozen houses, in some of which the owners

had been seated at their evening meal not an hour before. Five human beings perished by this catastrophe, the effects of which were still painfully visible in 1837. The covered bridge over the Rhine escaped almost by a miracle; that over the Serända was soon annihilated.

Splügen is the chief place in the desolate pastoral vale of the Rheinwald, and anciently belonged to the lords of Sax, in the vale of Misocco, on the S. slope of the Bernardine, but it afterwards joined the Grey League.

The atmosphere is very chilly here, and barley barely ripens.

The village prospers by the constant passage of goods and travellers to and from Italy. In autumn it is thronged with drovers; large herds of cattle and many horses then cross the Alps for the Milan market.

An excursion may be made from Splügen to the source of the Hinter-Rhein. It will occupy 5 hours—2 along the post-road, 2 on horseback, and 1 on foot: it is described in the Bernardine Route, p. 214.

ROUTE 88.

PASS OF THE SPLÜGEN,—FROM SPLÜGEN TO CHIAVENNA AND THE LAKE OF COMO.

To Colico 5 posts = 44¾ English miles.

A diligence goes twice a-week over the Splügen to Milan.

With post horses it takes 7½ hours to go from Splügen to Chiavenna, including stoppages.

N.B. Without an Austrian Minister's signature on the passport the frontier cannot be passed, and the traveller unprovided with it, will inevitably be turned back on the summit of the mountain. A toll of 15 batz is paid for 2 horses, between Splügen and the Austrian frontier.

The Splügen road, turning to the l. from the village of that name (p. 208) crosses the narrow wooden bridge over the Rhine, and quitting the river, begins at once to ascend. It is carried up the valley of the Oberhausen-bach, a small torrent which joins the Rhine at Splügen, by an entirely new line, the old one having been demolished by the disastrous tempest of 1834. Indeed this little valley presents one sweep of desolation; road and bridges having been entirely carried away, and enormous piles of broken rocks spread over its sides and bottom. The new line, however, on this side of the mountain, constructed by a Swiss engineer, employed by the canton of the Grisons, is, in every respect, a great improvement upon the old one. A little way above Splügen it is carried through a tunnel, 80 metres long, supported by a Gothic arch.

After surmounting the district of fir forests by an almost uninterrupted slope, the road reaches the summit of the pass, 6500 ft. above the sea, by means of 16 skilfully conducted zigzags, by which the face of the mountain is scaled. Along this narrow ridge, which is 4¾ miles from Splügen, and more than 1800 feet above it, runs the boundary line of Switzerland and of Lombardy. Almost immediately after surmounting it the road begins to descend. Upon this slope lies the first cantonièra, or house of refuge; and, lower down, a series of tourniquets conduct to the Austrian Custom-house and Passport-office—a group of buildings, including several very common taverns for the entertainment of travellers. Here passports are examined and luggage searched, and the traveller must often reckon upon no inconsiderable delay, especially if he arrives between 12 and 2, the douanier's dinner-hour. The custom-house stands at one end of a sort of oval basin, surrounded by lofty mountain peaks, among which, on the rt., of the road, rises that of the Splügen, and the glaciers which feed the rivers running towards Italy. It is a scene of extreme desolation; not a shrub of any kind grows here; no vegetation is seen but lichen, mosses, and a little coarse grass. The snow often reaches up to the windows of the first story of the houses.

The route of the Splügen was completed by the Austrian Government in 1823, to counteract the new Swiss road over the Bernardin, which, had the Splügen been allowed to remain in its original condition, would have withdrawn from it all the traffic into Italy. The engineer employed in this undertaking was the Chevalier Donegani. The old road, a mere bridle-path, proceeded from this elevated valley, or basin, direct to the village of Isola, through the defile of the *Cardinel*, a most perilous spot, from its dire and constant exposure to falling avalanches.

The French army of Marshal Macdonald, who crossed the Splügen between the 27th November and 4th December, 1800, long before the new road was begun, in the face of snow and storm, and other almost insurmountable obstacles, lost nearly 100 men and as many horses, chiefly in the passage of the Cardinell. His columns were literally cut through by the falling avalanches, and man and beast swept over to certain annihilation in the abyss below. The carriage-road very properly avoids the gorge of the Cardinell altogether, but the way to it turns off from the second wooden bridge crossed on quitting the custom-house.

Near the scattered hamlet Teginate, the descent re-commences, and soon after the road is carried through the first great gallery more than 700 feet long, 15 feet high and wide, followed by a second, 642 feet long, and, after a short interval, by a third, 1530 feet long. These galleries, the longest on any Alpine high road, are constructed of the most solid masonry, arched with roofs, sloping outwards, to turn aside the snow, supported on pillars or low windows like the embrasures of a battery. They were rendered necessary to protect this portion of the road from falling avalanches which ha-

bitually descend the face of the mountains, and which, if not warded off, would have swept away the road the first year after it was made.

From the entrance of the second gallery there is a most striking view down upon the roof of the houses of Isola, and the long line of zigzags, abandoned since 1838, by which the traveller originally descended to Chiavenna. At the village of Pianazzo, a cluster of pitch-coloured hovels, the new line, after descending 2 angular terraces, turns off to the left, and from this point is carried almost in one gradual slope to the village of Campo Dolcino. This alteration, by which nearly 3 miles of distance are saved, was rendered necessary on account of the injury done to the old line by the storm of 1834, and also by the great dangers from avalanches to which that part of the route, between Isola and the Cascade of the Medessimo, was exposed from avalanches which fall regularly into the savage glen of the Lira, below Pianazzo, producing an almost annual loss of life. In 1835 five peasants and eight horses were overwhelmed by the snow in this glen, as they were returning from conducting the diligence on a sledge over the mountain. The postilion being nearest the rock, which fortunately somewhat overhung the road, drew the horse he rode under the cliff as soon as he heard the crash; to this circumstance he and the animal owed their preservation. Although buried, like the rest who perished, they were rescued and dug out after an imprisonment of some hours.

Pianazzo stands at the same height above the sea as the bridge over the Rhine at Splügen. The road, after passing through it, crosses the little stream of the Medessimo, within a few yards of the verge of the precipice over which it throws itself in a beautiful fall 800 feet high. The only thing to be regretted in the new line of road is, that by carrying the traveller above this fall, it deprives him of the view of it, unless he choose to return by the old road from Campo Dolcino, to visit it. After crossing the bridge the road traverses a new gallery, 25 metres long, and thence gradually descends upon

2 Campo Dolcino, which, in spite of its sweet-sounding Italian name, is out a poor village, with a poor inn (Post), on a small dreary grassy plain, on the borders of the Lira.

A further improvement has been made in the continuation of the road, which, on quitting the gorge, threads the gorge of St. Giacomo; an inscription, by the road side, commemorates its completion by Carlo Donegani, in the reign of the Emperor Francis II. The sight of the tourniquets of the old road, painfully zigzagging out of the gorge below, which a heavy carriage could surmount only by the strength of 8 horses, will convince the spectator how great this improvement really is. It has been effected at considerable labour and expense, by cutting through the rock. The vale of the Lira presents a singular aspect of desolation, from the quantity and size of the masses of fallen rock which entirely fill the lower part of it. They are fragments of the neighbouring mountains, which are composed of a species of white gneiss, exceedingly brittle, and which, after exposure to the weather, assumes a red colour. It must have been a difficult task to carry a road through such a wilderness, between such a labyrinth of detached blocks; and it is, accordingly, in many places narrow, the turnings very sharp, and the terraces too short. The aspect of desolation in this fractured valley would be greater were it not for the rich dark foliage of the walnut-trees, which now begin to sprout out from among the rocks, so as to mask their barrenness. The tall white Italian campanile of the church of Madonna di Gallivaggio, amid such a group of foliage, contrasting with the tall precipices around, forms an agreeable picture. Near it, at the village St. Giacomo, whence the valley is named, the Lira is spanned by a bold bridge.

A mile or two farther on, the valley opens out, and Chiavenna expands to view, a picturesque town beautifully situated, under an Italian sun, surrounded by hills clothed with the richest vegetation, with vines, figs, and pomegranates.

1 *Chiavenna* (Germ. Clefen)—*Inn:* Conradi's, very good ;—*Post.*

Chiavenna (Clavenna of the ancients), a thriving town of 3040 inhabitants, is charmingly situated close under the mountains, which appear to impend over it, at the junction of the valley of St. Giacomo with that of the Meira, called Bregaglia. Beyond this beauty of situation there is very little here to interest the passing traveller. The town derives much benefit from its position on the Splügen road, and maintains several spinning mills for silk and cotton. An ingenious manufacturer, named Vanossi, at one time wove here a fireproof cloth of asbestus, a mineral, which abounds in the mountains of the neighbourhood. Opposite the inn is a picturesque ruined *Castle*, on the top of a rock, which once belonged to the Salis family: the present owners deny strangers all access to it. The principal *Church of St. Laurence* has a tall campanile standing within a square inclosure, surrounded by a cloister. On one side are two bonehouses, filled with skulls, and, adjoining them, in the octagonal *Baptistery*, is a curious ancient stone font, sculptured with rude bas-reliefs which will interest the antiquary. The citizens keep their Valteline wine in natural grottoes, at the foot of the mountains, which form excellent cool cellars, and are called Ventorali.

Near Pleurs, about 3 miles up the Val Bregaglia, memorable for the fate of its inhabitants, who were buried by the fall of a mountain (see p. 213), is a peculiar manufacture of a coarse ware for culinary purposes, made out of potstone (lapis ollaris). This stone is easily cut, or turned in a lathe, and is able to endure heat. Pliny calls it lapis Comensis, from its being exported from the lake of Como: the manufacture has greatly dwindled down at present.

The road up the Val Bregaglia and over the pass of the Malojia, and the description of Pleurs, are given in Route 89.

Chiavenna belonged to the Dukes of Milan down to the 16th century, when the Swiss became possessed of it, and it formed, with the Valteline and Bormio, a state subject to the canton of the Grisons. Napoleon added it to the kingdom of Italy, as lying on the S. side of the Alps; and the Congress of Vienna, by the same rule, transferred it to the Emperor of Austria.

The lower valley of the Meira, from Chiavenna to the Lake of Riva, is by no means pleasing in its scenery, and the low ground is occupied by marsh rather than meadow; so that it is at the same time very unwholesome.

Travellers should not stop for the night any where between Chiavenna and Colico. Malaria hangs over the district around the embouchures of the Meira and Adda, and the stranger who neglects this warning (§ 12) may pay for his temerity by a fever. Varenna, on the E. shore of the lake, where the Post is a good inn; Bellaggio, on the point of the promontory between the lakes of Lecco and Como, or Cadenabbia on the W. shore of the lake, are all safe and capital quarters, and the traveller ought not to stop to sleep till he reaches one of them.

1 Novate, a small village, to which the post station has recently been removed from the Riva, stands near the N. extremity of the Lago Mezzola, called also Lago di Riva. It is a most picturesque small lake, so walled in by mountains that, until a few years, there was no road by the side of it, and travellers were carried

across it by a tedious navigation in flat barges; rendered difficult and intricate by the annually increasing deposits of mud, which form shoals between this lake and that of Como, and prevent the steam-boat ascending to Riva. The naked and savage mountains around have a very peculiar outline. Their sides are furrowed with ravines, down which furious torrents precipitate themselves at some seasons, strewing the margin of the lake with wreck. The engineers who constructed the capital new road, finished in 1835, experienced the greatest obstacles in crossing the debris at the mouth of these ravines. The Codera, one of the most furious torrents, spreads out its waste of rocks and gravel in the shape of a fan, for a breadth of at least half a mile. This river at ordinary times trickles through the stones in 3 or 4 paltry driblets, crossed by wooden bridges, under which the water is turned by the construction of artificial canals, flanked by wedge-shaped dams and dykes. After traversing this desolate space, the road is carried through two galleries excavated in the rock, and soon after emerges upon the delta of the river Adda, flowing from the E. out of the Valteline into the lake of Como. There can be little doubt that the lake originally bathed the feet of the mountain on this side; but in the course of ages, the deposits brought down by the Adda and Meira have so far encroached on it as to form an extensive plain of swamp and morass breathing pestilence, through which the Adda now winds in a serpentine course. The new causeway stretches in a straight line across this morass, passing the Adda upon a long wooden bridge, too narrow for more than one carriage at a time. Near the centre of the plain the great road to the Stelvio branches off on the l. (See Handbook for South Germany.) The Spanish Fort Fuentes, built 1603, as the key of the Valteline, on a rock, once, perhaps, an island near the mouth of the Adda, is left on the rt., and the margin of the lake of Como is reached at

1 Colico, a village situated under the Monte Legnone, immediately S. of the embouchure of the Adda. It is less unwholesome than formerly, owing to the drainage of a large portion of the marsh-land. It is not, however, a good halting-place; there is no tolerable inn here.

The *steam-boat* from Como arrives off Colico every day about noon, and immediately returns. It will touch here to embark or disembark a carriage, if notice be sent to Domaso, otherwise it brings to at Domaso, on the opposite shore, and passengers are conveyed thither in boats. Boats may at all times be hired here to cross or descend the lake. The magnificent carriage-road of the Stelvio is carried along the E. shore of the lake, traversing several remarkably long tunnels excavated in the solid rock: it is well worth exploring, at least, as far as Varenna, the next post station from Colico.

A diligence goes once a week from Milan over the Stelvio to Innsbruck.

ROUTE 89.

CHIAVENNA TO ST. MAURITZ AND THE SOURCE OF THE INN, BY THE VAL BREGAGLIA AND THE PASS OF THE MALOYA.

8¼ Stunden = 27 Eng. miles.

A carriage-road up the Val Bregaglia and over the Maloya has been many years in progress, but remains down to the present time (1838) incomplete. At the point of departure from Chiavenna, a large bridge requires to be built, which is not yet begun; but after a mile or two the new road commences, and continues practicable for 2 horse carriages as far as Castasegna. Thence to Casaccia will probably be Macadamized in the course of 1838. Even now, the journey is practicable in a char.

The inns in the Val Bregaglia are bad; the best is probably that at Vicosoprano.

The road ascends by the rt. bank of the Maira, and about 3 miles above Chiavenna passes on the opposite side of the river (in face of a pretty cascade formed by the Acqua Fraggia descending from the N.) the grave of the village of *Pleurs*, buried with its 2430 inhabitants, by the fall of Monte Conto, on the night of the 4th September 1618. It was a beautiful and thriving place, peopled by industrious inhabitants, and contained numerous villas, the summer resort of the citizens of Chiavenna. It now lies beneath a heap of rocks and rubbish, 60 ft. deep. Every soul within it perished, and the long continued excavations of all the labourers that could be collected from far and near failed in rescuing anything, alive or dead, from the ruins. All traces of the catastrophe are now nearly obliterated, and the spot is grown over with a wood of chestnuts. The inhabitants received many previous warnings, which were unfortunately despised. Masses of rock fell the day before, rents and crevices were formed in the mountain, and the shepherds had observed their cattle fly from the spot with marks of extreme terror. For many hours after, the course of the Maira was dammed up by the fallen debris.

The Val Bregaglia (Germ. Bergell) is fertile and picturesque; it is shut in by high mountains. Many of its inhabitants emigrate, and adopt the profession of chimney-sweepers, which they exercise in some of the large towns of the continent. After passing through Santa Croce, and Villa (Pontella), the road reaches the Swiss frontier at

2 Castasegna. Above this, the white mulberry no longer flourishes, and this is therefore the limit of the culture of the silkworm. The ruined Castle of Castelmur on the l. bank of the Maira is conspicuous by reason of its tall donjon, 100 ft. high, from

which 2 walls, 15 ft. high and 10 thick, descend into the gorge to the river side. The valley was formerly closed here by a gate, and the castle formed the key of the valley.

2¼ Vico Soprano (Vespran), a village of 504 inhabitants on the l. bank of the Maira.

Casaccia (has an inn said to be tolerable), a village situated at the S. side of the Septimer, and on the W. of the Maloya, over both of which mountains the Romans conducted high ways in the age of Augustus.

The path over the Septimer 7360 ft. high, leads by the valley of Oberhalbstein to Coire, and was the ordinary highway between Italy and Switzerland, until the formation of the carriage-road over the Splügen, which being a lower pass, and 10 miles shorter, is of course preferred to it. On the Septimer are situated the sources of the Maira and the Oberhalbstein Rhine, and out of a small lake on its E. declivity, on the confines of the Maloya, the *River Inn* rises out of the small lake called Lago di Lugni. Thus, one single mountain distributes its rills between the 3 great seas which bathe the continent of Europe.

There has been a tolerable carriage-road over the *Maloya,* or *Maloggia,* *Pass* ever since 1823, but as the approaches to it, until very lately, were barely passable for the rudest kind of cart, it has been hitherto of little utility. The summit level is 6270 ft. high. A little way down the E. side of the ridge, the road falls in with the infant Inn (called Acqua d'Oen) here a mere torrent which hastens to pour itself into the lake of Sils, a picturesque mountain basin, extending as far as

2¼ Sils, the highest village of the Engadine. The most conspicuous building here is the villa of a chocolate manufacturer, named Josti, a native of Davos, who, having quitted Switzerland a beggar, made a large fortune in one of the capitals of N. Germany, a part of which he expend-

ed on this huge and unprofitable structure.

The lake of Sils is succeeded by two other small lakes of Silva Plana and of Campfeer, through both of which the Inn passes. At Silva Plana the Julier road (Route 82) enters the Engadine. About 3 miles lower down stands

1¾ St. Mauritz.   Route 82.

ROUTE 90.

PASS OF THE BERNARDIN, SPLUGEN
TO BELLINZONA.

5¼ posts = 45½ Eng. miles.

A diligence goes to and from Milan, twice a week.

The road over the Bernardin was constructed in 1822, under the direction of the engineer Pocobelli, at the joint expense of the Sardinian and Grison governments. About 6-7ths of the sum required was advanced by the King of Sardinia, who duly appreciated the advantages to his dominions to be derived from a highway, which should connect by a direct line, the port of Genoa, and the capital of Turin, with Switzerland and W. Germany.

The road, leaving the bridge of Splügen on the l., advances up the valley of Hinter-Rhein, whose stern and barren features have less of beauty than of wildness, along the l. bank of the Rhine through Nüfanen, a distance of about 9 miles, to

1 Hinterrhein—(*Inn:* Post)—the highest village in the valley, 170 ft. above Splügen, an elevation at which no grain but barley grows.

A multitude of streamlets trickle down from the crevices in the surrounding mountains, where deep snow rests almost all the year round, to feed the infant Rhine. But the *Source of the Rhine* lies about 10 miles higher up the valley, half of which distance can be performed on horseback, the rest on foot ; the latter part of the walk especially, is difficult and fatiguing, and the assistance of a guide is necessary to find the way. The river takes its rise at the very extremity of this frost-bound valley, from beneath a glacier ironically called Paradies, situated between the Moschal Horn and the Piz Val-Rhein, or Vogelberg (10,300 ft.), two of the highest mountains in the Grison range, forming part of the group called Monte Adula. At the end of about 4 miles the path begins to ascend, and is soon lost in crossing steep slopes covered with debris of rock, so that a previous knowledge of the direction will alone enable the traveller to reach the source. After skirting along the sides of a savage ravine called Hölle a steep descent leads down to the fountain head, in the glacier, which is sometimes hollowed out into a magnificent dome or cavern.

The road over the Bernardin bids adieu to the Rhine at Hinter-Rhein, crossing it by a stone bridge, the first which spans its current, after which it immediately begins to ascend, breasting the steep slope of the mountain by sixteen zigzags; many of its turnings are very abrupt.

A striking view opens out on the rt. over the head of the Rhine valley and the glaciers whence it bursts forth. On the rt. of the road rises the gigantic mass of the Moschel-Horn, and on the l. the black peak of the Mittag-Horn overhangs the pass.

This passage over the Alps is said to have been known to the Romans; it was called the Vogelberg down to the beginning of the fifteenth century, when a pious missionary, St. Bernardin of Sienna, preached the gospel through these remote Alpine valleys, and a chapel dedicated to him, on the S. side of the mountain, gave rise to the name which it still retains. It was traversed in March, 1799, by the French army of Lecourbe, at a season when winter still reigns on these elevations, and before the mountain possessed any other road than a miserable mule-path.

The summit of the pass, about 7100 ft. above the sea, and nearly 2000 above the village of Splügen, is partly occupied by a lake called Lago Moesola, the source of the Moesa, along whose margin the road runs. At this point a very substantial but homely inn, or house of refuge, has been erected.

A little way down the S. slope of the mountain the Moesa is crossed by a handsome bridge of a single arch, 110 ft. above the river, named after Victor Emanuel, King of Sardinia, who contributed so largely to the construction of this road. The carriageway is here covered over with a substantial roof, supported on solid buttresses, to protect it from avalanches and whirlwinds of snow, to which this gully is much exposed at times. A few straggling and stunted pines here make their appearance; a little lower down trees 40 or 50 ft. high may be seen clinging to the rock, with barely two feet depth of soil beneath them : their roots scarcely strike downwards at all, but spread far and wide in a horizontal direction, so that, when a tree is thrown down by the wind, roots and soil are peeled off at once, and nothing but bare rock remains below.

The S. face of the mountain is also far more abrupt and precipitous than the N., but the road is so skilfully carried down it, and so gradually, that a postilion, accustomed to it, trots quickly down the whole way, turning sharp round the corners of the zigzags. The traveller beholds the road almost beneath his feet, extending like an uncoiled rope below him, and as he moves backwards and forwards, following its turns, he appears to hover over the valley below, and might fancy himself fastened to the end of a pendulum and balanced in mid-air.

1¼ St. Bernardino — (*Inn :* Post, good)—is a post-house and village, the first and loftiest in the valley of Misocco, consisting of a few houses planted half-way down the descent on a small plain or ledge. There is a mineral spring here, having a temperature of about 40° Fahr. It is probably the highest warm source among the Alps, and annually draws a few invalids to the spot, where tolerable accommodation is afforded in two inns. The passage of the mountain from Hinter-Rhein to St. Bernardin is effected in about 3½ hours.

The descent from this into the lower valley of Misocco (in Germ. Maisox Thal; Ital. Val Mesolsina) is a scene of beauty scarcely surpassed among the Alps.

Near St. Giacomo there are quarries of gypsum; here there is also a fall of the Moesa. It is a continued descent as far as Misocco and the Ponte di Soazza, which is only a few hundred feet higher than Coire, in the valley of the Rhine. This will give some idea of the abruptness of the southern descent from the Alps contrasted with the northern.

1 Misocco—(*Inn:* Post, very dirty) —a village of about 900 inhabitants, called also Cremao.

In the neighbourhood of Misocco the luxuriant growth of the chestnut and walnut, the abundant crops of maize, the presence of the vine and the mulberry, which succeed each other within the space of a few miles, remind the traveller that he is indeed in Italy, and he soon becomes otherwise aware of this change by the altered language, the laziness, and filth of the inhabitants and their miserable habitations. The situation of Misocco is charming; a little way below it, in the middle of the valley, rises up the ruined *Castle of Misocco*, a feudal seat of the powerful Lords of Masox, sold by them, 1482, to the celebrated Milanese general Trivulzio, taken and destroyed by the Gräubündtners, 1526. The valley is here bounded by precipices, over and among whose rocky sides a number of waterfalls dash, assuming the shape of that which in Scotland is called the Mare's Tail. The knoll on which the castle stands seems

formed to command the passage u and down.

A very steep and difficult path ascends the E. side of the valley nearly opposite the castle, and crossing the ridge of the Alps, by the dangerous pass of the *Forcola*, descends at once upon Chiavenna.

Below Soazza the road crosses the Moesa twice, and reaches the bottom of the valley, the descent below this being inconsiderable. On the rt. close to the road, the graceful cascade of Buffalora precipitates itself from the top of a rock. At Lostalla the general legislative assemblies of the men of the valley are held annually.

1¼ Leggia. The post is either here or at Roveredo. At Grono the Val Calanca opens out from the W.

Roveredo—(*Inn:* Post, Il Canone d'Oro)—a village containing nearly 1000 inhabitants, with the ruined castle of Trivulzio in its vicinity. The Prior of Roveredo and 11 old women were burnt for practising witchcraft by Carlo Borromeo, in 1583, at his first visitation of the diocese. The rivers hereabouts are used to float down the timber cut in the forests of the higher transverse valleys.

St. Vittore is the last village in the Canton of the Grisons; below it we enter the Canton Tessin and the Val Levantina, and our road joins that descending from the St. Gothard (Route 34). Between the junction of the two rivers Moesa and Ticino stands *Arbedo*, memorable in history for the severe defeat which the Swiss sustained here from the Milanese, commanded by the celebrated generals Della Pergola and Carmagnola, in 1422. Near the Church of St. Paul, called Chiesa Rossa, from its red colour, 2000 Swiss lie buried under 3 large mounds, still distinguishable. Defeat was at that period so unusual to the Swiss, even from a greatly superior force, that they retired across the Alps abashed and discouraged.

The distant aspect of Bellinzona

surrounded by battlemented walls, which once stretched quite across the valley, and overhung by no less than 3 feudal castles, is exceedingly imposing and picturesque. It looks as though it still commanded (as it once did) the passage of the valley. The luxuriance of vegetation, and the magnificent forms of the mountains around, complete the grandeur of the picture.

1 *Bellinzona* (Germ: Bellenz)— (*Inns :* Aquila d'Oro, tolerable; Cerva, stag; Biscia, serpent: none very good or clean.)

Bellinzona, situated on the l. bank of the Ticino, and containing 1520 inhabitants, is one of the 3 chief towns of the Canton Tessin, and becomes the seat of government alternately with Lugano and Locarno, for 6 years together. It has all the character of an Italian town in its narrow and dirty streets, and in the arcades which run under its houses. It stretches all across the valley to the river, so that the only passage up or down lies through its gates. It is still a place of some commercial importance as an entrepôt for the merchandise of Germany and Italy, and from its situation at the point of union of 4 roads—from the St. Gothard, the Bernardin, from Lugano, and from Locarno on the Lago Maggiore. In ancient times, however, it was of still greater military consequence, as the key of the passage from Lombardy into Germany, and defended as it was by 3 forts and high walls, it must have been a place of great strength. It became the fruitful cause of intrigue, contest, and bloodshed between the crafty Italians and the encroaching Swiss. The latter first obtained possession of it, and of the Val Levantine, by a nominal bargain of 2400 florins paid to the Lord of Masox, and they obtained from the Emperor Sigismond a confirmation of their title. The Duke of Milan, Phillip Maria Visconti, whose ancestors had lost this territory, by no means acquiesced in this transfer, and, seizing a favourable opportunity, surprised the Swiss garrison of Bellinzona by a Milanese force under Della Pergola, and took possession of the town and valley. It was this event which led to the battle of Arbedo, in which the Swiss received so severe a check. They afterwards twice gained possession of Bellinzona and its subject valleys by hard-fighting, "by the help of God and their halberts," as they boastingly proclaimed, first from the Duke of Milan, and next from the French, who, in the reign of Louis XII., obtained temporary possession of these valleys.

From the beginning of the 16th to the end of the 18th century the Swiss maintained uninterrupted possession of Bellinzona, governing its territory, as a state subject to the cantons, with a rule as tyrannic as that of the absolute Dukes of Milan, their predecessors.

The *three picturesque Castles* which still seem to domineer over the town, though partly in ruins, were the residence of the 3 Swiss bailiffs deputed to govern the district, and were occupied by a garrison and armed with some pieces of cannon. The largest, called *Castello Grande*, on an isolated hill to the W. of the town, belonged to canton Uri, and now serves as an arsenal and prison. Of the two castles on the E. the lower one, *Castello di Mezzo*, belonged to canton Schwytz, and the highest of all, *Castello Corbario*, to Unterwalden; they are both unoccupied. The view from Castello Grande is very striking. A long *bridge* is here thrown over the river Ticino, which, however, in summer is shrunk to 3 or 4 of the arches. The banks are guarded against sudden inundations by a strong dyke called Tondo Ripario, constructed by the French under Francis I.

There remains little else to particularise here. The *principal Church*, in the square, is a handsome modern building faced with white marble, and has a pulpit ornamented with historical bas-reliefs. There are several convents here. The *Church of S. Biaggio* (St. Blaize), in the suburb Ravecchia, outside the Lugano gate, is said to be very ancient.

From Bellinzona the traveller has the choice of two roads to Milan: by the Lago Maggiore (Route 91) or by the Lago Lugano (Route 92).

The *steamer* on the Lago Maggiore departs from Magadino, the port of embarkation, 8 miles S. of Bellinzona, about 5 o'clock in the morning in summer, returning from Sesto in the evening.

ROUTE 91.

BELLINZONA TO MAGADINO AND LO-
CARNO, ON THE LAGO MAGGIORE.

	Ital. miles.	Swiss stund.	Eng. m.
To Magadino, 8	=	2¾	=	9¼
To Locarno, 11	=	3¾	=	12¼

The lower part of the valley of the Ticino, between Bellinzona and the lake, is a broad plain, from which the mountains recede to a considerable distance, but still give grandeur to the landscape. The country is highly cultivated, the slopes covered with vineyards, but the bottom becomes marshy lower down, and is therefore unhealthy.

There is a road practicable for carriages on both sides of the Ticino ; that on the l. is the most direct to Magadino.

On quitting Bellinzona, by the Lugano gate the dry bed of a torrent called Dragonata is passed. As its name would imply, it is at times a great scourge ; it carried off in 1768 the Franciscan convent outside the town, and threatens similar injury.

There are many country-houses on the outskirts ; and high upon the slopes of the hills are numerous buildings, now deserted, to which in ancient times the natives of Bellinzona used to resort for safety, when the plague was raging in the town. At Cadenazzo the road to Lugano,

over the Monte Cenere (Route 92.) turns to the E. out of our route.

Magadino. (*Inn:* Hotel Il Vapore, said to be good ; but the situation has the reputation of being unhealthy, owing to the neighbourhood of the marshes of the Ticino and the prevalence of malaria—a sufficient reason to make a traveller cautious in taking up his quarters here for the night. § 12.)

This little village was not long ago a small group of houses ; but it has gained some importance of late, to the prejudice of its neighbour Locarno, as the port of the Lago Maggiore, at whose N. extremity it lies, and as the station of the *steam-boats*.

The *steamer Verbano* sets out in summer from Magadino every morning between 5 and 6, touches at the principal places on the W. shore of the lake, and reaches Sesto Calende about 12. It sets off to return at 1. The fare for the entire voyage is 6 fr., 40 fr. for a landau, and 30 fr. for a calèche.

The road from Bellinzona to Locarno crosses the Ticino by the long bridge completed in 1815, in the place of one carried away by the fearful inundation of 1515, which did so much injury to the whole valley (p. 102). The road runs along the rt. bank. It passes under the Monte Carasso, and commands a good view of the opposite mountains, including the Monte Cenere, and up the valley over the romantic town of Bellinzona to the snowy Alps towering behind it. The low ground through which the now almost stagnant Ticino winds, being very marshy, is not so pleasing a feature, and the exhalations from it are unwholesome. At the bridge of Sementina a torrent, issuing out of a ravine on the rt., forms a pretty waterfall. In 1829 this stream, swelled with sudden rains, desolated the land around its mouth, and carried away the bridge. According to the superstitious notions of the peasantry, the upper part of this wild gorge is haunted by the ghosts of misers, who there do penance after death for their exactions from the poor while living. The latter part of the route, after crossing the torrent Verzasca as it winds along the W. shore of the lake, is splendid beyond description.

3¾ *Locarno* (Germ. Luggarus). *Inns:* Albergo Suizzero; Il Gallo.) This is one of the three capitals of canton Tessin; it has 1700 inhabitants, and is said to have once contained twice as many, but has decayed since the 15th century in population and prosperity. It is beautifully situated on the margin of the lake, on which it has a little port, at the foot of the hill surmounted by the church of Madonna del Sasso, and at the entrance of the converging valleys of Val Verasca, Maggia, Onsernone, and Centovalle, the last a primitive district scarcely ever visited by travellers. The climate, the vegetation, and the sky are all Italian; even the people are Italian in laziness and superstition. The groves of orange and lemon, the tall white steeples on the hill-sides, and the little white chapels peering out from among the trellissed vines, and mirrored in the glassy lake, are all the characteristic features of an Italian landscape, even though, as far as frontier-lines are concerned, we are still in Switzerland. The deposits of the numerous torrents here flowing into the lake have encroached considerably upon it, forming a flat marshy delta, which renders Locarno not altogether healthy.

The principal buildings in the town are the *churches*, and the convents, of the former it has three, besides that of *Madonna del Sasso*, on the height above it, a building well worth visiting, both for the exquisite view it commands over the blue lake, and the entrance of the valley of the Ticino, whose winding course may be traced flashing in the sun, and also because it contains, among the accumulated decorations of painting, gilding, and stucco-work, several valuable and interesting pictures in fresco, by *Bernardino Luini*, enclosed in medallions.

The *market* at Locarno, held once a fortnight, is frequented by the natives of the neighbouring valleys from far and near, and exhibits a singular mixture of costumes.

The traveller will be surprised to hear that in this little paltry town the distinctions of rank are more punctiliously observed than in many of the great European capitals. No less than seven grades or castes are numbered among its inhabitants. At the head stand the signors (nobili); next to them the borghesi, or burghers; below them the cultivators, terrieri, or old landholders: these 3 classes have the right of pasture on the common lands, an almost worthless privilege, owing to the neglect into which they have fallen. Below these, as to privileges, rank the oriondi (settlers from the villages), and the sessini; and the quatrini and mensualisti, foreign settlers.

The decay of the prosperity of the town is traced to the intolerance of its Romish inhabitants, who, instigated by their priests, compelled those among their fellow-citizens who had adopted the reformed faith to emigrate. In March, 1553, 116 persons, including women and children, who had refused to purchase the privilege of remaining by the sacrifice of their religion, were banished by a decree of the Swiss diet, and quitted their homes for ever. With them went industry and prosperity; they settled at Zurich, transferring thither the manufacture of silk, which is now of such vast commercial importance to that city. The day after the sentence of exile had been pronounced the papal nuncio arrived with two inquisitors : he indignantly objected to the mildness of the sentence, and urged the deputies of the diet, under pain of the pope's displeasure, to couple with it confiscation of the goods of the heretics and separation of them from their children, in order that they might be educated as papists. To this demand, however, the deputies did not yield obedience. The doctrines of the Reformation were preached here first by Beccaria, a pious Milanese monk, about 1534: he was soon expelled, and took refuge in the Val Misocco.

The criminal statistics of the district around Locarno show a large amount of crime in proportion to the number of inhabitants. The neighbouring valley of Verzasca is in evil repute for the number of assassinations committed in it. Bonstetten, who travelled through it in 1795, says that the men all wear at their girdle, behind, a knife a foot long, cal'ed *falciuolo*, to kill one another. He states that the average number of law-suits among a population of 17,000 souls was 1000 yearly. Whether this statement were true or not at the time, a great improvement has certainly taken place since ; at present the number of offences in the same district, whose inhabitants have increased to the amount of 3000 souls, shows an average of 100 crimes against person and property yearly. Acts of violence, murder, &c. are, however, still very common, and the people have the reputation of being very litigious.

There is a path up the Centovalli, a secluded and little-visited valley, very winding and narrow, to Domo d'Ossola on the Simplon (Route 59). The path is a bad one.

The *Val Maggia* (Germ. Mayenthal) opens out about 2 miles to the N.W. of Locarno, beyond the narrow pass of the Ponte Brolla. A tolerable cross carriage-road has been carried up it to Cevio, the chief village, and thence to Peccia. It cost the canton nearly 300,000 Swiss fr. The distance from Locarno to Covio is 9 Italian miles ; and thence to Fusio, the highest village, 10½ miles.

LAGO MAGGIORE.

The *steam-boat* from Magadir calls every morning off Locarno, Canobio, Canaro, Intra,the Borromea Islands, Belgirate, Arona, and Sest for passengers both going and returning. It quits Magadino between 5 and 6, in summer, and returns about 7, keeping near the W. shore.

Sailing-boats may always be hired at any of the ports on the lake to make short excursions.

The *Lago Maggiore*, the Lacus Verbanus of the Romans (Germ. Langen See, or Lager See), is about 52 miles (47 Italian = 12 German miles) long and about 9 miles wide at its greatest breadth. Only a small portion, at its N. extremity, which is often called Lago di Locarno, belongs to Switzerland. About 7 miles S. of Locarno, the Austrian frontier occupies the E. shore, and the Sardinian the W. The navigation of the lake is free to the three states which form its margin ; but the Austrians have established a sort of lake police upon its whole extent. The 3 chief rivers by which it is fed, are, the Ticino flowing from the St. Gothard ; the Tresa, which drains the Lago Lugano ; and the Toccia, or Tosa, descending from the Val Formazza, by Domo d'Ossola. The scenery of its upper end is bold and mountainous ; so is the bay of Baveno (to call by that name the W. arm, containing the Borromean Islands, and overhung by the snowy peaks of the Alps) ; but, towards the S. and E., its shores are less lofty, subsiding gradually into the Plain of Lombardy.

The principal places on the W. shore are Ascona, surmounted by a castle ; Brissago, a charming spot, conspicuous with its white houses, and avenue of cypress, leading to the church. Its inhabitants are wealthy and industrious. Terrace rises above terrace against the hill-side ; and the vine, fig, olive, pomegranate, and myrtle, flourish in the open air.

eyond this, the Swiss territory ends. anobbio, situated at the entrance of the Piedmontese valley Canobina, ontains a church designed by Bramante. The two islands off Canero ere, in the fifteenth century, the resort of five robber-brothers, named Mazzarda, who committed depredations all along the shores of the lake. ntra is a very industrious small town, ith several manufactories. A road as been commenced along this shore f the lake, by the Sardinian 'government, to connect Baveno, on the Simplon, with Bellinzona and the St. Gothard.

The places on the E. side of the Lago Maggiore are St. Abbondio Swiss); Macagno (Austrian); Luino, whence a good road runs by Ponte Tresa to Lugano (Route 93.); Porto and Laveno, nearly opposite Intra, whence a carriage-road runs o Varese and the Sacro Monte.

The Borromean Islands and the S. extremity of the lake are described n Route 59.

ROUTE 92.

BELLINZONA TO LUGANO AND COMO BY THE MONTE CENERE.

To Como, 5 posts = 33½ English miles.

To Lugano, 5⅛ Swiss stunden = 16 Italian miles = 17¼ English miles.

Diligences daily to Lugano.

This road turns out of the valley of the Tessin at Cadenazzo (p. 218.), about 4 miles below Bellinzona, and begins to ascend the Monte Cenere, a steep ridge surmounted by means of numerous zigzags. The top may be reached in 2 hours from Bellinzona. This part of the road was formerly infested by robbers, and, not long ago, the night diligence, in crossing it, was accompanied by an armed escort; but, since a guardhouse of carabineers has been established on the summit, there appears to be no longer danger. From the summit, a fine view is obtained over the N. extremity of the Lago Maggiore; but a far more interesting prospect opens out on the opposite descent towards Lugano. In front expands its beautiful lake, backed by mountains; and, on the rt., the Monte Salvadore, with the church on its conical summit, becomes conspicuous. At Rivera, the road falls in with the river Agno, which rises about 12 miles to the E., at the foot of the Monte Camoghè, and follows it through Bironico to Morone, where it turns to the l., and again ascends a slight eminence, at whose foot lies

2½ *Lugano* (Germ. Lauis)—(*Inns:* Albergo Suizzero, Post; Corona.

Lugano, one of the 3 chief towns of the canton, and the largest, most thriving in trade, and most extending in population, contains 4500 inhabitants, and is charmingly situated on the margin of the Lago Lugano. It deserves to be visited, were it only on account of the beauty of its site, and to explore the scenery of its lake. The hills and mountains around abound in all the productions of the luxurious vegetation of Italy; and numerous villas are scattered along its slopes and margin, embowered among vineyards and gardens, and backed by the dark foliage of the umbrageous walnut. The town contains 3 monasteries and 3 nunneries. The principal *Church*, or *Cathedral of San Lorenzo*, is planted on an eminence, commanding a fine view. The portal is richly adorned with sculpture, and the façade is said to be from a design of *Bramante*. A small chapel, attached to the sequestrated convent of S. Francisco, built by Bramante, has been pulled down. Near the cathedral is a curious bonehouse.

Santa Maria degli Angioli, founded in 1499, contains remarkable paintings by *Bernhardino Luini*; a Crucifixion, and a Madonna, over a doorway, are both works of first-rate excellence; a Last Supper, in the refectory of the convent, is of inferior merit.

The *Hospital* was erected previous to the year 1200. There is a *Theatre* here of recent construction.

There are considerable manufactures of silk in Lugano ; and the town further derives activity and prosperity from being the entrepôt of goods shipped across the lake from Italy, to be transported over the Alps, and *vice versâ.* A large fair is held here on the 9th October. No less than 3 *newspapers* are published here, chiefly advocating very democratic principles, and not unfrequently attacking the neighbouring monarchical governments of Austria and Sardinia. There are several printing establishments, which send forth cheap editions of works prohibited in Italy.

Environs.—Monte Caprino.—The mountain opposite Lugano is penetrated by [natural grottoes, which have been converted into cellars, called *Cantine.* Numerous small houses are built over them ; so that at a distance they have the appearance of a village. These are much resorted to in summer by the towns-people on account of their coolness.

A further inducement to visit this spot is the exquisite view that it commands.

The view from the top of *Monte Salvadore* is of no common beauty and extent, even though the mountain is only 1980 ft. above the lake. This mountain forms a promontory, washed on two sides by the Lake of Lugano. The view extends over numerous other lakes, and is bounded by the snowy chain of the Alps. Monte Rosa is seen in all its grandeur from hence ; and, according to some, the white needles of the Dom of Milan are visible when the atmosphere is very clear. Keller has engraved the panorama from this mountain. On the summit is a little pilgrimage chapel: the distance is less than 7 miles, and it may be reached on horseback or on foot.

" Monte Salvadore stands amid the intricacies of the Lake of Lugano, and is, from a hundred points of view, its principal ornament—rising to height of 2000 ft., and, on one side nearly perpendicular. The ascent is toilsome, but the traveller who performs it will be amply rewarded. Splendid fertility, rich woods, and dazzling waters, seclusion and confinement of view contrasted with sea-like extent of plain, fading into the sky—and this again, in an opposite quarter, with an horizon of the loftiest and boldest Alps — unite in composing a prospect more diversified by magnificence, beauty, and sublimity, than perhaps any other point in Europe, of so inconsiderable an elevation, commands."—*Wordsworth.*

Lugano is distant only 15 miles from Como and 12 from Varese : the Lago di Como, on the E., may be reached in 3 hours (Route 93.), and the Lago Maggiore in less. A good carriage-road runs to Luino, on its E. shore, described together with the Lago Lugano in Route 93.

The road to Como runs by the water-side, under the Monte Salvadore. The limestone rocks, composing its base, exhibit a singular phenomenon, highly interesting to the geologist. About 10 minutes' walk beyond the chapel of San Martino, a compact, smoke-grey limestone appears by the road-side, in beds about a foot thick. " The further we advance, the more we find the beds of limestone traversed by small veins, lined with rhombs of dolomite. As we advance, the rock appears divided by fissures, the stratification ceases to be distinct, and, where the face of the mountain becomes perpendicular, it is found to be formed entirely of dolomite, which becomes gradually purer and more white, until a little way from Melide, where it is succeeded by a dark augite porphyry." The celebrated geologist Von Buch considers that the gas discharged from this latter igneous rock, at the time when the

...ountain was upheaved by volcanic ...rces from below, has penetrated the ...ssures of the limestone, and changed ...e part of it nearest to the porphyry ...nto dolomite. The change in colour ...nd substance, from a grey limestone ...nto a white crystalline marble, like ...af-sugar, may be easily traced in ...s gradual transition by the road-...ide.

At Melide, a promontory projects ...nto the lake, from the point of which ... ferry-boat conveys passengers and ...arriages across it, in a few minutes, ...o Bissone, on the opposite side. ...Melide is the birthplace of Fontana, ...he architect who, in 1586, trans-...orted the Egyptian obelisk from ...he Colisseum at Rome, and erected ...t on the square in front of the Va-...ican.

After a delightful ride along the ...hore of the lake, the road quits it at ...Capolago, and soon reaches Men-...drisio, which, though a small town ...of 1700 inhabitants, contains 3 con-...vents. It is supposed to be the cradle ...of the once-powerful Milanese family ...Della Torre, or Torriani. The famous ...*tower*, from which they derived their ...name, was destroyed in the civil wars ...of the fourteenth century.

The inhabitants keep their wine in ...caves in the mountains, which form ...capital cellars. The Austrian cus-...tom-house and police-office is reached ...a little beyond Chiasso, and within ...2 miles of

2½ COMO.   See Hand-book for Italy.

ROUTE 93.

LUINO, ON THE LAGO MAGGIORE, TO MENAGGIO ON THE LAGO DI COMO, ACROSS THE LAGO LUGANO.

Luino, a small village, on the E. shore of the Lago Maggiore, has a tolerable inn. A good carriage-road leads hence to Lugano, a drive of 3 or 4 hours, ascending directly from the margin of the lake the steep

heights behind Luino, which com-mand a fine prospect. It then follows the rt. bank of the Tresa, upwards, at a considerable height above that river, through a beautiful valley, crossing the Swiss frontier about 3 miles from Luino, and 9 from Lu-gano.

Ponte Tresa, a village of 365 in-habitants, is named from an old wooden bridge which leads across the river into Lombardy. At the fur-ther end stands the Austrian toll and custom-house ; and, on this side, a Swiss toll is exacted. A great pro-portion of the cattle, with which Lombardy is supplied by Switzerland, pass over it. The village is prettily situated on a bay of the Lago Lu-gano, so completely land-locked as to seem a distinct lake.

Another of the winding reaches of the lake stretches N. about half a mile on the E. of our road, as far as

Agno, a village of 600 inhabitants, placed at the spot where the Agno, or Bedagio, empties itself into the lake.

One of the prettiest scenes on this very picturesque road is that pre-sented by the small lake of Muzzano, which lies on the rt. of the road to

Lugano (see p. 221.).

The *Lago Lugano* (called also *Ce-risio*) is exceedingly irregular in shape, making several very acute bends, so that the conspicuous moun-tain Salvadore stands on a pro-montory, washed on two sides by its waters: its greatest length is about 20 miles. Its E. and W., and one of its S. arms, terminate in the Austrian territory, and travellers must have an Austrian visa on their passports, to enable them to land there.

The scenery of this lake is exceed-ingly beautiful, and has a character distinct from that of its two neigh-bours Como and Maggiore, in being more gloomy, rugged, and unculti-vated. It at the same time presents great variety ; near Lugano its shores are as smiling, as frequently speckled with white villas and churches, and as richly fringed with vines, fig-trees, and walnut groves, as the more garden-like borders of the Lago di Como ; but, in penetrating its E. bay from Lugano to Porlezza, the mountains gradually assume a more wild and precipitous outline, and the darker foliage of the pine forests furnishes the predominating colour.

Boats for passengers and carriages may be hired at Lugano for Porlezza; it takes 3 hours to row thither, and the charge for a boat with two rowers is 8 fr. There is no road along this part of the lake.

Porlezza lies within the Lombard frontier, and is the station of the Austrian police and dóganiers. Chars may be hired here to go to Menaggio ; the road is bad and only prac-ticable for light vehicles. It tra-verses a very pretty valley, passing on the rt. the little lakes of Piano and Bene. It is a walk of about 2 hours to reach

Menaggio, an unimportant village on the W. shore of the Lago di Como. Instead of stopping here the travel-ler had better either proceed a little way down the lake to Cadenabbia, or cross it to the promontory of Bel-lagio, or to the opposite shore at Varenna, at all which places there are good inns. Near Tremezzo, a little way beyond Cadenabbia, is the *Villa Sommariva*, among terraces bordered with myrtle hedges and perfumed with citron groves. This palace contains several remarkable works of art—paintings by *Gauden-zio Ferrari, B. Luini*, and others ; also the Palamedes of *Canova*, and, above all, *Thorwaldsen*'s grand bas-relief the Triumph of Alexander, executed for Napoleon when Emperor, and de-signed by him to decorate the Sim-plon arch at Milan.

Bellagio is a charming spot, com-manding perhaps the most splendid views to be met with on any of the Italian lakes. The prospect is double, extending upwards, as well as down towards Como and Lucco. The best

points for enjoying it are the terrace and delightful gardens of the *Villa Serbelloni.*

The *Villa Melzi*, another palace in this neighbourhood, is a charming mansion, elegantly fitted up, chiefly visited on account of its beautiful flower-garden.

Varenna (where the Post-house is most agreeable quarters) may be visited on account of the remarkable galleries near it excavated in the solid rock, to allow that magnificent work of art, the *Road to the Stelvio Pass* to traverse the E. shore of the lake.

The Comasques emigrate all over Europe, as venders of Plaster of Paris figures, barometers, and looking-glasses.

A *steam-boat* starts every morning at 8 from Como, and ascends the lake to Domaso, returning the same evening, and touching at all the prin-cipal places on its shores. The fare is 5 fr. 22 c.

The steamer returns to Como about 5, corresponding, both in the hour of arrival and departure, with the omnibus (called Velocifera), which runs to and from Milan daily.

They who wish to explore the beau-ties of the lake at their leisure had better take a row-boat.

There cannot be a more delightful voyage than that along the S.W. arm of the lake to Como ; the shores are literally speckled with villages and with white villas, the summer resort of the Milanese nobility, dur-ing the season of the Villeggiatura.

The places most worth mention-ing on the E. shore are Nesso, back-ed by a dark wooded gully, out of which dashes a cascade, and near it the Villa Lenno, supposed to stand on the site of *Pliny's Villa*, which, from its sombre situation, he called *Tragædia*; an opinion confirmed by the discovery of broken columns, &c., in the lake. Beyond Lenno (Lem-nos), in a retired bay, is the Villa Pliniana, a square melancholy build-ing, so called, not because Pliny lived here, but because an intermit-

ent spring, rising behind it, is asserted to be the one minutely described
by him. Beyond the wooded promontory Torno is Blevio, near which
a monument is erected to Mr. Lake,
who was drowned here in 1833.
Nearer to Como is the Villa Pasta,
the residence of the celebrated singer.

On the opposite, or W. shore, beginning from Cadenabbia, we may
mention Balbiano, on a projecting
promontory, the Isola Concacina,
Urio, the Villa Passalacqua, with its
terraced gardens ; and near Cernob-
bia, the *Villa d'Este,* so named by
Caroline of Brunswick, Princess of
Wales, who resided here some time,
also the Villa Odescalchi, the largest
on the lake.

The Lake of Como, called by the
ancients *Lacus Larius* (te Lari Max-
ume !—*Virg.*), is about 40 miles
long, from N. to S. Its S. extremity
is divided into two branches by the
promontory of Bellagio ; at the bottom of one of these bays lies *Como*
(Comum), the birth-place of Pliny
and Volta ; and, at the extremity of
the other, on the E., *Lecco.* The
chief feeder of the lake is the Adda,
which enters it at the N., and flows
out at Lecco. The bay of Como has
no outlet, so that its waters must also
find their way out by the Adda.
Taken altogether, it perhaps surpasses in beauty of scenery, and in
the richness of its almost tropical
vegetation, every other lake in Italy.
It enjoys a classical reputation, as
the residence of the two Plinys, and
the scene of the scientific researches
of the elder Pliny, the naturalist.
Claudian describes the voyage up
the lake in the following elegant
lines :—

" Protinus umbrosâ quâ vestit littus olivâ
Larius, et dulci mentitur Nerea fluctu,
Parvâ puppe lacum prætervolat, Ocius inde
Scandit inaccessos brumali sidere montes."

SECTION II.

THE ALPS OF PIEDMONT AND SAVOY.

PRELIMINARY INFORMATION.

As the traveller in Switzerland, who has fully enjoyed the scenery of the Alps, and inhaled fresh spirit with the mountain air, must desire information upon such routes as are often or occasionally visited across the great chain of the Alps south of the Simplon, and which would lie within his summer's excursion, the following information upon such passes as debouche into the course of the route of the Simplon, furnished by a traveller who has himself examined all upon which he has written, will be found useful to those who are disposed, not only to examine the lateral valleys which fall into the Route of the Simplon, but such other alpine passes and retreats as the traverses of the great chain present, from Savoy and France into Piedmont — even to the Maritime Alps and the Mediterranean.

Piedmont has on its northern, western, and south-western sides, a clearly-defined frontier in the ridge of the great chain of the Alps. From the valley of the Toccia, which lies within its frontier, to the Col de Ferret, near Mont Blanc, the Pennine Alps divide it from Switzerland; from the Col de Ferret to Mont Tabor, the Graian Alps separate Piedmont from Savoy; from Mont Tabor to the Col d'Argentière, at the head of the valley of the Stura, the Cottian Alps separate it from France; and from the Argentière to the source of the Tanaro in the Monte Cassino, the Maritime Alps divide the southern Piedmont from the county of Nice. East of the Monte Cassino the great alpine chain passes insensibly into the Apennines.

The eastern boundary — the frontier of the Milanese and the States of Parma — is not within the object of this section, which is to furnish to travellers useful information for excursions in the Alps of Piedmont.

On the side of Italy, the Alps offer a striking difference in their appearance to that presented in the approaches from Switzerland, Savoy, or France. From these the intervention of secondary ranges, and the long valleys preclude any great extent of the chain from being seen at the same time; but from the plains of Piedmont, even as near as Turin — not 30 miles in a direct line from the nearest point in the crest of the chain — a range of the central peaks and passes, extending through 200 miles, is clearly seen.

A day's journey is sufficient, from almost every accessible part of the crest of the Alps, for a descent into the plains of Piedmont; whilst on the western side of the chain, two or three days of approach from the plains, in deep valleys amidst the mountains, are requisite for its attainment.

The rambler in the Piedmontese Alps will generally find *accommodation* equal to any in Switzerland, except perhaps in the beaten routes of the Bernese Alps, and sight-seeing excursions, as on the Righi. Crowds would find provisions short and want of room, but parties of two or three would fare well, be received with civility without obsequiousness, and meet with less extortionate hosts than in Switzerland. Fleecing the traveller has not yet grown into a system as among that *independent* people; and, generally, a traveller may devote more time, and visit more sublime scenes, at a less expense, and with nearly as much facility as in Switzerland. Piedmont only requires to be more known to turn the current of ramblers, and induce them to spend a part at least of their time and money among its romantic valleys and passes.

The *roads* skirting the Alps, and the approaches to them from the plains of Piedmont, are generally excellent. Wherever there is intercourse there is a good road adapted to the wants of the inhabitants : if fit for volantins or chars, these may always be obtained at moderate charges, usually 12 francs a day. *Mules* may readily be obtained in all mountain routes accessible to them, at charges varying from 4 to 6 francs a day ; and *guides* at 4 or 5 francs a day may be had in every alpine village of Piedmont. It is desirable to get men known to, or recommended by, the innkeepers or the Curès of their villages ; for they are so fond of the employment, that few scruple to avow their acquaintance with passes and places of which they really know nothing : their only use then to the traveller is to bear his luggage, and talk Piedmontese, a jargon which few travellers are acquainted with. In Piedmont French and Italian are often unknown ; among those, however, who act as guides, French is generally spoken, especially in those valleys on the frontiers of Savoy and France.

If mules, horses, or a char be taken across the frontier, a *boleta*, or permission to pass the douane, is necessary ; here the animal is registered, the course of the traveller stated, and money for the horse deposited as a duty upon the *entrée*, which is returned to the owner when he leaves the place on the frontier, indicated in the boleta, to return to his own country.

As there is much smuggling on the frontier of France, the traveller is often subjected to vexatious delay, but time will always be gained by submitting to it. The French can rarely be bribed — the Piedmontese easily — to facilitate the passage from one country to another.

It is almost unnecessary to advise a traveller not to sleep in the plains, if he can reach the mountains. His own love of that

"Health in the breeze and freshness in the gale,"

which is so exciting and invigorating in the mountains, he would seek for the pleasure and spirit of breathing it; but the suggestion is offered to induce young travellers to avoid sleeping near the rice grounds of Piedmont, or near the ponds, where in the summer the Piedmontese steep their hemp: these are deleterious, and may produce fever — fatal to the continuance and enjoyment of an alpine journey.

The *wines* of Piedmont are generally wholesome, often fine, nnd sometime of great celebrity; and there is scarcely a hut in a village on the mountain where *grisane* — a fine sort of biscuit, long, like pipes, and made of excellen flour, — cannot be obtained. The traveller should never fail to supply hi pockets with some of this, broken to convenient lengths; this, with a quaf from a fresh cold spring, having a dash of Kirschenwasser in it, will bear him, if taken at his intervals of rest, through a long day's journey.

The *money* of Piedmont is the same as of France; *i. e.*, of the same quality, denomination, and value.

The *measures of distance* are very difficult to understand. The mile of Italy, 60 to a degree, is sometimes meant; but more frequently the mile of Piedmont, 40 to a degree: the difference is enough to add a weary length to a day's journey, when the mile is nearly double that of the mile of England. The French league of 25 to a degree is a common measure by which they estimate distances; but all these are vague as applied to mountain rambles, and it is best to estimate distance by trial. There can be no mistake where from point to point is stated as so many hours distant; and what has been accomplished in a day or six hours by one traveller, may be safely recommended as the time required for another.

Pedestrian Tours of 6 Weeks or 2 Months chiefly in the Alps of Savoy and Piedmont.

** Carriage Road. * Char Road. † Mule Road. § Footpath. — All names following the marks indicated are the same as the last.

** Geneva to Salenches, or St. Martin. (115.)
* Chamouny.
† Tête Noire to Trient. (116.)
Col de Balme to Chamouny. (117.)
§ Breven.
§ Montanvert, le Jardin.
† Chamouny to Cormayeur, by the Col de Vosa, Col de Bonhomme, and the Col de la Seigne. (118.)
** Cormayeur to Aosta. (107.)

* St. Remy. (108.)
† Hospice of the Great St. Bernard.
Liddes.
* Martigny. (*see* Switzerland, Route 59.)
** Visp in Valais.
† Pass of the Mont Cervin. (106.)
Chatillon, Val d'Aosta.
Col de Jon. (104.)
Brussone.
Col de Ranzola.

Gressoney.
Col de Val d'Obbia.
Riva.
Varallo, Val Sesia. (101.)
Rocco. (102.)
Col de Colma.
Pella — Lake of Orta, boat to.
Omegna.
* Vogogna. (59. and 105.)
* Macugnaga — Monte Rosa.
§ Col de Moro.
Saas.
† Visp, in Valais.
* Pass of the Simplon. (59)
Arona — Lago Maggiore.
Borgomaniera. (101.)
Biella. (103.)
Ivrea. (107.)
Aosta.

† Cogne.
Pont — Val d'Orca.
Ceresol.
§ Col de Galèse, and return to Chapis.
† Col de Croix de Nivolet.
Val Savaranche.
Villeneuve — Val d'Aosta.
* St. Didier.
† The Crammont, the Belvidere and Pass of the Little St. Bernard. (114.)
* Bourg St. Maurice.
Moutiers Tarentaise. (122.)
** L'Hôpital Conflans.
Ugine.
Faverges.
Annecy.
Geneva. (53)

Six Weeks' Excursion.   If extended to 2 Months, start from

* Moutiers Tarentaise. (123.)
Baths of Brida.
† Pralorgnan.
Col de Vanoise.
Lanslebourg. (127.)
** Pass of the Mont Cenis.
Susa.
† Cesanne. (131.)
† Col de Sestrieres.
* Pragelas — Val Clusone.
Perouse.
† Val Germanasca. Protestant valley. (132.)
Balsille.
Col de la Fontaines.
Pralis.
Col Julian.
Bobbio.

* La Tour.
† Val Angrona.
Rora
** Lucerne.
Barge.
Peysanne. (133.)
† Crussoles.
§ Pass of the Monte Viso.
† Abries.
Coombe de Ouiras.
* Embrun.
** Gap.
Grenoble.
Chamberry.
Aix.
Annecy.
Geneva.

ROUTE 101.

ARONA ON THE LAGO MAGGIORE TO
VARALLO IN THE VAL SESIA.

An excellent carriage road leads in less than two hours from Arona (Route 59) to Borgomaniera, a large well-built town in the direct road to Vercelli and Turin, from Arona. From Borgomaniera a good carriage road lies through the village of Gozzano to Buccione, a village at the head of the lake of Orta (anciently the Lacus Cusius), which may be reached in an hour from Borgomaniera. The scenery on the road, especially the approach to the lake of Orta, where this beautiful lake is seen backed by Monte Rosa, is scarcely rivalled by any lake and mountain scene, from one end of the Alps to the other.   At Buccione boats may be had to take carriages to Omegna at the lower end of the lake, distant 9 miles, and thence to Gravedona in the route of the Simplon, beyond the Lago Maggiore.

From Borgomaniera there is an excellent road to the little town of Romagnano on the Sesia, where the inn is good.   From Romagnano the road up the course of the Sesia is singularly beautiful ; the mountains as they are approached offering richly wooded slopes, and the masses are relieved by castles, churches, and oratories.   The vegetation is most luxuriant ; several villages are passed.

The principal place before arriving at Varallo is Borgo Sesia ; here the valley becomes narrower, and the road offers some striking scenes, though the range of view is more limited in the narrow parts of the Val Sesia.   It opens again in the neighbourhood of *Varallo*, where the situation of this town, and the sanctuary on its celebrated Sacro Monte — *La Nuova Gerusalemme nel Sacro Monte di Varallo*, as the guide-book calls this extraordinary place of pilgrimage — form singular and interesting scenes.   The Grand Falcone is an excellent inn, and the best in a place where many are required to provide for the bodily wants of the spiritual visitors to the Sacro Monte, who, especially on the Festas of the Church, crowd here as devotees.

Varallo, from every point of view, is highly picturesque, but it is so in a striking degree when seen from the bridge across the Sesia, which is very lofty and narrow, having three arches. From the dry bed of the river below the bridge; the Sacro Monte seen through its arches, the old houses which overhang the torrent, and the richly wooded slopes of the mountains which descend to the Val Sesia, form

a tableau that few sketchers fail to possess.

The *Sacro Monte* is, however, the great object of attraction and pilgrimage.   It rises immediately above the town by a paved path, which winds up the side of the hill, and offers from every turn the most picturesque and beautiful scenes.   Just before the summit is attained, the visitor passes a chapel and crucifix, the *ex voto* of a pious German serjeant-major, as duly announced by an inscription, which informs the visitor that, in honour of God and the Virgin Mary, John Pschel raised this chapel.

A troop of vagabonds, always ready to serve the traveller, offer themselves as guides ; and to facilitate the visit to this extraordinary place, one is necessary, to point out all the chapels or oratories in the order of their numbers, an affair of research by no means easy ; for though the spot of ground which they occupy is small, it seems, from its varied surface, and its labyrinth-like arrangement, to be very extensive.

This remarkable place has fifty chapels, or oratories upon it, besides the great church, fountains, &c. These oratories contain groups of figures modelled in terra-cotta, painted and clothed, placed and composed on the floors.   They chiefly represent some of the principal events in the history of Christ, in the order of their occurrence.   These places are never entered ; they are merely frames or cases for the subjects grouped within them, which, seen from 2 or 3 peepholes in front, like those in rareeshows, excite the devotion of the faithful, and the disgust, except in a few instances where they exhibit skill as works of art, of the merely curious. Externally, these oratories are rich in the architectural display of façades, porticos, domes, &c: the figures within are the size of life.

The subjects are in the order of the numbers on the chapels.

1. The Fall of Man.

2. The Annunciation.
3. The Visitation.
4. The Angel announcing to Joseph the Miraculous Conception.
5. The Star of the East.
6. The Nativity.
7. Joseph and Mary adoring Christ.
8. The Presentation in the Temple.
9. The Angel advising Joseph to Fly into Egypt.
10. The Flight.
11. The Murder of the Innocents.
12. The Baptism in the Jordan.
13. The Temptation.
14. Christ and the Woman of Samaria.
15. Christ Curing the Paralytic.
16. Christ Raising the Widow's Son.
17. The Transfiguration.
18. The Raising of Lazarus.
19. The Entrance into Jerusalem.
20. The Last Supper.
21. Christ in the Garden.
22. Christ finds his Disciples Sleeping.
23. Christ Betrayed by Judas.
24. Christ in the House of Anna.
25. Christ in the Hands of Caiaphas.
26. The Repentance of St. Peter.
27. Christ in the House of Pilate.
28. Christ in the House of Herod.
29. Christ Reconducted to Pilate.
30. The Flagellation.
31. Christ Crowned with Thorns.
32. Christ again Conducted to Pilate.
33. Christ Shown to the People.
34. Pilate Washing his Hands.
35. Christ Sentenced to Death.
36. Christ Bearing the Cross.
37. Christ Nailed to the Cross.
38. The Crucifixion.
39. Christ taken down from the Cross.
40. The Pieta — the Women around the Body of Christ.
41. The Body wrapped in Linen.
42. San Francesco.
43. Christ Lying in the Sepulchre.
44. Saint Anna.
45. An Angel announcing to the Virgin Mary her Transition to Heaven.
46. The Sepulchre of the Virgin Mary.

In the first of these, representing the Fall of Man, Adam and Eve are seen amidst animals of all sorts and sizes, from the elephant to the rabbit. In the second, the series which refer to Christ, commences with the Annunciation. One of the large compositions, representing the Murder of the Innocents, No. 11., contains above 60 figures, the size of life, besides the painted groups on the walls; so arranged as to assist the composition. All the walls are thus painted, and many of the pictures are masterly productions, not unworthy of the reputation of Pelegrini Tibaldi, whose name is found in the list of those who were employed upon the works of the Sacro Monte di Varallo; together with that of Gaudenzio Ferrari, a pupil and companion of Raphael, Fiammingho, the famous sculptor of children, and many other artists of eminence, as painters, sculptors, and architects. The valleys of the Novarais, of which Val Sesia is the principal, are remarkable for the number of painters they have produced, and the names of many are preserved here as having proudly contributed to the embellishment of this singular sanctuary in their own country.

The subject of the Transfiguration is represented upon an enormous scale; the group in the foreground contains the demoniac boy; on the mountain, an immense modelled mass, are the three disciples, above them Christ, with Moses and Elias; over these, painted on the walls and ceiling of the dome, are the host of heaven; and above all, the Almighty. This vast composition occupies the highest and largest of these structures; and the height of the whole composition, modelled and painted, is nearly 100 feet.

Much effect is produced by the appropriate situation of some of the subjects. The access to the place where Christ is laid in the sepulchre is by a vault, where little light is admitted; and as it is difficult on entering from the open day to distinguish at first any object, the effect is very imposing.

Many of the figures are clothed in real drapery, and some have real hair, which appears very grotesque; yet the character and expression of the heads is, in many, finely modelled. There is in the subject of the Visitation the head of a female strikingly fine. The executioners conducting to Calvary, or otherwise employed in inflicting suffering on Christ, are, to increase the disgust for their characters, modelled with goîtres appended to their throats — a proof that these are not considered beauties here, in spite of the traveller's tale. The models are painted, but no offence to taste in their class of art arises from this, because, as the subjects can only be seen through peep-holes in front of the *prie-dieus* of the oratories, and not in passing from one of these to another, as much illusion is produced in seeing them as in observing a picture.

Among the objects of religious reverence here is a flight of steps, called the Scala Santa, recommended to the especial devotion of the faithful, who are informed by an inscription on a tablet at the foot of these stairs, that they have been built in *exact imitation* of the Scala Santa, at St. John Lateran, in Rome. Some of the numerous devotees and pilgrims may always be seen crawling to heaven up these stairs, encouraged by a concession of plenary indulgence granted by Pope Clement XII. to all who would climb these eight and twenty steps on their hands and knees, say an *Ave*, a *Pater*, and a *Gloria* on each step, and kiss each step devoutly!

This extraordinary place originated in the piety of the *blessed* (*i. e.* half saint) Bernardino Caimo, a noble Milanese, who obtained in 1486, from pope Innocent VIII., a faculty to found this sanctuary. Only 3 or 4 chapels were built in the time of the founder, but so great did its reputation for sanctity soon become, that princes and rich devotees contributed

to its accomplishment, to the exter now observed. St. Carlo Borome twice visited it, in 1578 and 1584 and the pallet *bedstead* upon whic this patron saint of Milan died, i preserved here as a holy relic for th adoration of the faithful.

The church is a handsome struc ture, and the cloisters, where th priests reside, are in a beautiful situ ation, commanding views of Varall and the Val Sesia below the town. A the entrance to the immediate site o the Oratories, the priests have kindly established booths or shops for th sale of *corone*, i. e. crucifixes, madon nas, beads, &c., which have acquired sanctity, and the power, *in some cases* of working miracles, by havin touched the blessed bed of the holy St. Carlo, or other miracle-working relics possessed by the fraternity of th Nuovo Gerusalemme. The body is however, provided for as well as the soul; and there are two booths within the sacred precincts for the sale of liquors, where the devotees may be generally seen preparing themselves for, or refreshing themselves after, the plenary indulgence at the Scala Santa, by plenary indulgence in *aqua vita*.

It is extraordinary that a place so remarkable, in a country so beautiful, should be so little known to English explorers of the picturesque: by them the Val Sesia and its lateral valleys of the Mastellone, and the Sermenta — the former leading by Fobello, the latter by Carcoforo, to Banio in the Val Anzasca — are rarely visited.

No valleys in the Alps surpass these for the grandeur and beauty of the scenes which they present; none are more easy of access to Alpine tourists; a finer race of inhabitants is nowhere to be found, except perhaps in the neighbouring valley of Anzasca. The cantons of Switzerland do not offer greater varieties of costume, than are to be found in the different transversal valleys of the Sesia. And Varallo is far enough in the heart of the country o be made head-quarters, whilst researches are to be made in its neighbourhoood; and not an unimportant part of these agrèmens, is the certainty of finding good quarters at the Gran Falcone, the chief albergo at Varallo, after the wanderings of a day or two in the mountains and valleys in its vicinity.

ROUTE 102.

BAVENO (Route 59.) TO VARALLO BY THE LAKE OF ORTA AND THE COL DE COLMA.

To those who would make an excursion to Varallo, from Baveno and the Boromean Isles, a more beautiful route than that by Borgomaniera and the Val Sesia offers itself. Immediately above Baveno rises the mountain ridge, which divides the Lago Maggiore from the Lago d'Orta, and a mule path leads across it to the town of Orta. The views of the Italian lakes, the vast extent of the plains, and the glorious boundary of the Alps, apparently in close proximity, presented in this short transit, is scarcely, if at all, surpassed by the views from the Righi. On the ascent, the Lago Maggiore in all its length lies spread out, from Baveno to Magadino, and the view in this direction is only bounded by the Lepontian and Rhetian Alps. Towards the little lakes around Varese, and to the plains of Lombardy, the view is boundless. Afer crossing the ridge, the Alps, and Monte Rosa in all her magnificence, burst upon the observer; and beneath him lies, in the repose of its deep locality, the beautiful lake of Orta, offering a thousand picturesque sites, yet scarcely known to the traveller, though it is within 2 hours of the route of the Simplon, a course followed by crowds of pleasure-loving ramblers, who seek their highest enjoyment in scenes like these, yet pass unwittingly the loveliest.

Those who do not choose to go by the mountain to Orta, may visit it in a char by an excellent road; that, at Gravellona, a short distance from Baveno, turns up the valley of Strona, into which flows the Negolia, the river that carries off the waters of the lake of Orta, which issue from it at Omegna. The Negolia, after its confluence with the Strona, rushes across the route of the Simplon, and falls into the Toccia, near Cossegno.

The route from Baveno to Orta by the mountain is the shortest, but it occupies more time than the drive, which may be made by Omegna in 3 hours.

At Omegna a boat may be taken to go to *Orta*, a town delightfully situated on the borders of the lake, where there is a good inn recommended by moderate charges. The facilities in the neighbouring mountains and forests for shooting, and on the lake for fishing, offer most agreeable inducements for a short summer residence in this cool and delicious retirement. Yet this spot so delightful is scarcely known; the traveller into Italy gallops along the shores of the Lago Maggiore, unconscious that a day or two, devoted to visiting the Lake of Orta, and Varallo, would be remembered as the pleasantest he had ever spent.

Besides the rambles amidst the beautiful scenes around the lake, the bathing, boating, and fishing on it; to the list of the recommendations of Orta, as a place of short sojourn, may be added, that it is within one day's ride or drive of Milan, Turin, Como, Bellinzona, Varallo, Monte-Rosa, by the Val Sesia, or the Val Anzasca, and of the summit of the Simplon.

It was at one time contemplated, to continue the great route of the Simplon along the shores of the lake of Orta; this was the plan of General Chasseloup, but the difference of level between the lakes Maggiore and Orta, the latter being considerably higher, induced the adoption of the present line. Such a road is still, however, contemplated by the Sardinian government, as a decoy from the Simplon-route, to Turin, of which, numerous travellers would avail themselves, for the sake of the beautiful scenes they would enjoy in skirting the mountains of Piedmont in its course. It is by no means a difficult journey to make even now. A good road leads to Omegna, where a boat may be taken for Buccione at the upper end of the lake, 9 miles distant; here there is a good inn; post-horses may be obtained, and the journey continued to Borgomaniera. To go this way from Baveno to Omegna, to visit Orta, the Isola Giulio, and other objects and places on the lake, would not occupy more than 7 or 8 hours; and from Borgomaniera to Turin, is only a long day's drive.

The Isola di San Giulio is an object of singular beauty in the lake; it lies between Orta and Pella. The church and town of San Giulio surmount a rock that rises out of the deep lake; the bright buildings on it, contrast with the blue waters with a fairy-like effect. The church has high antiquity; it was built on a spot rendered sacred by the retreat of San Giulio, in the 4th century; here his ashes are preserved in a subterranean vault; and the vertebra of a monstrous serpent, said to have been destroyed by the saint, is shown as a relic; how this relic of a whale was brought to such a retired spot it is difficult to conjecture, but it serves for the tradition. The church is rich in the materials of its structure; some columns of porphyry, a mosaic pavement, and bas-reliefs. There are vestiges on the island of ancient fortifications, used when Guilla, the wife of Berenger, the second king of Lombardy, took refuge here in 962, and defended it resolutely against Otho the First, emperor of Germany, who had invaded Italy, and deposed her husband. Otho restored the island to the bishops of Novara, who had long held it before it was seized by Berenger. The island gave a title

to a dukedom as early as 590, when Minulfo, duke of San Giulio, held it; he favoured the descent of the Franks by the Saint Gothard, for which treachery he lost his head, by order of Astolpho, king of the Lombards.

Behind the town of Orta a hill rises on which there is a sanctuary, dedicated to Saint Francis of Assise: over it are distributed 22 chapels or oratories, like those of Varallo. Some are elegant in their architecture; and they contain, as at Varallo, groups in terra cotta. The hill is laid out like a beautiful garden, a character which peculiarly belongs to the mountain slopes which surround this lake, and whence probably its name is derived. The views from the hill of the sanctuary are of singular beauty, comprising the lake, the proximate mountains covered with wood, villages which speckle the shores of the lake and the sides of the hills, and the whole surmounted by the Alps.

At Pella, the village on the shore near to the Isola Giulio, mules may be had for crossing the mountain of Colma to Varallo; and the ride is one of great interest, from the beautiful sites and views which it offers. A steep path leads up the mountain side to Arola, amidst the richest vegetation; vines, figs, gourds, and fruit trees, make the course a vast garden. Magnificent forest trees offer their shade, and the road in some places passes amidst precipices of granite in a state of decomposition, which offers an interesting study to the geologist; here, many of the specimens sold at Baveno are obtained. Above these granitic masses, the path continues through scenes resembling the most beautiful park scenery of England, and then opens upon the Col de Colma, a common, where a boundless scene is presented of the lakes of Orta, Varese, and the plains of Lombardy, and, towards the Alps, of Monte Rosa.

The descent on the other side, towards Varallo, is not less beautiful; it lies through the Val Dugia, the birth-place, in 1484, of Gaudenzio Ferrari, the pupil of Raphael. The Val Sesia is seen in the deep distance, richly wooded and studded with churches and villages ; the path leads down through pastoral scenes, which sometimes recall the most agreeable recollections of home to an English traveller; then changes almost suddenly to the deep gloom of a ravine, where there are quarries, formerly worked for the buildings of Varallo, buried in a forest of enormous walnut and chestnut trees. Issuing from this wild spot, the traveller shortly finds himself in the Val Sesia at Rocco, about four miles from Varallo. See page 230.

ROUTE 103.

ROMAGNANO (Route 101.) TO TURIN.

The road usually taken is that which leads by the course of the Sesia to Vercelli, but this is flat and unin-teresting, and descends to the riziéres, or rice grounds of Piedmont. A more pleasant route, especially since the completion of a new road to Biella, is one which crosses the Sesia and passes through the Canavais, a district celebrated for the quantity of hemp which it produces, and from which it derives its name. In the season it is singular to see the whole population engaged in stripping and otherwise preparing hemp ; whether walking or sitting, alone, or in groups in the streets before their houses, all are thus occupied.

After crossing the Sesia, the tra-veller passes through Gattinara, a town where there is an excellent inn, the Albergo del Falcone. It is a great recommendation to excursions in Piedmont, that tolerable inns are to be found in most of the little towns, and in many, especially in a line of intercourse, they are really excellent. Some of the Italian antiquaries, and

among them Denina, assert that the great battle of Marius and Catullus against the Cimbres was fought in the neighbourhood of Gattinara.

From Gattinara to Biella the route lies through Masarana and Cossata, and offers many beautiful views of the plains and the mountains as the road rises or falls over the undulating ground, which skirts the bases of the mountains that subside into the plains of Piedmont.

Biella, situated on the Cervo, one of the affluents of the Sesia, is 22 miles from Varallo, and about 12 from Ro-magnano. It contains a population of about 8000. It has some trifling manufactories of paper, common woollen goods, and hats. Its sanctuary of *Notre dame d' Oropa* is, however, an object of attraction, which brings crowds of visitors to offer their devo-tions to an image, one of the thousand dirty black specimens of bad carving, which, under the name of *Our Lady,* is worshipped for its miracle-working powers: that of Oropa is said to have been carved by Saint Luke, who is made a sculptor as well as a painter, and to have been brought by a St. Eusebius, from Syria, and pre-served by him in the then wild and desert mountain of Oropa, near Biella.

The sanctuary of Mont Oropa is 6 miles distant, and the access to it, high up in the mountain, was for-merly difficult, but the road now, though steep, is practicable for light carriages. Those, however, who hope for health from the miraculous power of the *block,* must walk up. A series of steep tourniquets leads to the church dedicated to the Virgin, which is a fine structure of the 14th and 15th centuries. Painting and sculp-ture have adorned and enriched it ; and among the artists employed are found the names of Gaudenzio Fer-rari and Luino. At the angles, in the zigzag ascent to the church, there are erected chapels, dedicated to the Virgin, and named after some event in her life, as, the Chapel or Oratory of the Annunciation — of the Purification — of the Assumption, &c. A few are dedicated to saints in the Romish calendar; and the whole number of these chapels exceeds 24.

One benefit to the traveller who may choose to wander by Biella, a little out of the high course from Varallo to Turin, arises from this miserable superstition, for it has caused the establishment of good inns necessary for the accommodation of the numerous pilgrims who visit it; and he will have no reason to complain of a want of comfort at Biella. There is a communication by diligence, three times a week, between Biella and Turin, distant 33 miles.

From Biella to Turin there are two roads, one by Saluzzola, Cigliano and Chivasse, the other by Ivrea; the distance is nearly equal; but by the former the traveller descends at once to the plains; by Ivrea, a more picturesque road leads across valleys and open commons, by Mongrando, and over the Monte Bolengo, famous for the vineyards on its slopes. The views presented from the heights, of the plains and valleys spread out below the traveller on the left, and of the richly wooded mountain slopes, the lowest buttresses of the Alps towards the side of Piedmont, on the right, well recompense the traveller for the worse road, and lead him to

Ivrea, at the entrance of the celebrated valley of Aosta, about 20 miles from Turin. See page 250.

ROUTE 104.

VARALLO (Route 101.) TO CHÂTILLON IN THE VAL D'AOSTA, BY THE PASSES OF THE COL DE VAL DOBBIA, THE COL DE RANZOLA, AND THE COL DE JON, CROSSING THE VAL DE LYS AND THE VAL CHALLANT.

From Varallo, the ascent of the Val Sesia can best be made on mules, though it is not altogether impracticable for chars as far as Riva, distant 9 hours. The Val Sesia offers scenes of less rugged grandeur than some of its lateral valleys; but in its course, many of great beauty are passed, chiefly rendered so by the fine wooding of the slopes, the grand forms of the trees, and the sometimes tranquil, often furious course of the Sesia. Before arriving at Scopello, the villages of Balmuccias and Rua are passed, and the wild valley of Sermento opens on the right.

At Scopello there are many smelting houses, where the copper ore, already washed and crushed, is reduced. About 50 tons annually are raised at Alagna, at the head of the Val Sesia, 4 leagues above Scopello.

There is not much variation in the scenery, though the whole is pleasing. The route passes by the villages of Campertongo and Mollis, to Riva, the chief of the high villages in the valley. Within the district known as the Val Sesia there are reckoned two bourgs and 30 villages, evidence of a thickly-populated country in the valleys of the Alps. Riva is situated at the confluence of the torrents of the Dobbia and the Sesia, and about half a league below the village of Alagna, where the mines of copper are wrought. From Alagna, a pass by the Mont Turloz leads in six hours from the Val Sesia to Pesterana in the Val Anzasca.

Riva is a miserable place of rest; the inn affording only wretched accommodation, and its inmates little civility, but there is no other. The church of Riva will surprise the traveller by its structure, its excessive decoration, and the real talent with which it is painted within and without, chiefly by one of the numerous painters which the Val Sesia has produced—Tanzio, or Antonio d'Enrico, a native of Alagna. The external paintings have a remarkable freshness, though they have been painted more than 200 years, and exposed to the weather in this high valley.

The view of Monte Rosa from

Riva is very sublime ; its enormous masses clothed in glaciers, close the head of the Val de Lys, and offer a scene of extraordinary grandeur.

The course into the Val de Lys from Riva is up the narrow ravine of the Dobbia, by a wretched and difficult path, in some places overhanging the torrent, in others disputing with the river the narrow course through which both must struggle. After passing the miserable hamlet of Grato, near to which there is a fine waterfall gushing out of the black ravine, the abrupt ascent to the Col de val Dobbia is up through a pine forest, and thence over alpine pasturages by a long and fatiguing path, which offers no object of particular interest to the traveller.

The distance from Riva to the Col, which is 8200 feet above the level of the sea, requires 6 hours. On the summit there is a stone hovel for the shelter of travellers who may be unfortunate enough to require it ; it existed in Saussure's time : it consists of two apartments, a chapel and a place of refuge within. It was built at the joint expense of the commune of Riva and of an individual of Gressoney named Luscos. Steep slopes of snow lie near the summit unmelted throughout the year. The view of Monte Rosa is concealed for some time from the traveller, but in the course of his descent the deep valley of the Lys, and the sublime masses of Monte Rosa, offer views rivalling any in the great chain.

From the summit to Gressoney requires three hours. At this retired village the traveller will be agreeably surprised on arriving at an excellent inn, kept by the family Luscos ; where a harpsichord, German music, a tolerable library of Latin, German, and some French authors, portraits of Joseph II. and Maria Theresa, and a formidable array of many generations of the Luscoses' half-length ancestors, in " curled white wigs " hung around to recal their virtues to the memory of their descendants—is an unexpected finding in a village so retired that it almost touches the glaciers of Monte Rosa.

It is a singular fact, that in all the communes at the heads of the Piedmontese valleys of Monte Rosa, the German language is spoken ; at Riva and Alagna in the Val Sesia, above Pesterana in the Val Anzasca, and at St. Giacomo in the Val Challant. The manners of these communities is as distinct as their language, from that their neighbours lower down the valleys, with whom they hold little intercourse : they encourage a pride of birth and birthplace which strongly keeps up the separation. At Gressoney, in the Val de Lys, this is perhaps more strongly exemplified than in any other of the valleys. Here their characters are distinguished for honesty and industry, and few communities have a higher moral tone. Crime is almost unknown among them, and if disputes arise the syndic or magistrate elected by themselves hears the complaint, and effects an amicable settlement.

They possess many of those comforts which an Englishman appreciates, and which are unknown to the lower inhabitants of the valleys. Their education and attainments are of a higher order than is usually found in such a class, especially in such a place.

Many of their young men have distinguished themselves by the abilities which they have displayed when they have gone abroad in the world. They have become merchants and bankers, and many from among them have become eminent for learning and science, and reflected honour on the little community located in this alpine solitude. Among these is Herr Zumstein, better known in the Val Sesia as M. De la Pierre, who has made several ascents of the Monte Rosa, and gave great assistance to Colonel Von Welder, in his topography of Monte Rosa. Zumstein holds the appointment of inspector of the forests of the Va Sesia.

From Gressoney St. Jean, the descent to St. Martin, in the Val d'Aosta, by the valley of the Lys, is a journey of about 26 miles; passing through many villages and hamlets—of which the principal are Gaby, Issime, Fontainemore, and Lillianes,—and through some scenes of wildness and beauty, which, however, become common to the traveller in the Val d'Aosta and its lateral valleys. Above Gressoney St. Jean are the hamlets of Gressoney la Trinitè, San Giacomo, and St. Pietro.

The excellent accommodations afforded at Gressoney St. Jean make it desirable head-quarters to those who would visit the magnificent glaciers at the head of the Val de Lys, or make excursions around Monte Rosa by the Col d'Ollen, which connects the heads of the valleys of the Sesia and the Lys, and the Col de Betta between the Val de Lys and the Val Challant. Excellent guides may be found at Gressoney, and there are few valleys in proximity with the glaciers which offer so many alpine wonders to the examination of the traveller.

In continuing the route direct to Châtillon, in the Val d'Aosta, it is necessary to ascend the steep forest-paths and slopes of the mountain on the side of the valley opposite to the Col de Val Dobbia: it is an extremely difficult and fatiguing path the whole way up to the Col de Ranzola, the summit of the ridge which divides the valleys of the Lys and Challant.

On emerging in the ascent from the pine forest, the finest perhaps of the views of Monte Rosa is presented, especially when taken in connection with the beautiful Val de Lys, which lies far below the traveller, with its quiet villages and fertile pasturages. The Lys, like a silver thread, may be traced up to its glaciers. On either side of the valley the vast mountains belted with forests offer, at the depression of their ridges, the paths by which the most frequent intercourse takes place with the neighbouring valleys. The scene is imperishable from the memory whilst any of the recollections of the Alps remain to the traveller.

After passing the Col de Ranzola the descent is gradual to the little hamlet of St. Grat. Nor is it either steep or difficult to Brussone, in the Val Challant. The distance from Gressoney to Brussone is 6 hours. In the descent, the Val Challant may be traced in its course far down towards Verrex, where it joins the Val d'Aosta; except at the lowest part of the valley it fails in striking objects of interest, but near its termination there are some fine scenes. Above Brussone the valley ascends through several hamlets to St. Giacomo d'Ayas, whence a pass leads to the head of the Val Tournanche and the pass of the Cervin.

At Brussone there is one of the most detestable inns in Piedmont. Filth and its accompanying goître, disgust in every direction, and the Cheval Blanc with its dirty hostess cannot be forgotten. Sleeping here may be avoided, as the journey from Gressoney to Chatillon in the Val d'Aosta may be easily accomplished in a day, and from Gressoney to Varallo may be performed in another, and thus the bad inns at Brussone and at Riva may be avoided.

From Brussone another mountain range must be crossed to reach the Val d'Aosta at Châtillon; or the traveller may descend to Verrex in the Val d'Aosta, which requires 5 hours, passing through Challant and Challard. The road across the mountain presents some glorious views, and Châtillon, by the Col de Jon, is reached as soon as Verrex by the Val de Challant. After crossing some meadows beyond Brussone, the road winds steeply up through a forest of pines and larches, and then opens upon one of the most beautiful pasturages in the Alps — the Col de Jon, which is a fine greensward, broad and luxuriant. On reaching the descent towards the

Val d'Aosta this beautiful valley is seen in all its length, from Chatillon to the Mont Blanc ; not traced quite to the base of the latter, for its summit only is seen towering over the lower abutments into the Val d'Aosta, and showing a glorious termination to this vast and beautiful view, which, in the descent, constantly varies. A series of steep tourniquets brings the traveller down to the forests of chestnut and walnut-trees, for which the Val d'Aosta is celebrated. These offer to him their shade and soon the vines and figs add their luxuriant foliage to the cool and refreshing path which leads through the village and baths of St. Vincent, and the valley of Aosta is entered at one of its finest points near Chatillon.

ROUTE 105.

VOGOGNA, I N VAL D'OSSOLA, TO VISP IN THE VALAIS, BY THE PASS OF THE MONTE MORO, AND THE VALLEY OF SAAS.

Vogogna (Route 59) is situated in the plain of the Val d'Ossola, 2 posts below Domo d'Ossola, and on the confluence of the torrent of the Anza with the Toccia. The valley of Anzasca leads directly up to the Monte Rosa ; the village of Macugnaga, the highest in the valley, is a day's journey from Vogogna ; thence the pass over the Moro, and by the valley of Saas to Visp, though long and fatiguing, may be accomplished in another day, or accommodation may be found, if necessary, at Stalden, 8 miles short of the whole journey.

On leaving Vogogna, a road, leading directly to the Val Anzasca, lies across the plain, and passes by the village of Pic di Muliera, at the foot of a steep ascent which leads to another village called Cima di Muliera ; these are situated on the left bank of the Anza.

The path rises high on the steep slopes which descend to the bed of the Anza, and the village of Castiglione overhangs the richly-wooded sides of the valley. On the lower slopes of the valley the vine flourishes, and the path for miles, with little interruption, is shadowed by trellices. On looking back, the views of the Val d'Ossola are beautiful, and greatly enriched by the luxuriant vegetation of the foreground. The buildings, especially the churches, are still Italian in character, and sparkle in the landscape ; and beyond the plain of the Val d'Ossola the mountains which divide it from the Lago Maggiore bound the view.

The road up the valley is scarcely any where level. The valley is remarkably narrow, and the path, accommodated to the sinuosities of the slopes, is carried steeply up and down, in and out, but offering from this cause an infinite variety of sites, whence the scenes of the valley are beautifully presented : its steep sides, however, offer few spots for cultivation. Forests, fruit-trees, and vines enrich the whole surface, and it is only on reaching high spots in the path that little plains and slopes of arable and pasturage, and village spires are seen above the belts of forest on the opposite side, and these again surmounted by the peaks of Monte Rosa at the head of the valley.

The descent to the village of Calasca offers beautiful views, and beyond it the path descends to the banks of the Anza, and for some time borders on the stream. Here the fine cascade of the Val Bianca bursts out, one of the celebrated waterfalls of Piedmont. Soon after the valley opens, a little above the Ponte Grande, where a single arch of large span and sweeping elevation, crosses the Anza, here two roads branch off ; that on the right bank of the river leads to Banio, a large village whence paths ascend to cross the mountains into the Val Sesia (Route 104.) The road to the Monte Rosa ascends by the left bank of the river ; in its course it skirts the village of St. Carlo, and the traveller soon after arrives at Vanzone, the chief place in the Val Anzasca, and halfway in his day's journey from Vogogna to Macugnaga.

Above Vanzone the same beautiful scenery prevails, and the route passes through many villages,—among them Ceppo Morelli, Campiole, and Morgen —to an abrupt and narrow defile which marks a distinction between the valleys of Anzasca and Pesterana, the latter being the name given to the upper part of the valley through which the Anza flows, from the plain of Macugnaga to the defile.

The beautiful valley of Anzasca has been described by Brockedon in his "Excursions in the Alps," and a quotation from that work will put the reader, and the traveller in these scenes, in possession of requisite information upon this interesting valley and its inhabitants :—

" After sketching the fine view of Mont Rosa from the door of the auberge, and collecting from mine host some information for my day's journey, and a confirmation of my guide's topography in the names of the places which we had passed, we left the retired little plain of Macugnaga. The valley soon narrowed to a deep glen; the descent was rapid, and in less than an hour brought us to the gold mines of Pesterana. There is an *El Dorado* sound in this, which excites high expectations; but there is no more appearance of it than in the pavement of St. Paul's Churchyard. The mines are explored to find this 'world's chief mischief,' combined, in very small proportions, in sulphate of iron; a kilogramme of ore yielding, by the process of amalgamation, an average of only six grammes, the richest ore only yielding ten. My landlord at Macugnaga had furnished me with the name of Professor Fantonetti, as the superintendent of the mines, and as the possessor of a collection of specimens of the minerals of the valley.

" I called upon this gentleman at Pesterana, and received the most courteous and obliging attentions from him. He sent a servant with me to the mills on the Anza, where the ore is crushed, and to the mines ; and directed the miners to give me assistance and information. The first was readily offered ; but the last was useless, as I could not understand a syllable of their jargon. I entered the mine about 300 yards, by an adit of slight ascent : here a shaft was sunk about 60 feet, and I saw several miners working on the lower vein of the ore. The quantity raised is not very considerable. Women are chiefly employed in pounding and picking the ore, whence it passes to the mills of granite, in which it is ground and prepared for amalgamation : the final process is in the hands of M. Fantonetti alone. On my return to that gentleman's house, he pressed me to take refreshment, and gave me some specimens of the ore of the mines, and two works which he had written, — one of them, on the mines of those valleys, in answer to a work of Rossini's, at Turin.

" I soon after crossed the Anza, over an alpine bridge, and continued to ascend above the right bank of the river. Numerous adits of mines, indicated by the earth and stones thrown from them, marked the pursuits of the inhabitants of this valley, who are nearly all miners. The mineral riches of these mountains—iron, lead, copper, silver, and gold—are worked at short distances from each other; and many of the mines of the inferior metals are very productive. The distinction between the continuous valleys of Pesterana and Anzasca, is strongly marked by a vast mass of the mountain, which, nearly closing the bottom of the former valley, leaves only a deep and savage gorge, through which the Anza escapes on the left side into the Val Anzasca. The path over this mass leads through what scarcely deserves the name of a village, Morgen, but which lies in a spot richly wooded by magnificent chestnut-trees. The descent into the Val Anzasca is very beautiful: the river is again crossed, over a fearful bridge, immediately below the defile of Pesterana; and the road continues on the left bank of the river, entirely through the valley. The first village in the Val Anzasca is Campiole, near Ceppo Morelli; it is the place which travellers who would avoid the valley of Macugnaga, or Pesterana, would arrive at by the path over the Mont Moro. The descent, my guide informed me, is longer than from the Macugnaga pass; but much distance is gained by travellers who would go from the valley of Saas direct to the Val Anzasca. Here the Piedmontese dialect began to prevail: though the German patois of my guide was understood even below Vanzone.

" The immediate scenery of the upper part of this beautiful valley, where from its depth the lofty mountains were hid from my view reminded me of some of the sweetest scenes of Devonshire. But the path soon rose above the left bank of the river, and attained a considerable elevation; and I perceived that, except in a few limited spots at the upper end of the valley, and here and there on the steep sides of the mountains, there was no land to cultivate. Extensive forests of chestnut and walnut-trees, fine in form and rich in colour, clothed the hills as far up as the eye could perceive them (except where lofty and distant mountains peered above), and descended far beneath the traveller's path, to where it met the opposite slope, scarcely appearing to leave room enough for the river to struggle through, and of which glimpses were rarely caught. This was the general character of the valley. From a chapel at Cimamorga, in the road near Ceppo Morelli, there is a very striking view: in it all the beautiful characteristics of the scenery seemed to be assembled—the river far beneath struggling through its narrow bed;

the majestic forests, which clothed the mountain sides, among which was sometimes seen a village church or group of cottages; and the vista towards the Alps terminated by the vast and beautiful peaks of Monte Rosa.

" I was much struck by the appearance of the inhabitants of this valley. I rarely saw a plain woman: their beautiful faces and fine forms, their look of cheerfulness and independence, and what in Piedmont was more remarkable, their extreme cleanliness, continually arrested attention. Their costume was peculiar, but pleasing: the hair braided; a vest fitted to the form, and buttoned high, over which was another, usually embroidered and left open; beneath, a silk or other cincture round the waist, and a petticoat reaching half-way down the legs: the feet generally bare; the sleeves of the chemise loose, full, and white as the snow of their mountains; with faces, hands, and feet, cleaner than those of any other peasantry that I ever saw. Sometimes I observed a loose coat, like that of the modern Greek, worn over their usual dress, as if going on a distant visit. Naked feet are rarely seen without the concomitants of filth and beggary, and among such persons a large proportion of the *gummy;* but here the feet, ankles, and legs, were models for the artist; and my admiration as a painter was demanded, in observing the elegant form and graceful appearance of one particularly beautiful young girl, near St. Carlo, who was bearing a vessel of oil on her head to the mines. All this I suppose will appear rodomontade to those who are only acquainted with the ugliness, filth, and wretchedness of the general inhabitants of the valleys of Piedmont; but another fact will support the claims of the Anzascans to distinguished superiority. I did not see nor hear of a goître or crétin in my day's journey of twenty-five miles through the valley — a strong confirmation of the opinions always given to my inquiries by mountaineers themselves, that the filthy habits of a people are the primary causes of goîtres and crétinism ; it is thus induced in the community of those afflicted by the dreadful scourge, becomes hereditary, and can only be removed by a change of habits in two or three generations. This valley differs not in the local causes, often cited as productive of crétinism, from other valleys which are marked by this scourge. The waters of the Anza flow from the glaciers of Monte Rosa as those of the Doire descend from Mont Blanc, and both are drank by the inhabitants. The proportions of labour, and the burdens borne, are at least equal in the Val Anzasca ; the degree of elevation and moisture is similar ; and it is parallel with those valleys which are the most remarkable for this curse, the Valais and the Val d'Aosta.

" The Anzascans are aware that they have a reputation for cleanliness and beauty, and they are justly proud of it. Whilst I was taking refreshment at Vanzone, the principal town in the valley, I mentioned to the innkeeper (rather, a sort of keeper of a chandler's shop) the impression which the people of the valley had made upon me. He seemed delighted at my having noticed the fine women and their cleanliness, and said that what I had seen was not sufficient to do them justice : ' Come,' said he, ' into our valley at a festa ; see our women on Sunday next at St. Carlo, the village below there, which you see in the valley ; all the world will be there : in Upper Val Sesia they boast of their women, but they are not to be compared to ours.' I spoke again of their cleanliness ; he said, ' Our women pride themselves upon the quantity, the fineness, and, above all, the whiteness of their linen ; and they are so scrupulously clean in their persons, that (I must use his own energetic expression) *il est plus facile de trouver une mouche blanche dans cette vallée qu'une vermine.*'

" I had not observed any beggars in the valley ; and there was no appearance of poverty : mine host said, that the great industry of the Anzascans enabled them to establish funds for their poor, which prevented their wants, and restrained their begging. Those who could not work were assisted, and those who could, were not permitted to be idle.

" Some time before we arrived at Castiglione a man had joined us, whose French was a relief to me from the silence of nearly all but gesture which my guide's patois imposed upon me. He relieved Jan, my guide, by good-naturedly carrying his burden, and was persuaded, with difficulty, to partake of some excellent wine of the valley, which we procured at Castiglione. He mentioned his intention of going to the Valteline. I picked up another companion, in a young man of respectable appearance going to Muliera ; from him I received much information, as we walked together, about journeys around Mont Rosa, and intelligence of the places and objects *en route.* It was evening when we reached Cima de Muliera, whence the descent is very rapid by a zigzag paved road to Pie de Muliera, which he kindly walked through, to put me in the right road across the valley to Vogogna. He pointed out a house in passing through Pie de Muliera, which formerly belonged to a superintendent of the gold mines, who had fantastically displayed his riches, or his occupation, by gilding the balconies, railing, and other ironwork of his residence. I think I can perceive in the Val Anzasca the location of the Ictymuli, whose gold mines were so extensively wrought, that Pliny says a law existed among them which forbad their employing more than 5000 men. D'Anville and Cluverius place the Ictymuli at the head of the Val Sesia : it has always been a subject of difficulty with ancient geographers ; but here, where, and where only in Piedmont, gold is still raised, the name of the Ictymuli may be traced in the villages of Cima de *Muliera* and Pie de *Muliera*, at the entrance to the valley where the mines are worked, and where yet, at the latter place, the receiver of the metal resides. This admitted, the commercial importance of the ancient pass of the Moro may be accounted for; its antiquity, and the excellence of what remains of it, carries it back to a remote period as a line of intercourse, at least coeval with that of the Great St. Bernard.

" My recollections of the scenes which I have passed through in the last three days, from Visp to Vogogna, induce me to think this pass the most wild, interesting, and beautiful that I have yet made ; and the Val Anzasca I have distinguished in my mind as the happy valley, not only for the blessings which its inhabitants possess, but the evils which they appear to have avoided, and which have rendered even the presence of priests unnecessary, — at least I saw none ; nor did I, during my descent through the valley, from Macugnaga to Pie de Muliera, meet or see a soldier, a douanier, or a beggar — a goître or a crétin."

At Macugnaga, an inn, which may be endured by an alpine traveller, and which may subdue an alpine appetite, offers all its bad accommodations with so much civility, as almost to reconcile the traveller to disgust, starvation, and want of rest. Myriads of fleas, and nondescript food do not promise well for rest and refreshment; but the little host who keeps the inn — of whom Æsop was the prototype—boasts of his having studied the *cuisine* at Lyons; he seems to have fitted himself for the service of Harpagon. Still the inn may be endured, for the sake of the palace of nature in which it is placed.

There is no scene in the Alps surpassing the appearance of Monte Rosa from Macugnaga ; at least it is better seen, than Mont Blanc is seen at Chamouny ; from its loftiest peaks to its base in the plain of Macugnaga, its vast masses are spread out before the observer. Its deep rifts are marked by lines of snow, and glaciers which stream from its summit to the vault of ice whence issues the torrent of Anza. The bases of the lateral mountains are clothed with dark forests of fir and larch, and the whole scene gives an impression of immensity, and excites the most sublime emotion.

The little plain of Macugnaga is the arena of an amphitheatre, of which more than three sides are inclosed by enormous mountains. On the left is observed the pass which leads over the Mont Turloz to Alagna and the Val Sesia (Route 104.), thence, sweeping round to the right, the eye marks the Pizzi Bianca, which mingles with the prodigious masses of Monte Rosa, and passes on to the Cima de Jazi, and the Col of the Monte Moro, a panorama of unmatched grandeur. The plain of Macugnaga — a league long, and half a league wide — is a luxuriant meadow, which produces abundance of food and fodder for the cattle : there are many little hamlets in it, some almost touching the glaciers. The church of Macugnaga is a building of more striking appearance and richer in its decorations than one would expect to find in such a situation.

The defile below Pesterana divides not only the valley of Pesterana from that of Anzasca, but even the language of the inhabitants. In the Val Pesterana and the plain of Macugnaga German alone is spoken, as in the other high valleys which commence in the deep rifts of Monte Rosa ; while in the Val Anzasca the language is Piedmontese and Italian.

The ascent to the pass of the Moro is very abrupt, and the traveller rises rapidly above the little plain and village of Macugnaga. The path lies at first through a straggling forest, but the Alps or pasturages are soon attained, and the scene thence presented is most magnificent — all the masses of this glorious mountain are open to his view, from its peaks still thousands of feet above him to the basin of Macugnaga, now thousands of feet below. Such a scene cannot be conceived, and once seen can never be forgotten. From the high pasturages the path traverses a stony and barren slope to the snow and glaciers, which it is necessary to cross. On the summit, amidst a heap of stones, a cross is placed, and the traveller looks down on the other side of the mountain towards the valleys, and into a scene of sterility which has no relief.

Before descending towards the valley of Saas it is desirable to walk along the crest of the Moro to the right, about a quarter of a mile, where, mounting some rocks, a glorious view offers itself; extending over the valley of Anzasca and Antrona, to the plains of Italy and the chain of the Alps, even to its subsidence in the distant Tyrol. The traveller who, in going from Visp by the Moro, wishes to shorten his route and avoid Macugnaga, may from the summit of the Moro descend to Campiole in the Val Anzasca by a tolerable path, but he would lose the finest views of the Monte Rosa.

The summit of the pass of the Monte Moro is 9100 English feet above the sea, and 4 or 5 hours are required to attain it from Macugnaga. The descent is at first difficult on the northern slope of the snow, but one soon reaches an ancient paved road which has been cut out of the face of the precipices, and fearfully overhangs a deep hollow into which the glaciers which stream down from the surrounding peaks seem to be poured. The spot is one of the most desolate in the Alps. Soon it is necessary to cross a very steep narrow slope of snow, which stretches down, below where it traverses the path, at least 500 feet; here a slip would be fatal, but the guides trudge across it, laden with the travellers' luggage, as if the

thought never occurred to them that it was possible to slip and fall into the deep and fearful gulf. At length the paved road is left, and no vestige can be traced of it — it has been destroyed by the masses which have fallen from the precipices above.

The path now winds down the vast talus formed by these repeated falls of rocks, to reach the scanty herbage of the highest pasturages. From below it is impossible to trace any path, or even in what direction the path lies, by which the descent has been made; yet it is not a century since that this was the road by which the courier from Piedmont to the Valais regularly passed.

The pass of the Moro, and another across the glaciers on the right into the Val Antrona, are mentioned in an old record of the date of 1440, as "*forts vieux passages*," and great expenses were incurred in 1724 and again in 1790 in the endeavour to restore them in order to facilitate the conveyance of salt and other articles of commerce, but the new repairs were soon destroyed by avalanches. As passes for commercial objects they are superseded by the Simplon, and they are now only traversed by the smuggler, or the peasant who despises the danger or difficulty if he find it the shortest path to a fair or a festa.

Amidst the desolation of the spot, upon which the traveller who has crossed the Moro first feels himself safe, he finds the alpine Ranunculus, Gentianella, and other mountain flowers ; but the debris of fallen mountains, and the enormous glaciers which surround him, give a fearful impression of desolation. In an hour, however, he reaches the *châlets* of Destal, and here he can get such refreshments as excellent milk, cheese, and eggs.

The traveller who leaves the Valais to cross the Moro and descend upon Macugnaga, naturally seeks the enjoyment of the magnificent scene of Monte Rosa, as it bursts upon the observer on the Moro. To obtain this is necessary to reach the *châlets* of Destal from Visp, of easy accomplishment in a day, in order to reach the summit of the Moro by 9 or 10 o'clock, before the mists of the valley rise and obscure the mountain; for by midday, even in fine weather, the Monte Rosa is often so belted by light clouds, that the enjoyment of the view is withheld from all but those who will exert themselves to pay a morning visit to the scene.

From Destal a difficult path crosses the mountains in the Val Antrona, a valley that debouches into the Val l'Ossola.

Soon after quitting the *châlets*, the path leads down to a dreary lake formed by the melting of the glaciers — a great glacier in fact dams the valley, and these waters accumulate within it. From the lower end of the lake the view of the northern side of the Cima de Jazi, and some of the peaks of the Monte Rosa, offer a scene of savage sublimity. It is necessary to skirt the dam of ice and descend below it — an affair of some difficulty; how the cattle are made to ascend and traverse it, which they must do to reach their pasturages, it is difficult to imagine. From below, this barrier of ice appears so effectually to close the valley, that it is impossible to imagine that any accessible alp lies above it.

From this barrier the path lies down the valley, still sterile and filled with rocks and stones; the Rhododendron, however, and a little brushwood give evidence of improved vegetation. About an hour brings the traveller to the village of Allmengal. From this village a path crosses the mountains on the eastern side, and leads to Antrona; and on the west another path leads over snows and glaciers to Zermatt in the valley of St. Nicolas. This presents a terrific appearance, but it is said to be without danger, though the traveller must be an hour and half on the glaciers.

Neither of these paths are indicated by Keller, whilst those laid down in his map from Eringerthal and Einfischthal, between the Valais and Piedmont, have no existence but in his map.

About an hour below Allmengal, lies the village of Micra. Before reaching it, larches and pines are passed, but they are stunted from their great elevation. After crossing a little plain, a rugged path leads down by a hamlet, and the traveller passes under Mont Fée, whose bright snows rising above a forest of pines give a singularly beautiful appearance to the mountain. Soon after he arrives at the little plain and village of Saas, the principal commune of the valley. Formerly the traveller's only place of refuge was the house of the curè, now an auberge offers its independent welcome; and Moritz Zurbruken, the innkeeper, is one of the best guides in the valley to the passes and objects of interest in his neighbourhood. A very interesting account was lately published at Geneva by Marc Viridet, of a hazardous excursion made by him and two friends, under the guidance of Moritz, across the Roth-horn and the glaciers of the Fletschorn to the village of Simplon.

The plain of Saas is beautiful amidst the wild scenery which surrounds it; it is nearly a mile long, and its verdant meadows are refreshing to look upon after the sterility of the upper valley and the pass of the Moro.

Immediately below the plain of Saas the valley becomes a defile, and rocks in the wildest disorder mark the desolating effect of winter upon the precipices which bound the valley. Some magnificent cataracts pour their unregarded volumes of water into this deep and desolate ravine — which in other situations would divide celebrity with the finest falls in Switzerland. The torrent of the Saas is often traversed in the descent, over bridges which tremble under the weight of the traveller, especially if he be on a mule, for this valley is accessible to mules even to the glaciers of the Moro above the *châlets* of Destal.

The valley of Saas is formed of a succession of ravines and little plains. About two hours below Saas, and below a rugged path in a narrow defile, the little plain of Aballa opens and presents its village and church, amidst meadows, gardens, and other evidence of a lower region and more favoured vegetation. Below Aballa the valley becomes again a gorge of the wildest character ; and in the two hours required from Aballa to Stalden the path lies almost continually amidst scenes nowhere surpassed in the Alps for the savage wildness of their character. How dangerous it has been to travellers, crushed by rocks that have fallen from above, or who have fallen over the precipices, along which the path is carried on the side of the ravine, into the black gulf below, is shown by the numerous crosses stuck in places of danger — more than 150 of these are placed between Saas and Stalden ; they mark where life has been lost. The initials of the victims, the date of the accident, and the P.P.N., *praie pour nous*, are cut on the cross, and ask the prayers for their souls, of the passengers.

" The valley of Saas," says Brockedon, " is the narrowest that I have yet passed in Switzerland ; the sides were excessively steep, and terminated in a deep, narrow bed, through which the river tore its foaming way. I had to cross it three times, and over bridges so ill constructed, with only a few pines laid across, that to me, who had been rather inured to such places, the sensation of crossing on a mule was horrible ; the planks moved loosely under the animal's feet, and the whole fabric shook as if an infant could have overthrown it. Some bridges in the valley are at fearful heights above the torrent : one of these, which I sketched, about two miles above Stalden, serves for communication between some cottages and the opposite mountain. Its height above the water is from 200 to 300 feet ; and the cottage are so placed on the cliff, that a line dropt from them would hang far over the torrent on the other side. I have no where else seen such rugged wildness ; the huge old larches which overhung the deep gorges of the river were of immense size, and their giant limbs and roots, thrown about in a savage grandeur, were quite in accordance with the surrounding scenery. The ravine slopes steeply to the torrent from Stalden to Saas, except at the little plain of Aballa ; and the small quantities of barley raised, is grown in such difficult situations, that one wonders that the labour is not an obstacle to any attempt to cultivate it."

Immediately before arriving at Stalden, the torrent of the Saas, and that of the Matter, or St. Nicolas valley, meet and rush with fury through the lofty arch of an alpine stone bridge : from which the scene is very grand.

A little below the confluence, and on the left bank of the river, the village of Stalden is situated : here there is a decent inn, where the traveller may find accommodation and rest, if the two hours, yet necessary for reaching Visp in the Valais, should add too much to his day's fatigue. Stalden is about 8 miles from Visp. After the *belles horreurs* of the valley of Saas, the scenery below Stalden is tame. At Visp (Route *59.*) there are two or three tolerable inns, and the village offers many picturesque points of view : the snowy peaks observed to bound the view on looking up the valley from the bridge, is generally pointed out as Monte Rosa, but the " queen of the Alps " cannot be seen from Visp. Those peaks are on the mountain of Saas, which divides the valley of Saas and St. Nicolas, and overhang the glaciers which are crossed in going from Allmengal to Zermatt by the path already mentioned.

ROUTE 106.

The first eight miles of this route takes the traveller back to Stalden, whence, ascending by the road on the right without crossing the torrent, he enters the Mattertal or valley of St, Nicolas. The road is carried along the steep slope of the side of the mountain which bounds and narrows the valley, where the furious torrent which descends from Zermatt foams in its deep course far below the path of the traveller. The vast buttress which, resting against Monte Rosa, stretches down towards the Valais, dividing the valley of the Saas from that of St. Nicolas, terminates at the confluence of the rivers which flow through these valleys. The slope at the confluence is richly wooded, and among its forests and pasturages, the village of Grenchen is seen on the left, in the valley of St. Nicolas; it is remarkable as the birthplace of Thomas Platter, the reformer, who was a physician of Basle. This village the guides rarely fail to point out.

The route to St. Nicolas is not so fearfully savage as the path up the valley of Saas, though, but for the immediate comparison, the Val St. Nicolas is wild enough to satisfy a lover of alpine scenes. In two hours the traveller from Stalden reaches the village of St. Nicolas, the chief place in the valley; it is agreeably situated amidst the orchards and forests which enrich its immediate vicinity : the house of the curè is usually resorted to by strangers, and his hospitality never fails.

The journey to Zermatt from Visp is a short one of nine hours only, and St. Nicolas is about half way. Starting at a very early hour from Visp, the traveller might cross the glaciers of the Cervin on the same day, and reach the *châlets* of Brieul :

but it is a wiser course to start in the morning from Zermatt, cross the glaciers, and reach the Val d'Aosta at Chatillon the same evening, that is, supposing the effort of the traveller be to reach Chatillon from Visp in two days ; the more frequent practice, however, is to go to Zermatt on the first day, to Val Tournanche on the second, and Chatillon on the third.

Above St. Nicolas the valley becomes much narrower, and the path in many places carried along a steep slope where a slip would hurry the unfortunate passenger to his certain destruction. The valley widens before arriving at Herbuggen, and passes near a fine glacier which descends from the Schallhorn. The next village above Herbuggen is Randor, and about an hour higher up is a larger village — Tesch, — where, if foul weather should overtake the traveller, he has little chance of comfort; the few unfortunates who have staid here have left their maledictions upon its dirty and miserable accommodations.

At Zermatt, two hours further, the house of the curè offers its hospitalities, and a worthier host than Jean François de la Costa cannot be found. In the little plain of Zermatt, situate amidst the grandest scenery of nature, surrounded by forests of pines and vast glaciers, is placed, with its neat church, this elevated and retired village, with more cleanness and comfort among its inhabitants than is to be found in many places of greater pretensions : this has perhaps been effected by the influx of strangers, for many mineralogists, botanists, and entomologists, come here to collect rich harvests in the neighbourhood. The intercourse with the Val d'Aosta by the Mont Cervin is not frequent enough to produce such effect upon the manners and character of the inhabitants, — the example of the worthy curè may however have done much. Here many days may be spent in excursions to the glaciers and points of view with which the neighbourhood abounds, and to which many of the inhabitants are excellent guides.

From Zermatt, a path already adverted to, leads to the valley of Saas, and another — rarely used except by the boldest mountaineers — lies directly across the glaciers of Monte Rosa, by a course known by the name of the Aréte-blanche, to Macugnaga ; this pass is better known by its German appellation, Weissen Thor. The distance from Zermatt to Macugnaga by this pass is twelve hours, and its highest point exceeds 12,000 English feet.

But the grand object of a visit to Zermatt is the Mont Cervin, which, from the village, is seen to rise in singular beauty and magnificence against the sky, of a pyramidal form, and more than 4000 feet of elevation above the bed of ice from which it seems to spring. In the whole chain of the Alps not one object offers so striking an appearance as this remarkable mountain, which lifts itself from an otherwise unbroken line of glacier, which is more than 11,000 English feet above the level of the sea : this scene alone would repay the trouble of a visit to Zermatt from Visp.

There is some confusion produced by names on the frontiers of states, each language giving its own : thus the Mont Cervin in French is the Monte Silvio in Italian, and the Matterhorn in German ; and the village of Zermatt is known on the Italian side of the mountain as Praborgne.

When the traveller in the Alps receives the hospitality of the curès of retired villages, where there are no inns, it is usual to leave with the housekeeper, or for her, a donation, which it is just should at least equal the cost of such accommodation at an inn ; the tax would otherwise be heavy upon the limited means of the host, and kindness and attention is thus insured to future travellers.

There is another cluster of huts and granges called Zmutt, still further up the little plain of Zermatt ; it lies close to the glaciers of the Breithorn but is passed on the left by the traveller who approaches the Cervin About an hour above Zermatt the path abruptly ends in a deep rift in the mountain, in the depths of which the torrents from the glaciers of the Cervin are seen to struggle and force their way into the valley of Zermatt. A path has been cut out of the overhanging rock to reach a wild alpine bridge by which the torrent is crossed, and the ascent to the Cervin abruptly commences by a path which passes by some granges and up a rugged course through a pine forest, in which, however, it does not long continue, but enters upon some scanty pasturages enamelled with flowers, and making a considerable *détour* to the right, soon leaves the traveller to wander up a trackless course of loose schist, sodden with the waters from the glaciers. Often it is necessary to traverse deep water courses cut by the streams, and this fatiguing ascent offers little variety until he reach the glaciers; and this is only after a fatiguing march of four hours from Zermatt, and two long hours to reach the summit are still required on the glaciers— which are free from danger, though deep rifts on the left, point out the risk of deviating from the true course.

From the summit of the pass, which exceeds 11,000 English feet above the level of the sea, the scene around is one of extraordinary magnificence ; the eye wanders over a vast intervening country to the Bernese Alps, sweeps round by the Breithorn and Monte Rosa, looks down upon a thousand peaks towards Piedmont, and rests upon the wonder of the Alps, the pinnacle of rock in immediate proximity — the Cervin—whose peak is 15,200 English feet above the sea. During the ascent this glorious object—the motive for his journey, the reward of his exertion— is constantly before the tourist.

On the actual crest there is some bare rock, and a little space so exposed that the snow cannot rest upon it. Here

Saussure remained three days with his son and attendants engaged in experiments at this elevation. Traces of the rude cabins in which they sheltered still exist, and also of a redoubt thrown up three centuries ago by the Valaisans, and known by the name of Fort St. Théodule: it never could have been intended for serious defence but placed there with a silly military swagger, of which the Swiss were at that time fond, to mark what they claimed as their frontier— the crest of the Alps.

From the summit the descent towards the Val d'Aosta still lies over the glacier for two hours, thence down the steep and loose Moraines, swampy and difficult of descent, for two hours more, before the traveller can reach the *châlets* of Mont Jumont, — the first on the side of Piedmont, without even any summer residence of man intervening between Zermatt, the last habitations in Switzerland, and this place, a distance of nine hours. About an hour below the châlets of Mont Jumont, is the plain of Breuil, where there are many granges, and a chapel, in which, once a year, during the resort to the pasturages in these high regions, service is performed. The plain of Breuil appears to have anciently been a lake. From its lower extremity the peak of the Cervin is seen on the side opposite to Switzerland, but still towering over its enormous bed of glaciers.

Below the plain of Breuil, the route descends by a wild and deep gorge, through which a torrent rushes, and scarcely leaves space enough for a path by the side of the rock; through this savage ravine, one of the wildest in the Alps, the traveller passes for about two hours, and then reaches the first village, which is composed of many houses scattered over the slopes of an amphitheatre of rich pasturage, surrounded by mountains. This, the highest village in the valley, bears also its name — Val Tournanche.

At this commune, the Piedmontese officers of the customs, or as they are called in Piedmont, preposè, are stationed. The difficult and dangerous passes into the Valais are the surest courses for smugglers. Formerly, in defiance of Napoleon, and his Berlin decrees, they passed these frightful solitudes laden with British muslins, tempted by a high reward; but sometimes they were shot by the preposè stationed at points of observation.

From the village of Val Tournanche to Châtillon is a journey of about six hours, generally deep in the ravine through which the Tournanche foams; two or three little hamlets are passed, the principal of which is Antey. On approaching Châtillon the road rises high up on the side of the ravine, and winds amidst enormous blocks of serpentine which have fallen from the mountains, whose sides and bases bound the gorge. The arid faces of the rocks, whence these have been detached, present the richest colours to the pencil of the artist, and the vast trunks and wild branches of the chestnut and walnut trees increase the picturesque character of the valley. Through a forest of these the path descends, and on emerging from it the Val d'Aosta opens, the old and new bridges of Châtillon spanning with their single arches the deep ravine of the Tournanche; and, beyond, on the opposite side of the Val d'Aosta, the ruins of the Château d'Usselle present those materials of the picturesque for which the valley of Aosta is so celebrated.

The bridges are among the most remarkable objects at Châtillon. That over which the high road now passes is a very fine single arch, thrown across a deep gulf. From it are seen, further down the torrent, the remains of a Roman bridge, also a single, and still an entire arch; and immediately over it another bridge, one which served its purpose for many ages, but it has now been superseded by the new bridge, and its improved approaches.

In the depth of the gulf, and a little up the stream, are forges, strangely placed there, for the sake of the water power in working the tilts ; a wild path leads down to them, and the view of the bridges from the bottom of the ravine forms one of the most striking scenes in the valley. Châtillon contains a convent of capuchins.

ROUTE 107.

FROM TURIN TO CORMAYEUR, THE VAL D'AOSTA.

The shortest route from Turin to Ivrea, at the entrance of the Val d'Aosta, is by Lemie, Volpiano, St. Benigno, and Foglis — all large villages or towns, containing from 1800 to 3000 inhabitants. St. Benigno has one of the most beautiful churches in Piedmont.

The road lies across the flat rich plains which extend to the bases of the Alps; and before arriving at Foglis, two of the torrents which descend from the Alps are crossed — the Malone and the Orca — on flying bridges, and between Foglis and Ivrea another river, the Chiusella, is crossed, near to where the road by Foglis falls into the high road from Chivasso to Ivrea. This spot has some celebrity, as the scene of a successful struggle of the French against the Austrians : it was the first battle in the war of 1800, and immediately preceded the victory of Marengo. In the combat on the Chiusella the Austrian General Salfi was killed. Two other villages lie beyond Foglis on this road, — Montalegno and Romano. The distance from Turin to Ivrea by this road is 12 leagues ; a better but longer road lies through Chivasso and Caluso.

Ivrea is a large walled town. The entrance is highly picturesque, across the deep bed of the Doire, which flows immediately below the *Port d' Turin*. It contains about 8000 inhabitants. Here large markets are held, to which cheese and other pastoral produce of the Alps are brought ; it is also a depôt for the iron which is obtained near Cogne, and from other mines worked in the valley; here also, some cotton works have been recently established.

The prison is a large building, with towers at the angles ; these, and the old walls, from many points of view, furnish most picturesque materials for the sketch-book. This town or city, as it is called, — and in English estimation, as the seat of a bishop, ought perhaps to be considered one — is said to be the southern gate to the Val d'Aosta. It is of great antiquity, and mentioned by many ancient authors under the name of *Eporedia*. Strabo says that here the unfortunate Salassi made prisoners by Terrentius Varro, when these brave people of the Val d'Aosta were subdued, were sold as slaves by public auction, to the number of 36,000.

On leaving Ivrea, on the right is a vast ridge of alluvium, the Monte Bolegno, which stretches into the plains. The road ascends on the left bank of the Doire, passes below the château of Montalto, and continues through the rich broad valley of the Doire — broad enough to constitute a part of the plain, for at Settimo Vittone, 3½ leagues, the ascent has been so gradual as scarcely to have been perceived. Nor is it in fact until the traveller reach Pont St. Martin, two leagues, that he may be said to have fairly entered this valley of the Alps.

At Pont St. Martin, however, all doubt is removed. The lofty arch which formerly sprung the torrent of the Lys, one of the finest Roman works of its class in the valley, is now being removed for another, better adapted to the improved intercourse of the inhabitants of the valley with the plains. The situation of this village is strikingly fine. The entrance to the Val de Lys offers a temptation to explore it, and a visit to the villages situated at the foot of the glaciers of Monte Rosa (Route 104.) will well repay the explorer of an alpine valley.

After crossing the Lys at a short distance from its confluence with the Doire, the road ascends to Donas, where a Roman work — a pierced rock — is passed through, and near to it is a Roman milestone cut in the rock, noting xxxii.

From Donas the road ascends abruptly for a short distance, and close to the Doire, which it steeply overhangs, to

Fort Bard, celebrated for the temporary check which its fort gave to the advance of the French army under Bonaparte, in 1800. It was garrisoned by only 400 Austrians, yet such was the strength of the position, that Bonaparte almost despaired of carrying it, and a few days more must have starved his army into a retreat; by a gallant manœuvre, however, in the efficient placement of a single gun, above the precipices of the Mont Albaredo, which overhangs Bard, they checked the battery which covered the approach to the town, and the army passed by night under the grenades and *pots de feu* thrown by the fort. Another gun was raised to a belfry which commanded the gate of the fort, and the Austrians, fearing an assault, surrendered. Upon such slight occurrences the fate of Europe turned. As the French army would have devoured all the supply of the Val d'Aosta in a few days, it must have retreated, and the battle of Marengo, one of the most brilliant events of French history, would not have been fought. Within a few years the fort has been greatly strengthened, and it is now considered invulnerable.

After passing through the steep and narrow streets of Bard, the entrance is seen, on the left, to the valley

of Champorcher, whence a path leads by the village of Pont Bosel to the Col de Reale in six hours, and by this pass and the valley of the Soanna to Ponte in the Val d'Orca.

Above Bard the valley is narrow, and offers little variety in ascending by the deep and rapid course of the Doire to

Verrex, 2½ leagues from Pont St. Martin, is situated at the entrance to the Val Challant (Route 104.). Here many improvements have recently been made, especially in the construction of a new bridge and a good inn — both were much wanted; but throughout the valley, the addition to the numbers of the inns, and of the accommodations which they offer to travellers have undergone an extraordinary improvement within a few years.

There is a large square keep of the old castle of Verrex, which overhangs the Val Challant; it is a picturesque object from below, and the scenes from it are worth a scramble to the ruins.

There is a convent of Augustins at Verrex.

Above Verrex the valley widens, and the little plain of the Doire shows the destruction which the torrent brings with it, in the sands and rocks left in evidence of its destructive violence in the spring.

About a league and a half above Verrex the road enters upon one of the most remarkable scenes in the valley — a deep ravine, through which the Doire has cut its way, or found such a gulf its natural channel. The road ascends steeply on the left of the river, and is cut out of the rock, in some places overhanging the foaming torrent, and where the rock equally overhangs the traveller. These rocks are surmounted by the ruins of the château of St. Germains, placed so as effectually to command the pass, when the brigand feudal proprietors robbed and maltreated the unfortunate passer-by. These ruins are an improvement in the morale as well as the picturesque.

The road cut out in so remarkable a way was probably a Roman work. It was some time since repaired by the Augustin monks of St. Bernard, as a tablet on the road records, but by a little manœuvre of Charles Emanuel III., king of Sardinia, in adding a bit above and a bit below, he has taken a large share of the credit to himself.   It stands thus : —

CAROLI EMANUELIS III. SARDINIÆ
REGIS P. F. INVICTI AUCTORITATE
INTENTATAM ROMANIS VIAM
PER ASPERA MONTIS IOVIS IUGA
AD FACILIOREM COMMERCIORUM
ET THERMARUM USUM
MAGNIS IMPENSIS PATEFACTAM
AUGUSTANI
PERFECERUNT A. MDCCLXXI
REGNI XLII.

This defile is called the pass of Mont Jovet. From the head of the pass the view down the valley is very striking. Immediately above it, the finest part of the Val d'Aosta extends to the *Citè* as Aosta is called. The wine in the neighbourhood of Mount Jovet is celebrated.

Nothing can exceed the beauty and richness of the scenery, and the magnificent character of the foliage ; the walnut and chestnut trees are celebrated for their grandeur and picturesqueness.

Before arriving at St. Vincent, a singular bridge over a deep ravine is crossed. It is called the Pont des Sarasins, and by antiquaries is recognised as a Roman work. From its parapet one of the most beautiful scenes in the valley is presented on looking up towards Châtillon, and including among its objects the Château d'Usselle and other ruins. Not far from this bridge is the agreeable village of St. Vincent, where there are mineral springs. About a league above is

Châtillon, which was mentioned in Route 106.   The distance from Verrex to this place is about ... leagues.

Above Châtillon the same fine rich character of scenery prevails, only interrupted by the occasional traces of destruction left by the torrents which in the spring rush down from the lateral valleys to fall into the great drain of this district, the Doire.

About a league above Châtillon is the village of Chambave, celebrated for its wine, one of the richest and most *recherché* in Piedmont. The wine of the Val d'Aosta has a great reputation, and the vine is cultivated on the mountain sides to an elevation of 3000 feet above the level of the sea. In the valley, hemp, Indian corn, and fruit trees, fill the plain like a vast garden.

Nuz, a poor village with the ruins of a château, is nearly halfway between Châtillon and Aosta. Before arriving at Nuz, a valley on the right bank of the Doire is seen to run up to the ridge of mountains which separates the valley of Aosta above Mont Jovet, from the valley of Champorcher. At the entrance of this valley is the picturesque château of Fenis. Above Nuz the road passes through the village of Villefranche.

In front of the inns in the road up the Val d'Aosta it is a common custom to trellice vines quite across the road ; the delicious shelter which this affords to the heated and weary traveller must be enjoyed to be fully valued : in this part of the valley the custom is most general.

On the approach to Aosta the château Quart is seen placed high on the mountain side ; a path leads up to it from near Villefranche, and down on the other side of its glen towards Aosta, so that a visit to it requires no retracing of steps, and the beautiful scenes presented in the ascent and at the château deserve the trouble of climbing there. Little more than a league further up the valley is

AOSTA, a city more interesting for its Antiquities and historical assoiations than any other claim it has to mportance. Its situation is indeed trikingly beautiful, near the confluence of the Buttier and the Doire, in a deep rich valley, surrounded by ofty and snow-capped mountains. The Civitas Augusti — or Augusta Prætoria — claims a much higher antiquity. It was known under the name of Cordèle, as the chief city of the Salassi : its history, earlier than its conquest by Terrentius Varro, a general of Augustus, is fabulous, but the antiquary of Aosta has no difficulty in fixing the date of its foundation 406 before that of Rome, 1158 B.C. ! By the army of the emperor it was taken 24 years before the Christian era, and its inhabitants reduced to miserable captivity. Augustus rebuilt the city, gave his own name to it, and established there 3000 soldiers from the Prætorian cohorts. The remains of large public buildings attest its importance at that time. A triumphal *arch* in tolerable preservation is one of the finest of the remains — nearly one fourth of it is buried in soil brought down by the torrent of the Buttier, near to which it is situated. Across this river there is a Roman bridge, now nearly buried in the soil accumulated around it during so many ages. There is also a remarkable gate or port, having two façades, with a quadrangle between them, each façade composed of three arches—that in the centre is much the largest. There are also the ruins of an *Amphitheatre*, of a barracks or Prætorian palace, towers, walls, and fragments of unknown former appropriation, now serving only to perplex antiquaries.

Aosta is the seat of a bishop under the archbishop of Chambery. A military commandant is also stationed here, and a numerous establishment of official inspectors ; fiscal, sanitory &c. ; a tribunal of justice, a royal college, an hospital for the military, and another for the poor.

Anselm, the notorious archbishop of Canterbury in the 11th century, was born at Aosta.

St. Bernard, whose name is immortally associated with the mountain pass from the valley of the Rhone to the valley of the Doire, was archdeacon of Aosta ; and his knowledge, from his situation, of the exposure and sufferings of those who traversed these regions, led to his establishment of the celebrated hospice, upon the permanent footing it has since held, and left him to be remembered as the " Apostle of the Alps."

The cathedral is deserving of a visit, though it has no high antiquity.

There is a column erected to commemorate the flight of Calvin from the city in 1541, with the following inscription : —

HANC

CALVINI FUGI

EREXIT ANNO MDXLI

RELIGIONIS CONSTANTIA REPARAVIT

ANNO MDCCXLI.

The inns at Aosta are now generally good, but the Eçu de Valais is excellent, for cleanness, comfort, and accommodation. A diligence passes daily between Aosta and Turin, going three times a week, and returning the alternate days : and chars may be had in all the intermediate towns.

The difficulties about distances in Piedmont, alluded to in the introduction to this section, is no where more strongly felt than in this route to the Val d'Aosta from Turin. With maps, post-books, descriptions of the valley, and the latest authority — the "*Dizionario Geografico Storico, statistico-commerciale degli stati di S. M. il re de Sardegna,*" and the last " *Carta Corografica delle Divisioni di Torino e di Aosta,*" published by authority of the government, before us, neither distances nor measures can be reconciled. Whether the miles are geographical, 60 to a degree, or of Piedmont, 40 to a degree, is not mentioned ; and no measure from the scales of three of the best maps will agree with either of the quantities described in the three best works, which ought to be of authority since they are sanctioned by the government; so that the distances named can only be approximations.

The valley of Aosta, more perhaps than any other in Piedmont, is afflicted in a horrid degree with crètinism and goître; from Châtillon to Villeneuve this blight seems to have fallen most heavily. Brockedon says, " Nowhere are goîtres and crétinisms more prevalent than in this beautiful valley. The peasantry appear squalid and filthy, a race of beings generally stunted and diseased. Of the whole population in the neighbourhood of Aosta, one in fifty is a crétin; and above half are more or less goîtred. Some of these are horrid objects. Tumours as large as their heads are appended to their throats, varying in number, size, and colour. The dirt, deformity, and imbecility of the inhabitants of this part of the valley, presented a scene so wretched, that it harrowed our feelings. Not a well-dressed or decent-looking person is to be met with : all bear marks of poverty, disease, and wretchedness; and this too amidst scenes for which nature has done so much. Surrounded by mountains, and high in their own locality, we saw nothing of the lightness, activity, and high spirits of the mountaineer. Something weighs upon the people like a curse. Many conjectures have been offered upon the cause of goîtres and crétinism. Labour, food, water, air, have all been offered in explanation; but none of these account for it satisfactorily. The opinion of our guide was, that it was chiefly owing to the villainously dirty habits of the people most afflicted with it. He said that among the mountaineers this was the general opinion ; and though it sometimes descended in families, and often was observed in infancy, yet it might be traced to the filthy habits of preceding generations."

On leaving the city to ascend th[e] valley, the drive for about four mile[s] lies through the open plain of th[e] Val d'Aosta, and through scenes o[f] its greatest richness in vegetation[.] At this distance from Aosta the roa[d] passes beneath the château Sarra, a[n] unpicturesque structure; nearly op[-] posite to it, on the other side of th[e] valley, is a queer building in villain[-] ous taste, the château of Aimaville[,] situated on a knoll in a commanding position, and thrusting its impudent pretensions into notice as if it were a work of high refinement.

Sarra is about halfway from Aosta to Villeneuve. Between these places the road passes, near to the latter place, through St. Pierre, where there is one of the most picturesque châteaux in the valley. Soon after leaving St. Pierre a fine scene is presented in the approach to Villeneuve, where the vast rock above the town is seen surmounted by the Châtel d'Argent, and beyond, the snowy alps at the head of the Val Savaranche. About a mile from St. Pierre the road turns towards the river, which it crosses by a stone bridge to reach the little town of

Villeneuve, where there is nothing of interest, and where the inn offers poor accommodation ; it is too near to Aosta to induce the owners to make it more agreeable in the hope of detaining travellers. Near to Villeneuve, the valleys of the Savaranche, and the Rhèmes, open almost together from the south, into the valley of the Doire. Above Villeneuve the valley narrows and becomes much more wooded, the walnut trees forming in some places almost a forest, especially near

Arvier, about 4 miles above Villeneuve. Here the vineyards are celebrated, every slope being terraced, and vines planted. A little beyond Arvier is the dirty narrow village of

Ivrogne. Until within two or three years this village was almost a arrier to the passage of carriages up ne valley, from the steepness and arrowness of its principal street. Now, however, this is altogether voided; a new bridge is made over ne torrent of the Grisanche, and a good road is carried behind the town nd falls into the old road above it, where this enters on the road cut out of Fort Roc, which has also been widened, and a good road is now carried through the defile which separates what is considered a distinction in the valley — the Val d'Aosta, from the valley of La Salle.

Here the road rises hundreds of feet above the bed of the Doire, which is seen foaming below through its restrained course ; and from the summit of this pass, Mont Blanc at the head of the valley closes the scene with its masses as a magnificent barrier. The view is strikingly beautiful. The road, thus carried over the precipices, crosses in some places deep rifts in the mountain side ; over these chasms, platforms are placed, which, being removed, would cut off all communication by this road, and oblige an army to make a considerable *détour* to descend by other points into the Val d'Aosta. A peep over the parapet wall, or through the platforms into the depth below, excites a shudder.

From Fort Roc the road descends rapidly to the Doire, which it crosses on a wooden bridge, and thence continues on the left bank to

La Salle. Before arriving at this village there is a fine view of Mont Blanc and the valley, presented, as the road passes into a deep ravine to cross a torrent near its head, thence winding round on the other side of this ravine, it rapidly descends upon La Salle, a dirty narrow village, where, however, the name is preserved of the ancient people of this valley, the Salassi. On a hill near La Salle are the ruins of an old feudal castle, there are many traces of its high antiquity found in and about the village. From Ivrogne to La Salle is about nine English miles ; thence to

Morgex, by a steep and rather narrow road, is about three miles. Nearly opposite to Morgex, it is in contemplation by the Sardinian government to form a good approach by the camp of Prince Thomas to La Tuille, and the pass of the Little St. Bernard. One of the most important benefits which the government could confer upon its subjects in the Val d'Aosta, and the Tarentaise. At Morgex two or three little inns have been lately built.

From Morgex, the road up the valley is better than that between La Salle and Morgex, and at the distance of a league a branch of the road descends to cross the Doire, and leads to the village and baths of St. Didier. Through the former the road to the Little St. Bernard passes, and about a league from the branch road to St. Didier, the traveller enters

Cormayeur, where he will find in the Albergo del Angelo a capital inn and a good table d'hôte, and where, during the summer, he may enjoy, *en pension,* this beautiful retreat in the finest part of the Alps.

Cormayeur, though considered as the head of the Val d'Aosta, is in reality in the Val d'Entrèves ; it is a large village with many good houses, situated near the confluence of the two branches of the Doire which descend from the Col de Ferret and the Col de la Seigne. At the foot of the southern side of Mont Blanc to which it approximates so nearly, that the glaciers and snowy crests of the great chain appear to hang over the valley. From the village, the summit of Mont Blanc is concealed by the Mont Dolina, but half an hour's walk discloses the chain, from the " Monarch," to the grand Jorasse. That part of the chain seen from the village to close the valley includes the remarkable peak of the Géant, and the whole course of the path, by which the passage may be made by the Col de Géant to Chamouny, is, on the side of Piedmont, to be traced from Cormayeur. This excursion, fatiguing and difficult, is seldom made. Mrs. Campbell, however, and her daughter, English ladies, crossed from Chamouny to Cormayeur, in company with a dozen guides, in the summer of 1823; an adventure not yet forgotten in the neighbourhood.

Cormayeur is a place much resorted to in the summer by invalids, for the sake of its mineral waters. There are different springs near it; that of La Victoire is half a league to the S. W.; its waters are impregnated with carbonic acid gas, sulphate of magnesia, and a little iron, and has a temperature of about 54. The spring of La Marguerite varies a little in the proportions of its components, but its temperature is 12 degrees higher. The Piedmontese have great reliance on the salutary effects of their mineral springs, and in their resort to them bring together many *agrèmens*. To them, the traveller to the head of the Val d'Aosta, and the tourist around Mont Blanc are indebted for an establishment which offers to them rest, and refreshment, and, generally, agreeable society, after their journeys.

The establishment of chars at Cormayeur is excellent. A tariff fixes the price; for 2 persons, at 12 francs; for 3, at 15 francs; and for 4, at 20 francs, for their conveyance to Aosta.

ROUTE 108.

MARTIGNY TO AOSTA.— PASS OF THE GREAT ST. BERNARD.

At Martigny (Route 59.) chars are generally hired for this excursion, to take the traveller as far as Liddes, whence the ascent to the hospice is made on mules, the road beyond being impracticable, at present, for any sort of carriage; but the spirit of the Valaisans will, if possible, overcome this difficulty. The same energy which has so much improve the roads in their canton, has alread made the difficulties of the forest St. Pierre to subside; and if the be encouraged by the Sardinian go vernment, or, perhaps, in defiance its blind policy, we may yet see good practicable char road on th side of Switzerland, carried to th hospice of the Great St. Bernard.

The length of route from Martigny or rather the village La Bâtie, whic lies in the route of the Simplon, nea Martigny, to the hospice, is nin leagues. It passes through the Bourg of Martigny, and shortly after crosse the Drance. The bed of this river still exhibits in the rocks and stones with which it is strewn, evidence of the devastation occasioned in 1818, by the bursting of a lake in the valley of Bagnes.

After crossing to the left bank of the Drance, the road leaves the path to the Forclaz, which leads to Chamouny, on the right, and continues up the course of the Drance to the miserable villages of Valette and Bouvernier. Soon after the river is crossed, and the road continues on its right bank in the deep valley of the Drance. In one part the defile is so narrow that it was found necessary to cut a gallery through the rock: beyond it, the road soon after recrosses the river, and ascends on the left bank to

St. Branchier, another dirty village situated at the confluence of the two branches of the Drance, one of which descends from the Val d'Entremont, and the Great St. Bernard, the other from the Val de Bagnes and the glaciers of Charmontane.

Above St. Branchier there are some fine scenes in the Val d'Entremont, but none strikingly grand; it has the general character of an alpine valley, and nothing that deserves to be particularly remembered. At Orsieres the path which leads to Issert and the Val de Ferret turns off on the right.

Beyond Orsieres the scenery improves a little in wildness. The torrent can seldom be seen in the deep gorge which it has made its course, and there is nothing striking in the scenery until the traveller arrives in the forest of St. Pierre.

Liddes and St. Pierre are the only villages on the road between Orsieres and the hospice; the former has a tolerable inn, (L'Union), where travellers can rest and refresh.

It is usually a journey of 10 hours to the hospice, from Martigny. The charge for a char to or from Liddes and Martigny is generally 12 francs, and for each mule from Liddes to the hospice 6 francs, and a *douceur* to the boy who returns with the mule. Between Liddes and St. Pierre chars are seldom taken, not that the road is impracticable, but it is, at present, very liable to disruption.

St. Pierre is a dirty wretched village, but it has fragments and inscriptions enough to support some claims to antiquity. A military column, dedicated to the younger Constantine, is placed here. De Rivaz says that it was originally on the summit of the pass of the Great St. Bernard, and replaced there the statue of Jupiter Penninus, which Constantine destroyed about the year 339.

On leaving St. Pierre the road crosses a deep abyss, through which the Drance forces its way into the valley below. The road to the hospice leaves on the left a torrent which descends from the Val Orsey, in which there is, not far from St. Pierre, a magnificent cascade.

The road formerly led through the forest of St. Pierre, by a path among the rocks and roots of pines, so steep and tortuous, that Napoleon's difficulties in transporting his artillery were here; perhaps, the greatest that he encountered from natural obstacles during his extraordinary expedition in 1800, across these Alps. Lately the spirited Valaisans have cut an excellent road along the precipices which overhang the deep course of the Drance, avoiding the steep rises and falls of the old road, and leading the traveller by a safe path, which their daring engineers have cut out of the rock, through a savage and appalling defile.

On leaving the forest, and rising to where the pines and larches are stunted from their elevation above the level of the sea, the traveller arrives at some pasturages, where there are many châlets. The enormous mass of the Mont Velan appears to forbid further progress, some of its fine glaciers, particularly that of Menou, stream down into the plain of Prou, where, amidst the shelter of surrounding mountains, numerous herds gather the rich herbage of this alpine pasturage.

On rising above this basin, the path enters another defile, and the scenes become more sterile and dreary as the summit is approached. At length, after passing some beds of snow, the solitary walls of the

HOSPICE appear, and the traveller reaches, on the very summit of the pass, this dwelling in the clouds, 8200 English feet above the level of the sea.

Here, in the practice of the most disinterested benevolence, lives this community of *Religeux*, who devote the best time of their lives, when man is most susceptible of his powers for its enjoyment, to the service of their fellow men; those whose pursuits oblige them to traverse these dreary fields in seasons of danger, when, without such aid and protection, hundreds must perish.

The Hospice is a massive stone building, well adapted to its perilous situation, which is on the very highest point of the pass, where it is exposed to tremendous storms from the northeast and south-west. On the northwest it is sheltered by the Mont Chenelletaz, and in an opposite direction by the Mont Mort. There is no mountain which bears the name of the St. Bernard. Like that of the St. Gothard, the name is only given to the pass. The chief building is capable of accommodating 70 or 80 travellers with beds: 300 may be sheltered; and between 500 and 600 have received assistance in one day. Besides this, there is a house near the hospice on the other side of the way; it was built as a place of refuge in case of fire — an event which has twice happened here since the foundation of the establishment. It bears the name of the Hôtel de St. Louis, which was given in compliment to the kings of France, whose protection was often extended to the hospice. It is chiefly used for offices, and by the domestics of the establishment.

Within a few years additional accommodation in bed-rooms has been added. The ground floor consists of stabling, store-room for wood, fodder, &c. A flight of steps leads up to the principal entrance in the first floor of the building, where a long corridor connects the offices, &c. with the chapel. Another corridor on the floor above leads to the dormitories, the refectory, the gallery of the chapel, &c. The *Drawing Room*, appropriated to the reception of strangers, especially ladies, is entered from the stairs between the two corridors. Here, the few brethren who are privileged to enter, do the honours to their visitors.

The *Clavandier*, (or Burser), an office which was, until lately, most courteously filled for many years by M. Barras, who resided nearly thirty years at this hospice, when he was removed, and placed at the head of his brethren, in the recently established hospice, on the pass of the Simplon. The Clavandier the commissary of the establishment, is the brother who usually presides at the hours of 12 and 6, dinner and supper. Formerly gentlemen dined or supped with all the monks in their refectory, but this is now discontinued.

The room appropriated to visitors

is large and convenient; it is hung with many drawings and prints, presents sent by travellers in acknowledgment of the kind attentions which they had received from the brethren. A piano was among the presents thus sent, by a lady. Attached to this room is a cabinet, in which a day, unfavourable for outdoor enjoyment, may be passed with interest and pleasure. It contains collections of the plants, insects, and minerals of the Alps, and many relics of the temple dedicated to Jupiter, which formerly stood on this pass, near to the site of the hospice. These antiquities consist of votive tablets, and figures, in bronze, and other metals and materials, arms, coins, &c., and are curiously illustrative of the early worship on this mountain, and the intercourse established over this pass. No trace whatever now remains of the temple, though these relics are found upon what is known to have been its site. Steps cut in the rock may yet be seen, which led up to the spot upon which the temple stood.

The chapel of the hospice is generally well attended on Sundays and Festas, when the weather is not unfavourable, by the peasants from the neighbouring valleys and Alp pastures. The tawdry ornaments of Catholic ceremony and worship in the chapel weakens the impressive character of the establishment and its devotees, for whom the most unfeigned respect must exist; but as their religious peculiarities are never obtruded upon strangers, and as their most valuable duties are performed in obedience to the dictates of their religion, no man has a right to make them a ground of offence.

After the battle of Marengo, where Desaix fell, Napoleon ordered a monument to be erected in the chapel of the convent, but it has within a few years been removed, and is now placed on the landing of the stairs, between the corridors.

In the chapel there is a box, where donations in aid of the funds of the establishment are put, and travellers who receive its hospitalities offer their acknowledgments in a sum not less than they would have paid for such accommodation at an inn. The money thus given by those who can afford it, ought to be in a more liberal degree, because that excess aids the monks to extend their assistance to poor and destitute travellers, a very numerous class of claimants upon them, from the great intercourse which exists by this pass between Switzerland and Italy.

There are usually 10 or 12 brethren here. They are all young men, who enter upon this devoted service at 18, and few survive the time of their vow, 15 years: the severities of the weather in the winter, at this height, impairs their health, and they are driven to retire to a lower and more genial clime, but often with broken constitutions and ruined health. Even in the summer, it has happened that the ice never melted in the lake on the summit, and in some years not a week has passed without snow falling. It always freezes early in the morning, even in the height of summer, and the hospice is rarely four months clear of deep snow. Around the building, it averages 7 or 8 feet, and the drifts sometimes rest against it, and accumulate to the height of 40 feet. In the summer of 1816, the ice of the lake, on the summit of the Great St. Bernard never melted, and not a week passed without snow falling. The severest cold recorded was 29° below zero, of Fahrenheit: it has often been observed at 18° and 20° below. The greatest heat has been 68°, but even in the height of summer, it always freezes in the morning.

The perilous passage of this mountain is more frequently undertaken in the winter than is generally imagined; it is difficult to conceive the necessity or urgency of affairs which can lead persons at such a season through scenes of such peril. They are generally pedlars or smugglers who traverse these dreary and dangerous solitudes in defiance of the snows, tourmentes, and avalanches, which always threaten and often overwhelm them. During the severe cold, the snow at this elevation falls like dust; the particles are frozen so hard that they do not attach and form flakes as in lower regions, nor consolidate on the surface where it lies; a storm of wind, therefore, lifts it, and the air is filled with a mist of snow which the eye cannot penetrate; and the poor wretch exposed to it wanders from the land-marks, which in clear weather would guide him, to some fatal spot where he is destroyed. These are the tourmentes so much dreaded. Avalanches are less frequent, but they are often fatal; snow, in large masses, accumulates on the steep slopes of the mountains, until its weight overcomes its support, or, submelting, loosens it; then it suddenly slides off, and soon acquires a degree of inconceivable violence, which sweeps away everything in its course: these avalanches often happen in the winter, and render the approach to the hospice, especially on the side of Switzerland, very dangerous.

To assist travellers, amidst the perils to which they are here exposed, is the duty to which the kind brethren of the hospice and their assistants devote themselves. Undismayed by the storm they seek amidst these dangers the exhausted or overwhelmed traveller; they are generally accompanied by their *Dogs*, animals of peculiar sagacity for this service. These often roam alone day and night through these desolate regions, trace out the victim buried in the snow, lie on him to impart warmth, bark and howl for assistance, or if the distance be too great, return to obtain it. There are usually five or six of these noble animals kept at the hospice, but their duties sometimes lead them into fatal danger. On the 17th of December, 1825, a party, of three Maroniers, domestics of the convent, one of them was Victor, a worthy man, well remembered by alpine travellers, went out with two dogs, on the side of the Vacherie, to search at a dangerous time for travellers; they met one with whom they were returning to the convent, when an avalanche overwhelmed them, and all perished except one of the dogs, whose prodigious strength and activity enabled it to escape. The bodies of poor Victor and his companions were only found after the melting of the snow in the following summer.

The *Morgue* into which the bodies of the victims who had perished on these mountains used to be placed for recognition, has been altered within a few years; the bodies which had long been left in the morgue have been removed, together with the bones of hundreds, the accumulation of ages, which, until a short time since, had remained within a walled enclosure attached to the morgue. These relics of mortality might have continued there without offence; it was a *memento mori* of the deepest interest. Scarcely ten years ago Brockedon described it thus: — " There is one scene of melancholy interest usually visited on the St. Bernard — the *morgue*, or receptacle for the dead. It is a low building, a few yards from the eastern extremity of the convent, where the bodies of the unfortunate victims to storms and avalanches in these mountains have been placed. They have generally been found frozen, and put into this horrid receptacle in the posture in which they perished. Here, many have " dried up and withered," and on some even the clothes have remained after eighteen years; others present a horrid aspect, some of the bones of the head being blanched and exposed, whilst black

integuments still attach to parts of the face: among the latest victims were a mother and child. The air passed freely through the grated windows, without bearing to the nostrils of the observer the foul evidence of its transition through this dreadful place. From the rapid evaporation at this height, the bodies had dried without the usual decay. In a walled enclosure on one side of the morgue was a great accumulation of bones, white, broken, and apparently the gathering of centuries. Upon this rocky and frozen soil they could not bury the dead, and, probably, as they dry up without offence, they are placed here for the chance of recognition."— *Passes of the Alps.*

The system of purveyance for the hospital seems to be well regulated; supplies come from Aosta and the neighbouring villages. Their winter store of hay for their cows is so valuable, that the mules which ascend from either side with travellers, are required to bring their own hay. Wood for firing is one of the most important necessaries to them. Not a stick grows within two leagues, and all the wood supplied to the convent is brought from the forest which belongs to it, in the Val de Ferret, a distance of nearly four leagues. The consumption of wood at the convent, is considerable, for, at the great elevation of the hospice, water boils at about 190 degrees, which is so much less favourable for the concoction of meat than at 212 degrees, that it requires five hours to effect that, which, at the higher temperature, may be done in three hours. They have now adopted stoves for warming the convent with hot air.

Visitors universally acknowledge the kind and courteous attention which they receive from those excellent men, particularly at table. They are freely communicative about their establishment, and conversation has no restraint, but in the respect which their characters demand. The language used by them is French, though there are Italians and Germans among them. They are well informed upon most subjects, and intelligent upon those in which their situation has been favourable to their acquiring information. The periodical works of some academic bodies and institutions are sent to them, and they have a small library, which is chiefly theological. During their short summers, their intercourse with well-informed travellers is extensive, which is shown in the names and notices left by travellers in the albums preserved carefully by the brethren at the hospice ; this intercourse gives to their inquiries a propriety, and an apparent interest in the affairs of the world.

A report had prevailed, that the funds of the convent had suffered much upon the fall of Napoleon, who had especially patronised the establishment. In reply to inquiries upon this subject, the prior answered, that their funds were in a flourishing condition ; that Bonaparte rather impoverished than enriched them. It was true that he had assisted them with donations, but his claims upon their funds had exceeded his benefits ; that they had had forty men quartered upon them for months together, and 60,000 had passed in one season, and all these had been assisted. Their funds, he said, from the facilities which peace gave to travelling, were now increasing, because visitors to the convent, who can afford it, are usually donors.

The monks are of the order of St. Augustin, and the distinguishing badge of that order is a white slit band passed round the neck, the ends before and behind being tucked into the girdle. The dress is a black cloth robe, which reaches nearly to the ankle, buttoned from top to bottom ; a black conical cap, with a tuft at the top, completes a costume which is gentlemanly and becoming.

Travellers who wish to stay at the hospice for a few days, must do it with leave of the principal. It is understood that the object of the establishment is only to assist the passing traveller ; but a stay of some days for scientific research, or excursion in the neighbouring mountains is readily acceded to. One of the brethren has twice ascended the Mont Velan, and made excursions across the glaciers which divide the Combin and the Velan, and separate the Val Pellina from the Val Orsey.

" The scene from the western end of the hospice, looking towards Italy, is sterile and dreary ; patches of snow are seen on the sides of the mountains, which sweep down to the lake ; and the *Pain de Sucre*, a pinnacled mountain on the other side of the Vacherie, with its rocks and snows, adds to its wildness and desolation.

" A column opposite to the middle of the water, marks the boundary of Piedmont and the Valais ; above, and beyond it, is the little plain of Jupiter, where a temple formerly stood, and from which a Roman road led down on the Piedmontese side of the pass. This road may be easily traced in the hewn rock, and the remains of a massive pavement ; but not a vestige of the temple is left above the surface.

" The period of the foundation of the temple of Jupiter, which was formerly on the summit, is unknown ; but many of the bronze votive tablets, which have been found in its ruins, appear to be of great antiquity ; they were placed in the temple and on the altars by travellers, in gratitude for escape from perils * in their journey across the Alps ; some are inscribed to Jupiter, some to the god Penninus. This difference probably arose from the nation of the devotee ; for when the Romans be-

* A custom which is continued in the Catholic Church, as every traveller in France Italy, and Catholic Switzerland may have noticed.

came acquainted with this pass, the worship of Jupiter for that of Penninus was a change only in name and Penninus was preserved with, that of Jupiter long after the Romans had extended their conquests beyond these Alps. The religion, if not the temple, had long been established upon these heights; from the fragments, however, which have been found of the temple, it appears to have been a Roman work of a time probably not earlier than that of Augustus. The period of the substitution of a military column for the statue of Jupiter, under the younger Constantine, in the year 339, was probably not that of the destruction of the temple; for medals of the children of Theodosius, fifty years later, have been found there. It has been conjectured by Chrétien de Loges, in his " *Essais Historiques sur le Mont Saint Bernard,*" that it was destroyed by the Huns and Vandals during their ravages; for it was not in existence when the Lombards passed the Alps in 574.

" The name of this mountain, or rather of this range of the *Pennine* Alps, is generally admitted to be of Celtic origin, from *pen*, or *penn*, a height (this term is still preserved in Cornwall and Wales as *Pen*dennis, *Pen*maenmawr), and not from the Pœni, who crossed the Alps with Hannibal. The territories of the Veragri extended to the summit of this pass, which was the barrier between them and the Salassi, a people of the Val d'Aosta. On this mountain, Livy states that the Veragri worshipped a god of the Alps, Penninus, or Jupiter Penninus, and one of the earliest names for this passage of the Alps, was Mons Jovis, or Mons Jovis Penninus; this was gallicised into Mont Joux, by which it was generally known before it acquired that of St. Bernard.

" The first foundation of the hospice has been attributed by some to Louis the Debonnaire, by others to Charlemagne, whose uncle *Bernard*, an illegitimate son of Charles Martel, led a division of the invading army of Charlemagne over the Great St. Bernard when he went to attack Lombardy. The present name of the pass, Saussure supposes, might have been derived from this *Bernard;* but there was another of the name, an illegitimate son of Pepin, to whom Charlemagne left the kingdom of Italy. To him may rather be attributed the original establishment of the hospice, from the interest which he would have in preserving the communication with Gaul by this passage of the Alps, and with it have given his name, for there is historical evidence that a monastery existed on the Great St. Bernard before the year 851; for Simler mentions, that Hartmann, abbé and almoner of Mont Joux, who was made at that time bishop of Lausanne, had been chief of the monastery. De Rivaz mentions even an earlier abbé of this convent, Vultgare, in 832; and the annals of Bertin state, that Lothaire the second king of Lorraine, in 859 made a treaty with his brother, the emperor Louis II., by which he ceded to him Geneva, Lausanne, and Sion, but reserved particularly *L'Hospital de St. Bernard*, which proves, says Saussure, the importance of this passage, and the name which it bore. But its history at this period is obscure, because in the year 390, it was devastated by Arnaud, who destroyed the monuments and records.

" The present hospice was founded in 962, by Bernard, who was born of a noble family of Savoy, at the château of Menthon, on the lake of Annecy. A determination at an early age to devote himself to an ecclesiastical life, induced him to desert his home and go to Aosta, of which city he afterwards became archdeacon. A coincidence of his name with that of the monastery probably influenced his determination to re-establish the hospice on Mont Joux, of which he ecame the chief. He founded at nearly the same time the hospice on the Little St. Bernard, and gave to them the name, and placed them under the protection of his favourite saint, Nicolas de Myre, as tutelary patron of these establishments. By degrees the name of the devotee was joined to that of the saint, and after the canonisation of Bertrand, his name superseded that of all others, and has continued attached to the hospice since 1123. The attempt of Constantine to destroy the worship of Jupiter had not entirely succeeded; but St. Bernard rooted out the remains of paganism, and founded an establishment for active benevolence, to which thousands have been indebted. He died in 1008, after having governed the convent upwards of 40 years. For some time after the death of St. Bernard, the hospice was exposed to frequent outrages from barbarians who traversed the mountains; and its records of the 11th century present a succession of calamities. The Saracens overran the country, carrying fire and sword into the alpine valleys; the monastery of Mont Joux was burnt, and its ruins became a station of brigands, who plundered or exacted an exorbitant payment from all passengers through a barrier which they established at the south-west extremity of the lake. The Normans having determined to expel these marauders, broke down the barriers and killed the guard. Still outrages continued; and Canute, king of England and Denmark, among others, complained to the pope and the emperor of the horrors and violence committed in the Alps upon his subjects going on pilgrimages to Rome, who seldom ventured to traverse these mountains unless in companies of 400 or 500. His complaints were regarded; the tolls of the passage were abolished; and Canute, in consequence, wrote to his bishops and prelates, informing them that he had secured the safety of the

pilgrims in the route of the Pennine Alps. The brigands were driven out, good order succeeded to outrage, and the convent was re-established.

"In the contests of the emperor Frederic Barbarossa with pope Alexander III., and Humbert, count of Maurienne, diplomas of protection were given by them to the convent, for the security of persons and property belonging to the monastery. It was one of the very few objects in which emperors, sovereign pontiffs, and other distinguished persons, disputed the glory of fostering and protecting a foundation so important to humanity. It soon acquired great celebrity and opulence. As early as 1177, it had, in various dioceses 88 benefices, in priories, cures, châteaux, and farms; it had lands in Sicily, in Flanders, and in England. Its climax of riches and importance was in 1480, when it possessed 98 cures alone. Subsequently, however, the reformation, political changes in the states, loss of distant property, disputes with the popes, with the neighbouring states, and with each other, drove the monks of St. Bernard to seek even eleemosynary assistance. The very land upon which their noble duties are performed has been the subject of disputes between the neighbouring states. Sardinia claimed it as within a frontier extending to the bridge of Nudri, on the northern side; but the Valaisans established a claim to it as within the diocese of Sion, by bulls of the popes from Leo IX. to Benoit XIV. The hospice, therefore, stands within the canton of the Valais; but its authority extends only to the middle of the lake, on the borders of which a column is fixed as a line of demarcation; and the excellent brethren of St. Bernard had not only all their property within the state of Sardinia taken from them, but they were actually taxed by this state for the use which they made of the summer pasturage of the Vacherie. Very little property in land still belongs to the hospice; a vineyard at Clarens*, and a farm at Roche, in the Pays de Vaud, are the principal: their resources are small, and in aid of them, collections are regularly made in the Swiss cantons; but this has been sometimes abused by impostors, who have collected as the agents of the hospice." — *Brockedon's Passes of the Alps.*

On leaving the hospice to descend to the Val d'Aosta, the path skirts the lake, and passes between it and the Place de Jupiter. A little beyond the end of the lake, after passing through a short defile, the scene opens towards Italy, into the vast basin of the Vacherie, where the cows of the convent are pastured. The road turns abruptly to the right, and sweeps round the basin to descend gradually in the plain below. A short cut downward is always taken by an active mountaineer, and is generally safe to the less practised traveller, but let him beware of short cuts in the ascent; in the former case the course is obvious, and the path is generally traceable, but in an ascent all is concealed in the rugged and broken ground above, and the unwary traveller is decoyed into danger before he is aware of its extent.

The view on first looking out upon the Vacherie, from the gorge in the Mont Mort, is very fine, the mountains on the opposite side being sublime in form and elevation; the most striking in the scene being the *Pain de Sucre*, celebrated by Saussure.

---

* The 22d note of the 3d Canto of Childe Harold contains, to the disgrace of Lord Byron, a sneer at the establishment of St. Bernard, for having, he says, cut down the "Bosquet de Juliet," with brutal selfishness, that the ground might be inclosed into a vineyard for the miserable drones of an execrable superstition; " he would thus, for the sake of Rousseau, set the worthlessness of this; ' Bosquet' against the utility and value of a vineyard, the most valuable sort of property near the lake of Geneva, which was to be employed so entirely in the service of humanity.

At the lower end of the Vacherie the path winds down by a series of zigzags, and thence the descent is rapid to St. Remy, a dreary little village, but where there is now an excellent inn. Here return chars to Aosta may generally be obtained for 10 francs. Travellers who leave Aosta to visit the hospice, in a char for St Remy, and intend to return, let it await them there for four or six hours, and pay 20 francs for the char for the day, with a buono-mano to the postilion. But it generally happens that the traveller crosses the mountain, in which case he pays from 12 to 14 francs for the char, and the postilion waits till the evening for customers descending from the Great Saint Bernard, and it is seldom that they are disappointed in a fare.

From St. Remy the road descends with little interest in the scenery, to St. Oyen, where the Piedmontese custom-house is placed, and where the passports are examined. These require great regularity, or the permission to pass is withheld. Beyond St. Oyen, at Etroubles, another examination takes place. The Piedmontese officers are usually very courteous, an advantage, which the good temper of the traveller is sure to obtain.

At Etroubles, the St. Bernard branch of the Buttier is crossed, and the road descends to the village of Gignod, where the vegetation begins to luxuriate, and the Italian side of the mountain is felt and seen. Here there is a fine peep into the Val Pellina. From Gignod to the city of Aosta, the richness of the scenery is constantly increasing. Trellised vines and Indian corn mark the approach to the Val d'Aosta; and the first view of the city and the valley, in the descent from the St. Bernard, where the background is filled with the magnificent forms and snowy summits of the mountains above the Val de Cogne; is perhaps, one of the finest in the Alps.

ROUTE 109.

ST. BRANCHIER TO AOSTA BY THE
VALLEY OF BAGNES, THE GLACIERS
OF CHARMONTANE, THE COL DE
FENÊTRE AND THE VAL PELLINA.

(Two Days.)

From St. Branchier (Route 108.),
a good mule track leads up the valley
of Bagnes, which is very fertile, to
Lourtier, passing through many villages, especially those of Chable, and
Morgnes. The valley is narrow,
abounding in gorges, and offering
many fine scenes to the pencil of the
traveller. Above Lourtier this character becomes more striking, and the
pass increases in difficulty to Mauvoisin, a hamlet not far below the
glaciers of Getroz. The descent of
these glaciers from the Mont Pleureur
was the cause of the interruption of the
waters of the Drance, which formed
a lake and burst its bounds in 1595,
and carried off in its destructive course
more than 140 persons from the valley, besides houses and cattle. A more
recent inundation, that of 1818, from
a similar cause, has left fearful traces of
its overwhelming power. Among the
boulders brought down by that event,
is one which contains above 1400
square feet; and the height which the
waters then attained is yet distinctly
marked, where the land, then covered,
is even now desolate.

"Vast blocks of stone," says Brockedon, in his "Excursions in the
Alps," "which were driven and deposited there by the force of the
waters, now strew the valley; and
sand and pebbles present an arid surface, where rich pasturages were seen
before the catastrophe. The quantity
and violence of the water suddenly
disengaged, and the velocity of its
descent, presented a force which the
mind may calculate, but cannot conceive.

"In the accounts which have been
given of this event, the object of the
writers has been merely to describe

the catastrophe, and the extent of its
injuries; but in reading the account
of M. Escher de Linth, published in
the *Bib. Univ. de Genève, Sci. et
Arts*, tom. viii. p. 291, I was most
forcibly struck with the unparalleled
heroism of the brave men who endeavoured to avert the evil, by opening
a channel for the waters, which had,
by their accumulation, become a
source of terror to the inhabitants of
these valleys.

"In the spring of 1818, the people
of the valley of Bagnes became
alarmed on observing the low state of
the waters of the Drance, at a season
when the melting of the snows usually
enlarged the torrent; and this alarm
was increased by the records of similar
appearances before the dreadful inundation of 1595, which was then occasioned by the accumulation of the
waters behind the débris of a glacier
that formed a dam, which remained
until the pressure of the water burst
the dike, and it rushed through the
valley, leaving desolation in its
course.

"In April 1818, some persons
went up the valley to ascertain the
cause of the deficiency of water, and
they discovered that vast masses of
the glaciers of Getroz, and avalanches
of snow, had fallen into a narrow part
of the valley, between Mont Pleureur
and Mont Mauvoisin, and formed a
dike of ice and snow 600 feet wide
and 400 feet high, on a base of 3000
feet, behind which the waters of the
Drance had accumulated, and formed
a lake above 7000 feet long. M.
Venetz, the engineer of the Valais,
was consulted, and he immediately
decided upon cutting a gallery through
this barrier of ice, 60 feet above the
level of the water at the time of com-
mencing, and where the dike was 600
feet thick. He calculated upon making a tunnel through this mass before
the water should have risen 60 feet
higher in the lake. On the 10th of
May, the work was begun by gangs
of fifty men, who relieved each other,

and worked, without intermission, day and night, with inconceivable courage and perseverance, neither deterred by the daily occurring danger from the falling of fresh masses of the glacier, nor by the rapid increase of the water in the lake, which rose 62 feet in 34 days—on an average nearly two feet each day ; but it once rose five feet in one day, and threatened each moment to burst the dike by its increasing pressure ; or, rising in a more rapid proportion than the men could proceed with their work, render their efforts abortive, by rising above them. Sometimes dreadful noises were heard, as the pressure of the water detached masses of ice from the bottom, which, floating, presented so much of their bulk above the water as led to the belief that some of them were 70 feet thick. The men persevered in their fearful duty without any serious accident, and though suffering severely from cold and wet, and surrounded by dangers which cannot be justly described, by the 4th of June they had accomplished an opening 600 feet long ; but having begun their work on both sides of the dike at the same time, the place where they ought to have met was twenty feet lower on one side of the lake than on the other : it was fortunate that latterly the increase of the perpendicular height of the water was less, owing to the extension of its surface. They proceeded to level the highest side of the tunnel, and completed it just before the water reached them. On the evening of the 13th the water began to flow. At first, the opening was not large enough to carry off the supplies of water which the lake received, and it rose two feet above the tunnel ; but this soon enlarged from the action of the water, as it melted the floor of the gallery, and the torrent rushed through. In thirty-two hours the lake sunk ten feet, and during the following twenty-four hours twenty feet more ; in a few days it would have been emptied ; for the floor melting, and being driven

off as the water escaped, kept itself below the level of the water within ; but the cataract which issued from the gallery melted, and broke up also a large portion of the base of the dike which had served as its buttress : its resistance decreased faster than the pressure of the lake lessened, and at four o'clock in the afternoon of the 16th of June the dike burst, and in half an hour the water escaped through the breach, and left the lake empty.

" The greatest accumulation of water had been 800,000,000 of cubic feet ; the tunnel, before the disruption, had carried off nearly 330,000,000 — Escher says, 270,000,000 ; but he neglected to add 60,000,000 which flowed into the lake in three days. In half an hour, 530,000,000 cubic feet of water passed through the breach, or 300,000 feet per second ; which is five times greater in quantity than the waters of the Rhine at Basle, where it is 1300 English feet wide. In one hour and a half the water reached Martigny, a distance of eight leagues. Through the first 70,000 feet it passed with the velocity of thirty-three feet per second — four or five times faster than the most rapid river known ; yet it was charged with ice, rocks, earth, trees, houses, cattle, and men ; thirty-four persons were lost, 400 cottages swept away, and the damage done in the two hours of its desolating power exceeded a million of Swiss livres. All the people of the valley had been cautioned against the danger of a sudden irruption ; yet it was fatal to so many. All the bridges in its course were swept away, and among them the bridge of Mauvoisin, which was elevated 90 feet above the ordinary height of the Drance. If the dike had remained untouched, and it could have endured the pressure until the lake had reached the level of its top, a volume of 1,700,000,000 cubic feet of water would have been accumulated there, and a devastation much more fatal and extensive must have been the consequence. From this greater danger the people of the valley of the Drance were preserved by the heroism and devotion of the brave men who effected the formation of the gallery in the dike, under the direction of M. Venetz. I know no instance on record of courage equal to this: their risk of life was not for fame or for riches — they had not the usual excitements to personal risk, in a world's applause or gazetted promotion, — their devoted courage was to save the lives and property of their fellow-men, not to destroy them. They steadily and heroically persevered in their labours, amidst dangers such as a field of battle never presented, and from which some of the bravest brutes that ever lived would have shrunk in dismay. These truly brave Valaisans deserve all honour !"

But the skill of M. Venetz was not limited in its application to emptying the lake: his abilities have been properly directed to the prevention of such another catastrophe, for the liability to its recurrence was obvious. Not one twentieth part of the ice which formed the barrier, had been removed when the dike burst, and fresh masses were still falling from Mont Pleureux and Mont Mauvoisin, the mountains of which the bases formed the buttresses to the dike ; in fact the dike was again accumulating so rapidly, that at the end of 1819 the barrier was almost as complete, as before its bursting from the pressure of the lake.

It became therefore an important object to prevent a repetition of the former catastrophe, by the adoption of such means as would prevent, or at least diminish, the increase of the barrier. Blasting by gunpowder was found impracticable, from the difficulty of firing the powder at considerable depths in the ice, and from the comparatively small masses removed by this means. After much consideration and many trials, a mode has been adopted and put in execution by M. Venetz, which promises the greatest success.

"M. Venetz had remarked that the glacier could not support itself where the river was of a certain width, but fell into it and was dissolved ; whereas, where the river was comparatively narrow, the ice and snow formed a vault over it, and consequently tended to the preservation of any portion falling from the glacier above. Perceiving also the effect of the river in dissolving the part it came in contact with, he formed and executed the design of bringing the streams of the neighbouring mountains by a canal to Mauvoisin, opposite the highest part of the glacier where it touched that mountain. From hence it was conducted by wooden troughs on to the glacier in a direction parallel to the valley. The water was divided into two streams : one falling nearly on the one edge of the Drance, and the other on the other ; and having been warmed by the sun in its course, soon cut very deep channels in the ice. When they reached the river the troughs were removed a few feet, and thus the stream produced the effect of a saw, which, dividing the ice, forced the portion between them to fall into the Drance.

"When the weather is fine, these streams, which are not more than four or five inches in diameter, act with extraordinary power, piercing a hole 200 feet deep and six feet in diameter in 24 hours. They are calculated to remove 100,000 cubical feet of ice from the barrier daily, and it is supposed that if the weather is fine the whole will be removed in three years.

"At the end of the season of 1822 the Drance remained covered only for a length of 480 feet; whereas, at the commencement of the operation, it was covered over a length of 1350 feet. M. Venetz estimates the quantity of ice removed in 1822 as between eleven and twelve millions of cubical feet." — *Bib. Univ.* xxii. 58.

The châlets above Getroz can be reached in good time in one day from Martigny; and those who wish to cross the glaciers of Charmontane can sleep at the châlets, and, starting early the next morning, push on to the extremity of the valley, cross two glaciers, and attain the summit of the pass of the Col de la Fenêtre in time to reach Aosta on the following day.

These enormous glaciers have a greater extent, commanded at one glance, than perhaps any other in the Alps. With crampons on the feet, the traverse, it is stated, by one who has recently passed, is neither dangerous nor difficult, but very fatiguing from their great extent. As they are seen to stream into their channel from the lofty peaks of the Combin and the Velan, they offer to the enterprising traveller one of the grandest views in the Alps. The elevation of the Col de la Fenêtre exceeds 9000 English feet, and the view from this crest extends over the southern mountains which bound the Val Pellina, to the peaks of the Iseran and the Cogne.

From the Col de la Fenêtre the descent is long and fatiguing to Balme, the first hamlet, and to Ollomont, where there are traces of an aqueduct built by the Romans for the supply of water to Augusta Prætoria. Thence the road descends through e village of Valpellina, and still lower that of Rogniant, near to where the Buttier is crossed, and the path leads into the city of Aosta. (Route 107.)

ROUTE 110.

MARTIGNY TO CORMAYEUR BY THE COL DE FERRET.

At Orsieres, in the Val d'Entremont (Route 108.), a path turns off on the right, enters an agreeable valley and continues on the banks of an alpine river, and, after pursuing a tolerable road to Issert, the principal village in the Val de Ferret, 3 hours distant from Martigny, ascends rapidly towards the higher hamlets of Pra le Fort, and Branche. The mountains which bound the valley towards the west are lofty, and crowned with the northern extremity of those vast glaciers of the chain of Mont Blanc, which, divided on the crest, descend towards the Val de Ferret, as the glaciers of Salena, Portalet, and Neuve; and, on the other side, towards the west, form the glaciers of Trient, du Tour, and d'Argentière.

There is nothing, however, remarkable in the scenery of the Val de Ferret. The route leads up a succession of rather flat divisions of the valley, from Issert to the Châlets de Folie, distant 2 hours. On the right, the short transversal valleys, or rather crues, in the side of the mountains, are the channels for these glaciers.

Above the Châlets de Folie, the usual path to the Col de Ferret leads up through the Châlets of Ferret, by the detritus of a mountain which fell in the year 1776, burying the pasturages of Banderai. Near to these châlets the two paths separate — that on the left leading over the Col de la Fenêtre to the Great St. Bernard, that on the right to the Col de Ferret.

Instead, however, of ascending by Ferret and the Châlets of Banderai, the guides now take a shorter path directly up the pasturages on the right, above the Granges of Folie; but, without a guide, this may lead into scenes of danger, towards the deep crues and precipices which form the eastern side of the great chain of Mont Blanc — scenes of impressive grandeur, from their vastness and utter sterility.

The ascent by the shorter path is very steep and fatiguing to the Co de Ferret; but the view when near the summit well repays for the trouble of attaining it, the time required from the Châlet de Folie being about two hours.

From the ascent, the whole Val de Ferret is seen, bounded on either side by lofty mountains, and the distance is limited only by the Bernese Alps.

The woods and pasturages of part of the Val de Ferret belong to the Convent of the Great St. Bernard, and at this distance from the hospice — 4 or 5 leagues — the brethren obtain all their wood, and some hay.

From the crest of the Col de Ferret, the view along the south-eastern side of Mont Blanc, towards Piedmont, is one of the scenes celebrated by Saussure. The eye is carried through the Val d'Entrèves and the Allée Blanche to the Col de la Seigne, an extent of 40 miles. Numerous glaciers are seen on the right, streaming down into the valley from the great glaciers of Mont Blanc; but the " Monarch " himself is not seen, the enormous masses of the Grand Jorasse and the Géant conceal him in this view.

The descent is over a soft slaty soil, in which the tracks of sheep and cattle have cut deep trenches, in which if a man stand he is half concealed. Ten minutes below the Col a cross is placed on the edge of a precipice which the path passes; it serves to guide the course of the ascending traveller, though from below it seems to be placed on a pyramidal mass of rock which it would be impossible to attain. Far in the deep valley, the stream flowing into Italy appears like a thread of silver.

An hour and half of fatiguing descent brings the traveller to the Châlets of Pré de Bar, famed for being the dirtiest in Piedmont.

Near Pré de Bar the vast glacier of Triolet sweeps down from the crest which divides this glacier from the masses, which, on the other side, form the glacier of Talefre. Below the glacier of Triolet the road descends by a most fatiguing path, amidst rocks and stones and bushes, presenting a scene of alpine desolation. The valley is very narrow, and each rift on the mountain side towards

Mont Blanc has its glacier hanging down from the summit. Not less than seven distinct glaciers are passed in the course of this valley, before reaching the village of Entrèves, near to Cormayeur. These chiefly descend from the masses which form the Grand Jorasse, and the remarkable peak of the Géant. A few miserable villages in the Val d'Entrèves are passed. The highest is Sagion; those below are Pré-sec and Plan-pansier. More than half the length of the valley is passed, on the descent, before Mont Blanc is seen: when its prodigious mass opens to the view, the effect is overwhelming. The ruggedness of the descent is increased by passing over the débris of a mountain fall beneath the Géant. This passed, the river, which descends through the Val d'Entrèves, is crossed, the village of Entrèves is left on the right, and, winding along a path by the side of the mountain, Cormayeur (Route 107.), is reached in 15 or 16 hours from Martigny.

ROUTE 111.

AOSTA TO PONTE IN VAL D'ORCA, BY COGNE, FENÊTRE DE COGNE, THE COL DE REALE, AND THE VAL SOANNA.

(Three Days.)

From Aosta (Route 109.) a road leads directly down to the river Doire, which is crossed on a wooden bridge, and a path ascends on the right bank through the rich plain of the valley, and through the villages of Gressau and Joveneau to Aimaville, about a league and a half, where one of the most fantastical offences to good taste in building, spoils one of the finest sites in the valley. A knoll jutting out into it is surmounted with a squab, square mass of masonry, a modern antique, worse than any cockney attempt to decorate a garden with a castle. At Aimaville there formerly existed an ancient pagan temple, which was succeeded by an establishment of knights templars; and within the present queer structure is an ancient armoury of the barons of Aimaville. It is now inhabited by the Contessa di Rocca.

From the château the ascent is steep to the hamlet of St. Martin. The view from the crest above it is perhaps the finest in the Val d'Aosta, in the richness of its plain, studded with villas and châteaux. The city is seen as in a glorious frame, and beyond it, towards the great chain, the peaks of the Monte Rosa close this unmatched scene of the beautiful and magnificent in nature.

On turning the brow of the mountain which forms the southern side of the entrance to the Val de Cogne, a path at an elevation of at least 2000 feet above the torrent of the Cogne, leads into the valley. Soon after losing sight of Aosta; deep in the valley beneath the path, the tops of the cottages of Pont d'Ael are seen clustered with a few trees, and near it a white line which crosses the ravine. This is well worth an examination, and a path leads down to this remarkable village, where the line crossing the gulf will be found to be a road over an aqueduct, which now serves as a road. This is one of the most remarkable of the Roman structures remaining in the Val d'Aosta, from the times of the empire. This aqueduct is raised 400 feet above the torrent, which it crosses by a single arch; immediately above the arch is the ancient road or gallery, lit through slits in the wall. This gallery is 180 feet long, 14 feet high, and 3 feet wide. The vault is composed of the slabs which formed the bed of the ancient water-course. The gallery is entered by arched ports at either end; there are two, one on either side, at the village of Pont d'Ael, and at the other end the port opens down the valley. This singular work is in perfectly sound condition, though built, as a still legible and even sharp inscription indicates, by

Caius Aimus and his son, of Padua, in the thirteenth year of Augustus. This inscription is inaccessible; it is placed on a tablet just over the arch on the lower side towards the valley of Aosta. Though it cannot be reached, to which fact it probably owes its preservation, yet it can be readily read from the brink of the precipice on the side of Pont d'Ael, and the following is the inscription : —

IMP. CÆSARE AUGUSTO XIII.
COS. DESIGN. C. AVILLIUS C. F. C. AIMUS
PATAVINUS PRIVATUM.

Their name is still preserved in the village and château of Aimaville.

Travellers in the Val d'Aosta should not fail to visit this interesting work of antiquity, which is placed in a situation where it is impossible to imagine that any benefit could ever have arisen commensurate with the expense of the structure. The surrounding scenery is very grand.

In ascending the valley of Cogne, it is not necessary to retrace one's steps to regain the path high upon the mountain side. A shorter cut from Pont d'Ael leads to it; the valley for a long way above Pont d'Ael is a fearful ravine, utterly impracticable in its depth, which, except at two or three points, is equally impervious to the eye. In some places the narrow path on the edge of the precipices, wretchedly guarded by poles and trees, which a child might throw over, is so obviously dangerous, that none but a practised mountain traveller could pass some places without a shudder. Opposite to one spot, where the path turns suddenly into a deep rift or crue in the mountain side, is a slide, down which trees cut in the forest above are discharged, for the chance of the torrent bringing them down to the Val d'Aosta. Not one in ten escape being broken into splinters; these, however, serve for the usines and founderies for working the iron raised in the Val de Cogne, and which is celebrated in Piedmont.

The difficulties of constructing a road by which the productions of the valley could be brought down, is obvious on observing its precipitous character. The valley, however, opens a little near some usines, and from where the river is crossed to its left bank, a tolerable road leads to Cogne. This road has been made by two brothers, iron-masters, who have recorded its formation on a tablet, in a rock. There is very little cultivation in the valley, the products of the mines giving occupation to its inhabitants; every stream drives its tilt hammer, and almost every person is employed in working, smelting, or forging the iron raised.

The hamlets of Silvenoir, Epinel, and Crela, are passed before reaching the village of Cogne, where a villanous inn is the only place of rest; either, in anticipation of an early start across the mountains from Cogne, or, after having traversed them during the long fatiguing day's journey from the Val d'Orca, for the six hours required between Cogne and Aosta, is too much to add to such a day's work either way.

On leaving Cogne for the pass, a good road continues up to the place where the iron ore is brought down from the mountain. The track by which the miners ascend and the ores lowered, is distinctly seen. In the "Journals of an Alpine Traveller;" the scene has been thus described : —

"On our approach to Cogne, I was struck by the appearance of a great quantity of iron ore, heaped upon the roadside, which was here of good breadth and kept in tolerable condition. On the opposite side of the valley, in a mountain, is a mass of iron ore celebrated for its extraordinary richness : the mines are worked at a great height in the mountain side, and I was surprised at the laborious mode adopted for bringing the ore down into the valley, thence to be taken to the founderies and forges. Zigzag paths are made from the adits, upon which barrows on sledges are placed filled with the ore, and these are in succession pushed off by a conductor. When the sliding-barrow has acquired sufficient impetus down the inclined plane forming each line of the zigzag descent, the man who directs it leaps adroitly into the barrow and descends with it, and before the load has acquired an uncontrollable velocity, it is brought up by a bank at each angle of the zigzag path or slide. The conductor then gets out, turns the barrow in the direction of the next slide, pushes it forward, and again, while it is in motion, leaps in, and is taken down to the next angle; and thus, in a series of turns, at last reaches the bottom in the valley. The men have, it appears, to walk up the mountain again, and their empty slides are dragged up. . I never saw power so misapplied or wasted."

On leaving the little plain of Cogne the road ascends by a steep path on the mountain side, leaving on the right the valley of Vermiana, into which descends an enormous glacier from the mountain called the Grand Paradis. The steep path passes over what appears to be a vast dike in the valley, the torrent flows round it to escape through a ravine at one extremity. On crossing the ridge, the traveller finds himself on a more wild and open ground, leading to the alps and pasturages of Chavanes. Some of the lower châlets are soon reached : further up on this fine alp, which feeds large flocks and herds during the summer, numerous châlets form the cluster known as the Châlets of Chavanes. Here the scene is rich in the pastoral groups and beauty of the herbage, and sublime in the magnificence of the amphitheatre of mountains and glaciers.

Immediately in front is the great glacier of Cogne, by which an active mountaineer can cross and reach Ponte, in the Val d'Orca, in a day. A less dangerous road, however, is found by leaving the glacier, and turning to the left up a steep and difficult ascent to a narrow col, called the Fenêtre de Cogne, a mere notch in the crest of the mountain. From this place the view of the Alps, which bound the Val de Cogne on the west, is magnificent from the grandeur of their forms and the vast extent of their glaciers.

In the opposite direction, the glaciers which crest the northern side of the Val d'Orca are not less striking and are perhaps more impressive from their greater proximity. They form a vast barrier to the right of the Val Champorcher, which opens into the Val d'Aosta (Route 108.), at Fort Bard.

The descent is extremely difficult, from the steepness of the path and looseness of the soil. This difficulty ends before reaching a little chapel or oratory, built probably as an *ex voto* by some grateful Catholic for a merciful preservation here. This oratory is placed on the brink of one of several little lakes, formed by the melting of the glaciers. No spot can be more savage than this, or give a more impressive idea of dreary solitude.

The path now skirts, as it leaves it on the right, a dark and enormous mountain mass, and descends rapidly down the valley, but nothing habitable appears. The valley deepens considerably on the left below the path: the eye can trace its course down towards Bard, and a path across the valley is also seen which leads from the Val Champorcher by the Châlets of Dodoney into the valley of Fenis.

After crossing a buttress of the mountains which the path skirts, and which is called the Col de Ponton, it leads to the bank of a torrent just where it issues from a great glacier; then crossing another ridge over a beautiful pasturage, it descends to the borders of a little lake at the foot of the Col de Reale.

From this spot to Fort Bard down the valley of Champorcher, is about 6 hours.

Turning abruptly to the right, the path leads to the Col de Reale in less than an hour, and from this crest one of the finest alpine panoramas is presented. Not only, upon reaching the crest, is the plain of Italy and the far stretch of the maritime Alps, to the southward, spread out like a vast map, but in an opposite direction the entire mass of Monte Rosa is better seen than from any other point of view. Every peak, and glacier, and valley, and pass, from the sharp pinnacle of the Cervin (Route 106.), to the Col de Val Dobbia (Route 104.) are seen, whilst the intermediate range of mountains above Dodoney, and the deep valley of Champorcher below, serve as a foreground to this sublime scene. The black and scathed rocks which bound the crest of the pass complete this extraordinary panorama.

Nothing can be imagined more beautiful than the view towards the plains where the deep valley of the Soanna sinks into darkness, whilst about the mountains which bound it, and far over and beyond, the plains of Italy stretch away into indistinctness, and are lost in the distance.

From the crest the descent is rapid. Passing to the left under a beetling mountain, the path skirts a deep ravine, leaves on the right some old adits of a mine worked unprofitably for silver, and, after a tortuous descent of two hours, passes by some châlets. The level of the pine forests is soon reached, and deep in a little plain is seen the church and village of Val Pra, which, instead of being the highest church and village in the Val Soanna, is usually placed, in the authorised maps, nearly as far down as Ronco. If the traveller arrive late at Val Pra, the worthy old peasant Giuseppe Danna will give him his best welcome.

At the opposite extremity of this little plain, the path descends by a stunted pine forest, and through the depths of the valley, to the village of

Peney, and by one or two little hamlets to the village of Cardonera. There is nothing peculiar in this part of the valley, until just before reaching the hamlet of Bosco del Ronco : there are the remains of a slip from the mountain, which took place in 1833, and strewed the little plain with rocks and stones.

At Ronco there is an inn, which hunger and fatigue may make endurable ; below it, a bridge, in a wild and striking situation, leads across a ravine to the village of Ingria. Before reaching it, however, the opening of the valley of Campea is passed, which leads directly to the glaciers of Cogne, shorter by seven hours than the route by the Col de Reale. The only village in the Val Campea, above Ingria, is Campiglia.

The inhabitants of this valley wear a singular sort of shoe or boot ; it is made of coarse woollen, tied tight round the ankle, but half as broad again as the foot ; it gives an awkwardness to their gait.

Below Ingria, the valley becomes a ravine of singularly wild and grand character. Vast precipices, gorges and forests, offer alternately, sometimes together, their magnificent materials for alpine scenery. Soon the old towers of Ponte are seen in the valley of Orca, beyond the depths of the ravine. Enormous overhanging masses close the proximate part of the valley, whilst above and beyond Ponte the plains of Piedmont appear.

A path down through a forest, and near some quarries, leads to the Villa Nuova of Ponte, the cotton works established by the Baron Du Port, and about half a mile beyond is the town of Ponte, six hours from Val Pra in the mountains.

Nothing can exceed the picturesque situation of this place, at the confluence of the Soanna and the Orca, rich in vineyards, inclosed by mountains, offering in combination with the surrounding scenery, the towers and ruins of two feudal castles in the most striking situations, and the head of the valley closed by the snowy peaks of the lofty range which divides the Val d'Orca from the Tarentaise.

There are many spots about Ponte which offer views of singular beauty. Few places are so rich in the picturesque : these, too, offer a remarkable variety, for besides the views of Ponte and the valley, from the villages on the surrounding mountains' sides, both the Orca and the Soanna present retreats in their deep and retired courses, which are no where exceeded for picturesqueness. A walk down two or three meadows between Ponte and the Orca, leads to one of these, well worth the traveller's visit, where the bright deep waters of the Orca seems hemmed in by lofty and forest-crowned precipices. Of its tranquillity and beauty, no idea can be formed.

Ponte is a singular old town, with long arcades, beneath which there are shops, and the markets are held. It has a tolerably good inn.

The establishment of the *Fabrica*, the first cotton works known in Piedmont, has given employment to several thousands of men, women, and children, as printers, spinners, weavers, and dyers ; the goods being prepared within the walls of the Fabrica, from the raw material as imported from Genoa, to the completion of every article for the market. The prohibition to the exportation of machinery from England, leads to their obtaining it, at a great cost, from Mulhausen, in Alsace.

Ponte is distant six hours from Turin, to which city, a diligence goes three times a week. There is an excellent carriage road to the capital, which passes through Courgne, a large town on the western side of the Orca ; Valperga, celebrated for having one of the noblest campaniles in Piedmont ; Rivarolo ; Lombardore, where the river Mallone is crossed ; and Lemie ; besides numerous villages. All those places named, are towns, and some are large. They are situated in the richest part of Piedmont, amidst Indian corn, vines, mulberry and fig trees. Those which are placed on the subsidences of the Alps, a little above the plains, are in the most beautiful situations, surrounded by vine-covered hills, and backed by lofty ranges of mountains. Little idea can be formed of the richness and beauty of Piedmont, except by those who have skirted the mountains on the borders of its rich plains. The traveller who enters it abruptly, by the usual routes, at right angles, across the chain of the Alps, sees too little of its actual and picturesque richness to estimate justly this fine country.

ROUTE 112.

PONTE TO VILLENEUVE, BY THE VAL D'ORCA (DÉTOUR TO THE COL DE GALESE), THE COL DE CROIX DE NIVOLET, AND THE VAL SAVARANCHE.

(Three Days.)

On leaving Ponte to ascend the Val d'Orca, the road continues on the left bank of the river throughout its course. The scenery is very fine; the forms of the mountains vast and grand, rugged and broken, clothed with magnificent chesnut-trees, and frequently exhibiting the effects of disintegration in the enormous blocks which have fallen from the heights, in many places in such quantity, that the road is carried over or around the *débris* with such sinuosity and undulation, that the variety of views they aid to present gives a peculiar character to this valley.

About three miles from Ponte is the village of Sparone. Many little hamlets lie on the road, and many usines are worked for small iron wares, with tilts, and no stream is allowed to remain idle, where, at a small cost, and with simple machinery, it can be made to tilt a hammer, or move a saw.

Beyond Sparone the same character of scenery prevails to Locana, a little town about four or five miles above

Sparone. In these villages, many of the weavers for the Fabrica are employed. The streets of Locana are narrow and dirty, and its inn worthy of such a place. The "Three Pigeons" is not likely to be forgotten by any traveller who has had the misfortune to enter there.

Above Locana the valley soon becomes dreary, and the road more rugged. About half way, near some smelting houses and forges belonging to M. Binna, the road, which he keeps in order below, ceases to be practicable for a charette. Above, there is only a mule path, which winds up amidst the enormous masses of fallen granite and serpentine, some of which have blocked up the course of the torrent, and compelled it to find another channel — these and the savage mountains which now domineer in the valley, give it great wildness. Yet the tortuous road rising over these *éboulemens,* often leads to beautiful little plains between them.

There are several hamlets above Locana, as St. Marco, Arsone, and La Frera, but each is more and more miserable, until 6 or 7 miles from Locana. The climax of wretchedness is found at Novasca, which has pointed a proverb —

> Novasca, Novasca,
> Poco pane, lungo tasca.

Yet this spot offers to the traveller some of the most sublime horrors encountered in the Alps. Here a grand cataract bursts out from a rift in a mountain mass of granite, where all is denuded to absolute sterility. Below it, a thousand enormous masses of granite are bouldered by the materials brought down and thrown upon them by the fall. The passage across the river, among these rocks, is unmatched in alpine bridge-building: poles and planks are placed from rock to rock, and almost under the spray of the cataract. Beyond the passage of this torrent the road still ascends on the left bank of the Orca.

About a mile above Novasca is a terrific gorge, called the Scalare de Ceresol, where enormous precipices overhang the course of the Orca, which tumbles through a succession of cataracts between these herbless precipices. The path which leads to the summit is cut out of the rocks, and a flight of steps (Scalare), practicable for mules, is carried up through the gorge ; sometimes on the actual brink of the precipice which overhangs the foaming torrent; in others, cut so deep into its side, that the rocky canopy overhangs the precipice. In some places there is not room enough for the mounted traveller, and there is the danger of his head striking the rocks above him. This extraordinary path extends half a mile. In its course, crosses are observed, fixed against the rock to mark the spots of fatal accidents : but as three such accidents happened in company with an old miscreant who lived at the foot of the Scalare, suspicions were entertained of these having been murders which he had committed there. He underwent severe examinations ; yet, though no doubt existed of his guilt, there was not evidence enough to convict him. It is believed that, at the spots where the crosses are placed, he pushed his victims over in an unguarded moment, where a child, unheeded, might have destroyed a giant.

The termination of this wild road is like a winding staircase, in which it is difficult for a mule to turn : near here the peep into the ravine is perfectly appalling.

On emerging from this singular path and fearful defile, the traveller finds himself on a plain, where there is barley grown, and an abundance of rich meadow land. Immediately before him is the snowy range which divides the Val Forno from the Val d'Orca, and across which a col leads to Gros Cavallo, in that valley, in a few hours.

A little way within the plain, the valley turns to the right, and leads up under a mountain, where the Comte d'Aglie has some silver mines. The ore is smelted in the valley, and near the works there is a spring of water slightly ferruginous, but so highly carbonated, that the gas escapes from it in a sparkling state. The peasants have fitted a wooden tube into the hole, through which it ascends ; a little canal of reed fixed to the top of the tube enables them to fill bottles, which are instantly corked and tied, and abundance of this water is thus taken to Turin. It is almost tasteless, when drunk at the spring it is delicious.

The mountains of Levanna, on the left as the traveller ascends the valley, are very grand ; pinnacled, glaciered, and utterly inaccessible. Three of the peaks, near together, bear the name of the *trois becs*. The valley widens near Ceresol, the highest of its church villages, about eight miles above the Scalare. Here he may rest in what a mountaineer would call an *assez bon gîte* — none but a mountaineer, however, would think it so.

To shorten the next day's journey, it will be better, however, to ascend the valley yet higher by three hours, to the Châlets of Chapis, and, if mules are required, to engage them at Ceresol to come up the following morning to Chapis early enough to insure arrival, in good time, at Villeneuve, in the Val d'Aosta, in the evening of the same day. Fatigue only, however, is spared — no time is gained by riding.

From Ceresol, the extraordinary pass of the Galese at the head of the Val d'Orca, is first seen, above a perpendicular streak of snow, called the Grand Coluret, which must be climbed to cross the ridge of glaciers which surmounts it, and by which a passage may be made into the valley of the Isere in the Tarentaise.

From Chapis there is a walk of two hours and a half to the highest châlets in the valley—those of Serue—

which are passed by the traveller who would go to the Galese. Beyond Serue the scene perhaps surpasses in sterility and savageness any other in the Alps. A narrow path leads along the steep slope of the Mont Iseran, until it stop abruptly at an inaccessible gulley in the mountain called the Little Coluret. To ascend above this it is necessary to climb along the face of a fearful precipice overhanging, at a great height, a lake at the head of the valley. Having climbed round it, the plain of Belotta is attained. This plain is the bed of an ancient lake, now filled with an enormous glacier, which streams down from the left. The bottom of this glacier must be crossed by a very steep ascent up a vast mass of ice, and above it, up the gulley of the Grand Coluret, at least 1500 feet from the glacier. Precipices, fringed with icicles, overhang the traveller, and having climbed up close to the rocks, on the right side, it is at last necessary to cross the snow itself that lies in the hollow; this is not dangerous to a steady head, but a slip would precipitate the unlucky traveller at least 2000 feet. On the other side the footing is firm, but climbing among overhanging masses of rock requires a steady head and firm foot. Having passed these, he will reach the steep back or upper edge of a glacier, forming a precipice of ice about 40 feet high When this is passed, the traveller reaches the top, about 10,000 feet above the level of the sea, where one of the most glorious views in the Alps rewards him: he looks out over the head of the Val Isère, upon La Val, and Tignes. To this valley the descent on the side of the Tarentaise is not difficult. In returning, there is little danger in the descent, less than in the ascent, though it seem more dangerous, for the feet sink deep and firmly in the loose soil of both the Colurets. The Little Coluret can be safely descended, though, from the looseness of the soil, the ascent is impracticable.

At the Châlets of Serue refreshment of milk, cheese, and butter may be had: bread must be taken there; of this necessary and wine, the traveller must stock himself when he visits these wild valleys; and he is especially cautioned against wandering there without a careful and well-recommended guide. At Novasca, or Ceresol, Giuseppi Bruscha, better known by the name of Muot, from the loss of one hand, may be heard of; he is a good guide, an active mountaineer, a capital chasseur, and a good-tempered, intelligent fellow.

The traveller to the Val d'Aòsta is recommended, if he reach the Châlets of Chapis, to give a day to the Col de Galese, and return to sleep at Chapis, before he cross to the Val Savaranche.

To go to the Val Savaranche, it is not necessary to go to the pasturages of Serue. Before the abrupt ascent to the Alp of Serue commences, a torrent is seen descending from the right. Up the left bank of this torrent a difficult zigzag path ascends, and at the end of two hours leads to some châlets even higher than those of Serue. The scenes presented during the ascent, of the vast ranges of the Levanna and the Iseran, are of the most sublime character. Above these châlets, the path is a series of flights of steps rudely cut in the rock. Beyond this a scene of frightful sterility is presented: numerous alpine lakes or tarns are seen, but no prospect of escape, no path from this cul de sac seems to offer itself; yet in the most improbable of all directions there is one, which actually lies up and over the rugged and pinnacled crest of the boundary to the left, offering a path a thousand times more difficult than that of the Gemmi, without the protection of its parapets. The summit attained, the scene around, viewed from this crest, known by the name of the Col de Croix de Nivolet, is one without parallel in the Alps for the wild peculiarities observed on looking back into the savage valley just left. In at many lakes appear, and the brow above the last châlets, cuts abruptly against the deep haze of the Val d'Orca, which is surmounted with the enormous range of the Levanna.

On looking on the other side of the col into the Plan de Nivolet, which is the head of the valley of Savaranche, many lakes are also seen at the foot of the glaciers of the Nivolet, the same mountain which, towards the Tarentaise, is known by the name of the Iseran, and directly across the head of the Plan de Nivolet, is seen a still higher col than that upon which the observer stands; it is called the Col de Rhemes, and leads through the Val de Rhemes to Villeneuve, by a shorter course than the Savaranche.

The descent towards the Plan de Nivolet is much easier than towards the Val d'Orca; and having attained the banks of the lakes, a nearly level path leads through the fine pasturages at the head of the Plan de Nivolet; yet not a tree or shrub grows here, and the plain is exposed to fearful storms in winter.

In about an hour from the lakes the châlets of this plain are reached. The want of other fuel than dried cow-dung gives a filthy aspect to these châlets. Below them the ground of the plain becomes boggy, and broken up into thousands of knolls. At the end of another hour, these are left, to descend by a path lying over bare and smooth granite, like that on the route of the Grimsel, above Handek. After a considerable descent, the traveller suddenly finds himself on the brink of a vast precipice, and overlooking the village of Pont, in the deep valley, thousands of feet below him. Here, on the edge of the precipice, a cross is placed, which is seen from below; the spot is called the Croix d'Aroletta. From it, one of those sublime scenes which occasionally bursts upon the traveller, in the Alps opens upon him. The three vast peaks of the Grand Paradis, breaking

through their enormous vestment of glaciers, lies before him; and on the right, a black mountain, that overhangs the path by which he must descend to Pont. Down these precipices he must wind for more than an hour to reach this village, the highest in the Val Savaranche, passing on his descent a magnificent cataract.

But here the striking and peculiar scenery of this pass ends; the valley below Pont is narrow, and with very little cultivation at the bottom. On the left a path leads over the mountain of Causelles to the Val de Rhemes; and another on the right crosses to the Val de Cogne. (Route 111.) Gioux, or Val Savaranche, is the principal village in the valley, and here refreshment may be obtained.

There are many little communes in this valley. Near to one of these, Pesai, an avalanche fell in 1832; it destroyed some cows, and three men perished. Crosses mark the spot where their bodies were found.

Before reaching Gioux there is a picturesque spot in the valley, where two villages are perched opposite each other, Tignietti and Crettom; and here the mountains are seen which bound the valley of Aosta on the side opposite to the Val Savaranche.

In the lower part of the valley, the path continues at a vast height above the course of the river-bank, on its right; as it approaches the Val d'Aosta, a magnificent view of Mont Blanc, towering over all the intermediate mountains, opens to the traveller. Here the Val de Rhemes joins the Val Savaranche, and both enter the valley of Aosta. The end of the Val de Rhemes appears like a table land on the mountain side, studded with villages, rich in meadows and vines, walnut and chesnut trees.

From this elevation, the descent to Villeneuve is rapid, fatiguing, and difficult; and the journey from Chapis to the Val d'Aosta (Route 107.) will be found to be quite enough for one day.

ROUTE 113.

IVROGNE TO BOURG ST. MAURICE, IN
THE TARENTAISE, BY THE VAL DE
GRISANCHE AND THE COL DU MONT.

(16 hours.)

The entrance to the Val Grisanche
by the torrent which flows into the
Val d'Aosta, is utterly impracticable.
It is necessary to cross the torrent by
the new bridge, and immediately behind the little dirty town of Ivrogne
to pass a mill, and ascend through
orchards and meadows that appear to
lead away from the Grisanche.   At
the head of these the path arrives abruptly below some precipices; thence
turning and ascending along their
bases, the traveller shortly finds himself in the path which is carried high
above the left bank of the Grisanche,
and which leads up the valley.

For about four hours the scenes
have a striking character.   The river
roars so deep in the gorge as scarcely
to be heard; and the rocks which
bound its course are so nearly perpendicular, that the tops of lofty and
enormous pines, rooted in the rifts
below, can almost be touched by the
hand of the traveller in passing above
them.   Overhanging the path, the
mountains so close in, that the light
of day does not half illuminate this
deep and savage defile.   On a sort of
terrace, on the opposite banks, the
ruins of a feudal castle are seen frowning over the black ravine, and fitted
for tales of romance.   From it, the
view into the valley of Aosta must be
beautiful, but what access there is to
these ruins cannot be traced, or even
imagined, from the opposite bank,
though this is so high above the torrent, that the path seldom approaches
it nearer than 200 feet.

This narrow defile continues during
an ascent of more than two hours.
Sometimes the path is formed of terraces, rudely and perilously formed of
loose stones placed across rifts in the
precipices; in others, the buttresses of
rock are cut away to make the road

high and wide enough to pass a point
of danger; this in some places has
been done with a mass of rock, which,
having fallen from above, and rested
on the line of communication, has required boldness and skill to form a
path, by it; thousands of these masses
have fallen into the gulf below, and
only rendered the torrent more furious by the interruption.   Numerous
cataracts stream into this valley; and
it is necessary in passing beneath one
of these, which descends from a great
height, far up the gorge, to go
hastily across over the rude bridge
formed of trunks of trees laid rudely
across, and scarcely guarded by a rail,
that offers very slight security.   On
looking up, as nearly as the spray
can be approached, another such
bridge is seen to span the top of the
fall, and which connects some forests
or pasturages above.

At length, at the upper extremity of
the defile, the valley opens at the village of Seris, a place which furnishes
only the most miserable accommodation.   The passage up the Grisanche
to Seris is all in the valley really worth
a visit from the Val d'Aosta, and it
well deserves from the tourist in that
valley, an examination, as far as Seris.
To those, however, who would cross
into the Tarentaise, a further description of the route is necessary.

The sterility of the Val de Grisanche above Seris is striking; it is
rugged and strewn with enormous
blocks which have been detached
from the mountains, often from precipices so steep that no vegetation
rests upon their surfaces, where
still impending masses threaten the
passing traveller, and numerous
crosses record the frequency of fatal
accidents.   Deep rifts in the sides of
the precipices are channels to cataracts that pour their white foam from
the dark recesses; in some places,
the black precipitous slopes of the
mountain are always wet and herbless, and reeking as if from some
recent avalanche.

For more than two hours up the valley from Seris the same character of scenery prevails; some miserable hovels and a few fields of stunted barley are found in the bottom of the valley; on its sides there is only the dark precipice or black forest of pines. The head of the valley is bounded by the immense glaciers of Clou. Over these, however, the bold mountaineer finds a pass to St. Foi, in the Tarentaise.

At Fornel, the highest village in the valley, the route to the Col du Mont leaves the Val de Grisanche, ascends a steep path on the right by a torrent, and reaches some châlets on a small but fine pasturage. Above these the path skirts the brink of precipices over a deep gorge, and enters a basin in the mountains — a scene of the most frightful disorder; it is filled with rocks and stones constantly brought down from the surrounding mountains, the summits of which are crested with glaciers, some so precipitous that the ridge of the mountain is surmounted by one of translucent ice, which presents, when the sun shines through it, a most brilliant appearance. The ascent is very steep for three hours up a trackless, loose path, and up slopes of snow, steep, and many hundreds of feet across. It is fatiguing and difficult. From the Col the scene is very fine, not only of the deep valley of stones towards Piedmont, but also towards Savoy, where nature presents a gentle aspect in the mountains which bound the Val Isère; for the Col is so narrow both can be seen from the summit.

The Col du Mont was the scene of some desperate conflicts during the wars of the revolution, between the French and the Piedmontese. General Moulins, who commanded the former, after many efforts, succeeded in gaining the position by advancing during a snow storm, when such assailants were not expected, and retained it in spite of not less than ten efforts to repossess it. The height

of the Col, from the absence of all vegetation, must exceed 8500 feet.

After passing down a steep path, leaving on the left, black precipices — the haunts of the chamois — the pasturages belonging to the commune of St. Foi appear in a deep basin, bounded below by a forest. It is almost impossible to imagine a contrast more striking than the wretched and desolate hollow, filled with rocks and stones, on the side of Aosta; and this, one of the most beautiful pasturages in the Alps on the side of the Tarentaise. In little more than two hours the châlets in this basin are reached, and in another hour it is traversed. Beyond it the road winds steeply down through a forest, and at length emerges to cross a torrent and enter the village of Muraille, where another bridge over a deep ravine leads to the hamlet of Massure, thence traversing a brow on the mountain side, the road descends to the village of St. Foi, in the Val Isère. The approach to St. Foi is strikingly fine, for one of the most beautiful mountains in the Alps, the Chaffe-Quarré, bounds the opposite side of the Val Isère. From its base in the torrent, far below the terrace where St. Foi stands, to its summit, which is peaked with a triangular pyramid of snow, the entire height of this stupendous mountain is seen. St. Foi is only two hours from St. Maurice, and offers little accommodation to the traveller, at least when compared with the comforts of the inn at St. Maurice, *chez* Mayet.

From St. Foi the descent by a paved road is very steep to the banks of the Isère. Before reaching the river a torrent is crossed, which forms, a little way up the valley, a fine cataract. It is difficult to get a view of it. This is the stream which from above descends between the villages of Massure and Muraille.

From the bridge the path lies across meadows for some way, and on the banks of the Isère. Soon after, rising, it leads to the village of Scez, at the foot of the Little St. Bernard, and thence, across cultivated ground, to a new bridge thrown over the torrent of the Reclus. Here there is abundant evidence of the destructive character of the torrent after storms, in the sand, rocks, and stones, which mark its course at such times. Soon after the road passes by some coarse woollen cloth-works, and some usines for making small iron ware. Then across the winter bed of the furious Versoi, which descends from Bonnaval, and below an old round ower belonging to the village of Châtelard. From this place the road to St. Maurice is wide and excellent, and ere long, it is to be hoped, a road of the same width and excellence will lead from this valley to the Val d'Aosta by the pass of the Little St. Bernard.

ROUTE 114.

CORMAYEUR TO BOURG SAINT MAU-RICE, BY THE PASS OF THE LITTLE ST. BERNARD (DÉTOURS TO THE CRAMMONT AND THE BELVIDERE).

To go to the little St. Bernard from Cormayeur, it is necessary to return by the great road to Aosta (Route 107.), about a league, to where the branch from it leads to St. Didier ; or a shorter course may be found by scrambling down the slopes which lead to the Doire, and crossing it higher up the river, than by the bridge which forms part of the high road.

St. Didier is a tolerably large village, having the importance of a *post aux lettres*. It has two inns : l'Ours is decently appointed. Like that at Cormayeur (though very inferior to it) its chief support is from the pensionnaires, who stay to take the waters of its mineral springs: these at St. Didier are hot, having a temperature of 92° of Fahrenheit.

Between the village and the springs, there are some beautiful meadows, the source of its common name, Pré St. Didier ; these are sheltered by the base of the Crammont, and by the enormous precipices of bare rock which overhang the source of the mineral waters, and form one side of a deep inaccessible gulf, through which the torrent from the glaciers of the Ruitor and the Little St. Bernard forces its way.

The hot spring lies up this gulf almost as far as it is accessible ; from this spot it is led through tubes to a building niched in beneath the precipices. Within ten years, however, this has been deserted for baths, to which the water is now conducted, in the meadow, where a rather elegant structure has been raised — Pavillon, as it is here called. It has been built at the expense of the Province of Aosta, as a decoy to the royal family to make it a place of their frequent resort. To this a wing has been lately added, which contains new baths for the public, which are more convenient than the old ; and there are several houses in the village where, for very moderate charges, bed and board may be obtained.

The view of Mont Blanc from the meadows is a glorious scene ; and, from beneath the precipices near the source, magnificent foregrounds may be obtained.

The road which leads by the valley above the gorge at the springs of St. Didier, and to the Little St. Bernard, is a steep zigzag, presenting at each turn new and striking scenes of the valley below, and of Mont Blanc. On reaching the level ground above, that overhangs the deep rift in the mountain, through which the branch of the Doire from La Tuille bursts through into the plain of St. Didier, the scene is fine. It borders a pine forest, of which some vast old trunks hang over the precipices, and help to conceal the deep torrent which roars in its course beneath.

Up through this forest a steep

Path leads to the Crammont, an excursion which no visiter to St. Didier or Cormayeur should fail to make, if the weather be favourable, for no spot in the Alps will afford him so fine a view of Mont Blanc, or a more glorious panorama.

The ascent up the forest to reach the Crammont lies for an hour amidst the pines, then, emerging into fine pasturages, the path leads up through several clusters of châlets; at the last of these it is usual to leave the mules, if any have been employed, to await the return of the traveller. The opening scenes of the valley below, as he rises, excite and encourage his efforts to attain the summit, which is usually accomplished in four hours from St. Didier; the chief difficulties lie in the extreme smoothness of the sward, and the steepness of the slope which make the footing insecure, and much time is lost by slipping back, particularly over some of the rounded knolls, where the effect of looking back is enough to make the unpractised traveller shudder, for the ground is seen to cut abruptly against some objects in the valley thousands of feet below, with as impressive an effect as if it were the ledge of a precipice of that depth, over which a slip would precipitate the shrinking observer. Nearer the top, however, the footing is more secure; thousands of marmots have burrowed and loosened the soil, and traces of these animals are found even to the summit.

The highest point of the Crammont is the outward edge of a large flat mass of rock, dipping towards the Crammont about 20°; the upper end of this mass actually overhangs the rocks below, so that a stone dropped from it would fall perpendicularly hundreds of feet, and then striking the precipitous sides of the mountain would bound into the abyss below, broken into thousands of fragments. This experiment is generally practised by visiters, who witness the

motion given to the stones in the channels below, and hear with astonishment the roar which ascends from the commotion and disturbance. In this savage hollow, chamois are generally seen.

Here the whole of the enormous mass of Mont Blanc is open to the observer, midway of its height, (for the height of the Crammont is about 9200, and that of Mont Blanc 6500 English feet above the peak of the Crammont,) from the peaks which bound the Col de la Seigne to those of the Grand Jorasse, every aiguille and glacier through this vast line of nearly 40 miles, is seen, within an angle of 150 degrees, lying like a picture before the observer from the Crammont. The depths of the Allée Blanche are concealed by some low intervening mountains, which may be considered the western bases of the Crammont.

Towards the N. E. and E. the Val d'Aosta presents a beautiful portion of the panorama. The mountains which bound it sweep down to the Doire, and leave between them, the channels which are the courses of its affluents. In the valley, the Doire appears like a thread of silver. Looking S. E., directly down the line of ascent to the Crammont, the Camp of Prince Thomas, and the table land above the precipices of the valley of La Tuille, appear to be immediately beneath. Above and beyond it lies the enormous glacier of the Ruitor, one of the finest objects within the view: this is connected with the glaciers, at the head of the valleys of Cogne, the Savaranche, and the Grisanche.

Towards the south is the pass and plain of the Little St. Bernard, guarded by the Belvidere, the Valaisan, and the other mountains which bound that pass.

Towards the Great St. Bernard, the course may be traced of the path which leads by the pass of the Serena from the head of the valley of Aosta to St. Remy. The hospice cannot be seen, but the Mont Velan and the Combin are seen beyond it.

All visiters to the Crammont, who have seen it in favourable weather, speak of it with rapture; and Saussure thus records his second visit there : —

"Nous pâssames trois heures sur cette sommet ; j'y en avois aussi passé trois dans mon premier voyage, et ces six heures sont certainement celles de ma vie dans lesquelles j'ai goûté les plus grands plaisirs qui puissent donner la contemplation et l'étude de la nature."

The descent requires more care than the ascent, at least to guard against slipping : the guides usually sit down, and slide with great speed over the dry grass.

The traveller who proposes to make a visit to the Crammont a part of his day's journey to St. Maurice, should start very early, and direct that the mules, if he take any, should, from where he left them, be sent across the pasturages, to châlets which lie in his way to the village of La Balme. He will thus gain time in ascending the valley, though the descent to the hamlet of Evolina, down a steep and rugged path over loose stones, is very fatiguing.

La Balme is in the valley, about an hour's walk above where the path up through the forest leads to the Crammont; and there is no object of interest missed between the two places.

A little above La Balme the torrent is crossed, and a path winds steeply up on the mountain side ; it being impracticable in the depth of the valley, which is here a ravine, to form a road. This is carried on the right bank to a great height above the bed of the torrent. There are occasional peeps offered of the river, and there is one of particular interest — it is where the avalanches which descend from the Crammont fall into the ravine, sometimes in such quantity that the snow remains, under the shadow of the mountain, unmelted for the year. This is the spot, in the opinion of those who have most

carefully examined into the subject, where Hannibal and his army, in their descent from the Alps, found the road, by which they could have descended into the valley, destroyed. The road formerly lay on the left bank of the river. Within these 60 years the present road, to avoid this liability, has been made on the other side, high above all risk from such an accident.

Not far from this spot the road turns abruptly to the left, and the alpine bridge and village of La Tuille, and the glacier of the Ruitor, open upon the traveller. The bridge is crossed, and wine and refreshment may be found in the little auberge of La Tuille.

A short way above La Tuille the stream from the glacier of the Ruitor may be crossed, and a path taken to descend into the valley of Aosta, by some beautiful pasturages, and through a forest that overhangs the precipices above St. Didier, whence the view of Mont Blanc is inferior only to that from the Crammont ; after crossing the camp of Prince Thomas, the path descends down the steep mountain side on the right bank of the Doire. It is nearly in this course that the Sardinian government contemplates the formation of a good road over the Little St. Bernard, to connect the Pays d'Aosta with the Tarentaise.

From La Tuille the road ascends rapidly to Pont Serrant—the last village towards the Little St. Bernard,— and after crossing a very deep ravine over a wooden bridge, a striking scene, and passing the village, the road becomes more steep, but presents little interest except to the geologist. About two hours above Pont Serrant the col is reached — a fine pasturage on a plain about a league long, and half a league wide, bounded on the left by the Belvidere and the Valaisan, and on the right by the Belle-face, at the foot of which mountain lies a little lake — the Vernai, which is left in its deep basin on the right, in ascending to the Col of the Little St. Bernard.

After passing the ruins of some mural defences thrown up during the war of the Revolution, when France and Sardinia struggled for possession of these summits, the road enters upon the plain, and the traveller sees before him, at the opposite extremity of the plain, the hospice lately rebuilt.

On the plain, however, there are objects of high antiquity. A circle of stones on the highest point of the plain bears still the name of the Cirque d'Annibal. The stones are rude masses, varying in size, none very large; they are about 10 feet apart, and the circle measures nearly 260 yards round. The tradition is, that Hannibal here held a council of war. That he staid on the summit of the Alps, and waited for his stragglers, is an historical fact; and, independent of other and abundant evidence, no plain on the summit of any other of the alpine passes is so well adapted for the encampment of his army as this.

Near to the circle there is a column standing, the Colonne de Joux, supposed to be of Celtic origin. It is nearly 20 feet high, and 3 feet in diameter. It is composed of Cipolino, a variety of marble which abounds in the Crammont. About a mile and half from the Colonne de Joux is the hospice, situated at the south-western extremity of the plain. Here formerly a peasant, appointed by the government, used to administer hospitality; but since it has been rebuilt, some brethren of the Hospice of the Great St. Bernard have taken this duty upon themselves.

If the traveller determine to visit the Belvidere, and has already visited the Crammont, it will be too much for one day, and he will do well to sleep at the hospice, and either ascend the Belvidere in the evening, or on the following morning. It is of easy accomplishment: the ascent may be made in an hour. Mont Blanc, which is also seen from every part of the Col of the Little St. Bernard, is from the Belvidere a more magnificent object. The view is of great extent, commanding the mountains far south of the Tarentaise, and looking down upon enormous glaciers streaming into the valleys east of the Belvidere; but the scenes are very inferior to those discovered from the Crammont.

The *Hospice* was founded by St. Bernard, but nothing of its history is preserved. The Great St. Bernard has absorbed all the interest, though, if the veil of the obscure history of the Little St. Bernard could be removed, it would perhaps surpass in early importance that of its great rival, for celtic remains still exist there, and the foundations of a temple constructed of Roman brick are traced on the col, near the column.

From the hospice, the road winds down the mountain side, and in two hours the traveller reaches the village of St. Germains. Thence a zigzag path descends to a stream called the Reclus, which is overhung at the point of passage by an enormous bank of gypsum, bearing the name of the *Roche Blanche.* In situation it perfectly agrees with Polybius' account in the passage of Hannibal, of such a rock, and the events which occurred there. This is one of the chief points of evidence, and, taken with the others, furnish a mass which must force conviction on the minds of unprejudiced inquirers — that by this pass of the Alps, Hannibal entered Italy; General Melville, in his examination, the basis of De Luc's treatise; Wickham and Cramer from their researches; and Brockedon from his repeated visits; all travellers in the Alps, who have examined the other passes also, in reference to this question, have come to the conclusion that, on this line, only can the narrative of Polybius, the only worthy authority upon the question, be borne out.

Below the Roche Blanche the ancient road by the Reclus is avoided, from its constant exposure to destruction by falls from the Mont de

Scez. It now passes by cultivated fields through the hamlet of Villars to the village of Scez (Route 113.) and thence to Bourg St. Maurice.

ROUTE 115.

GENEVA TO CHAMOUNY.

Crowds of voituriers loiter about the streets of Geneva, and especially in the neighbourhood of the principal inns, ready to start at a minute's notice for Chamouny, or any other excursion upon which the traveller may determine. Few travellers take their own carriages from Geneva to Chamouny. A light char with a pair of horses, to take four persons, may be hired for twenty francs, to go to Sallenches or to St. Martin, where another, and lighter vehicle, can be taken to convey two or three persons to Chamouny. In Savoy the charges are regulated by tariff; the expenses are now moderate, and imposition is immediately punished upon complaint to the syndic. A diligence goes every day, in the season, to Sallenches.

If the traveller have a carriage, and intend after visiting Chamouny, to cross, by the Tête Noire or Col de Balme, to Martigny, on the way to the Simplon, he should direct his carriage to be forwarded to Martigny, from Geneva, to await his arrival there. The daily steam-boat from Geneva to Villeneuve, if it do not greatly reduce the expense of such conveyance, will insure its arrival in time at Martigny.

Geneva is left for Chamouny, at the Port de la Rive; and the road, though hilly, is good to Chesne, half a league from the city, and one of the largest villages in the republic. The road offers some fine views of the Voirons, Mont Salève, and the range of the Jura. Soon after leaving Chesne, the road crosses a little stream, the Foron, which has its source in the Voirons. This stream is the boundary, of the canton of Geneva and the Sardinian frontier; and a little beyond it, at Annemasse, is the station of the Sardinian douane. Here the greatest civility is shown if the passport be *en réglé ;* and no search or trouble is given about baggage in passing this frontier of the Sardinian states. On the first rising ground beyond, the Mole, a sugar-loaf mountain, is seen in all its height, 5800 feet, partly concealing the only hollow in the range of mountains beyond, by which the course to Chamouny lies.

Beyond Annemasse the road runs high above the valley of the Arve, in which the blanched stones mark by their breadth how furious the river must be in its winter course. Suddenly the road winds round the brow of a hill that overhangs the valley, and turns into an abrupt and steep hollow, to pass the Menoge on a good stone bridge, then, rising steeply on the other side, the road passes over an elevated plain, and soon reaches the village of Nangy, about three leagues from Geneva. A little beyond there are some ruins on the right; and, after passing Contamines, are seen those of the Château of Faucigny, that gives its name to the province of Faucigny, of which Bonneville is the chief place. The road now passes so near to the Mole, that this mountain is an imposing and beautiful object. Upon it an obelisk has lately been built — one of the points in a trigonometrical survey of Savoy. Beyond Contamines the road declines. The mountains which bound the Arve present a bold aspect, and the entrance is striking, through an avenue of trees, to

Bonneville, five leagues from Geneva, which is generally travelled in a char in four hours. Here the horses are usually rested; and the traveller, who will find the Couronne a better inn than any at Cluses, generally takes a lunch or early dinner.

This is the chief place in the province of Faucigny; it is in the diocese of Annecy, and has a prefecture. Its nhabitants were formerly 3000; at present they do not exceed 1300.*

There is a good stone bridge at Bonneville, which was built in 1753. It crosses the Arve; and near to it is a column not long since erected in honour of Carlo Felice, and in gratitude for his having added to the security of their town by the formation of strong embankments, to restrain the furious Arve.

This column, which is surmounted by a statue of the King, is 95 feet high.

The bridge is crossed in pursuing the route to Cluses. On the left, the Mole is flanked, and the road lies between the base of this mountain and the Mont Brezon, the range that on the right bounds the valley of the Arve, which is here rich in cultivation. The road, after some time, undulates, and passes through the villages of Vaugier and Scionzier; beyond the former, the valley widens where the Arve is joined by the Giffre; a torrent that descends from the Buet, flows through the valley of Samoëns, and by the town of Tanninges, then, joining the Risse, below St. Joire, enters the valley of the Arve at Pont Marigny.

The road continues close under the Brezon until its precipices frown over the route near Cluses. Here, crossing the Arve on a stone bridge, it enters the town of Cluses, turns abruptly to the right, and passes between vast mountains, through a defile, in which Cluses is built, and the passage of which it entirely commands.

Cluses, an old town, eight leagues from Geneva.

* The inhabitants of a place seem to have as great a desire to claim antiquity for it, as for their families. Documents that only record their existence for five centuries, are despised. The people of Bonneville say, that their town was an important place in the time of the Romans; that it was sacked by the Franks, &c. When the Barons of Faucigny built their castle is uncertain: in the 13th century, however, a few houses near it, bore the name of Burgum Castri, which was changed by Beatrix, sovereign of Faucigny, in 1283, into Bonneville, and granted to its inhabitants certain privileges.

Inns : — Parfaite Union, Eçu de France.

Many privileges were granted to Cluses. One of the earliest recorded, is by Hugues, dauphin of Vienne, Baron of Faucigny, who, in 1310, bestowed many municipal advantages; but in consideration of them, the inhabitants owed him military service: this, exercised in feudal times, and the almost impregnable character of their town, made them pugnacious and mischievous to their neighbours. They often attempted to burn Bonneville; and in 1340, sacked it. When, however, Faucigny passed into the hands of the counts of Savoy, it gained its object against Bonneville, in becoming the seat of the assembled states of Faucigny, and of the administration of provincial justice. Its history is however chiefly made up of the plagues and fires it has suffered. Those in 1310 and 1490 entirely destroyed it.

The population is about 1800. A large proportion of these are employed in watchmaking, for which this town has been celebrated above a century. They prepare *movements,* watches in a rough state, for the watchmakers in Geneva, and in Germany. Thirty years ago, above fourteen hundred persons were thus employed in Cluses. Maglan, Scionzier, and other villages in the neighbourhood; of these above a thousand persons were employed at Cluses.

For so retired a spot, its relation with commercial men is extraordinary. Their early habits of business, and fitness for conducting it, has led to the establishment of many natives of Cluses, in Alsace, at Augsburgh, Strasbourg, and Lyons, as bankers and manufacturers. The town is miserable enough in appearance, and excites not the least suspicion that rich men were ever born there.

On leaving Cluses, the road is carried through the defile on the borders of the river, and beneath precipices, that mark the first grand entrance into an alpine ravine. The valley is very narrow, nearly all the way to Maglan, and, in some places, the road is straitened in between the river and the bases of precipices, which actually overhang the traveller. From some of these, a little out of the road, the steep talus of rocks and stones which have fallen from above, spread out to the river, and the road rises over the ridges. The banks of the river are well wooded, and the scenery is as beautiful as it is wild.

Before arriving at Maglan, the precipices on the left, retire a little, forming an amphitheatre, which is filled, nearly half-way up, with the *débris* of the mountain. At the top of this talus, 800 feet above the valley, the grotto of Balme is seen, to which a mule-path leads, which is undistinguishable below. At a little hut in the hamlet of La Balme, mules are kept for a visit to the grotto; and whilst these are getting ready, *limonade Gazeuse*, and other temptations to the thirsty traveller, are offered. A little beyond La Balme, those who are amateurs in pure water may taste from a spring which bursts out close to the road in large volume. Saussure conjectured that it might be the embouchure of the channel which empties the lake of Flaine, in the mountains above.

Those who intend to go on to Chamouny, should not waste any time here; but if the day's journey be only to St. Martin or Sallenches, the grotto is worth a visit. Its depth is great: it enters the mountain more than 1800 feet; but the view from it, owing to the narrowness of the valley, is limited. The peaks, however, of Mont Douron, seen on the other side of the valley, are remarkably fine in form.

Maglan lies below the lofty mountains on the right bank of the Arve; the Commune which is straggling, contains nearly as many inhabitants as Cluses,—they, too, are distinguished for their establishment in foreign countries. Beyond Maglan the same character of scenery prevails, but the valley widens. About a league and a half beyond Maglan, the road passes close to one of the highest waterfalls in Savoy, that of Nant d'Arpenaz; the stream is small, and before it reaches half its first descent it is broken into spray. After storms, however, its volume falls on the rock, on which it breaks; after reaching the slope or talus, formed by the soil and stones it has brought down, it rushes across the road beneath a bridge, and flows into the Arve. The rock of brown limestone, from which it descends is remarkable for its tortuous stratification, forming a vast curve, and the face of the rock is so denuded that its structure is perfectly seen. The route from Geneva is so much frequented by strangers in this season, that it is beset by all sorts of vagabonds, who plant themselves in the way openly as beggars, or covertly as dealers in mineral specimens, guides to things which do not require their aid, dealers in echoes, by firing small cannon where its reverberation may be heard two or three times. These idle nuisances should be discountenanced.

Between the fall of Arpenaz and St. Martin, the valley increases in width, and rich fields spread up the base of the Douron from Sallenches; the peaks of the Varens, which rise nearly 8000 feet above the level of the sea, and immediately over the village of St. Martin, which now opens to the view, and shortly after the traveller enters the bustling inn-yard of the Hôtel des Mont Blanc. Here, in the season, he never fails to meet numerous travellers going to or from Chamouny; the latter imparting their impressions of the wonders of Mont Blanc, and their adventurous scrambles in the presence of the "Monarch" to the listening expectants of such enjoyment; — all is excitement.

Within a hundred yards of the inn a bridge crosses the Arve, and leads to the town of Sallenches, half a league from St. Martin's. On this ridge one of the noblest views on the Alps is presented of Mont Blanc: its actual distance to the peak is more than 12 miles in a direct line, yet so sharp, and bright, and clear in every part of its stupendous mass, that the eye, unused to such magnitude with distinctness, is utterly deceived, and would rather lead to the belief that it was not one third of the distance. On looking up the valley over the broad winter-bed of the Arve however, objects recede, and give the accustomed impressions of distance; above this rises the mountain of the Forclaz, its sides clothed with pines, and its summit with pasturage. Over these, are seen the Aiguille de Gouté, the Dome de Gouté, and the head of the loftiest mountain in Europe, propped by ridges of aiguilles, and the intervals of these filled with glaciers. This one view, the first usually enjoyed by travellers from England to Chamouny, is so impressive as to be generally acknowledged a sufficient reward for the journey.

Sallenches, about 36 miles from Geneva, is a little town containing about 1500 inhabitants. Though above half a league further, the tariff for chars, mules, and guides, are the same as at St. Martin; these may be referred to upon hiring either, and thus all disputes are avoided; a *pour boire* to the postilions is at the will of the employer, and their civility almost always insures it. A char to Chamouny, without return, is 12 francs.

The pedestrian who intends to visit Chamouny and return by Geneva, is advised to go from St. Martin up the right bank of the Arve to Chede, Servoz, and Chamouny, and return by the Col de Forclaz, and the baths of St. Gervais. If, however, the traveller should not intend to return by the valley of the Arve, the most agreeable approach to Chamouny from St. Martin is by Sallenches, and the baths of St. Gervais to Chede.

From Sallenches the distance along a level road to the baths is a good league, it there turns abruptly on the right into the gorge of the Bourant, a stream which descends from the Bon-homme. At the upper extremity of a little level spot, a garden in the desert, are the baths, the houses *en Pavillon*, for lodging and boarding the invalids who retire to this delicious spot, and find in their absence from the stirring scenes of society, a repose which restores the mind and body to its energies; the credit of this is, however, given to the waters, which are at 90° temperature; the heat of Bath with the qualities of Harrowgate. In the Journals of an Alpine Traveller, he says, on leaving St. Martin's,—

" Went in a *char-à-banc*, a sort of carriage like a sofa placed on wheels, to the baths of St. Gervais. This is so little out of the usual route, by Chede, and so pleasant a deviation, that all visitors to Chamouny should go or return by it; it is a little fairy spot, in a beautiful valley, where excellent accommodation may be had *en pension;* hot mineral baths for the sick, and delightful walks around this little paradise for the convalescent. At the back of the house, a little way up the glen, there is a fine cataract; and one of the pleasures of this place is its solitude, amidst scenes so beautiful and wild, that it would be difficult to find it, without a guide."

The glen is a *cul-de-sac;* there is no leaving it upward; it is necessary to return to the entrance, where two roads branch off— one very steep, leads up to St. Gervais, a beautiful village in the Val Mont Joie, through which the Bourant flows, until it falls into the gulf behind the baths; above St. Gervais, this road continues through the villages of Bionay and Tresse to Contamines, and the pass of the Bon-homme. (Route 118.)

The other road, at the entrance of the glen of the baths of St. Gervais, after skirting a little way the mountain base below the Forclaz, leads across the valley of the Arve, and falls into the shorter road by Passy to Chede. Passy is a village a little on the left out of the road; it is remarkable for some Latin inscriptions, which were found in building the church; they have led to many conjectures upon its antiquity, and the supposed acquaintance of the Romans with this retired valley.

Chede is a little hamlet, where the road steeply ascends above the broad plain of the Arve, which from Salenches to this abrupt rising off the valley, forms a vast level, that, when filled by winter torrents, resembles a a lake in its extent. Near to Chede there is on the left a fine cascade, which travellers, who start at 5 A.M. for Chamouny, generally visit for the sake of the beautiful iris that then plays over it.

At length, after attaining a considerable height above the plain of the Arve at St. Martin's, the road passes, what, until within a very short period, was a little lake, the Lac du Chede; from which, as from a mirror, a fine view of the summit of Mont Blanc, towering over the lower range of mountains was reflected; this was one of the little "lions" in the excursion to Chamouny; but a *débâcle* of black mud, and stones, has descended and filled it, and the lake of Chede is no more.

Pictet, in full encouragement of the little vagabonds that infest the route, at least from Cluses to Chamouny, advises travellers to provide themselves with small coin to give to the numerous little children, who serve as guides to the cascade, the lake, &c.

The road, still rising above the spot where the lake was, turns into a deep curve to cross the bed of a wild torrent. This usually furnishes the first alpine adventure to the traveller, for the road can seldom be kept in good condition for a week: every fall of rain alters it, and varies the apparent peril to those who follow.

From this wild spot the road passes through what is called a forest, and soon reaches the village of Servoz, where there are now two inns, offering very tolerable accommodation to travellers overtaken by storms. Here the horses of the chars are usually rested; and if St. Martin have been left before breakfast, this is a capital place to obtain one, good enough to satisfy an appetite given by the freshness of the morning air in the mountains. Tea and coffee, eggs, milk, butter and bread, and the delicious honey of Chamouny are ample materials; to these chicken or a ragoût of chamois can often be added.

At Servoz there is a shop where the minerals of Mont Blanc are sold, but these are usually bought by travellers at Chamouny, where the collections are larger, and the purchase is a reminiscence of Mont Blanc.

At Servoz, guides may be had to accompany the traveller to the Buet, one of the sight-seeing summits near Mont Blanc, and offering a fine view of the "Monarch;" and, from its elevation, nearly 10,500 feet above the level of the sea, a vast extent of horizon is presented, bounded on the east by the mountains of St. Gothard, and on the west by ranges which extend and subside into Dauphiny, the lakes of Geneva and of Annecy are partly seen, and the whole line of the Jura mountains bounds that part of the horizon.

The Buet is a dangerous mountain to visit without a good guide: the fate of a young Danish traveller, M. Eschen, is still remembered; he perished in August, 1800; his fate arose from his disregarding the advice of his guide.

Servoz is the best side on which to ascend the Buet; the usual way is to proceed up the mountain, and sleep at some châlet; then starting early, reach the summit of the Buet, and descending by the Val Orsine, arrive at Chamouny in the evening.

Those who, returning to Geneva,

would vary their route, may, from Servoz, enter the valley of Sixt at its head, and descending by Samoëns and Tanninges, pass on the northern side of the Mole, by St. Joire and Baillard, and enter the high road from Chamouny to Geneva, near Nangy; this excursion is detailed by Captain Markham Sherwill, whose ascent of Mont Blanc in 1825, and frequent visits to Chamouny, and residence there, have made him perhaps better acquainted with the neighbourhood of Mont Blanc than any other Englishman: he says in a private letter, describing the visit to the valley of Sixt, —

" You must start early in the morning from Chamouny, walk or ride, if an opportunity offers, to Servoz; breakfast here, and lay in a moderate supply of cold meat and bread, with wine, or brandy and water; the latter is preferable. Take the footpath that leads to the Col d'Anterne. Be sure you engage a guide at Chamouny, who is acquainted with the pass, or it would, perhaps, be better to take one from Servoz. After having ascended as far as the last châlets, you bear to your left, instead of continuing to the summit of the Col d'Anterne, and direct your course amidst the terrific *débris* of the *écroulement* of the Montagne des Fys. The path is rugged, but when the pedestrian has reached the top of the mountain, which he must attain through a forked-like opening, he will contemplate with great satisfaction the magnificent view of Mont Blanc, and a thousand other stupendous objects. Having rested here an hour to enjoy a scanty meal, the descent on the northern side is gradual, and you arrive in about an hour at some châlets, which bear the name of Les Châlets des Sales, properly so termed, for they are a cluster of huts, containing the most dirty, filthy, and savage (in appearance) set of women that can be imagined. Here you will find milk and cheese, with tolerable good water, of which there is none on the Montagne des Fys. Near these huts are fossil shells. On quitting this spot, where women, children, and swine pig together, you continue to descend rapidly during nearly four hours through a narrow gorge, whose beauties and luxurious appearance are very striking after the barren and bleak pass of the mountain: cascades, rushing streams, and forests of dark and imposing feature are amongst the varied objects worthy of attention. At Sixt there is a very tolerable auberge, where most delicious trout are to be obtained in great abundance, the water of this valley not being too cold, as at Chamouny, to prevent a good supply.

" The second day you ascend the valley towards the mountain, called the Tête Noire, or Fer à Cheval, which terminates the valley. This semicircular and perpendicular horseshoe mountain is ornamented with seven cascades, produced by the melting of the snows on its summit, over which there is a dangerous path known but to few, that leads to the Pic du Midi, and on to St. Maurice in the valley of the Rhone. During this walk in the valley of Sixt there are various objects of great interest. On your right the Buet raises his snowy head to the clouds; from hence the ascension of this interesting mountain is more easily made than from Valorsine, being an excursion of about four hours to the summit. (See M. de Luc's account.) After having passed the old monastery of Sixt, coeval with the former priory of Chamouny, the very fine fall of La Gouille presents itself on your left, than which nothing can be more rich in alpine accessories. The mines at the end of the valley are difficult of access; most of the miners live at Sixt. There are exterior communications from shaft to shaft along the perpendicular face of the mountain, highly dangerous for those who are unaccustomed to narrow paths and precipices. It would require much time to enumerate all the objects of curiosity to be seen at short distances from Sixt, where I stayed four days. Before quitting this spot, I will add, that it is possible for ladies to arrive at Sixt on mules ; but in that case, on quitting Servoz, you must continue the path that leads to the summit of the Col d'Anterne ; and when there, take the left-hand mule road, which will lead you towards Sixt ; but be sure your guide is acquainted with the mountain d'Anterne, for should he take the right-hand path, you will have a good chance of sleeping at the foot of the glaciers of the Buet. This is a fatiguing day for ladies.

" The third day you descend towards the beautifully situated village of Samoëns ; then passing through Tanninges, you arrive at St. Jeoire at the foot of the Mole, a mountain so well seen from the ramparts of Geneva ; an excursion to the summit of which will amply repay, and is by no means difficult. The panoramic view from its point is one of infinitely varied beauty. From St. Jeoire, whose noble château has been the cradle of so many eminent cardinals, generals, and statesmen, you proceed to Nangy and Geneva. This third day may be accomplished without sleeping at St. Jeoire, where there is a good inn, provided you can meet with a char, which is not likely, either here or at Nangy. The safer way is to sleep at St. Jeoire, and reserve the fourth day for an easy journey to Geneva.

" A *char-à banc* may go all the way from Geneva to Sixt : the road throughout is good.

" If you ascend the Mole from St. Jeoire on the fourth day, you may descend to Bonneville, hire a carriage, and return very conveniently to Geneva."

The mines mentioned by Captain Sherwill are now worked by Englishmen, who have established themselves there.

From Servoz the road, after cross-ing the torrent of the Dioza which descends from the Buet, lies close under the foot of the Breven, between this mountain and the Arve, which issues at Pont Pelissier from one of the finest gorges in the Alps. The valley between this bridge and Servoz was once a lake, produced probably by a mountain fall damming up the valley of Châtelas, by which the Arve descends to the valley of Sallenches. Near the Pont Pelissier, on a mound, are the ruins of the château of St. Michael. Chapels and monasteries on elevated places are frequently dedicated to the archangel, and most châteaux in such situations bear his name.

After crossing Pont Pelissier, the road ascends by a very steep path to a ridge, the Montets, which separates the valley of Chamouny from the Vale of Servoz. From several spots, especially near the crest, the peep down into the now inaccessible ravine through which the Arve finds a passage, is a depth to shudder at.

From the Montets, the enormous mass of Mont Blanc, now in close proximity, is magnificent ; and it is impossible to describe the emotions it excites : but the summit can no longer be seen ; it is concealed by the vast Dome de Goût.

The descent from the Montets lies through some fine meadows to Ouches, the first village in the valley.

Soon the white lines of glaciers are seen to extend themselves into the valley. The first is that of Taconey, which is two miles up the valley above Ouches : it is, however, so mere a line compared with the vastness of other objects around, that the traveller never fails to be disappointed in its apparent size. Numerous torrents are passed, which descend furiously from the glaciers of Mont Blanc, and cut deep channels, which are difficult to cross, or to keep in repair the passages over them— they are disrupted by every storm.

About half a league beyond the

stream from the glacier of Taconey, is
the hamlet of Bossons, and near it
the glacier of that name, which reaches
further out into the valley than any
other; but this too, like that of the
Taconey, disappoints, unless the traveller visit it, when he will find that
from its height, the *Moraine*, — i. e.
the rocks and stones that are thrust forward by the ice, and form a huge embankment to the glacier,— is difficult
and fatiguing to climb, and the white
and apparently unimportant mass of
ice, of which the lower extremity of
the glacier is composed, is really
formed by enormous masses split
into a thousand fantastic forms —
some are fine pinnacles 60 or 80 feet
high, others immense blocks broken
or melted into fantastic forms, and so
impending, that they excite a shudder,
but the colour, the deep and beautiful blue colour of the ice in its
depths, offers effects of which no description can convey an idea.

A little above the glacier of Bossons the Arve is crossed, and the road
continues on its right bank. At the
head of the valley is seen the Glacier
du Bois, the largest in the valley, the
terminus, in fact, of the Mer de Glace.
This lies, however, a league beyond
the village of Chamouny — now a
large and important community,
which displays almost the bustle of an
English watering-place in the most
retired, heretofore, of the alpine valleys.

Chamouny. Here there are several
good inns, of which the principal are
the Hotel de Londres et d'Angleterre,
the Union, and the Hotel du Nord.
The former is the oldest establishment, and has never forfeited the reputation of being one of the best held
and appointed inns to be found in the
Alps; where Victor Tairrez and his
excellent wife are so practised in
their acquaintance with, and their
provision for, the wants of travellers,
especially English, that more *comfort*
will be found there than in almost
any other inn out of England.

The customary charges at the inn
are, — dinner, 3 to 4 francs; breakfast 1½ to 2 fr.; bed, 1½ to 2 fr. —
Mineral warm baths may be had at
the inns; these offer the most refreshing and agreeable luxury, after
the fatigue of mountain excursions.

At Chamouny and elsewhere, the
travellers' books at the inns are great
sources of amusement; often containing, in the remarks of preceding travellers, useful information. A most
disgraceful practice has too often prevailed, of removing leaves for the sake
of autographs; it is difficult to imagine any act more unworthy, for this
selfish gratification they destroy what
would be pleasure to hundreds.

The village of Chamouny, or La
Prieuré, as it is sometimes called, from
a Benedictine convent established here
about the end of the 11th century,
was known earlier than is generally
imagined. The original act for found-
ing the priory was lately discovered
by Captain Sherwill, among some old
documents which had for ages been
neglected. This act bears the seal of
Count Aymon, and a reference to
"Papa Urbano regnante;" this can
only refer to Pope Urban II., and
fixes the period between 1088 and
1099 — probably about 1090. The
gift which accompanied this deed was
of the Vale of Chamouny, from the
Col de Balme to the torrent of the
Dioza near Servoz — about 7½ leagues
in length, by about 3 in breadth,
including the mountain sides and
slopes. From this document the origin of the name of Chamouny may
be discovered. The words *Campus
Munitus*, champ muni, or fortified
field, from perhaps its mountain
boundaries; this name does not occur
after the adoption of *Prieuré* — this
probable conjecture is Captain Sherwill's. The documents furnished also a
slight history of the progressive settlement of its inhabitants, and the occasional intercourse of important strangers with the priory. The first visit
recorded, that of the bishop of Geneva,

within whose diocese Chamouny lay, was in the 15th century ; when, after visiting the abbot of Sallenches, " he continued his perilous journey to Chamouny, where he arrived as late as the 4th of October, in the year 1443. He was accompanied by the abbot, his two officiating clerical attendants, and some menial persons. The visiting party performed the journey on foot. They remained several days at the priory to repose ; and after having visited this most secluded part of his diocese, the bishop returned to Geneva, by way of Annecy," whether by Megeve from Sallenches, or from Bonneville, the document does not mention. Captain Sherwill has published a little pamphlet, " A brief historical Sketch of the Vale of Chamouny," which contains the result of his researches, and brings down the history of the priory and the people to the time of Wyndham and Pocock's visit in 1743. Since that time constant intercourse has been recorded. Captain Sherwill's memoir contains an interesting account of a visit made to Chamouny by St. François de Sales, when bishop of Geneva, in July, 1606.

The first knowledge of Chamouny was clearly not a discovery of Wyndham and Pocock's. With Geneva and with Germany, the natives of Chamouny had long had much intercourse, and their fairs, held at the priory, brought many strangers. The *ordonnance* for establishing these fairs, was granted by Philip of Savoy, Comte of Geneva, and bears date, 3d of November, 1530, and three years later, he gave permission for the establishment of a market, to be held every Thursday. This weekly market still exists.

Messrs. Wyndham and Pocock's excursion to Chamouny, and their report of it, led, by its publication in the *Mercure de Swisse*, in the months of May and June, 1743, to the excitement of great interest in these retired wilds, amidst the most sublime scenery in nature, and at the foot of the loftiest

mountain of Europe, where thousands have made their pilgrimage. Unlike other places, merely fashionable, and crowded by idlers, no extent of participation can lessen the sublime emotions and impressions made by the scenery of the vale of Chamouny. More than 3000 strangers have visited it in one season, and of these, hundreds of the vulgar and unfeeling *parvenues*, whose exclamation of " how rural !" recorded by Lord Byron, would have shocked refinement elsewhere, here cannot lessen the enjoyment offered in this glorious temple of nature.

The guides, mules, and all affairs that can be regulated by the state, to guard against disputes, is here in the hands of a syndic, who, as guide *en chef*, has a code of laws, and tariff of charges, which all must obey. *All disputes are referred to him, if they should arise ; to him application must be made for guides, who, each in turn, must attend the traveller who needs his services. If, however, a particular guide, out of turn, be taken, three francs extra must be paid for each course. Courses are certain excursions ; thus, the Montanvert is one course, the Flegère another : if both be done in one day, the compromise is ten francs. A particular guide cannot be chosen. This regulation is subsequent to 1821, when forty men were enrolled, selected for their intelligence, and the excellence of their certificates, which had been given to them by their employers when satisfied with their conduct.

The chief receives his salary from the government, but Captain Sherwill thinks that the new system has serious disadvantages. " The guides do not now, as formerly, seek to instruct themselves. Before 1821, a man was chosen for his ability, his courage, his prudence, and his general knowledge : now, a guide knows, that, being placed on the list, his turn must come to attend a stranger, and that no one can deprive him of the benefit of his appointment; he therefore sits quietly down by the side of his fire, where he waits only the call of the chief guide, and abandons all books of instruction. Therefore it is to be feared, that when the original race of guides has passed, and that there appears no longer on the list the names of Coutet, Payot, Paccard, and Balmat, we shall see at Chamouny a comparatively ignorant race of guides, capable, no doubt, of conducting strangers in all ordinary cases, but not possessing that agreeable information and useful knowledge, which render a walk over the most dreary mountain still more engaging, and which often draws from the pocket of the pedestrian an extra franc, as an acknowledgment of the additional pleasure he has received from the conversation of his guide."

The price allowed by government for the services of a guide, was seven francs per day, which they voluntarily reduced to six francs, the old French crown.

Jacques Balmat, the most daring skilful and experienced of the guides who made the first ascent of Mont Blanc, and was 70 years old, disappeared in 1835. He went out with a hunter of Valorsine to chase the chamois, parted from him near the Pic de Medi, having proposed an ascent which the other thought too dangerous; but poor Jacques was from his youth a goldfinder; one who believed that it would be possible to become suddenly rich by such a discovery. He always preferred to follow this phantasy to acting as guide, and he paid for it the forfeit of his life. The spot from which he fell, over the precipices of the Mortine is known, but to recover the body was considered impossible.

EXCURSIONS AROUND CHAMOUNY.

"——— Above me are the Alps,
The palaces of Nature, whose vast walls
Have pinnacled in clouds their snowy
 scalps,
And throned Eternity in icy halls
Of cold sublimity, where forms and falls
The Avalanche—the thunderbolt of snow!
All that expands the spirit, yet appals,

Gather around these summits, as to show
How earth may pierce to Heaven, yet leave
 vain man below."

It is impossible to imagine the bustle and excitement of a visit to Chamouny. The arrival and departure of travellers, the presence of the guides and their tales of adventures, the plans for to day or to-morrow, the weather, not here the commonplace substitute for having nothing else to say, but the most important source of enjoyment or disappointment to the traveller. On looking out in the evening upon Mont Blanc, from the windows or the yard of the Hotel de Londres, with a plan for to-morrow, with what anxiety all indications of a change are watched; how every body is consulted; groups of ramblers arrive from Geneva, from the Valais, from Piedmont, or from visits to the surrounding points of view; success is envied — failure pitied.

The Montanvert.—This is generally the first, often the only excursion made from Chamouny, with the intention of returning to it. The object of this excursion is to visit the Mer de Glace, the enormous glaciers which terminate in the Glacier du Bois, and the source of the Arveron, in the valley of Chamouny.

To go to the Montanvert it is necessary to cross the Arve and the opposite meadows, by a path which leads across the valley to the foot of the Montanvert, where the path rises above the valley, through the forest of pines which skirts the base of the mountain, in some places very steep, and to ladies, or unpractised travellers, mounted on mules, apparently dangerous; but as the guide is generally in attendance in all places of difficulty, and there are really none of danger, confidence is soon possessed.

After a scramble amidst rocks, and the roots of pines and larches, occasional openings among the trees afford peeps into the valley, and mark the great height so rapidly attained. Sometimes *crues* are crossed — the channels of avalanches in the winter, which sweep down every thing in their course. Here the guides generally perform the *mystery* of desiring silence, lest a whisper should disturb the slumbering snows above, and bring down destruction by displacing a rock. The step from the sublime to the ridiculous, is here reduced to the smallest possible interval.

Until within a few years, the path beyond this place was impracticable for mules ; now, however, it is made good to the pavilion, or house, on the Montanvert, which is reached from Chamouny in 2½ hours. This was originally a rough inclosure of four dry walls, covered with a roof for shelter, which was built at the expense of an Englishman, and named the Château de Blair ; this has now become a cowhouse or stable ; and even the pavilion, built afterwards at the expense of a M. Desportes, by M. Jaguet, to extend the benefits of the Château de Blair, is so improved, that refreshment, accommodation, and beds, in the season, await the visitors to the Montanvert, the Jardin, and other spots of interest to which it leads.

From the Montanvert, the Mer de Glace is seen to an extent of two leagues up the valley, towards the Mont Periades and the Aiguilles of Lechaud, on either side of which, a branch continues ; that on the S. W. forming the great glacier of Tacul, and that on the E. and N. E. the glaciers of Lechaud and Talèfre. The view of this enormous sea of ice is one of the most striking in these scenes of wonder, but its great extent, from the vast size of every object about it, is very deceptive. Directly across the Mer de Glace are some of the finest of those pinnacled mountains which form so striking a feature in the Chamouny scenery. The nearest is the Aiguille du Dru, and still further on the right, is the Aiguille du Moine. A thousand nameless pinnacles pierce the clouds between them, and seem to

prop the loftiest of this stupendous mass which is the Aiguille Verte, that rises more than 13,000 feet above the level of the sea, and nearly 7000 feet above the Montanvert.

Those who do not intend to cross the Mer de Glace, should, at least, descend upon it, to have a just idea of its character, and by walking far enough upon it, two or three hundred yards, to observe the beauty of its purity and colour in the crevices, which cannot be conceived when looking down upon it, for the stones and soil are rejected to its surface, and thrown over at its edges, forming what are called the *moraines* of the glacier.

The Jardin.—Those who wish to cross the Mer de Glace, and visit the Jardin or Courtil, on the Glacier de Taléfre, should sleep at the pavilion, for, to a fatiguing day's journey, two hours and a half makes an important addition. The accommodation now offered at the pavilion enables the traveller to sleep comfortably and start early. No person would venture without a guide, and with one, a description of the course is scarcely necessary. The great object of the excursion is to enter more into the heart of Mont Blanc, to penetrate into its profound valleys, and witness scenes of wilder horrors and more savage solitude ; and there is no excursion from Chamouny that excites these sublime emotions more powerfully. The guide should be provisioned for this excursion, and in fact any other where the visitors are not numerous enough to insure an establishment for refreshment. Bread and cold meat, and wine, should be taken by the guide to the Jardin, the Mont Breven, the Chapeau, and such other places as the guide may advise.

The course taken, is to follow the S. W. side of the Mer de Glace, and reach the base of the Aiguille de Charmoz, where, from there being fewer crevices, the Mer de Glace can be crossed with greater safety. Several ridges of *moraines*, called arrêtes, which lie in the direction of the glacier, are crossed, and that part of the glacier called Lechaud is ascended a little, to attain the lower extremity of that of Talèfre, which here presents an awful appearance, from the disruption of the ice, and the vast and wild masses and pyramids into which the glacier has broken, from its abrupt descent into the glacier of Lechaud. These hang *in terrorem* over the traveller who dares to approach them.

To pass these glaciers it is necessary to climb the rocks of the Couvercle, the base of the Aiguille du Talèfre. This, which is difficult from its excessive steepness, is not dangerous. A part of the path lies in a little gulley in the rock, to climb over which, in some places, the hands are required, as well as the feet. This part of the passage is called the Egralets. Above it, where the path is less steep, and where there is some herbage, the traveller reaches the bed or level of the Glacier du Talèfre, which leads to an oasis in this desert — an island in the ice — a rock which is covered with a beautiful herbage, and enamelled, in August, with flowers — this is the Jardin of this palace of nature, and nothing can exceed the beauty of such a spot, amidst the overwhelming sublimity of the surrounding objects, the Aiguilles of Charmoz, Blétière, and the Geant, and the enormous glaciers of Tacul,'all vindicate the truth of the poet's glorious description, —

" Mont Blanc is the monarch of mountains,
    They crown'd him long ago,
On a throne of rocks, in a robe of clouds,
    With a diadem of snow."

In returning from the Jardin it is not necessary to descend by the Egralets ; a steep path leads down from the glacier of Talèfre to the glacier of Lechaud, and then by the path to the base of the Charmoz, to Montanvert, and Chamouny.

It requires five hours to go from the pavilion to the Jardin, and seven or eight to return from the

Jardin to Chamouny, for though the descent may be made quicker, the traveller is more fatigued, and, allowing for rest and enjoyment, the journey is one of sixteen hours, from and to Chamouny; the gain of three, therefore, by starting from the Montanvert, will obviously lessen its fatigue.

The Flegère. — This point of view of Mont Blanc is that which is most generally attained by ladies, because it may be accomplished on mules the whole way, and it is one of the finest in the valley. It was from the Croix de Flegère that Mr. Burford took his panoramic view of Mont Blanc, lately exhibited in Leicester Square. The point attained lies exactly opposite the Glacier du Bois, or Mer de Glace ; and from no point are the remarkable group of Aiguilles, which surround the Aiguille Verte, so finely seen. The Montanvert is visited for the sake of its proximity to the Mer de Glace ; the Flegère, to enjoy a view of Mont Blanc with its attendant objects. It is an excursion which requires only two hours and a half, from Chamouny to the Flegère. The road that leads to it, lies up the valley, to the hamlet of *les Près*, where it turns off to the left towards the Aiguille de Chalanods, one of the Aiguilles Rouges, where a steep path commences, which leads up to the pasturage of Pra de Viola. Thence a good hour is required to attain the Croix de Flegère, which commands a view of the whole range, from the Col de Balme, to the furthest glacier that, below Chamouny, streams into the valley, which lies in a great part of its extent in delicious repose beneath the observer.

Within two minutes' walk of the Cross are the châlets of Flegère, which afford shelter in unfavourable weather, and where refreshment may be had : for sight-seeing is turned to good account in every place in the neighbourhood of Chamouny where the visitors are numerous enough to ensure a sale of the provision made.

The height of the Croix de Flegère is about 3500 feet above the valley.

If the traveller be pressed for time, and can only visit one of the spots of interest around Chamouny, it should be the Montanvert; if two, this and the Flegère; if three should be the

Breven. — This excursion requires five hours from Chamouny to the summit of the Breven; it is fatiguing and difficult for ladies, yet many go there; for if they can bear the fatigue, their guides either avoid danger, or protect them when exposed to it; and the confidence which the names of Balmat, Coutet, Tairrez, Davassoud, and others, inspire, is so great, that the adventurous dame who begins with the Flegère often ends with the Jardin or the Breven.

It is fatiguing, however, to reach the Breven and descend in one day, about 12 hours; for this reason, many go in the evening to the châlets of Planpra, or Pliampra, the path to which lies behind the church of Chamouny, and leads directly towards the base of the Breven.

This mountain and the Aiguilles Rouges form the north-western boundary of the Vale of Chamouny, nearly throughout its extent. It is strikingly distinguished, however, from its neighbour, by its ridge being unbroken, and even rounded, though it offers on the side of Chamouny a vast line of precipices, apparently inaccessible.

About one third of the ascent to the Breven may be accomplished on a mule; another third will attain the châlets of Planpra, where there is a glorious view of Mont Blanc and the valley of Chamouny. In this wild spot the meadows and pasturages are beautiful.

Above Planpra, either a fatiguing path may be taken, which is cut in the rocks, or one, that leads directly up the pasturages, which, when dry, are very slippery; it is a choice of labour and difficulty without much difference: many patches of snow are passed, and it is not uncommon to observe the red fungus upon it, such as Captain Parry noticed in the high latitudes of his northern voyages. At the end of an hour from Planpra, the path reaches the base of a steep rock, which it is necessary to climb, by a sort of open chimney about 50 feet high. To clamber up this perpendicular gulley is one of the feats of which travellers boast; those, however, who do not value the glory it confers, or will not set it against the risk, go on half a mile, and find a convenient path by which this precipitous rock can be surmounted. Above it the path lies up a gentle slope, neither fatiguing nor dangerous to the summit of the Breven; this has an elevation of about 8500 English feet above the level of the sea, or 5000 above Chamouny, yet not more than two fifths of the height of Mont Blanc above the valley. This elevation, however, offers the finest view of the whole mass of Mont Blanc, of all the numerous sites whence it can be seen. The vale of Chamouny alone separates them, and this proximity is so great that every peak and glacier, and even crevices in the glaciers, can be distinguished; every pasturage and châlet, in that band on the mountain side, which lies above the pine forests and below the eternal snows.

When adventurous travellers ascend Mont Blanc, numerous visitors crowd the Breven to watch their progress, for the course lies like a map, from the village to the summit, and, with a good glass, every step they take may be observed. From the Buet, 2000 feet higher, there is a more extended horizon, but the Breven conceals all the lower belts of Mont Blanc, and as the Buet is double the distance from the peak of the "Monarch," he is not so distinct, nor offers a scene half so grand as the view of the entire range from the Col de Balme to the Col de Vosa, for the cross on one, and the pavilion on the other may be seen from the Breven.

The return to Chamouny may be varied by passing on the western side of the Breven, above the valley of Diozas, near to a little lake, then descending by the châlets of Calaveiran, towards the village of Coupeau, a path leads down to les Ouches, in the valley of Chamouny, and thence up the valley to the priory.

Source of the Arveron.—This affluent of the Arve issues from below the vault of ice with which the Glacier du Bois, the Mer de Glace, terminates. It is a delightful walk of an hour, along the plain of the valley, crossing beautiful meadows, and a little forest. The road to the Col de Balme, and up the valley, is left at *les Près*, where that to the source of the Arveron, turns off to the right, and passes the hamlet of *Bois.* The vault of ice varies greatly in different seasons, and the author, at different times, has remarked a change of from 30 to 100 feet of height in the arch. It may be entered, but this is dangerous, and some have suffered for their temerity. The guides generally prohibit entrance, but many walk thus far without their aid, and their folly has no restraint. The danger is, that blocks of ice may detach themselves from the vault. In 1797, three persons were crushed. One, a son of M. Maritz of Geneva, perished; his father and his cousin escaped with broken legs.

The scenery around the source is very grand, the deep blackness of the depth of vault, the bright and beautiful azure where the light is transmitted through the ice. The enormous rocks brought down by the glacier from the mountains above, here tumble over, and are deposited in the bed of the Arve. Here, too, the dark forest, and the broken trunks of pines, add to the wild character of the scene.

The advance and recession of the glaciers seem to depend upon the seasons. If it be hot, the ground melts the subjacent ice, and the glacier advances,

and a wet season by depositing a greater quantity of snow, increases its weight and force. Sometimes the difference is many hundreds of feet. It is not more than thirty years since it reached the forest of pines, now passed through in approaching to it.

A path, steep and difficult, brings the visitor from the Montanvert, down through the forest to the source of the Arveron, of which many who are active and strong avail themselves, and thus return to Chamouny.

The Chapeau is easier of access than the Montanvert. It is one of the points of view on the Mer de Glace, the side furthest from Chamouny: from it the Aiguilles of Charmoz, and le Blatière are seen immediately under Mont Blanc, with the vale of Chamouny, the Breven, and other vast and interesting objects; but its chief interest lies in its proximity to the Mer de Glace, where the glacier begins to break into pyramids and *obelisques* of ice; and here avalanches are frequently seen, where these toppling masses fall over with frightful effect. Captain Sherwill thus describes the Chapeau : —" I should advise travellers who have not seen the source of the Arveron to visit this and the Chapeau on the same day, which may be done either in going to or returning from the latter : this plan is far more preferable, and much less fatiguing, than to descend to the source by the path of La Filia, usually recommended by guides on quitting the Montanvert, and which is very inconvenient to ladies, the mountain being extremely rugged, and the descent so rapid that mules never go that way.

" A visit to the Chapeau may be accomplished either on foot or with the mules : if you go direct to it, you must continue along the valley as far as the village of Les Tines ; and, after having passed this picturesque spot, ascend a narrow road on the right hand that leads to the scattered hamlet of Lavanchè, continue through this latter by a good mule path beside the glacier, until you arrive at the foot of the ascent to the Chapeau. Here it is necessary to leave your mules in care of a boy, while the guide conducts you to a cavern, above which is the grass mound properly called the Chapeau : strangers in general are satisfied with a visit to the cave, from whence the view is perfectly unique, and very astonishing.

" On your return from the Chapeau, you descend by the same path as far as Les Tines, from whence there is a road on the left that leads to the hamlet of Les Bois, situated at the source of the Arveron. This excursion may be accomplished in about five hours, and will prove one of the most agreeable and least fatiguing of those that surround Chamouny.

" Pedestrians who feel themselves capable of undertaking difficult passes may, on quitting the Chapeau, continue to ascend by the side of the Mer de Glace, and arrive opposite to the hut on the Mantanvert ; but to accomplish this there is a very dangerous rock to pass, known by the guides by the name of ' *Le Mauvais Pas.*' I took with me two guides, Joseph Coutet and the Giant, as he is called ; and having arrived opposite the Montanvert, we traversed the Mer de Glace. This is dangerous ; but the traveller will have a far better idea of the grandeur of this frozen ocean than by merely visiting a few of its waves from the usual point near ' La Pierre des Anglais,' so termed at the ascent of Dr. Pococke and Mr. Wyndham in 1741.

" In the month of July, when the weather permits, a large quantity of heifers are driven from Chamouny, each attended by its owner, to the hut on Mantanvert, for the purpose of being conducted across the Mer de Glace, to pass their summer of three months on the slopes of the mountains that are near the Aiguille Dru. Before they are launched upon the sea of ice, a number of peasants precede them with hatchets and other tools, in order to level such places as are thus rendered less dangerous, although accidents generally attend this transit. At certaim intervals men are stationed to point out the line of march ; the operation, which requires several hours, and is truly picturesque to witness, is worthy the attention of the stranger, if he should be at Chamouny at the time : it is a kind of *fête* or holiday, for men, women, and children, attend the procession, passing the whole day on the mountain in the full enjoyment of this extraordinary and Herculean task. One man remains on the opposite side of the Mer de Glace, as guardian to the herd, that wander about in search of the rich but scanty pastures of those untenanted mountains. He carries with him sufficient bread and cheese to last one month, which is renewed at the expiration of that period, carried to him by some one interested in his well-doing, and is the contribution of all those whose heifers are under his care. He is allowed one cow, which furnishes him with milk : knitting is his chief employ, and thus he passes his time of expatriation in making stockings and contemplating the wonders of nature that surround him during three months of the year."

The Ascent of Mont Blanc is attempted by few ; of these, the records are to be found at Chamouny. When Saussure ascended to make experiments at that height, the motive was a worthy one ; but those who are impelled by curiosity alone, are not justified in risking the lives of the guides. The pay tempts these poor fellows to encounter the danger, but their safety, devoted as they are to their employers, is risked for a poor consideration. It is no excuse that the employer thinks his own life worthless : here he ought to think of the safety of others ; yet scarcely a season passes without the attempt. One Englishman went to the summit, only to say that he had been there. For long before the arrival the guides were certain that all view would be shut out by clouds; yet he went, and now boasts that he did it in half an hour less than it has been done by any other scrambler.

One of the latest who succeeded in attaining the summit was the Comte de Tilly, the first Frenchman who had been there; his pamphlet, giving an account of it, published at Geneva in 1835, is one of the most ridiculously *national accounts* ever read.

When Messrs. Fellows and Hawes went up in 1827 they took a course to the left of the Roches Rouges, and this has greatly lessened the danger of the ascent by avoiding the most dangerous part of it. All who have succeeded have advised no one to attempt it; they admit, however, when again in safety, that the fatigue and danger was infinitely exceeded by the gratification.

The excitement of sleeping out in the mountain is part of the interest of the adventure. This may, however, be enjoyed by going to the *Grands Mulets*, an excursion in which there is little danger, and sleeping there; choosing a moonlight night and fine weather to enjoy the extensive view, the bright sky, and the thunders of falling avalanches. Or, another excursion may be made to enjoy a night out, by crossing into Piedmont, over the Col de Géant. This adventure requires three or four guides. It was performed in the year 1822 by two English ladies, Mrs. and Miss Campbell, who, with eight guides, started at mid-day, August 18th, slept out one night on the mountain, and descended the next day to Cormayeur. Saussure remained out many successive nights and days engaged in experiments on the Col de Géant: and during the prohibition of English goods by Bonaparte, this was a common path for smugglers who crossed it from Switzerland to Italy laden with British muslins.

ROUTE 116.

CHAMOUNY TO MARTIGNY, BY THE TÊTE NOIRE, TRIENT, AND THE COL DE FORCLAZ.

There are two roads which lead from Chamouny to Martigny; one by the Tête Noire, the other by the Col de Balme. Travellers are often perplexed which to choose of these two passes. The general scenery of the Tête Noire is superior; but the Col de Balme has *one view* which far surpasses any in the Tête Noire.

The route to the Val Orsine and Tête Noire lies up the vale of Chamouny, by *Les Prés*, where the path to the Arveron divides; thence the main route of the valley continues to the chapel and hamlet of *Tines:* here the valley narrows, and the road ascends steeply on the banks of the Arve, opposite to the bases of the Aiguilles Rouges, to some pasturages, and the hamlet of *Les Isles,* beyond, the Arve is crossed, and the village of Argentière is left on the right hand; this is the third and highest parish in the valley, and is two leagues from the priory; here the magnificent glacier of Argentière is seen streaming down from between the Aiguilles d'Argentière and du Tour.

Soon after passing Argentière the road turns to the north, leaving the path to the hamlet of le Tour, and the Col de Balme on the right. The path rises rapidly to the miserable hamlet of Trelefan, passing what is called the Montets by a sterile gorge, and at a short league from Argentière the summit of this pass is attained; the streams on either side take different courses, that through Chamouny to the Arve, and that towards Martigny to the Rhone.

A little beyond the crest, a savage and sterile valley opens to the left, through which the Eau Noire, the torrent of the Val Orsine, descends; and on looking up this valley, the snows of the lofty Buet lying behind the Aiguilles Rouges, are seen. After passing the hamlet of Couteraie, the road descends rapidly to Val Orsine, the chief village of the valley. Its church having been more than once swept away, a strong rampart of masonry and earth has been raised to defend it from similar catastrophes.

Below Val Orsine, the valley narrows to a gorge, abounding, in season, with wild fruits: through it, the torrent forces its way into the more open valley below, acquiring in its course fresh force, from the contributions of numerous waterfalls and streams which descend from the glaciers above.

In this gorge, a sort of barrier marks the frontier of Savoy — it is utterly useless as a defence: soon after the torrent is crossed, near to where a mill and some pleasant meadows contrast with the generally savage character of the deep valley. In a wild part of the ravine the road passes under an overhanging rock, which bears the name of the Roche de Balme: an inscription contains some compliments to Lady Guildford, which, having been nearly obliterated, has been *restored*, with mistakes, " too numerous to mention," but very amusing.

Considerable improvements within a few years have taken place in this route, on the side of Switzerland. Formerly, a fearful path led from the depths of the valley by a zigzag course, over loose and dangerous slopes to gain the Tête Noire, up what was well known by the characteristic name of the Malpas; now, instead of descending into the valley, to rise again, the road is carried over the mountain side, and at one place a gallery is pierced through a rock, in a situation of singular grandeur, where it overhangs precipitously the dark valley beneath.

This improvement, which removes all danger from the pass, has not been extended to the side of Savoy : the government of Sardinia seconds no efforts of improvement thus spiritedly begun by its neighbours. On the contrary, the steep and rocky path left like steps, is only practicable for mules — and for these in many places difficult ; and it is to be hoped that the time is not distant when a good char road will lead into the valley of Chamouny from Martigny. The latest improvement is an extension of the road, on the part of the Valais, almost to the frontier of Savoy, by cuttings, and the construction of terraces, on the side of the valley of the Eau Noire, by which the violent undulations of the old road will be avoided, and carry the traveller below the rock of Lady Guildford.

A little beyond the gallery, there is a house where shelter in foul weather may be had, and a glass of *schnaps* to warm the wet and cold traveller. Near this spot the road turns abruptly into the dark forest of Trient, passing round the brow of a mountain covered with dark forests : this brow is called the Tête Noire, beyond which the road through the forest continues for half an hour. In the depths below the forest, the torrent of the Trient is heard forcing its way into the Eau Noire, which it joins before their streams fall into the Rhone.

On leaving the forest, the valley of Trient opens, and in about six hours after his departure from Chamouny the traveller reaches the little auberge in the hamlet, where he may rest and refresh. Here, a new room has been built as a *salle à manger*, but the dormitory is wretched : it must, however, be worse before weariness refuses even such accommodation.

The little valley of Trient is deeply seated amidst pine forests, the débris of the surrounding mountains, and the fearful precipices from which these have been detached. In the plain of the valley some barley is grown, and the meadows are luxuriant.

A little way beyond the hamlet,

the torrent which descends from the glacier of the Trient is crossed, and a steep path leads up through the forest, which clothes the mountain side of the Forclaz : little more than half an hour is required for this ascent. On the way, another port or barrier is passed : it is left in a wall which closes the passage between the mountain and the precipice. Near it are the ruins of a redoubt : this is another specimen of playing at soldiers among the Valaisans. On the right a path is passed, which, in crossing the valley from the Forclaz to the Col de Balme, avoids the hamlet of Trient.

From the Col de Forclaz the descent is by fine pasturages, and two hours are required to reach Martigny : the view of the valley of the Rhone seen in the descent from Martigny to the St. Gothard is one of the most celebrated in the Alps. The path is much sheltered by pines and beeches, and lower in the valley by the pear and apple trees : in the neighbourhood of these are numerous cottages, and many are passed before the path falls into the route, that leads from Martigny to the Great St. Bernard, and the valley of the Drance. (Route 106.)

ROUTE 117.

MARTIGNY TO CHAMOUNY BY THE COL DE BALME.

This road is recommended to those travellers, who have not been to Chamouny, but who enter it for the first time from the Valais : for the sake of the first impression which the view of Mont Blanc makes upon them when seen from the Col de Balme.

On leaving Martigny, the route over the Forclaz is repassed ; but, in descending to the valley of Trient, a path to the left leads towards the glacier of Trient and the dark forest, up through which lies the ascent to the Col de Balme.

Deep in the valley on the right, the

hamlet of Trient lies in repose amidst its beautiful meadows; and before and above the traveller, on the opposite side of the valley, are the precipices of the Aiguille, from which poor Escher de Berg fell in 1791, when, in defiance of the advice of his guide, he tried some fool-hardy feat, and paid his life for the attempt.

The path through the forest of the Forclaz, at length emerges higher up the valley of Trient, than where it was crossed from the Tête Noir ; and the traveller has to pass over the detritus of winter torrents, which must be crossed before the forest that leads up to the Col de Balme is entered. The path through it is excessively steep and fatiguing, often intercepted by the entangled roots of the pines, which form steps two or three feet in height, and it is a subject of wonder how mules get up or down such places. At length, after climbing about an hour and a half up the mountain side, and through the forest, the traveller emerges upon the pasturages and châlets of Herbageres. Above these, the ascent is gradual to the summit, where one of the finest scenes in the world bursts upon the traveller. Mont Blanc, from his summit, to his base in the vale of Chamouny, lies like a model before him, surrounded by the Aiguilles of La Tour, L'Argentière, Verté, de Dru, Charmoz, Midi, &c., &c. ; and each divided by enormous glaciers, which as they stream into the valley clothe the steep course of their descent. How glorious is the "Monarch," thus seen, attended by all his peaks like guards. Below, the eye sweeps its course entirely through the vale of Chamouny, to the Col de Vosa, at its other extremity. On the right, the Aiguilles Rouges are the nearest : beyond these bounding the valley, lies the Breven, and behind it is seen the Mortine, which supports the snowy summit of the Buet. It is a magnificent scene to dwell upon, and those who do not arrive at Chamouny by the Col de

Balme, ought to make an excursion from the Prieuré, expressly to enjoy this most glorious view.

There is a house of refuge on the Col de Balme, where shelter and refreshment, with excellent wine may be had, and 5 or 6 tolerable beds are ready to receive travellers overtaken by a storm.

On the descent, the source of the Arve is passed, at least the highest of its springs; the path lies down over fine pasturages, and by the châlets of Charamillan, to the hamlet of La Tour, where cultivation, though scanty, is reached, and barley, oats and flax are raised. About a mile below La Tour, the path falls into the road to Chamouny from the Tête Noire (Route 116.) The time from Martigny to Chamouny, by the Col de Balme, is nine hours. To go in one day from Chamouny to Trient, by the Tête Noire, and return by the Col de Balme requires 12 or 13 hours. When this is intended, to gain time it is desirable to take a char as far as Argenture, the road being good enough to go over it with great despatch from Chamouny.

ROUTE 118.

CHAMOUNY TO CORMAYEUR, BY THE COL DE BON-HOMME, AND THE COL DE LA SEIGNE.

(Two or three Days.)

In leaving Chamouny the road lies down the valley to Ouches, where it leaves the route to Servoz on the right hand, and proceeds by the hamlet of Foully. A little beyond this, another path, which on the right leads by the mountain of Vaudagne and the Forclaz of St. Gervais, is avoided, and one is taken that leads up through a forest of larches, and by a steep zigzag course to the châlets. From the Col de Vosa, where a pavilion has been placed, there is a fine view of the valley of Chamouny, Mont Blanc, &c., which extends to the Col de Balme.

From the Col, a very steep path leads down by some châlets towards the deep course of the torrent that issues from the glacier of Bionnassai, which lies before the traveller, and presents amidst its rocks and snows a most savage aspect. Without going far up, it is difficult to ford this torrent; but having crossed it, some cottages are passed at the head of the forest that clothes the mountains which bound the eastern side of the Val Mont-Joie, into which the path now descends. On the opposite side of the valley is seen the beautifully situated village of St. Nicolas de Veros, on its fine terrace on the mountain side, and backed by the vast mountain of Hermance, the northern buttress of the Mont Joli.

The route to the village Bionnay in the Val Mont-Joie, leads too far down the valley. Much distance is saved to those who would ascend it, by taking a path to the left, which through Le Champel, and other hamlets, over well cultivated fields, and by rich meadows, in the valley, leads to Contamines, a large village beautifully situated: it has a handsome church, though this is scarcely remarkable in Faucigny, where it is generally the pride of the village.

The view of the valley presented to the traveller in descending from Bionnassey to Contamines is of its whole length, seen up to the peaks of the Bon-homme.

At Contamines there is a tolerable inn; but if the traveller wish to reach Cormayeur the next day, it is desirable that he should go on to Nant Bourant, and start thence early on the following morning.

The passage from Chamouny to Cormayeur is easily made in three days. The travellers may go on the first after 12 o'clock from Chamouny to Contamines, the following day from Contamines to Chapiu or the Hameau de Motet, the third to Cormayeur.

It is, however, very often done in two days by going to Chapiu or Motet the first day, as often, too, by making the second the long day, starting from Nant Bourant, and reaching Cormayeur.

From Contamines the view of the Val Mont-Joie is very fine. One o fits finest features is the beautiful Mont Joli, the bases of which, on the right, bound the valley.

On leaving Contamines, which lies on rather high ground above the river Bourant, which flows through the Val Mont-Joie, the path, after passing another village, descends and crosses the torrent to the hamlet of Pontet: above this, the valley narrows until it end in the little church-village of Notre Dame de la Gorge, most singularly situated in a deep dell which lies at the foot of Mont Joli. Up the ravine the course is impracticable, as it terminates in a cataract of the Bourant.

At Notre Dame de la Gorge, there is a *fête* on the 15th of August which is attended by hundreds of peasants and others, who come from the neighbouring villages to attend mass: a sort of fair is held, and the scene is very animated.

Close to the church a wooden bridge crosses the torrent, and a very steep and rudely paved path leads directly up the mountain side and through a forest: the denuded face of the granite on the path, and the large stones which fill up the interstices, make this a difficult road for mules, and a fatiguing one to men. It leads to the châlets and pasturages of Nant Bourant, where the torrent is crossed by a stone bridge: the gulf through which it rushes has a fearful depth, and a little way down, below the bridge, the water falls into a still blacker and deeper ravine, forming the *Nant* or cataract of the Bourant: it is difficult even from above to get a view of its furious descent.

At the châlets of Nant Bourant a tolerably convenient place for sleep-ing has, within a few years, been erected, and this is the best place to rest at, when a succeeding long day's journey is determined upon.

Above the châlets the valley is very narrow, the road passing through the forest, which belts and clothes the base of the Mont Joli; at length it enters upon the pasturages, which are rich, though scanty from the quantity of stones and rocks that abound: after rising above the *débris* which have fallen from the mountains, the path winds up to the châlets of Mont-Joie, where the traveller usually rests and obtains the refreshment of a draught of milk. Between Nant Bourant and these châlets, huge masses of glaciers extend down the crues on the south-western flanks of Mont Blanc; but immediately above the châlets is the vast glacier of Trelaulai. This, and the black rocks which support it on one side of the valley, and the precipices and *débris* over which there is a pass to the valley of Haute Luce on the other, almost inclose these châlets as in a deep basin. Upward, the valley is closed by the Bon-homme; and, on looking back, the whole length of the Val Mont-Joie is seen bounded by the peaks of the Varens above St. Martin's.

From the châlets of Mont-Joie, the path leads up a steep acclivity which overhangs the depths of the valley: its appearance is appalling, as the traveller looks down from his mule, and sees his foot overhanging the slope beyond the path. As the mountain is ascended, it becomes more and more sterile; the pine does not grow so high as the châlets of Mont-Joie, and on the next terrace above the châlets, on the Plan des Dames the rhododendron is the largest shrub that flourishes. On the Plan there is a cairn, a heap of stones, which has existed from time immemorial. Tradition says, that a great lady with her suite perished here in a storm, and gave name to the fatal spot; every guide adds a stone to the cairn, and requests the traveller to do so from some feeling of awe associated with it as a duty.

From the Plan des Dames, the path leads up herbless slopes and over some patches of snow, to reach what, from below, seems to be the col. On the left, wild and abrupt precipices rise : and two of the peaked rocks there, bear the name of the Bon-homme and the *Femme de Bon-homme.*

The crest, however, which lies close to these pinnacles is that of the Col de la Gauche, across which a path lies that leads down to Maxime de Beaufort, and the whole course of the valley of Beaufort to the Bourg is seen before and below the traveller. On looking back, too, the valley of Mont-Joie is seen in all its length, and these glorious scenes of alpine valleys, with the thousand peaks which crest the chains of mountains that divide them, offer displays of alpine scenery no-where surpassed.

The path of the col de Bon-homme turns on the left from the Col de Gauche, behind the pinnacles of rock, and extends by a loose, swampy, path-less slope to the col, distant an hour from the Col de Gauche. The height of the Col de Bonhomme exceeds 8000 English feet above the level of the sea : from it, the beautiful mountain of the Chaffe-Quarre, in the Val Isère (Route 113.), is finely seen.

From the Col two roads branch off; that on the right leads down in two hours to the châlets of Chapiu over a broken swampy ground ; and from Chapiu in three hours, the traveller can reach Bourg St. Maurice, in the Tarentaise, by the valley of Bonnaval.

It requires six or seven hours to go from Nant Bourant to Chapiu. The state of the weather makes an import-ant difference in the time: the journey should never be undertaken but in fine weather, or with a good prospect of it. On the 3d of September, 1830, two English gentlemen perished in a snow storm whilst crossing it—the Rev.

Richard Braken and Augustus Camp-bell, the former at the age of 30, the latter 20 ; they were on their way from Chapiu : their guides, who were capi-tal mountaineers, would have insured their safety, but the travellers wanted resolution to meet the danger, and sunk from terror and fatigue.

At Chapiu some of the châlets are fitted up in a rude way to receive tra-vellers who may be disposed to come here and sleep, thus dividing the jour-ney to Cormayeur. From Chapiu a path leads in two hours up by the stream of the Versoi (which descends through Bonnaval) to the hameau de Glacier, so called from its promixity to one of the glaciers of Mont Blanc, and half a league further, to the châ-lets of Motet. This miserable spot divides with Chapiu the honour of entertaining travellers. Those who reach Motet direct, cross the Cime du Fours, to which the path on the left, on the Col de Bon-homme, leads an hour sooner than by the *détour* to Chapiu, but the road rises 1000 feet higher, and the descent is much more fatiguing; the accommodations, too, at Motet, are much worse than those at Chapiu: it is, however, gener-ally taken, for the sake of gaining time by those who go to Cormayeur from Nant Bourant in one day. The ha-meau de Glacier is, perhaps, a better place to rest in for the night, because it is lower ; but there is no choice of comfort.

The pasturages of Motet belong to the people of the Tarentaise and are generally occupied by a family from St. Maurice.

The steep path which winds up the mountain side to the Col de la Seigne is in many places dangerous from the softness of the soil over which the path passes, and the nar-rowness of the path, carried as it is along the steep slope; so steep, that in some places the bottom of the valley cannot be distinguished immediately below.

The author of " Excursions in the

Alps " mentions his passage of this col to Cormayeur, from Chamouny, and gives a vivid picture of the danger real or pretended; we shall quote him to Cormayeur : —

" From these châlets the ascent to the Col de la Seigne is very steep and fatiguing; and in one place the idea of danger was strongly excited by our guide, who lay on his back towards the mountain slope, where a very narrow path skirted a precipice, and held our coats until the mules were beyond the point of danger. The path was slippery, from the wet and loose slate of which it was composed; but the precaution was appalling, and, I think, unnecessary; though we certainly could not see the bottom of the valley immediately beneath us as we passed this spot.

" After ascending about an hour and a half from Motet, we attained the summit of the Col de la Seigne, about 8000 feet, where an alpine view of extraordinary magnificence burst upon us. We looked upon Mont Blanc, and along the course of the valleys which divide Piedmont from the Valais, and extend nearly 30 miles on the eastern side of its enormous mass, through the Allée Blanche, the Val Veni, and the Val d'Entrèves, to the Col de Ferret. Two immense pyramids of rugged rock rear from the valley their scathed heads, and appear like guards to the "monarch of mountains;" beyond and below them lay the little lake of Combal, whence issues one of the sources of the Doira Baltea; and down the sides of Mont Blanc appeared to stream the glaciers of the Allée Blanche and the Miage; whilst the distant peaks which overhang the western side of this long valley or valleys (for different portions of it, from the Col de la Seigne to the Col de Ferret, bear different names) give a peculiarly grand and severe aspect to the scene: among these the Géant and the Grand Jorasse are distinguished. The eastern side of the valley is formed by the Cramont, and a range of mountains which extend to the Col de Ferret, and terminate the vista in Mont Velan and the masses which surround the pass of the Great St. Bernard. The summit of Mont Blanc was occasionally enveloped in clouds, and the changes which these produced upon the scene were often strikingly beautiful. Most travellers, whose expectations have been formed upon the descriptions in guide-books, are led to believe that the eastern side of Mont Blanc is one vast precipice, from the summit down to the Allée Blanche: it is certainly much more abrupt than towards the vale of Chamouny; but no such anticipation will be realised in the magnificent view from the Col de la Seigne.

" From this col, leading across the great chain of the Alps, we began our descent over some beds of perpetual snow, which, lying on the northern side of the path, remain unmelted. Though steep, these are not dangerous, as the feet sink two or three inches and give firmness to the step. Scarcely any melting takes place on the surface of the snow, unless where the soil has been washed over, or fallen so as to cover it. Generally, the snow melts below, in contact with the earth; and this is one of the causes of avalanches, where the mass which slips acquires momentum enough to rush on. Caution is generally necessary near the edges of these beds of snow, where it is thin, lest the traveller should sink through, perhaps two or three feet. After a tedious descent to the first pasturage, at the base of the two immense pyramids which formed so striking a feature from the summit, we sat down upon the short and soft grass of the pasturage of the châlets of the Allée Blanche, to rest the mules and ourselves, and took refreshment, which we had brought with us. The life and spirit of such enjoyment as this is only known to alpine travellers. The sward around us was enamelled with beautiful flowers : of these, the broad patches of the deep blue gentianella were the richest in colour ; the alpine ranunculus, and a hundred other varieties, embellished the place where we rested ; being surrounded by, and in the immediate vicinity of, the loftiest mountains in Europe.

" Soon after leaving this delightful spot, we skirted the little lake of Combal by a very narrow and dangerous path. The mule on which my friend rode attempted, in order to exhibit his obstinacy or his courage, to turn upon this narrow way ; but there not being sufficient room, his tail overhung the water, whilst his fore-feet were resting in a nearly erect posture against the rocks which bordered the lake : a blow from Michael was the only applause that he received for his feat, and he then wisely and safely resumed his route. After passing the lake at the lower extremity across an embankment of great thickness and strength, the path descends on the left side of the torrent, which struggles with horrid violence in continued cataracts down the ravine for several miles, particularly where, in passing by the glacier of Miage, our route lay amidst rocks and stones, the débris of the mountain, brought down by the glacier, of which it concealed the base and sides. The ice being covered by the stones and soil, the path was so dangerous that we followed the advice of our guide, and descended from our mules. We were occupied nearly two hours in passing this *moraine*, as the guides here call these terminations of the glaciers. Sometimes we were at the water's edge, at others on a pathless ridge, some hundreds of feet above the Doire, walking over loose stones, and these rendered less secure by the numerous streams which, falling from the heights above us, crossed our path to increase the torrent foaming beneath. At length we escaped from this fatiguing part of our route, and entered the beautiful meadows of the

Val Veni, which are separated from the Val d'Entrèves by a high ridge that skirts the forest of St. Nicolas. There are no châlets in the Val Veni, but several granges, in which the great quantities of hay made in the meadows and slopes of this valley are stored.

" The forest of Saint Nicolas, which we traversed on our way to Cormayeur, is opposite to some extensive buildings at the foot of the Glacier de Brenva : these were formerly occupied by miners, who prepared the lead and copper ores raised near this place : but the expenses having exceeded the profits, these buildings are now falling to decay. Across the valley we saw the beautiful glacier of Brenva appearing through the enormous larches and pines of the forest, presenting to us a scene deservedly esteemed one of the finest in the Alps. We now rapidly descended by a narrow road which fearfully overhangs the lower range of the glacier of the Brenva, whose sides were covered with masses of granite and rocks of great magnitude. The torrent which we had seen rushing through the valley passed beneath the glacier, and reappeared increased by a stream, which issued from an arch at the termination of the glacier, like that of the Arveron in the Vale of Chamouny.

In the valley below us lay the village of Entrèves ; and towering high above it, on our left, were the Géant and its pass. The road improved as we approached Cormayeur ; and we soon got into excellent quarters at the Albergo dell' Angela. (Route 107.)

ROUTE 119.

SALLENCHES TO L'HOPITAL CONFLANS.

From Sallenches (Route 115.), a new route is being constructed, which if it proceed with spirit, will one day open a char or carriage communication between the valley of the Arve and that of the Isère, in the Tarentaise.

The road which has been made or improved to Megève rises directly up the steep side of one of the slopes of Mont Foron, to the village of Comblou, about an hour's ascent. Its gay spire is seen from the road to Chamouny, near Passy, and also from the valley of Maglans in approaching to it. From Comblou there is a most beautiful prospect, well worthy the traveller's walk from Sallenches or St. Martin's. It commands the valley of Maglans on one side, and the Varens, and the upper valley of the Arve on the other. The Aiguilles de Varens rise in great grandeur directly *en face* of the spectator, and on the right of the upper Arve, all the peaks and glaciers of Mont Blanc, and its extreme summit, are as distinctly seen as in a model. Few spots for such prospects can vie with the village of Comblou.

A little beyond Comblou the highest part of the road to Megève is passed : thence to the latter bourg, the distance is a league, over a road nearly level. Here are two miserable inns. From Megève a road leads to the Pas Sion, a col which divides the valley of Haute Luce from the valley of the Arly, and leads by the shortest course to Beaufort.

From Megève, the road descends the valley of the Arly in two hours to Flumet, a little town of Upper Faucigny, containing about 1000 inhabitants. Here, on a rock, are the ruins of a château, in which the first baron of Faucigny resided.

Flumet is seated near the confluence of the Flon and the Arly : the former river descends from the hamlet of Gietta, by which a path traverses the Col des Aravis and the Grand Borand to Bonneville.

Below Flumet the road is only practicable for mules; it is excessively hilly and wild. The valley of the Arly is a gorge, deeply seated; and bears the name of the Combe of

Savoie. In two hours from Flumet, it leads to Heri, a village situated in a most agreeable spot, surrounded by high mountains covered with pine forests.

Below Heri, the path, in many places cut out in the mountain side, overhangs the deep bed of the Arly, and alternate spots of savageness and beauty are found throughout this valley. Its richness in walnut trees is celebrated, and the oil which the nuts furnish is an important article of commerce.

Ugine is a large ill-built town, containing 3000 inhabitants, famous for its fairs of cattle and mules. To the north of the town, on a steep lime rock, there are the remains of a lofty square tower, flanked by other towers, which defended a château attacked in the 9th century by the Saracens. The château was destroyed in the 13th century by Humbert, first dauphin of Vienna. It is situated on the right bank of the Arly, and lies in the road now opened between Faverges and Annecy, — a road which will be noticed under Route 120.

From Ugine an excellent carriage road continues down the Arly to l'Hôpital Conflans, through a deep and rich valley. Before arriving at l'Hôpital, one sees on the other side of the Arly the valley of Beaufort, where the Doron, which flows through it, falls into the Arly. The valley of the Do:on leads by a mountainous mule road, in about 4 hours, to Maxime de Beaufort, a town famous also for its cattle fairs. The inhabitants are rich and independent, from their commerce in cheese, butter, and cattle : their pasturages are the most valuable in Upper Savoy. Beaufort communicates with Megève by the valley of Haute Luce and the pass Sion, by the head of its valley with the Col de Bon-Homme, and by the valley of Roselen and the Col d'Allée with the valley of Bonnaval (Route 113.) in the Tarentaise.

Beaufort is one of those retired

spots in the Alps, whence the inhabitants issue in the winter to seek employment in foreign countries. Some, periodically return, content with their gains; others realise great wealth, and remain to die where they obtained it. Among these are remembered M. Viallet, a great planter in St. Domingo, whose fortune before the revolution was valued at a million and half francs ; M. Cornu, a rich banker of Paris; Bouchage, a banker of Toulouse; Favre, a celebrated silk merchant of Lyons ; and Jean Mollie, who died about 1780, and left to his descendants the enormous sum of, it is said, 400 millions of francs.

At present Beaufort is one of the most independent communities in Savoy. They were permitted by Charles Emmanuel, duke of Savoy, to free themselves from feudal rents by purchase ; and in 1772 they paid to M. Villecardel de Fleury, marquis of Beaufort, 100,000 francs for their emancipation. The old families of Beaufort in England and France had their origin here.

Near Beaufort, on a hill at the entrance to the valley of Haute Luce, are the finely situated ruins of the château de la Salle. This château received Henry IV. and his courtiers in October 1600 : the pranks played there by them furnished some scandalous traditions.

L'Hôpital and *Conflans* are divided only by the Arly : the former being situated on its right bank, the latter on the rocky slopes above it on the other side.

Conflans is an ancient little town, with about 1300 inhabitants. It was formerly surrounded by strong walls and defended by two very strong forts. It resisted the troops of Francis I. in the war of 1536, when it was partly burnt, and its two forts demolished. A little below Conflans, near the banks of the river, there is a royal smelting-house and foundry, where the silver from the ore raised in some mines in the neighbourhood is re-

duced : it is seldom worked, and the *Fonderie* Royale is a worthless appendage to Conflans.

L'Hôpital, with its wide streets and clean appearance, is one of the nicest little towns in Savoy ; it has about 1500 inhabitants, and lying in the high road, by which communication is held with Ugine, Annecy, and Sallenches, with Chamberry, and with Moutiers Tarentaise, it has, since the establishment of good roads, been daily increasing in importance. A diligence by Faverges to Annecy, and another between Moutiers and Chamberry, which passes through l'Hôpital, have been established. The little town contains excellent inns, and that held by the frères Geny is not surpassed in comfort by the inns at Chamouny.

ROUTE 120.

GENEVA TO CHAMBERRY BY ANNECY

A diligence goes every day from Geneva to Chamberry, but on alternate days by two different routes — one by Annecy, the other by Rumilly.

On leaving Geneva, the road, common to both as far as

St. Julien, passes through the Plain Palais, crosses the Arve, and continues through Carouge and the richly cultivated plain of the Arve, until it rises to the village of St. Julien, on the frontier of Savoy, where the baggage and the passports of travellers are examined.

Here the road continues to ascend a long hill to the Mont Sion, a ridge which runs nearly at right angles with the Mont Saleve. From its height, about 3300 feet above the level of the sea, the views of the Lake of Geneva, the Jura, and the deep valley of the Rhone flowing into France form a fine panorama.

It is a pleasing drive, but there is nothing remarkable in the scenery. Its course is generally high, though it undulates until it rises to

Cruseilles, 2¾ posts, a little town possessing 1300 inhabitants, the ruins of an old castle, and a dirty inn ; opposite to which one of those crosses is placed, so common within the archbishopric of Chamberry, which invites every body, under a promise of 40 days' indulgence, to say an ave and a pater and make a genuflexion, as a set-off against crime ! The inscription on this, in bad French, is as follows : — "Monsenior Irene Yves de Solle, avaque de Chambery et da Geneve, accorde 40 jours indulgences a lous gens qui feront un acte de contritions et disont un pater et une ave davant cette croix crussoles, le 23 Août, 1810.

From Cruseilles the road to Annecy rapidly descends to cross the stream of the Usses in a deep defile, which can only be traversed by a considerable détour up the deep valley to rise on the other side to a level with the road from Cruseilles. A lofty bridge, built of brick, once crossed this ravine, about half-way down the valley. This has long been impassable, except to the foolhardy pedestrian : it was too narrow ever to have been safely passed in a char. The Sardinian government has, however, decided upon throwing an iron wire suspension bridge over this ravine, to carry the road directly across, where the shortest connexion will be continued ; this will require as great a length and have nearly as much elevation as the suspension bridge of Freybourg in Switzerland.

It is a pleasing drive by the villages of Alonzier, Caval, Pringy, and Metz, through a hilly country, often presenting fine points of view ; at length it crosses the Mont des Bornes, and descends a hill side which overlooks the plain and lake of Annecy, and the fine mountain scenery which surrounds it. There is a singular beauty in the views thus presented, and a charm in the approach to Annecy which is likely to be long remembered. At the Pont de Brogny the river Fier, which falls into the Rhone at Seissel, is crossed, and in half an hour the traveller finds himself at

Annecy, 2 posts. Inhabitants about 6000. Inns tolerable, the best is the Hôtel de Geneve. This city is in a beautiful situation at the extremity of a great plain, and on the borders of a lake, which is discharged by canals, that cross its streets, and which is led by the canal of Thiou, to fall into the Fier at Cran.

Annecy is a curious old town, the shops in many of its streets are under arcades, and there is an air of respectable antiquity about it — though this, the ancient capital of the duchy of Geneva, is only the modern town. In the 12th century it was known as *Anneciacum novum*, to distinguish it from *Anneciacum vetus*, which formerly existed on the slopes of the beautiful hill of Annecy-le-vieux. Numerous medals of the Roman emperors of the two first centureis of the Christian era have been found here, and inscriptions, sepulchres, urns, and fragments of statues, and of a temple attest the presence of this people. It rests upon little more than conjecture, that it was known to them as *Civitas Bovis*, or according to some bewildered antiquarians, as *Dinia or Dignitia ;* no monument, or MS., authorises one or the other.

The earliest mention of Annecy is by the emperor Lothaire, who gave it, under the name of Annesiacum, to his wife, Tietberge, as proved by a document, bearing date January 11. 867.

In the 12th century, the present Annecy was distinguished from Annecy-le-vieux, by William I. Comte of the Genevais. When the house of Geneva became extinct, Annecy passed into that of Savoy. In 1412 it was totally burnt. To assist in restoring the inhabitants to their town, Amadeus VIII. duke of Savoy, gave them many privileges, and enabled them to establish flax spinning works, which have continued to be its principal manufacture. In 1630, the plague almost depopulated the town, and destroyed or dispersed the workmen. Victor Amadeus I. afterwards established here four silk mills; these were destroyed by fire during the war of 1691.

In 1724, during violent disputes among the different manufacturers of Annecy, a large establishment for the manufacture of hats, which had existed for a century and half, was destroyed, as well as others for the production of worsted stockings. At the same time were destroyed the manufactory *of the fire arms of Collin,* famous in its day, and extensive works for scythes, reaping hooks, and cutlery; perhaps there is no town in Europe whose history has been so long associated with manufactures as Annecy. The linen bleacheries established in 1650, which have always sustained a high reputation, are still flourishing. Encouraged by Napoleon, when Savoy was under the French government M. Duport, now the Baron Duport of Turin, established here the first cotton works; these still flourish. He subsequently established those at Pont in Val d'Orca (Route 111.)

Even now the manufactures of Annecy are not all enumerated; there are others of black glass — of sulphuric acid, of printed cottons, &c., and in the neighbourhood, a fine vein of coal is worked, at Entreverne, — and at the village of Crans there are oil, corn, and fulling mills on the Fier, and mills for the manufacture of paper.

The active inhabitants of Annecy have always sought new channels for their industry — they found this to be necessary in order to procure subsistence for the population of the city, when its numerous convents were suppressed. It has now substituted industry and independence for idleness and beggary.

There are many objects of interest among the public buildings of Annecy — the ancient château, the residence of Genevois-Nemours — the old Bishop's palace — the Cathedral, with its sanctuary, where are deposited the relics of Saint Francis de Sales, and the Mere (Sainte) Chaptal : scandal has been busy with their names. The translation of the relics of the former was made on the 28th of May 1806, with great ceremony; the following day those of Sainte Jeanne-Françoise Frémiot de Chantal were transferred with equal solemnity.

" The tender friendship that long subsisted between St. Francis de Sales and La Mere Chantal, has given to their memory, and relics, with pious Catholics, a degree of interest similar to that excited by the remains of Abelard and Eloise.

" St. Francis de Sales was descended from the noble family of de Sales in Savoy; he was born in 1567, having devoted himself to the church, and evinced great zeal and eloquence in its defence. He was ordained prince and bishop of Geneva, by Pope Clement VIII., for the popes assumed the right to confer these titles long after the reformed religion had been established at Geneva. Annecy being made the bishop's seat when the Genevese expelled the chapter from their city, St. Francis de Sales died at Lyons in 1622, and was buried at Annecy. His canonisation took place in 1665; but before that event his remains were so highly valued by the inhabitants, that when the city was taken by the French in 1630, one of the six articles of capitulation stipulated that the body of the venerable Francis de Sales should never be removed from the city."—*Bakewell's Tour in the Tarentaise.*

At the lower extremity of the lake there is a beautiful promenade, where fairs and public amusements are held. The views from it of the mountain and the lake are fine. The level of the lake is about 1400 feet above that of the sea; it abounds in fine fish; among those least known to travellers re the lotte, and a fish peculiar to his lake, the *vairon*.

A good road carried along the south-west shores of the lake leads to Faverges. About two thirds of the distance is the Château Duing, placed on a neck of land which runs out into the lake —here many strangers come to board and lodge during the summer, and enjoy the most delightful excursions in its delicious neighbourhood.

The best way to get to the Château Duing is by the lake : a boat may be hired for a few francs, and a boatman to row there. In ascending the lake, an opening in the lofty mountains which bound its north-eastern side, discloses the Château of Menthon, on the delicious slopes of a recess : here St. Bernard, the "Apostle of the Alps," was born, and the place of his nativity, independant of its local beauty, cannot fail to interest the traveller. (Route 108.)

A road leads up by Menthon, and across the mountain above into the valley of Thones, one of the most retired, and unfrequented, by strangers, in Savoy. It may be visited in going from Annecy to Bonneville, on the road to Chamouny, for a road leads there in 8 hours through Thones and Entremont, an excursion offering much beautiful scenery, and very little known. Opposite the Château Duing, is Talloires, the birthplace of the celebrated chemist Berthollet.

From the Château Duing, the road to Faverges continues up the valley of Eau Morte about three miles ; it is so nearly level, that the plain of the valley is often inundated.

Faverges has a population of about 2000, it is beautifully situated amidst wooded slopes and mountains ; it is well cultivated, and abounds in rich meadows. It was known in the 12th century as Fabricarium, a name arising from its numerous forges for copper and iron. Its reputation has not decreased ; there are now silk mills established there, manufactories of cut-lery, and tanneries ; and since the completion of the road by Ugine into the Tarentaise it is daily improving. Its old castle is finely situated.

A slight elevation divides the head of the valley of the Eau Morte from that of the stream of Monthoux, which runs into the Arly at Ugine (Route 119.). The valley of Monthoux is richly wooded and picturesque. There is, however, a much shorter way than by Ugine to l'Hôpital Conflans ; two hours may be gained by going there over the mountains by the Col de Tamie.

If the traveller have time, a short excursion may be made from Annecy to Annecy-le-Vieux ; where, on the inner and southern angle of the tower, will be found the following inscription : —

JOVI. . . O. . . MAXIMO.
L. VINICIUS SEVERUS . . . . .
SUO ET L. VINICII LATINI PATRIS SUI
NOMINE DAT. ARAM.

The establishment at Cran of the hydraulic machines for the drainage of the lake, are also deserving of a visit.

From Annecy to Aix there is nothing remarkable. The road passes through the villages of Vieugy and Balmont to

Alby, a village containing about 800 inhabitants. It is situated on the Chèron, and one of the most remarkable objects between Annecy and Aix is its fine bridge—a single arch of great height and span, which is thrown across the Chèron, at Alby. This village was more important formerly when the Comtes of Geneva surrounded it with a wall and castles, of which some traces exist, which were built on both sides of the river to defend the passage of the valley. Beyond Alby the route is without particular interest, except at

Albens (2½ posts), a village of 1000 inhabitants, where coins of Claudian, Antoninus, Gallienus, and other emperers have been found. Beyond Albens the road soon descends, and overlooks the plain of Aix, where that town, the lake of Bourget, and the basin of Chamberry, bounded by the Mont du Chac, the Mont d'Azi, the Mont Granier, present a scene of singular beauty.

Aix les Bains. Inn, Hôtel de la Poste. There are numerous boarding-houses; that of M. Guillaud and the Maison Vernat, are recommended. Charges, board and lodging, 6 fr. a-day; baths in the house at 1 fr. 20 c.; douches 1½ fr.

This watering place was known to the Romans under the name of Aquæ Gratianæ, and it is still resorted to on account of its mineral springs, and of the attractions of the beautiful country round it, by more than 2200 visitors yearly. The town itself is situated at a little distance to the east of the pretty Lac de Bourget, and contains 2000 inhabitants; in itself it has little to recommend it, and little or nothing has been done to promote the accommodation or amusement of strangers. It contains several *Roman Remains*, a *Triumphal Arch*, in a debased Doric style, probably of the 3d or 4th century, raised by T. Pompeius Campanus, a portion of an Ionic *Temple* of Diana or Venus, and a *Vapour Bath*, lined with bricks and marble, with hypocaust, and pipes for the water, in a tolerably perfect state.

Its *Mineral Springs* are warm and sulphureous; they have a temperature varying between 110° and 117° Fahr. The *Alum Spring* (incorrectly so called, as it contains no alum) issues from beneath an antique arch; it is partly employed in douching horses.

The *Sulphur Spring* is exceedingly copious; it is drank at the source, and is good for correcting derangement of the digestive organs. These waters, however, are chiefly employed for baths, and above all for douche baths. A handsome bath-house has been built by a former king of Sardinia, into the apartments of which the hot water is introduced in streams which descend from a height of eight or ten feet upon the patient. After undergoing the douching process, which consists in having the water applied to various parts of the body, while they are, at the same time, subjected to brisk friction by the hands of two attendants, the patient is wrapped up, dripping wet, in a blanket, carried home in a sedanchair, and put into a warm bed. A brisk perspiration succeeds.

Balls are given twice a week during the season in the room at the *Cassino*, where there is also a reading-room. Gaming is prohibited.

A portion of the time not occupied in the bathing process may be agreeably employed in rides and walks in the neighbourhood, whose varied and beautiful scenery cannot fail to afford pleasure and amusement. The favourite excursion is to *Haute Combe* on the opposite or north-west shore of the Lac de Bourget (Borghetto). This monastery, beautifully situated by the side of the lake, and at the foot of the Mont du Chat, was founded in 1125. Its Gothic chapels were the burial-places of the princes of Savoy, canons of Citeaux, &c. Among them is an archbishop of Cantorbury, son of Count Thomas of Savoy, who died in 1270. The building was pillaged and desecrated at the French revolution; the coffins were opened and rifled, and the monuments, paintings, and stained glass broken and effaced. It was, however, restored by Charles Felix, king of Sardinia, as nearly as possible to its original condition; the tombs have been renovated, the walls painted afresh, and the windows replenished with Bohemian glass. About half a mile behind the abbey is an intermittent spring, called *Fontaine des Merveilles.*

The west shore of the lake consists of a tall precipice of limestone, rising almost perpendicularly from the water's edge, and extending from Haute Combe to the castle of Bordeau. One of the meditations of Lamartine, that entitled "Le Lac," was inspired by the scenery of this spot. Behind Bordeau commences the ascent of the Mont du Chat, the probable route of Hannibal ; the old Roman road has been recently replaced by a fine causeway, skilfully conducted in zig-zags up the hill.

At the south extremity of the lake was the castle of Bourget, the residence of the ancient counts of Savoy, down to the time of Amadeus V. or the Great, who was born in it in 1249. He sent for the painter Giorgio di Aquila, a pupil of Giotto, to deco rate its interior ; and some fragments of fresco, now nearly effaced, in a cabinet formed in the thickness of the wall of one of the towers, are probably a part of his work.

CHAMBERRY (2 posts), the route from Aix, is very beautiful as it passes below the finely wooded slopes of the Mont d'Azi, and Dent de Nivolet, its undulations often presenting views of the lake of Bourget and the fine range of the Mont du Chat. The approach to Chamberry (Route 127.) is highly picturesque, and offering some beautiful views.

ROUTE 121.

GENEVA TO CHAMBERRY, BY RUMILLY.

There is so little to interest the traveller in this route, that it is generally avoided by strangers, who prefer going by Annecy, though it is a little further round.

From St. Julien, the point at which the route by Annecy separates from that by Rumilly, the latter takes a more westerly course toward the Rhone ; it rises over the ridge of the Mount Sion, but, at a place 1200 feet lower than the point of passage to Annecy. Hence it descends into the beautiful little valley of the Usses, at *Frangy*, 4 posts, a neat little town, with good houses, and tolerable inns. Many Roman antiquities, in coins, medals, and inscriptions have been found here.

The road rises steeply from the vale of the Usses, and is carried over a country where the valley of the Rhone can be traced, which is, at one point, only a few miles from Seissel ; there it takes a course, up, and high above the valley of the Chéron, and presents many and extensive views into and over this valley. This is the most picturesque part of the route.

Rumilly, 3 posts. Here the Chéron, near its confluence with the Elpha, is crossed. In every village along this route, Roman coins and medals have been found. At Rumilly, these and other relics have been dug out. The antiquity of Rumilly, *Rumilliacum,* is high ; it lay in the principal road from Aix to Geneva, but nothing is known of its early history ; and of later, traces of a fire or a plague alone mark the progress of time in the history of most of the Savoyard towns of this class. It has now a population of nearly 4000 inhabitants.

From Rumilly to

Albens (1½ post) the drive is very beautiful, especially under the hill of Chautagne, where the village of Bloye is situated. At Albens the road by Rumilly and Annecy from Geneva to Chamberry unite.

ROUTE 122.

CHAMBERRY TO LANSLEBOURG BY L'HÔ-
PITAL CONFLANS, MOUTIERS, TIGNES,
AND THE COL D'ISERAN.

Montmeillan, 2 posts. (Route 127.) Here the routes to the Mont Cenis and the Val Isère divide : the former crosses the Isère to enter the valley of the Arc at Aiguebelle, and continue in it to Lanslebourg ; the latter ascends by the entire course of the Val Isère and, after crossing the Col d'Iseran, descends by the valley of the Arc to Lanslebourg.

This is a post road to l'Hôpital, the distance being 4½ posts. The first post station from Montmeillan is Gressy, 2¾ posts. Thence to l'Hôpital, 1¾.

Montmeillan is left, after having ascended through its steep streets to where two roads branch off: one, on the left, leads to Aix; the other, on the right, proceeds along the mountain side, on the right bank of the Isère, to

St. Pierre d'Albigny, a neat little town with a good inn. There is nothing worthy of notice before reaching St. Pierre. The Isère flows through a portion only of its broad winter bed, leaving the blanched stones to mark its extent at that season. The slopes around Montmeillan and St. Pierre are celebrated for the wine they produce.

A little beyond St. Pierre is a fine feature in the scenery of the valley, the Château de Miolans. It is built on a mass of rock jutting out of the mountain side in a most commanding situation. The ascent is gradual to the platform, which on the top of the rock is extensive enough for the castle. Its elevation is about 800 or 900 feet above the Isère, commanding extensive views up and down the valley, and across into the valley of the Arc; for it is nearly opposite to the confluence of the Arc and the Isère.

" The old towers of the Château de Miolans overhang inaccessible precipices, four or five times their height. The look out upon the beautiful scenes in the valley below, from the slits which serve as windows to the cells in the towers, must often to the poor prisoners within (for this was the state prison of Savoy) have created a desire for liberty, and at the same moment have crushed the hope of its attainment.

" The château originally belonged to one of the most ancient families in Savoy, distinguished as early as the ninth century. Between that period and the sixteenth, many of the barons of Miolans were celebrated as soldiers, and other members of the family were eminent in the church, as bishops of the Maurienne; but the male line becoming extinct in 1523, the château was bought by Charles III., duke of Savoy, and converted into a state prison, which continued to be its appropriation until the events of the French revolution united Savoy to France, when the castle of Miolans was dismantled. However strong it might have been as a prison, as a military station, at least since the use of cannon, it must have been defenceless. Now, it is interesting only to the painter and the antiquary; rank weeds fill its courts, its drawbridges are decayed; its walls are crumbling to the earth, and bear to oblivion in their ruin the names written upon them by the soldier in the guard-room, and the captive in his cell. Where formerly the sighs of the poor wretch once pierced the walls of the dungeon, blasts of wind have now passed through a thousand rents, and whistled the requiem of feudal tyranny." — *Journals of an Alpine Traveller.*

A path on the northern side of the road leads down through meadows and vineyards to the village of Fraterive in the road beyond Miolans; thence through the village of Gressy, and the hamlets of St. Vial and Fronteney to l'Hôpital Conflans (*ad Publicanos*). (Route 119.)

At l'Hôpital the Arly is crossed to pursue the course to the upper valley of the Isère, a district distinguished as the Tarentaise. The journey to Moutiers, distant about 16 English miles, is through a picturesque valley. The road lies on the right bank of the Isère, through a succession of beautiful scenes. The direction of the valley in ascending from Montmeillan to Conflans is N. E., but from Conflans to Moutiers it is a little east of south.

Above Conflans the valley is much narrower; the lower ranges of the mountains are more richly wooded, the valley retired and pastoral in its character. The ruins of châteaux are often seen, on heights that jut out on rocks in commanding situations from the rich backgrounds of forest trees.

The first village that is passed is La Batie (*Oblimum*), and the next of any importance is Roche-Cavins, which is about halfway between Conflans and Moutiers. About 10 miles from Conflans, near the hamlet of Petite Cour, there is a fine cataract, which dashes down amidst immense rocks, — a spot forming a striking contrast to the general fertility and repose of the valley. About three miles farther, the valley opens into a rich little plain, where the pretty village of Aigueblanche is situated. Here the road rises, and having passed its crest, descends into a deep defile that leads to Moutiers, by a road terraced on the steep slope of this ravine, from which it abruptly enters the basin of the Val Isère, in which Moutiers Tarentaise (*Daren-tasia*) is situated on the confluence of the Isère, and the Doron of Bozel.

Moutiers. —Inn : Poste. Chez Genard. Inhabitants 2000. This capital of the Tarentaise derives its present name from an old monastery, which was built at a little distance from the ancient Darentasia, which was destroyed many centuries since. The ancient city was the seat of the bishops of Darentasia ; and it is highly probable that in this city, which gave its name to the bishopric as early as the year 420, and to the province of the Tarentaise — having been destroyed at an unrecorded period — its bishops built, at a little distance, another church, and a monastery for the clergy, who came to fix their residence in the present Moutiers ; and preserved the primitive title of their seat, which has not varied for thirteen centuries. That no vestiges of the ancient city should have been found, is not very extraordinary, when it is considered that the Ostragoths, and the Lombards in the seventh century, and the Saracens twice in the ninth century, having penetrated into the valleys of the Maritime, Cottian, and Grecian Alps, destroyed the habitations, and ruined the towns and villages. It is often afterwards mentioned in local archives connected with the church, and in the wars of the sixteenth and seventeenth centuries, and in 1630, when it was almost depopulated by the plague. The history of its church is perfect from its first archbishop in 420 to its last in 1793, a period of 1373 years. The city now contains an hospital for the poor, which was founded in the tenth century, and an *E'cole des Mines,* with a laboratory for practical examination of the productions of the mines of Pesey.

But its salines are now the distinguishing feature of Moutiers. They are admirably conducted, and produce nearly fifteen hundred tons of salt yearly, extracted from a saline source which is only impregnated to the amount of 1·83 per cent., even in the strongest of its three springs.

These springs rise at the base of a vast mass of limestone, in the deep ravine of the Doron, about a mile above its junction with the Isère. The water rises with force from its source, and emits carbonic gas and a little sulphuretted hydrogen. The springs are warm, and that of the strongest 99° Fahrenheit. During the great earthquake of Lisbon, the salines of Moutiers ceased to flow for 48 hours : when the reflux took place the quantity was increased, but the saline impregnation was weaker. The salt-works at Bex (Route 56.) are conducted in a similar way, but with a vast difference in the saline strength of the water. At Moutiers it has scarcely half the strength of that of sea-water ; yet it is worked to some profit by the simplicity of the process, and the use of water as the motive power for the pumps.

Besides common salt, the water contains, in small proportions, sulphate of lime, sulphate of soda, sulphate and muriate of magnesia, and oxide of iron.

There are four great evaporating-houses filled with faggots of black thorn. The water from the mines is pumped to the top of the first and second of these, which are uncovered, and then allowed to pass through perforated canals, slowly dropping and spreading over the extensive surface of the branches. By this process the sulphate of lime attaches itself to the wood, and the water loses so much by evaporation, that the proportion of salt, after the operation, is increased nearly one half: *i. e.* to about 3 per cent. It is then pumped above the third house, constructed in the same way, except that it is covered, to prevent the saline solution from being again weakened by rain. In this, the evaporation leaves the solution of the strength of 12 per cent. A fourth house now receives it, and in favourable weather it there acquires a strength of 22 degrees. The process of pumping, after percolation and evaporation, is carried on by the force of a canal of water, detached from the Doron, and the machinery scarcely ever requires interference.

When the brine has acquired the strength of 20 per cent. it is conducted into a large building, where there are boiling pans, and the salt is crystallised in the usual manner.

So much fuel is saved by this system of evaporation by the air, that only one sixteenth of the fuel is consumed which would be required for evaporating the brine as it comes from the springs. The faggots are changed once in about 5 or 6 years : they decay soonest in the first evaporating-houses, where the solution is weakest : those in 3d and 4th are more durable, from the coating of selenite they acquire, which, when broken off, resembles the stems and branches of encrinites.

There is another mode of evaporating from cords, invented by an ingenious Savoyard, of the name of Buttel. It consists in suspending cords from the roof, and fixing them tight at the bottom : they are about 16 feet long. These cords are placed as thickly as possible, consistent with free ventilation ; and the upper ends are so fastened, that the water pumped over them trickles down, only by these cords, very slowly. By repeatedly allowing the brine thus to descend, the whole of the water is evaporated, and the cords left incrusted with a cylinder of pure salt, which is detached by a particular instrument. This practice of completing the process, by evaporation in the air, is discontinued now, though the cords are used for getting a higher concentration of the brine than heretofore : this strong solution is sent, like the rest, to the boiling pans. The weak solution used to rot the cords ; but, by only using them after 5 per cent. had been obtained in the solution, they have been known to remain 30 years in use, without being changed ; some of these, originally $\frac{1}{2}$ an inch in diameter, are coated with gypsum 2 or 3 inches thick. These works belong to the government, though they yield an annual profit of only 50,000 francs = 2000*l.*

From Moutiers to Bourg St. Maurice the road again takes a N.E. direction ; and, on leaving the little basin of Moutiers to ascend the Isère, it passes through a gorge which continues a short way, and then opens at the village of St. Marcel. The scenery around is very fine and picturesque. The road, which formerly passed on the left bank of the Isère, now rises high on the right bank, and is carried over a neck of rock at a great height above the torrent. The view looking down and back upon St. Marcel from the rock is very fine. This road was made by Victor Emanuel, Duke of Savoy, in 1766. The defile at the base of this rock is only wide enough for the torrent of the Isère.

The valley opens above this defile ; and immediately beyond it, below the road, is seen the village of Centron, still preserving the name of the Centrones, an alpine people who inhabited this valley.

About 10 miles from Moutiers is *Aime* (Axuma), one of the chief towns of the Centrones, and, according to inscriptions found there, was evidently called Forum Claudii before the name of Axuma was given to it. On a hill above it, there are the remains of Roman fortifications; some round towers of great antiquity, both in the town and on the site of the ancient fort are still standing, the masonry having been strong enough to hold the masses together through so many ages. There is also a subterraneous communication which traverses the town, from some ruins, supposed to have been a temple, to the fortress; the vault of this passage is supported by columns of stone, each shaft of a single piece. Here some inscriptions have been found, particularly one in honour of Trajan:—

IMP CÆSARI
DIVI NERVÆ F. TRAIANO.
AUG. GERM. DAC.
COS. PONTIFICI. MAX.
TRIBUNI. POTEST.
XII IMP. VI. COS. V.
P. P.
DEVICTIS DACIS
FORO CLAUDII PUBL.

An ancient communication between the town and the fort may also be traced in steps cut out of the rock upon which the latter stands. That the former extent of Aime greatly exceeded its present boundaries, was shown by some discoveries of subterraneous structures opened in forming a new road into the Upper Tarentaise in 1760.

Above Aime the formation of a new carriage road is in rapid progress, and the inhabitants hope that their Government will soon open it across the Little St. Bernard, and make this a high road to Turin. The beauty and interest of such a route cannot fail to lead to a great influx of strangers, besides the benefit of communication between different communities of the same state.

Generally, the valley of the Isère, from Aime to Moutiers, is wild and dreary, and not picturesque. The vine grows as far as the village of Bellentres, which is nearly opposite to the village and valley of Laudri, that lead to the mines of Pesey, the most celebrated in Savoy. They are situated near the foot of the glacier of the Chaffe-Quarre, and more than 5000 feet above the level of the sea: the ore is a fine-grained sulphuret of lead; it contains about 60 ounces of silver per ton. These mines in 1785 yielded annually about 4000 marks of silver, and 40,000 quintals of lead: they are now less productive. The height of the mines is a serious obstacle to their being worked to great advantage.

As the valley is ascended, the pass of the Little St. Bernard opens to the observer a more obvious course than that of the road up the Isère, which turns again from St. Maurice to the W. and S. S. W., and continues in this direction to its source in the Iseran.

Bourg St. Maurice (Berigentrum). Excellent Inn: Hotel de Voyageurs. Chez Mayat. (Route 114.) Thus far up the Val Isère there is a good char or carriage road, but beyond St. Maurice it is necessary, in order to go further up the valley, to go on horseback or on foot; it requires one day to go from Bourg St. Maurice to La Val, and another across the Col d'Iseran to Lanslebourg and the Mont Cenis.

From Bourg St. Maurice to St. Foi (Route 113.). The approach to St. Foi from the meadows below it offers one of the most beautiful scenes in the valleys of the Alps. Having climbed the tortuous and difficult chaussée which leads to the village, the route continues for a long way by a wild and lofty path on the mountain side high above the torrent, through the village of La Tuille to Brennieres. Nothing can exceed the savage

grandeur of this route ; — the deep
ravine is too narrow for the structure of a path lower down towards
the torrent.   On the opposite side
the enormous glaciers that stretch
from the Chaffe-Quarre along the crest
of the mountains, offer the grandest
scene of its class to be found anywhere in the Alps.   The most magnificent view thus presented is opposite to the village of La Gure, of
which the spire seems to touch the
glaciers.   More than once this village
has been destroyed by the fall of ice
and rocks ; but the danger is defied
for the sake of the little land which
its terrace above the Isère affords.
From the glaciers a hundred lines of
cataracts, from the melting of the
glaciers, seem to stream down upon
the village.

Soon after passing La Gure the
road yet ascends to a ridge, which
being crossed, the path leads steeply
down to the Isère in the depth of the
ravine.   Here alpine horrors await
the traveller.   The overhanging rocks
darken the pass, and a fragile bridge
only in a wild situation, over a lateral
stream, enables the traveller to ascend the valley.   A little beyond
this bridge the defile opens into the
plain and village of

Brennieres.   Here the Isère is
crossed, and the path ascends on the
other side through a rugged pine
forest, where the path is carried very
high to avoid a ravine.   The eye
cannot penetrate to its depth, though
the roar of the torrent is heard in
these solitudes.   In passing over this
ridge, there is one spot where a cleft
in the mountain side can only be
passed upon the trees, rocks, and
stones, which the peasants have
jammed into it, to form a path, which
thence descending almost to the river
side, continues a short way only,
before another expansion of the valley
forms a little well-cultivated plain,
in which there is a large village, —

Tignes.   The approach to it, issuing from the defile below, is very
striking.   The inhabitants are robust
and independent, and are great breed-
ers of mules and cattle.   Directly opposite to Tignes is a valley, where
one may pass by the Col de Large to
Entre-deux-Eaux (Route 123.).

On leaving the plain of Tignes a
steep rugged path leads up the mountain side, to pass another of those
ravines, which in this valley so singularly alternate with the little plains.
This, the last, separates the plain of
Tignes from that of La Val.   The
forest trees, from their greater elevation, are more stunted, the rocks more
denuded, and the whole passage between the two villages is unmatched
in apparent danger from falling rocks,
and in savage wildness.   In the midst,
a fragile bridge crosses the torrent,
and soon after the traveller finds himself in the plain of LaVal, where barley is raised, and where irrigation is
so well managed, that there is an
appearance of luxuriant vegetation.
This is the highest church village in
the Val Isère :   it is surrounded by
lofty mountains, crested with snow
and glaciers.   At the head of the
valley, the Col de Galese above its glaciers can easily be seen. (Route 112.)

A miserable hovel called an inn is
the only place of reception at LaVal.

To cross the Col d'Iseran the path
ascends gradually from the valley, by
a stunted pine forest.   There is a
hamlet called Forno, further up the
valley on the route to the Galese, but
this is avoided, and by the time the
traveller arrives opposite to it he has
attained a great elevation.   The way
to the Col requires a guide from
La Val, as the course is trackless,
and only known by bearings :   the
ascent is easy.   Some crosses mark
the loss of life in these solitudes ;   in
one instance by murder, in another a
poor soldier was found dead from cold
and exhaustion.   Near the summit, the
soil produces myriads of flowers, and
of great variety.   The view, on looking back upon the ridge of the great
chain is exceedingly grand, but not

o fine as from the Col d'Iseran, and the descent on the other side. Here the traveller looks over a thousand peaks, whose black and scathed precipices appear to spring out of the sea of glaciers which extends from the Levanna (Route 112.) to the Roche Melon (Route 127.).

From the col, the course lies down a high valley over a lofty pasturage, which terminates at the bottom in a defile, across which a cataract falls. The descent from this ravine is very difficult and fatiguing down to the plain below, where the pasturages and châlets of St. Barthelemi, belonging to the inhabitants of Bonneval, offer abundant summer resources to the herds and flocks of the proprietors.

From these pasturages the descent is very steep and fatiguing. The valley of the Arc is seen below, and on the left, looking up to the head of the valley, the glaciers of the Levanna seem to fill it; across these a path leads in 5 hours to Gros Cavallo in the Val Forno, and thence in ten hours to Lanzo.

The first village reached in the valley of the Arc is Bonneval: here the inn is detestable; so, in fact, are all in the valley, until the traveller reach Lanslebourg, yet four hours down the valley from Bonneval.

After crossing the Arc, the road descends to Bessans, passing on the left the valley of Averole, by which the Col de Lautaret and the valleys of Viu and Lanzo on the side of Piedmont may be reached,—one of the wildest passes in the Alps.

At Bessans the Arc is again crossed, and a high ridge is passed which divides the Commune of Bessans from that of Lans le Villiard, a village about a league above Lanslebourg. From Lans le Villiard a path leads into the great route of the Mont Cenis. If the traveller have started early, he may reach the posthouse on the mountain on the day of his departure from La Val; if he be late, it will be better to proceed down the

valley to Lanslebourg, and enjoy the comfort of an excellent inn there — the Hôtel Royal.

ROUTE 123.

MOUTIERS—TARENTAISE TO LANSLE-
BOURG, BY THE COL DE VANOISE.

A char may be taken as far as Bozel for this journey, but beyond, it is necessary to take a horse or proceed on foot. It requires two days, and the place of rest is Pralorgnan.

The road passes by the salines of Moutiers (Route 122.), and ascending on the right bank of the Doron, reaches in a quarter of an hour the Rock of Salins, situated opposite to the confluence of the valley of Bozel, or the Doron, with that of St. Jean Belleville. Ascending the latter, there are two mountain passes, — one leads to St. Jean Maurienne, the other to St. Michael, both in the valley of the Arc — either an easy day's journey.

The Château de Salins was anciently the residence of the archbishop of the Tarentaise; its ruins are situated immediately above the salt springs, in the valley below. These are guarded with great care, to prevent the people of the country stealing any of the water and making their own salt!

Salins is conjectured to have been the site of the ancient Darentasia. Of the castle of Salins some ruins exist. There are records of its importance in 1082, when the tyrant Aymeric, of Aigueblanche, was defeated by Humbert II., whose succour had been solicited by the oppressed subjects of Aymeric. Humbert retained, at their request, the government in his own hands, and established at the town and the Château de Salins the tribunals of his new province; and documents bearing date 1358, show that these still existed, though it is known that the town was destroyed about the end of the 14th century, by a fall from the mountains on the west. This fall of rocks and stones so filled the valley, that the lower town was buried beneath the mass. All that remained were the parts most elevated. Subsequent falls destroyed what remained, except the castle, and this has been demolished. A few miserable houses, rebuilt around the Salines, await a similar fate from the threatening appearance of the rocks above.

The castle, however, remained long after the destruction of the town in the 14th century. Books still exist, which were printed at the château very soon after the discovery of printing. It is supposed that the first press in Savoy was established there, and that Maurice Mermilliou was the Caxton of the Tarentaise.

Salins lies south of Moutiers. From the confluence, the road into the valley of Bozel takes an easterly direction through scenes which are rich in wood and highly cultivated, and where there are many beautiful points of view.

At the village of Brida or La Perriere, which is reached in an hour from Moutiers, there are mineral springs, and establishments *en pension* for the invalids who resort to them, — coffee and reading rooms, jeu de billiards, and other resources for the convalescent. The waters are so much impregnated with sulphuretted hydrogen as to be perfectly detestable to the taste.

At Brida the Doron is crossed, and a tolerable road leads to Bozel. Between the two villages the country is rich in cultivation : vines and fruit-trees in the valley, corn-fields and pasturages on the belts of the mountains, and above, pine forests, surmounted by snows and glaciers, the valley being closed at the head by the mountains of Pesey, and one of the most beautiful, in form, in the Alps, the Chaffe-Quarré.

At Bozel mules can be hired for continuing the journey. Above this village the valley widens, and the scenery increases in grandeur, except, that in passing under the intermediate

mountain of Plagny, this conceals the Chaffe-Quarré.

The ascent to the village of Champagny is deep in the valley, and on the banks of the Doron, of which the broad stony bed marks its wider winter course. On approaching Champagny, the road is distinctly seen which leads up to the mines of Pesey. (Route 122.) It is a good mule-path, and leads across the col to the valley which descends to Landry in the Val Isère. The lateral valleys of the Doron abound with beautiful scenery, and most of them lead to points of view in the mountains, where some of the finest alpine scenes are presented, particularly in the valley of Allues, and at the châlets of Châtelet, near the Col de Forclaz, whence Mont Blanc can be seen, and a vast extent of the peaks of the great chain.

At Champagny the road to Pralorgnan lies up that branch of the Doron which flows from the south. After passing the village of Villard Goitreaux, thus named from the prevalence of goître among the inhabitants, the road ascends by a steep path to a narrow valley. On the right there is a cataract, formed by the fall of the Doron into the gorge at Bellentre. As the valley widens it has the character of park scenery that terminates in the little plain of Pralorgnan, which is backed by the glaciers and scathed peaks of the Vanoise.

The beautiful meadows and calm retirement of the valley of Pralorgnan is very striking. On entering the village, a narrow lane on the left, leads to the only inn or house of reception for strangers, where miserable accommodation only can be obtained. The innkeeper is a large proprietor, having between 200 and 300 cows in the mountains.

From the inn door the path to the Vanoise lies directly up on the right, and the châlets in the mountains are reached in an hour. Each step becomes more and more dreary, until it arrive at the bases of the bleak and streaming glaciers of the Aiguille de la Vanoise. On reaching the *moraines* it is necessary to climb them on foot, and let the mules scramble as they may, or as the guide can assist them. At the base of these *moraines* there is, in the winter, a lake formed. To its basin there is but one entrance: within, nothing can exceed the savage solitude of the spot, surrounded by black precipices and glaciers; it seems to be impossible to get out, except by the way one gets in. No trace of a path appears. Under the advice of the guide, however, the glaciers may be climbed and traversed—a most fatiguing and difficult task. Having surmounted the difficulty, the traveller, after crossing a few patches of snow, enters upon an open plain, covered with rich pasturages, but bounded by enormous glaciers and inaccessible peaks. On the plain of the col, which is now gradual to the summit, poles are placed to guide travellers when snow conceals the track. The path is long and tedious, across these solitudes, from the glaciers of the Vanoise to the summit. Three little lakes are passed, the source of streams which descend, on one side to the Doron, and on the other to the Arc. On the right, enormous glaciers are seen, which extend to the Roche Chevrière, the vast mountain which is seen from the ascent to the Mont Cenis, overhanging Termignon.

From the col, the descent towards the châlets of Entre-deux-Eaux is rapid and difficult. The long sterile valley above these châlets, which leads by the Col de Large to Tignes, in the Val Isère (Route 122.), is seen below the traveller, who finds the descent so fatiguing, that the rest, and refreshment, bread, meat, and wine, which he must bring with him from Pralorgnan, will here be most welcome. Milk, cheese, and butter, perhaps eggs, may be got at the châlets.

After an hour's rest, as refreshing to the traveller as to his mule, the torrent is crossed, but instead of pursuing its course through its deep gorge to Termignon, a path is followed which leads up on the opposite mountain to the Plan de Loup, a long pasturage, not so wild or high, but about the breadth of the Col de Vanoise. The scene, looking back upon the valley of Entre-deux-Eaux, and the Col de Vanoise, is very sublime, and seems, when thus spread out before the observer, of a much greater extent than can be imagined by those who pass them.

On the col of the Plan de Loup, another small lake is passed, then a long and most fatiguing descent commences, which leads down to the hamlet of St. Marguerite. Soon after the path enters a pine forest, through which a miserable road leads down to the valley above Termignon, into which there are some magnificent peeps. There is still, however, a long and fatiguing descent to make before that little town can be reached. There is a path which, going from the hamlet of St. Marguerite, skirts the Mont Parouffa, behind Lanslebourg, and leads directly to the latter town, but, though a shorter, it is even more fatiguing than the route to Termignon, and one which it is difficult to pass with a laden mule. At Termignon the path from the Vanoise falls into the great route of the Cenis, which in an hour takes the traveller to Lanslebourg (Route 127.).

ROUTE 124. (*See* Route 127.)

ROUTE 125.

PONT BEAUVOISIN TO AIX BY THE MONT DU CHAT.

The road to the Mont du Chat leaves Pont Beauvoisin to follow a course on the right bank of the river Guiers Vif., through the villages of Belmont and Tramonex to St. Genix, a large village near the confluence of the Guiers with the Rhone, thence turning abruptly up the latter river, it continues on its left bank for about 10 miles, through some fine scenery, until it reach

Yenne, a little town most agreeably situated on a rising ground above the Rhone, nearly opposite to a fort, finely placed on a rock above the Rhone, called St. Pierre Châtel, which, on the French side of the river, defends the passage.

Yenne existed in the time of the Romans, under the name of Ejanna, and, according to some authorities, Epaona. It lies in the ancient route from France to Italy, by the Mont du Chat, which was much used before the opening of the Grotto near les E'chelles. The whole neighbourhood is very rich in cultivation. Corn, wine, and fruit-trees abound. The white wines named *Marètel,* and *Altesse,* grown at Lucy, on the banks of the Rhone, a little north of Yenne, owe their excellence to plants which were brought here from Cyprus, by a duke of Savoy, or the lords of his court.

From Yenne, a road, which is not in a very praiseworthy condition in the plain, though it is the route of a daily diligence from Lyons to Aix le Bains, leads directly towards the Mont du Chat, by Chevalu, distant four miles from Yenne. This village is situated at the foot of the mountain. The extreme richness of the country cannot fail to draw the attention of the traveller, and when, beyond Chavelu, the road ascends and rises high enough above the surrounding country, its excessive fertility is its striking feature.

The road over the mountain is well constructed. The summit of the Mont du Chat rises on the right ; on the left, steep slopes and precipices descend to the base, ending in rich pasturages, in which there are some little lakes or tarns. Many tourniquets in the road give a gradual ascent, and at the end of an hour the summit is attained. The scene, on looking back towards France, is one of the most fertile in the world; studded with villages and towns, and so extensive, that where the distant mountains of Tarrare do

not limit the horizon,— it subsides into indistinctness. Immediately below, on the same side, are the rich pasturages of the western slopes of the Mont du Chat. Beyond these are the valley of the Rhone, and the hills and plains which extend to the Ain.

On the summit of the pass there is a level, about 300 yards across. The road passes on the southern side of a large mass of rock which is upon it. The summit of the pass is covered with stones, rocks, and brushwood. A temple formerly stood here, of which the foundations may be traced, and many of the stones around, made part of the building. The stones have been well cut, and the cornices of many are yet tolerably perfect. An inscription was found here by Dr. Cramer, which has given rise to the idea that the temple was dedicated to Mercury. "We have said," he observes, "that the temple on the summit of the Mont du Chat was reported to be dedicated to Mercury, but the inscription itself hardly bears out this opinion. M. Albanis de Beaumont, in his description of the Alpes Grecques, calls this mountain the Mons Thuates, but without giving his authority. Now, Theut and Thait, in Armoric, are the names of the deity who presided over highways, and who was much worshipped by the Gauls ; hence Cæsar says, that the people principally worshipped Mercury, who had the same office among the Roman deities. The name, therefore, of Mons Thuates, would argue a passage here of very high antiquity, and the temple, if really dedicated to Mercury, would tend strongly to the confirmation of this opinion." — *Dissertation on the Passage of Hannibal.*

It has been satisfactorily shown by De Luc, and by Wickham and Cramer, that the army under Hannibal here encountered its first difficulties in passing the Alps. After having ascended the Rhone as far as Vienne, he led his army across the country of the Allobroges, by Bourgoin, les

Abrets, and Aouste (Augusta Allobrogum), now a village on the left bank of the Guiers, nearly opposite to Yenne, thence by Chevalu (Leviscum), across the Mont du Chat to Chamberry (Lenimcum).

The form and character of the Mont du Chat agrees entirely with the account, by Polybius, of those events which could only in such a peculiar locality occur, but the inquiry cannot be condensed into the space that could be afforded here. It has been clearly shown by the above authors, that the army passed the Mont du Chat to Chamberry, thence to Montmeillan, and up the Val Isère to Conflans, Moutiers, and St. Maurice, and passed into Italy by the Little St. Bernard.

From the summit of the Mont du Chat, 5000 feet above the level of the sea, the view on the eastern side is one of surpassing beauty. It appears to overhang the lake of Bourget, into whose deep blue waters it seems only a leap. Beyond is the rich valley of Chamberry, extending from Albens to the Mont Granier; the town of Aix seems to be at your feet across the lake: on the right, the city of Chamberry lies like a model; hundreds of hamlets and villages speckle the beautiful valley, which is bounded on the opposite side by the rich slopes of the Mont d' Azì, and the Dent de Nivolet, far beyond are seen the mountains which bound the Val Isère, and the snowy summits of those which extend to the Dauphiny Alps.

The descent is peculiarly exciting. The road is safely and finely made, which winds down the steep side of the mountain, but in many places the parapet is seen to cut abruptly against the deep blue lake, and suggests the idea of its being thousands of feet, *a plomb*, below.

On reaching the base, however, there are fields, rich woods, and villages on the steep slopes which rise from the lake, but this extends only to Bordeau, beyond this village there is no path by the lake: its shores are too abrupt, at least as far as Hautecombe. If the traveller would go direct to Aix, a path on the left leads to the village of Bordeau, where a boat can be hired to cross the lake to the opposite shore, and a walk of twenty minutes leads to Aix, and the comfortable pension of Maison Vernat.

The direct road continued to Chamberry from the Mont du Chat, passes through Bourget, where the plain of Chamberry commences, this is traversed for about seven miles to the city from Bourget through the villages of Motte and Bissy, and amidst a luxuriance of vegetation which cannot be imagined.

ROUTE 126.

PONT BEAUVOISIN TO CHAMBERRY, BY AIGUEBELLETTE.

About a mile and a half from Pont Beauvoisin the high road to Les Échelles is left; and at the village of Domessin a narrow road turns off to the left, and leads over a low hill well wooded, and thence through a remarkably rich plain, that extends to those limestone precipices which are a continuation of the ridge of rocks that make so formidable a barrier at les Échelles. Avoiding the principal road to La Bridoire, and crossing the plain direct from near Pont Beauvoisin, the path abruptly approaches these precipices. Close to their bases a zigzag path, very steep, leads up the talus formed during many ages by the *débris ;* in some places, however, the path is so narrow, that the wall of the precipice can be touched by one hand, whilst the other overhangs the steep and dangerous descents below: in some places two persons cannot pass each other. A little time is gained by this short cut, and there is some chance of adventure, and the situations are striking, but it is scarcely worth the fatigue. It leads to the same hamlet, Bridoire, which is highly picturesque in its situation, its cottages, and its water-mills. From this place the road ascends, crosses a ridge, and enters upon the basin of the lake of Aiguebellette, a rich open valley, finely wooded; and, where a view of the lake is obtained, the whole scene is beautiful.

The road undulates amidst the magnificent walnut trees which abound here, and passes through the village of Lepin, offering some very fine views. There is a singular character of tranquillity and retirement in the spot: the scenery resembles that of the most beautiful of our Cumberland lakes; but the visit of a traveller is so rare an occurrence, that instead of a crowd of visitors, and a season for visiting, a year may pass away without any other stranger being seen than a little *négociant* making a shorter cut to Chamberry than by the great road to Les É'chelles.

A ridge divides the village of Lepin from that of Aiguebellette; at the extremity of the ridge on the left, overhanging the lake, is a château, in a most romantic and beautiful situation; the road on the other side of the ridge descends to Aiguebellette, and passes the ruins of the castle of its barons: it is of high antiquity; its foundation is unknown, and it is therefore attributed to the Romans: it is recorded to have been repaired in the 11th century. It was burnt and demolished by one of the dauphins of Vienne, in the 15th century.

Aiguebellette is a poor little village, in a most beautiful situation; it has a miserable little inn, which cannot furnish even decent wine and refreshment in a country so abundant — not even fish from the lake: these are taken and sent to distant markets. The government claims a beggarly tax upon the right to fish of about 12*l.* a year; the lake is celebrated for the excellence and abundance of its carp, trout, and other fish. The lake is about three miles long, and two wide; its depth varies, but it is generally about 150 feet deep. Around the lake are fields and meadows, but most of the slopes of the surrounding mountains are wooded. Oats, barley, potatoes, Indian corn, and flax are grown in the spots cultivated.

It is curious that a tradition exists here that Hannibal passed with a part of the Carthaginian army by Aiguebellette; and the inhabitants also speak of a distinguished stranger who lived long in retirement in this beautiful solitude, and left many proofs of his benevolence, but died without leaving a name.

On proceeding from Aiguebellette the path skirts the churchyard, and enters a line of meadows beneath magnificent walnut trees. Soon, however, it begins to ascend the mountain side, and rises over the intervening trees, presenting views of the lake, the villages around it, and the distant hills which slope down and border the Rhone. The road now becomes very steep, ascending in zigzags, sometimes sunk in the crues of the mountain, at others rounding the projections, and increasing, as the observer rises above the lake, the beauty with the extent of the view. At length, after a very fatiguing ascent for an hour, the summit is attained, and a glorious view is presented over the basin of Chamberry, similar to that which is seen from the Mont du Chat; but, though not so elevated, it is, perhaps, superior; the idea of a fall into the lake of Bourget does not, as there, make the traveller shrink from the parapet. Instead of looking down into the lake, it is seen, at its nearest point, about eight miles off, resting at the base of the steep Mont du Chat; and opposite to it are the houses of Aix.

Chamberry seems, from the Aiguebellette, to be just below the observer; and, in the road to it from Les É'chelles, which may be seen, the cascade of Couz is distinctly observed; its bright white line forming a very small speck amidst the extent and scale of the surrounding objects. The valley, too, between the Dent de Nivolet and the Mont Granier is more opened, and the richly-wooded and cultivated scene more extended: few such glorious views are presented as that offered to the eye of the traveller from the mountain of Aiguebellette.

The descent from the summit of the col may be made by two routes: that on the right seems to have been the old Roman road, but it is now impracticable for horses. There are traces of its having been a well-constructed road, in the remains of high and very thick dry walls, which supported, towards the plain, its terraces. Albanis de Beaumont says that, after half an hour's descent by this road, there are many stone coffins found at the foot of the lateral rocks, with slabs which formerly covered them, upon which some characters are seen, though they are too much effaced to be read: blocks, too, of cut stone are found, and he conjectures that they are the ruins of a chapel dedicated to St. Michael, which was attached to an hospital that existed here in the 9th century, and, probably, under some other denomination, even in the time of the Romans.

The road at present used from the summit of the Col d'Aiguebellette to Chambery is the best, though only practicable for pedestrians or cattle: it might easily be rendered fit for the passage of chars; but, as there is little intercourse across it, there is no sufficient motive for its improvement.

The first village reached after an hour's descent is Vimine, ingeniously conjectured by Beaumont to be derived from *Via Minima*, because it lay on the shortest route from Lemincum (Chambery) to Vienna, Allobrogum (Vienne, on the Rhone). In going to or from Chambery by this route, instead of that by Les É'chelles, the pedestrian will gain two hours; the whole distance from Pont Beauvoisin requiring about eight hours.

From the village of Vimine to the hamlet of Cognin is a short hour's walk over a bad road, but through beautiful scenes: thence, in half an hour, the traveller will reach Chambery.

ROUTE 127.*

PONT DE BEAUVOISIN TO TURIN, BY LES ÉCHELLES, CHAMBERRY, AND THE PASS OF THE MONT CENIS.

Postes 37¾, about 180 English miles.
Diligences go three times a week.

Pont Beauvoisin (Inn : la Poste) is the last village in France; it lies on the bank of the Guiers Vif; here crossed by a bridge, at one end of which are stationed French, and at the other Sardinian, custom-house officers, ready to scrutinise the passports and the baggage of travellers arriving from either side.

After passing for a mile or two across the plain, the road begins to ascend, to a height from which a fine view is attained over the fertile fields of France, and then, bending round the shoulder of the hill, enters the grand gorge of La Chaille. The highway is here formed either by blasting a passage through the solid rock, or by supporting it upon terraces of solid masonry along the edge of the abyss. On the opposite side rises a bare escarpment of limestone, forming cliffs several hundred feet high; and in the depths of the gorge below rushes the white foaming river. The spot has been described by Rousseau in a passage which deserves quotation:—

" Non loin d'une montagne coupée, qu'on appelle *le pas des E'chelles*, audessous du grand chemin taillé dans le roc, et à l'endroit appelé Chailles, court et bouillonne dans des gouffres affreux une petite rivière qui paraît

---

* Route 124. is incorporated with this Route.

avoir mis à les creuser des milliers de
siècles : on a bordé le chemin d'un
parapet, pour prévenir les malheurs ;
cela faisait que je pouvais regarder le
fond et gagner des vertiges tout à mon
aise.   Bien appuyé sur le parapet,
j'avançais le nez et je restais là des
heures entières, entrevoyant de temps
en temps cette écume et cette eau
bleue, dont j'entendais les mugisse-
ments à travers les cris des corbeaux
et des oiseaux de proie qui volaient de
roche en roche et de broussailles en
broussailles, à cent toises au-dessous
de moi. Dans les endroits où la pente
était assez unie et les broussailles assez
claires pour laisser passer des cailloux,
j'en allais chercher d'aussi gros que je
pouvais les porter ; je les rassemblais
sur le parapet en piles, puis, les lan-
çant l'un après l'autre, je me délectais
à les voir rouler, bondir, et voler en
mille éclats avant que d'atteindre le
fond du précipice."

2. Les E'chelles. (Inn : Poste.) A
village also situated on the Guiers,
which here descends from the mountains of the Grand Chartreux, to which
a road leads from Les E'chelles.

The valley beyond this village is
a complete *cul-de-sac* — a wall of
limestone 800 feet high stretches
directly across it ; and from Les
Echelles the eye in vain seeks at first
for the means of exit.   At length a
little hole, like the entrance to a bee-
hive, may be discerned in the face of
the precipices halfway up, towards
which the road winds.   On a nearer
approach, this is discovered to be the
entrance to a tunnel of large dimensions, pierced directly through the
mountain. It is 25 feet high and wide,
and nearly 1000 long, excavated in the
limestone rock.   This noble work
was commenced by Napoleon, and
finished by the king of Sardinia in
18:7.   There exist two older roads ;
the most ancient of these, however,
by no means deserved that name — it
was a mere path, of the most rugged
and difficult kind, partly conducted
through a cavern by means of ladders

placed one above the other.   This was
called the Chemin de la Grotte, or
les E'chelles, from which the neighbouring village derived its name. The
difficulty of the passage was increased
at times by the mountain torrent,
which, when swollen, took its course
through the cavern.   It was utterly
impassable for beasts, travellers were
sometimes carried through it seated
upon an arm chair, attached to the
backs of stout Savoyard peasants,
who performed the service of beasts
of burden, as the South American
Indians do at the present day, on
some of the passes of the Andes.

The approach to the old road from
the side of France was by a deep fissure
low down in the corner of the valley,
on the right hand of the Gallery.

An improved road was made in
1670, by Duke Charles Emanuel II.
of Savoy, at considerable cost, by removing vast masses of rock, so as to
render it passable for carriages.   Napoleon, however, with his usual originality and penetration, struck out a
new line, and boldly pierced through
the mountain, forming a carriage-way,
along which two diligences fully loaded
may pass abreast.   On issuing out of
the Gallery, the old road is seen on
the right.   By tracing it downwards
about half a mile, the traveller may
approach the old roads, on the side
of Savoy, the most ancient is now
blocked up and impassable.   A pomp-
ous inscription, written by the Abbé
St. Réal, commemorating the enterprise of Charles Emanuel in forming
his road, — which, though steep and
narrow, and very inconvenient, was a
grand undertaking for the period, —
may still be seen on the face of the rock.

Our route is now carried through a
rocky and narrow ravine, which gradually expands into a pretty valley.

1½ St. Thibeaud de Coux.

Not far from this a little waterfall descends from the cliff on the
right, described by Rousseau, in his
usual strain of exaggeration, as "La
plus belle que je vis de ma vie."

Another contracted ravine must be passed to reach

1½ *Chamberry* (Italian Ciamberi). Inns : le Petit Paris ; la Poste.

Chamberry, the capital of Savoy, is an archbishop's see, and contains about 10,000 inhabitants, and is situated within a circle of mountains.

Several towers and other fragments exist of the ancient *Castle of the Dukes of Savoy.* The Gothic *chapel* built within its enclosure (1415) survived the conflagration of 1798 : it is passed on the left hand as you enter the town from Lyons. That valuable relic the *Santo Sudario* (holy napkin), now at Turin, was for a long time deposited in it. Francis I. of France made a pilgrimage on foot from Lyons to see it : there is another of these holy impostures kept in St. Peter's at Rome, and shown to the populace on all great displays of the *relics.* The infallible popes should settle which is genuine : in the meantime both are worshipped.

Before the French revolution, there were 20 convents in Chamberry: there are still seven, four of which are nunneries.

Among the most conspicuous buildings at present are the *Three Barracks.*

There is a *Public* Library containing 16,000 volumes, an incipient museum, and a few pictures, none of them calculated to afford the stranger much gratification : there is also a *Theatre.*

The *Royal College* is placed under the control of the Jesuits, who fill the offices of teachers in the various branches of learning and science.

St. Réal, author of the "Conjuration Contre Venèse," was born at Chamberry, 1639 ; and the Comte Xavier le Maîstre, author of the "Lépreux d'Aoste," is also a native. This town also boasts among her citizens a counterpart of the Man of Ross in General de Boigne, who, having made an immense fortune in the British East Indian service, bestowed the greater portion of it, to the amount of 3,417,850 fr., in benefiting his native place. He founded two hospitals, and set on foot many improvements. A new street has been named after him, and a monument has recently been erected to his memory. He died 1830.

Chamberry is, on the whole, a dull town, with little to interest the traveller : it is celebrated for a peculiar manufacture of silk gauzes.

About 20 minutes' walk to the south of the town is *Les Charmettes,* the residence of Rousseau and of his friend Madame de Warrens. There is nothing in the place at present worth notice independently of its connection with J. Jacques : the house has the appearance of a poor farmhouse, and Rosseau's room was the one over the entrance.

Those who have time on their hands, and desire an agreeable two hours' walk, may visit the ravine called Le Bout du Monde. The road to it turns out of that to Turin at the end of the Faubourg de Montmeillan, follows the left bank of the Leysse by the side of the great dyke, as far as the village of Leysse, where it crosses the stream, and, passing on the right the picturesque castle of Chaffardon, enters the gorge of the Doriat, which is closed in on all sides by high cliffs, forming the base of the Dent de Nivolet, and has no outlet. Behind a paper mill, built by one of the Montgolfiers, the stream falls in a pretty cascade over the wall of rock here formed of remarkably regular and thin horizontal strata, through some of which the water forcing its way forms singular supplementary jets at a distance from the main fall. A pleasant excursion of a day or two may be made from this spot to the baths of Aix, and the Lac de Bourget (Route 120.).

In the course of the next stage we pass, on the left, the castle of Bâtie, and farther on, close to the road, that of Chigneir, links of a line of forts extending through the country, on whose towers watch-fires were lighted to alarm the inhabitants, in time of war, in case of foreign inroads. For these rude means in the middle ages, telegraphs have been substituted. Up the valleys of the Arc and Isère, the chain of old castles continues almost without an interruption. The mountain seen on the right is the Mont Grenier, 5700 feet high. The side facing Chamberry is a perpendicular escarpment, produced by an immense mass of the mountain having broken off in 1248: it overwhelmed the country at its base with ruin, and buried sixteen villages. The marks of this catastrophe are still visible in the series of hillocks, now covered with vineyards, called Les Abymes de Myans. The Mont Grenier stands in the angle between the valley of Chamberry and that of Gresivandan, which leads to Grenoble : it is traversed by the Isère. On the left bank of the river, a few miles down, stand the ruins of the *Château Bayard*, the cradle of the illustrious knight, "sans peur et sans reproche."

2 Montmeillan. (Inn not good.) This little town stands on the right bank of the Isère, at the junction of four roads : that of the Mont Cenis, issuing out of the valley of the Maurienne ; that from the Tarentaise and Little St. Bernard (Route 122.) ; that from Grenoble down the fertile and beautiful valley of Gresivandan ; and that from Chamberry. The Castle of Montmeillan was long the bulwark of Savoy against France. Henry IV. while besieging it in 1600, was nearly killed by a cannon shot from its walls, which covered him with dirt, and made the king cross himself devoutly; upon which Sully remarked, that he was happy to see that his Majesty was so good a Catholic. It was bravely and skilfully defended for thirteen months against Louis XIII. by Count Geoffrey Bens de Cavour. The works were finally demolished by Louis XIV., who took the place in 1705. A few scanty fragments of wall, partly overgrown with briars

and nettles, crowning the rock above the town, are the only remains of the former bulwark of Savoy, and the key of its Alps.

A good white wine is grown near Montmeillan.

The bridge over the Isère, crossed in proceeding towards the Mont Cenis, commands, in clear weather, a fine view of Mont Blanc, which is seen from no other point in our route. The road then pursues a course towards the Arc ; then, taking that river for its guide, enters the valley of the Maurienne, which extends up to the Mont Cenis.

1½ Maltaverne. A good inn.

1½ Aiguebelle. The country hereabouts is dreary and unhealthy from marshes which produce malaria and its consequences, goître (§ 19.). The *Castle* above the town, called *La Charbonnière*, was the birthplace of several counts of Savoy.

2¾ La Grande Maison.

2 St. Jean Maurienne. (Inn : Hotel de l'Europe, clean and comfortable.) The chief town in the valley contains nothing remarkable.

The vineyards of St. Julien, grown on the *débris* and gravel-beds brought down by the Arc, produce a wine of some repute.

2 St. Michel. Inn : Hôtel de Londres.

2½ Modane. The last scene of Sterne's " Sentimental Journey " is laid here.

The scenery of the valley now becomes interesting. The road ascends high above the Arc, and the gorge, in whose depths it flows, serves as a natural and tremendous fosse to the fort Lesseillon, built on the opposite height, and commanding, with its many-mouthed batteries, rising tier above tier, the passage to Italy. A light bridge, spanning the black gorge which separates the fort from the road, is a striking object : it is called the Pont du Diable.

2 Verney. Near this, Horace Walpole lost his lap-dog, which was car-

ried off by a wolf pouncing down upon it from the forest.

At Termignon the path from the Col de Vanoise (Route 123.) joins our road.

2 *Lanslebourg.* Inn: Hôtel Royal, good. This village lies at the foot of the Mont Cenis. After passing a large barrack, the road crosses the Arc, and bidding adieu to that stream, begins to ascend the mountain by easy and well-constructed zigzags. Extra horses are necessary to reach the summit; and it takes about 3½ hours for a carriage to mount from Lanslebourg to the posthouse of the *Mont Cenis.* It is possible to walk up in a shorter time, avoiding the zigzag and following the old road, which debouches near the 20th *Refuge.*

Between Lauslebourg and Susa there are twenty-three houses of Refuge planted at intervals by the road side, occupied by cantonniers, whose duty it is to take care of the road and assist travellers. Each house is numbered, beginning from the Piedmontese side of the mountain. Near No. 22. avalanches sometimes fall: the dangerous spot may be passed in three or four minutes. No. 20. is called La Ramasse. Here sledges are kept; and in winter, when deep snow covers the inequalities on the sides of the mountains, travellers may descend in one of them to Lanslebourg in ten minutes! The sledge is guided by a peasant, who places himself in front; and, from the experience gained in collecting (*ramasser*) and transporting wood in this manner, they are so skilful, that there is little risk in this extraordinary mode of travelling. The perpendicular descent is 600 mètres — nearly 2000 feet.

The 17th Refuge is the barrier of Savoy: here a toll of 6 francs per horse is levied, and goes to keep the road in repair. Soon after the point culminant of the pass is reached, 6780 feet above the sea level; thence the road descends to the plain of Mont Cenis; and a person may arrive at the posthouse from Lanslebourg, on foot, in 2 hours and 20 minutes. The road passes near the margin of a considerable lake, which is generally frozen during six months of the year: it is famed for its delicious trout: the fishery belongs to the monks of the Hospice.

3. Posthouse of the *Mont Cenis* (Monte Cenisio), a tolerable inn, where travellers may regale on the excellent trout of the lake, and sometimes on ptarmigan, for which they will, however, pay handsomely. This magnificent road, another monument of the genius of the imperial road-maker, Napoleon, was commenced by his orders in 1803, and finished in 1810, at an expense of 300,000*l.* The engineer was the Chevalier Fabbroni. It is one of the safest roads over the Alps, and the most practicable in winter time.

About half a mile beyond the Post, is the *Hospice*, originally founded by Charlemagne, who crossed the Mont Cenis with an army in the 9th century. The existing edifice, built by Napoleon, is now occupied, half by a corps of carbineers, who examine the *passports* of all travellers crossing the mountain; the other half by monks of the Benedictine order, who exercise gratuitous hospitality towards poor travellers. The house contains two or three neat bed-rooms for guests of the higher class.

At Grande Croix, an inn at the lower extremity of the plain, is a group of taverns occupied by carters and muleteers: there the descent begins. The road, as originally constructed, skirted along the sides of the mountain; but, owing to its fearful exposure to avalanches, this portion of it has been abandoned, and a new line, supported on a lofty causeway, and reached by winding tourniquets, descends directly through the midst of the plain of St. Nicolas, quite out of the reach of avalanches, except between the 3d and 4th Refuges, where they still sometimes fall in spring. A gallery cut in the rock where the old road passed, is now abandoned: it exhibits a most singular scene of confusion, the roof having partly fallen in.

The barrier of Piedmont stands in the midst of the little plain of St. Nicolas. On issuing from this plain, a magnificent mountain on the left is seen—the Rochemelon: on its summit is the chapel of Notre Dame des Huges, formerly visited by pilgrims, but of late abandoned on account of the risk and difficulty of the ascent. From its top a view may be obtained of a part of the plains of Italy. These are not visible from any part of the Mont Cenis road above Molaret. The new road no longer passes through Ferrière and Novalèse, but proceeds directly to

3 Molaret, the first Piedmontese village, near which there is a small inn. A new gallery has been cut in the rock between this and

2 Susa. Inn: La Posta, very comfortable. This little town of 2000 inhabitants, planted at the point of junction of the roads over the Mont Genèvre (Route 130.) and the Mont Cenis, is chiefly remarkable on account of its antiquity, having been founded by a Roman colony in the reign of Augustus, under the name of Segusio. The only thing worth notice is the *Arch of Triumph*, of the Corinthian order, erected about eight years B. C., in honour of Augustus: it is outside the town, in the governor's garden. The inscriptions upon it commemorate the names of the various tribes ruled over by Cottius, the barbarian sovereign of this district, from whom the neighbouring Alps were named Cottian. He was a prince of great bravery; and, having bid defiance to the Roman arms in his fastnesses, was at length gained over as an ally by Augustus.

Here was formerly a fort of great strength, which commanded both the valleys, called the fort of Brunette: it is now demolished.

Susa is situated on the Dora Riparia (Duria Major), and our road was by the side of it all the way to Turin, where it joins the Po.

1½ St. Giorgio.

1 St. Antonia.

1 St. Ambrogio.

1 Rivoli. Not to be confounded with the place of the same name on the Adige, near which Napoleon gained a great victory.

There is an ugly palace of the king of Sardinia here.

1¾ Turin. See Mrs. Starke's, and the Handbook for Northern Italy.

ROUTE 128.

Mont Cenis to Susa, by the little Mont Cenis and the Col de Clairée.

(Ten or twelve Hours.)

Those who would make an excursion by the Little Mont Cenis, a singularly wild route, instead of quietly descending by the high road from the Mont Cenis to Susa, may accomplish it easily in twelve hours.

The posthouse of the Mont Cenis (Route 127.) is left by a path which descends directly to the lake, then skirting its upper border and across the meadows, it soon ascends rapidly towards the pasturages which lead to the châlets of the Little Mont Cenis, which are distant from the posthouse two hours. The mountain slopes around the plain of the Mont Cenis offer some of the richest pasturages in the Alps; those which lead to the Little Mont Cenis are of great extent.

A very little way beyond the châlets of the Little Mont Cenis, the col is attained, and the valley which descends to Bramante in the valley of the Arc, and which lies at right angles with the path across the col, is seen through a great part of its length. On the opposite side of this valley rises the peak of the Grand Vallon; and a little on the left, from a deep turn in the valley below, called the Combe d'Ambin, rises one of the finest peaks in the Alps, the Mont d'Ambin: on it, though its accessibility seems a miracle, is the station used in the triangulation and measure of an arc of the meridian across the great chain. The entire crest of the Ambin is covered with glaciers, and every crue is traced by a white bed of snow that rests within it. At the lower extremity of the valley of Bramante the mountains of the Vanoise close the view.

To ascend this valley it is necessary to mount from the col of the Little Mont Cenis directly up some rocks, and continue for a short time on that side of the mountain ; the path afterwards descends among vast rocks which strew this sterile-looking valley ; and, after leaving on the right the turn in the ravine below, which forms the Combe d'Ambin, through which a stream like a thread of silver flows, the path ascends up a rugged and broken course until it reaches the châlets of Savines. Here there is a rich little spot of meadow land, and a scanty herbage on the slopes of the valley. On the left, a rugged path leads across from the posthouse on the Cenis, by some little lakes in the mountains of Bard, to this valley, above the châlets of Savines : it is rather shorter, but more fatiguing. Wolves are so common in the forest of Bramante, lower down the valley, that the dogs kept at the châlets of Savines are of great power, having their necks armed with spiked collars. The wolves here are probably the successors of those various rascals that gobbled up Walpole's poor little dog Toby, as his master passed with the poet Gray at the foot of the forest on his way into Italy. The herdsman, who always has his rifle ready, is prepared, when he hears the alarm from his dogs, to go and destroy the marauder.

Having ascended above the meadows of Savines, the path rises amidst rocks and stones, and at length reaches a little lake in an elevated plain, in which all seems desolate, solitary, and sterile. The black precipices of the mountain of Bard on the left hand, and those of the Mont d'Ambin on the right, bound its sides ; from the Ambin enormous glaciers sweep down to the lake, and small cataracts, from the melting of the ice on either side, mark their courses by light lines of foam that stream down the precipices, and make their dark masses still blacker. Amidst this apparent sterility thousands of gentianella, ranunculus glacialis, violets, and a hundred other alpine flowers, grow and bloom unseen, in every swampy spot, and between the stones with which the plain and col are covered.

This lake is filled by the meltings of the glaciers of the Mont d'Ambin. It is called the Lac Blanc, or Lac de Savines : it is about a mile long. At its upper extremity is a low ridge, certainly not a hundred feet above the level of the lake ; this is a crest of the great chain, the Col de Clairée : across it two paths lie : that on the right, by a wild and difficult course, leads over the Col de Touilles to Salabertrand in the Val d'Exilles.

The route to Susa lies on the left ; by it the descent from the Col de Clairée is down a steep and rocky hollow, which terminates at the crossing of a bright stream near a pasturage. This spot, where wine may be cooled in the stream, is a delicious place of rest, and where the refreshment, which it is necessary for the traveller to take with him from the inn on the Mont Cenis, will be fully enjoyed. From this place of rest a steep slope leads down to the pasturage seen from the resting-place. It is a flat, surmounting enormous precipices, which seem to forbid any attempt to descend from them. And there will be little disposition immediately to seek a path, for from this spot one of the most glorious views in the Alps is presented. Immediately below is the deep basin and narrow valley of the Clairée, which is almost always filled with vapour that seems to boil as in a caldron ; when the clouds from it rise high enough to catch the current of air, they disperse.

Beyond this valley, the mountain above Chaumont, in the Val d'Exilles, bounds the view; but, turning towards the left, the Combe of Susa is seen over the intervening mountains, even to its termination in the plains of Piedmont, stretching away to the horizon far beyond the hill of the Superga.

On the right, are the precipices which must be climbed, though they seem to be utterly impracticable, by those who would go from the Col de Clairée to the Col de Touilles.

So abrupt are the edges of the precipices that divide the lower valley from this pasturage, that descent seems hopeless. "We stood," says one who has travelled much in these unfrequented passes of the Alps, "on the brink of enormous precipices, their outlines at our feet cut abruptly against the clouds, into which, through occasional openings made by the wind, we could see the black, deep, and shadowed valley. The scene was most impressive. Our guide was puzzled for a short time by the clouds which obscured the point for which we should make. At length he led us down the precipice by a most extraordinary path, which it was difficult to discover: it was like winding steps which had been rudely cut in a crevice: it seemed like a descent through a chimney. Below this rift, a steep, difficult, stony, and most fatiguing path brought us to some Piedmontese châlets.

"Though the caldron of clouds seemed to sink as we descended, they sometimes in their changes enveloped us; and we were glad to hear the voice of a boy, who, having heard us, shouted to us from the châlets, to tell us what direction we should take.

"A still more difficult path led us further down to some other châlets, below which there were extensive pasturages on a steep slope. Having crossed these, we entered a wood, down through which the most abrupt and fatiguing part of our route lay, which would scarcely have been practicable but for the entangled roots. From the wood we emerged upon a rocky slope, and, after a march of eight or nine hours, reached a few scattered stone huts at the head of the Val de Clairée. On looking back, we appeared to have descended the face of a precipice, down which the numerous streams of the Clairée ran from the summit, as if they issued from the sky, to the torrent by which we rested, the white lines were traceable through three or four thousand feet of their descent.

"The pass of the Clairée is, on the Italian side, the steepest that I have ever traversed. This was one of the many difficult passes by which the Vaudois, in 1687, under their pastor and captain, Henri Arnaud, returned to their valleys. They had, after entering Savoy, wandered by a course rather difficult to trace, until they had crossed the Col de Bonhomme, whence they descended into the Tarentaise, traversed the Mont Iseran into the valley of the Arc; thence by the Mont Cenis, the Little Mont Cenis, and the Col de Clairée, into the valley of the Clairée. Here they encountered the troops of the Grand Duke of Savoy, who prevented their entry into the valley of Exilles by the Clairée, and they were compelled to return and cross the Col de Touilles, from which the southern branch of the Clairée, called the Ciauri, flows. The account of their sufferings, before they cleared these mountain passes, and so signally defeated their enemies at the bridge of Salbertrand, forms a part of one of the most interesting narratives ever published; it was written by Henry Arnaud himself, their colonel and pastor, and translated not long since by the late Hugh Dyke Acland, from a rare copy, under the title of "The Glorious Recovery by the Vaudois of their Valleys." An account of these interesting people, and of this, their most remarkable adventure, has been lately given to the world by Dr. Wm. Beattie, in his history of the Waldenses, recently published by Virtue, and which contains engraved views of the eventful scenes through which they passed.

" The recollection of their perilous adventures," says the author of " Excursions in the Alps," " was vividly recalled whilst sitting on a spot which they also had visited, resting ourselves from a fatiguing descent which they had encountered, and in sight of the savage mountain of Les Touilles, by which they were compelled to retreat, and encounter yet farther dangers. The few miserable huts near us were uninhabited, and neither afforded shelter nor food. Continuing our route, we kept close to the torrent, from which a large stream was separated for irrigation. By the side of the channel of this stream we continued some way; then the road sank below it; afterwards we ascended rapidly by a steep path cut out at the foot of precipices, which rose in unbroken grandeur directly over us.

" Along the face of these rocks the channel for the watercourse was cut; and though at our greatest elevation above the valley of Clairée, we were at least a thousand feet higher than the natural bed of the torrent, we were still below the head of the artificial channel whence its waters flowed rapidly towards us. It was difficult to believe the fact before our eyes; and, as we looked back into the short, deep, narrow valley that we had left, and whilst we saw the Clairée foaming down its course, the aqueduct seemed to *ascend* steeply from the valley. This water is led round the brow of the mountain to irrigate the meadows above Jaillon. From the highest point of our passage the view up the valley of the Doire to Exilles was very fine; and immediately after passing this point, the Combe of Susa opened to us from between

the Roche Melon and the Col de Fenêtre, to the plains beyond Turin. We soon fell into the high road from the Mont Cenis (route 127.); and about seven o'clock reached the Hôtel de la Poste at Susa."

ROUTE 129.

GRENOBLE TO BRIANÇON BY BOURG D'OYSANS, AND THE COL DE LAUTARET.

(Two Days.)

Grenoble (Gratianopolis) is the chief city in the department of the Isère; it is an important place, beautifully situated, and having a population of 25,000. It is celebrated for its public institutions, and for the great interest of the objects in its neighbourhood. These will be detailed in our future Handbook for France. It is here only mentioned as the starting point for an excursion across the Col de Lautaret to the pass of the Mont Genèvre.

There is a good road from Grenoble by Vizille Gap and Embrun to Briançon, and a diligence goes to the latter town three times a week from Grenoble; but it is 50 miles further and through a road that is generally uninteresting, whilst that by the Col de Lautaret abounds with some of the finest scenes in the Alps.

To save this distance Napoleon commenced the construction of a new road by this pass, and many magnificent works were completed upon it, but since his abdication it has been abandoned. The new line was called " *Route d'Espagne en Italie.*"

On leaving Grenoble for Vizille, after crossing the long rich plain formed by the alluvium of the two rivers the Isère and the Drac, the road rises steeply to the village of Brie; the views of Grenoble and its neighbourhood on looking back are very fine. After proceeding along the elevated ground for some distance the road descends towards Vizille, and presents fine views of this town, on the Romanche, near its confluence with the Drac, and of the surrounding mountains.

Vizille, 3½, leagues has about 2000 inhabitants. It is considered as the cradle of the first French revolution, for here the parliament of Dauphiny, first made a declaration fatal to the power of the Bourbons.

Here was the château of the celebrated constable of the seventeenth century, Lesdiguières. It had since the revolution become the property of M. Pérrier the brother of the minister, who had established cotton or flax works here ; but it was destroyed by fire in 1825, and it yet remains little more than a heap of ashes.

A char may be used as far as Bourg d'Oysans. The high road to Gap crosses the Romanche. That to the Col de Lautaret ascends by the right bank of this river through a narrow, but beautiful and well-wooded valley, which runs with nearly the same wild character into the heart of the mountains for 6 or 7 leagues. In some places the valley widens enough for the establishment of a village or a hamlet. Of these Chichiliane, Gavet, and La Clavet are the principal. Near Gavet there are some iron-works. This remarkable ravine or combe, which is also an English or rather Celtic name for a defile, bears the name of the Combe de Gavet and extends from the plain of Vizille to the plain of the Bourg d'Oysans, which is a fertile valley surrounded by lofty mountains. It is within record that a large lake was formed in the eleventh century by the falling of the neighbouring mountains at the entrance of the Combe de Gavet; this dammed the river, and the waters accumulated in the plain above, and formed a large lake, of which the surface was three leagues long, and one wide, and its depth from 60 to 80 feet. This lake existed for about 200 years. At length, in September 1229, it burst its barrier, rushed into the Combe of Gavet, swept away in its fury every thing that it touched, rapidly passed into the Drac, and thence into the Iseran, then flowing over the plain below the two rivers, submerged a great part of Grenoble.

Bourg d' Oysans, 7½ leagues from Vizille, is situated on the left bank of the river, and near the upper extremity of the plain. The vegetation of its valley is remarkably rich ; the lofty mountains that surround it offer in some places precipitous faces that present extraordinary instances of tortuous stratification. On approaching the Bourg, the enormous Mont de Lens, wrapt in glaciers, closes the head of the valley, and divides the torrent which flows from the dark gorges of the Vençon, which descends from the valley of St. Christopher, from that of the Romanche, which flows through the Combe of Malval.

The inn at Bourg d'Oysans *chez* Ratoux is the only endurable one on the route, it is therefore necessary to divide the journey here, and rest, at 11 leagues from Grenoble.

From Bourg d'Oysans, the road is practicable throughout only for mules. In many places a good char-road remains ; but from point to point the road has been allowed to fall so entirely to decay that it is now become impracticable.

A little beyond the Bourg, the road twice crosses the Romanche, and ascends by its left bank very high above the *Infernets*, as the inaccessible combe of Malval is called, and at least 800 feet over the torrent. The ancient road — for this course was known to the Romans, from Briançon to Grenoble—passed much higher behind Mont Lens, where there is a village of this name, 4200 feet above the level of the sea. In carrying the new road along, above the torrent, where the escarpments of the mountains are bare, smooth, and nearly perpendicular ; wherever it has been possible to cut away the rock in open day, to terrace the road, this has been done; but where masses which could not be removed projected, these have been boldly cut through, and a gallery has been made, in one place, 200 feet longer than that of Gondo, in the route of the Simplon. (Route 57.) Three lateral openings were found to be necessary to light the gallery, from either of these a sight of the foaming course of the torrent, 800 feet below, is most appalling. At the further end of the gallery, the road sweeps down to the banks of the river, and then passes nearly on its level through another gallery. Such are the extraordinary works on this route, now useless to the world, for the want of doing something more to make them available.

From the last gallery, the road rises up through a sterile valley filled with rocks and blocks of enormous size that have fallen from the mountains above; in the midst of such a desert lies the hamlet of

La Dauphine, 4 leagues from Bourg d'Oysans: here refreshment may be had at a miserable auberge. Above La Dauphine the same savage and rocky character of the valley prevails. Numerous streams are crossed which descend in falls from the glaciers that crest the precipices, and foaming over the steep talus formed on the sides of the valley by the disintegration of the mountains, cross the road and add to the fury of the Romanche. Not far from la Dauphine, on the left, a magnificent cataract gushes out from the top of the precipice, and falls in a large volume into the valley below; this is called *La Saut de la Pucelle.* The universal story of a peasant-girl, leaping down unhurt, to escape the violence of a chasseur is applied to this fall also.

So vast are some of the blocks that strew the valley, that one among others measures 50 paces in length, and against several, stone huts and châlets are raised and sheltered; for though there appear to be little herbage here, what there is is rich enough

to induce those who have herds to send them here to pasturage.

Still further up the valley, on the left, are the lead-mines of La Freux, belonging to M. Marat de l'Ombre, where many workmen are employed to rise the ore and smelt it. The adits are seen high up the precipitous sides of the mountains; and ropes and machinery extend into the valley below; these mines are said to be worked to advantage. The completion of this road to Grenoble, would be to the proprietors a measure of great importance.

At the head of this savage valley the road rises to the miserable village of La Grave where there is a wretched inn. The author was once detained there in a storm, and the filth and misery of such a *gîte* cannot be imagined. It is rare to find bread there. Eggs, however, may be had, and good wine.

The situation of La Grave is very fine, directly opposite to the vast glaciers of the Mont de Lens. During the winter the cold precludes the burying of the dead, the ground is too hard: the bodies are, therefore, suspended in the granges until the returning spring; so wretchedly are they off for fuel that dried cow-dung is chiefly used.

On leaving La Grave, the path descends to pass some rocks; then rising, it leads abruptly to a turn in the valley that overlooks a very fine fall of the Romanche, all its waters being poured into a deep abyss; to flank this abyss the road makes a little détour, rises above the head of the fall, and soon after the traveller reaches

Villard d'Arène, a village as wretched and as filthy as La Grave. Here the mountain of the Lautaret commences, or rather the mountain ridge or barrier that divides the valley of the Romanche from that of Monestier or the Guisanne. This pass rises to the height of more than 6000 feet above the level of the sea; the col is covered with the most beautiful pasturage, and is one of the richest spots in the Dauphiny Alps for the harvest of the botanist.

On the summit, two leagues from Villard d'Arene, there is a *Maison Hospitalier*, one of those founded by Humbert II. in the eleventh century; this is kept by a peasant appointed to the duty; but travellers are cautioned not to trust to getting fed there, though wine always, and bread and curds may sometimes be found on the Lautaret.

The scene from the col is most sublime: immediately above it on the right is the Mount d'Arcines, scathed, and pinnacled with rocks, and clothed with enormous glaciers, ending on side of the Romanche, in the glacier of Tabuchet, whence this river has its source; on the other side, the river Guisanne is seen tumbling down the Mount d'Arcine, from its glaciers, to flow through the valley of Monestier.

From the Col de Lautaret a steep road descends into the sterile and miserable valley of the Guisanne, to the first hamlet La Madelaine, thence to La Lozet, where there is a more tolerable inn than any since Bourg d'Oysans; still lower is the village of Casset at the base of the glacier of Lasciale; and at the end of three hours, or four leagues, from the Col de Lautaret, are the

Baths of Monestier, fourteen leagues from Bourg d'Oysans: here there is an inn, to which the filth and privations of those passed *en route* reconciles the traveller, and almost persuades him that it is tolerable.

The mineral waters here are both drank and employed in baths, and are so abundant that they are employed to turn a mill. Below Monestier the valley exhibits cultivation; barley is grown, and the meadows by irrigations are very productive; and after the naked and sterile route from La Dauphin to Monestier the appearance of trees is hailed as giving the highest charm to the scenery.

The whole course of the Guisanne can be seen to Briançon, where the forts of this frontier town are seen, piled above each other; beyond is a chain of lofty mountains, over which is seen the peak of the Monte Viso— this is a magnificent scene.

There are several villages in the Val Monestier below the baths; the principal are La Salle, Chantemerle, so named from the number of blackbirds that frequent it; and St. Chaffrey. The approach to Briançon is strikingly fine, its walls and forts rising as they do to the highest *l'Infernet*, which is placed on a peak, nearly 10,000 feet above the level of the sea: the broad rich valley of the Durance below the town, and the mountain boundaries to the valley make this one of the most picturesque towns and scenes in the Alps.

Briançon, 4½. Inhabitants 3000. This town has gates, walls, and regular defences, and every strong position is occupied with a fort or battery; it guards the frontier of France by the pass of the Mont Genèvre and the valley of the Durance.

It is a city of high antiquity. Pliny attributed its foundation to the Greeks, who were chased from the borders of the lake of Como; others have given its foundation to Bellovesus or Briennus. Ammianus Marcellinus calls it Virgantia Castellum; it held a Roman garrison. St. Ambrose was here on his way to Vienne in Dauphiny when he heard of the death of the emperor Valens, whom he was going to baptize.

So strong was the position of Briançon, or so small the community, that the barbarians who dismembered the Roman empire appear to have respected or despised it; for no mention is made of their desolating presence in this little city. This was probably due to the strength of its position. After the Roman power had ceased, Briançon became a republic, until it voluntarily placed itself under the Dauphins. It was in part burnt in the wars of Calvinism, at the end of the sixteenth century; but it was destroyed by fire in 1624, and again in 1692, its archives were consumed, and with them the records of the civil and military history of the Cottian Alps.

Numerous bas-reliefs, inscriptions, and medals, have been found here, which give to Briançon a high antiquity.

This little city is one of the smallest in France, having less than 3000 inhabitants. The streets are narrow and steep; but many of the houses are well built. It boasts of a Grand Place, and its old church is worth a visit.

The city itself is strong from its position and mural defences; but the seven forts which guard it render it almost impregnable. Between the city and some of these forts there is a bridge over the deep bed of the Durance, which foams beneath vast precipices: the bridge is of bold construction, a single arch of 130 English feet span and 180 feet above the torrent: it was built in 1730, under the direction of the Maréchal d'Asfeld.

ROUTE 130.

BRIANÇON TO SUSA BY THE PASS OF THE MONT GENÈVRE.

On leaving Briançon for the Mont Genèvre, the valley of the Durance is ascended by a narrow gorge for more than a league, just to La Vachette, a little hamlet at the foot of the Mont Genèvre; here, on the left, in a striking contrast to the valley of the Guisanne, opens the Val de Neuvache, a large and productive valley. It is also called the Val des Près from its rich meadows; its mountains are clothed with forests; through it the river Clairée flows for 10 leagues, and then loses its name in a less important torrent—the Durance, which has scarcely run two leagues from its source in the Mont Genèvre. At the foot of the Mont Genèvre is a fountain which formerly bore the

name of Napoleon, and served to commemorate the construction of the new route; this was removed by the Bourbons, lest some thirsty way-farer should bless his memory.

The ascent commences through a pine forest and by a series of admirably constructed zigzags leads the traveller up to the col, and presents at every turn a variety in the views of Briançon, and its forts, the valleys of the Durance and Neuvache, and the surrounding mountains; these so much relieve the tedium of ascent that the summit is attained before the traveller has an idea, that he has accomplished a distance of nearly two leagues.

The plain of the Mont Genèvre is remarkable for the culture of barley on its summit, nearly 6000 feet above the level of the sea, and there are fine pasturages on the slopes of the neighbouring mountains. On the plain there is a village, called the

Bourg Mont Genèvre, three leagues from Briançon, which is inhabited all the year: here is the custom-house, a troublesome place to those who enter *la belle France.*

On the plain, and almost from a common source, two rivers rise — the Durance, which flows through France, into the Mediterranean, and the Doira-Susana, which flows into the Po and the Adriatic.

On the summit of the plain an obelisk was erected, to commemorate the construction in 1807 of this fine road over the Alps; it is 60 feet high, and had on its pedestal inscriptions to record the event: these the Bourbons removed. Is it possible that the wicked and the weak who ordered the destruction of such memorials as these, and the record on the fountain at the foot of the Mont Genèvre, can have thought that with their removal the fame of Napoleon would be forgotten? Some retribution has already fallen upon such folly and injustice.

On leaving the col of the Mont Genèvre, the course of the river is followed for two leagues down a series of tourniquets, made in the loose soil on the side of Mont Chaberton, along which the road is carried, until it reaches the bed of the river, and crosses it about two miles from Cesanne; the road then continues to this village, where the stream from the Mont Genèvre falls into a larger branch which descends from the lofty mountains that bound the Protestant valleys of Piedmont.

Below Cesanne, the course lies down a principal valley to

Oulx, three leagues, a large village at the entrance to the valley of Bardonneche, whence there is a pass by the Col de la Rue, to Modane, in the valley of the Arc. From Oulx, it is about two leagues to Salabertrand, a place memorable for the battle fought and won by the Vaudois, under Henri Arnaud, on their return to their valleys after expatriation, in 1689, when they were opposed by 2500 regular entrenched troops, three times their numbers, and commanded by the Marquess de Larrey, who was wounded in the action: every spot around has interest in connection with that event: especially the mountains in proximity, that by which they had descended on the night of the battle; and that on the opposite side of the valley, which they crossed, by the Col de Sou, to go into their valleys after their victory.

Beyond Salabertrand the valley narrows considerably, and forms, a good league below, near the fort of Exilles, a deep defile; in the midst of this the fort is placed, which perfectly commands the valley; here the river is crossed, and the road thence continues on its right bank, beneath the heights of Chaumont,— a spot rendered memorable by the fate of the Comte de Belleisle, who fell here on the 9th of July, 1747: his desperate valour, which had been excited by the promise of a Bâton de Mareschal of France, if he succeeded in forcing the pass, was checked, after he had received many severe wounds,

by a *coup de grace* from a grenadier of the regiment of Monserrat.

The valley, in and below the defile, is richly wooded, and preserves nearly the same character for three leagues, from Salabertrand to Susa, (Route 127.), 22 miles from Cesanne.

ROUTE 131.

CESANNE TO PIGNEROL, BY THE COL DE SESTRIERES.

From Cesanne, the road made by order of Napoleon to descend into Italy, is more direct than that by Turin; but the miserable policy of the Sardinian government has allowed this road beyond Cesanne to fall into decay, and thus almost compelled travellers to pass by Susa and Turin.

The route by the Sestrieres from Cesanne, crosses the Doire, and the ascent to the col immediately commences, by a series of zigzags like that of the descent from the Mont Genèvre, each can be seen from the other across the valley of the Doire, a lengthened snake-like course. The road from Cesanne soon reaches the hamlet of Champlas; still the road continues to ascend over fine pasturages, till it reach the Col de Sestrieres and its châlets: the plain of the col is nearly two miles long. On the side towards the Val Pragelas the view is wild and fine, of the valley and the Mont Albergian. Above the fort of Fenestrelles, the road leads down by tourniquets to the banks of the Clusone, and to the first village, Sestrieres, four leagues from Cesanne, and thence to Traverse: the broad bed of the river beneath the dark pine forests opposite to Pragelas, gives rather an appearance of sterility to the valley.

Fenestrelles, four leagues, a village of 800 inhabitants, with a tolerable inn. The fort of Fenestrelles is a place of great strength, which guards the approach to Piedmont by this valley; it rises, from the defile formed by the base of the Mont d'Albergian, and the mountain which commands the left bank of the torrent; up the latter an immense line of connected fortifications rises, and a gallery leads up through these defences from terrace to terrace by 3600 steps to reach the highest battery. On the summit is a basin covered with verdure, called the Pré de Catinât, from that celebrated general having encamped there. Not far from the summit is the Col de la Fenêtre, which looks out upon the combe of Susa and the valley of the Doire: there are remains of old forts on the base of the Albergian, but they are neglected as unnecessary. The village of Fenestrelles lies in the middle of the defile below. The fort of Fenestrelles is used as a state prison.

From Fenestrelles to Pignerol there are eight leagues, nearly the whole of which lie in the valley of the Clusone: there is little interest in the valley, or variety in the scenery: it is generally narrow, but where there is cultivation, corn and wine abound. The mulberry, for silk-worms, flourishes in the valley, and fruit and forest trees luxuriate, as they are almost always found to do on the side of Piedmont. Formerly, this valley was filled with a Protestant community, but their living in it is now prohibited; the Vaudois churches are not permitted out of the valleys of Rora, La Tour, St. Martin, and Angrona. The valley of La Tour is known also as the valley of Lucerne, and the Val Pelice.

Below Fenestrelles, the route passes through numerous villages and hamlets — Montole, Rouse, Villaret, and Chapelle — before reaching Perouse, the principal town in the valley; which is sometimes called the valley of Perouse. It is situated directly opposite to the valley of St. Martin, or the Germanasca, one of the most interesting of the

PROTESTANT VALLEYS. A good road ᵃᵃds up by the torrent of the Germanasca to *Pomaret* and *Perrier*, through scenes of great richness and beauty.

Above Perrier two branches meet; that to the S.W. leads to *Rodoretto* and *Pralis;* that on the N.W. has, above a defile on its opposite side; amidst fruit-trees, corn, and pasturages, the commune of *Maneille.* A little beyond, the road enters a deep ravine of the Germanasca, which is singularly wild and beautiful; at its upper extremity it opens into the valley below the Commune of *Marcel,* nearly opposite to the valley which leads across the Col de la Fontaine to Pralis.

Continuing up the valley of the Germanasca, the house of M. Tron, the Syndic of Marcel, is passed; a singularly handsome structure in such a situation. He is a man remarkable for his hospitality; but this virtue does not extend to his wife and family, and the stranger who expects to receive it will fare ill in his absence. About a league above this spot is the hamlet of Balsille; and immediately over, the celebrated Castella, a terrace on the side of a peaked mountain, where the Vaudois entrenched themselves under Henri Arnaud. Here the little handful of brave men, only between 600 and 700, struggled for their fatherland, and fought, for three days, the united armies of France and Sardinia, amounting to 22,000 men, when the latter, found it necessary to bring up artillery, which was accomplished with excessive difficulty, the heroic Vaudois, foreseeing that against the cannon they could not hold their position, retreated during the night without losing a man; and the following day their sovereign, of Sardinia, having quarrelled with his allies, agreed to restore them to their valleys and their hearths. No history exists, so replete with wonderful adventures as that of the simple peasants of these valleys, who fought and suffered, and reconquered, for liberty of conscience.

Above the Balsille, one of the grandest assemblages of materials for alpine scenery is to be found, in cataracts, ravines, and mountains: from the head of the valley there is a pass by the Col de Pis, to Pragelas in the valley of Clusone. The author has crossed from Pragelas to Perouse in one day, and he knows no finer traverse in the Alps.

From Perouse to the Balsille, and return to Perouse, may be accomplished easily in a day.

On the route from Perouse to Pignerol, some fine quarries are passed, where stone is raised for the public works of Turin; nearly opposite to these is seen another of the Protestant churches, *St. Germano*, and the little valley which leads to *Pramol;* still further down is the church of *Prarustin*, nearly opposite to where the valley widens, and the road enters upon the plains, through the hamlets of Port and Abadia, to Pignerol.

ROUTE 132.

PIGNEROL TO EMBRUN, BY THE VALLEYS OF THE VAUDOIS, AND THE COL DE LA CROIX.

From Pignerol to La Tour a diligence travels daily; the distance is not more than 10 English miles: the route lies through St. Secondo to Bischerasco, 5 miles, and 3 miles farther to the first Protestant community at

St. Giovanni. Here a new church was built whilst Piedmont was under the government of Napoleon. Upon the restoration of the house of Sardinia, the Catholics, whose church is on the other side of a little stream, complained that the voices of the Protestants in singing disturbed their devotions, and an order was given to shut out the abomination by a large barricade of wood, which the Vaudois were compelled to erect before the door of their church. This has now, however, dropped away bit by bit, and little remains of this evidence of intolerance. The church is of a singular form—a horse-shoe—but it is not favourable to the preacher or his congregation.

A short league beyond St. Giovanni, through a fertile country lies *La Tour*, the principal town of the Protestant communities; their church, St. Marguerite, is situated, about a mile from the town, near the rock of Castelluzzo, celebrated in their history.

There are excellent inns at La Tour: the Canon d'Or, kept by Bartolemo Revel, is on the St. Giovanni side of the torrent, which flows from the Val Angrona. The town of La Tour is situated on the other side of the river.

At La Tour a hospital has been established for the sick and poor among the Protestants, by funds raised chiefly in Holland, Russia, and England; more recently, a college has been established there for the education of young men for the ministry of the Vaudois churches, and they have thus removed the necessity which had hitherto existed of sending them to Geneva. This institution was opened in the year 1837; it is chiefly endowed by funds raised in the above countries, but owing in a great measure to the liberality, the exertions, and the zeal for the cause of the Vaudois, of Colonel Beckwith, and Dr. Gilly. To the latter, the Vaudois are under the deepest obligations for the interest he has taken, and the influence his writings have excited in their favour.

There is no part of the Alps that, for richness and beauty in the lower valleys, and for wild and magnificent scenery in the defiles and mountains, surpasses the valleys of the Vaudois. Easy of access, by good roads from Turin, La Tour, their principal town, is reached in six hours from that city. Twice a day there are diligences from Turin to Pignerol, and daily from Pignerol to La Tour, over fine roads, and through a country luxuriant in vegetation. There are good inns at La Tour, to make head quarters for excursions; and the civility of all classes to strangers, especially English, ought to be a recommendation to ramblers in their country. Of the

Vaudois generally, but especially of the mountaineers, it has been justly said, that " they are far superior in moral character to the Roman Catholic inhabitants; they are from ancient habit, honest, civil, and quiet; and from their situation and necessity simple and laborious."

One of the most interesting excursions from La Tour, is into the valley of *Angrona*, which is surrounded by lofty mountains and pasturages. It is richly wooded down to the deep defiles of its torrent, and presents every variety of scenery, but some of its wild scenes are associated with their history: as the *Barricades of Pra del Tor*, which defended by them, gave security to their families who sought refuge within this grand and most picturesque defile. Above it in the recesses of these mountains, concealed from the world for many ages, their Barbes, or teachers, held their institution for instruction, and fitted their pupils for the ministry. Every foot of ground in this valley is sacred in the history of this extraordinary people. In the Pra del Tor there has lately been erected a Catholic church, but the heart of the valleys is not the heart of the people.

The excursion may be varied by following the high road to the village of Angrona, which offers from many beautiful points of view the plains of Piedmont. The return may be made through the defiles, or on the steep slopes that bound the river. A day given to explore the Val Angrona, will be remembered with pleasure.

From La Tour, up the valley of the Pelice, the road passes by the hamlet of St. Marguerite, where is situated the Protestant church of La Tour. Beyond this hamlet, the ascent of the valley is rich and picturesque. About an hour and a half from La Tour, the village of *Villar* is passed, and thence to *Bobbio* is scarcely another hour.

From Bobbio a pass up the mountains leads by Serra le Cruel, and the Col Julien to

Pralis. From La Tour this is a day's journey, but there are few excursions that offer more striking scenes, especially from the Col Julien. Near the summit — " Alps o'er alps," are seen piled in the most sublime confusion, and, surmounting all, the Monte Viso. So near does the latter appear, that the path to the Col de Viso, on the side of France, can be distinctly traced. The descent towards Pralis is very long and fatiguing. From Pralis the author went in one day's march across the Col de la Fontaine to the Balsille, and through the valley of St. Martin to Perouse.

On leaving Bobbio, a long wall is seen, an embankment, made to guard the village from the inundations of the Pelice; it was built by a grant from Oliver Cromwell, during whose protectorate one of these fearful calamities had nearly destroyed Bobbio. A little beyond, the river is crossed, and the mountain ascent begins; soon, on bending to the left, the scenery becomes wild and savage. The last view down the valley towards Bobbio is very fine.

After a long course amidst strangely situated hamlets, where rocks and trees of the wildest character make up a rapid succession of picturesque scenes, the path reaches a dreary mass of rocks, over which is poured the torrent of the Pelice, and further progress seems forbidden. Up, amidst these rocks, however, a path is found, which enters a deep ravine, within which are the ruins of the fort of Mirabouc, built against the steep escarpments of the mountain. The ravine is utterly impassable on the side opposite to the fort; nor is there a path on the side where the ruins of the fort stand, that does not pass through the line of its former gates. The fort was demolished after the wars of the French revolution, in 1796.

Above the fort Mirabouc, a path through a narrow and sterile valley enters upon the meadows and pasturages of the Bergerie de Pra — the highest hamlet in the valley, situated in the midst of fertile pasturages, and where barley and potatoes are raised. This is the station of the Sardinian custom-house on the frontier.

The ascent to the Col de Croix is by a steep and difficult path, made in zigzags, up the abrupt side of the col, towards Piedmont. This, however, is soon surmounted, and from the highest point which overlooks the side of Italy, the defile of Mirabouc is a savage scene. The col is nearly level for half an hour, and then the path, traversing the side of a hollow, gradually subsides to the valley of the Guil, within the territories of France. On the col there is a station of the douane, and at La Monta, in the valley of the Guil, travellers are examined; thence the distance through the hamlet of Ristolas to

Abries is about 4 miles, where there is an inn, rather better than one might expect to find in the mountains. At Abries the torrent from Valprevaire flows into the Guil, and a path up its course leads to several mountain passes. Below Abries the road through the valley of the Guil leads, in about two hours, to the fort of Queiras, passing in the descent, those valleys in which there are still Protestant communities, particularly that of St. Veran, in a valley which joins from the left the valley of the Guil, at Ville-vielles; and the valley of Arvieux, which enters that of the Guil near Queiras. To these, and the Val Frassenières, on the other side of the Durance, the name of the *Pays de Neff* has been given, to commemorate the services rendered to these communities by this young Swiss Protestant minister, who devoted his life to renovating and sustaining the religious worship of the primitive Christians that had existed in these valleys from time immemorial. Neff seems to have taken for his model Oberlin, the good pastor of the Band la Roche, near Strasbourg, for he not only regarded with the deepest interest the religious faith and practice of these people, but he established schools, and taught them reading, writing, arithmetic, agriculture, and the elements of much useful knowledge, not before possessed by them. He died in 1829. His name throughout these valleys is remembered with the deepest reverence and affection.

The Château de Queiras is finely situated in the valley: it is garrisoned, and entirely commands the pass, and from every point of view presents a most picturesque object. There is a tolerable inn at Queiras.

Below the château the road skirts the deep bed of the river for a short way, then descending to the torrent, which it crosses, it continues for nearly two hours, through one of the finest defiles in the Alps. In some places the mountains seem to close in above the traveller; and it is often necessary to cross the Guil to find a path on one side, which is forbidden on the other by projecting rocks or perpendicular precipices of vast height, whose bases sink like a wall in the torrent. Sometimes, when both sides forbid a passage in the depth of the ravine, the road runs high above the river, and on these higher paths the yellow rind and tortuous branches of the stone-pine overhang the gorge, and enrich its sublimity, with a touch of objects in such situations beautiful: some hamlets are passed in this savage ravine. At length the road emerges, winds up a steep and rugged path, crosses the torrent of Seillac, and descends upon Guillestre, a little bourg which was one of the stations, during the war, for English prisoners.

A little below, the road passes beneath the fort of Mont Dauphin, which guards this entrance to France — a garrison singularly placed on a rock that is insulated at the mouth of the Guil, at its confluence with the Durance. Here the great route from Grenoble to Briançon is entered; and the course down the valley to Embrun (2 hours) is by an admirably formed and well-kept road.

ROUTE 133.

EMBRUN TO SALUZZO OR SALUCES, BY THE COL DE VISO.

From Embrun to Abries (Route 132,)

After passing Ristolas and ascending the valley of the Guil to La Monta— where the path to the Col de Croix turns off to the left— the route to the Monte Viso continues up the valley to the highest village, l'Echalp, about a mile and half above La Monta. At l'Echalp guides may be obtained for excursions either across the Monte Viso to Saluzzo, or into the valleys and recesses of this remarkable mountain.

The valley of the Guil above Abries is narrow and savage: bare and precipitous escarpments descend to the torrent, and form its left boundary: the bed of the Guil is filled with enormous rocks. The path to the Col de Viso ascends above the right bank over steep acclivities and pasturages. Above these the head of the Monte Viso is continually presented, filling the open space in the view, formed by the sides of the valley of the Guil. After a long and fatiguing ascent to the châlets and the Bergerie de Monviso, the pasturages are at length left, and the ascent lies over the remains of a road rudely paved with large rough stones, so destroyed in many places by the rocks which have fallen from the impending precipices, that the ascent is dangerous and impracticable for mules — the danger lies in their liability to slip between the rocks and stones, and thus break their legs. This paved road formerly reached to the Gallery of the Traversette, which pierced the mountain 250 feet below the present crest, but its entrance has been closed by the débris of the precipices which overhang the pass; masses from these have fallen and destroyed the path within its range. From the last traces of the road, the traveller must scramble up the trackless slope, towards the mountain which overhangs him; this steep ascent, over beds of snow, keeping close to the impending rocks, leads up to the col of the Viso, 5 hours distant from Abries.

From the col, the view down the valley of the Po and over the plains of Piedmont, is one of the most magnificent in the world. This vast expanse, seen from a height of 10,150 English feet above the level of the sea, commands a view, which extends to 100 miles distant in the horizon. The rocks and vast precipices in the foreground and on the col, the deep subsidences of the mountains which bound the valley of the Po immediately below the observer, till they sink lower and lower into the plains, are most impressive. On the plain, bright but indistinct masses, mark the positions of the towns and cities of Piedmont within the view, and this indistinctness contrasted with the sharp and defined forms of the enormous peak of the Viso, rising yet 3000 feet higher and in close proximity to the observer, produce an indescribable effect upon his mind and feelings; this view extending to an indistinct horizon, is one of the most magnificent and sublime scenes in the world. The traveller who would enjoy it should leave Abries so as to be on the Col de Viso by 10 o'clock or earlier. This can only be made certain by starting soon after 4 in the morning from Abries; before mid-day, vapour generally rises in the plains and the valley of the Po, and obscures the prospect.

The col is a mere ridge, so narrow that it is traversed in a few paces. On it are the remains of a redoubt; and here, during the wars of the Revolution, many struggles were made and battles fought for the possession of this position.

Some, with no better foundation than the fact that the plains of the Po could be seen from the col, have supposed that this was the route of Hannibal; but the same authority that records his having shown the plains to his army, states that the army encamped on the summit, and waited three days for stragglers. Here, 100 men could not have encamped, and the pass must then have been impracticable to elephants, and even horses,—for the gallery, which pierced the mountain 250 feet below, to avoid the traverse of the last and steepest part of the crest, was only made in the 15th century; but this too was imputed to Hannibal, as if a mountain could be pierced more rapidly by an army than by as many men as could be brought to apply their labour efficiently upon a point so limited.

But the question about the construction of this gallery has been recently settled by the discovery of documents at Saluces. It had been attributed to Hannibal — to Pompey — to the Dauphin Humbert of Vienne — to the Saracens — and to Francis I., and the advocates for each found arguments to support their opinions. It was, however, executed under the orders of Ludovico II., Marquis of Saluces; who, with a spirit beyond his age, undertook this extraordinary work for the commercial interests of his people, by making a route three days shorter than any other from Saluces to Dauphiny. By treaty with René, king of Provence, who contributed towards the expenses on his side of the mountain, this road was opened to receive from France by laden mules, salt, drapery, and metal wares, in return for nut oil, wine, rice, and flax from the marquisate of Saluces. By means of this gallery, and the roads constructed as approaches, this intercourse was open 6 or 8 months in the year.

The length of the gallery was about 250 English feet, and 10 feet high and 10 wide. It was begun in 1478, and was completed in 1480; — an extraordinary work to accomplish in that time, especially as they could only labour, at that height, about 7 or 8 months in the year.

At present not a trace of the gallery remains: the rocks have fallen and buried the entrance on both sides. This had frequently occurred — in 1620, 1676, 1798, and 1812 — and the fallen masses had been removed by the people of the communes on either side of the mountain. In 1823 a mass fell, and so entirely closed the entrance on the side of Piedmont, that where it was, cannot be clearly seen; it had some time before been buried on the side of France. It has ceased to be important for commercial objects since the opening of the route by the Mont Genèvre, and it will now in all probability remain for ever closed.

The ascent to the col on either side, but particularly on that of Piedmont, was greatly relieved by the gallery; for though the perpendicular difference of height was not more than 300 feet, this was the most difficult part, for even now, in the descent towards Piedmont, its inclination exceeds 45 degrees.

Down this steep and difficult path the traveller has to proceed towards the valley of the Po. To descend thither he moves beneath precipices that every moment threaten to bury him, and these subtend such vast angles above him, that the precipices are a thousand times more impressive than loftier ones at a greater distance.

About 1000 feet below the col, a mass of rock is turned abruptly, and on the right there lies a scene unsurpassed for the immensity of the objects above, below, and around the observer. On looking up to the right towards the Monte Viso, this mountain rises in all its magnificence on one side of a deep valley, in which are some little dark lakes, the source of the Po, which below them is seen to trickle in a silver line down the black rocks, from the base of the Viso into the valley below. Nothing can exceed the impression of solitude and sublimity made by this scene; the glaciers, the beds of snow which must be traversed in the descent, and thousands of rocks and stones piled in wild confusion, amidst which a path must be found to reach the lower valley which, hid by projecting rocks and masses, seems dark, obscure, and doubtful, and where the steep descent seems to lead to nothing certain. At length, however, all these sublime horrors are passed, and vegetation is soon after reached, in a beautiful little plain covered with the richest herbage. This spot is called the *Piano del Re;* in it there is a delicious fountain, from which the traveller rarely fails to quaff.

A short descent from the Piano del Re leads to another little plain, the *Piano di Fiorenza,* so named from its beautiful flora, with which it is enamelled. Nearly two miles below is the first hamlet, *Piana Malze,* a name derived from the forest of larches which is near it. The wretched appearance of its inhabitants is sickening; here is the station of the Sardinian douane. About three miles further down the valley is the highest village, Crissolo, which for filth, poverty, and discomfort, is unmatched even in Piedmont; beds, except of the filthiest description, cannot be obtained; and for bread they depend upon a supply of *grisane* from Paesana.

Whoever would pass the Viso, should start early enough to cross from Abries to Paesana the same day: he should arrive on the Col de Viso before the ascent of the vapour, and avoid the filth and starvation of Crissolo.

Below Crissolo there are some fine wild scenes in the valley of the Po, and after having passed the confluence of the Lenta with the Po, the village of Oncino is seen in a striking situa-

tion, between the two rivers. From Oncino the view of the valley of the Po, and the plains of Piedmont, is singularly fine. The inhabitants of Oncino have some celebrity as brigands; at least their neighbours give them that character.

Paesana is distant from Crissolo about three hours. It is a large town with 5000 inhabitants. Here there is a very tolerable inn.* From Paesana a good road branches off to Barge, and passes through a beautiful and rich country to Lucerna and La Tour (Route 134.).

From Paesana to Saluces is about 14 miles, passing through the town of Sanfront; inhabitants above 5000, and the villages of Gambasca and Martiniana. At the latter, the valley, which had widened to the plains from Paesana, is altogether left by the traveller, and the remaining distance of six or seven miles after skirting the mountain, enters upon the plain, over a level road, to Saluces.

ROUTE 134.

ST. DALMAZIO TO EMBRUN, BY BARCELONETTE AND THE COL D'ARGENTIÈRE.

The Stura, one of the largest affluents of the Po, which the traveller to Nice crosses near Coni, issues from an open valley opposite to St. Dalmazio, where the high road to Nice is left (Route 136.); and the course up the valley of the Stura is by a very good road for a light carriage, which extends as far as Venadio — greatly facilitating the intercourse with this place, which is the principal bourg in the valley, and offering a temptation to invalids to visit the mineral springs in the neighbourhood, which are much frequented. The distance from St. Dalmazio to Venadio is nearly 8 leagues.

In ascending the valley, the first hamlet is that of St. Martino; and

* Desiderio, king of the Lombards, who was defeated by Charlemagne, and kept prisoner for a long time at Vienna, in Dauphiny, was permitted at last to take up his residence at Paesano.

soon after passing it the Stura appears in its deep course in the valley; and beyond it, rising abruptly amidst some pinnacled rocks and precipices, lies the village of Rocca Sparviera. The traveller interested in the adventurous career of Francis I. will trace here the course of his chivalrous companions in arms, who passed the mountains by this village when they went to capture Prosper Colonna, the celebrated Roman general, at Villefranche.

Colonna had been sent by Leo X. to join the Swiss in Piedmont, and defend its frontiers against the invasion threatened by Francis. He was stationed at Carmagnole, with 500 men at arms, and some light horse. Francis, who was waiting on the Dauphiny side of the Alps, having been informed of his situation, and thinking it would be a gallant enterprise to attack Colonna at Carmagnole, sent some of his bravest officers upon the expedition. Amongst these were the chevalier Bayard, Imbercourt, la Palisse, and d'Aubigny. The army of Francis was not yet ready to start; but these gallant soldiers crossed the Argentière, and descended the valley of the Stura to Rocca Sparviera. Here they left the course of the Stura, and, under the guidance of the Signor de Morete, crossed, by a difficult path amidst the rocks of Sparviera, into the Val de Grana; thus avoiding the Swiss troops stationed at Coni to guard any débouché by the Val Stura into the plains. Having reached in safety the town of Savigliano, the French party proceeded to attack Colonna at Carmagnole. It is probable that he had received some information of their intention, for he hastily left Carmagnole to join a body of Swiss troops under the cardinal Schinner at Pignerol. On his way thither he stopped to dine at Villefranche, where the French surprised him and made him prisoner. The gallant party then fell back upon Fossano to await the descent of the French army under Francis; who, whilst other passes from France were carefully guarded, descended by this from the Argentière. The Swiss, who were at Coni, hastened to join Schinner's troops at Pignerol. Their defeat at Marignano by Francis soon followed, and their long-sustained reputation for invincible soldiers was there lost.*

Soon after passing Rocca Sparviera the road winds down to the river, crosses the Stura, and continues on its left bank almost throughout the valley. The cultivated land which borders the Stura is very rich and luxuriant: the chestnut trees are of great magnitude; and the forms of the mountains which bound the valley are highly picturesque.

About four leagues from St. Dalmazio the traveller reaches

Demont, a town formerly remarkable for its fort, which guarded the valley of the Stura and the communication with France by the Col d'Argentière: it was built by Charles Emanuel I. in the sixteenth century, upon the ruins of an old castle which had been razed by the Austrians in 1559. It has been memorable for its sieges in almost every war between France and Sardinia. In that of 1744, when the Spanish and French armies, commanded by the Infant Don Philip and the Prince of Condé, invaded Piedmont, they forced the narrow pass of the Barricades, descended the valley of the Stura, and took the fort of Demont by the use of red-hot shot. Afterwards they besieged Coni, and fought a battle which they won from Charles Emanuel III., who succeeded, however, in throwing supplies into the city, which was gallantly defended. After a long and tedious investment, the storms of autumn and the want of supplies — which were cut off by the Piedmontese peasantry — compelled the allies to raise the siege and recross the Alps

---

* Sismondi has made sad rigmarole of the topography of this adventure.

towards the latter end of November, when they suffered the severest privations from cold, hunger, and fatigue. Though pursued by the troops, assailed by the peasants, and exposed to storms, yet they returned to France, over frozen roads and through deep snow, with all their artillery, and with a few guns taken from their enemies, — the miserable trophies for which they sacrificed thousands of lives and millions of treasure: on their way, they destroyed the fort of Demont. It was again restored, but finally demolished in 1801; when Piedmont, having become a part of France, the forts that guarded the defiles on the frontiers of Dauphiny were razed. Since the restoration of Piedmont the reconstruction of many has been contemplated, some are begun, and this among them. The mound upon which the ruins stand is situated in the middle of the valley, — the river passing on one side, and the road on the other. Further up the valley, and not far from the fort, is the bourg of Demont, where there is a tolerable inn. From Demont to

Venadio, the scenery is in many places highly picturesque, — a charm for which it is much indebted to the magnificent old trees which form foregrounds to beautiful views of the river and the mountains; and these are heightened by the festoons of vines and gourds which decorate the branches. From the town of Venadio the scene down the valley is very fine. Here it is necessary to leave the char; but mules may be hired for continuing the journey up the valley, and across the Argentière into France.

Above Venadio the change is rapid to wild and alpine scenery, varying from a road by the stream which ripples through quiet meadows, to narrow paths which overhang the course of the torrent — a course, too narrow in the ravine for a path by the river, it is therefore carried on ledges of the precipices above, and forms in some places fearful mule paths for the traveller's ascent of the valley. Such scenes are observed near Zambucco. Above are the villages of Pied de Port and Pont Bernardo. At a place called the Barricades — a narrow defile, where defences of the valley were formerly erected, and which was often the scene of desperate conflicts — the road is carried along a shelf of rock above the river, and has been cut out of the precipices which darken and overhang the ravine, and offers an almost impregnable barrier to the passage of the valley. Above the Barricades the road, or rather path, lies amidst the *débris* of the mountains which bound the valley, and offer a scene of wild desolation. Above it lie the villages of Praynard and Bersesio; the latter is the principal place between the Barricades and the Col d'Argentière; here accommodation may be found, after a long day's journey from Coni, preparatory to another from Bersesio, across the mountain to Barcelonette.

Bersesio. Above this village the scenery is wild and rugged, the mountains presenting a thousand pinnacles of rock, blighted and scathed. Still in the valley barley is cultivated, and the pastures are rich; and the villages of Argentière and La Madelaine are found. Soon after passing the latter of these the path leads abruptly to the Col d'Argentière, 7200 feet above the level of the sea. Before arriving at the crest, the path skirts a little lake, the source of the Stura, called La Madelaine: it is about 600 or 700 feet across. This lake is supposed to be the source also of the Ubayette a stream on the side of France; for, at a short distance from the col on that side, and a little below the level of the lake, a spring — the source of the Ubayette—gushes out: this spring, it is believed, communicates with the lake.

From the summit the view is very extensive, especially towards France, looking down the course of the Ubayette towards L'Arche, the frontier station of the French douane. Below L'Arche there is little interest in the scenery. The road descends through the villages of Certamusa and Meyronne to the junction of the Ubayette with the Ubaye, where two roads lead into the Embrunnais, — the principal following the course of the Ubaye to Barcelonette, the other leading by the camp of Tournoux, the village of St. Paul, and the Col de Vars, to Guillestre and the valley of the Durance.

The scene is fine from where these roads separate. Châtelard, in a well-cultivated little plain, is left on the right, and the road passes on through Jausier. There is not much interest generally in the scenery except at Pont de Cluse, near Jausier, where the rocky defile through which the Ubaye struggles offers some fine points of view.

Barcelonette has 2200 inhabitants, and a very decent inn. The town is larger and better built than one would expect to find in a valley so sequestered, and having so little communication with the rest of the world.

It is chiefly inhabited by the proprietors, of the Alps and pasturages of the valley. More than 100,000 sheep are pastured in its communes: from their wool, some coarse goods, consumed chiefly by the inhabitants, are made; there is much corn also grown in the valley; but for almost every thing else they are indebted to strangers, in other valleys or other countries; it is not long that the cultivation of potatoes has been practised among them.

This valley was known to the Romans, but there is little of its history to be relied upon, except in connection with that of Embrun, which has been better preserved. It is known that it was subjected to irruptions by Saxons and by Saracens, who made their way from Marseilles; these were defeated by Charles Martel. Under Charlemagne France had the benefit of a protecting government. In the

sixth century, a convent of Benedictines established here did much to ameliorate the condition of the inhabitants of the valley; but all the wars in which Provence has been engaged have extended their horrors in this valley, and it was often liable to the irruptions of the Saracens, particularly in the tenth century. From the fourteenth century, it was alternately subjected to Savoy or France: Amadeus conquered it in 1388. It was re-attached to Provence by René of Anjou in 1447; it was again taken by the duke of Savoy, Charles III., in 1537. In the middle of the sixteenth century, the inhabitants adopted the reformed doctrines, but they were shortly after either forced to abjure them, or were expelled their country.

Napoleon contemplated the construction of a new road through the valley of Barcelonette to pass the Col d'Argentière and enter Piedmont, by the Val de Stura. Since his abdication the idea seems to have been abandoned; but its benefits to 20,000 inhabitants of the valley, by the greater development of their energies and the increased prosperity of Barcelonette, ought to have some weight with the government of France.

There are many communications with the neighbouring valleys, by passes in the mountains; as with Embrun by the Col de la Vacherie, and with Colmar and Allos by the valleys of the Tinea and the Varo, which discharge their streams near Nice.

Soon after leaving Barcelonette near the village of St. Pons, the ruins of an old castle are seen in a fine situation.

The roads down the valley of Barcelonette are in so wretched a state, that the want of embankments exposes the inhabitants of the valley to the frequent loss of communication, from the destructive effects of the torrents. Not far below Barcelonette, it is necessary to ford the beds of the Bachelar, the Rio Bourdon, and other torrents, for want of bridges.

The first large village below Barcelonette is La Thuiles, and the next after crossing the Ubaye by a wooden bridge, Méolans, thence down the valley, there is a tolerable char road. Amidst dreary and wild scenes, the general character of the valley of Barcelonette, there is, however, a striking exception in a village beautifully situated, called

La Lauzette, the Goshen of the valley. It is agreeably wooded: near it is a little lake which abounds in fine trout, and in the immediate neighbourhood are fruit trees and a fertile soil. A little way, however, below the village, the scene changes again to sterility. After crossing a ridge, a series of tourniquets leads down the pass of La Tour, or, as it is called, the *Chemin Royal:* a part of the road in the valley admirably made; but, unconnected as it is with the country above or below by any road so good, it is worthless.

Below these tourniquets the valley offers some of its most wild and grand scenes. On looking back from the path carried along the brink of the precipices high above the torrent, the Ubaye is seen in its deep course issuing from the defile of La Tour, and beyond, the grand forms of the mountain of *Cugulion des Trois E'vêques,* which divides the valley of Barcelonette from that of the Var, the scene is one of savage dreariness.

The road continues on the left bank of the river high above its bed; until, leaving the side of the hill upon which the fort of St. Vincent is placed, a very difficult path leads down into the river, which is crossed to arrive at the little village of Ubaye.

From this place, one road passes down by the river to its confluence with the Durance at La Brioule; and another, up the side of the mountain to the Col de Pontis, which leads to Savines on the Durance, in the high road from Gap to Embrun, which is distant from Savines, 8 miles (Route 185.).

From the ascent to the Col de Pontis, on looking back towards the valley of the Ubaye, the hill of St. Vincent is a strikingly fine object, surmounted by forts which formerly guarded the entrance to the valley of Barcelonette, when it was under the dominion of Sardinia. By a wise arrangement, it was ceded to France in exchange for the valleys of Pragelas and Exilles, when the states of France and Sardinia prudently agreed upon the chain of the high Alps as their line of demarcation.

ROUTE 135.

PASS OF THE COL DE TENDE FROM TURIN TO NICE.

27½ Posts, = about 115 English Miles.

The road quits Turin by the Porto Nuovo, and continues by the side of the river Po, to

2¼ *Carignano.* This town, of 7200 inhabitants on its left bank, has long been an appanage to the younger branch of the royal family of Sardinia, who purchased it from the Marquises of Romagnano; the son of the king bears the title of Prince of Carignan. The objects best worth notice here are, the Church, the marble tomb of Blanche of Montferrat, and the equestrian statue of Jacques Provana.

The Po is crossed a mile or two after quitting the town.

2¼ *Racconigi,* a town of 10,000 inhabitants, on the banks of the Maira. The *Palace* of the Prince of Carignan, recently fitted up, and the park attached to it, merit notice.

1½ *Savigliano,* a town of 15,000 inhabitants, still retaining its ancient fortifications, though no longer a place of strength. At the end of the principal street is a Triumphal Arch, erected in honour of the marriage of Victor Amadeus with the Princess Christine of France.

2¼ *Centallo.*

1½ *Coni,* or *Cuneo.* Inn: La Posta, a good sleeping place. An episcopal city, with a population of 18,000 souls, and once a strong fortress, of which conspicuous mention is made in all the campaigns of Italy, down to the time of the battle of Marengo; after which its fortifications were demolished by the French, and converted into agreeable promenades (Route 134.).

The fatality of the cholera at Coni, in 1835, was greater than in any other part of Europe.

About 6 miles beyond this city, the road quits the great plain of the Po and its tributaries, to dive into the recesses of the mountains. The ascent thus far from Turin is scarcely perceptible. Near San Dalmazzo, distinguished by its ancient Benedictine abbey, the Monte Viso is seen in clear weather towering over the intervening Alps, and the general line of the range in colossal elevation. Its snow-clad peak, rising more than 12,000 feet above the sea level, is a truly magnificent object.

From San Dalmazzo a road turns off on the west to the Col d'Argentière, and to Barcellonette in France. See Route 135.

1¾ Robillante.

1 *Limone,* the station of the douaniers, who annoy travellers coming from Nice, though it is under the same government, as much as if they came from France or the Milanese. Here a bridge of nine arches was built by Victor Amadeus, to carry the road over the torrent of the Vermenagno.

The next stage comprises the ascent of the col, which is surmounted by skilfully constructed terraces, forming a series of zigzags. About half-way from the summit, an attempt was made by the former princes of Savoy, and continued down to the French occupation in 1794, to bore a tunnel through the mountain, and thus avoid altogether the tedious passage over its crest. If completed, it would have been more than a mile and a half long, and would have surpassed every similar work in the Alps. The culminating point is a narrow

ridge, 6162 feet above the sea. On the north and west it commands a fine view of the Alps from Monte Viso to Monte Rosa; while, on the south, the Mediterranean may be faintly discerned. Near the top there is a house of refuge: a succession of more than fifty zigzags conducts the road down to

4 *Tende* (Inn, Hôtel Royal, good), a little town on the Roya. Here are the picturesque ruins of a castle, the residence formerly of the counts of Tende.

The narrow defile of the Roya presents some striking scenes, especially near Saorgio, where a fort perched on a rocky knoll commands the passage of the gorge. It was taken by the French in the campaign of 1794. Below Saorgio there is a very savage defile, through which the road passes on the banks of the Roya to

2¼ *Ghiandola.* At the little inn on the Roya here, excellent trout may be procured. This is the best sleeping quarters between Coni and Nice. This village is very pretty, and most beautifully situated in the vale of the Roya, though overhung by abrupt and barren peaks.

The road now crosses the Col de Brovis, a spur or off-set from the main chain of Alps, 4277 feet high. At its south base, close under the hill lies

2½ *Sospello,* deep sunk in the little vale of the Bevera, which abounds in thick woods, in olives, and figs. The Bevera forms a junction with the Roya about 12 miles below Ghiandolo, and thence flows 4 miles further into the Mediterranean at Ventimiglia. Inn detestable; musquitoes in myriads.

Another minor ridge, called the Col de Braus, 3845 feet above the sea, remains to be surmounted before the traveller descends into the valley of the river Paglione, to reach

2¼ *La Scarena.*

The sudden transition from the bleak and bare ridges of limestone, traversed by the road. to the luxuriant vegetation and high cultivation of the Riviera, is very striking.

2½ Nice, in Route 136.

ROUTE 136.

NICE TO GENOA, BY THE CORNICE OR RIVIERA.

35¾ Posts, = about 130 Eng. Miles.

This road, commonly called the Riviera, is decidedly one of the most interesting routes into Italy. It is less a pass of the Alps than a road by which they may be avoided, as it is carried all along the shores or on slopes of the subalpine chain, just before it dips into the sea. It is not liable, like other passes into Italy, to be obstructed by snow, on which account it is to be preferred to all other roads to or from that country in the winter season.

This route along the Maritime Alps was the earliest passage frequented by the Romans : it was called the Via Aurelia, and was the first which they carried out of Italy beyond the Alps. Cæsar entered Italy, this way when about to encounter Pompey, and cross the Rubicon,—a circumstance alluded to by Virgil : —

Aggeribus socer Alpinis, atque arce Monœci, Descendens, gener adversis instructus Eois.

The Cornice is, as its name implies, a ledge cut in the sides of the mountains which overhang the sea in this route, and combines the advantage of alpine scenery possessing all its grand and savage features on one side, with the deep blue of the Mediterranean sea, of which it seldom loses sight, on the other. It is carried along the shore round capes, on turning the sharp angles of which, the most exquisite prospects unexpectedly burst into view : sometimes it ascends a spur of the Alps in order to avoid a détour, and then an extensive view is displayed of the long curve of the beach, with receding bays and advancing headlands stretching out

one beyond another in the distance. Numerous antique towns, abounding in curious relics of architecture not yet described in any English work, stud the margin of the shore, and picturesque white latteen sails sparkle along the dark blue sea.

Nice. (Ital. Nizza.) Inns : Hôtel des Etrangers ; Hôtel de Yorck ; Pension Anglaise; Hôtel de l'Europe.

Nice, a town of 20,000 inhabitants, is less remarkable for anything which it contains than for its situation on the shore of the Mediterranean, and at the foot of the Alps, which shelter it as with a wall from most of the cold winds, except the *bise* or west wind. All the rich vegetable productions of a southern climate — oranges, figs, olives, pomegranates, capers, myrtles, and even palm trees — flourish around, and in the open air. On account of these peculiar advantages of climate, it is annually resorted to by invalids in the winter season, and the English usually form a predominating colony here.

Nice is built on the banks of the river Paglione, and along the margin of a little bay : it is provided with a small port and pier, at which the steamers to and from Marseilles and Genoa touch. The ground plan of the town is in the shape of a triangle. The language of the lower orders is a singular dialect, in which Latin, French, and some words of Teutonic origin are intermixed. The quarter called Croix de Marbre is that in which the English chiefly reside, though its situation is not well chosen for invalids : a row of houses built under the shelter of the *old castle*, on the opposite side of the river, would be far preferable. Nice is most agreeable as a residence during the months of November, December, and January. In February, the Vent de Bise begins to blow, and drives away the invalids. Persons in bad health ought to avoid the heights above the town, which are much exposed to cold blasts from the Alps: from these the town itself is sheltered.

The rocky eminence crowned by *Fort Montauban*, and bearing at the extreme point of the promontory a lighthouse, commands a very extensive and beautiful view all along the coast westward to Antibes, in France, and Cannes (where Lord Brougham and Sir Herbert Taylor have built themselves villas), and eastward it extends to Mentone, and the picturesque castle of Monaco; the island of Corsica, more than 90 miles off, is also visible in clear weather. On the east side of the promontory of Montalban lies the little town of Villa Franca, the place for quarantine, and a station for galley slaves, situated at the end of a nearly oval harbour, deep and large enough to hold 100 ships of the line, but exposed to the south, where it is entered by a narrow mouth. The east slope of the hill is so much more sheltered than even Nice, that aloes and lemon groves flourish in the open air at Villa Franca. Outside the bay there is a considerable *Fishery of Tunny*, which begins in April.

The eminent naturalist, M. Risso, who resides at Nice, has published a most valuable description of its geology, natural productions, &c.

Very pretty boxes, toys, &c., in the style of Tunbridge ware, and even larger articles for household furniture, are manufactured at Nice from the olive wood. From the wood of the fig tree, turned in the lathe, baked in a furnace, and covered with a black varnish, light cups, and other utensils capable of holding hot water, are formed. The stalks of the palm leaves are converted into walking-sticks.

The journey to Genoa along the Riviera may be performed in a light calèche, with post-horses, in 2⅓ or even 2 days, halting at Oneglia. Few travellers, however, will be willing to pass over its interesting scenes in

so hurried a manner. It is a country to be dwelt upon: the artist may enrich his sketch-book at every step, and the architect or antiquary will find ample field for the most interesting researches. Persons travelling in a heavy carriage, which requires four horses, should be cautioned that in some places the road is steep and narrow, and runs along the verges of precipices, whose bases, 200 or 300 feet below, are washed by the Mediterranean: parapets are not always provided in such spots; and, unless the horses are very quiet, and accustomed to the road, there is some danger. With a heavy carriage, the traveller should compel the postilion to drag down every hill, and the drag-staff should be let down always in ascending the hill; lest the horses should back over the precipice. With a light calèche there is little to fear on this score; and, indeed, since the opening of the road only one carriage has been overturned down the precipice. With Vetturino horses the journey may be made in four days, and may be thus advantageously divided. Start from Nice in the afternoon, or earlier to visit Monaco, and rest : —

1st night at Mentone, where there is a very comfortable little inn.

2d, Oneglia — good inn.

3d, Savona — capital inn; and in the morning of the

4th, To Genoa.

A long and laborious ascent leads out of Nice to an elevation of 1500 or 1600 feet above the city. On this height the road is carried along for some distance; and offers a series of views of extraordinary beauty, extending over Nice and Villa Franca, which appear at the feet of the spectator; while, if he look back along the coast of France, he may discern the Estrelles, Cannes, Antibes, and the castle of the Isle S^{te}. Marguerite, the prison of the Man in the Iron Masque, and the Islands of Hyères, rising against the horizon. Further on the road, Eza appears below, singularly perched on a rock; and at the sea side, the castellated Monaco, also crowning a rocky promontory.

At Turbia (a corruption of Trophœa Augusti) stands the remarkable ruin of a Roman *monument* erected to commemorate the conquest of the various tribes of the Maritime Alps by Augustus; a design which would have long since been frustrated by the destruction of the inscription, had the fact not been recorded by Pliny. It is a vast circular structure surmounted by a tower. The village has been built out of its fragments and masses: the ground is strewn with blocks and inscriptions, and bas-reliefs are built into some of the walls.

. We now enter the principality of Monaco, which, though only eight miles long by five broad, is yet governed by a sovereign prince, under the protection of Sardinia, who levies duties and taxes, and is occasionally very troublesome to travellers, by means of his douane and police officers. His revenues are derived chiefly from oranges and lemons, which grow abundantly in his territory. The principality was founded in the tenth century, in favour of the Grimaldi family; but when the male line became extinct, it descended through the females to the family of Matignon. The reigning prince resides chiefly at Paris.

Monaco, the capital, is a singular town, fortified, and containing 1200 inhabitants. It is built on an elevated rock, a promontory above the sea, on the shore of a little bay, on the right of our road. It is said to have been founded by Hercules, and was known to the ancients as " Portus Herculis Monœci." It has the honour of having been mentioned by Virgil. Close to the castle cactuses grow in profusion.

6 *Mentone*, also within the principality, is a much larger place, of 3000 inhabitants, provided with a port. Mentone, though counted 6

posts from Nice, is not more than 20 English miles distant.

Near Mentone a fine arch has been thrown across the gorge of the Baussi Rossi, on the high road to Ventimiglia. The traveller should not fail to alight, enter a vineyard on the right hand close to the bridge, and examine this extraordinary structure, in such a situation, it is called the Pont St. Louis.

1½ Ventimiglia (*Albium Intemelium*). Inn: Hôtel de Turin. This small town has been recently fortified.

Near Bordighiera, and in other places along the coast, palm trees grow in the open air; but they will scarcely be recognised as such at first, owing to the practice of swathing their branches to protect their leaves, which form an important article of commerce, being exported to Rome and other large cities of Italy, to be used in the religious ceremonies of Palm Sunday.

3 *St. Remy*, or *St. Remo*, is a considerable town, of 11,000 inhabitants, situated on the slope of a hill. It exports large quantities of oil, dried fruits, and lemons.

2¼ St. Stephano. The scenery falls off in interest between Porto Maurizio and Oneglia. The route is chiefly on the shore, and is a wretched, uninteresting portion of the route.

2¾ *Oneglia*, a town of 5000 inhabitants, the birthplace of Andria Doria: i is famed for good oil. It was taken by the French in the campaign of 1792-4.

4 Alassio.

1½ *Albenga*, a very ancient and interesting town. The *Albium Ingaunum* of the Roman itineraries contains many interesting relics of the middle ages, such as a circular baptistery. Several remarkably lofty towers, and the whole of the ancient feudal fortifications still remain.

The streets of many of the old towns through which the road is carried are so narrow, that the walls of the houses on both sides are grooved by the marks of the axletree. From the scarcity of ports in some parts of the coast, vessels of 30 or 40 tons burden are drawn up high and dry on the beach. Several of the torrents descending from the Alps require to be forded ; a process attended, at times, with some risk, owing to their sudden increase after rain : they subside, however, equally fast.

The views of the bay of Albenga, from either of its headland boundaries, are singularly beautiful.

The last hill on the road remains to be surmounted before reaching Finale. Its ascent is not less than three miles long, and the descent by zigzags, on the east side, two miles. To avoid this unnecessary labour, the government are at present constructing a new line close to the sea. In 1838, at least 400 workmen were employed in opening a tunnel through a part of the mountain for it to pass, and thus preserve its level without ascent or descent.

3 *Finale*, a town of 7000 inhabitants.

Soon after leaving Finale, the road passes the western headland of the little bay of Noli, by a gallery cut in the rock, 500 feet long. The effect of looking from it, on emerging upon the deep blue sea, is very striking.

The little fishing town of Noli, once a republic ! is supposed to be the Ad Navalia of Antoninus. The town is deeply embayed between the capes of Noli and Vado. The road round the latter is very fine to

Vado, which is passed a short while before reaching Savona ; it was the Roman Vada Sabatia.

3¾ *Savona.*

Savona (Sabatium), an episcopal town of 12,000 inhabitants, was at one time the most important seaport on this coast next to Genoa, and excited the fear and jealousy of her citizens, who, to keep down so formidable a

rival, ruined the harbour for a time by sinking two old vessels laden with stones at its mouth, in 1525. The French afterwards repaired the damage, and it is once more a flourishing port, carrying on a considerable export trade of sail-cloth, cables, soap, fruit, and lace. There are several fine *churches* here. The Duomo, richly decorated, contains paintings by Albano.

Between Savona and Genoa the magnificent new road is conducted on a perfect level, near the sea, partly along arched terraces, partly through cuttings and blastings by gunpowder in the solid rock. As a work of engineering, it is not surpassed on any alpine pass.

Cogureto, or Cogoleto, a humble village, would be passed unnoticed, except for a claim which it sets up of being the birthplace of Christopher Columbus. The generally received opinion, founded on Columbus's will, is, that Genoa was the place where that great man first drew breath. Here, nevertheless, is shown the identical house by the sea side ; and it is marked by more than one inscription to commemorate the fact. The will, it must be observed, does not express that he was born in the *city* of Genoa, but that he was a Genoese, — " *Siendo yo nacido in Genova*," — being, as the will was written in Spanish and in Spain, as applicable to the state as to the city. At Cogoleto the torrent Leone is crossed by a ford : it is at times a dangerous stream, when swollen by rains.

4½ Voltri.

The tall white tower of the lighthouse of Genoa, seen at a long distance off, announces the approach to that proud and stately city.

3¼ GENOA.

See Handbook for NORTHERN ITALY.

INDEX.

₊ In order to facilitate reference to the Routes, most of them are repeated in the Index twice : — thus, GENEVA to Chamouni, is also mentioned under the head Chamouni * to Geneva ; such *reversed* Routes are marked in the Index with an asterisk to distinguish them.

THE END.